BING
CROSBY

Swinging on a Star

THE WAR YEARS
1940–1946

BING CROSBY

Swinging on a Star

THE WAR YEARS
1940–1946

———

Gary Giddins

LITTLE, BROWN AND COMPANY
New York   Boston   London

Little, Brown and Company
Hachette Book Group
1290 Avenue of the Americas, New York, NY 10104
littlebrown.com

First Edition: October 2018

Little, Brown and Company is a division of Hachette Book Group, Inc. The Little, Brown name and logo are trademarks of Hachette Book Group, Inc.

The Hachette Speakers Bureau provides a wide range of authors for speaking events. To find out more, go to hachettespeakersbureau.com or call (866) 376-6591.

Library of Congress Cataloging-in-Publication Data
(Revised for vol. 2)
Giddins, Gary.
   Bing Crosby : swinging on a star : the war years, 1940–1946
Gary Giddins. — 1st ed.
      p.   cm.
   Discography: p.   Filmography: p.
   Includes bibliographical references (p.) and index.
   ISBN 978-0-316-88792-2 (hc)
   1. Crosby, Bing, 1904–1977. 2. Singers—United States—Biography.
   I. Title.
ML420.C93 G53 2001
782.42164'092—dc21
[B]   00-044403

10 9 8 7 6 5 4 3 2 1

LSC-C

Printed in the United States of America

For Deborah, Lea, and Alice

Some have spoken of the "American Century." I say that the century on which we are entering—the century that will come out of this war—can and must be the century of the common man.

—Henry Wallace, The Price of Free World Victory (1942)

Neither appealing to the listener nor ignoring him, the cool performer speaks to him from inside the listener's head. The voice may be Olympian or diabolical, but it is always superior and always calm. It is often ironic. It knows the listener inside out.

—Evan Eisenberg, The Recording Angel (1987)

He had read almost all the important plays and novels in the world; compared to them, the new plays and books seemed thin. But movies seldom disappointed him; moreover, he liked the despised Hollywood pictures. Their repetitiousness, their total emptiness of intellectual content, their copybook moralities, their large implausible lying, their naïve licentiousness, did not bother him at all; in these childlike qualities they exactly resembled the Arabian Nights, and like the Arabian Nights, Hollywood pictures seemed to him part of one ever-running endlessly involuted rainbow-hued dream.

—Herman Wouk, Youngblood Hawke (1962)

That is the substance of remembering—sense, sight, smell: the muscles with which we see and hear and feel—not mind, not thought: there is no such thing as memory: the brain recalls just what the muscles grope for: no more, no less: and its resultant sum is usually incorrect and false and worthy only of the name of dream.

—William Faulkner, Absalom, Absalom! (1936)

It's a pretty old air, said Mr Dedalus, twirling the points of his mustache. Ah, but you should have heard Mick Lacy sing it! Poor Mick Lacy! He had little turns for it, grace notes that he used to put in that I haven't got. That was the boy who could sing a come-all-you, if you like.

—James Joyce, A Portrait of the Artist as a Young Man (1916)

CONTENTS

Part Three

DER BINGLE

BING CROSBY

Swinging on a Star

THE WAR YEARS
1940–1946

INTRODUCTION

Bing Crosby was born Harry Lillis Crosby on May 3, 1903, the fourth of seven siblings, in Tacoma, Washington. Three years later, the family moved inland to Spokane and a two-story house across the way from Gonzaga University. His father, Harry Lowe Crosby, a bookkeeper whose Danish-Anglican family had deep roots in America, almost as far back as the *Mayflower,* was depicted by his son as a hail-fellow-well-met character who liked to sing and strum a mandolin. His mother, Catherine Helen Crosby (née Harrigan), was a devout Catholic and a hard-line disciplinarian whose Irish ancestors went to Canada in 1831 and gradually moved to the United States and westward to Washington. Bing won his nickname in third grade as a dedicated fan of a syndicated feature, "The Bingville Bugle," which parodied a hillbilly newspaper in drawings and news flashes. At Gonzaga's high school and university, he excelled in elocution, Latin, English, history, and Christian doctrine. He held a series of before- and after-school jobs, including altar boy and sweeper at a skid-row flophouse, and he found his passion in sports and entertainment.

Crosby dropped out of Gonzaga in his last year of law school when he began earning money as a performer. He had been scouted by a high school kid, Al Rinker, to play drums in his band, the Musicaladers. He offered to sing, too. They built a dance-hall following, and when the band broke up, Rinker (a pianist) and Crosby found work as a duo. With Al's sister, the jazz singer Mildred Bailey, beginning her career in Los Angeles, they bought a Model T and drove down the coast. With her encouragement, Bing ditched his drums, and the two men found work on West Coast vaudeville circuits. Betting on a hunch, the formidable Paul Whiteman hired them to work with his orchestra, bringing them to New York, where they flopped until they found a third partner, songwriter Harry Barris, and called themselves the Rhythm Boys. They were a Jazz Age phenomenon, swinging, funny, hard-playing, hard-drinking. Whiteman brought them back to Hollywood to appear in the film *King of Jazz.* On their own, they triumphed at the Cocoanut Grove, where Bing met his future wife, starlet Dixie Lee, and the fabled Mack Sennett, who in 1931 featured him in a series of two-reelers. That year he was also recruited by CBS to star in a network series, the success of which led to his record-breaking tenancy at New York's Paramount Theater and the national obsession with a new microphone-savvy style of singing called crooning. At Dixie's insistence, Crosby stopped drinking. Paramount's 1932 picture *The Big Broadcast* launched him as a film actor; NBC's *Kraft Music Hall* reinforced his eminence on the air; a handshake agreement with Jack Kapp led to the formation of Decca Records and Crosby's unrivaled career as a recording artist. He became the voice of the Depression and the recovery. At the start of a new decade, he and Dixie had four sons and a majestic home. He had a new movie partner in the recently imported Broadway comedian Bob Hope. Crosby was rich, powerful, beloved. His life was exemplary. All the fan magazines said so.

PRELUDE

Pilgrim's Progress, 1927–1937

May 1927. From a letter to Bobbe Brox, on tour in Philadelphia with the Brox Sisters, written in New York while Bing Crosby worked with the Paul Whiteman orchestra:

> I'm sick of this town, the inhabitants thereof, and the appurtenances thereto. Work day and nite, with no opportunity for any healthy recreation and only able to find amusement in the solace of rum with its subsequent discomforts. I got a strong yen on to get from here, preferably coast work and unless things take an unlooked turn for the better shall gratify said yen.
>
> Business at the club is a bit sad and the same is true of the show. It appears as tho the 1st of June will find both jobs terminated, praise God! And then I believe we go into the Paramount for 10 weeks. Imagine the unalloyed pleasure of 5aday in Midsummer in New York. No golf, no ball games. Odzooks! Tis most disconcerting.
>
> I might run down there next week if I can make it. If you come to town don't neglect to call me. Hope the surroundings in staid Phillie have quieted down your urge for companionship and revelry.
>
> Lotsa Love
> Bing[1]

May 1928. Letter to Edgie Hogle, Spokane, written on hotel stationery:

Hotel Gotham
John R. St. at Orchestra Pl.
Detroit, Mich.
Monday 1928
Dear Edgie—

I know that I am away behind in my correspondence with you and must owe you plenty of letters. We have been pretty busy during the last few months and have been jumping in and out of New York with little chance of getting set anywhere so my duties in this respect have fallen into a sad state. However I have received all of your cheery epistles and was indeed glad to hear from you.

This Detroit is probably the boss town of them all with every facility for having a good riotous time at first hand. Right across the river from Canada, but no need to go over there as the spots on this side give plenty of good satisfaction.

I have been setting comfortably on the wagon for some two weeks, but I fear the congenial surroundings here are going to necessitate a temporary descent. I hope it is only temporary. My drinking hitherto has been spasmodic, but when occasion demands, it is usually for a protracted spell. Don't crack around home tho....

The Band and ourselves have switched to Columbia Records exclusively, leaving Victor because of a better proposition. The talk in the East and the trend of the stock market seems to indicate that Columbia in a couple years will pass Victor in popularity and sales.

Their new machine has the Victor orthophonic stopped and they are turning out some great recording. As a result of the sudden switch, our last two weeks in New York was plenty feverish grinding out enough records for Columbia to full up the catalogue....

From here we play Buffalo, then into New York for some more records and jumping to Minneapolis then Chicago, Kansas City etc. There is a possibility I may get home around August if we get a vacation after Chicago. I hope so even if it's only for a week.

Best wishes to Maudine and your Mother and Sisters. And hello to the gang.

Your friend
Bing
c/o P. Whiteman
1560 Broadway
New York City[2]

February 1929. From a letter to Mrs. H. L. Crosby, Spokane, written on
hotel stationery:

The Seneca
Rochester, N.Y.
Friday—15th
Dear Mother—:

I received your letter today, it having been forwarded here from
~~Rochester~~ Syracuse, and am enclosing money order for ~~of~~ a C,
which you can split with Dad.

...The [Rhythm Boys] are verily the "stormy petrels" of show
business, particularly myself. At present we are in a frightful imbroglio with the Columbia Company. Victor Company, Keith Albee and
Whiteman claiming us contractually obligated to each of them....
Pending a satisfactory arrangement we have been working but spo-
radically and jumping all over the East Coast. Shortly after our
return we landed a show which augured very well for us with good
parts and a nice salary. But while up in Pennsylvania the agent
neglected to close the deal and we returned to find the chance lost.
This is but one instance of a dozen similar incidents...the Savoy
Hotel in London made overtures for our services and finally made
us a highly attractive offer. I found a loophole in our Whiteman
contract and being dissatisfied with the way things were breaking
over here, partially accepted. We were getting quite fed up with this
part of the country, and our material and manner of working had
been so extensively pirated that the novelty had begun to pall. I
figured a change of locale, new surroundings, new audiences, etc.
coupled with the reputed avidity of the English for anything jazz
and American would afford just the break to put us into something
worthwhile....We were convinced that over the proposed six
months period, we could net ourselves about $350 a week with
excellent prospects of an even greater return if the angles were
worked properly. Now Whiteman has proved the fly in the ointment.
He has become convinced of the impracticability of touring any-

more and has arranged to stay definitely in New York with the Zieg-feld Roof, "Whoopie Show" [*sic*], radio and recording supplying the necessary angles. This, of course, is precisely the type of work for which he needs us the most, and he is fuming plenty about injunc-tions, suits of law and any other means of preventing our early departure. Further, I personally have been offered a nice contract for exclusive recording and radio work. This, of course, would necessitate disbanding the trio which I am reluctant to do. I guess the thrill of the footlights and the glamor of the greasepaint has got into my blood, for unquestionably an arrangement such as has been tendered to me, would provide a definite and lucrative future far in excess of present prospects, but without the attendant glory, and association peculiar to show business. Then too, Rinker would be left without anything, and having started with him, breaking away now, hardly seems the right thing to do.

So you can understand things are in a turmoil. Truthfully, I don't know which way to turn. We are going into New York Sunday and, as we are expected to sail Friday next, some conclusion will have to be reached quickly although not too sure of myself I am reasonably convinced that my talents, if any, are above average, and there is a niche somewhere for me in this field. The difficulty lies in finding out where and connecting at once. I want you and Dad to believe that my chief desire is making out in a big way quick and doing something for you that will really matter. I realize fully that what measure of success I have attained is directly attributable to your guidance and upbringing and I know too, that your prayers and those of the sisters must have played no small part.

I have thought a great deal about Bob and now believe if you can wait until the present difficulties are definitely settled, (say until early spring) I can do something definite.... I know I owe you and Dad a great deal more than I can ever repay, and I hate to see him growing up doing himself irreparable harm just through his own willfulness. (As I did)....

I will be at the Belvedere hotel next week in the event you should write.

Love to all

Harry

P.S. Regarding your query concerning our vitaphone. Whiteman doesn't wish his name used in a talking picture, short or otherwise, until he has made his first. Hence we are holding off. There is plenty of time and we'll probably get more dough when we do.[3]

January 1932. From a letter to a fan, Mr. A. C. Collins, written in New York:

In response to your kind letter, I want to thank you very much for your interest in my broadcasting. Having no contact with our unseen audience, any applause or critical comment is greatly welcomed and appreciated.

Both Mrs. Crosby (Dixie Lee) and myself wish to thank you for your kind invitation to spend a vacation in Canada, as we can think of nothing that would be more pleasant. However, I feel, as you must know from your experience, that the luck I am having right now will not hold up forever, and I want to take advantage of it and make all I can while I can, and do not think I will get a vacation until late in the summer, at which time I expect to go back to California and do some picture work.[4]

September 1937. Bing Crosby's handwritten list of his employees and their salaries:

House: housekeeper (Alice Ross, 100), nurse (Eve Waldorf, 100), chauffeur, maid, cook (all 75), watchman (120), gardener (80). Ross, nurse, maid, cook live in house.

Ranch: caretaker (125) and two laborers (100 each) for horses, caretaking, etc.

Stable: trainer (Albert Johnson, 200), and five labor (100, 80x3, 40). Equal 6900.

Office: Everett Crosby manager, Larry Crosby publicity (200), HL Crosby secty (200), Ruth Clark asst (120), clerk (100), bookkeeper (Clay Johnson) 100, EE Wyatt, clerk (100), Mary R Crosby clerk (25).[5]

Part One

———

TIME
OUT

1

MEANWHILE

Expert in cascading cadenzas and euphonious ululation, proud paterfamilias, acme of all virtues—that's how we'd describe Bing Crosby if we had his vocabulary. But in plain English: swell singer, happy husband and father, grand guy.

—*Radio and Television Mirror*, 1940[1]

Shortly before supper on an evening near the close of 1940, the thirty-seven-year-old Bing Crosby entered the palatial yet intimate home he had built a few years before at 10500 Camarillo Street, in North Hollywood's Toluca Lake district, and stepped into a too-familiar din. Turning the latch, he could hear his wife, Dixie, a few weeks into her twenty-ninth year, upstairs ranting at their four sons in a pitch verging on hysteria. He climbed the grand staircase that spiraled up to the first-landing bedrooms and stepped down the three shallow treads into Dixie's dressing area. Sitting upright on a settee, she had the boys arrayed at her feet: seven-year-old Gary, the five-year-old twins, Phillip and Dennis, the not-quite-three-year-old Lindsay. She turned, disrupted and dazed, to her husband of ten years and instantly fell silent. Without a word, he put one arm around her back and the other beneath her legs, gently lifted her, and carried her to the bed.[2]

It was not the final straw, just one of many that weighed him down, triggering his resolve to make a startling change in his picture-perfect life—a life symbolized in magazine stories and on a bestselling postcard depicting their twenty-room Georgian Colonial. Fronted by a six-pillar colonnade with balconied entablature, it evoked Mount Vernon as modified by the architect of Tara. Beyond the showcase entrance hall, it served primarily as a doggedly private retreat where show business and its machinations could be held at bay. At the same time, it walled in Dixie's growing dependence on alcohol, which made the retreat less than a haven.

Bing spent that day, as he did most of December, at Paramount Pictures competing with Bob Hope for wisecracks on the set of *Road to Zanzibar*. As usual, as the skies cleared (record-breaking rains drenched Los Angeles all season), he stopped at Lakeside to play nine or more holes before returning home to whatever new calamity awaited him. He kept his restlessness to himself. Crosby appeared to almost everyone as the most creditable of entertainers, his voice and personality incarnating continuity in volatile times, at once princely and familiar, imperturbable. *Road to Singapore*, his biggest picture yet, had kicked his career onto a new plateau in early 1940, and in the fall he dominated recording sales with three straight number one hits ("Sierra Sue," "Trade Winds," and "Only Forever"), a return to form after a relatively sluggish 1939. His weekly radio hour, *Kraft Music Hall* (*KMH*), placed reliably in the top ten of network programs. He wore his success blithely. His private life was thought to be idyllic and deserved. His wife, formerly a promising star in her own right, epitomized a rare combination: Hollywood-beautiful and girl-next-door-approachable. She was smart, charming, droll, athletic, fiercely loyal, and sometimes as sharp as a thorn—in the words of one besotted admirer, "altogether nifty."[3]

Bing lived like a king with relatively disciplined appetites. He didn't own a plane, a yacht, or a Rolls; had never been to Europe; kept no mistresses in hidden-away apartments; and thus far had erected no statelier mansions than the monument of Americana on Camarillo. At Rancho Santa Fe, California, where he ran a thoroughbred farm and administered a pro-am golf tournament, he surprised his trainers by arriving at the stables with the rosy fingers of dawn. He knew horses almost as well as they did. Paramount reproached him for working alongside his laborers when he renovated the property, since it meant the makeup department had to disguise his blistered hands. He loved singing, which had made him famous; golf and fishing, which he could well afford; and thoroughbred racing, which strained his holdings, not just because of the buying and training of horses and the maintenance of a stable, but because of the wagers he usually lost. Still, he had no addictions beyond the need to keep busy and no desire to flaunt the proof of his achievements. He owned a vast wardrobe, a hundred or so suits, but no one could tell that from his willful informality. He developed a head for business and a tight fist, but he remained a rich man with working-class manners, preferring Hawaiian shirts and khakis to full dress, and a library of books, recordings, and pipes to an entourage. Impatient with introspection, he communicated in a language of joking camaraderie: stoic, manly, rarely nostalgic, never sentimental, and often flippant. Admired for his intelligence, quick wit, and ability to converse about anything, he could not always resist the urge to sermonize. He was a devout Catholic, confident, independent, obstinate, and unaffectedly modest.

As Dixie's bouts of drunkenness increased, the Crosbys appeared in public often enough to allay rumors of marital discord, or at least restrict them to the Hollywood community, where they were rife. A week at El Mirador in Palm Springs; a trip to Mamaroneck, New York, when Bing competed in the U.S. Amateur Open Golf Championship; a party at Café La Maze the day his horse Don Mike finished first in the $10,000 handicap at Santa Anita; various restaurants and nightclubs; a boxing match. They were spotted at a corner table at Perino's Sky Room quietly singing to each other like young lovebirds as the John Kirby Sextet played songs from Bing's pictures. Dixie's friends noticed her growing reclusiveness. Her sons observed that at times she slurred her words. She often isolated herself in her room, unavailable to them. She fainted more than once. When she collapsed in the upstairs hallway, the housekeeper, who usually covered Dixie's tracks, shooed the boys away. Bing later assured them she was fine. No need to worry.

Not until four or five years later did Gary draw the connection between his mother's failings and alcoholism, a subject that people in those years tended to ignore, deny, or burlesque. "I'll tell you something about my mother," said Gary, whose own life and career were torpedoed by alcoholism. "For my mother to get up on that stage, she would have to drink. Because she was an alcoholic from birth, I don't care what anybody says. She had no self-esteem, didn't think she was pretty, didn't think she was anything. And it didn't get easier when she walked away from her career. When you feel that way, you've got to have something to get out there."[4]

This was the era—not yet sobered from the binge that was Prohibition—when W. C. Fields enjoyed his last tottering hurrahs, when stolid MGM tuned its Thin Man franchise to the rattle of a martini shaker, and when Craig Rice, now forgotten but then characterized as the Dorothy Parker of detective fiction, wrote comical mysteries solved in a mist of rye and gin that landed her on the cover of *Time*. The Twelve Steps as framed by Alcoholics Anonymous had yet to find much traction. Its membership barely topped one hundred. Among those most skeptical about classifying excessive drinking as an infirmity were the medical men in the Crosby circle. The surgeon Arnold Stevens, a family friend and himself an alcoholic, told Dixie, "You're very run down," and advised brandy and milk. Dixie once told a columnist that during her pregnancies, brandy was all she could keep down. Decades after her death, which occurred three days before her forty-first birthday, her internist George "Jud" Hummer, who practiced in the Crosby Building on Sunset Boulevard and counted himself and his wife among Dixie's dearest friends, refused to concede she had had a drinking problem. Joseph Harris, her obstetrician at Cedars of Lebanon who took her through three pregnancies, never thought—any more than most of his colleagues would have—to warn her of prenatal drinking. The term *fetal alcohol syndrome* didn't appear until 1963.[5]

An exception was a psychiatrist, Anthony Sturdevant, who specialized in young people but saw Dixie regularly in the Crosby home. For short periods, he kept her off the booze. Yet seeing a psychiatrist had its own stigma, generating as much suspicion as alcoholism. Patients had to endure the stereotypes attached to analysis: presumptions of weakness, dark undercurrents, madness, electroshock. Bing encouraged Dr. Sturdevant's ministrations, though they ultimately failed.[6] A paradigm of self-discipline who thought depression treatable by exertion of will, Bing had proved by example that drinking was merely a bad habit. You just stopped, or you moderated it when it got out of hand. "He is the only one in the family I never saw drunk," Gary marveled.[7]

Yet ten years earlier, Bing drank his way through the speakeasies of one city after another, waking in strange bedrooms, bathrooms, hotels, cafés, under tables, and failing to show for professional and personal engagements, incurring suits, threats, dismissals. He joked about leaving a "trail of broken bottles," not hearts, after years on tour with Paul Whiteman's orchestra in that woozy interval before he established his name on radio and in movies. Dixie forced him to reform. When her arguments and pleas had no effect, six months into their 1930 marriage, she flew to Agua Caliente and threatened a divorce. He pursued her and promised to turn his life around. Despite occasional missteps, he exceeded everyone's expectations. His career flourished, as did the marriage. As far as the public knew, their union was not merely solid, it was exemplary, an article of faith, like the widely held belief that FDR stood on his own two legs or that George VI was an adept orator.[8]

In the spring of 1940, millions of Hearst readers opened the *American Weekly*, a Sunday supplement, to "Those Hollywood Divorces," by Adela Rogers St. Johns. A Hollywood insider, St. Johns had a reputation for peeling away the tinsel; in truth, she merrily shoveled it on. This week her mission was to praise those couples who are "so happy they never make news" (the Harold Lloyds, the James Cagneys, the Crosbys) and to refute the argument that a woman's devotion to her career poisons love. Her "research into the matter" included a discussion with Joan Crawford, "the most honest woman I have ever known," who revealed that her marriage to Franchot Tone foundered not on the shoals of mutual careerism but because her relentless domesticity, ironing shirts and darning socks, got on his nerves. St. Johns then reversed her defense of working women by describing the "ideal" marriage of the Crosbys, which friends credited to the fact that Dixie had "abandoned her performing career and devoted herself entirely to being a good wife and mother."[9]

That fall, *Life* ran a similar (unsigned) article, "The New Hollywood," in which the stars "build homes, live quietly and raise children." This new housebroken Hollywood was illustrated by a picture of the serene Crosbys: Baby Lindsay, seated on Bing's lap, is turning to exchange a smile with his mother, who is standing behind Bing; surrounding them are the older boys, in matching uniforms. ("Like many movie children, they go to a military school.") A caption acknowledges the hoary Hollywood precept that women prefer their matinee idols to be unmarried. "Bing Crosby's family is perhaps Hollywood's best. This rare photograph, taken by George Strock, would have been inconceivable ten years ago, when it would have wrecked an actor's career. Besides being Hollywood's proudest father, Bing runs a horse ranch, a race track, and an office building."[10]

The Paramount Pictures publicity engine, with which Crosby seldom cooperated (hence the rarity of *Life*'s photograph), pushed this narrative hard. Fans seeking parenting advice wrote him letters, and Bing, a meticulous correspondent, responded. He shared an anecdote with a member of the Catholic Sportsman's Guild: "One time I found it necessary to spank my oldest boy, Gary, age six, and afterward when I was attempting to make up with him, he said, 'I'm going to get a farm and have a lot of pigs and make you take care of the pigs.' Whereupon I said, 'I'm going to get a farm and on it I'm going to have a lot of skunks.' 'Doggone,' said Gary, 'I forgot about skunks.'" To another correspondent, Bing wrote of his boys: "So far in their lives we have tried to make them self-reliant and have tried to instill in them a correct appreciation of values, and a knowledge of the difficulties necessary to attain financial security."[11]

A week or so into the new year of 1941, shortly after Bing carried her to her bed, Dixie drove the six blocks from Camarillo Street to Kitty Sexton's house on Cartwright Street to tell her devoted friend that Bing had demanded a divorce. She had hardly made it through the door before breaking down. Bing had it all planned, she explained, weeping. He'd instructed her to go to Sun Valley with the younger children and Kitty—he trusted only Kitty to travel with her—in order to establish residency and expedite the proceedings.

Of the exclusive, gated neighborhoods where Hollywood's elite

gathered, Toluca Lake had a peculiarly checkered terrain, strad-
dling North Hollywood and Burbank with great patches of manicured verdure divided by freeway inlets as gray as smog. Mansions
routinely went up and came down, plush modern showplaces, lush
haciendas, and multi-gabled legacies that wore their age with patri-
cian forbearance until the bulldozers arrived. The Crosbys' stylish
Colonial villa, one mile south of Lakeside Country Club, represented new blood and new wealth, but there were also suburban
enclaves with boutique houses like the Cape Cod–style cottage that
Kitty Lang had bought to be near them.[12] After a botched tonsillectomy killed Kitty's young husband, the outstanding guitarist Eddie
Lang (Bing's accompanist and confidant), Bing and Dixie had persuaded her to leave New York and stay with them as long as she
desired.[13] Kitty gratefully gave Bing Eddie's precious Gibson L-5 guitar and soon found her own one-bedroom house, the Cape Cod, and
refurbished it, adding a staircase and an attic bedroom for her niece,
who lived with her. She enclosed her yard with a white picket fence
to keep in her two dogs. When Kitty married her dogs' veterinarian,
Bill Sexton, he moved in and the menagerie grew with another dog,
chickens, pigs, and a cat. They had a son, Tim.

Kitty remained an essential presence in the lives of the Crosbys.
She helped Dixie through her pregnancies, bringing Eddie's religious medal to each birth (the medal's final resting place would be
Dixie's coffin). Kitty shopped for the necessities and hired a nurse
who cured Gary's colic. She spent so much time with the infants
that Bing named one of his first horses Aunt Kitty. "I was so proud
that I couldn't sleep," she recalled.[14] She and Dixie placed bets on
Aunt Kitty in her first two races, which she lost. When the trainer
assured them she had a better than even chance in her third race,
Dixie decided they ought not to bet to avoid a jinx. But Bing fluttered twenty dollars, and Aunt Kitty came in by a head, after which
he took Kitty Sexton to the Santa Anita paddock and presented her
with a lock of the horse's mane. Kitty, a former Ziegfeld girl, had
worked as Dixie's stand-in at Paramount and Monogram, and Dixie
urged her to return to show business as her own career lurched to
a finish. With Dixie and Bette Davis singing backup, Kitty made a
steel-disc recording so dire that the three women ceremoniously

buried it in the Crosbys' garden. After Dixie's death, she did return to show business as the beloved wardrobe mistress for casinos in Reno. "Reno's Auntie Mame," a reporter called her.[15]

Kitty, along with the other women in Dixie's circle, recognized Dixie's problem at least as early as 1933. She knew full well how Dixie had forced Bing to deal with the issue of his drinking and assumed that Bing was now attempting a turnabout, his own intervention. He did not really want a divorce, she said. But Dixie bought none of it—no, no, no, she wailed. She had thrown her arms around his neck and begged him to reconsider and he had removed them and said he no longer loved her. She promised to stop drinking, but he insisted that she "would have to prove it to him first."[16] Kitty told her that she needed to get permission from her husband, Doc Sexton, to accompany her to Sun Valley, at which point Dixie promised she would be "a good girl"—their code, meaning Dixie would not drink if Kitty made the trip.

Kitty agreed, calmed her down, and went alone to Camarillo Street to talk with Bing. He took her into the backyard, where they walked as he unburdened himself. He could not take it anymore. They had no home life. He worried about the boys. They saw things they shouldn't see, especially when he was away, which he had been virtually every day in December, filming *Road to Zanzibar*, broadcasting *Kraft Music Hall*, and making no fewer than twenty-two sides at seven sessions for Decca Records. Kitty urged him to give Dixie the "hope of reconciliation"—"Tell her you love her." He said he could not do that, not right now. He thanked her for agreeing to chaperone Dixie and raised details for the trip. Kitty told him they would require only a nurse for Lindsay, as she could take care of the twins and Gary was at school. A week into the new year, he drove the two women and three of the boys to the station. Upon arriving at Sun Valley Lodge, Kitty phoned him to say they were fine. Dixie had not taken a single drink.[17]

Kitty continued to believe that the whole exercise was a test to save the marriage. She was confident that Bing loved his wife and she knew intimately the pressures on him not to divorce; his fiercely Catholic mother might have accepted that mortal sin in his siblings, but however much she derided Dixie (who was not born to the faith, no more than Bing's father, Harry, was), Bing was another story, the boy she had once imagined in the priesthood and the man who would soon personify Catholicism to his massive public. Also, Kitty hadn't heard a whisper of another woman in Bing's life. Yet Bing was determined enough to warn John O'Melveny, the power-house attorney and abiding fixer behind his career, about his plans, and he in turn notified Todd W. Johnson, the lawyer-accountant whom Bing once described as "my tax-man who handles the intricate and sometimes extremely delicate matters in this field."[18]

The Crosby party had a large suite at the Sun Valley Lodge, with Dixie and Kitty sharing one room, a second bedroom for Phillip and Dennis, and a third for the nurse and Lindsay. They had a spacious living room with a fireplace and a veranda overlooking the skating rink. At a time when most states permitted divorce only when one spouse accused the other of a "fault," Nevada and Idaho pioneered quick splits with a residency requirement of six weeks before filing suit. They offered amusements to make the weeks pass pleasantly. Reno operated the busiest divorce mill in the nation, but the recently constructed Sun Valley Lodge provided a tonier alternative for those who could afford to avoid the crowds and ill repute associated with Nevada. Devised by W. Averell Harriman, the railroad heir and future New York governor, Sun Valley invented the idea of a Western winter resort while generating a raft of new customers for the Union Pacific Railroad, of which Harriman was chairman. He opened the lodge in December 1936 and offered such enticements as chairlifts and heated pools and celebrities—Clark Gable and Errol Flynn were the first in a stream of famous tenants that included Ernest Hemingway, Gary Cooper, and Bing. One lawyer who facilitated Sun Valley divorces from the 1930s into the 1970s said of potential clients, "We want only the carriage trade, not the bus trade."[19]

Idaho was liberal with divorce but not with liquor, which visitors could buy only if they obtained a license. Dixie purchased one along with a bottle of scotch that she promised not to open; she just wanted to know "it's there on the table."[20] She recruited a bellboy to take the twins skiing, skating, and hiking and spent much of her time knitting and conversing with Kitty by the fireside. She seemed reasonably content, even put on a few pounds, though she insisted she would never forgive Bing for saying that he no longer loved her. She did not want the divorce, she said, but whatever happened, a

breach now existed. Bing had a faithful lookout in Kitty. She periodically excused herself in the evenings and headed downstairs to
call him with assurances that all was well; Dixie had not taken a
drop since their arrival.

This continued for two weeks, at which point Bing phoned to say
he would come up the next day with Gary. Dixie was utterly
unnerved. The next morning, she uncorked the scotch. "Why now?"
Kitty asked as Dixie downed one shot after another. Dixie said she
didn't want to give him the satisfaction of knowing she had
abstained all that time; "He hurt me deeply when he said he no
longer loved me."[21] She was loaded when Bing got off the train.
Kitty intercepted him, told him Dixie "had been so very good" until
she learned he was on his way. Bing waved away her fears. He had
changed his mind; he no longer wanted a divorce. He had consulted with a Jesuit priest, who asked him, "If Dixie was drowning
and raised her hand up to you for help, would you refuse her?" The
identity of the priest is unknown, but the likely candidate is Father
Arthur Dussault, Bing's classmate at Gonzaga University who
became its public relations director and later a vice president of the
university and who would remain Gonzaga's primary link to Crosby.[22]
The priest's position found despotic support closer to home. Bing
confided to his brother Ted that when he'd told their mother of his
intention to divorce Dixie, she said, "No. You're not."[23]

He stayed the weekend, secluded with Dixie, and when they
came back to Camarillo Street late on Sunday, they were determined to make the marriage work. A few weeks later, in mid-
February, Bing took time off from *Kraft Music Hall*—the press
explanation dwelled on his frustration over the ASCAP strike,
which forbade him to broadcast songs by ASCAP songwriters[24]—
to return to the Sun Valley Lodge with Dixie and the boys for a
proper family vacation. The cool, dry mountain weather must have
been a relief from the torrential rains that peaked in February,
causing floods and making 1941 the wettest year Los Angeles had
experienced since 1884—a record that stood until 1977, the year
of Bing's death.

The tax man Todd Johnson was relieved. On Tuesday, January
21, he wrote Bing a long letter (nearly twelve hundred words):

Dear Bing,

Jack O'Melveny informed me this morning that you had adjusted your domestic affairs so that you no longer contemplated a separation and property settlement with Dixie. I am certainly glad to hear this for many reasons. I will mention some of the financial reasons hereafter in this letter. Leaving aside the personal reasons which are always considered sufficient by the parties involved, a separation and property settlement would indeed be an expensive one for you, considered only from an income tax standpoint....I have spent the last several days in analyzing the tax changes and tax matters which must be considered in such an event and I will briefly summarize those which I think will still be of interest to you.[25]

Johnson's conclusions refuted popular assumptions shaped by annual newspaper accounts of the best-paid Americans. Bing had ranked near the top for the previous three years. In 1940, he placed fifth, after MGM's studio chief Louis B. Mayer, the heads of IBM and Lever Brothers (soap, detergent), and Paramount's Claudette Colbert. A financial reporter estimated his salary at $400,000 to $450,000 at a time when only six hundred and fifty people in the country earned $75,000 (about $1.29 million in today's currency).[26] Weeks before springing the divorce ultimatum, Bing had made headlines because of his exceptional new contract with Paramount: he would star in nine films over three years at $175,000 per film. Bing had a five-year contract with Decca Records that averaged $60,000 per annum and a $200,000 salary from *Kraft Music Hall* on a contract that ran through 1943. His base expectations for the next year came to $785,000. Add to that his investments in real estate, the Del Mar racetrack, Rancho Santa Fe, and a contractual right (hard won from Paramount) to produce one independent film a year, and he was surely looking at a million.[27]

Johnson painted a different picture. He knew that Bing had decided he would not produce a fourth independent feature. His investments had not been successful, the track cost him more than it earned, and his pro-am tournament at Rancho Santa Fe was strictly for charity. Johnson's "rough but comparatively accurate estimate" of Crosby's 1940 *net* income, $526,000, exceeded the gross income estimated by reporters, but his own analysis focused on liabilities. Bing's federal and state taxes for 1940 came to $377,000, leaving him a total of $148,000 for "personal purposes." Should he and Dixie separate, his tax bite would increase by $55,000, leaving him $93,000. Bing's proposed settlement of $30,000 a year to Dixie would reduce his take-home to $63,000 — a hefty number that nonetheless justified Johnson's conclusion that it would be "expensive for you to assume the status of an unmarried taxpayer." More alarming was Johnson's estimate for 1941. He predicted a federal tax increase that would shrink Bing's income by another $30,000 and averred that he did not want to seem nosy ("your personal expenditures [are not] within my employment"), but would Bing please notify him of potential deductibles?[28]

He then laid out the immediate threat: Bing owed $377,000 in taxes for 1940, but as of December 31 of that year, the total of his available cash, other than what he had in his personal accounts, came to $167,000. Had he lost his ability to earn income at the start of 1941, he would have to sell assets to meet the shortfall. "You can see the position your estate would have been in had you died on January 1, 1941," Johnson continued, "or should you die in the future." Promising to cooperate with O'Melveny on all matters, he concluded with the recommendation that Bing purchase a half a million dollars in life insurance to handle "accrued income tax and inheritance taxes on your estate should you die unexpectedly."[29]

Marriage was not the only Crosby battleground. Pervasive dissatisfaction roiled him at thirty-seven, as he reckoned his achievements and the restraints they put on him. After a fifteen-year ascent from the fringes of vaudeville to the peak of Paramount's mountain, he felt cramped by the very successes he had struggled to attain. Champing at the bit, he contemplated severing both his marital ties and his career ones — especially with *Kraft Music Hall*. Of all his professional associations, radio was most like marriage; it tied him down in a way records and films never did. He loved to record and could do so when he liked, piloting the session at his own pace. When shooting a film, he relished the challenge of working with people he admired for a rigorous schedule of several weeks, after which his time was his own.

But radio, which paid far less than movies, held him in place week after week with script consultations, rehearsals, and live broadcasts. It required him to answer to absentee masters, people beyond the producer, director, writer, announcer, costars, guest stars, and orchestra conductor who worked on the show; these included the sponsor, the advertising agency, the network, and the FCC. Radio imposed an irksome domesticity. Yet he would ultimately stick with it—despite his front-page rebellions before and after the war—when everyone else, including Kraft, ran off to television. Radio, as Bing knew better than anyone, had ripened and refined his persona, influencing the characters he played on-screen and increasing the diversity of his recorded songs. In May 1940, when the press reported his demand for a sabbatical, a fan wrote Bing pleading with him to reconsider. "Radio made you what you are today," she wrote; why not take time off from making movies instead? Bing wrote her back as if she were a disapproving prioress, thanking her for her concern and explaining that he needed the twenty-one-week layoff for summer travels.[30]

Crosby delegated his brother and manager Everett to explain to the picture studios eager for his independent film that he was pulling back there as well. After the project to which he was presently committed (at Universal), Bing would no longer make outside pictures unless they had outstanding stories. Privately, Everett advised him, "I am afraid that if this war situation gets any worse it would be difficult to get a good deal and there is liable to be a curtailment program to go into effect, so we better not wait too long."[31]

For the first time since the speakeasy days of the 1920s, Bing seemed distracted, irresolute; he knew what he wanted *now,* but he did not know if he would want the same thing tomorrow. He negotiated hard contracts and put off signing them. In this, he mirrored the country's irresolution. As the nation rebounded after the nightmare of the Depression, it chafed beneath a cliché as old as Homer, heard everywhere: *the storm clouds of war.* The entertainment industry quailed. When Kraft picked up Bing's option in June 1940, it inserted an opt-out clause to be used in the event the United

States declared war. As the storm clouds broke and Bing soared to greater heights of popularity, the cheese maker's fear seemed hapless and panicky. Another vogue phrase also caught the mood of vacillation: *phony war*.

A few weeks after Germany launched the Second World War with a blitzkrieg on Poland's eastern border and a day after the Soviet Union invaded Poland from the west, Senator William Borah, the blustering Republican isolationist from Idaho, told a reporter, "There is something phony about this war." His remark made international headlines. The mocking British press called the slack eight months that followed the Allied declaration of war a *sitzkrieg,* or a sitting war. Britain dispatched planes to Germany to drop leaflets rather than bombs (launching another epithet: *confetti war*) as France hunkered behind its supposedly impregnable Maginot Line. Borah perceived an upside in Europe's feeble response, reasoning that if the combined might of the Nazis and Red Army proved "too big a bite to chew," the Allies would fold their hand and back off from further involvement in the conflict.[32]

For the United States, the stalemate continued long after Hitler bestirred Europe in April and May of 1940, invading Denmark, Norway, the Low Countries, and France, the last commemorated with the führer's little jig. On September 7, his Luftwaffe initiated the first of fifty-seven consecutive nights of bombing London, killing more than forty thousand civilians. In America, the twenty-seven months between the subjugation of Poland and the attack on Pearl Harbor required patriotic double-bookkeeping, waving the flag while opposing foreign entanglements.

Rage disfigured urban and rural America. Thugs took anti-Semitism to the streets of Boston and New York while diplomats sanctioned it in the State Department, particularly during the tenure of the vile quota-spouting assistant secretary of state Breckinridge Long. Roosevelt ignored anti-lynch legislation for fear of losing his reliable Southern support. On May 3 (Crosby's birthday, coincidentally), an act of Congress decreed the third Sunday in the month I Am an American Day. Then as now, Congress considered that a decent day's work. Was the country leaning toward war? Certainly not, the president said. Yet it could not renounce its responsibility to help friends. Roosevelt cannily addressed the press corps on neighborliness in terms that exceeded the folksiness of his Fireside Chats. Refining an analogy he had used as early as 1916, when as assistant secretary of the navy he had stumped for President Wilson's reelection, he evoked something more akin to a *Kraft Music Hall* skit than a strategic argument and delivered it in the spirit of a top banana. "Suppose my neighbor's home catches on fire and I have a length of garden hose four or five hundred feet away," he proposed. "If he can take my garden hose and connect it up with his hydrant, I may help him put out the fire. Now what do I do? I don't say to him before that operation, 'Neighbor, my garden hose cost me fifteen dollars; you have to pay me fifteen dollars for it.' No! What is the transaction that goes on? I don't want fifteen dollars—I want my garden hose after the fire is over."[33]

Three months later, FDR's garden hose morphed into a bill permitting him to "sell, transfer title to, exchange, lease, lend, or otherwise dispose of, to any such government" any defense article he deemed vital to the defense of the United States. Churchill called the Lend-Lease Act the most "unsordid act in the history of any nation." Yet at least four-fifths of the American public opposed intervention and would have parted with the garden hose only for cash on the barrelhead. As isolationists on the Right and Left accused him of warmongering, Roosevelt pursued a program of aid and preparedness. He urged rearmament, chose a revered Republican as secretary of war, sent castoff destroyers to Britain, reconfigured the navy as three fleets, posted "Liberty ships" in support of Allied convoys, relegated Axis ships to "protective custody," and froze Japan's assets, all in the name of making America the "arsenal of democracy" without making war.[34]

Americans went about their business, which, for the vast majority, included one or more weekly visits to movie theaters, and shrugged off the nation's first peacetime draft, signed into law in September 1940. All men between twenty-one and forty-five were required to register for a one-year commitment, decided by lottery. Within a year, the period of commitment doubled. Would we or wouldn't we? Meanwhile, the entertainment industry scattered its own versions of phony wars, all of which, it turned out, involved Crosby at the center or on the margins. On the lighter side, there were phony feuds, played for laughs and facilitated by the immediacy of live radio. Bing exchanged quips with his contemporary Bob Hope in what became a thirty-five-year-long joke that spread to pictures and television; he would later accede to a more delicate fake spat with the first singer to challenge his dominion, Frank Sinatra, who played the amiable aspiring son to Bing's breezily tolerant father.

Far less playful was the scuffle Bing initiated with *Kraft Music Hall* that occupied him for much of 1940 and 1941 and proved to be a warm-up for his postwar assault on the authority of network radio. He would soon play a significant if ancillary role in the pointless battle occasioned by ASCAP's arrogant demand for tribute in the form of hiked licensing fees. This aggression triggered a network strike that lasted well into 1941, altering the terrain of American music while doing little to increase the standing of ASCAP's songwriters. Bing's reluctant compliance with the strike hastened its end. More detrimentally, in 1942 the American Federation of Musicians followed with a recording ban that created long-lasting havoc, though it ultimately boosted Decca's footing as Bing recorded a hit with a choir instead of musicians ("Sunday, Monday, or Always"), and Decca's chief, Jack Kapp, made peace with the union a year before the other record companies followed suit. A darker struggle unfolded beneath the radar of the public as new technologies were suppressed by broadcast monopolies in order to outlast competitive copyrights. The networks reneged on promises to the FCC to make television commercially available by the end of 1940. They stymied the implementation of higher fidelity frequency-modulation (FM) radio to protect their AM fiefdoms. The pioneering inventor Edwin H. Armstrong demonstrated the advantages of FM radio and was ruined by RCA's nuisance suits. These ended after the network finagled its own FM copyright, at which point Armstrong had already taken his own life. Biding his time, Bing would eventually help to democratize broadcast technologies, but that effort, also, would have to wait out the war.[35]

A remarkable thing happened in that dangling will-we-or-won't-we interim between the phony war and Pearl Harbor: a brief but glorious cultural regeneration, which most people took for granted at the time and later forgot about or conjoined in memory with the broader canvas of the 1940s. The two-year interregnum of creativity coincided with a burst of optimism epitomized by the New York World's Fair. Despite the faltering economy and hovering war clouds, forty-five million people traveled to Flushing Meadows to experience the World of Tomorrow with its hydroelectric Democracity and Con Edison's City of Light ("wonder city of the modern world") and General Motors' Futurama, which predicted how life would be in 1960. When the fair shut down in October 1940, Bethlehem Steel carted away four thousand tons of the fair's structural steel and alchemized it into ships and armaments.

In retrospect, the promised futurity is far less dazzling than the vibrant highs of American civilization at its irreverent best, as it was in 1940 and 1941, especially in its songs. It is impossible to educe from this flurry of musical invention the static of the America First Committee, the German American Bund, and other unholy alliances of those years. Were these new melodies any less real than the hatreds and fears of the era, any less indicative of the time and place? It wasn't only music. The fiction of 1940 suggested a level of accomplishment and promise that virtually vanished in the four years that followed Pearl Harbor. When jurors for the Pulitzer Prize convened to honor a novel for 1940, they found nothing worthy. Yet their rejects included Ernest Hemingway's *For Whom the Bell Tolls,* William Faulkner's *The Hamlet,* the last bow of Willa Cather (*Sapphira and the Slave Girl*), a benchmark of genre fiction (Raymond Chandler's *Farewell, My Lovely*), and three first novels that endured as classics: Richard Wright's *Native Son,* Carson McCullers's *The Heart Is a Lonely Hunter,* and Walter Van Tilburg Clark's *The Ox-Bow Incident.* Publishing itself undertook a revolution unmatched until the advent of e-books, as the paperback line of Pocket Books went into full production and, exploiting a Hollywood hit, made an unlikely bestseller of *Wuthering Heights.*

At the same time, Hollywood ramped up its creative energy by importing Alfred Hitchcock from England (*Rebecca*), Orson Welles from radio (*Citizen Kane*), and promoting John Huston (*The Maltese Falcon*) and Preston Sturges (*The Great McGinty*) from the ranks of its screenwriters. Old-line directors flourished too, Ernst Lubitsch with *The Shop Around the Corner,* Charles Chaplin with *The Great*

Dictator, ~~William Wyler~~ with *The Letter*, John Ford with *The Grapes of Wrath*, Michael Curtiz with *The Sea Wolf*, Frank Borzage with *The Mortal Storm*, Frank Capra with *Meet John Doe*, Howard Hawks with *His Girl Friday*, and Walt Disney with *Fantasia*. The fact that Victor Schertzinger's *Road to Singapore*, which introduced the team of Bing and Bob, topped the 1940 box office indicated the remoteness of war and the surplus of irreverence. Yet the army was fast encroaching on Hollywood; a year later, two fugitives from vaudeville, Bud Abbott and Lou Costello, broke house records with *Buck Privates*, the first of the service comedies that portrayed the armed forces as year-round summer camps with free smokes and frequent visits from the Andrews Sisters. The top-grossing movie of 1941, *Sergeant York*, honored an ambivalent World War I hero played with hillbilly humility by Gary Cooper, incarnating the nation's reluctant resolve to meet the moment.

Yet nothing in this grace period proved more astonishing than the American output in music. If the country was whistling past the graveyard, it had a hell of a repertoire. No *sitzkrieg* here; who could sit still surrounded by the thumping of swinging four-beat rhythms and the whirling helix of eight-to-the-bar boogie-woogie? When we speak of the Great American Songbook, we refer to songs composed from the mid-1920s, when a generation of songwriters shucked off the contrivances that made Tin Pan Alley a factory of greeting-card platitudes, to the 1950s, when musical styles rocked into a new phase. In that quarter century, songwriters gauged their accomplishments against the inventiveness of their interpreters, writing not for amateur singers and pianists in bourgeois parlors (the target arena for their predecessors), but for performers who could mine every nuance in an urbane lyric and a showy harmonic sequence. They flattered the tastes of an eager and discerning new audience that would rather listen to professionals than participate in amateur musicales. If the 1930s brought pop songwriting to a summit, the deluge of songs in 1940 and 1941 represented a capstone, an onslaught that combined pop and jazz, Latin American and country music, folk and blues.

Nearly a hundred standards emerged in this calm before the storm, so many that the most zealous jitterbugs could not keep up; some of the best-known titles had to wait years to get a proper hearing—four years for "Lover Man," which found its voice in Billie Holiday; ten for "Because of You," which Bing sang superbly on *Kraft Music Hall* but unaccountably did not record, allowing it to hibernate until 1951, when it launched Tony Bennett's career. Only time and diverse interpretations could do justice to "How High the Moon," "I'll Never Smile Again," "Fools Rush In," "Blueberry Hill," "It Never Entered My Mind," "Blues in the Night," "Polka Dots and Moonbeams," "I Don't Want to Walk Without You," "The Nearness of You," "Imagination," "Taking a Chance on Love," "I Concentrate on You," "Walking the Floor Over You," "You Don't Know What Love Is," "You've Changed," "I Understand," "Boogie Woogie Bugle Boy," "Key to the Highway," "When You Wish Upon a Star," "You Are My Sunshine," "Chattanooga Choo Choo," "My Ship," "Take Me Back to Tulsa," "Deep in the Heart of Texas," "Bewitched, Bothered, and Bewildered," "The Last Time I Saw Paris," "How About You," "I Could Write a Book," "Goin' to Chicago," "Bésame Mucho," "You Stepped Out of a Dream," and, though no one paid attention to it until 1942, "White Christmas"— all created within two years. Most significant about this list is not the number of songs familiar to devotees of American song but the fact that almost anyone, no matter how hidebound by twenty-first-century biases, is likely to know at least a few.[36]

Then there were the hugely popular instrumental numbers, every bit as emblematic of the era: "Frenesi," "After Hours," "Moonlight Cocktail," "Tuxedo Junction," "String of Pearls," "Snowfall," "Pennsylvania 6-5000," "Harlem Nocturne," "Solo Flight," "What's Your Story, Morning Glory," "Blue Flame," "Tickle Toe," and dozens more, not least Jay McShann's "Swingmatism," which introduced a young saxophonist from Kansas City named Charlie Parker. Glenn Miller's recordings (eight number one hits in 1940) did so much to juice the economy that RCA Victor manufactured the first gold record to certify the million copies of "Chattanooga Choo Choo." Tommy Dorsey peaked. Jimmy Dorsey peaked. Gene Krupa peaked. But the most dazzling achievement in orchestral music belonged to Duke Ellington, who, after a dozen years as the acknowledged master of big bands, reached a pinnacle where he could do no wrong. In addition to songs that thrived in the pop marketplace ("All Too Soon," "I Got It Bad and That Ain't Good," "Don't Get Around Much Anymore," "Do Nothing Till You Hear from Me"), he wrote concise instrumental masterpieces that reformed the mood, texture, and ambition of American music: "Cotton Tail," "Jack the Bear," "Ko-Ko," "Conga Brava," "Harlem Air Shaft," "Warm Valley," "Blue Serge," "In a Mellow Tone," "Jump for Joy," "Just A-Sittin' and A-Rockin'." His brilliant young protégé Billy Strayhorn, spurred by the ASCAP strike that hobbled Ellington, added major pieces of his own, including the band's theme song, "Take the A Train." Every one of these records made money.

While swing enjoyed a lock with the public, two other jazz idioms shot into view, exploring its past (the New Orleans revival) and anticipating its future (modern jazz, or bebop, cobbled together at after-hours jam sessions in Harlem). A more conspicuous antithesis to swing was embodied by a songwriter who experienced as liberating a rebirth as Ellington while remaining in every other respect his total opposite: the wandering troubadour from Oklahoma, Woody Guthrie. As the Popular Front inspired politically active singers and songwriters to create anthems for the labor movement, boosting a new brand of folk music that contrasted with the slick urbanity of Tin Pan Alley, Guthrie showed up like the answer to a prayer. He wrote songs as easily as talking, never more effectively than in 1940, when he composed "Pastures of Plenty," "Union Maid," the Dust Bowl ballads, songs celebrating the Bonneville Dam, and dozens more, including "This Land Is Your Land." He thrived in New York. He'd have had a harder time in his home state. In Oklahoma City that year, a mob torched Woods' Progressive Bookstore and its inventory, including stacks of the Constitution and the Declaration of Independence. No one was arrested, but the store's owners were sentenced to ten years (overturned in 1943) for displaying subversive literature.

Another kind of folk song, rarely considered in that light, also made inroads into pop music, a vein of timeworn evergreens, handed down from generation to generation. Mixed in with ballads from early Tin Pan Alley and newly Anglicized songs from South America, this eclectic tapestry—much of it in the public domain—included Latin classics like "Green Eyes," "Maria Elena," and "Amapola"; laments by minstrel and abolitionist composers, from "De Camptown Races" and "Carry Me Back to Old Virginny" to "Darling Nelly Gray" and "Beautiful Dreamer"; and a fusion of parlor and slave songs as varied as "On Moonlight Bay," "Sleep," "On

Top of Old Smokey," "When You Were Sweet Sixteen," "John Henry," "My Gal Sal," "Frankie and Johnny," "Wait Till the Sun Shines, Nellie," "Jimmy Crack Corn," "I Know Where I'm Going," and "My Melancholy Baby."

In 1940, the music industry moved fifteen million copies of sheet music, but it sold seventy million records. A year later, the number of records increased by nearly 90 percent, to 130 million records—heavy, brittle shellacs that revolved around a spindle seventy-eight times per minute and usually featured one song per side. In 1934, when Jack Kapp started Decca Records, the recording business was thought to be dead, beyond resuscitation, buried by the free music emanating from its hated rival radio. Now the three leaders—RCA Victor, Columbia, and Decca—competed for artists, distribution, packaging, and pricing. It was not just the industry's best year since the crash; it was its best since 1921.[37]

This was the terrain Bing stepped into at the start of a new decade, as different from the cloistered temper of the Depression as it was from the carousing excesses of Prohibition. Yet this would be the decade he most fully inhabited. He would explore the delicious motley of pop music more deftly and comprehensively than anyone else and in the process become an essential voice of the home front. In the summer of 1940, the year he recorded an astonishing sixty songs, Everett informed him, "Kapp has a pretty nice surprise for you when he goes to the coast in the way of a royalty check over and above your guarantee."[38] Whatever frustration, boredom, or despair he experienced he kept hidden. Even as he contemplated familial and professional ruptures, the public could see only the steadfast strength and reliability celebrated in countless magazine and newspaper stories. His discontents aside, idleness was never an option for the man whose persona hinged on the pretense of laziness—who walked, talked, sang, and acted as if tranquillity represented moral certainty, the virtue of the unflappable. He was about to do his bit in ways he could scarcely imagine, mirroring and defining the times more astutely than he and all but a few men and women had ever done. But first there would be an intermezzo of restless muddle as he tried to figure how an aging crooner might continue any kind of meaningful career at all.

2

INDEPENDENCE

Ay, in the very temple of Delight
Veil'd Melancholy has her sovran shrine.
　　　　　—John Keats, "Ode on Melancholy" (1819)

The year that ended with a threat of domestic crack-up had opened unassumingly on the genesis of a new Crosby. At the start of 1940 no one could have predicted the enormous success of *Road to Singapore*, let alone its transformative power in effecting a makeover in Bing's persona—and a decade-long ascension in his standing as an entertainer. His primary commitment in the months before its March premiere involved starring in and coproducing his third independent picture, away from Paramount, following *Pennies from Heaven* (Columbia, 1936) and *East Side of Heaven* (Universal, 1939). The happy experience of the last inclined him to stick with Universal and the director David Butler, a friend who shared Bing's affection for the outmoded byways of American show business. They decided to make a picture that would document a few of the old-timers before it was too late. Butler contrived a blatantly routine plot as a pretext to mount a vaudeville show within the picture, allowing them to corral a handful of vaudevillians whose occasional movie appearances from decades past were long (in many instances, permanently) lost. Bing later recalled the film solely in terms of those players—"Names I had seen in vaudeville [as] a young man growing up, and when I later played vaudeville myself, I worked with some of them."[1]

If I Had My Way underscored his role as a link to a fading America steeped in traditions of minstrelsy and variety. It provided counterpoint to the cheeky comedy he did with Hope and fell in line with other, better-known pictures that attempted to slake an apparently unquenchable nostalgia for a quaint tradition: *The Story of Vernon and Irene Castle, Lillian Russell, Ziegfeld Girl, Tin Pan Alley, Yankee Doodle Dandy,* and several more. These movies presented a harmonious masquerade, a polished past that eradicated all but the sweetness. They initiated a still-prevalent commercial ritual in which the songs of one generation are profitably marketed to them a generation later as remnants of the best years of their lives. Bing made four such pictures in the early years of the war, starting with *The Star Maker* (1939), a tribute to Gus Edwards's turn-of-the-century "schooldays" troupes, followed by *If I Had My Way, Birth of the Blues* (1941), and *Dixie* (1943). None did as well as Bing's present-day escapades, which set box-office records. But they reinforced his stature as the performer who personified unbroken continuity from then till now.

Crosby developed a trusting relationship with Butler on *East Side of Heaven*. This was essential. The business of coproducing a film made for a different on-set dynamic; no longer just the insouciant star, occasionally standing up to blockheaded producers, he now personally scrutinized the budget, approved minute as well as big decisions, and fought over release dates and promotion. As it turned out, *If I Had My Way* involved one studio altercation too many, inclining him to forgo his right to star in another outside film until after the war.

Bing and Dave Butler went back a long way. Butler directed Dixie as a Fox starlet and introduced her to Bing when he was one of the Rhythm Boys crooning at the Cocoanut Grove—or so he claimed until the day he died. Like Bing, he grew up in the Northwest (he lived through the San Francisco earthquake), bred horses, golfed, and liked to laugh. He performed in the Crosbys' elaborate Marching and Chowder Club parties, where guests cavorted in loosely rehearsed and fully costumed vaudeville shows. He had acted onstage as a child and appeared in dozens of silent pictures before directing his first feature, in 1927. His fascination with the worlds of entertainment informed the subjects of nearly half the sixty-five pictures he directed. His assurance with musically gifted children—he guided Shirley Temple to stardom at Fox—made him perfect for *If I Had My Way*. As keen as Universal was to banner the name Bing Crosby, the studio foresaw longer-term residuals in its new contract player Gloria Jean, a thirteen-year-old soprano whom the studio publicized as eleven.

When it came to singers, movie studios favored the white American vernacular: Crosby at Paramount, Fred Astaire at RKO, Dick Powell at Warner, Alice Faye at Fox. The ever-pompous MGM could not resist classical sopranos if they came with impressive cleavage, yet even there, the waning of Jeanette MacDonald had made way for the domesticated belting of Judy Garland (until Kathryn Grayson upped warbling by an octave after the war). Universal was a bit different; it cultivated operatic teenage girls, having taken on the fourteen-year-old Deanna Durbin after MGM dropped her. Durbin's several hits saved Universal from financial ruin. By 1940, however, she outgrew training bras, underage parts, and the requirements of her masters. So the producer Joe Pasternak went to Manhattan to audition girls for the starring role in Universal's forthcoming *The Under-Pup*. He discovered Gloria Jean Schoonover, of Scranton, Pennsylvania, who came to the tryouts chaperoned by her music teacher. Gloria later surmised that Pasternak liked her because, unlike the other contestants, she did not wear makeup or Shirley Temple curls (she preferred pigtails) and had the nerve to point out that the piano needed tuning.[2]

Pasternak dispatched Gloria and her mother to Hollywood, where she was told she would have to sacrifice her last name and shave two years off her age, the latter a fiction the studio maintained for two years. *The Under-Pup* scored big, and for her second picture Gloria was recommended as costar in *If I Had My Way*. Bing liked her from the start and approved of the casting, a happy pairing for them both. He was amused that she, too, had gotten her start on radio from Paul Whiteman, when his band passed through Scranton. Her winning smile and twinkly eyes radiated unspoiled likability and her nimble instrument easily handled the ornamental trills required of a juvenile movie coloratura.

Vaudeville aside, *If I Had My Way* rehashed the same hackneyed plot points from Crosby's two previous independent films. This time he is a fearless if slightly plump ironworker laboring in a rivet gang on the New Deal's most august construction projects: the Golden Gate Bridge, Bonneville Dam, Boulder Dam. But in line with the earlier films, he is once again a surrogate father to an orphaned girl and finds himself obliged to make good with a failing restaurant. *Variety* reported the deal he wrangled from Universal as "unique," allowing him to finance all or part of the picture with a dollar-for-dollar return on the net profits. The Crosby Investment Corporation, launched by John O'Melveny for *East Side of Heaven,* assumed a quarter of the $810,000 budget.[3] Bing accepted the treatment by Butler and James V. Kern, formerly a member of the singing Yacht Club Boys,[4] and a strong supporting cast, including the veteran scene stealers Charles Winninger and Nana Bryant.

The first of the ex-vaudevillians recruited by Butler became the third lead after Bing and Gloria. El Brendel, a Swedish dialectician associated with the phrase "Yumpin Yiminy," did not have an ounce of Swedish blood to his name, which was Elmer Goodfellow Brendel. Born of Irish and German stock, he started in vaudeville parodying Germans until America entered the war. Glowing reviews brought him to Hollywood, where he scored in two of Butler's early hits. By 1940, he was relegated to two-reelers, yet Butler cast him as Bing's relentlessly mugging sidekick. "They thought he was the funniest thing," a baffled Gloria Jean recalled. "When he was filming we could hear Bing laughing in the background, off set." Of the other bygone stars, three—the singer Grace La Rue, the comedienne and suffragette Trixie Friganza, and the female impersonator Julian Eltinge, a top liner whose career was obliterated by municipal edicts banning cross-dressing—delivered cameo lines. Blanche Ring got to revive her 1909 hit "I've Got Rings on My Fingers," probably because she was married to Charlie Winninger.[5]

The only artist who truly validated the initial concept ultimately undermined the picture's durability: the silky-smooth blackface minstrel Eddie Leonard, singing and gliding through "Ida." Blackface is obviously more nettlesome than a travesty of Swedish, but in 1940, it was Brendel's routine that discomfited audiences, not Leonard's. In what is thought to be his only surviving film appearance, the resilient song-and-dance man provides an authentic peek at his heyday in the 1890s and presages the revival of minstrelsy that gathered strength throughout the war and immediately after. In the film, Crosby introduces him as "sixty-four years young," but he was actually seventy and died within the year. No mere symbol of antiquarian show business, Leonard conjures the racial irony that conflated mockery and tribute, but without the demeaning stereotypes. He toned down his makeup from the darker cork and exaggerated features favored by Al Jolson and Eddie Cantor, demonstrating blithe techniques that anticipate not only Crosby's blackface indulgences (in three films made between 1942 and 1944), but also Ray Bolger's soft-shoe, Hank Williams's yodel, and Michael Jackson's moonwalk.

Not five weeks before *If I Had My Way* went into production, Bing's brother Larry, his publicist and general factotum, wrote him a two-page memo about the film's music, conceding at the outset that Universal knew "I have no authority, except when you give me your opinions." Expressing a lack of confidence in Butler and "his yacht club boy assistant" (Kern), he wanted Bing's support in negotiating the picture's songs with the studio. He argued that Butler and Kern had examined three hundred songs for a Kay Kyser programmer, yet none of their final choices made "the popularity standings." Homing in on his real motive, he pointed out that none of the Gus Edwards songs favored by Paramount in Bing's *The Star Maker* achieved success either, though all the new songs written for that picture and *East Side of Heaven* by Bing's songwriting team of lyricist Johnny Burke and composer James Monaco made the top ten. In short, Larry wanted Burke and Monaco in on the deal for *If I Had My Way*. Larry's advocacy displayed a thin understanding of songwriting. Only three good lyricists write "commercially," he contended: Burke, Al Dubin ("who can't be handled"), and Johnny Mercer ("I know you think he writes very smart lyrics...but the folks don't buy"). He also noted that Burke turned down a seat on ASCAP's board of directors "to come back with us," so he ought to have the "authority to advise on musical matters as well as to write lyrics."[6]

At the time Larry wrote his testy memo, there was no reason to assume Burke and Monaco were not on board for the new film. But he worried for good reason. The Burke/Monaco catalog was controlled by the publisher Santly-Joy-Select, which enjoyed a pipeline to Bing's movie songs since the Crosbys held a financial interest in the company and Larry maintained personal friendships with its partners Lester Santly and George Joy. Wanting to maintain the status quo, he fretted over Bing's friendship with rival songwriters, particularly Mercer. He had been hearing rumors for months about a change but evidently did not know that the discontent lay with Burke, not Bing. In 1939, Burke met the man he believed to be his ideal match: a twenty-six-year-old Syracuse-born Broadway-song plugger who had just begun to display a rare melodic talent in songs like "Darn That Dream" (written with Eddie DeLange) and "I Thought About You" (written with Mercer). Born Edward Chester Babcock, he changed his name at sixteen to Jimmy Van Heusen. He had authority, facility, and charm to spare, and Burke was determined to have him move to Los Angeles and partner with him as the new Crosby songwriting team. First he had to convince Bing.

That took the better part of a year, and his first attempt at persuasion did not bode well. In 1939, Burke and Van Heusen wrote a memorable song, "Polka Dots and Moonbeams," tailored for Bing and presented it to him as proof that Johnny and his New York friend had the right chemistry. Bing, inexplicably, didn't go for it. One might like to think that, reading the lyrics off the lead sheet, he winced at "Now in a cottage built of lilac and laughter / I know the meaning of the words 'ever after' / And I'll always see those polka dots and moonbeams / When I kiss my pug-nosed dream." Yet he had recorded worse in songs that had nothing comparable to the elegant simplicity of Van Heusen's tune, which cemented the song as a pop and jazz standard. Of all the standards in the Burke–Van Heusen songbook, "Polka Dots and Moonbeams" is conspicuous by its absence in the Crosby songbook; not only did he decline to record it, but he never once sang it on the air. It's not unlikely that Bing, in 1939, might have thought recording it an act of disloyalty to Jimmy Monaco, whom he liked and admired. But a year later, he was as gung ho for Van Heusen as Burke, and even after the song became a hit for Tommy Dorsey's boy singer Frank Sinatra, he continued to ignore it. In the 1950s, when his syndicated radio show obliged him to record dozens of songs he had neglected the first time around, he skipped over "Polka Dots and Moonbeams."[7]

So in the early months of 1940, Burke kept his head down,

fulfilling his obligation to write two scores with Monaco and doing excellent work, knowing better than to announce his dissatisfaction to anyone but Bing. By midyear, Bing was on board for the change, but they had to do it quietly and with finesse. Everyone liked the gentle Monaco, and the split-up of a successful songwriting team could be as harrowing as a zapped marriage. Yet no one could miss the tension. Burke and Monaco fought with and taunted each other while Burke surreptitiously promised the moon to Bing, Van Heusen, and, undoubtedly, himself; Jimmy Monaco was twenty-three years his senior—twenty-eight years older than Van Heusen. Burke saw the younger, hipper, jazzier man as a ticket to greener pastures. He was, of course, quite right.

Bing treated Larry's nervous opportunism as usual, by quashing or ignoring it. His standard deal for independent pictures provided for only four people. He paid himself $150,000, his brother-manager Everett $15,000, and "his favorite songsmiths," Burke and Monaco, $20,000.[8] That's the way it stood. Moreover, Bing knew better than to accept Larry's analysis of old versus new songs. Jack Kapp, his mentor at Decca Records, had taught him the shortsightedness of ignoring the array of classic evergreens. The title number of the current picture, "If I Had My Way," written in 1913 and quickly embraced by barbershop quartets everywhere, had produced a magnificent Crosby recording a year earlier. Three of the four songs Burke and Monaco wrote for the picture ("April Played the Fiddle," "Meet the Sun Halfway," "I Haven't Time to Be a Millionaire") also produced hits. Yet they signified a generic songwriting style that restated passé Depression sentiments—look to the sunny side of life; who needs money?—and did far less well than the barbershop number.

Three weeks before he recorded the *If I Had My Way* score, Bing emphasized the point by introducing an unknown ditty that had nothing to do with the movie. "Sierra Sue" had been gathering dust since 1916. It isn't known if Bing, Kapp, or someone else uncovered it, but after Bing recorded the plaintive song, Kapp cannily postponed its release until the Burke/Monaco numbers fell off the charts. Kapp, like Bing and surprisingly few others, understood something crucial about the temper of the phony-war interval. Despite a proliferation of great new songs, the public craved old-fashioned diatonic melodies from the period preceding the Depression, melodies outfitted with platitudes that were at once wistful and soothing. They served as comfort music, a balm, a melancholy medicine for melancholy. Only Crosby could administer them in that vein, reestablishing them as the core of abiding values.

Bing's mood remained upbeat during the filming of *If I Had My Way*. Observers thought he radiated contentment. He enjoyed the cast and crew, especially Gloria Jean and the buoyant Butler, and the Monaco-Burke songs delighted him. The forty-day shooting schedule began February 13 and progressed swimmingly. The studio worried about keeping to its original budget, in part owing to schooling and recreational requirements for Gloria, which reduced her workday to three and a half hours. Butler evaded those restrictions by settling Gloria in the studio's schoolroom between takes, keeping her on call for a full eight-hour day and pulling her out when he was ready to shoot. Gloria didn't mind. She didn't think of it as work and she adored Butler, so "patient and understanding."[9] Once, he adjourned a scene to help her complete an art project. The studio grumbled about "letting Crosby go each Thursday at noon for his broadcast appearance."[10] Costs escalated and hysteria set in when they were forced to shoot around Bing and Gloria for three days after they picked up a contagious skin disease that required the constant salving of facial lesions. They lost half a day after Gloria filmed a scene with a squirrel named Crack that clawed her back.[11] In the end, the ever-efficient Butler, averaging two to three script pages a day, completed the film on time and only five thousand dollars over budget.

From the first, Bing took a protective interest in Gloria, who "loved the man, so sweet and so kind, always cracking jokes and pulling gags. You have favorites when you work in the industry, and Bing was one of my favorites."[12] The day they started filming, he said, "First I want a hug." They laughed about their mutual inability to read music and their experiences with Pops Whiteman. She thought Bing's implacable poise hilarious, especially at prerecord sessions when he parked his gum on the microphone, remarking, "This is one of my bad habits." Gloria began chewing to imitate him. They would run through the song and he would ask her if she thought she knew it and she'd say, "I think so," and he'd say, "Me too," and they'd nail it in one take. He repeatedly advised her to stick close to family and beware the sharpies who would try to exploit her.[13] He told her to memorize her lines and marks but not to take things too seriously: "We're going to have fun with this. Throw it away and don't try to act," he instructed before a scene. "He was wonderful with me,"[14] she said.

If tension roiled Bing at home or in his disputes with the imprudent new studio head Nate Blumberg, it was apparent to no one, though he occasionally disagreed with Butler over the staging of his scenes. When it came to songs, he brooked no interference about blocking or interpretation. Yet when Butler had a good idea, Bing nodded and said, "I like that better," and redid it Butler's way. At quitting time he vanished to play golf. Bing spoke to Gloria about his boys and brought Dixie to the set. Gloria thought his family life as idyllic as the fan magazines stated: "Things looked so perfect then. Dixie was lovely, a lovely girl, always smiling and hugging Bing. He doted on the boys. They ran around and everybody loved them. Bing didn't seem strict at all. I overheard some prop men say, 'Bing's gonna have trouble with this one and that one,' and sure enough he did when they got older."[15] Gloria's kid sister, Bonnie, the same age as the twins at the time (six), visited the studio and became friendly with Dennis. She remembered the boys as "well behaved and darling."[16] Gloria heard gossip about Dixie's drinking, but she never saw it—"not like W. C. Fields, who was funny and nice, but out-and-out drunk."[17] Toward the end of the shoot, Bing gave Gloria and Bonnie a dog, Patsy, a "niece" of the celebrated Thin Man dog Asta.

On April 14, the last Friday of filming, Gloria turned fourteen (twelve, by Universal's lights) and Bing threw a party at the studio, bringing his family and inviting her parents and three siblings. She had told him of her crush on Basil Rathbone (who three weeks later starred with Bing in *Rhythm on the River*), so he bought her a gold charm for her bracelet with Rathbone as Sherlock Holmes engraved on one side and on the other: FROM BING, IF I HAD MY WAY, 1940. A *Time* reporter, researching the Crosby cover story that ran a year later, came to the studio that day with a photographer who took pictures of Bing and Dixie and the boys. He wired his editor: "We tried to photograph this same idea at Crosby home but couldn't get everyone together. Would like you to know that this is a very valuable set of pictures since it is practically impossible to even *grab* a shot of Crosby and family. Director David Butler is great personal friend of Bing's, raises horses. It's no gag that Crosby likes Gloria Jean. He really wanted to give her a party, had a great time making a picture with her."[18]

Bing's good feelings prevailed at the Decca recording sessions; his performances are interpretively and rhythmically much heartier than the clip-clop arrangements by John Scott Trotter, his music director on *Kraft Music Hall* and dozens of records. He even prepared a surprise. After recording "The Pessimistic Character," the score's wittiest song and the only one that didn't make the charts, he asked to do a second take. Midway, he offhandedly called the eponymous pessimist a "dirty bastard." Usually this was his way of signaling a reject. But after Trotter conducted the instrumental interlude, he resumed with a parody lyric he wrote as a gift for Butler, whom he called "the old laughing loser," because when he lost a race, "instead of getting angry, he'd start laughing as he tore up his tickets."[19] Decca pressed copies for Butler and friends. It captures better than the legitimate recordings the sanguinity of the moment. Bing's verse alludes to Butler's wife, Elsie, Gloria ("the singing kid"), and a horse named Alice Faye, after the Fox actress who starred in another film Butler made for Universal, *You're a Sweetheart*. As an inducement to get her to do a demanding stunt, he had offered to name a filly for her. Two years later, during the shooting of *If I Had My Way*, the horse Alice Faye won at Santa Anita, paying forty-three dollars on the dollar. This created mayhem at Fox, where everyone had had a bet down. The studio head Darryl F. Zanuck told Butler, "Please don't name your horses after any of the stars. We've lost two hours."[20]

> *Here's the mighty Butler, big time sport,*
> *Floatin' like a zephyr on the tennis court,*
> *Can anybody use him around the place,*
> *The old laughin' loser with the crabapple face.*
> *When he gets a tip on Alice Faye,*
> *He gets so darned busy, forgets to play.*
> *Horse comes in at a fabulous price,*
> *The old laughin' loser with the double-six dice.*

[....]
C'mon Elsie, get your things,
Looks like no one wants us here at Bing's
Let's get the singin' kid and go someplace,
The old laughin' loser with the crabapple face.

Bing displayed a subtler discernment after Butler commissioned an additional ballad from Burke and Monaco. Burke brought the result, "Only Forever," to the studio and played it for a jury consisting of Bing, Butler, the screenwriter James Kern, and the recently installed president of Universal, Nate Blumberg. Johnny remembered: "When I finished, they all looked at Bing. Someone asked him, 'What do you think?' 'I don't know,' he said, looking unhappy. 'We don't really need a song like that.' 'That's what I thought,' said the studio head. 'Let's forget it.' I felt horrible. It was the first time in four years Bing had turned down a song of ours. Then on the way out, Bing stopped me and, lowering his voice, said, 'That song's terrific, but they don't need it. Let's save it for the next show.' So it went into *Rhythm on the River* and was a big hit." It emerged as one of the bestselling Crosby records of 1940 and earned an Academy Award nomination.[21]

Blumberg made another bad call. Bing expected to begin filming at Universal in January, after *Road to Singapore* wrapped in December, but the start-up got delayed by a few weeks, which meant *Singapore* went into release as they were shooting—and instantly broke box-office records. Blumberg, formerly an RKO Theaters executive, knew nothing about making pictures, but he knew a lot about exhibition and recognized a publicity bonanza when it was handed to him. He ordered an early release for the picture for the same reason that Bing opposed it: it would compete with *Road to Singapore*. When Bing learned of Blumberg's plan, he fired off a telegram to Everett in New York, where Blumberg kept his office: UNDERSTAND UNIVERSAL CONTEMPLATES APRIL 27TH RELEASE DATE THIS WOULD BE TWO MONTHS TOO SOON. I WANT YOU TO SEE BLUMBERG AND TALK HIM OUT OF IT. IT IS VERY IMPORTANT AND I DONT WANT YOU TO LEAVE NEW YORK UNTIL YOU HAVE TAKEN CARE OF IT.[22]

Flush with confidence, Blumberg could not be persuaded. Universal released *If I Had My Way* two weeks after Gloria's birthday party, and Blumberg doubled-down on his defiant campaign. He put out ads featuring Bing, Gloria Jean, and the female lead, Claire Dodd (to indicate a romantic angle for Bing, which did not exist in the film), plus the vaudevillians Eddie Leonard and Blanche Ring, under a banner: "You'll get a Bang out of Bing...AS HE SENDS YOU THAT 'SINGAPORE' SWING." His push backfired. The film seized no business from *Singapore*, but it did garner bad word of mouth from those who saw both, one startling in its irreverence, the other an agreeable low-rent programmer. Like all Crosby films, it benefited from cross-promotion with *Kraft Music Hall* and earned a tidy profit. Yet reviewers complained it ought to have been released as a B picture, not an A doubled with cheaper fare from other studios (*Charlie Chan's Murder Cruise* and *King of the Lumberjacks*, among others). Blumberg rued crossing his star when *Variety* reported Bing's plans for another "outside job this year," possibly at Warner or RKO, because "Universal rushed the release of *If I Had My Way* ahead of its original schedule and placed it in direct competition with his Paramount film, *Road to Singapore*."[23] Had he known that Bing did not intend to exercise his freelance option until after the war, Blumberg might have enjoyed a less stressful summer.[24]

If I Had My Way never recovered from its reputation as trifling (*Variety*: "Bing Crosby will likely want to forget this cinematic adventure just as quickly as possible"[25]), a reputation underscored when Universal rereleased it in 1946, to leech off his immense postwar success, as a true B feature, deleting Gloria Jean's big solo ("The Little Grey House in the West," a World War I song) and the entire vaudeville sequence. For sixty years, no one could see the uncut picture; even prints at the Library of Congress, the Museum of Modern Art, and Crosby's personal library ran fourteen minutes short. A slight film, to be sure, but Crosby is in superb voice and an infectiously happy mood, and the script is an instructive period amalgam of public works, Lend-Lease politics, pacifism (Crosby's character proclaims, "One reason this is a great country is because we build bridges instead of bombing them"), unionism, the greedy rich, vaudeville lore, and social wish fulfillment à la Capra.

The conflation of old and new played out similarly on Bing's radio show and in his recordings. In choosing songs for *Kraft Music Hall*, he created a time-traveling montage, ignoring songs with which he had no personal affiliation. This neglect is unique to the prewar period. In previous and subsequent years, he used radio partly as the medium for singing songs he liked but could not record, either because they didn't fit in with his or Decca's plans or because they were sewn up by other performers. Young singers, especially Sinatra, covered Bing; he hardly ever covered them. A few exceptions in the *KMH* lineup reflected Bing's affiliation with the songs' writers or publishers. In particular, he helped to launch two classics by lyricists from the Crosby fold, though he did not plan to record either of them: Johnny Mercer's "I Thought About You" and Johnny Burke's "Imagination." They had in common the same composer, Jimmy Van Heusen, who would soon enter the Crosby circle. "I Thought About You" generated a hit for Benny Goodman with a vocal by Mildred Bailey, who in 1925 had encouraged Bing's career. By singing the song on the air twice (he never recorded it), he boosted Mercer's and Van Heusen's ASCAP royalties, but he left the recording field to Mildred.

"Imagination" prompted a more intriguing legacy. When Burke approached Jimmy Van Heusen, the younger man had recently found a solid interpreter of his songs on his home turf: Frank Sinatra. Jimmy's lifelong friendship with Sinatra began in the days when he demonstrated new songs (not his own) for a Tin Pan Alley publisher. Frank, largely unknown and sporting a yachting cap in imitation of Bing, visited the office in search of material.[26] They hit it off. Then everything changed for Frank. Harry James hired him to sing the vocal choruses on a handful of records, which caught the attention of Tommy Dorsey. Dorsey's band, a pop powerhouse fueled by superb arrangements and jazz soloists, proved an ideal showcase for Sinatra. Yet while Dorsey helped find songs Sinatra could make his own, he also had him cover one Crosby record after another—his film songs and an occasional ringer like "Devil May Care," a middling job by Burke and Harry Warren, an old friend of Bing's. Frank needed songs of his own and Van Heusen, working with the more accomplished Burke, submitted two beauts. "Polka Dots and Moonbeams," the song Bing passed up, turned out to be Sinatra's first hit record and a permanent part of his repertoire; "Imagination" did better. The four songs he recorded with Dorsey at a session in April illustrate his dilemma. Two ("April Played the

Fiddle," "I Haven't Time to Be a Millionaire") were from *If I Had My Way*. "Yours Is My Heart Alone" was an adaptation of a Franz Lehar melody that Bing recorded three weeks before. "Imagination," by the team that would soon become inseparable from Crosby, was the song that bounced Sinatra into the top ten.

It had some help from Glenn Miller, whose version rocketed to number one a few weeks before Dorsey's, and from Bing, who liked "Imagination" so much that he sang it on three *KMH* shows in May and June. The song is still largely associated with Sinatra, but Bing never let it go. He cut a lovely Decca record in 1947, languorous and wistful, and deepened his interpretation of it in 1954 for his General Electric radio show a week after Sinatra appeared on the program to sing duets with Bing. For Bing, the song remained a contemplative ballad of love and loss, harmonically flecked with minor and diminished chords, melodically confined to his mid-range. Sinatra revived it in 1961 as a finger-snapping swinger; Bing adhered to the songwriters' intention: "Slowly, with a lilt."[27]

"Imagination" roused Bing's interest in Van Heusen. Not everyone recognized Burke and Van Heusen's potential to emerge as the 1940s' quintessential songwriting team, but the two most popular male singers of the decade did. When Burke, backed by Bing, offered Jimmy the chance to relocate to Los Angeles, he needed little persuading. Burke worked for Bing Crosby and Paramount Pictures, the top of the heap; Frank was Tommy Dorsey's chattel. Nearly fifteen years later, after Burke quit Hollywood, Van Heusen would sign on as Sinatra's primary composer, teaming with the lyricist Sammy Cahn to kick-start a new career for himself and the singer. In the interim, he and Burke created the new Crosby songbook.

When Bing wasn't plugging his movie songs and Decca recordings on *KMH,* he was idling in another era, often another century: "Juanita" (1850), "De Camptown Races" (1850), "Old Black Joe" (1860), "Silver Threads Among the Gold" (1873), "Carry Me Back to Old Virginny" (1878), and songs introduced when he was in elementary school, like "When Irish Eyes Are Smiling," "On Moonlight Bay," "The Missouri Waltz," "Ballin' the Jack," "Indian Summer," and "Alice Blue Gown." This, of course, fit in with Jack Kapp's Americanist strategy for Bing, a distillation of his style into its purest components—the peerless Crosby baritone as national security blanket. The troubadour approach especially befitted a year commercially dominated by Glenn Miller, who mooted the distinction between hot and sweet bands by creating a romantic sound in love with itself, neither passionate nor erotic. Jazz flowered in the orchestral swing of Duke Ellington, Count Basie, Louis Armstrong, Benny Goodman, Artie Shaw, and Jimmie Lunceford, yet cuteness and honeyed sentiment held dominion. The most successful black group, the Ink Spots, a vocal quartet formerly devoted to hot rhythms, now styled its ballads by alternating the florid high tenor of Bill Kenny (the castrato sound in American pop) with intervals delivered in a deep-bass Southern Negro parlando by Hoppy Jones. The Ink Spots jolted sales for Decca Records. White audiences could not get enough of them during the war.

In the year Bing recorded Earl Robinson's cantata *Ballad for Americans*, dueling for sales with Paul Robeson, he exemplified its hymn to liberal diversity by roaming through musical niches past and present. He recorded cowboy songs, country songs, Hawaiian songs, Irish songs, Mexican songs, the ultimate Lend-Lease canticle ("A Nightingale Sang in Berkeley Square"), and, to keep the pot stirred, two-beat jazz with his friend Connie Boswell[28] and his kid brother bandleader Bob Crosby. He explored each trail vigorously. From the 1913 Mexican waltz "Marcheta" to the 1934 Sons of the Pioneers theme "Tumbling Tumbleweeds," he reinvigorated his upper mordents, that signature ornamental twist with which he buttered good lyrics. His conviction occasionally inspired John Scott Trotter to complement him with loping bass patterns, tight muted brasses, and efficient strings. He was lighthearted in duets with Johnny Mercer ("On Behalf of the Visiting Firemen"). He rewrote and privately recorded a version of "The Girl with the Pigtails in Her Hair" as a birthday gift for Kapp's daughter Myra. Jack liked it so much he asked Sammy Cahn and Saul Chaplin, the songwriters he kept on salary, to revise it for commercial release, which Bing caroled with playful flourishes.

Another aspect of Bing's nature also resurfaced: the undertow of loss and fear, the threat of unremitting loneliness. In the 1930s, his voice did double duty between candidly swinging jazz and the counterpoint of plangent ballads. He was the bard of longing, broken connections, love that almost was or might have been, in recordings of "Home on the Range," "The Last Round-Up," "The One Rose," "My Isle of Golden Dreams." He now looked to an earlier time for even darker elegies, none more so than the practically suicidal "I'm Waiting for Ships that Never Come In" (from 1923), which he recorded as a favor to its lyricist Jack Yellen, whom Bing had met on his first film, *King of Jazz*. The ethereal delicacy of his performance may reflect his memory of the first time he heard it sung—by Mildred Bailey at Jane Jones's speakeasy in the Hollywood Hills, shortly after he and Mildred's brother Al Rinker made their way from Spokane to Los Angeles and she took them in hand, teaching them the ropes.[29]

Jack Kapp heard in Bing's performance the mood of the multitudes. However much the public loved swing, it had another yearning that needed attention. The great novelist and critic Albert Murray wrote at length about blues music being a means of keeping the blues at bay. That's what Kapp understood and what Crosby could convey, the sadness that undermines sadness. To give sorrow words, they reached back to Stephen Foster, that master of lamentation. In this, Kapp had dual motives, both of which placed Decca a year ahead of its rivals. Early in 1940, ASCAP announced its intention to double its licensing fees. Kapp knew this would instigate calamity. While the rest of the industry took a wait-and-see attitude, he prepared for the worst and stocked his shelves with songs in the public domain, particularly Foster's, which he served to Bing, Louis Armstrong, the Mills Brothers, and less significant players on Decca's roster. He fortified his company long before the other record labels followed suit. After the 1941 ASCAP strike curtailed broadcasting of every A-list songwriter in the nation, Foster's nineteenth-century sonnets of parlor and plantation infused the air—one could hardly turn on a radio without hearing someone dreaming of Jeanie's light brown hair.

Some dismissed the Foster revival as sentimental; others found a kind of moral suasion in classic songs that bound generations. The astute critic Otis Ferguson of the *New Republic* wrote, "There is always something lovely and arresting to the heart about a plain song, when it comes unannounced from some place or time where people lived and worked by it."[30] Like Kapp, he heard those songs as a new foundation for Crosby's everyman authority, especially "Jeanie with the Light Brown Hair," the forlorn daydream of a man whose love has strayed, and "Beautiful Dreamer," one of Foster's last songs and his entreaty to a muse even more vaporous than Jeanie. Crosby's performance of the latter is impeccable, perhaps the most convincingly demotic interpretation ever recorded. The song later devolved into a cloying cliché, sung by performers as unalike as Al Jolson, Marilyn Horne, the Beatles, and Jimmy Spice Curry. Bing sang it as written. Composed in an unusual 9/8 meter, it alternates measures of three eighth notes and two quarter notes with measures of nine eighth notes, creating a patient, darting rhythm to which Bing— backed by Trotter's orchestration of strings, clarinet, and flute— brings solemn poise. It's a savory yet little-known recording, for despite Foster's sudden ubiquity (between 1940 and 1942, his songs were featured in at least sixty films), he generated sporadic record sales. "Surely," Otis Ferguson wrote of Bing's record, "if there is anyone Foster himself would like to hear singing those deep-chorded harmonies, it is this man with a voice which seems to indicate the chord change with each note, so free of pretensions and so full of the original wonder, so artless, homely, and right."[31]

At that same session, Bing mined the 1916 elegy "Sierra Sue," by one Joseph Buell Carey, and struck gold. No less depressing than the Foster laments, "Sierra Sue" had the advantage of obscurity. Evidently the only song Carey published, it had lain dormant for a quarter century. Trotter provided a responsive orchestration, laying out in the first bar of each eight-measure episode and enhancing the piece with a nicely rolling lilt that belies the lyrics: "Sierra Sue, I'm sad and lonely / The rocks and rills are lonely too" and "The roses weep, their tears are falling / The gentle doves no longer coo." Bing's stately midrange allows for dramatic low dips, perfectly turned mordents, and modulations that underline the tune's shifting melody. The a cappella measures work like a springing coil. "Sierra Sue" was Bing's first number one hit in over a year, dominating sales in the summer and fall, and his luck persisted with consecutive number ones, "Trade Winds" and "Only Forever." Kapp was right again: forlorn emotion beats no emotion at all.

3

GHOSTS

He really had the capacity of complete calmness. I've never worked with anyone in my life that had this rhythm, easy, easy rhythm. His whole body was singing because of his perfect rhythm. Whether it was a fast song or it was a slow song, it was just a completely natural way of singing.

—Mary Martin (1987)[1]

Four days after he introduced "Imagination" on *Kraft Music Hall* and on the day *If I Had My Way* opened in New York, Bing reported to Paramount to begin shooting *Ghost Music*, the picture released in August as *Rhythm on the River*. This schedule offers one explanation for his mounting restlessness and, specifically, his demand from Kraft for what some considered an unreasonably long summer layoff: fatigue. From 1933 on, Bing usually made three pictures per year, but he took breaks of two to four months between them. This year he had one month between finishing *Road to Singapore* and commencing *If I Had My Way,* and during that month he allowed his fourth annual pro-am golf tournament—a three-day event in January at Rancho Santa Fe—to be filmed for a two-reeler, "Swing with Bing," produced by his friend Herb Polesie and distributed by Universal.

The tournament made news in the sports world for its record three hundred and fifty competitors, including Ty Cobb, and the thirty-six-hole card held by the winner, Ed "Porky" Oliver, who came in nine strokes under par. For "Swing with Bing," intended as a golf promotion and approved by the PGA, actors Andy Divine, Bing's fishing chum, and Mary Treen delivered cringe-inducing comic narration; Bing's dad and his brothers Larry and Ted took bows. Bing had no lines, but he executed the entrechat he had developed in his days with Mack Sennett and recorded a new, soon forgotten Burke/Monaco song, "The Little White Pill on the Little Green Hill," lip-synching, with descriptive hand gestures that are the best part of a frivolous project. The only lasting significance of the venture is that during the prerecord, Bing was accompanied by a young pianist named Buddy Cole who would play a major role in his postwar radio work.

After *If I Had My Way,* the May 6 start-up of *Ghost Music* allowed him only three weeks to recoup and prepare. He considered attending the Kentucky Derby on his last free Friday but ended up spending that night at the dentist. Such, at least, was his explanation for not showing up at a party to launch the Pirates Den, a restaurant in which he and a dozen celebrities—among them Bob Hope, Errol Flynn, Rudy Vallée, Johnny Weissmuller, and Tony Martin—invested a thousand dollars each. The noxious columnist Jimmie Fidler, another investor, took a break from attacking films that were critical of the Third Reich to invent a battle of the baritones between Bing and Martin, a new star at Decca, taking aim in his column: "One more snub from Bing, says Tony, and he (Martin) will start punching."[2] Neither singer would take the bait or play the game. Martin had adored Bing since college, when he drove from St. Mary's, near Berkeley, to see the Rhythm Boys at the Cocoanut Grove. He could hardly believe they were now friends and golfing partners. When he started out playing saxophone, Martin studied Crosby's records to learn how to phrase. "To listen to Bing was taking lessons. He was the master, and a very friendly, charming man," he recalled. "Almost like Will Rogers—he never met a singer he didn't enjoy. He could do it all. Bing sang jazz; he could have sung classical. He had the knowledge and he had a way to do it. He had a wonderful lower pitch too. He was no mouse—he could *cut* that wax. I think if he were at it today, he'd still be a lead singer on the charts. He could do anything."[3] Not much room there for a feud, no matter how fake.

The Pirates Den, on North La Brea, near Beverly Hills, had a clanging ship's bell at the entrance, pirate waiters, and a brig, where a woman customer would be hauled and obliged to scream for release, at which point she received an official scroll for the Best Scream of the Season. There were mock battles featuring bull-whips and "mystifying" drinks served at a Skull and Bones Bar. A year later, patrons were invited to hurl bottles at dummies of Hitler and Tojo. This was an era rife with theme restaurants, most of them short-lived. The Pirates Den hit Davy Jones's locker after an irate mother complained that her son and two friends were charged $6.50 for three sandwiches and Cokes, a piratical price in 1940.

Ghost Music began as a treatment written in Berlin by the Galician-born émigré from the German film industry Billy Wilder. He worked on it with Jacques Théry, whose wife introduced Wilder to the woman who became the first Mrs. Wilder. In October 1939, Paramount bought it strictly as a vehicle for Crosby. Should Bing decline to make it, Paramount would have no obligation to fulfill the contract.[4] Moving the project forward, the studio hired Théry to write the script but quickly dismissed him in favor of Wilder and his current partner, Charles Brackett, a sought-after team thanks to two recent triumphs: Mitchell Leisen's *Midnight* at Paramount and Ernst Lubitsch's *Ninotchka* at MGM. They labored on the script for barely a month, when it was taken away and handed to Dwight Taylor, known for his work on RKO's Astaire-Rogers musicals. Bing brought in his favorite gagman Barney Dean to punch it up.

This was a blow to Wilder, not least because of his admiration for Crosby; he had been a fan of Bing and the Rhythm Boys since hearing their records with Paul Whiteman. After the war, as an A-list director, Wilder fashioned *The Emperor Waltz* around Bing. He even provided a bit part for another Rhythm Boy, Harry Barris, in *The Lost Weekend*. But Wilder's and Brackett's labors on *Ghost Music* were scrapped, and in later years, he denied that he deserved the story credit given him and Théry. "All he did," Wilder's agent Irene Heymann related, "was sell a story to Paramount, which they completely changed. He said they messed it up completely. It wasn't at all like his own story."[5] Wilder told Cameron Crowe for the book

Conversations with Wilder, "It was a good story, and I sold it, but then they used just one little detail. And that was it." Five decades after the fact, he had no difficulty recalling details of his original treatment:

> The full story was of a man in New York who was a kind of Cole Porter. He did the words and the music; he was the number-one man in the country. We see now, through the backstairs, there comes a young man and he...is the ghostwriter for the music. Then we see a girl, who comes later, without knowing the man. She brings him the lyrics. In other words, the Cole Porter character has got two people who are ghostwriting for him, because he's suffering from writer's block. The boy and the girl meet...they're going to stay together and make a name for themselves: "Goodbye, Mr. Porter." And now the two get married, and she's pregnant, and they cannot get a job—because they're good ghostwriters, they keep their mouths shut about what they did previously....They cannot sell anything. They sound too much like Cole Porter! Now the third act was—which they did not use—about a great writer, an Irving Berlin type, who comes up to see them....[He] becomes the ghostwriter for the two. That was the story. They made *Rhythm on the River* out of it.[6]

Wilder protested too much. Except for the pregnancy and third act, his description is a fairly accurate rendering of the film Paramount released, albeit as a chaste romance with a softer edge than in Wilder's telling. Taylor's script is wreathed with clever lines of a kind that reflected the humor of *Kraft Music Hall.* The film's glossy look honors the Paramount house style: ritzy art direction, bright lighting, and extended two-shots that encourage the illusion of an improvised give-and-take. In 1964, Wilder revisited the songwriting angle and a roundelay of false identities in his Las Vegas sex farce *Kiss Me, Stupid,* a coarser picture lacking the gentleness and insider humor of *Rhythm on the River.* Rarely has the songwriting world been shown with a more knowing wink than it was by the director Victor Schertzinger (then flying high with *Road to Singapore*), who lived part of its story. Schertzinger had been a successful composer and lyricist who suddenly lost his ability to write songs. The movie seemed to give him a musical lift. In the brief time left to him (he died in 1941 at age fifty-three), he wrote his three most durable songs, "I Don't Want to Cry Anymore" (used in the picture), "I Remember You," and "Tangerine." Bing, too, took the story personally and made it a jazzy tour de force.

Rhythm on the River triggered a brief picture career for Mary Martin and a longer if spotty one for Oscar Levant while hastening the breakup of Burke and Monaco. It changed the status and look of the movies Bing made for Paramount over the next fifteen years. His earlier films offered ample pleasures: strong scores and supporting players, solid productions. Their reliable profits buttressed his standings at the studio and in the industry. Still, few of those films were considered important; they were Bing Crosby vehicles, as opposed to pictures starring Bing Crosby. Despite the Crosby clause in his contracts, which prevented the studio from billing him alone or above the title (he figured he would get the acclaim for a hit no matter the size of his billing, while a flop would be charged to his costars), most of the actors he worked with were relatively unknown. A few had the talent and staying power to become genuine stars (Carole Lombard, Joan Bennett, Martha Raye); most of them quickly faded (Kitty Carlisle, Mary Carlisle, Shirley Ross, Madge Evans, Louise Campbell). It was considered wasteful to pair him with a box-office draw. The audience lined up for Bing as it later did for Elvis Presley. The costars were interchangeable.

Road to Singapore helped to alter the equation. Beyond his and Bob's paranormal chemistry, it was a mild comedy, but it spawned a franchise that got funnier and edgier with each outing, supplanting Crosby's usual crooning romances. The film's unforeseen success, the annoying interest of other studios wanting to poach Bing, and Crosby's impatience with the quality of his material stirred Paramount to give *Rhythm on the River* the full benefit of its particular gloss, typified by the shiny, multidimensional, satin-draped art direction of Hans Dreier. If George Robinson's stargazing cinematography in *If I Had My Way* flatters Bing more than Ted Tetzlaff's objective approach does in *Rhythm on the River*, Tetzlaff's affluent look emphasizes Bing's easy command of screen space. *Rhythm on the River* was a better picture than *Singapore* and his other recent outings. It promised him entrée to smarter films and stronger ensembles in future.

He was not the kind of actor whose middle age would lend itself to family comedies (Bing as dad with wacky kids) or thrillers (Bing as detective, cop, spy) or Westerns (Bing with a holster), options taken by his contemporaries. Despite his seductive charm, he emanated a willful aloneness that resisted romantic clinches. As Crosby's days of serenading the girl in close-up vocals waned, a new persona emerged: the character who achieves success reluctantly and whose aloofness borders on neurotic reclusiveness. The tendency had always been there, but with reason; his characters were self-absorbed because of alcoholism (*The Big Broadcast*), egotism (*We're Not Dressing*), devilry (*Here Is My Heart*), or irresponsibility (*Sing You Sinners*). In the 1940s films, his brooding isolation is enigmatic. Beset by a dark, drizzly November in his soul—tuned in, fed up, put out—his character believes he might be content if he abandoned his talent (he was often cast as an artist who depreciates his art) for a catboat or an out-of-the-way inn or a religious vocation. Indeed, on May 14, eight days after he began work on *Rhythm on the River,* partially set at a getaway called Nobody's Inn, Paramount closed a deal with Irving Berlin to provide songs and a basic plot for a project titled *Holiday Inn.*

Mary Martin, who grew up in Weatherford, Texas, listening to Bing for hours at a time, spotted shyness as a component in his transformation. "He was always very breathy, very sexy. It didn't matter if he just said hello, everybody would like it. I did. No one in the world could make that sound," she recalled. Yet when they began shooting, "he was absolutely terrified of any love scenes, any close-ups, any kissing. He was even more shy than I was. I felt pretty romantic. I mean, you know, with him singing to me. He really was a very shy man and he would put the love scenes off until the very last minute. That had to be done at the very end of the picture, and then he'd get on his bicycle and ride off as fast as he could."[7] Bing was probably not responsible for casting her, though he had full contractual approval of his leading ladies. He did not even realize that he had attempted to further her career a few years back. At a time when she was making the rounds of the studios, accumulating rebuffs for a "neck too long, cheeks too thin, nose too round, hair wrong color" and a smile "that photographed like a chipmunk," she landed a job singing the midnight-to-dawn shift at a nightclub called the Casanova.[8]

Mary's repertoire included an arrangement of a song that was hot in 1936, "Shoe Shine Boy," by Sammy Cahn and Saul Chaplin, a team that specialized in writing rhythm numbers for black bands. It was one of their early vaudeville novelties, revamped for Louis Armstrong in the New York stage show *Hot Chocolates*. Audiences loved it and Armstrong's luminous recording inspired notable versions by Bing (with Jimmy Dorsey's band), Fletcher Henderson (featuring Roy Eldridge), and Count Basie (his first recording, featuring Lester Young). Mary liked the tune and so did a steady customer: "This man kept coming in all the time with a group of people and he'd ask or send a note, would I sing 'Shoe Shine Boy.' He looked familiar, and finally I found out it was Bing Crosby, and practically had a stroke because he came in so often, always sending a note, would that girl sing 'Shoe Shine Boy.' Naturally, I loved doing it."[9]

During the first week on the set of *Rhythm on the River*, between shots, Harry Barris, cast as a jazz musician in the picture, sat at a piano and played to break the monotony. Mary asked if he knew "Shoe Shine Boy," and as he went into it, she sang along. Bing wandered by and mused about a girl who used to sing it that way in a club; he'd listened to her many nights, even took the trouble to arrange a screen test, but when he'd tried to contact her, she had left the club for another engagement and he was unable to locate her. "I often wonder what happened to her," he said. Martin told him, "I'm that girl." Having reunited over "Shoe Shine Boy," they wove their missed connections into the script: Bing meets Mary in an elevator and flirts unsuccessfully. When they meet again, he is indifferent, though she thinks he's stalking her.[10]

For Mary's one previous film, *The Great Victor Herbert*, Paramount had modeled her makeup on Claudette Colbert's and Jean Arthur's, both of whom she vaguely resembled, while costumers had mummified her in crinoline. According to Martin, she attended a dinner party one night and sat next to Colbert's husband, who, until she began speaking, did not seem to notice she was not his wife. *Rhythm on the River* restored her sense of self: "Making movies with Bing almost made Hollywood worthwhile. He is the most relaxed, comfortable, comforting man. No matter what happens he can ad-lib, cover up, and carry on. He can even sing with gum in his mouth, he just parks it over on the side."[11] Bing fought for her at Paramount and eventually hired her as a cast member on *Kraft Music Hall,* where she replaced Connie Boswell. Martin was happily married (though she and her husband were thought to be gay) and the absence of sexual tension between Mary and Bing enhanced their mellow magnetism. A sly alertness, a mutual sparkle in their eyes, bound them as neatly as their voices.

Oscar Levant, the pianist, wit, memoirist, and professional neurotic known chiefly for his wisecracks on the radio show *Information Please,* also got a second lease in Hollywood as a result of his mordantly funny turn in *Rhythm on the River.* A lifelong nicotine fiend, he makes his entrance in a cloud of smoke as Billy Starbuck, assistant to the songwriter Oliver Courtney. Basil Rathbone, the Shakespearean actor turned matchless villain and Sherlock Holmes impersonator, imbues Courtney with a fussily distracted narcissism. Learning of his lyricist's death, he paces the floor mumbling, "Croon, spoon, tune, soon." He was the only film star in the production other than Bing. The studio signed Levant because of his popularity on radio: "When I informed them that I couldn't act, my modesty beguiled them and I was signed for three pictures."[12] He thought Rathbone a "stuffed shirt," yet they display a fine, ironic rapport. He got along well with Schertzinger, whose musical talent he genuinely admired and who allowed him to inject his own dialogue. With Bing also ad-libbing, they foster an atmosphere of offhand kibitzing. Levant waged a battle with Schertzinger's assistant director, Hal Walker, to avoid prerecording his piano. He won, for good and ill. Live playing gave him the opportunity to insert fragments of Rachmaninoff and Chopin, but his absurdly ornamental accompaniments were intrusively overmiked. He could pretty much do as he liked; in one shot, he reads his memoir, *A Smattering of Ignorance,* and grimaces. Bing first met Levant, the son of Orthodox Jewish immigrants, in 1920s New York when he played piano with Ben Bernie's orchestra. Bing sat in one night and Levant accompanied him on "It All Depends on You." After *Rhythm on the River,* Bing often recruited him as a guest for his radio show.

The picture brims over with allusions to *KMH* involving appearances by his bandleader John Scott Trotter and his announcer Ken Carpenter, who hawks, instead of cheese, a beauty cream that also functions as a salad dressing and a motor lubricant. Crosby filled the cast with cronies and acquaintances, his personal repertory troupe of actors who showed up in uncredited bits year after year, among them the silent-screen villain Brandon Hurst (ten Crosby films) and the Prohibition-era dancer Richard Keene (fourteen Crosby films). In addition to casting Harry Barris, whose songwriting ("Mississippi Mud," "I Surrender, Dear," "Wrap Your Troubles in Dreams") had done so much to launch his career, Bing insisted on parts for his old friend William Frawley and his devoted jester Barney Dean. He hired Jimmy Cottrell, his classmate and a former welterweight champ of the Pacific Northwest, as property man, which led to Cottrell's long career at Paramount and his lifelong friendship with Oscar Levant. "I'd rather have their collected correspondence on my bedside table," Bing wrote, "than the exchange between George Bernard Shaw and Ellen Terry."[13] He insisted on the film having a strong jazz component.

The New Orleans–born, language-mangling trumpet player and vocalist Wingy Manone, who began recording the same year as Bing (1926) and enjoyed the unlikeliest hit record of 1935, a croaking riff-laden rendition of "Isle of Capri," found a new audience with *Rhythm on the River* and subsequent appearances on the Kraft show. With his broad Armstrongian trumpet sound and gravelly voice, Manone served as a standard-bearer for traditional small-group jazz in a world of swing. Bing liked his playing, his jivey lingo, and his outlook: anything for a laugh. He was also a walking repository of high-grade pot, which he stored in the prosthesis that replaced his right arm, lost in a childhood streetcar mishap.[14] Dixie reveled in the moonfaced jazzman's antics and encouraged him to discard his manners when playing at posh clubs and parties in Palm Springs and Del Mar—he felt obliged to sound pretty, and she insisted on gutbucket blues.[15] In *Rhythm on the River,* Wingy leads an unemployed band, its instruments in hock. Bing's character, Bob Sommers, hires him to help audition his songs.

He'd been told to be on the film set at eight a.m., and Wingy rankled at having to hang around until his few scenes came up. For three days, he played cards with Harry Barris and filmed random shots, wearing the requested blue pinstripe. On the fourth day, he showed up in brown and was sent home to change. The director was mildly upset. He reserved his tantrum for the day he called Wingy in to do the "Rhythm on the River" jazz number, an outstanding set piece in which Bing sings and paradiddles his drumsticks (the only time he did this on film) on the walls and counters of a hockshop before leading the high-stepping band out the door. Bing was not needed that day, as he didn't have to be in every shot, but Manone said, "Let's wait till the boss gets here." Schertzinger angrily insisted that *he* was the boss. Manone finally relented and later boasted that Schertzinger so liked the scene—often singled out as the best in the picture—that he invited Wingy to sit in his box at the Hollywood Park races.[16]

The pawnshop jam session's "Rhythm on the River," with Bing demonstrating a preternatural ability to use props (Fred Astaire's toy-store number in *Easter Parade* borrows from this scene), is as close as the film gets to a production number. The song's unusual ten-bar melody unleashes the jazz band. Everything else is a solo or a duet, rarely more than a chorus in length, accompanied by solo piano and often interrupted by extraneous noises, as when Bing drolly sings "When the Moon Comes over Madison Square," a cowboy parody, over the shouting of a music publisher.[17] As Bing's ghostwriting love interest, Cherry Lane, Mary Martin burnishes "Ain't It a Shame About Mame," a rare example on film of the expressive wit that would make her a Broadway legend, the first genuine rival of Ethel Merman, who once observed, "She's okay, if you like talent." No less unusual than the unceremonious presentation of songs is Bob's chaste pursuit of Cherry. The film hasn't a single embrace or kiss.

Rhythm on the River represented a change for Bing's film identity, a retreat from the braggadocio he nurtured in most of his 1930s roles. In its place is cheerful conviction exemplified in his nonchalant use of props: flipping the whetstone, lighting a match on his thumb, stroking a dog, manipulating a ladder, playing the precise rhythmic accent on a cymbal he barely glances at. For most of the film's running time, Bob Sommers flouts authority, at the end accepting it grudgingly as the price of indulging his dreams of irresponsibility. Imperturbable, pipe in hand, stain on shoulder, jest at the ready, he is as content to be a ghostwriter as Courtney is to be a fraud. Yet in teaming with Cherry, he trades ghostly indifference for pragmatic clout, forcing Courtney to accept them as artists as long as they accept the charade of Courtney's bogus reputation. He remains self-reliant but is no longer cocky and somehow no longer whole. Yet the new Crosby persona's desire for a reclusive independence deepened. *Rhythm on the River* is a rehearsal for the more obstinate attitude displayed in *Holiday Inn* and *Blue Skies*.

A week before the premiere, Paramount arranged for a press screening of *Rhythm on the River* at the Del Mar racetrack, preceded by an hour-long radio broadcast emceed by Pat O'Brien to present cast and score. The day began gloomily on the golf course when a doctor from San Diego had a heart attack and collapsed and died in Bing's arms. Several hours later, Bing and Mary and other cast members, enthusiastically backed by Trotter's orchestra, romped through the movie's songs at the track. Paramount used the occasion to release an ominous photograph of the Crosbys that newspapers invariably captioned as a rare family shot. Spokane's *Spokesman-Review* gave it a perplexed headline: "Bing Crosby and Family Make Interesting Group." Bing, with his youngest son, Linny, on his knee, wears his straw hat low on his forehead and looks grim, as does a clearly fatigued Dixie. Gary and Phillip appear bored. Only Dennis grins.

In late August, the film premiered on both coasts. At New York's Paramount Theater, the show was topped with Will Bradley's band, singer Dinah Shore, comedian Ken Murray, and the Mexican singer Tito Guízar, who introduced several songs that Bing successfully Anglicized, including "Solamente una Vez" ("You Belong to My Heart"). At Los Angeles's Paramount Theater, the show was on the bill with Count Basie, whom one reviewer described as "African as the gnu."[18] Most critics liked the film. In the *New York Times,* Bosley Crowther contrasted it with the year's "supercolossal" duds; Paramount's picture seemed shot "'off the cuff'—and, behold, it turns out to be one of the most likeable musical pictures of the season," with Bing's "apparent" ad libs "beautiful to behold." The *Chicago Tribune*'s pseudonymous Mae Tinee wrote, "It's gay! It's provocative! It's casual as a breeze and friendly as—Wendell Willkie." *Time* swooned over Levant, the "first-rate crooning by Crosby and Martin, lively trumpeting by famed one-armed Swingster Wingy Manone," and "Scenarist Dwight Taylor's smooth lines." *Variety* reported, "Some may tab this as the best picture Crosby has appeared in for several years," a sentiment echoed in *Film Daily*. The trades noted better-than-average box office, and "Only Forever," a million-seller, beat "God Bless America" as radio's most plugged song.[19]

Bing, however, was in a funk. The columnist Sidney Skolsky contacted him as he left for Del Mar and requested a comment for his series "Actors Looking at Themselves." Exceeding his usual diffidence about his "modest" achievements, Crosby revealed spasms of doubt. "I'm bad," he told Skolsky. "I'm awkward. I underplay everything. After I see myself I wish I could do it again." Of his singing, he groused, "It sounds the same all the time. I wish I sang louder. And I wish I took off some weight."[20]

Uncertainty also prevailed in the snake pit of music publishing. In *Rhythm on the River*, Cherry Lane says you have to have something to hold yourself together. Bob Sommers asks what holds *her* together, "Polka dots and moonbeams?" It was probably intended innocently, a reference to a hit song that broke for Dorsey and Sinatra weeks before the scene was shot and an insider's nod to Burke. Yet it may have disconcerted Monaco, who had received a similarly approving salute from Crosby in *East Side of Heaven*. Johnny Burke and Jimmy Monaco were coming undone in the belligerent divorce Bing had hoped to avoid. Their tempers had never matched; Monaco placid and flexible, Burke proud and confrontational. The music publisher Santly-Joy-Select had a lot at stake. Lester Santly fretted over Johnny's tendency to "rile himself up at Jimmy, whose simple habits seem to offend [his] very active mental mechanics." He wrote George Joy that Monaco "is as intent on quitting Burke as Burke is on quitting Monaco except that poor Jimmy is very sweet about it and wants out because he doesn't want to cause anybody any trouble." Heartened by Larry Crosby's affection for Monaco, Santly hoped they could keep the two as a team. To do that, he figured they would have to keep Bing ignorant of the quarrel. Fat chance.[21]

Intent on securing the publishing rights to future Burke/Monaco scores—including a reputedly brokered assignment for a Kay Kyser picture—Santly tried to fend off Johnny Mercer and his publishers, "for there is no doubt that if Bing heard about this controversy

he may want to do Mercer that favor…and a crisis of this kind
between the writers would only make Mercer that much more
important." Confident that Select would have the inside track if
they could keep Burke and Monaco together and unaware of
Burke's determination to land Jimmy Van Heusen as his partner, he
hoped "the boys" would cool down in the summer.[22] It was not to
be. Mercer landed the Kyser film. When Bing needed a song for
Birth of the Blues in 1941, he assigned it to Mercer. But in helping
Mercer, Bing was buying time until Van Heusen committed to
Burke. Paramount informed Crosby's office, with Bing's foreknowl-
edge, that it would not renew Monaco's contract (Bing continued,
all the same, to record his songs).[23] In the end, when Larry realized
that Van Heusen was ready to go to Hollywood, having agreed to
work with Burke on a Jack Benny film (costarring Mary Martin), he
submitted to the inevitable and cut himself in. He signed Van Heusen to his agency with an understanding that Select would share in
the team's publishing rights.[24] The way was paved for the new team
to embark on Crosby's next picture, *Road to Zanzibar*—as soon as
Bing sorted out another tempest, on the radio.

4

PREWAR AIR WAR

*I am not fond of acting, but it's a living. I can't help sing-
ing. My preference is radio first, then screen, and stage if
I must.*

—Bing Crosby (1939)[1]

After his New York stage triumphs of 1931 and 1932, notching all-
time house records at the Paramount Theaters in Manhattan and
Brooklyn, a synchronous phenomenon stemming from his breakthrough on network radio, Bing jettisoned concerts entirely. He
divided his performing life into thirds: records, pictures, broadcasting. Records were easy and movies paid best, but radio was the
arena he loved—and griped about—most. It was the sole achievement that brought him to the brink of boasting, not of his own
contribution, but of having brought to the air the "Blue Book of the
loftiest talent in show business"[2] while collaborating with "some of
the best writers and producers I ever had the pleasure of working
with."[3] Radio was in his blood, and by 1940 he incarnated the very
heart of American broadcasting. He helped define the medium and
remained loyal to it long after his peers left for television. Radio
had inaugurated the Bing persona when he aired locally in Los
Angeles and refined it when he went national in New York. Bing
changed the attitude and bearing of radio from oracular to cracker-
barrel, lampooning its highfalutin mid-Atlantic pretensions with
his singular version of the everyman vernacular. Radio and a theat-

rical satire of it led directly to the feature film (*The Big Broadcast*, 1932) that initiated his two decades of stardom at Paramount. After he took over *Kraft Music Hall*, in 1936, NBC promoted its Thursday schedule as Bingsday.

But radio made onerous demands on his time. Unlike James Cagney and Bette Davis, Bing never declared war on his picture studio to command better parts; unlike Frank Sinatra and Sarah Vaughan, he never fought his record company for better songs. He did wage wars on radio about everything from the freedom to choose songs and guests to the freedom *not* to have a studio audience and a pompous announcer. The biggest battles involved the advertising agency and network that broadcast his longest-running program, *Kraft Music Hall*, and the ultimate outcome revolutionized radio, converting it from a live to a recorded medium, a transformation that influenced the development of television. If the second of these battles, in 1946, had that transition as a specified motive, the first one, in 1940, reflected a muddle of contrary objectives.

That year proved to be a turning point in the expansion of radio. When Bing first sang on the air with Paul Whiteman, in 1928, local stations had been up for barely a decade, and networks were in the mewling stage. Millions of families rushed to buy radios as the price of consoles fell, but the vast majority of those families were urban, Northern, and white—factors reflected in network programming. Radio sales plummeted at the start of the Depression but picked up markedly a few years later. From the time he debuted on *KMH*, with eighty-five stations relaying the program around the United States and most of Canada, he knew exactly what kind of show he wanted. When his listeners sent him letters complaining that he didn't sing enough, lacked an on-air audience (a live laugh track, in effect), or featured types of music they didn't understand, he wrote back to explain his ideas. "I am sure you would tire of me if I sang at you for a full hour...We are not using a studio audience as cheer leaders, preferring to entertain listeners at home in a direct and personal way....Maybe we can all stand a little education and come to like things we do not now understand—as grand opera or jazz."[4]

By 1940, radio reached a near-saturation point with urban whites, approaching 95 percent, while rural America averaged a mere 18 percent. Manufacturers of radios had every reason to expect the numbers to continue rising, but war shut them down a year later when the government halted the manufacturing of home receivers in favor of electronics needed for military operations. Receivers vanished from store shelves and were not restocked for the next five years.

Encouraging the networks' sociogeographic bias were the authoritative Hooper ratings. Hooper created a percentage system calculated from random phone calls to listeners in no more than three dozen American cities, ignoring small and poor rural areas. A Hooper rating of 16.1 meant that 16.1 percent of the radio audience tuned in to a particular broadcast. Most programs ranked well below 9 percent, dozens below 3 percent. Double-digit ratings indicated a better than respectable success; a rating of 20 points, let alone the 30 points achieved by very few programs, indicated a smash hit, a broadcasting staple. The stars who could pull that off walked on rose petals and, if their shows were produced by the J. Walter Thompson advertising agency, sported orchids, which were dispatched as accolades by Thompson's innovative chief of radio production, John U. Reber. Bing once described Reber as "a crafty and dour-faced Pennsylvania Dutchman." His power reflected the fact that the airwaves were largely controlled by the agency clients, who coveted hit shows to promote their goods.[5]

American radio was "owned" by four highly unequal networks, two of them operated by NBC: the prevailing Red network, which broadcast nine of the ranking top-twelve shows in the early 1940s, and the second-tier Blue network, the home of commentators Walter Winchell and Lowell Thomas, the quiz show *Information Please,* and the situation comedy *The Aldrich Family.* In 1943, after years of antitrust litigation, the FCC forced NBC to divest itself of the Blue network, which remained a second-tier network, in 1945 rebranding itself as the American Broadcasting Company, ABC. CBS, NBC's only real competitor, had two of the top-twelve shows. The fourth network, the Mutual Broadcasting System, debuted almost a decade after NBC and CBS and organized its affiliates as a cooperative; it aired mostly news commentary and did not score significant ratings until it latched onto *The Lone Ranger* and *Superman* during the war. Altogether the four networks offered some three hundred and seventy nationally sponsored programs, along with hundreds if not thousands of local shows created by affiliate stations, ranging from insomniac after-hours talkfests to five-minute fillers. Radio was a live medium; *one* sponsored network show, on Mutual, played recorded music. NBC and CBS prohibited recordings on network broadcasts.

More than fifty women's serials ran roughshod over the daytime schedule, but prime time was dominated by variety shows, of which there were nearly a hundred, emphasizing music or comedy or blending the two. In January 1940, twelve shows could boast ratings of 20 points or higher. Here they are in order of their Hooper ratings:[6]

1. *The Edgar Bergen and Charlie McCarthy Show.* Comedy variety, NBC (34.6)
2. *The Jack Benny Program.* Comedy variety, NBC (34.1)
3. *Fibber McGee and Molly.* Comedy variety, NBC (30.8)
4. *One Man's Family.* Family drama, NBC (28.7)
5. *The Lux Radio Theater.* Prestige drama, CBS (26.9)
6. *The Pepsodent Show Starring Bob Hope.* Comedy variety, NBC (25.0)
7. *The Kraft Music Hall* (Bing Crosby). General variety, NBC (23.3)
8. *The Fitch Bandwagon.* Musical variety, NBC (22.4)
9. *Major Bowes' Original Amateur Hour.* Amateur variety, CBS (21.6)
10. *Kay Kyser's College of Musical Knowledge.* Quiz variety, NBC (21.2)
11. *Pot o' Gold.* Variety giveaway, NBC (21.1)
12. *Walter Winchell's Jergens Journal.* Commentary, NBC Blue (20.0)

In the 1940s, Crosby earned an average annual Hooper rating of 20.2, though individual broadcasts fluctuated greatly. This meant that *KMH* ranked in the area of seventh- to twelfth-most-popular show on the air; it peaked at number three in 1945, by which time all radio ratings began an irreversible decline soon to be accelerated by the advent of television. In the realm of general or musical variety, Crosby was way out in front, and on July 4, 1940, when the

show began airing at nine p.m. EST instead of ten, his number
jumped three points, to 26.5, despite having to compete with the
popular Major Bowes. His ratings were especially impressive because
KMH was a one-hour show—one of three on the list; the other two
were Major Bowes's show and *Lux Radio Theater*—and had been
on the air longer than most. Although it achieved its greatest success in the Crosby years, it was an institution that existed before
and, for a short time, after him. The extraordinary diversity of his
guests gave the show a unique status, particularly with the press,
generating more daily newspaper previews, reviews, news briefs,
and best-picks than any other variety show ever had.

Before America entered the war, Bing's Hollywood guests were
often characterized as middling celebrities, booked from a stable of
well-known character actors. Several major stars held themselves
aloof from the airwaves or were enjoined from appearing on *KMH*
by studios that didn't want them playing second fiddle to the prince
of Paramount. Even so, the guest list from any period during Bing's
tenure is dazzling. From January to May 1940, for example, performers who participated in *KMH* sketches included Humphrey
Bogart, Maureen O'Hara, John Garfield, Basil Rathbone, Ida Lupino,
Frank McHugh, Lon Chaney Jr., Madeleine Carroll, Johnny Mercer, Gloria Jean, Randolph Scott, Lucille Ball, Joan Bennett, Ralph
Bellamy, Marlene Dietrich, Sabu, Errol Flynn, Kay Francis, Walt
Disney, John Payne, Raymond Massey, William Boyd (Hopalong
Cassidy), Brian Donlevy, Wendy Barrie, Geraldine Fitzgerald, Olivia
de Havilland, and select directors, writers, and sports figures who
knew how to stand at a mike and read lines.

In those same five months, the songs were handled almost exclusively by Bing and his backup group the Music Maids, plus a customary parody or bazooka solo by the show's resident hillbilly
comedian, Bob Burns. Yet *KMH* presented far more music than
that. Bing's flair for getting the masses to sit still for classical music
had been much praised during the 1930s. Now, with dance bands
appearing everywhere else, he raised his ante in the classics,
encouraging performers to lighten up in the *KMH* spirit. So Mischa Levitzki played "Valse" and accompanied Bing on an Italian
wedding song. Holland's Coolidge String Quartet played Tchai-
kovsky's "Andante Cantabile" and Percy Grainger's "Molly on the

Shore." While propagating classical music, these performers also brought internationalism to American radio. The musicians included Catalan cellist Gaspar Cassadó, the teenage Czechoslovakian pianist Robert Virovai and soprano Jarmila Novotná, Austrian harpsichordist Alice Ehlers, Norwegian soprano Kirsten Flagstad, Russian husband-and-wife piano duo Vitya Vronsky and Victor Babin, Swiss pianist Rudolph Ganz, German sopranos Lotte Lehmann and Elisabeth Rethberg, German harpist Mildred Dilling (whose pupils included Harpo Marx and Bob Hope), and Oscar Levant, who played Scarlatti and Debussy when he wasn't doing comedy sketches.

All in a typical five-month span. A prime-time twenty-first-century TV show with comparable reach on network or cable is unimaginable, but neither was it an easy achievement in the 1940s.

According to Bing, his association with Kraft began when Reber, who had launched the most successful stable of radio programs of any agency (Rudy Vallée, Burns and Allen, and Eddie Cantor were among the most resilient), convened a meeting to discuss who should replace Paul Whiteman as the emcee of *Kraft Music Hall*. At that August 1935 meeting, the producer Herb Polesie, a Crosby friend, proposed Bing and was met with a chorus of general agreement. Reber sent Polesie and the agent Tommy Rockwell to Saratoga, where Bing was attending the races, to offer him the job at three thousand dollars a week. Polesie described his idea for staging the show with a proscenium arch modeled after the Palace, New York's premier vaudeville house. Bing nodded, but added one proviso: "No audience. None of that phony bowing and applause."[7] When Reber heard this, he exploded. He would not work with "a performer who didn't abide by the rules of radio," which mandated "applause and reaction from the studio audience."[8] Yet weeks later, Crosby signed a twenty-six-week contract with J. Walter Thompson, pledging his exclusivity to the "Kraft-Phenix cheese program," to broadcast at ten p.m., "New York Time," from a studio in Los Angeles or New York. Reber paid no attention to the final line regarding locations, to his eventual regret.

It was understood that Bing would "sing and act as master of ceremonies," "participate in dramatic scenes," and attend rehearsals. Reber insisted on another point: "Mr. Crosby will not improvise or use extemporaneous material."[9] This didn't bother Bing, but

Thompson's unwillingness to hire an announcer did. Weeks before the January 1936 debut, Reber promised to look into it but noted that NBC provided "entirely satisfactory" announcers and Thompson had no money to hire one as a dedicated cast member for *Kraft Music Hall,* to which brother Everett Crosby responded by telegram: SORRY TO LEARN FIRM SHORT OF MONEY STOP WITH PROPER INTEREST MAYBE WE COULD LOAN YOU A LITTLE.[10]

Bing got some of his own back: "It is understood that there is to be no audience for rehearsals or the broadcast. Mr. Crosby will have the right to select the songs he is to sing."[11] The dramatic scenes never materialized, and extemporization or its simulacrum quickly accounted for much of the program's singular charm. A month into Bing's tenure, the agency hired the announcer Ken Carpenter, who stayed with Bing for the entirety of his radio career. The no-audience clause was breached, inevitably, by invitations to family, friends, and friends' friends, who begged for coveted tickets. Observers figured Bing's closed-door policy reflected his refusal to dress up and wear a toupee; his worn green hat, Hawaiian shirts, and unmatched socks were much discussed by guest stars who admired his sartorial insouciance, an extension of Bing qua Bing. The true reason for his not wanting an audience did not fit the Bing persona—he balked at having to entertain and elicit laughs. He had given up doing live performances because he preferred radio's anonymity. He imagined himself as a singer with a standardized script. If he happened to say something droll, well and good, but he couldn't be *expected* to amuse the customers.

In this he was the reverse of Bob Hope, who would not work without an audience, who relied on the audience to perfect his timing, to react and laugh and love him. Bing would have to be eased into loosening up and enjoying the audience, which, in addition to friends and insiders, soon included soldiers and sailors, whom he could hardly refuse admittance. Carroll Carroll, a writer on Thompson's payroll since 1932, was dispatched to create a radio personality for Bing that was drawn from the crooner's genuine irreverence and flair for slang. In no time, the show was associated with hearty laughter, despite its directive to function as a music hall. Welcoming applause was discouraged; impulsive applause had to be tolerated. Bob Burns, warming up the audience, requested that visitors mute their enthusiasm—and, lo, the silence gave the show a brisk, even-keel tempo that complemented Bing's carefree delivery.

Given the show's successful maiden year, the balance of power shifted, as the Thompson executives learned in January 1937, when Reber sent Bing substantially the same two-page contract. This time it had options to carry their association through 1940, at which point Bing would earn four thousand dollars per show. Three weeks went by with no response, prompting *KMH*'s director, Cal Kuhl, to write Everett: "What the hell are your solicitors DOING to our little agreement? Hand lettering it on parchment? Illuminating it with real gold leaf, and colors wondrous rare, brought from Samarkand and other foreign strands? Are they raising sheep in order to make the parchment?"[12] When Bing's revision was returned for countersignatures, it had grown to seven pages. It added a proviso that Bing always be billed on top in Kraft publicity, in a font as large as that used for any other artist. No one could argue with that. It went on to permit Bing, with a month's notice, to absent himself from as many as eight non-consecutive shows per year, without compensation. It stipulated that rehearsals not require his presence before one p.m.; gave him right of approval for lines "spoken by him on any such program"; allowed him to appear "solely for charity" on six non-Kraft shows a year; and "if at any of said times the Artist shall be in or near the City of New York, New York, said broadcast may be made from a station in said city to be designated by the Company."[13]

More surprised than angered by the implication that he did not safeguard Bing's interests, Reber immediately wrote Kuhl a twenty-two-hundred-word letter complaining how unrealistic and unfriendly it was for Crosby's lawyers to turn a simple statement of agreement into a document nitpicking "every conceivable" contingent. After all, up till then, there had been no major differences with Bing, so where did all this legalese come from? In the Kuhl letter, Reber addressed the new demands point by point. He would permit outside appearances on a drama series like *Lux Radio Theater* (a J. Walter Thompson program), but not on a variety show that would cheapen Bing's value as an exclusive Thompson artist. He was incensed that Bing would consider appearing on a show sponsored by a tobacco company, as it would alienate "millions of people in this country who do not think cigarette smoking is a good thing." *Of course* Bing would be the principal figure in Kraft advertising, but Reber would not sign a guarantee to that effect, as he could not police every printout for every Kraft event.[14]

He was aghast at the idea of Bing asking the agency to produce shows in New York and assumed that only lawyers unfamiliar with show business could make such a request. Bing never would, Reber insisted, because he knew that to do so would involve contracts with the cast, the orchestra leader, the announcer, and other members of the production. He acknowledged that his secretary had called his attention to the New York phrase in the original contract, but he could not imagine how it got there—"obviously it should not be that way so we are changing the opening paragraph to provide for Hollywood origination only."[15] Reber agreed to the eight nonconsecutive weeks off, however much they might "interfere with sales operations," and okayed afternoon rehearsals as well as "the entirely unnecessary" provision regarding Bing's approval of dialogue—as if they would ever "ask Bing to do any lines that he did not feel were...in good taste."

Reber addressed the revised contract to Bing personally (the Crosby version did not mention lawyers, only Harry L. Crosby Jr., J. Walter Thompson, and Kraft-Phenix) and asked Kuhl to forward it with a request that he sign it in timely fashion. Kuhl sent the agreement to the Crosby office, enclosing a copy of Reber's letter, which turned out to be a shrewd move. Along with the other points, Reber explained why Thompson could not guarantee the requested number of guest tickets for each show. But Bing never asked for that; Everett, who wanted them for himself, had put that in. Other provisions were also unknown to Bing, while the one dearest to his heart had been omitted. Bing penciled on Kuhl's cover note: "Ev, I wish you would close this up. The only objection in present form is *Maximum vacation* period—which should read *13 weeks not eight*."[16]

The contract was amended to grant him thirteen weeks off, consecutive or intermittent. He was still enjoined not to "improvise, extemporize or use unapproved material," but by this time, Carroll had found ways to get around that, and everyone knew that it was Bing who made his scripts work—scripts vetted three times before going into rehearsal, first by Bing, then by the Thompson office, and finally by a representative of NBC, who, as Bing recalled, "had absolutely nothing to say as to the content of the program." Still, network brass reserved the right to ensure good taste. "In other words," Bing recalled, "each network had its own censor," and in the event NBC disapproved of anything, a representative came "to our office to smooth our ruffled feathers."[17] If the program's panache lay in the illusion of spontaneity, no illusion was necessary concerning the merrily buoyant disposition of Bing's songs. He refused to rehearse them.

Bing argued for a better contract for his original bandleader, Jimmy Dorsey, but that became unnecessary when Dorsey opted to join the Swing Era, facilitating the entrance of John Scott Trotter— a musically conservative choice but a stylistically diverse one, and a perfect personality fit for Bing. Trotter was a tireless workhorse (he went 186 weeks without a break at the start of his *KMH* tenure) who wrote a staggering amount of music, maintaining quality while mastering the art of invisibility: orchestral accompaniment that frames the singer without calling attention to itself. Bing could forgo rehearsals because he trusted Trotter absolutely. At one point the agency suggested changing Bing's theme song, "Where the Blue of the Night Meets the Gold of the Day," or modernizing the arrangement, an idea Bing rejected as ludicrous. By the melody's third note—a comely half note, preceded by two eighth notes in a guileless rhythmic and diatonic buildup—everyone recognized it as heralding Bing. Why in the world would you mess with a theme that effective? When his option came up in 1938, Bing was so sanguine that he allowed print ads for Kraft Macaroni and Cheese Dinner to include his signed photo, providing he okayed the picture.[18] In turn, Thompson responded favorably to his concerns about up-and-coming technologies; should anyone offer Bing a commercial radio-television series, the agency had sixty days to tender a competitive television deal, or Bing could cancel his contract at year's end.

The 1938 agreement included a schedule of options through which Thompson hoped to control Crosby and freeze his salary (at five thousand dollars per show) through 1950, a commitment that dwarfed the infamous seven-year contracts of the picture studios.[19] Surprisingly, Bing let it go; perhaps he understood that this twelve-year extension, verging on indentured servitude, would work in his favor if and when he did sue for his release. He also shrugged off the agency's refusal of an eminently fair raise. Larry Crosby pointed out that other sponsors had offered to double his salary and Kraft's production budget. Bing didn't care. The *KMH* stint had become so pleasant, why roil the waters? Larry asked for permission to explore other options. Bing responded brusquely: "No change contemplated now, while show goes well, Kraft budget is their affair, not mine."[20]

Bing reiterated his affection for radio in a letter to a stranger. Although well known for cold-shouldering the press, Bing reserved part of most days for answering mail, especially from young fans— especially young fans at Catholic seminaries. In response to Miss Margaret Duffy, a student at Our Lady of the Valley, in Newark, asking which area of entertainment he preferred, Bing wrote: "I am not fond of acting, but it's a living. I can't help singing. My preference is radio first, then screen, and stage if I must. If one has the vocation, such a life can be a good one. It requires experience, except those lucky breaks in pictures, and an education is a real help in this or any profession." In 1940, his attitude changed entirely.[21]

Bing's show now originated in a state-of-the-art, modern setting. A year earlier, NBC erected the West Coast's first and most self-conscious art-deco-meets-WPA monument to broadcasting: Radio City of Hollywood, a three-story white office building that fronted the intersection of Sunset and Vine with a cornerstone on which the letters *NBC* soared vertically, framed by three deeply inset rectangular windows a full story taller than the habitable part of the building. Commanding more than two acres, it contained eight studios, four of which could seat three hundred and fifty people. Pilots flying into Los Angeles could not miss the roof, a knotty maze of aluminum domes of various sizes. Bing's process remained unchanged. Invited to attend a *KMH* rehearsal with a select audience ("scads and scads of movie folks"), one reporter made his way to Studio G on Thursday at one thirty p.m. and marveled as Bing and the show's guests, Frances Langford, Lloyd Nolan, and William Frawley, "went through their clever stuff, most of which never got over the ether." This dry run, blocked in nonconsecutive sequences without benefit of the orchestra, served as the only preparation for the show heard that evening.[22]

As the 1940s began, NBC considered itself invincible. It bought a page in *Variety* to crow about the results of a readers' poll conducted by the *New York World-Telegram*. Programs on the Red network won fifteen categories, programs on the Blue won four; a mere four categories went to "all other networks"—aka CBS. Winning personalities were Bing, Jack Benny, Lowell Thomas, Arturo Toscanini, Guy Lombardo, and Nelson Eddy. Yet the trade papers reported discontent on the Crosby front. For the first time, Bing publicly feuded with the network and sponsor, asking for a twenty-one-week summer layoff instead of the contracted thirteen weeks (he wanted a month at Del Mar and four in South America, mostly in the horse-breeding mecca of Argentina). He was also dismayed by the irrational strike threatened by ASCAP for 1941, which would bar him from singing just about every copyrighted song anyone ever heard of. Another problem arose about getting good guests. Picture studios recognized the advantages of synchronous promotion, but theater chains owned by those studios complained that radio kept prospective moviegoers at home. Larry questioned the effectiveness of guest turns by their usual character actors, especially after skits involving Joseph Calleia and Lloyd Nolan proved "sad," in his estimation. He thought the answer lay in more music, including featured numbers by the Music Maids, whom Larry managed.[23]

Everything was in flux and the trade papers had no more understanding than Miss Margaret Duffy of the brooding irritation that now undermined Bing's devotion to the airwaves. Reber added to the chaos in June 1940 when he appended to the 1941 option a "war clause": in the event the United States declared war, J. Walter Thompson could terminate its agreement with thirty days' notice.[24] Everett knew Bing could not get a renewal without accepting that clause, but John O'Melveny convinced Reber to expand the wording to stipulate that, for it to take effect, NBC's facilities would have to be unavailable and the sponsor seriously impaired owing to a national crisis caused by war. Everett reminded Bing of bad experiences he had had with despotic sponsors before he hooked up with Kraft and urged him to sign the addendum. Instead, Bing wrote on the memo, "Not going to sign this just now."[25]

He was preparing for his vacation. He would postpone Argentina until 1941, since he could wrangle only two weeks more from the agency, allowing him to depart after the August 8 show and return for the one on November 14, his longest sabbatical from radio since

1935. Bing could do nothing about ASCAP's suicidal behavior, but before boarding a train to New York, he gave a couple of candid interviews regarding the threatened strike.

For a quarter of a century, American music was ASCAP music, and its monopoly predictably spurred bold increases in licensing fees, more than 400 percent for broadcasters during the Depression and its aftermath. The 1940 declaration to double those fees could only be interpreted by the networks as deliberate provocation. Radio responded by launching its own agency to collect royalties, BMI (Broadcast Music Inc.), and calling for an embargo of ASCAP songs. ASCAP's grievances were not entirely without merit. Its members resented radio's capacity to use their music without permission and blamed it for a decline in sales of recordings and sheet music. Yet they aggravated the conflict.

With radio and ASCAP boycotting each other, a catalog of 1,250,000 songs would vanish from the air. ASCAP figured the networks and their affiliates would plead for mercy, a delusion encouraged by the cockiness of millionaire members like the impresario and lyricist Billy Rose. He was certain that radio could not survive without ASCAP songs and advised the organization to trim its sails and subsist on $2.5 million for one year instead of the anticipated $6 million: "It's nothing for songwriters to pinch their belts and be a bit hungry."[26] Larry Crosby told Variety how much hunger was involved: "There are 1,100 authors writing ASCAP numbers...available through 137 publishers," to which Bing added that BMI could not possibly "supply 137 publishers by the first of the year."[27]

Of course, BMI had no intention of functioning as ASCAP's interim substitute. It anticipated creating a rival operation to adjudicate and collect performance fees for its members, who would include unsatisfied ASCAP songwriters and plenty of new songwriters who had been rejected by ASCAP. These were the left-outs, the young and disenfranchised who recognized the strike as a chance to get their songs published and, better still, performed by radio entertainers desperate for non-ASCAP material. It was the last thing ASCAP wanted, but the upside of its assault on radio was a deluge of music from rural America, especially the South: untapped talent working in the genres of country and western, blues, rhythm and blues, Latin, and diverse "foreign" styles. The Crosby office launched one of the first important BMI songwriters, Cindy Walker.

A twenty-two-year-old Texan who started writing songs at the age of twelve but had not yet sold any, Cindy accompanied her parents on a trip to Los Angeles. She had written a song for Bing, "Lone Star Trail," and was determined to play it for him. As her parents drove down Sunset Boulevard, they passed the distinctive three-story Crosby Building, with its protruding semicircle fronts on both sides, opaque glass squares running up and above the entrance, and triple-peaked roof—one of the most appealing structures on Sunset for sixty years. Cindy pleaded for her father to stop, raced in, convinced Larry to let her audition a song, and ran back to the car to retrieve her mother to accompany her on piano. Larry, who later published the song after finagling a copyright percentage,[28] got her a pass to enter Paramount, where Bing had begun shooting *Rhythm on the River*. Bing listened to her during a break and was impressed. He sponsored her to travel to Spokane to perform at a Gonzaga fund-raiser; a newspaper heralded her as a "new radio and screen discovery, a blonde with a Texas drawl."[29] He also arranged for her to audition for Dave Kapp (Jack's brother and Decca's producer of country music), who signed her to the label. In December, Bing recorded "Lone Star Trail" and scored a hit. It was the first of five hundred songs, including "You Don't Know Me" and "Dream Baby," that together earned Walker a place in the Nashville Songwriters Hall of Fame, the first woman to be admitted.[30]

One hit, however, could not carry Bing through the ASCAP ban. He told reporters that he would not return to the air in November if the conflict remained unresolved, which triggered ledes like "Radio will have to get along without Bing Crosby unless he is permitted to sing tunes turned out by the American Society of Composers, Authors and Publishers"[31] and "Bing Crosby, known to Hollywood as 'The guy who never worries,' tonight admitted he was at least perplexed over the falling out of songwriters and broadcasters."[32] He claimed a willingness to leave the air: "It's not that I'm taking sides in this battle. I'm a peaceful person and I don't crave to fight anybody. But how am I going to get enough songs to sing when I eat up five tunes a week on my program?" If BMI couldn't provide him with hit songs, he ran "the risk of having my listeners think Crosby is losing his stuff, if he ever had anything on the ball. Rather than run that risk, I'll drop out of radio until the situation is untangled."[33]

With Dorothy Lamour and Bob Burns serving as *KMH*'s interim co-hosts, Bing traveled with Dixie and Lindsay to New York's Mamaroneck golf course, where he competed in the U.S. Amateur Open, failing to qualify by five strokes. That fall, the country writhed through election-year crusades, this time with the unparalleled novelty of a presidential third term. Roosevelt's enemies and even some admirers cried dictator, but his Republican opponent Wendell Willkie declined to pander to his party's isolationist belligerence. Crosby supported Willkie and placed a thousand-dollar bet on him after getting the election odds from a bookie named Butch working out of Lindy's in New York. Yet in September, Crosby drew a crowd of five thousand to a golf match at the Philadelphia Country Club to raise money for British War Relief. He played a match for refugee children in Boston. All the while, he kept his eye on the main chance; in Boston, he tried to purchase Casey Stengel's Boston Bees (now the Atlanta Braves) and was barred by baseball's commissioner owing to his involvement in racing. When not on the road, he maintained a suite at the Waldorf Astoria, where Larry cabled him that the clock had run out on his Kraft option, since he had refused to sign John Reber's war clause.[34]

The Thompson executives recognized that they were having serious trouble with their most prominent star. It wasn't money trouble, which could always be adjusted one way or another, but something else: indifference, loss of affect, burnout, perhaps even despair and depression, conditions that Crosby could never accept in himself or in those around him. Just as no "other woman" figured in his contemplation to fold his marriage, no rival figured in his inclination to quit radio. Rather, like the characters he played in his movies, he was sick of the game and longed for seclusion or an exotic road trip.

At first, the depth of Bing's anxiety was not fully clear to Reber, Carroll, and the higher-ups who met with him in New York, although after a few meetings, they knew changes had to be made and fast—in time for Bing's November 14 return. A couple of personnel changes had been made already. Kuhl left to produce *The*

Chase and Sanborn Hour for Edgar Bergen and was replaced by a young man, Robert Brewster; Carroll reluctantly accepted the forced assistance of a still younger man, writer Ed Helwick. They would play significant roles in remodeling the show.

Helwick had begun in Thompson's New York office as a delivery boy and was known around the office as a dandy. At six foot three, with wire-frame glasses, a high-rise pompadour, a camel-hair overcoat, two-tone shoes, and glen plaid suits, he was described by one pundit as a "delivery boy in the Adolphe Menjou manner."[35] He wrote sketches at night, and after two were accepted for broadcast, Thompson sent him to Hollywood. Carroll told him to read his old scripts to learn the Crosby lingo and assigned him to the memory spot, a feature created by Carroll in which Bing was routed to a bygone year to sing a nostalgic love song. He also assigned Helwick to write *KMH*'s trademark station breaks. NBC had the most annoyingly constant station identification in radio (and later television): three chimes, each bong underscoring a call letter, the middle bong at a higher pitch than the others. Every half hour, all day long, a staff announcer cued station identification, whereupon affiliates had twenty seconds to identify themselves. To relieve the monotony of the breaks, Carroll and Ed wrote a few lines to segue into the chimes (struck by hand until someone created a push-button recording), complete with sound effects. For example, the announcer gallops in on horseback like Paul Revere, breathlessly shouts, "N [*bong*], B [*bong*], C [*bong*]," and speeds away in a motorboat. When the ASCAP strike prevented the use of "Where the Blue of the Night," Johnny Burke wrote a university fight song, "Hail *KMH*," as the interim theme, adapting the chimes in the song's closing line: "With a hey-nonny-nonny and a hot-cha-cha / Hail K [*bong*], M [*bong*], H [*bong*]." Carroll, ever jealous of his turf, refused Helwick's more ambitious stuff at first, but when he had to take off two weeks for medical reasons, Ed wrote two whole shows and received two Reber orchids. At twenty-two, he was promoted to cowriter, the youngest in network radio.

Bob Brewster was only four years older than Ed, but with his Princeton background and social polish, he appeared relatively mature and experienced—an advertising lifer with the right palaver and a man whose career would extend well into the television era. Unlike Kuhl, who involved himself in every aspect of the program and wrote acerbic postmortems after each broadcast, Brewster functioned as most producers did: he made sure the program as approved aired on time and finished on time without loss of a commercial (always a danger when a guest overstayed his or her welcome). Brewster was happy to serve as Bing's mediator. While shooting *Road to Singapore,* Bob Hope told Bing that the "Eastern sachems at Thompson" prohibited him from mentioning Bing's name on his show. Bing wrote Brewster: "We are at present engaged in the concoction of a picture, scheduled for Spring release, and it would be greatly helpful to its exploitation if the 'Gestapo' could be induced to raise this mysterious ban. After all it's my name and it has been mentioned in spots of more questionable décor, and in terms considerably less adulatory. See what you can do."[36] What Brewster did, in effect, was clear the way for the most enduring fake feud in American entertainment. Brewster got along with Bing, but at one rehearsal he harangued the baritone Richard Bonelli for missing a cue. Bing stepped in to let him know that disrespect to an artist was unacceptable.

Bing now proposed a "radical revision" of the show for his November return, assuming he did return, and Brewster convened a September meeting with Everett and a Thompson executive to review it. They agreed with Bing that there ought to be more music. Realizing that instrumental numbers ("even the best such as Trotter's") drove listeners to their tuning knobs, they proposed adding a woman singer, preferably Connie Boswell. That meant cutting back talk, as a solo by the new singer and a duet with Bing would eliminate six minutes of scripted chat. They agreed that the station-break routines verged on "childish" but thought they should be retained. They agreed that some guest stars ("the glamour girls and boys") had been dismal on *KMH* and resolved to "book people for what they could do, rather than for what they were"—they felt certain Bing would be pleased by an increase in sports figures. Concert spots would be reserved for "the finest in their field," and it would be acceptable to have two concert performers if one was a Kirsten Flagstad and the other a Wingy Manone. In short, the show would "look new without seeming strange."[37]

Yet three days later, while Bing remained in New York, Reber wrote to remind him that in July, Thompson had picked up his 1941 option, incorporating language that Bing and John O'Melveny requested regarding the eventuality of war, and Bing had yet to sign or acknowledge the agreement. Everett assured Reber that the delay had nothing to do with the war clause, and he casually dropped a bomb: Bing wondered whether Kraft would consider letting him out of the contract. Reber, dumbfounded, wrote Bing that no one at Kraft or Thompson would agree to that. Kraft, "a loyal and considerate sponsor," had made business plans for 1941 based on Bing's involvement. He wondered "what could have led you to consider such a possibility." He urged him to sign the addendum so they could move forward.[38]

Instead of signing, Bing took an extraordinary step. He made an appointment with Reber and then skipped it, deciding that if he was going to expose his feelings, he would do so once—with the man on top, the one above Reber and above the J. Walter Thompson agency. With Everett in tow, he went to see Thomas H. McInnerney, creator and head of Kraft-Phenix, the largest dairy outfit in the country. Bing received a shipment of horses from South America, which he escorted to the coast on Monday, October 14. Before boarding the train, he spent forty-five minutes with the man who paid Reber's bills. An erstwhile pharmacist, McInnerney began his corporate rise with the purchase of an ice cream company, Hydrox Corporation. In 1923, he founded National Dairy Products, marketing such brands as Breyers Ice Cream and Breakstone Brothers cottage cheese. In 1930, he acquired his primary company, Kraft-Phenix. Three years later, he began advertising on radio, sponsoring *The Kraft Program*, which was soon renamed *Kraft Music Hall*.

When Bing left his office, McInnerney called Reber and recounted their meeting word for word. Despite Everett's recent query about Bing severing his contract, Reber could hardly believe his ears. He dictated, in Everett's presence, a long confidential letter—seven pages, single-spaced, half procedural strategy, half fly-on-the-wall exposition—and entrusted it to the discretion of four people: Carroll Carroll, Bob Brewster, and the top Thompson executives on the West Coast, Danny Danker and Willard Lochridge.

He began by noting that Bing was simply fed up and that Mr.

McInnerney, with his "remarkable understanding," considered it "entirely possible to make alterations in the Kraft program which will make it wholly acceptable to Bing and insure his enthusiastic cooperation for the future." Promising personally to meet Crosby's requests "without subterfuge or evasion," Reber set about re-creating Bing's meeting with McInnerney.[39]

Bing thought the program "worn out and disintegrating" and did not want to sink with it to the bottom. Five years was enough. He no longer merited the money Kraft paid him: "He had lived out his usefulness and wanted to be let out." Still, he realized he was under contract and, unless McInnerney agreed to the parting, would not run out on the show. McInnerney took the position that they would alleviate Bing's concerns by revamping the show. He raised the ASCAP battle, and Bing, contrary to his recent public statements, insisted it "didn't bother him particularly. He'd have to do the best he could while the fight was going on." He realized the strike was a matter of money and therefore the sponsor's problem. Bing's main issue was simple: he wanted to leave Hollywood between pictures to play golf and attend races in various parts of the country, and he wanted to take his wife and children with him. McInnerney asked about the boys' schooling. Bing conceded that he hadn't thought about that.

Asked to describe his ideal show, Bing said it would be a half an hour with a good orchestra, lots of strings, a small choral group, a girl singer for duets, and less talk. McInnerney didn't rule out the half-hour idea, but he asked Bing to help formulate a follow-up show, as Kraft wanted to maintain its hour of prime time. McInnerney volunteered that Bob Burns had "outworn his usefulness"; when Bing asked the comedian a question on air, McInnerney, listening at home, could answer it before Burns did. He had not favored renewing his contract (which paid him the same amount per show as Bing). Bing leaped to Burns's defense. No one could be funny fifty-two weeks a year, he said, and no man should be on as frequently as Burns—"a comic has one of the toughest jobs on the air." He had advised Burns to take longer vacations to prevent the public from tiring of him. Then Bing about-faced and said that in future he didn't want to do *Kraft* or any other show with a comedian; he disliked begging the studio audience for laughs.[40]

Bing called himself "the laziest man in the world" and said he worked only because he needed money. McInnerney, amused by this, proposed a company benefit for Bing, then griped about having to pay $200,000 in taxes on his $150,000 salary, whereupon Bing suggested a benefit for both of them. McInnerney asked if he wanted more money from *KMH*. Bing said, "No, what was the use?"

Reber suddenly revealed an uncharacteristic tentativeness of his own, hemming and hawing about when and how he might meet with Bing, suggesting that perhaps Carroll ought to sound him out first. He spoke of making this or that adjustment, found himself arguing with Bing's downbeat assessment of the program, then corrected himself: "Let me state as plainly as I can that WE MUST NOT DO THIS." Bing had mulled over his ideas for years and it was his (Reber's) and McInnerney's position that by going along with Bing, they could "have as good a show and perhaps a better one." Nonetheless, "we must be very careful not to lean over backward in our attempt to please Bing." Bing's "admitted laziness" would give them "the opportunity" to provide him with more commercial material, though "this does not mean we are to play tricks on him." He agreed to eliminate Bob Burns ("you must take every precaution to prevent Bob or William Morris from knowing about this letter") and the studio audience, though he would have to get authority to stop printing tickets for people involved with NBC, Kraft, Thompson, and the Crosby office. Finally, Reber noted that McInnerney, rather incredibly, had told Bing he would be able to broadcast the show from various places. Reber began to detail the complexities of such an operation and then thought better of it. He would leave the details for later. He apologized "for not working out this letter in better sequence, but I think it is very important to save even a day or two so I am sending it off and trusting it to your tender mercies."[41]

Crosby's meeting with McInnerney remained a secret from everyone other than those in the tiny circle convened around Reber's letter. Neither the fact of the meeting nor any of its particulars entered the sphere of rumor, let alone public discourse. Yet Bing was not averse to confessing aspects of his distress to *Variety*, which bannered them on the front page. Within days of returning to Los Angeles, after confirming with O'Melveny that he was bound to Thompson for another five years, he told a reporter that if the agency "insisted," he would fulfill his contract, but that he wanted to take it easy for a year or two and that might mean quitting radio or appearing only as a singer, as "he was tired of doing so much crosstalk every week."[42]

Reber's document allows two different interpretations. Either Bing was entirely sincere concerning his dejection, despite his "preference" for radio, or he gave McInnerney—an audience of one—the performance of his life. Either he was genuinely sick of the grind, or he set out to strengthen his hand for subsequent arbitration. His genuine distress would seem to be borne out by his nearly simultaneous decision to terminate his marriage, his resolve to limit his film work, and the tortured, inconsistent reasoning of his argument against radio. In fact, he did not use this rumpus as a negotiating tactic. He did not ask for more money ("what was the use?"), and he did not receive more, though he was certainly in a strong bargaining position. He made it clear, via Variety, that he was unavailable to competing sponsors; Everett refused offers from Lucky Strike and Campbell Soup and declared himself unauthorized to submit Bing to a rival company. All the changes instituted at KMH after his long break might have been achieved through customary conciliation. Most had been accepted prior to his sit-down with McInnerney.

The more cynical interpretation is perhaps warranted by his ultimate devotion to the air—even when he finally broke with KMH, after the war, he continued his alliance with the medium, producing five-minute filler shows into the 1960s—and the utterly uncharacteristic nature of his complaint. His gloom did not extend to his activities as a sportsman or his often-inspired work as a recording, film, and radio performer. Despite the prickly comments to Variety, he presented to the public and co-workers the usual, unruffled, laid-back, funny Bing of legend. One might chalk that up to sheer professionalism. McInnerney, however, was privy to a side of Crosby few would ever see—not the determined Bing who knew what he wanted and took it, come hell or high water, but a Bing flinching from life, in confessional mode, wanting big nebulous changes and not knowing precisely what they would entail.

The day before the November 14 show, Thompson confidently announced Bing's return for the 1941 season, and three weeks later, Bing signed a contract not unlike its predecessors except for two changes: more vacation time and no war clause. The latter came about after Bing told the trade papers he would not continue on the air in 1941 if he could not sing ASCAP songs, and he expected a clause allowing him to cancel his contract if the "supply of music failed to meet his requirements." Thompson blinked; it would drop the war clause if Bing dropped his ASCAP clause. He soon announced that of course he would sing the new BMI songs. "I can't keep on singing those old ones," he said.[43]

In the months Bing remained off the air, he delivered only one sentence on radio, on the night before the election. For Willkie's final broadcast appeal, staged at the Ritz Theater in New York, he was patched in from Hollywood to say, "I personally am against the third term," adding the names of actors—Clark Gable, James Stewart, Lionel Barrymore—who had asked him to represent them. Roosevelt won in a landslide. The next day Bing memoed his father, whom he had put in charge of small financial tasks, "Dad, Send $1000 [on account of] election bet—Air Mail will be fast enough."[44]

The election had been a historic event for broadcasting. The *New York Times* called radio "one of the most powerful weapons in the political arena," estimating that the two parties together spent more than $1.5 million to reach nearly thirty million homes; they also received free coverage provided by microphones that documented every electioneering event. Rallies at Madison Square Garden were televised in experimental transmissions from the Empire State Building and reached an estimated forty thousand viewers. A broadcast-ready voice and a gift for showmanship would now be essential political assets, and in that arena no one could touch the president, whom *Variety* called "the biggest figure in show business," with a matchless rating that peaked at 38.7. An estimated 90 percent of American newspapers opposed the third term, but Roosevelt brought his case to voters via the airwaves and mooted them all.[45]

While most of the nation tuned in for the November 4 election results, Bing returned to Paramount to begin *Road to Zanzibar*, and the *KMH* staff deliberated about Crosby's modified program. Bob Brewster reminded his fellow Thompson executives that a year earlier, critics of the trenchantly funny Fred Allen had convinced him to change his format. His ratings plummeted until he resumed the structure that had made him famous; too much novelty can be a dangerous thing. For another example of that, Brewster might have pointed to an underreported news story that flashed from Italy on November 11. The British Royal Navy successfully launched a novel aircraft attack on Italian battleships anchored at Taranto, the first ever all-air strike on a naval port, sinking a fleet in harbor. It played very well in Japan.

Three days later, with fanfare and high expectations, Bing came home to *Kraft Music Hall*. At some point in the late 1940s, when Bing reached an apex of popularity, a myth evolved regarding his return program and the election. Barry Ulanov reported in his 1948 Crosby biography that Bing declared on air, "As we say in this country, 'the best man won.' Now we must all get behind the President with renewed vigor and faith in him and in our country."[46] That almost certainly did not happen.[47] Yet what Bing and Carroll Carroll actually brought to the show may well have pleased the president more than a postmortem endorsement. Four months before Roosevelt passed Lend-Lease, they dramatized the moral necessity for it by reenacting the last scene from Alfred Hitchcock's film *Foreign Correspondent,* starring Joel McCrea. Hitchcock and his producer Walter Wanger evaded the Production Code and censors by describing their picture as a thriller without political content. It would have been hard to argue that after *KMH*'s adaptation.

The guests were Connie Boswell, making her first appearance in a two-year engagement as a cast member; two pals who worked on *Rhythm on the River,* Wingy Manone and Bill Frawley; and Joel McCrea. Bob Burns was back, and, despite the bother about sketch comedy versus music, the script proved persistently chatty. After Ken Carpenter's introduction, Bing sang "That's for Me" and welcomed Boswell back to the show after a three-year hiatus; Connie sang "Blueberry Hill" and re-created with Bing their famous 1937 duet on "Basin Street Blues." Bing, who rarely mentioned the sponsor's products, segued to the first of the three commercials by tossing the ball to the announcer: "Ken, suppose you get in a little of what it takes to keep us working steady." After Carpenter's fervent ode to Philadelphia brand cream cheese, Bing sang a haunting Polynesian ballad, "Trade Winds," his current number one hit. Unusually, he had recorded it three days *after* Dorsey and Sinatra did, but he won the race, the song doubtlessly enhanced by Dick McIntyre's steel guitar and a dreamy tempo that empowers Bing's full range and tenderly confident reading.

Bing introduced McCrea, at which point Burns also appeared for a lame tête-à-tête-à-tête concerning the actor's tallness, generating gratuitous insult jokes about Trotter's girth, leading Bing to cite a line from Edmund Spenser—or, as Bing called him, "That guy Spenser, Ed Spenser, Spenser with an s...seems to me he was the fella who said, 'He that strives to touch a star often stumbles on a straw.'" McCrea responded with an epigraph from Browning, and Burns came up with one from his uncle Glut, setting up jokes about bubble gum and bubble dancers that convulsed the musicians and few others. Finally, Carroll's script turned to the state of the world.

> McCREA: Kind of does something to you nowadays, doesn't it, to pick up a newspaper and read how the rest of the world is living—if you can call it living.
> CROSBY: As the newspaper editor said in that vital document of our times, the picture *Foreign Correspondent,* that you and Alfred Hitchcock helped Walter Wanger dream up—what is it he says about Europe, "There's a crime going on over there"?

With Carpenter announcing over sound effects (air-raid sirens, explosions, crowd panic) that they are in London, Johnny Jones (McCrea) of the *New York Globe* reports to America, as he does in the film, that "a part of the world as nice as Vermont and Ohio, Virginia, California, and Illinois, lies ripped up and bleeding like a steer in a slaughterhouse." Bing urges him to continue: "They're listening in America, Johnny." As the music swells, Johnny warns, "This is a big story—and you're part of it...Keep those lights burning there...Build a canopy of battleships and bombing planes around them." After the scene, Crosby tells McCrea he has "a hunch that as long as we realize what those lights mean to us, we'll keep them burning." The script then obliges McCrea to effect a bizarre transition, pointing out that the world is shrinking thanks to radio and airplanes—"Things we didn't have back in, well, back in 1906." Ah, 1906, a good year, Bing says, the year George M. Cohan wrote "You're a Grand Old Flag," which he sings after observing, "America's

defense is America's unity and the hearts of a hundred and thirty
million people are inseparably bound together in peace, freedom,
and democracy...We've got to hold on to the lights."

At the thirty-minute mark, which Carpenter observed by saying he
was so pleased to have Bing back on the air, he just had to ring bells
(bong, *bong*, bong), Bing sang "You Are the One," the only song—and
quite dreadful it is—by Carroll and Trotter. Burns did his monologue
and played piano and bazooka. Bing, Connie, and Trotter riffed about
double-talk, setting up Bing's introduction of "that quondam professor of polemics, whilom torrid trumpet player, *Kraft Music Hall* alumnus extraordinaire, a man I have the honor of supporting in a picture
called *Rhythm on the River,* J. Wingstone Manone...Tell me, Wingy,
are you solid?" There followed several pages of hepcat lingo, after
which they performed the film's title song. Frawley, whose gruff
humor made him a favorite on radio and in dozens of character parts
before he found stardom on *I Love Lucy,* entered for more jive. A
man-on-the-street routine enlisted the entire cast to pummel a convoluted joke at the expense of one Denby Danks (Carroll's petulant
revenge on Danny Danker, the vice president at J. Walter Thompson
who fought him on a salary raise) and finished with Bing and friends
singing special lyrics to "If I Had My Way." Trotter conducted "Alexander's Ragtime Band," Bing sang "Only Forever," and the hour concluded with a plea on behalf of the Red Cross.[48]

The transcript does little justice to the delivery, apparently,
because the broadcast was an unqualified smash. Along with sending the orchids, Reber wrote Carroll: "Quinn and I listened at home
of G.E. executive. It was a great show. Proud of it before those we
were glad to impress. Did have to explain [the bubble-dancer joke].
Naughty boys. Bing sounded great. Love, John."[49] *Variety* gave it a
glowing review, acknowledging "the usual half-truth, half-publicity
reports" about the show's remodeling: "More music and more singing there may have been. But it would take a stop-watch to tell the
difference. [Instead] of stressing that the show was 'different,' it
might be truer to describe it as 'better.' It gave every evidence of a
thoughtfully put together entertainment wherein a master-stylist of
song was visited by sundry personalities and all of them talked like
Carroll Carroll," whose "sharply witty" patter might assist H. L.
Mencken's work on "the American slanguage." This surely pleased

Carroll's ego, which was bruised by the addition of Helwick, whom Bing plainly liked better than Carroll.

The review does not mention McCrea, though he dominated much of the show, but it does issue a warning about the lurking menace in "polysyllabic gab," which went unheeded by Carroll and Bing. Bing had apparently changed his mind about working with a comedian; in the weeks Burns took off, he riffed as usual with such comedic foils as Lynne Overman and Benny Rubin. He did increase the percentage of music by featuring members of Trotter's band in solo numbers, allowing them to "get out in the clear and really take their best shots." He introduced the pianist Charles LaVere as a "handy human at a hot session."[50]

Listeners believed it was all spontaneous—that the quicksilver delivery, wheezer jokes, and long setups were made up on the spot. The ratings rose steadily in the next few months, and some observers, including Ed Helwick, who admittedly was biased toward the 1940 to 1942 seasons to which he contributed (before the draft claimed him), considered this to be *KMH's* golden era, a pinnacle in the history of sixty-minute variety. Helwick called it "the least rehearsed program on the air," an observation echoed by a *Time* reporter who told his editor, "A rehearsal never includes complete, dress, all-the-way-through rehearsal, probably the only major air show which does not."[51]

The *Time* field reporter followed the show's production for weeks. The script was delivered to Bing Tuesday afternoon, "the only time he is assuredly home." Bing spent the rest of that day and evening going over it and making changes. Trotter conducted musical numbers with the orchestra on Wednesday, without Bing. By Thursday noon, scripts incorporating Bing's alterations were distributed for a rehearsal that usually began with Bing and the writers lunching at the Brown Derby on Vine Street, followed by a dialogue run-through. Bing sang only a few measures of each song, mostly to cue his faithful audio man Murdo MacKenzie for the actual broadcast. If he didn't know a song, he'd slip out to a restaurant on Sunset that had a comprehensive jukebox and play a recording of it a couple of times. That was all he needed. By the time the invited audience shuffled into Studio B, "everyone connected with the program except Bing is dripping fright and sweat. During the rehearsal he is completely insouciant," the *Time* reporter noted. He described Bing's apparel, including a green hat that precluded the need for a "frontispiece," and observed, "It is inescapably obvious that he enjoys every moment of the rehearsal. He is constantly making cracks at the man in the control booth, jigging across the stage, waving his oversized hips, having great good fun with wheel-chaired Connie Boswell. She is obviously completely taken with Bing, plays up to him across the table and double-sided mike, laughs at all his jokes and capers."[52]

Still, the journalist couldn't quite make up his mind about Crosby. One moment, he wondered if his nonchalance wasn't sometimes a cover for his gastritis—a consequence of eating too much of the wrong foods—or his shyness. The next he reported that "today Bing's nonchalance is apparently completely natural, but indicates no lack of conscientiousness," concluding: "The point is he is a showman from toe to bald head, and things just fit in with his easygoing slick management." He admired Bing's wit, "his natural quickness," especially his few genuine ad libs, as when Jackie Cooper dropped his drumsticks on the air and Bing covered the mishap with the line "Hold the phone, there's been a nasty accident." He thought that Bing might be the only man as fast as Bob Hope: "We do know he can make Hope look sick when his stomach is in it."

Comparing original scripts with those bearing Bing's changes, he found instances of Bing enlivening the chat. After Trotter said, "I didn't want to be tarred and feathered," Bing was supposed to say, "Can't blame you," but he changed it to "There ain't that many feathers." Bing added to the program's verbal antics with slang ("society slats" for skis), alliteration ("Aeolian andiron" for Burns's bazooka), and archaisms ("mugient" for bellowing, "latration" for barking). They might not sound funny on the page, the reporter conceded, but they made "the script run smoother and more Crosby-like than the original writer could make it." *Time's* man surely would have been astonished to learn that four weeks to the day before Bing returned to the air, he'd done his damnedest to get rid of crosstalk and laughter. But the reporter would have found ample confirmation for all his observations had he visited Paramount Pictures, where Crosby and Hope, in clover and native mufti, gleefully jammed on the road to Zanzibar.[53]

5

RIGHT ALL THE WAY

*Then such mellow old songs as he sang, in a voice so
round and racy, the real juice of sound.*
— Herman Melville, *Omoo* (1847)

Road to Zanzibar needed to be a blockbuster. Unlike *Road to Singapore*, it opened to a primed, expectant audience. An average success would have been considered a disappointment, hardly injurious to Bing's standing in movies or to Bob Hope's, though his relatively brief tenure made him more vulnerable, but detrimental to them as a team. As it turned out, it established a motion-picture franchise—with decades of radio and television augmentation in the form of ready-made jokes and allusions—that blithely continued despite career skids. *Zanzibar* outsold *Singapore* by three million tickets; each of the next three Road trips nearly doubled *Zanzibar*'s receipts, and the two that followed them made enough money to warrant discussions of yet an eighth. In the 1970s and after, as audiences turned against Hope for his perceived espousal of the carnage in Vietnam, against Crosby for his (posthumous) reputation as a cold man and a callous father, and against both simply for being back numbers, the Road pictures were endlessly recycled on television and at repertory theaters, still fresh, still funny.

Road to Singapore displayed the affinity between the top-billed Bing and third-billed Bob, the alluring facility with which Dorothy Lamour joined them as one, and the wiggy irreverence and spontaneity of its radio-style humor. But it was a conventional film with the conventional backstory of a rover coming to terms with his plutocrat family amid hints of romantic melodrama, including an affable pal who loses the girl to his best friend. *Zanzibar* cashiered most of that, providing a true template for the series. Hammering cracks into the fourth wall, it asked the audience to participate in the jokes. Counting on everyone to remember the patty-cake routine, for example, it provided winking variations rather than repetitions.

The names of the characters played by Bing and the now-second-and-soon-to-be-co-billed Bob changed with each film, but their lopsided relationship remained the same. It involved relentless betrayals and exploitations—Wilfrid Sheed observed, "Not since the plays of Ben Jonson has comedy gotten any blacker"[1]—in a one-upmanship that invariably favored Bing's reliable mode of romantic earnestness over Bob's fractured daftness. Thus Bing kept winning Lamour in a rivalry that began anew at each outing. But *Zanzibar* also rehabilitated their rapport in a way that prevented Bob from becoming Bing's stooge. Bing is ostensibly the one with the brains, the schemer. Yet he is no less gullible; he scams Bob while competing tricksters scam Bing. Given the grounding of the characters, *Zanzibar* could dispense with logic and reality—good-bye to backstories. In a world of ripping lunacy, the only thing we have to fear is tedium. Fear, sex, and violence are jokes, and death—the threat of death, anyway—is the biggest joke of all.

Censorship was no joke, but it provided a foreplay of wits as the Breen office recoiled and the suitor obediently removed one groping hand while reaching around with the other. The producers were by no means meek in dealing with the Catholic qualms of Joseph Ignatius Breen, who, from 1934 to 1954, personally superintended the Production Code Administration, decreeing what his fellow Americans were mature enough to see and hear at the movies. His very presence indicated a particularly self-conscious fear on the part of Jewish studio chiefs who worked hard to moot and sometimes deny their ethnicity. Breen sympathized with the Falangists in Spain and the Nazis in Germany. He associated Jews with Communism and perversion: "The vilest kind of sin is a common indulgence hereabouts and the men and women who engage in this sort of business are the men and women who decide what the film fare of the nation is to be," he wrote to a Jesuit priest in 1932. "Ninety-five percent of these folks are Jews of an Eastern European lineage. They are, probably, the scum of the scum of the earth."[2]

Now, since Breen took their money, he had to watch his step, but he kept the others minding their steps as well. Filmmakers fought back and won skirmishes, but they had already conceded the war. It's a wonder that Paramount, the studio with the daring continental touch, could sneak so much past him, given the biases of its PCA liaison, Luigi Luraschi. A Paramount executive charged with developing foreign markets, Luraschi later bonded with CIA Red-baiters. In 1952, he worked up a campaign to deny the "un-American" *High Noon* the Academy Award for best picture (it went instead to Cecil B. DeMille's circus film *The Greatest Show on Earth*). Yet in his negotiations with Breen, Luraschi loyally fought to protect the wishes of Paramount producers.

Breen was the type of censor who insisted that a scene in which Arab slave traders auctioned Caucasian women be scrupulously monitored for the "costuming of these girls and the display of their physical charms," while expressing no qualms about depicting a public slave market in modern-day Zanzibar. When the writers Don Hartman and Frank Butler submitted the *Zanzibar* script for PCA approval in October, they expected a ream of objections about language and insinuation. They were not disappointed. Breen informed Luraschi in boilerplate fashion that it appeared to meet Production Code requirements. "However," the boilerplate continued, "we call your attention to the following details."[3]

> Scene C-2—Please change the underlined words: "You're a <u>pook-faced</u> old drizzle puss."...
>
> Scene C-9—Political censor boards frequently delete the showing of people being hit over the head with a chair as described in this scene...Scene D-1—There must be no evidence of the slave trader pointing up the breasts of the slave girl when he says, "Sambo wocky-dockies," and Hope's reply, "I'll say she has"...
>
> Scene D-25—There must be no suggestion in this scene that Fearless [Hope's character] is goosing the Turk.
>
> Scene D-31—The following dialog should be changed to get away from the present vulgar inference: "And there's no chance of

winding up married to a dog." "With your pedigree, I wouldn't be too sure."

Also in this scene, please make sure that there is no unnecessary exposure of the boys when one gets into the shirt and one gets into the pants of their only set of pajamas.

Scene E-2—Please change the underlined expression: "She's on the <u>make</u> for me."

Breen held firm in ensuing letters, which Luraschi passed to the producer, who passed them to the writers, who revised or ignored the complaints, adding purposely crude lines that they would graciously delete, hoping the lines they really wanted in could be overlooked in the spirit of compromise. But Breen wasn't in the business of compromise; he demanded obedience and usually got it. Noting with irritation that the writers had failed to alter several items, he added more to the list, which ultimately ran into the dozens.[4]

This interference had an upside: an incentive to be deviously amusing. The writers aimed not only to make scripts funny but also to bamboozle censors. As Bing and Bob crisscrossed the set between takes, like fighters going to their corners, they would receive whispered zingers from personal gagmen, each star looking to unbalance the other; the constant comic rigor roused players and crew. Breen had no knowledge of the ad libs or of how scenes would play. Two weeks into shooting, Luraschi returned to his office after screening daily footage and wrote a memo to the film's producer, Paul Jones: "In today's rushes there is a scene of Lamour working in her room in her teddy. Later, she puts on a dressing gown when Una Merkel enters. There was no indication in the script that the scene would play this way so we could not anticipate it. I don't know how much of this scene we can sell Breen before she puts on her dressing gown (I'll do my best to sell him all of it), but he generally cuts scenes of this type. If Lamour had been wearing what is commonly known as a slip we would stand a better chance."[5] Most of Breen's objections involved Bob's character; an ogling clown was more likely to err on the side of vulgarity than a supervisory wheeler-dealer was.

The general air of travesty accurately mirrored the fact that, like *Road to Singapore*, which began as a buddy adventure, *Zanzibar* originated as a drama—but this time, the genesis was factual. On returning from his vacation, Bing approved a gagged-up version of an original screenplay by Sy Bartlett, *Finding Colonel Fawcett,* concerning two men who investigate the 1925 disappearance in the Amazon of the controversial English explorer Percy Fawcett. Bartlett's script was considered unproducible because a romanticized film about better-known explorers complete with happy ending had reached theaters the previous year (*Stanley and Livingston*). Given the success of that picture and the ongoing Tarzan series, *Finding Colonel Fawcett* virtually begged to be burlesqued, which Don Hartman did, targeting Rio as the setting. Perhaps coincidence placed all but one of the Road movies in a protectorate: British (Singapore, Zanzibar, Hong Kong), French (Morocco), Dutch (Bali), or American (Alaska, in *Road to Utopia*). Rio was the exception, but the film had to be delayed until 1947, as the studio worried about upending the recently revived Good Neighbor policy by offending Brazil. Ordered to change the setting, Hartman chose a spot on Africa's eastern coast, one with a mellifluous, trisyllabic name that had been the site of one of Lon Chaney's most strenuous sadomasochistic exercises, *West of Zanzibar*.[6] Even so, the studio insisted that the safari chant (set to Jimmy Van Heusen's two-hundred-bar "African Etude") be "in a language at which no nation could take umbrage." Bing liked to say it was written in Esperanto and that Johnny Burke even made it rhyme.[7]

The producer Paul Jones first teamed Hartman with a Marx Brothers writer, Robert Pirosh, who brought to the project none of the madness he had laced through *A Day at the Races*.[8] Their draft includes a racist stage direction ("a big black buck of a conductor asks for the fares") and begins as Bing and Bob are chased from Atlantic City, accused of bank robbery; they hide in the rumble seat of a car driven aboard an ocean liner bound for Africa, where they help the distressed Lamour and outmaneuver a swindler searching for a "lost" diamond mine.[9] Jones brought back *Road to Singapore's* Frank Butler to reteam with Hartman, and in two months, they had a workable script. Now Bing and Bob were introduced, playing a carnival in South Africa, where they have been hustling for five years to earn passage back to the States. Lamour and Una Merkel[10] play a rival team of scammers. The diamond mine is merely a contrivance to get them all on safari.[11]

Hartman shared the story credit with Bartlett and the screenplay credit with Butler, earning a handsomer salary than either of them, but Butler—thanks to seniority and the alphabet—received first billing, a point Hartman unsuccessfully contested with the front office.[12] Uncredited writers were also paid; these included the quondam vaudeville hoofer and now gagman and kibitzer Barney Dean, a loyal friend and mascot to Bing and Bob, who finagled him a writer's salary, though he never actually wrote anything. They competed for his quips and slipped him into the dialogue. When Fearless Frazier (Bob) complains he wants to go home, Chuck Reardon (Bing) tells him, "Yeah, you'll wind up back there in Barney Dean's beanery blowing up bloodwurst." Hope received $5,000 as "special payment" for his writers, though that and a $12,500 "bonus" were apparently intended to enhance his per-picture salary of $56,875—which was way better than Lamour's deal ($23,333.34), but not close to half of Bing's salary. The audience embraced the team *as* a team long before Paramount followed through with financial and billing parity. Hope's contract stipulated that his name could be preceded by Bing's and that of any "recognized female star in the industry."[13]

Victor Schertzinger returned to direct. This time, knowing what to expect, he let the boys strut their stuff and worked with the producer Paul Jones to bring the picture in $63,000 under budget.[14] Jones's contribution is difficult to quantify, but it undoubtedly extended beyond bean counting. An unassuming, well-liked, skillful catalyst, Jones is little remembered today, yet he presided over an inventory of outstanding comedy classics, including the three best Road movies (*Zanzibar, Morocco, Utopia*), Hope's best solo vehicles, and the best films of Preston Sturges and the team of Dean Martin and Jerry Lewis. Hope's longtime collaborator Melville Shavelson emphasized Jones's "ability to laugh": "If you could make him fall out of his chair, you knew you had a good scene."[15] If a scene didn't work, he would call a break and lead everyone to the racetrack, charging the expedition to the studio. Weighing his résumé against that of Schertzinger, it seems probable that Jones suggested a stylistic facet that distinguishes *Zanzibar* from its predecessor and the Roads to come. Instead of their usual easygoing banter, Bing and Bob engage in high-velocity raillery in the mode of Howard Hawks's *His Girl Friday* (released fifteen months before *Road to Zanzibar*) and the recent films by Preston Sturges (*The Great McGinty, Christmas in July, The Lady Eve*). The pace of the dialogue between crooner and comedian is impeccable, unforced, and funnier than the actual lines.

Bing sailed through the film, which wrapped in late December, despite an exceptionally busy recording schedule (seven sessions in four weeks), the resumed weekly radio hour, daily golf, heavy rains, and a contemplated and then rescinded divorce. During Christmas week, he appeared at a holiday party for the venerable African American Ascot Avenue Elementary School (which replaced the one-room Vernon Street School, built on a land grant in 1876), along with Dorothy Dandridge and the dazzling twenty-one-year-old jazz pianist Nat King Cole, who had recently recorded his first significant vocal performance for Decca, "Sweet Lorraine." The King Cole Trio elated black audiences at a time when few whites paid attention. The drummer Bill Douglass, who attended Ascot Avenue, recalled Cole's visit as "just the greatest thing that ever happened around here."[16] Bing first championed Cole in 1938 after hearing him at Jim Otto's Steak House and excitedly returning with Johnny Mercer in tow. Mercer signed Nat when he founded Capitol Records, and, in 1944, "Straighten Up and Fly Right" raced up the charts, leading to his first appearance with Bing on *Kraft Music Hall*. A week after the Ascot Avenue event, Bing inaugurated the radio career of Michigan's all-American halfback Tom Harmon, who played his last game on New Year's Day and appeared on *Kraft Music Hall* the next evening. Bing had begun to plan Harmon's future when the athlete wrote him two years earlier, and he lined up Everett to manage him. Harmon's movie career wilted with a travesty called *Harmon of Michigan*. After serving heroically in the U.S. Army Air Corps, he married Elyse Knox (a star of B movies), fathered three children who grew up to be actors, and enjoyed a long run as a radio and television sportscaster.[17]

On the set, Bing and Bob partly improvised a couple of the funniest bits they ever shot. In one scene, effortlessly stretched to five minutes, Dottie[18] is bathing naked in a lake and they come across her clothes, gnawed by leopards. Assuming the worst, they alternately grieve and berate her as a double-crosser. As they bury her shredded garments, Bing suggests they say a few words, perhaps recite a poem. Bob launches into "The Shooting of Dan McGrew," which Bing nixes to orate a couple of lines from "The Face on the Barroom Floor." All this nineteenth-century doggerel is oddly apt in a film that parodies the traditional South Seas romance, a narrative popularized by Herman Melville in the 1840s: two white men, one intrepid, the other more jocular, jump ship, go native, savor nature's abundance while fearing their hosts' rumored cannibalism, and finally escape back to civilization. The first desertion is invariably followed by the second.[19]

Bing and Bob inadvertently summon the cannibals when they wander into a cave filled with drums—a "jungle telegraph," Bing surmises—and extemporize on the skins, drawing hundreds of black extras to their lair (the great composer and bass virtuoso Charles Mingus, only eighteen at the time, claimed to be one of them). Contemplating the giant pot, Bing ruminates: "That's life. Here today and just a burp tomorrow." The movie judiciously finessed the fine line between parodying and stereotyping African natives except for the offensive caricatures commissioned for the opening credits, depicting spear carriers with white minstrel lips, which were also used in Paramount's newspaper ads. To play the zanily Westernized tribal chiefs Joe and Sam and the medicine man Harry,[20] the filmmakers recruited three eminent veterans: Noble Johnson, who had appeared in well over a hundred movies since 1915; the Broadway fixture Leigh Whipper, who founded the Negro Actors Guild and broke the color barrier at Actors Equity; and Ernest R. Whitman, whose distinctive basso-buffo voice would soon become known to every black serviceman and thousands of white ones as that of Ernie "Bubbles" Whitman, the jovial host of the Armed Forces' *Jubilee* broadcasts.[21]

Charles Gemora, the stunt man turned makeup artist who was famed for playing gorillas in costumes of his own design, first worked with Bing (as a gorilla) in a 1933 Mack Sennett short, "Sing, Bing, Sing," and would later play a bear in *Road to Utopia*. He got the biggest laughs of his career trouncing Hope and his conspicuously bearded stunt double in *Zanzibar,* a prelude to the entire tribe knocking itself out with patty-cake anarchy. Bing rarely took his kids out of school to watch a shoot, yet that week he brought Gary, who never forgot the gorilla sitting on Bob and cratering the ground. After Dottie sang the coquettish "You're Dangerous" to Bob, he waddled away on his knees, sending her into a fit of laughter; they shot it again and kept the knee-walk. Lamour recalled Bing bringing relatives to the set and spending so much time with them that Hope tipped the assistant director to announce, "Quiet! Mr. Hope is ready to work as soon as he can find a certain untalented millionaire." Lacking a Barney Dean to feed her lines, Lamour rarely got one that was not scripted, yet she cracked up Bing and Bob by smiling at the end of a scene so only they could see that she had blacked out her front teeth. A frequent visitor to the set was the twenty-two-year-old contract actor William Holden, who bicycled from the stage where he was filming I Wanted Wings to watch the trio work. His director, Mitchell Leisen, would "have to come and grab me by the collar and drag me back to my own set." Holden recalled "much warmth in their teasing of" Lamour and thought they could have made "the funniest motion picture you've ever seen [by releasing] the on-set, off-camera scenes."[22]

As usual, the final film is littered with in-jokes, including a revival of the dueling conductors routine Bing and Bob had improvised at New York's Capitol Theatre when they first worked together, in 1932. Bob mocks Bing's gum-parking habit by parking his own wad on a cannon from which he is to be shot, then he pops his head out to request a "photo finish." (Unprepared for that Deanism, Bing could only murmur, "Okay.") References to high taxes and the draft convey the topicality of weekly radio, and the delayed entrance of Lamour and Merkel underscores the series' sexual reticence: the boys constantly talk about women, but faced with one, they choke. Bing even indulges in femme sashaying, wearing an oversize flouncy hat—anything to avoid the toupee. As a prelude to Bing's ballad "It's Always You," he and Dottie share a canoe (she does the paddling) and deride movie scores like the one Bing cues by running his hand through the water. Ken Carpenter's voice comes out of nowhere, narrating their trek as depicted on an animated map. When a heavy foils their patty-cake rumpus, they marvel that he must have seen their previous picture.

In Zanzibar, Bing and Bob develop a new twist in screwball

comedy in which the romantic rounds and class divisions that drive the repartee in comedies by Lubitsch, McCarey, and Sturges (and *Road to Singapore*) are replaced with competitive wisecracking by two men on a road to perennial vaudeville. Comebacks whiz by. Bing buys an octopus to wrestle Bob, who objects that it squirts ink. Bing: "Great, you can wrestle him and write a letter home." The octopus squirts Bing. Bob: "Write a letter." This kind of thing goes on for half an hour before Lamour appears, and it's over an hour before Bing's first ballad. In the two men's darkest scene together, Bob decides he has had enough of Bing's manipulations and walks off. As a dramatic actor, Hope rarely had a better turn— he is so convincing that the picture shudders to a halt. But it quickly cuts to Bob returning, the quarrel forgotten, and on they go: Bing carried by natives and sleeping in a bed, Bob legging it and cramming himself into a cot; Bing getting Lamour, Bob not even getting Una Merkel, though he does get the last laugh line.

They could not have foreseen how far their one-upmanship would take them. Of all phony wars, theirs was the most lasting— the longest-lived in show-business history. Fake feuds began with the literati. Before he began to sign his work as Mark Twain, Samuel Clemens initiated a humorous battle with a rival reporter, Clement Rice. With that feud in mind, New York columnists Mark Hellinger and Paul Gallico went at each other in a 1920s newspaper battle that Bing avidly followed during his years with Paul Whiteman. Maxwell Anderson and Lawrence Stallings made the friendly feud between two Marines the animating factor in their 1924 Broadway smash *What Price Glory?*[23] Walter Winchell switched media by launching a radio feud with bandleader Ben Bernie, the two of them pretending to loathe each other to boost their ratings. The puppet Charlie McCarthy took on W. C. Fields, and Fred Allen went after Jack Benny. On Wednesday nights, Allen lambasted Benny's violin playing; on Sunday nights, Benny exacted revenge. Fans tuned in to both shows to see how far they would go.

Bing and Bob played up their pretend rivalry on radio, at charity golf matches, on their respective USO tours, in interviews, and eventually on television. They trusted each other not to pick at any real scabs. "I knew him well," Bing said. "He started kidding me—I was a little ample in the waist in those days and he called me, you know, pot belly, said I was the only pot he ever saw that didn't have a rainbow over it. And then I'd kid him about his nose and his bad jokes. And it got to be a sort of pseudo-feud like Winchell had with Bernie or Fred Allen and Jack Benny.... The feud developed and got funny."[24] In the 1950s and 1960s, Bob often began his monologues with soft political jokes as the audience softly chuckled. Then he mentioned Bing, and before he delivered the setup, the audience guffawed in anticipation, ready to burst out in real laughter. It never failed. Presidents came and went, but the tit-for-tat Bing-and-Bob jokes played reliably from 1939 until Bing's death. "Bing's my oldest friend," Bob said in a monologue. "We often play golf together, you know. But that's all over. Would you play golf with a guy who cheats? A guy who picks up the ball when nobody's looking and throws it toward the hole? Of course you wouldn't. Neither will Bing."[25]

Three weeks into *Zanzibar*'s shooting, another film set up shop on a Paramount soundstage, a low-rent B musical starring the fallen comedian Bert Wheeler, struggling after the death of his partner Robert Woolsey, and the never-risen Constance Moore and Phil Regan. All *Las Vegas Nights* had going for it was a new Frank Loesser song, "Dolores," and the feature-film debut of the Tommy Dorsey orchestra, revitalized that year with the addition of the arranger Sy Oliver, the drummer Buddy Rich, and a couple of singers, Jo Stafford and Frank Sinatra. The band performed its current hits, including "I'll Never Smile Again," which featured Sinatra, who like the other sidemen received fifteen dollars a day and no screen credit.

Tommy was one of Bing's oldest friends in the music business. They had both worked with the composer-bandleader Victor Young, now the music director at Paramount in charge of *Las Vegas Nights* and *Road to Zanzibar*. Bing and Tommy recorded together with Paul Whiteman as early as 1927; Tommy soloed on Bing's 1931 radio debut, conducted by Young; Bing squared the ledger by appearing on Tommy's show in 1938. Tommy coined Bing's enduring sobriquet "the Groaner" and hired Bing's kid brother and would-be singer Bob Crosby when he was starting out. He unveiled his new band at the Paramount Theater on the same New York bill that debuted *Road to Singapore*.

Bing created a stir by showing up on the *Las Vegas Nights* sound-stage to welcome him out west and invite him to appear on *Kraft Music Hall*. Typically, he had ascertained Dorsey's schedule and probably knew better than Tommy when he would be filming. Most mornings, band members, exhausted from working long nights at the Hollywood Palladium, arrived on the set at five and slept wherever they could stretch their legs, waiting for their call. Two decades later, a tabloid reporter named Don Dwiggins wrote a paperback quickie called *Frankie: The Life and Loves of Frank Sinatra* in which he described Bing's visit:

> Sinatra earned a tribute that day, one he never forgot. When the camera moved in, as he stood under the hot lights, a man in a sport coat and slouch hat strolled over and listened approvingly. After the take, he walked up to Frank and shook his hand. He was Bing Crosby, Sinatra's first inspiration to become a minstrel.
> "Real nice, Frank," Crosby smiled. "You're gonna go far, boy."[26]

This story became lore, repeated with variations and rarely if ever sourced to the forgotten Dwiggins, who presumably based the story on the recollection of a witness. Whether or not it happened that way, or at all (there is reason to doubt it),[27] Bing had undoubtedly familiarized himself with Frank; they had in common "Imagination" and Jimmy Van Heusen, not to mention Frank's habitual covers of Bing's songs. In 1943, when Sinatra was the hottest new thing in the business and the fan magazines initiated the Bing versus Frankie war, Frank told Louella Parsons that Bing attended his 1939 opening night with Harry James's band at the Victor Hugo Club in Beverly Hills. They did not meet, but that evening Harry told Frank that Bing had remarked to him, "Hang on to your singer. I think he has something." Sinatra added, "His praise took the place of dessert in those days."[28]

In any case, Bing visited the *Las Vegas Nights* set specifically to see Tommy and meet his ingenious arranger Sy Oliver, who had created the puckish two-beat swing of the Jimmie Lunceford orchestra, a style he now adapted to Dorsey's band. The three men spent much of the week in one another's company, and Sinatra had no part in the socializing. One day they gathered in Bing's office to listen to a transcription disc of Victor Young's arrangement for the song that opens *Road to Zanzibar,* "You Lucky People, You." It was the first tune written by Van Heusen and Burke expressly for Bing, who was slated to prerecord it the next day. "Obviously he didn't like the arrangement," Sy Oliver recalled, "and before I could stop him, Tommy said, 'Hey, Sy, why don't you knock off an arrangement for Bing!' So I wrote one overnight, and Bing was so pleased that he said he wanted to do something for me in return, like introduce a song of mine on his radio show, the *Kraft Music Hall*." Sy demurred, but Tommy persisted. "Come on, Sy, you always have something extra in your briefcase." Sy pulled out a lead sheet he had written five years earlier for Lunceford, who had rejected it as sacrilegious, a faux-gospel lampoon of holy-roller preachers called "Yes Indeed!" That week, Bing sang it on the air as a duet with Connie Boswell.[29]

Of the two collaborations, "You Lucky People, You" produced the more immediate effect. The music critic Will Friedwald, in a justifiable fit of hyperbole, once described its introduction as "one of the greatest openings of any celluloid epic since Lumiere"[30]—an observation likely to bewilder anyone not in sync with the brio of a jazz band in full cry, in this instance Dorsey's band anonymously adding its heft to a studio orchestra. As the Paramount logo appears, we hear brasses and percussion, but when the credits roll, Victor Young's strings take over in his arrangement of the film's ballad "It's Always You," inducing a lulling conventionality. Then, when Ted Tatzlaff's cinematography credit pops up, we hear Bing sing the first phrases of "You Lucky People, You" as the Dorsey brasses riff spirited support. When Bing appears, in straw boater and bow tie, we realize the song is part of his carnival hoopla and never wonder about where that incredible music is coming from. It is enough to hear him, robust and grand, complementing the rhythm in his inimitably tranquil way. After the last bar, he mumbles under his breath, "That's for nothing, folks, and probably well worth it."

Movie audiences delighted in Bing's startling entrance, but the song, not one of Van Heusen and Burke's best, had little chance of success, as it could not be promoted over the air owing to the ASCAP strike. Nor was it helped by the curiously lackluster recording Bing made a month later, employing a lethal Trotter arrangement that opens with extraneous alto saxophone and interpolates an instrumental chorus for honky-tonk piano and strings. (Beginning with this session, which also produced "A Nightingale Sang in Berkeley Square," Trotter delegated many Crosby orchestrations to a young arranger named Ted Duncan, whose influence would be felt on Bing's recordings over the next two years, most famously on "White Christmas.") Dorsey's cover did no better. He retained Oliver's glowing score, augmented by his own trombone interlude, but Sinatra's mannerly phrasing failed to make an impression. The much anticipated arrival of Van Heusen had proved anticlimactic — none of the *Zanzibar* songs received airplay, and the next films scheduled for Crosby (*Birth of the Blues, Holiday Inn*) didn't call for Van Heusen and Burke. Their potential would have to simmer until late 1942, when *Road to Morocco* signaled their indisputable arrival as major players in 1940s popular music. "Yes Indeed!," however, created an enduring commotion.

On the Thursday after Sy showed him the lead sheet, Bing sang it on *KMH* in an arrangement that began with half a minute of ersatz minstrel badinage with Connie. Bing was in a congenial mood at that November 28 broadcast, which guest-starred Dorsey and Charles Boyer. His teenage protégée Janet Waldo, who had won a 1937 contest he presided over in Spokane (the prize was a Paramount screen test), recalled that during the rehearsal, her agent Larry Crosby requested a publicity photo of her with Bing and Boyer: "So Bing said to Charles, 'I'll wear mine if you'll wear yours,' and I thought, *What are they talking about?*"[31] She quickly realized they were talking about hairpieces, which they affixed and wore during the broadcast. Introduced mischievously by Bing as Jimmy's brother — the Dorsey brothers feuded, sometimes violently, all their lives — Tommy acted in a sketch with Minerva Pious (Mrs. Nussbaum from Fred Allen's show) as a crazed swing fan and played a trombone chorus on "Yes Indeed!" The radio audience took to the song, which Bing and Connie repeated on four subsequent programs, a good run for a new tune unaffiliated with a Crosby picture.

As it was a BMI number, it was especially welcome. After the ASCAP strike went into effect, Bing rediscovered Stephen Foster and songs like "Darling Nellie Gray" and "I Don't Want to Play in

Your Yard," as well as a few songs with connections to BMI *and* ASCAP, like Bing's 1938 hit "Mexicali Rose" and the Ink Spots' "Do I Worry." Some weeks, pickings were so lean, they resorted to the almost unthinkable; on one show, Connie brought out the cello she rarely played for a performance of Godard's "Berceuse."

The strike haunted Decca too, though Bing came up with an idea that paid large dividends in the long run. He asked Jack Kapp to schedule a session in early December with an orchestra conducted by Victor Young, on whom he frequently relied for projects especially dear to him. In a time of rampant bigotry, often directed against or perpetrated by the Irish (the anti-Semitic ravings of Father Coughlin were as familiar to radio audiences as Crosby's baritone), Bing decided to flag his own ethnicity. In the 1930s, he had emphasized his paternal English heritage on film and in his private life. He now undertook a rebranding that would define his life, career, and legacy to a degree he could not have foreseen in 1940. It was a decision of profound importance to him, an autonomous act of solidarity, his first public embrace of his mother's Catholicism.

The makeover began gently at a session designed to evoke ethnicity and the longing for a vanished world: four songs, two of them lullabies of Hibernia, two of them retrospections of the American Negro as conjured by Stephen Foster. Kapp's regrettable choice of the latter was not without a certain logic. Foster was an American classic, and Bing had recently found favor with two of his nocturnes of lost love. Black artists, including Paul Robeson, performed Foster's songs without altering the epithet *darkies* or amending the risible nostalgia for plantation life. If there was a pair of American melodies that every citizen knew, it was "My Old Kentucky Home" and "De Camptown Races." Neither had yielded a hit record since the 1910s, nor did they in 1940, though Bing interpreted them as fastidiously as he had "Beautiful Dreamer." Bing knew they were dubious choices to honor the cultural heritage of African Americans, and he did little to plug them on the air. He sang "De Camptown Races" only twice on the radio and didn't sing "My Old Kentucky Home" at all until 1944, when he performed it with the Charioteers, altering "Tis summer, the darkies are gay" to "Tis summer and everyone's gay."

The Irish songs were thematically consistent: lost love, lost world, loss. The lyricist Jimmy Kennedy is said to have enjoyed more hits in the United States than any British or Irish songwriter before Lennon and McCartney, though he rarely crossed the pond except to visit Mexico. Bing recorded his share: "Red Sails in the Sunset," "South of the Border," "Isle of Capri," "Harbor Lights," "My Prayer," even the novelty "Constantinople" (with Whiteman, in 1928). Yet "Did Your Mother Come from Ireland?," written by Kennedy and Michael Carr in 1936, languished until Bing sang it at this session, yearningly sculpting every phrase, with no sign of the brogue he later adopted for Irish songs. In this instance, the brogue would have mocked the earnestness of the occasion. When he revisited the song for his 1954 Decca retrospective *A Musical Autobiography,* he recalled that the actor Pat O'Brien requested it of him at parties, only to complain afterward that, while Crosby's rendition was "adequate," it was not as good as William Scanlon's or John McCormack's. In truth, neither of them recorded it (Scanlon died in 1898 and didn't record anything), but O'Brien might well have kidded him about James I. Russell's "Where the River Shannon Flows," which Bing also recorded that day. Bing had grown up with McCormack's 1913 record, had played it repeatedly on the phonograph his dad bought for the Crosby parlor in Spokane.

Kapp, unconvinced by Bing's enthusiasm, briefly delayed releasing the Irish songs, figuring he had a safe bet with the week's other session. Yet when Bing and Connie recorded "Yes Indeed!" two weeks after introducing it on the air, it failed to click. "Just about everything Bing recorded in those days became a hit record," Oliver observed. "But not 'Yes Indeed!' Don't ask me why."[32] The session, under Kapp's personal supervision, had promise. Bob Crosby, whose Dixieland swing band usually buoyed Bing's spirits, had just completed six weeks in San Francisco and committed to three sessions with his brother. At the first one, on December 13, he used the Bob Cats, a smaller contingent, to back the duets with Connie. Yet the first piece, "Tea for Two," came off as desultory, even sedated, with a key change midway that was too low for Bing and uncomfortable for both. "Yes Indeed!" was more engaging, abetted by Bob Haggart's popping bass and Muggsy Spanier's vigorous trumpet solo, but the performance feels too self-conscious and arch to bring the material fully alive. The afternoon ended on a sentimentally grateful note as Bing, Connie, Bob Crosby, Victor Young, and Jack Kapp recorded a three-minute Christmas greeting to Decca's New York staff. After a Dixieland prelude of "Jingle Bells," Kapp expressed gratitude to every employee, especially given mounting problems in the industry, at which point Bing began to hum "Hearts and Flowers."[33]

Connie continued on *KMH* for a year, but this was her last recording with Bing, ending an intermittent series that stretched back to 1931 and included such winners as "An Apple for the Teacher" and "Bob White." "Yes Indeed!" had a long life, however, as Tommy instantly encouraged Sy to write it up for his orchestra with Sy and Jo Stafford sharing the vocal; that record rocketed onto the charts and stuck there for five months, a swing-era classic, later covered by Harry James, the Charioteers, Peggy Lee, Ray Charles, Frank Sinatra, Hank Mobley, and others.[34]

Whatever disappointment they harbored over the "Yes Indeed!" session was offset three days later when Kapp and the Crosby brothers reconvened to record a milestone for Bing and for country music. The day dawned brightly as the trade papers reported that Bing and Paramount had signed a three-year contract, raising his per-picture rate to $175,000 for nine films; this, combined with the Decca renewal (negotiated, according to Kapp, in forty-five seconds during a break on the *Zanzibar* set) and the Kraft contract, guaranteed him a minimum of $2,300,000 (about $40.4 million in today's dollars) by December of 1943. The Paramount contract also gave him absolute approval on scripts, casting, music, directors, cameramen, and other personnel, rendering him—to the degree he exercised control—the de facto auteur of his films. His option to make another film outside the studio would end June 1, 1941, after which his cinematic services belonged exclusively to Paramount Pictures. The bump in his income did not mitigate his tax liabilities or allay his worries about his secretly contemplated divorce, but it might have helped put him in a particularly songful mode on December 16.

He began the session with an odd choice, covering a country-and-western song, "San Antonio Rose," that was presently amassing a million sales for Bob Wills, the King of Western Swing. Wills, who combined swing-band arrangements with a steel guitar, violin, and his own falsetto *ah-ha*s, had first recorded the tune without vocals as a protest against Irving Berlin's publishing company issuing an unauthorized rewrite of his lyrics. With Berlin himself backing Wills in the dispute, however, the company reissued the song with the original lyrics as "New San Antonio Rose," prompting a new recording that brought Wills national renown and his only gold record.

Where Wills and his vocalist Tommy Duncan rode the song at a medium-up-tempo clip, Bing took a poised and discerning approach, though lighter than the deep-night wonder he brought to such Western precursors as "Mexicali Rose" and "The One Rose." Faithful listeners who traced the stately, revelatory classicism in his Western songs back to 1933's "Home on the Range" could not fail to spot a change in Bing's vocal mask and style. In later years, observers puzzling over the adjustment in Bing's attack between the 1930s and the 1940s arrived at a medical explanation. They figured he must have had his vocal-cord nodules surgically removed. He hadn't. The laryngeal growths that contributed to the balmy throatiness considered so appealing in the early days of the New Deal disappeared naturally. But the stylistic change was deliberate. He softened the self-conscious artistry that had defined his ballads, muting the baroque elements of his technique—the tremolos, rhythmic fillips, shifting dynamics. His upper mordents continued to peg notes for emphasis, but he trusted the splendor of his instrument to convey the tale, replacing ardent mannerisms of youth with a matured clarity. This reinforced the illusion that singing was easy, nice work if you could get it—virile, natural, and honest. The sage crime novelist W. R. Burnett caught the flavor of the new Bing in his 1940 novel *High Sierra*, when the gangster Roy Earle and his girl pull into a roadside juke joint:

> The music stopped and one of the fellows put in another nickel. A new record swung up off the turntable and a mellow baritone voice filled the little room.
>
> "Crosby," said Marie. "He's sure swell."

"He sure is," agreed Roy. "He's about the only singer I like. I hate singers. They ought to have on skirts. But not that guy. He's got a real voice and I hear he's right all the way."[35]

Bing's version of "San Antonio Rose" outsold Wills's: 84,500 discs in the first three days, and eventually 1.5 million. The second of his twenty-three gold records and his first since "Sweet Leilani" in 1937, it marked a rare instance of back-to-back gold for the same tune. The performance might well have pleased Roy Earle, given Bing's sincerity, the emphasis on his masculine low notes, neatly patterned mordents ("Alamo-oe"), and a stirring reentrance after the interlude when he harmonizes "Ohhh" in tandem with a high-note trumpet. It certainly pleased Wills, who credited Bing's record, rather than his own, for making him a national figure. An heir to "Beautiful Dreamer" in its lamentation for an old love, the song crossed genre boundaries, its wistful melody timed to a reassuring two-beat. In 1942, Wills and Crosby sang it together into a wire recorder for the crowd on the eighteenth green of Tulsa's Southern Hills Country Club, auctioning the wire to whoever purchased the most war bonds. The president of Oklahoma National Gas claimed it for $250,000.[36]

Still, Bing's "San Antonio Rose" is far from electrifying; the performance is flawless but unadventurous, stretched thin by a long chorus structure (sixty-four bars) and dimmed by a brief and listless tenor saxophone solo by Eddie Miller that suggests the dutiful mooing of a wedding band. The real gem of the session is on the B-side, "It Makes No Difference Now," a 1938 BMI song written and introduced by another Decca artist, Floyd Tillman. This side became a hit in its own right, as consumers flipped the disc, encouraged by Bing's radio performances. As an ASCAP song, "San Antonio Rose" made its way without help from *Kraft Music Hall*, but he could sing "It Makes No Difference Now" whenever he liked. The recording features Bob Crosby's band at its best, especially the formidable Eddie Miller, who improvised an outstanding solo. Driven by the grooving tempo, Bing shapes and shades each phrase. The two-sided hit roused the country-music business on two counts. It proved to Jack Kapp, his brother Dave (who created a matchless country catalog at Decca), and rival producers that country music had mainstream appeal, and it paved the way for suave country balladeers like Jimmy Wakely and Eddy Arnold, who unabashedly took Bing as a mainstream model.

It was a good day for both Crosby brothers. Without Bing, Bob recorded two of his finest straight-swing (as opposed to his signature Dixie-swing) numbers, featuring the always distinctive pianist Jess Stacy: "The Mark Hop" and "Burnin' the Candle at Both Ends." Neither became hits, but people paying attention knew how good they were. At their third session in ten days, Bob sang ballads that also did not sell, deservedly. (Whose bright idea was it to record a vocal version of "Big Noise from Winnetka"?) For Bing's songs, "Dolores" and a whither-my-Indian-maiden antique, "Pale Moon," which Bing had sung with Al Rinker back in Spokane, Kapp featured the brothers and the Merry Macs, a close-harmony quartet. Neither the songs nor the arrangements were first rate, yet "Dolores," from *Las Vegas Nights,* sold nearly as well for Bing as it did for Dorsey and Sinatra. For a week, Dorsey's version was the nation's number one record, followed by Bing's at number two.

Bing's last 1940 Decca outing was almost laughable in its producers' desperation to dig up songs that would not be embargoed during the strike, bottoming out with "I Only Want a Buddy, Not a Sweetheart," by the blind country singer Riley Puckett. (Bing privately recorded a parody version to demonstrate his contempt for the material.) Victor Young's backing on "Chapel in the Valley" is deadlier than the tune. Yet Bing made lovely recordings that day of two 1920s evergreens associated with, respectively, Paul Whiteman and Al Jolson: "When Day Is Done (superbly revived in 1935 by Mildred Bailey) and "My Buddy." It did not escape Bing's notice that the former had been adapted from an Austrian tune by Buddy DeSylva, who was about to become head of production at Paramount Pictures. Neither song scored a hit, but both satisfied his yearlong inclination to resuscitate ballads of inexorable cheerlessness.

The upshot of all this activity—he did not record again until May—was that, come April 9, 1941, when *Road to Zanzibar* premiered at New York's Paramount Theater on a bill with the Benny Goodman Orchestra, Bing had four concurrent bestsellers: "San

Antonio Rose," "It Makes No Difference Now," "Did Your Mother Come from Ireland?," and "Dolores." When 1941's numbers were tallied, he did not score as well as Jimmy Dorsey ("Amapola," "Maria Elena," "Green Eyes") or Glenn Miller ("Chattanooga Choo Choo," "Elmer's Tune"), but Bing's ability to remain on the charts *every week* after more than ten years had no precedent. April marked the tenth anniversary of his first major hit as a solo artist, "Out of Nowhere." That milestone was generally ignored in the excitement over *Zanzibar*.

Excepting *Variety*, which thought the movie lacked "the compactness and spontaneity of its predecessor,"[37] reviewers united in a choir of hosannas. Paramount publicists went into high gear with parties, nightclub events, and benefits. They leaked a story about a leopard escaping during filming that got recycled in the columns (although it never happened) and made much ado about Lamour's nude swim (she wore a body stocking and stood in murky water up to her shoulders). Hollywood's cameramen allegedly voted her one of their favorite undressed women, and the studio's ads depicted her as a fern-covered Eve.

The world market might have shrunk (*Zanzibar* did not play Germany and Japan until 1950), but the studio needed no ploys to seize the box office. Opening-day receipts exceeded Paramount's confident estimates. House records were broken around the country. A month after the film opened, *Variety* reported on business in DC: "If the tourists are still in town they're touring the monuments and Government buildings, not clamoring to get into the picture houses. Except for *Zanzibar*."[38] The staid *New York Times* reviewer Bosley Crowther was no less tickled than the always breathless Louella Parsons. He predicted it would ruin the "Dark Continent for any future cinematic pursuits," because "never again will we hear those jungle drums throbbing menacingly but what we envision Bing and Bob beating a gleeful tattoo"; "the heart of darkness has been pierced by a couple of wags...farce of this sort very seldom comes off with complete effect, but this time it does."[39]

Another ecstatic review ran in the *New Republic*, courtesy of Otis Ferguson, who had been keeping tabs on Bing for a decade. In an essay called "Safari, So Good," he described *Zanzibar* as "the funniest thing I have seen on the screen in years. Years." Noting that "so many comedies now feel the need for a theme and a near-meaning," he lauded this one for its "free and happy air of the spontaneous." He applauded the leads as "two comedians without straight men happy in playing two straight men in search of a comic" and as show-business characters who, "for once...are allowed to talk in character." He thought the merriment "so knowing, veteran, and kindly [and] so happily infectious within its own strict demands of trouping" that it evoked commedia dell'arte.[40]

Executives at Paramount might have thought twice before bartering two sugar cubes for a notice in the *New Republic*. But when *Time* alerted them to its forthcoming major Crosby story, cued to the new picture, they delayed the release a month in order to synchronize with the publication. The picture was ready in March, at which time they liberally screened it for the trade press, waiting for more information from the magazine and wondering if Crosby would be featured on the cover. In any case, this would be a triumph to savor. *Time* initially treated the Crooner with disdain, cautiously coming around (he wasn't, the magazine conceded, going away) before finally clambering onto the bandwagon. Bing was one of three Hollywood actors, along with Gary Cooper and Rita Hayworth, to score a *Time* cover in 1941, but he was the only male popular singer to make the cut since Morton Downey in 1931. The seventeen-hundred-word article, entitled "The Groaner," demonstrated the inability of *Time* reporters—who interviewed Bing's teachers, priests, childhood pals, rivals, colleagues, sporting acquaintances, employers, and employees and observed him at work for a year—to find a chink in his armor. *Time* sanctified the view of the fan mags: Crosby was all things to all men for all time and even more so to all women.

The cover—captioned "BING CROSBY: He is still falling uphill"—underscored the gender issue with a black-and-white, head-and-shoulders etching of Bing squinting sunward and wearing an unflattering wide sailor collar against a background of two dozen women, teens to grandmothers, who stared at him warmly, maternally, longingly, thoughtfully, seductively, wistfully, or adoringly. The story quickly produced its hook: "Out of the Paramount Studio in Hollywood last week came some of the most uninhibited, daffy nonsense to hit the U.S. screen since the heyday of Harold Lloyd.

It was *Road to Zanzibar,* and its principal assets were two recruits from radio who bounced gaily through its inanities like a pair of playful puppies. For one of them, Bob Hope, it was the tenth film in a new and rapidly rising movie career; for the other, Bing Crosby, a dulcet, broken-toned singer who has confounded all the rules of show business for more than ten years, it was his 24th feature-length picture."[41]

Duly noting his singular reputation (the Crosby clause) for "having important stars around him while his contemporaries were fighting for single billing," it made a claim for Bing's picture work — he "has played every type of character" — that Bing, who refused *Time* an interview, would have disputed. In tracing his improbable rise and noting his carefree attitude toward work and life, which made "a bum out of Horatio Alger," the article listed his achievements and statistics, some of them inaccurately reported. He had not "sold 3,500,000 discs this year"; that was last year, and those sales broke (as *Variety* reported) a record held by Enrico Caruso, which would be broken by Crosby *this* year when he sold five million. *Time* chided those "gloomy souls who prophesied" a speedy demise to his career, neglecting to mention that *Time* itself once led the pack, but no matter. The naysayers failed to notice Bing's most "important" talent, which was to please "all ages, all sexes." It placed him on a Rushmore of pleasure-giving beside Babe Ruth and Bill Tilden. He was America's favorite because he "sings every song — whether it is 'Mexicali Rose' or 'Silent Night, Holy Night' — as though he felt it was the best song ever written." Despite its shoe-leather reporting, *Time's* article offered nothing new and a lot that wasn't quite true. It confidently depicted his personal life:

Harry Lillis Crosby, "The Groaner" to his friends, is also happily married to a trig, blonde lady who was once an actress. He lives in a sunny, 14-room house with an adjoining tennis court and swimming pool where he roughhouses in off hours with four shiny, beaming sons. [If] he isn't working he likes to get out to the track for the early-morning workouts, squeeze in 18 or 36 holes of golf in the morning, hurry back to the track for the afternoon racing. Except for an occasional nightclub outing with Dixie, he spends his evenings at home with the family telling the boys bedtime stories in Crosbyesque slang. One night Little Red Riding Hood finally gets "hep" that the wolf isn't grandma; the next night Goldilocks makes a "three-bowl parlay" on the bears' porridge.[42]

In addition to not interviewing Bing, they did not interview Dixie or the shiny, beaming sons. Public relations execs at Paramount Pictures must have been over the moon, because the story read as though they had written it, though they would have replaced the archaic *trig* with a different word—say, *trim*. During the year that *Time* shadowed him, Bing threatened to capsize his broadcast career, flinched at and then girded himself for the ASCAP strike, abandoned independent filmmaking, and recorded a series of laments out of character with the colloquial comedy of *Kraft Music Hall* and the bounding farce of his recent movies. Between the completion and the premiere of *Road to Zanzibar,* Bing had stunned his wife by telling her he no longer loved her, had asked her to establish residency in Sun Valley, then had attempted to make amends with a family vacation in that same sunny setting. None of this entered the *Time* story or the public's consciousness. He was, as far as anyone could see, unshakable, implacable, and still falling ever upward.

6

COVENTRY

If I'm a hard disciplinarian I'm going to be one until they're twenty-one, and then at twenty-one, I'll see if that kind of discipline bears fruit. I don't think it's going to hurt 'em any. Can't possibly hurt 'em, can it?
—Bing Crosby (1952)[1]

The fragility of the Crosby marriage bruised the four sons. They learned to harmonize their emotions with those of their parents, who, whether stonily remote or intrusively concerned, almost always demanded obedience. They imposed what seemed like an endless litany of rules on everything—deportment, table manners, weight, schoolwork, curfews—and employed penalties to enforce them. Bing framed his idea of child-rearing in line with his admitted inability to openly display love and other raw feelings, which, even in his most expressive singing and acting, he fanned at low flame. Measured and sure, steady as you go; that was part of his appeal. His songs of loss were ripened by restraint. His comedic chops fed on it, evoking the wary ballet of a silent-era comedian thrust into a shape-shifting reality he will equably master. As paterfamilias, he had scant patience for the kind of willful independence that worked well enough for him when he was growing up. Bing could not know it then, but nothing would suit his theatrical bent better than a clerical collar, a protective talisman holding him aloft. As priest, he would be everyone's ideal father: mellow and wise, immune to temptation, dispensing Old Testament regulations with New Testament liberality. But when it came to his own kids, Bing had nothing like the unflappable sagacity of Father O'Malley.

The Bing known to the public and to actors and musicians who adulated him differed markedly from the man who came home in early evening, at times as reproving as a drill sergeant or inclined to retreat to his study, worn out by a day of being Bing Crosby. Dixie could be loving and nurturing, but when she withdrew into alcoholic reclusiveness, her absence implied a punishment—as in, *You have not behaved well enough to see Mother today.* The Dixie her friends knew to be an enchanting, generous, waggish, impeccably turned-out woman, not yet thirty in the spring of 1941, was only intermittently available to her boys.

The first thing the children of celebrities learn is that their parents exude magnetism that attracts strangers of a curious kind, those whose admiration is muddled by desire. What is it they want—a touch or blessing that will impart the contagion of fame, talent, assurance, beauty, wealth? Not content to admire, these people demand acknowledgment of their veneration: a smile or a handshake or a souvenir such as a photograph, letter, signature, fetish. They feel as entitled as feudal serfs to a little noblesse oblige, and when they don't get it, their esteem turns to bile. To Gary, the eldest and most rebellious of the sons, it seemed that outsiders spoke of and approached Dad as if he were God. Gary thought him God Almighty, the magistrate who never raised his voice, his self-control looming as a churning reminder that the boys were merely boys, children. Bing wanted them humble, hardworking, and normal, though nothing in their lives portended normality. In the lexicon of postwar psychology, he might have been called a behaviorist. He surely had a mission. But as he makes clear in his 1953 memoir *Call Me Lucky,* proudly recounting his inflexible parenting, he considered himself a traditionalist, whacking compliance into his boys as the priests at Gonzaga and his mother had whacked it into him (his father had no heart for it). He took the job seriously, enforcing rules, inspecting homework, and allocating privileges.

Contrary to B. F. Skinner's teachings, however, he made a point of tempering his praise. There would be no swollen heads on his watch. *Call Me Lucky* earned him popular and critical approval for his allegiance to an old cross-stitch motto, "Never kiss a baby unless he's asleep," held over from a time when parenting experts warned that displaying too much love for a baby would instill an unquenchable appetite for sex. Bing expected his approach to be validated by the upright young men it cultivated—an attitude targeted for obsolescence by the 1950s child-rearing savant Benjamin Spock, Bing's contemporary almost to the day. Spock's counsel to cherish and cuddle awake babies held sway at the time *Call Me Lucky* appeared. Uncountable readers who bought Bing's book or read the *Reader's Digest* abridgement found in it an old-school rejoinder to Spockism; they had been spanked, and they had turned out all right, hadn't they?

Bing granted the "special problems" facing the children of celebrities, especially among their friends. The "well-grounded kids" paid them no mind. But always lurking about were those "bubbleheads who make a fuss over a boy whose father or mother's name is known in the entertainment world." He regarded unmerited praise from friends and parents as ruinous. He was, after all, the entertainer who had banned welcoming applause from *Kraft Music Hall* because he had done nothing to earn it. In recording his memoirs, Bing expounded on discipline shortly after conveying a wartime anecdote involving General Eisenhower, which was fitting. Bing's parenting was military, manly, and unemotional: "When I want to be especially flattering to one of my offspring, I say, 'Nice goin',' and let it go at that."[2]

He took corporal punishment so casually that, with the help of a freelance gag writer, Bert Lawrence, he worked it into the film he was shooting in April 1941, *Birth of the Blues*. His character, Jeff, is introduced as a young clarinet prodigy who steals off to the docks to hear and perform "darkie" music. His prosperous father is scandalized: "Did you ever hear any white folks play that low-down drivel?" "No, sir, only me," Jeff tells him. And he won't stop, because "this music makes you feel like the circus is coming to town. Kind of turns you loose inside." When Father offers to withhold a leather-belt whipping if he promises to practice scales and avoid the levees, Jeff wordlessly bends over the parental knee. We are encouraged to smile at Jeff's spirit and accept the old man's concerned if futile punishment. Yet Bing apparently perceived few parallels between that futility and his own patriarchal rigor. He wanted Gary to play the part of little Jeff, his boyhood self, and arranged a screen test, but Gary photographed as too young and didn't get the job.

In *Call Me Lucky*, which Bing initially composed aloud on thirty-six or so dictation belts prodded by questions from the magazine writer Pete Martin, he muses at greater length on parenting than on acting and singing. Dixie, he says repeatedly, shares his attitude and not only administers her own spankings but taunts him for being too soft. She complained "I was too lax, that I wasn't strict enough, and that I forgot their transgressions too soon. She used to reproach me with, 'You punish them; then ten minutes later you're taking them out to a movie. That's bad. You should let the memory of their punishment linger so they'll remember it.'" Defending himself against the charge of forbearance (at times, he says, "I couldn't tell if I was Captain Bligh in a Hawaiian sport shirt or the cream puff of the world"), he maintains, "I'll bet they remember the spankings they got when they were younger. I laid in a big leather belt—similar to the one I'd backed up to at Gonzaga in the hand of Father Sharp—and when they did something particularly outrageous—for example, going into Dixie's room, taking her canary out of its cage, and giving it what they called a summer suit by plucking its feathers—I summer-suited them by taking their pants down and fanning their rears. They remember that all right."[3]

They definitely remembered the canary, a misadventure too traumatic to be diminished by time or gallows humor. Bing softened the description for publication, making the prank less gruesome and the punishment less severe, and so did Gary, four decades later, in *Going My Own Way*. He thought the incident took place in 1940. His brother Phillip correctly recalled the year as 1941, for it partly triggered the recruitment, that autumn, of the formidable housekeeper, nurse, and governess Georgia Hardwicke, known to all as Georgie. According to Gary, the twins persuaded him to sneak out of bed (Linny slept through it) and into their mother's verboten sanctuary to pet her canary, perched high in a cage. One of the twins climbed onto a divan, reached into the cage, and gripped the bird too tightly. Gary flew back to his room, the others in tow, with Dennis sobbing, "I guess we killed it." Gary bore the brunt of the punishment because, as Bing chided him, "You're the oldest. Why didn't you take care of your brothers?" In Gary's version, there are no plucked feathers and no leather belt: "The only question was whether [the spanking] would be from the back of Mom's silver hairbrush or from Dad's hands. I remember his hands very well. They were short and stubby, not muscular, but extremely strong."[4]

In the unedited transcription taken from the *Lucky* dictation belts, Bing described the incident and others to Pete Martin with untroubled bluntness:

> Well, when they were young we used to spank them and spank 'em pretty good. I hope I don't get a reputation for being cruel by describing how we used to spank 'em but I had a big leather belt with some steel studs in it and when they did something particularly bad, for instance, one time the twins took the liberty of going into their mother's bedroom when she had a canary and opened the cage and plucked the canary clean. [Martin asks, "Alive?"] Alive! I took them in the bathroom, took their pants down, got the belt with the studs on it, and I took turns and I left some pretty good welts there. I might have even drawn a little blood in a few places. Sounds pretty cruel, I know, but I don't think I ever did it more than four or five times in their whole lives, because they certainly remember that. I did it to Gary and I did it to Linny, too—Linny least of all. Once or twice was all he needed it. All I had to do was just start for the belt and they were full of penitence.

He had been brought up the same way and accepted it with a certain pride, not unlike Dr. Johnson, who, when asked how he had acquired his expertise in Latin, answered, "My master whipt me very well. Without that, Sir, I should have done nothing."[5] Bing tolerated his father as a cheerful gadabout—Happy Harry—and mimicked him in the Bing persona relished by the public. But he did not fear him and consequently did not fully respect him. The only person Bing would ever fear was his mother, and though his submissiveness may have been more dutiful than loving (Bing's brother Ted didn't think any of the siblings really loved her), he sought from his sons a comparable deference. When Martin mentioned in the course of the interviews that his mother had paddled him with her hairbrush and then withdrew privileges, Bing chimed in with a scene out of *Jane Eyre*: "My mother did that when I was young. I had to stay in a dark room for a couple of hours. That was the worst part of punishment. I used to get that. But more than anything else, when we were real young she used to get a stick of kindling wood and belabor our behinds. She never could get Dad to do it. He was always over the hill. He'd say, 'Hell, they'll be all right,' and he'd walk out and she'd have to do it. At least, that's what she tells me now."[6]

Punishment united the recollections of his grown sons, though they rarely agreed on specifics. Phillip insisted he had never read Gary's book but he knew it to be all lies (they never conversed civilly after a widely reported fistfight in late 1959[7]). His memory of the canary and his upbringing contradicts Gary's in every detail but supports the basic narrative of a dead canary and much paddling. He thought the cage hung in the living room, not Dixie's dressing area, and confessed to being the one who climbed up a stepladder, not a divan, and grabbed the bird, then found it no longer moved. Phillip's worst moments occurred the next day, when the corpse lay on Bing's desk and Dixie told Phillip, "Go away. I don't ever want to see you again." Gary said both parents imposed the silent treatment for a week or so; in Bing-speak, "expulsion to Coventry" for a fortnight, ignoring the boys beyond giving them intermittent warnings: "Watch your step. Just watch your step."[8]

Coventry—"the silent bit," in Gary's phrase—defined the relationship between Bing and Dixie as far as he could see. In a good mood, Bing was forever singing and whistling, learning and figuring out songs, keeping his voice limber. Dixie, too, generally maintained a busily chipper attitude, droll and playful. When Bing walked in, she would announce: "The romantic singer of songs you love to hear has arrived!" She chided and joshed him, and he responded in kind, keeping it light. He teased her by using her real name, Wilma. But he resorted to silence when things went awry. "At the far end of the hall was a chasm," Gary said. "She was on one side and he was on the other, and any communication between them was superficial, except maybe at night when we weren't around. He was the greatest man in the world at writing I love you and acting I love you and singing I love you, but he couldn't sit down with one member of his family and say, 'I love you more than anything or anybody in the world.' I never saw that happen. He was married to a woman with an inordinate need for that kind of thing, but it was very tough for him to be demonstrative or affectionate. It was like: here's what I've got to offer and if you don't want it, okay, see you later." The boys never heard their parents battle, raise their voices at each other, or discuss divorce. The boys knew nothing about that; they recalled the Sun Valley trip as a happy family vacation. "Sure, he loved her," Gary insisted. "Of course he loved her. He just never knew how to show her."[9]

Phil remembered the leather belt with the studs, but not in connection with the canary and not in the hands of Bing, whom he steadfastly defended: "I just don't see there was any way you could have asked for a better father. It's funny, all that crap Gary said about getting whacked by Dad. Our mother was the one who did the disciplining." Bing, he argued, did not want to have to address their bad behavior after a "hard day's work or a bad day at the golf course, though he did not have many of those, and I think Mom just thought, well, she knew that was her job. She was strict as hell."

One strap she had was a Western belt. Gary said it had studs a quarter of an inch out and surrounded by silver but I think it was more they were shaped like diamonds and pressed into the leather so it was smooth, very smooth, and just a couple of whacks and that was it. She used the strap on all four of us and there was never one time she used it we didn't deserve it. She also had a pretty good right hand and a very good left hook! [Laughs.] But the earliest I remember were those spankings, the way she'd grab us and hold us. She always used that "This hurts me more than it hurts you" line or "I don't like to do that, but when you've been naughty and ugly and mean at school and you do something around here, why, I have to."[10]

Gary placed the studded belt only in the hands of Bing, describing the improbable regimen of a dozen licks or until a spot of blood showed. But he also acknowledged Dixie's whippings and her connoisseurship in switches, which she made him retrieve from their backyard. "I had to be sure to make the right choice. The branch couldn't be dead. It had to be limber, with plenty of spring still in it."[11]

He rolled up his pants and she flogged up and down his legs with the switch: "She was drunk when she was doing it and if you yelled or screamed it made her crazier. So she would cry and cry because she was doing it, and yet still do it more and more and more. So you had to get used to just standing real still and taking it, because you didn't want to excite her, you know?"[12] When she offered Gary the choice of a whipping from Bing or from her, he always chose her, not because she hurt less, but because he couldn't bear to wait until six p.m., when the "romantic singer" returned from the studio.

The secrets of the Crosby home forced the brothers to rely on one another for entertainment, which involved much roughhousing. They were discouraged from inviting friends over, except on birthdays, because, Gary said, "Mom might be loaded" and cause a scene that would become fodder for the kids at school. Conscious of their baronial isolation, he worried about discomfiting his friends, who did not live "in a twenty-room mansion with a swimming pool, tennis court, and half a dozen servants."[13] The fierce competition between the three older boys extended to the point where if one of them got away with something, he figured he'd scored points against those who got caught. Unlike Bing and Gary, Phillip recalled only one instance of bloodletting, when Dixie went after Denny with the wrong end of the belt, nicking him with the buckle. The incident stood out because Denny was rarely punished. If something broke, Phillip said, his twin "would blame it on me and I'd get a good scolding or whatever, and I'd say, 'but Mom, Denny did it, why don't you get him,' and she'd say, 'Because Denny's the only one who always tells me the truth' and Linny and I would go almost in unison, 'He's the one that lies to you *every time.*'"[14]

Dennis, whom the siblings thought of as Mom's favorite, later judged the punishments as justified, though, along with Lindsay, he applauded Gary's book for shattering the perfect-family myth. Phillip, who lived longest of the four boys and yet led the most consistently dissolute life, generally praised his father as ardently as Gary derogated him. Dennis and Lindsay, who ended their lives as suicides, remained neutral, conceding Gary's intense anger while mostly accepting his published revelations. Dennis looked back placidly, claiming to be comfortable with who he was, "even if I had the hell kicked out of me."[15] Lindsay, considered by the other boys to be Dad's favorite, never ceased shedding tears for him and insisted he was "on the button with all the important things."[16] The twins and Linny remembered good times, usually involving sports—Bing took them to Rose Bowls and World Series. Gary's memories were cinders. Yet of the four, he maintained the most considered admiration for Bing's professional brilliance, artistic control, and generosity to other performers.

Phil dismissed Gary's complaints as the mewling of a crybaby, yet he recalled a grim episode from right after the war when Gary attended seventh grade at a Catholic military school, St. John's. Fed up with the school's complaints about Gary's behavior, Bing—golf clubs slung over his shoulder, Dixie by his side—confronted Gary in the downstairs hallway. He told him to lower his pants and assume the position. Holding a driver by the club head, he swung three times at his behind. Dixie softly said, "Bing," to indicate that was enough. The other boys cheered him on: "Give him one more, Dad. Give him one more!" Phil observed, "I don't know why we said that. We didn't hate him, but we loved to see him get knocked around." When it was over, there were welts but no blood, and Gary went upstairs to soak in the bath. Phil said Bing wasn't trying to hit Gary hard. Gary remembered seventh grade at St. John's as the time he found a measure of self-esteem in sports; he never mentioned the golf-club incident in his book or interviews.[17]

"Our fucking lives were so confusing," Gary said. "We didn't know what we were supposed to be, who we were supposed to be, when we were supposed to be it. Dad was afraid we were going to turn into Hollywood kids, and he didn't want any Hollywood kids in the house. He kept impressing upon us that we shouldn't be that way, shouldn't act like rich kids, shouldn't be around rich kids, only normal, ordinary kids."[18] Except for the children of his parents' friends, who were mostly in show business.

Gary thought of his mother's circle as two halves. The "good group" consisted of nondrinkers who looked out for her. Most of them had, like Dixie, left the business; these included her chief confidante, Kitty Sexton; her high-school friend Pauline Weislow, who had briefly danced in chorus lines and whose husband, Saul, was a contract lawyer working for Crosby Productions; Midge Polesie, the wife of producer Herb Polesie; Alice Ross, who helped out as an assistant and whose husband, Hugh, handled Bing's insurance; Julie Taurog, considered a martyr, according to Phillip, for staying married to the director Norman Taurog, who had been banned from the Crosby home for a forgotten trespass; and Sue Ladd, formerly Sue Carol, Dixie's companion at Fox (Bing and Dixie honeymooned at her home), who became an agent and married her client Alan Ladd. In their presence, Dixie limited her intake because she knew they would stand up to her if she didn't. With one drink in her, she was hilarious, salty, generous, adorable, great fun. After a few more, she grew maudlin, morose, angry, obscene.

Gary called the other group "the drunks." Dixie regularly visited Joeby Arlen, the wife (and in *Wings,* the costar) of Richard Arlen. As Jobyna Ralston, she flourished as a spirited silent-film comedienne, but the talkies revealed an intractable lisp, which reduced her to supporting Rin Tin Tin until even those parts vanished. The Arlens lived nearby in Toluca Lake and Dixie drank with her by the pool through long afternoons, often joined by the beautiful, tipsy Virginia Bruce. Dixie would bring Gary along to play with Joeby's son, Ricky, and Virginia's daughter (by John Gilbert), Susan Ann. "We were a trio," he recalled, "and the game was that Ricky and I were hot for Susan Ann. We were six or seven, but we were supposed to be hot for her."[19]

Bing's attempt to eradicate a sense of specialness and privilege in his sons was routinely foiled by the phenomenon of Hollywood birthday parties, which doubled as publicity coups for the stars. Competitive in all things, Hollywood's leading players financed an industry of party planners, caterers, bakers, horse wranglers, magicians, and circus performers. An affecting series of photographs taken on a March Sunday in 1939 captures a party Edward G. Robinson orchestrated for his six-year-old son; the boy's name, Edward G. Robinson Jr., could serve as a trope for the delusive milieu in which these kids attempted to forge personalities. He was a Junior to a stage name, and his nickname, Manny, was a remnant of his father's birth name (Emanuel Goldenberg), which had been jettisoned for the marquee.

The party had a law-and-order theme, suitable for the son of Hollywood's preeminent gangster. Wearing a Marshall Field's mini-police-chief uniform, complete with knee-high black boots, little

Manny imprisoned his friends successively in a specially built jail and posed with them on a Black Maria delivered from the Warner lot. He was surrounded by other Juniors wearing Western hats; one photo taken before the black, gabled single-cell jail shows him with Jack Haley Jr., Sandra Burns (George Burns and Gracie Allen's daughter), Wesley Ruggles Jr., Stanley Bergerman Jr. (Carl Laemmle's grandson), and Gary Crosby. No one smiles. They disregard the camera and one another, grim as if facing the last mile. Gary— in chaps and a leather jacket, revolver in hand (they all hold toy guns)—stares at a wood plank beneath his feet. The other guests, who also included the Crosby twins, John Barrymore Jr., and children of Melvyn Douglas and David O. Selznick, had been subpoenaed with invitations printed on authentic State of California forms. They were entertained with pony rides, hay rides, hiking, and contests, but for Manny, himself a tortured memoirist later on (at twenty-four, he was the first in a notably prolific generation of Hollywood offspring), nothing surpassed the jail in which he locked up guests.[20] The jail loomed in Gary's memory as well: "When it got to be our turn, the twins and I entered the cell like we were told. [Manny] snapped the lock shut, unzipped his trousers and started to pee on us through the bars."[21]

Phillip did not recall being peed on, nor did anyone else, nor is it credible that Manny gunned them down like that in the presence of his parents and photographers. But Gary's recollections were often intensified by skeptical elaborations. He was sure that the party Bing threw for Gloria Jean involved Judy Garland and Mickey Rooney, which was not true but fit his conviction that nothing occurred without calculation—why would Dad be nice to Gloria Jean, a comparative nobody, unless star power figured into it? Gary was hardly alone in dreading the photo-op birthday parties. Others remembered reluctantly dressing up so that family chauffeurs could deliver them in proper outfits or costumes. Jane Fonda (another memoirist beset by a sadistic father and a suicide mother), younger than the Crosby twins by two years, hated having to wear frilly frocks to the parties of Christina Crawford (the epitome of literary Furies) or Marlo Thomas, where Bing "loudly" presented his sons, and Lana Turner, "invariably drunk, [fussed] over her infant daughter."[22]

"We had to go to those things," Gary said, "and when they were over we were supposed to go back to being with regular kids. But when the regular kids see a rich kid coming, they team up to beat the shit out of him. I hurt them so they wouldn't do that anymore, and then I'd become part of the gang. Hell, I thought fighting was the way you made friends."[23]

The Crosby birthdays were relatively private affairs held at the house with a few friends. Gary found no cause to complain; relaxed strictures, ample presents, not a photographer in sight. Indeed, he was proud of the old man for not playing the publicity game. Dodging the press was second nature to Bing, especially after the one time he allowed it to invade the family's privacy. On Christmas Day 1938, NBC planted hidden microphones in the Crosby living room for a fifteen-minute broadcast as Gary and the twins opened their presents, squealing, giggling, and ignoring the network's timetable. "Sound seasonal sentiment," reported *Variety.* "It's a cinch no actor at any time anywhere got such favorable national publicity." Perhaps, but Bing was chagrined and in future displayed his family only when all the Crosbys were in on the joke.[24]

Two interrelated themes are ubiquitous in the memoirs of Hollywood children: neglectful parents and all-powerful nannies. They get a twist in the Crosby story. During and after the war, Bing was often away, yet despite disappearances for USO tours, golf, racing jaunts, or location shoots, he could not be faulted for indifference. He was too much in his sons' faces, even when a little neglect might have been wished for—at least by Gary, who, when asked if Bing was away a lot, replied, "Not enough." On another occasion, though, he looked back in loneliness: "He was away a lot on location. Sometimes we didn't see him for months. But when he was home, it was like my whole world was there. He was tremendously sensitive and he cared deeply. He just had a rough time showing it."[25]

From the time Bing received warnings of threats to kidnap his children, a year after the Lindbergh kidnapping, he kept his first son guarded and monitored. Gary's high-school friend Robert Dornan recalled Bing as "obsessed with the boys being kidnapped, so he was uptight about letting them loose. Bing spoiled the heck out of them, in addition to being a disciplinarian, which is a rough mix."[26] Publicly, Bing dismissed those threats as "overplayed." When a newspaper ran a story about watchmen patrolling the house on Camarillo, he denied it; he hired no security beyond the usual staff, he said, appearing "unworried, although he admitted he had talked with G-men."[27] Yet he hired surrogates to look after them when they went to school or the ranch, and at home he supervised them relentlessly. He said he could not understand parents who "wanted to get rid of their kids, or get them out of the house so they can have a ball themselves or something. I know lots of parents in the West, in the towns in which we particularly live, who think nothing of letting" kids stay out till dawn, and if "they phone, they have no idea even where they are."[28]

Strictly speaking, the Crosby boys didn't have nannies but a succession of housekeepers obliged to watch them and who, in Gary's words, "goddamn nearly drowned us and beat us to death." For succor, they turned to the black help: Wilma, the affectionate cook who made her kitchen a pleasurable sanctuary; the chauffeur Teddy, who stopped in the kitchen to read the paper and tell them stories; the upstairs maid Rose, a pretty young woman they called the Shadow in recognition of her favorite radio show. The white minders were the ones to beware. Overbearing, capricious, and cruel, they wielded immoderate power, encouraged by Dixie's retreats into her closed bedroom. The worst of them, Mrs. Hughes, dragged a miscreant into the bathroom, filled the bath, and repeatedly submerged his head under the water. The boys' terror was intensified because they assumed that she operated with parental permission — until the afternoon when Dixie walked in on her dunking a head. "If Mom had had a gun," Gary said, "she would have shot her right then. It was the angriest I remember her. She kicked her out of the house, didn't even let her pack. So Mom got tired of nurses and she got Georgie, who just took over everything."[29]

Georgia Hardwicke, who arrived in the early autumn of 1941, became Dixie's lieutenant and nurse, recommended by Kitty Sexton; Georgie had worked for Bill Sexton's family. After the episodes of Sun Valley, the canary, and Mrs. Hughes, Bing wanted Georgie to shield the boys from Dixie's alcoholic lapses. Some of Bing's relatives speculated that she reminded him of his mother. Georgie belonged to a vanishing breed. A stocky, Boston-born, Irish Catholic spinster in her middle forties, frizzy hair, tight face, five feet two at most, she ran the household with invincible rectitude: dutiful, hard as nails, quick to use force, greatly admired by outsiders. Gary despised her and Lindsay found her abusive. Phillip described her as "a saint," "practically a nun," and "our second mother." Gary said she beat them with wire hangers. "Ha," Phillip countered; they were *wood* hangers, heavier than balsa but easily broken, and as she chased the boys over their beds, paddling away, the hangers splintered and the fragments flew across the room. Which proves what a liar Gary was, Phillip observed, just trying to be another Christina Crawford.

Georgie lived with the family long after Dixie's death, devoted in her fashion to all the Crosbys, but not as much as she had been to Dixie. Bing's second wife, Kathryn Grant, referred to her as Mrs. Danvers and eventually dismissed her. "Georgie would have killed my father if my mother said, 'Kill him,'" Gary joked. Gary accused her of eavesdropping on the boys' bedtime banter and barring them from idling in the kitchen. They sneaked in when she was elsewhere. Wilma, the cook, laughed behind Georgie's back but snapped to at the sound of her clacking footsteps while the boys lammed out the back door.[30]

What Gary, who called her a "bulldog" and a "monster," most hated was the way she prepared lists of the boys' depredations and presented them to Bing when he came home, expecting him to deliver punishments—though "she was also given the right to punish us. She believed in the letter of the law and if we broke the rules, she could whip us, too, which she did. She beat the shit out of us if Mom was passed out." Lindsay at first figured she was carrying out Dixie's orders but soon doubted that and came to resent her. This picture contradicts the observations of outsiders, as well as Phillip—who in later years sent her money and helped provide for her in a nursing home—and fails to explain her standing in the family, which was higher than any other Crosby employee.[31]

The daughter of Leo Lynn, the Gonzaga classmate who became Bing's stand-in and driver, remembered Georgie as "a really nice woman. Dixie really liked her, and she always seemed to, from all appearances, take very good care of the boys." Women in the Crosby office spoke well of her. The secretary Nancy Briggs thought Georgie "could be a lot of fun but was a no-nonsense woman who really did run that household, no doubt about it, and kind of raised the boys." Dixie's friends admired Georgie for seeing she ate the right things and giving her sedatives to put her to sleep. Georgie sent the boys presents when they were away in the summer. In later years, Bing entrusted her with dispensing their allowances.[32] She was the only servant other than the ranch hands who was regularly mentioned in the boys' letters; they thanked her for her packages of cookies and lollipops, though only Gary included her in his salutations—"Dear Mommy and Daddy and Linny and Georgie."[33]

The problems at home coupled with the ASCAP strike began to tell on Bing's work. He limited record sessions to summer months, completing thirty-five sides, as opposed to sixty in 1940. Except for lulls when the American Federation of Musicians' strikes shut down the business, this was his least prolific year for commercial recordings between 1935 and 1955, his last year with Decca. A few gems alleviated the diet of public-domain heirlooms, and overall sales remained strong: nineteen hits in 1941, though none topped the charts. As the country went gaga over *Road to Zanzibar,* he delivered a reticent if much praised performance in *Birth of the Blues,* the first feature film about the dawning of jazz, though the word *jazz* isn't mentioned in it. The script favors the terms *blues* and *darkie music,* which—though the latter was abhorrent by 1941—have a certain historical validity. The movie, though racist in its very concept, counters racism by emphasizing the theme that American vernacular music—specifically swing as popularized by whites—has its foundation in black music. This idea, commonplace in Europe and accepted by jazz aficionados, represented a step forward for Hollywood, where blacks were usually depicted as maids, porters, and fools, and for the United States, where jazz was lauded, if at all, as the music that whites (George Gershwin, Paul Whiteman, Benny Goodman) refined from unlettered Negro folk music.[34]

Birth of the Blues is invariably described as one of Crosby's favorite films, because Bing says so in *Call Me Lucky*. The unedited type-script of that book shows that Bing said nothing of the kind; Pete Martin added the line because it was one of *his* favorites. Bing recalled it indifferently except for the music, and even there his memory proved shaky. He admired the (uncredited) arrangements by his friend Joe Lilley, "a very gifted guy" who had worked on the Paramount music staff nearly five years yet never received a credit until *Holiday Inn* later that year—at Crosby's insistence. Lilley won him over with his arrangement of "Wait Till the Sun Shines, Nellie," a duet for Bing and Mary Martin, later reprised for a lively Decca disc that did count among Bing's favorites; "a very big record that did us both a lot of good," he said, though its sales were actually average. He told Pete Martin that Hoagy Carmichael wrote the only new song in the picture, conceived as a trio for Bing, Mary, and the trombonist-singer Jack Teagarden, called "The Waiter and the Porter and the Upstairs Maid." In fact, the song was written by Johnny Mercer. The unwitting slip may have reflected Bing's on-and-off exasperation with Mercer.

In 1941, that song's assignment meant a great deal to Mercer. Bing stood up to his own music publisher and to Paramount's publishing wing to award it. Mercer needed the boost, and their friendship flourished. "Dear Gate," Bing wrote him, "When you coming home. Dixie can beat you now at tennis" and "I alluz knew Hollywood's loss would be Gotham's gain" and, via telegram, WILL BE LOOKING FOR-WARD TO SEEING YOU ANYTIME YOU CAN GET DOWN CALL ME AT RANCHO-SANTAFE. But then it cooled, owing to Mercer's drinking, which intensified his festering envy. It was bad enough he couldn't make it as an actor, but he also faltered as a singer; his sole successes until he founded Capitol Records had been duets with Bing. And worse, the constant presence of Johnny Burke in the Crosby fold meant that he would never be Bing's principal lyricist. He socialized with the Burkes as well as the Crosbys but, with drink in him, sneered at the mention of Burke's name. According to Mercer's wife, Ginny (an early Crosby flame who never forgot his romantic and "very erudite" letters), the break came when Bing accused him of making a drunken pass at Dixie. They would continue to work together and Bing often promoted him as a singer and never hesitated to record his songs, but after that, the socializing tapered off.[35]

The concept for *Birth of the Blues* originated with Paramount's new head of production, Buddy G. DeSylva, recruited in February after the abrupt exit of William LeBaron. Paramount's Byzantine politics resulted in a succession of production chiefs, all of whom reported to the official studio head, Y. Frank Freeman, who understood movies strictly as profit-and-loss projects, caring little for them as entertainment, let alone as art. Barney Balaban, Paramount's president, hired DeSylva because he had a background in musicals and could be counted on to strengthen LeBaron's genial association with Bing. DeSylva had conquered most aspects of show business, displaying an uncanny grasp of when to cut and run for greener pastures. With composer Ray Henderson and fellow lyricist Lew Brown (Phil Silvers observed that Lew Brown, a gagman at heart, "needed DeSylva to edit and harness his ideas to make them work"), Buddy formed the most prosperous songwriting team of the Prohibition years, creating a cycle of Roaring Twenties anthems that combined effortless hook-laden melodies with risqué or maudlin lyrics. Crosby performed at an event honoring him in those years, back when he was but a Rhythm Boy and DeSylva was the toast of the town. DeSylva quit the team and the songwriting trade right before the market crashed, forsaking flappers and sheikhs to produce Depression pictures at Fox, including five starring Shirley Temple. When moppet futures flagged, he hastened back to Broadway and, in one season, mounted three eminent hits, two with scores by Cole Porter and one with a score by Irving Berlin.[36]

Then Balaban called, and DeSylva said good-bye to Broadway. He lorded over Paramount through 1944, when his heart convinced him he could take no more and then gave out anyway, in 1950, when DeSylva was fifty-five. He ran the studio zealously and intrusively, enjoying power and extending himself on behalf of his A-team — Crosby, Hope, Gary Cooper, and the new finds of his tenure, Alan Ladd and Veronica Lake. He protected the studio's directors, a daring bullpen that included the old right-wing buccaneer Cecil B. DeMille, the old left-wing aesthete Frank Tuttle, two irreverent young hotshots, Billy Wilder and Preston Sturges, and, on loan from RKO, the esteemed Paramount veteran Leo McCarey, who had been driven from the studio for refusing to destroy his masterpiece *Make Way for Tomorrow* with a happy ending and losing money to boot. DeSylva had caprices. Short, natty, chinless, he lived in clouds of smoke, which he rolled around his tongue like the caterpillar in Wonderland. He did not mind being kidded, but he guarded his autonomy. Sturges's bluff independence rankled him—they fought bitterly over Sturges's insistence on casting Ella Raines in *Hail the Conquering Hero*—to the point where he pushed him from the lot. Yet DeSylva faced down Freeman ("Y. Frank Freeman," Wilder famously mused, "a question nobody can answer") to protect *Going My Way, Sullivan's Travels, Double Indemnity,* and *The Lost Weekend.* At the same time, he seized another arena of the entertainment business, privately investing with Johnny Mercer and Glenn Wallichs to create Capitol Records.[37]

Settled behind Paramount's arched gates, he launched his reign with an idea that charmed Bing even as it augmented his own ASCAP royalties. "The Birth of the Blues," a prized item in the Henderson/DeSylva/Brown catalog, written for Harry Richman and *George White's Scandals of 1926,* is not a blues song. But it skillfully depicts the obstetrics of blues as a "new note" that is pushed "through a horn" and nursed and rehearsed until the word goes out that "the Southland gave birth to the blues!" A director named Monta Bell had once paid a thousand dollars for the title, expecting to use it for a film. DeSylva now bought the title back and made Bell the picture's producer.

DeSylva's idea was to fictionalize the beginnings of the Original Dixieland Jazz Band, the first white band to leave New Orleans. They created a sensation in Chicago, New York, and Europe, before rapidly fading with the rise of a more serious and accomplished generation of musicians that included King Oliver, Jelly Roll Morton, Louis Armstrong, Bix Beiderbecke, and Duke Ellington. The ODJB used the word *Jass* instead of *Jazz* in its name until vandals crossed out the *J* on their advertising posters. Its members worked alongside and studied black musicians in New Orleans, but up north the band became known for pandering to audiences with low comic antics. Still, the ODJB played the real thing and, in 1917, made the first successful jazz records, spawning numberless imitation bands with *New Orleans* in their names no matter where they hailed from. These early white bands incarnated a social-sexual aggression that Duke Ellington (echoing Hamlet by way of a 1923 bestseller) immortalized as "Flaming Youth." DeSylva's story, set entirely in New Orleans and entirely fictional, paid homage to black music while documenting the phenomenon of white outlaw musicians who breached the racial divide. In the ODJB period, pundits blamed jazz for every kind of moral dissolution, including an uptick in rape. Unsurprisingly, the film's trumpeter Memphis (played by Brian Donlevy) is found in a jail cell. Most white jazzmen were born of immigrants (the ODJB members were Italian and Irish), a point omitted from the picture. The thorough whiteness of the wailers accentuated the insurgent claim, new to movies, that black music was an American birthright in which everyone could proudly partake.

In a widely noted sequence, Betty Lou (Mary Martin) discloses that she can carry a tune. Unfortunately, she cannot make it swing, a fact made appealingly clear when she warbles a British music-hall ditty, "Waiting at the Church," in a droll faux-operatic style— Martin at her adorable best but of no use to a blues band. So she seeks advice, not from Jeff (Crosby), but from his pal and erstwhile family retainer Louey, played by Eddie "Rochester" Anderson, on the grounds that "you have been a colored man a long time." She tells him: "I want to sing like the colored folks." He judges her rendition of "Wait Till the Sun Shines, Nellie" corny, and he teaches her what a bass line is. This makes the difference—not that he is allowed to hear the result. He is barred by a black doorman (Ernest Whitman) from the club that hires her. In an approving column in the *California Eagle,* L.A.'s African American paper, Earl J. Morris deemed Betty Lou's tête-à-tête with Louey "very funny." He was also pleased to see the role of Louey's wife played by Ruby Elzy, the original Serena in *Porgy and Bess*; Elzy was an artist Eleanor Roosevelt had provocatively invited to the White House to entertain the Supreme Court. "Elzy," he wrote, "solidly chirps the 'St. Louis Blues' as W. C. Handy meant it to be sung."[38]

The film's closing montage, meant to show how the renegade music of old New Orleans provided the foundation for the famous musicians of the 1940s (Armstrong, Ellington, vaudevillian Ted Lewis, both Dorseys, and, inevitably, Whiteman, Gershwin, and Goodman), is explicit: modern American pop was born of Southern blues. When Betty Lou refers to Jeff's "blue music," he demurs and tells her "That ain't mine. That's gonna be everybody's blue music." Morris applauded the inclusion of Armstrong and Ellington in the montage and lamented the absence of Count Basie and two white bands, Will Bradley and Bob Crosby.[39] We also might wonder at the absence of Jimmie Lunceford, Artie Shaw, Glenn Miller, and Cab Calloway. But the picture's choice of stock footage aims for a broader scope than swing; it balances audience recognition against an aesthetic in which the blues element exists as an indispensable if sometimes remote ingredient seasoning all of American vernacular music.

Earl Morris described a scene in which the white characters avenge Louey, who is almost killed by the bad guys, as an instance of "interracial amity at its height." Yet amity is sorely tested by scenes like the one on the levee where black musicians are played by the ubiquitous Mantan Moreland and Sam McDaniel as jovial nitwits who inspect the bells of their horns as if they have no idea where their music comes from and—the insult squared—are outplayed by a white boy. These are plot points that would recur in jazz-themed movies over the next twenty years, beginning months later with Warners' *Blues in the Night*. Other clichés born here: white musicians are idealists who care nothing about money; they seek authenticity by imitating blacks who disappear after (figuratively or literally) passing them their art; they work for gangsters who threaten to kill them if they resist lifelong contracts or get too jazzy; they worship high notes; they share one girlfriend, a singer, who ends up in the arms of the film's top-billed star.

Birth of the Blues is musical comedy, and so the white musicians and the thugs are portrayed as knuckleheads. But their idiocies, including ODJB stage shtick, are merely tiresome, not excruciating. The depiction of black musicians, at least in the first reel, seems designed to allay the fears of Southern distributors—a point specifically addressed in caveats issued by the censor Joseph Breen. "It is very questionable as to how the people of the South will react to these scenes showing a white boy playing with the Negro band," he wrote Luigi Luraschi in a letter burdened with anxieties. "Any suggestion that the colored girl is acting 'flirtatiously' toward Jeff, a white man, should be avoided." Most of his qualms concern sex (brothels cannot be brothels) and piety ("We urge and recommend that you change 'prayin' ' to 'hopin' '"). He blue-penciled one scene in which a white bouncer kicks a "colored man" out of a barroom: "We think it would be better to have a white man kicked out." Surely, he was less alarmed by racial callousness than he was by the implication of an integrated clientele.[40]

The script went through several drafts in March and April.[41] At one point, Breen requested a meeting to discuss "innumerable" improprieties. Interestingly, he didn't get a meeting. In the end, he won small points and lost big ones. No one could look at this film and fail to realize that the "darkies" were instructors and whites their willing acolytes. Yet as late as August, during postproduction, he called for edits, cutting some four feet of "Mr. Brian Donlevy moving his hands down Mary Martin's back" and snipping shots of extras getting "clunked" with bottles and chairs. "We cleaned the bordellos up," Bing later lamented, but "it had some wonderful music."[42]

Birth of the Blues was the fourth and last film Victor Schertzinger directed with Bing—he died two weeks before it premiered.[43] He finished it under budget (around $850,000), in spite of last-minute alterations that deleted much of Betty Lou's backstory and, to Bing's evident relief, downplayed the romantic angle, which is handled even more chastely than the one in *Rhythm on the River*. Bing ignores Mary's one attempt at a clinch; she impulsively grabs his shoulders, he steadily delivers his line. He does hold her hand in their final scene. Bing expertly works his conman persona from the Road pictures, speaking glibly while pocketing cash, informal to the point of indifference. Unwilling to glue on the scalp doily more than absolutely necessary, he sported a "lucky hat" for most scenes. His muted performance is not unimpressive (the National Board of Review named him one of the year's best actors for *Birth of the Blues* and *Road to Zanzibar*)—emotion-free, yet superbly timed. Brian Donlevy, who bothered to create a character with a wolfish grin, seems marooned in the wrong picture. Everyone else is a friend of Bing, taking it easy, especially the eminently mellow Teagarden—legato in song, slurred in speech.

Bing knew him in the speakeasy era, when Jack worked with the Ben Pollack orchestra and was widely recognized as the first white musician to achieve a genuine mastery of blues. He was hired to play a small role, just one of the musicians, but his part was built up with the dialogue of a character dropped from the script. Mercer's song "The Waiter and the Porter and the Upstairs Maid" places him on equal footing with Bing and Mary, its lyrics echoing the plot in describing sexual intrigue among the help. At the same time, Teagarden's orchestra performed nightly at Hollywood's Casa Manana, so the film recruited his musicians, notably trumpet player Pokey Carriere, to dub the playing of Donlevy's character, and clarinetist Danny Polo, to dub Bing's. Other Teagarden sidemen appear in the film as musicians or extras along with the unfailingly energetic Harry Barris, as a bassist who accidentally invents pizzicato, and the guitarist Perry Botkin, Bing's accompanist for decades to come.

Bing insisted on Mary as leading lady although she was three months pregnant, a surefire way to hurry things along. She had decided the baby would be named Heller, boy or girl. As they filmed a scene in which the band takes her home in an open beer wagon, the conveyance hit a bump and she bounced off. Bing jumped after her, looking horrified but singing, to the melody of the title song, "The Birth of Heller." For the second take, used in the picture, she sits demurely and Bing tumbles off—an improvised pratfall evoking his time with Mack Sennett. Her pregnancy caused no distress for *Birth of the Blues* (or vice versa), which was Martin's favorite project with Bing, fortifying their friendship. She admired what it brought out in him, his "love for New Orleans music and black people and the way they did it, the way they sang it. He had that style, too, in his singing, and that's hard to get. His voice was sexy. It didn't matter if he [just] said hello. The only people who had that quality were Nat 'King' Cole and Bing."[44] She recalled how happy he was with Teagarden, Barris, and the rest. Wingy Manone, though not in the film, hung around the set, playing practical jokes to unsettle the sedate Teagarden and sharing the herb stored in his prosthesis.

Everyone expected "The Waiter and the Porter" to do well, and it did, but audiences responded most to older numbers (assembled under the supervision of Robert Emmett Dolan, who received the picture's only Academy Award nomination), which provided a series of enchanting episodes: Bing and Mary's duet on "Wait Till the Sun Shines, Nellie," complete with Teagarden solo (a price tag hangs from his jacket sleeve); Bing's rendition of the title song during the decorative credits; his too-brief take on "Memphis Blues"; his "My

Melancholy Baby," crooned to a child (Carolyn Lee) and backed by Botkin; Teagarden exhibiting his celebrated knack for playing with a slide and a water glass (the latter replacing the trombone bell and tubing); Ruby Elzy's blistering "St. Louis Blues," tears streaming down her face. A sequence dear to Bing re-created his apprenticeship at the Clemmer Theater in Spokane, when he would sing an entr'acte number to a slide show before the featured film. Monta Bell secured an excerpt from a 1925 picture that played at the Clemmer, *The Golden Princess,* to set the stage. Schertzinger devised the idea of photographing the authentic color slides *in* color—a bit of wizardry achieved by shooting Crosby singing "By the Light of the Silvery Moon" in black-and-white against a blank screen and double-printing his scene and the color slides on Technicolor film stock.

Shooting continued through the first days of June, absent Bing for most of Wednesday and Thursday, when he rehearsed and aired *Kraft Music Hall.* Bob Burns, Connie Boswell, and the Music Maids continued as regulars, along with John Scott Trotter's orchestra. They and the music guests, including Mary Martin, Teagarden, Ethel Waters, the Ink Spots, soprano Josephine Tuminia, harmonicist Leo Diamond, and Tahitian percussionist Augie Goupil, made the best of an ASCAP-free diet: Stephen Foster plus Brahms's "Lullaby"; "Clementine"; "Blues My Naughty Sweetie Gives to Me"; "The Friendly Tavern Polka"; "Amapola"; "Carry Me Back to Old Virginny"; "Dance of the Hours" as a bazooka solo; and so forth.

Duke Ellington circumvented his ASCAP affiliation in two appearances, playing a duet with his fabled bassist Jimmy Blanton on "Jumpin' Punkins," credited to his then-ununionized son Mercer Ellington, and two debuts that he never recorded commercially: "Stomp Caprice," also credited to Mercer (though it was actually an excerpt from the Ellington revue *Jump for Joy,* duly heralded in his scripted chat with Bing), and a largely improvised "Jive Rhapsody." The Ellington piece that really attracted attention was a flashy piano concerto based on the folk song "Frankie and Johnny," pairing Ellington with the Trotter band. It became a popular wartime showcase for him, yet he never recorded it with his orchestra beyond the disc transcribed from his radio performance.[45]

By that time, Bing had inadvertently put his mark on the Ellington orchestra. Ever since Duke recorded with him in 1932 ("St. Louis Blues"[46]), the bandleader insisted he would not hire a male vocalist until he could find a Crosby-range baritone. After playing the Apollo Theater on the same bill as an all-black Western called *The Bronze Buckaroo,* he invited its star, Herb Jeffries, to make a tour with the band. In his memoirs, Ellington recalled that Jeffries was initially "inclined to the falsetto [but] between shows, while everybody else was playing poker, Herb would be ad-libbing and doing imitations all over the place." When Ellington and his young collaborator Billy Strayhorn heard him do Bing, they shouted "Just stay on Bing!" Jeffries recalled, "Duke thought Bing was one of the greatest baritones of all time. He used to talk so much about the mellow, rich, baritone voice of Crosby, and I began to lower my range. Then I started listening to his records, and he became sort of my guru. One day Ellington heard me doing an impersonation on 'Where the Blue of the Night,' and he said, 'That's the voice I want you to record with!' So I started using that timbre [but] I also developed a dramatic voice with a little more volume to avoid an impersonation." At RCA during Christmas week of 1940, the band recorded Strayhorn's arrangement of a pop song, "Flamingo," featuring Jeffries's vocal. It sold millions, lifting the band's fortunes and ensuring that Ellington would have carte blanche in his RCA contract.[47]

Bing varied the usual *KMH* cast of character actors and occasional stars with sports figures and writers, including John O'Hara (who boasted glowingly of the experience in *Newsweek*), Ogden Nash, and James Hilton. These shows have not survived beyond the scripts and transcriptions of select musical numbers, yet historic poignancy attaches to at least one of them. Paul Robeson and Lew Ayres appeared on the February 6 show, broadcast the week Bing dispatched Dixie to Sun Valley. Within a year Robeson would be honored as a national treasure for organizing benefits for the war effort while Ayres, the movies' Dr. Kildare, would be vilified for declaring himself a conscientious objector and enlisting in the medical corps. A few years later, Robeson would be Red-baited, his passport confiscated and his name blacklisted, as was the patriotic cantata *Ballad for Americans* that he and Bing had recorded — separately but with equal success — and that had been used to open the Republican presidential convention of 1940.[48]

7

SOUTH AMERICA, TAKE IT AWAY

*Hollywood [is] no longer in Hollywood but is stippled by
a billion feet of burning colored gas across the face of the
American earth.*
> —William Faulkner, *The Wild Palms* (1939)

In May 1941, Bing turned his attention to Decca, conveniently located directly across Melrose Avenue from the Paramount gate. Determined to take his delayed South American trip that fall, he scheduled eight sessions for spring and summer, stockpiling platters to last out the year. The government had involved itself in the ASCAP strike but to no avail, and so he slogged through "Nell and I," "The Old Oaken Bucket" (from 1826), "Old Black Joe," "I Wonder What's Become of Sally," "Dear Little Boy of Mine," "Oh, How I Miss You Tonight," and "Mary's a Grand Old Name." Even by Jack Kapp's nostalgic lights, this stuff was rough going. The affecting sorrow, the honest sense of loss that previously informed Bing's evocations of similar material, disappeared, replaced by an impassive sense of duty. The records sold anyway; if the public preferred a beat, it also maintained its hankering for the comforts of the past. Bing's "Lights Out 'Til Reveille," a placid portent of the gathering storm, was hailed by *Time* as "the only US war song to date that seems tuneful and honest enough to outlast the war"[1] and held to the pop charts for three months; a disc that combined Brahms's "Lullaby" and Meredith Willson's sedate "You and I" also did well. Bing attempted to shake things up with Dixieland renovations of Gene Autry songs ("Be Honest with Me," "Goodbye, Little Darlin', Goodbye"), but the material held him in check. He sang in Spanish ("No Te Importe Saber") and French ("Darling, Je Vous Aime Beaucoup") and returned to Ireland ("Danny Boy"), with little joy. Most dishearteningly, he revisited his breakthrough number of 1928, "Ol' Man River," without the upbeat élan that made his first foray electrifying. His recording of "The Birth of the Blues" lacks the energy of the movie version.

There were exceptions. Backed by Teagarden's band, he re-created the wit of "The Waiter and the Porter," with Jack and Mary. (He didn't record "Wait Till the Sun Shines, Nellie" until the following year, after their radio performances upped its popularity.) Bing's version of "You Are My Sunshine," with a nifty Perry Botkin guitar intro, did more than the one by its composer Jimmie Davis to establish it as a standard, and it is rumored to have elicited a fan letter from Winston Churchill.[2] He is in rotund voice and a droll mood on "Clementine," which has two tempos and two time signatures and Bing's verbal embellishments: "Do I sound like Gene Autry / Could he sue me, Clementine" and "Plant you now, dig you later, like a tater, Clementine." But it's still "Clementine." He recorded and helped write a lively sixty-second promotional fanfare for the Del Mar racetrack based on a phrase coined by Dixie's friend Midge Polesie: "Where the Turf Meets the Surf." (His recording kicks off its races to this day.) After a pair of disappointing sessions with Woody Herman, to which Burke and Van Heusen contributed two uninspired songs, he recouped with a marvelous romp through "I Ain't Got Nobody."

Yet Bing's most touching performance from this strange interlude is his treatment of the deathless 1911 college fraternity song "The Sweetheart of Sigma Chi." Sentimental though it is ("The girl of my dreams is the sweetest girl / Of all the girls I know"), the song's elongated vowels, chromatic phrases, and canny use of diminished chords work well with Bing's unruffled ardor. It is an outstanding example of his ability to sing a song almost exactly as written, with few ornaments, and yet stamp his imprimatur on every note and syllable. A warm-up take affords his audiences a glimpse into his procedural method. Jack Kapp preserved an unusual number of rejected takes from the 1941 sessions. These alternates hold little interest except for the one-minute rundown of "The Sweetheart of Sigma Chi" in which Bing is backed by Trotter's piano and Botkin's guitar. He voices each pitch squarely at a fast tempo and utterly devoid of feeling. Bing is rehearsing, testing the intervals. And then, with Trotter's orchestra behind him, he comes fully alive, transforming the tatty tavern paean into something very like an art song.

As the summer wore on, Bing focused on plans for the South American horse-buying foray and the development of his next picture. With the windfall receipts from *Zanzibar*, Paramount extended him rare latitude; in 1941, he completed, start to finish, only one film. The new project would have to start rolling shortly after he returned from his vacation. What would it be? The trade papers were rife with rumors. Reports included *Road to Moscow*, though Paramount instantly sent out a correction; the next port of call, when they got around to it, would be Morocco. The studio assigned Delmer Daves to adapt a William Bowers radio play for Bing and Mary Martin, but it was shelved after several treatments failed to jell. William LeBaron, now at Fox, hoped to obtain Bing's independent picture deal for *Caribbean Cruise*, costarring Alice Faye and Carmen Miranda, but Bing quietly permitted his free-agent clause to lapse, pledging Paramount exclusivity for the next three years.

In truth, his next picture had been in contractual development since February. Back in 1933, Irving Berlin wrote the song "Easter Parade" for *As Thousands Cheer*, a revue conceived with Moss Hart in which each song was tied to a news event or celebrity. Berlin suggested they follow up with a holiday revue — sixteen national holidays, each triggering a Berlin song — but Hart lost interest and Berlin went onto other projects, including breakthrough RKO musicals for Fred Astaire and Ginger Rogers (*Top Hat* and *Follow the Fleet*), directed by Mark Sandrich. A chance encounter in Washington between Berlin and Sandrich in 1940 got the ball rolling again on the holiday idea, which Berlin, who never failed to protect his inspirations, had already submitted for copyright.

Sandrich told Berlin he had left RKO for Paramount to work with Jack Benny and that, having directed and produced three successful pictures (including the megahit *Buck Benny Rides Again*), he hoped to return to his forte, song-and-dance musicals. Berlin told him about his revue idea, called *Happy Holiday*. Sandrich said it might be ideal for Bing Crosby if Irving could fashion a storyline—revues did not work in pictures.

Berlin and Sandrich opened discussions with Paramount during the LeBaron regime and offered a story about a reluctant entertainer (in the first treatment, Berlin described him as "Bing Crosby without Crosby's ambition") who decides to work only on holidays, leaving his partner in the lurch. As they talked it through, Sandrich suggested they enlarge the role of the ex-partner for Astaire, who had left RKO to freelance and bowed at Paramount with a dud, *Second Chorus*. Desperate for a partner who did not make audiences long for Ginger, Astaire signed on to do a film for Columbia with a gorgeous contract player, Rita Hayworth, whose jubilant dancing skills had yet to be recognized. Beyond that, he had nothing going and relished the prospect of working for the first time with "the great Cros."

In February, as Sandrich completed work on a romantic comedy, *Skylark*, Buddy DeSylva entered the picture, an agreeable development: "I for one feel that it is a very shrewd move on the part of the company," Sandrich wrote to Berlin. "[DeSylva] certainly evidenced tremendous vitality in his first days on the job"—and he seemed particularly interested in their holiday film, so much so that he assigned another RKO emigrant, Ben Holmes, who wrote and directed short subjects to help with the story. Sandrich added, "I can't seem to bury my anxiety and excitement about getting into our project."[3] He had cause for anxiety when DeSylva nixed Fred.

It was a question of money. The combined salaries of Astaire and Crosby, plus Berlin's price (which included 10 percent of the gross and musical rights), would raise the budget to the danger point. Why waste two stars on one picture? "I can get George Murphy for $50,000," DeSylva observed at an executive meeting. "Why do I need Astaire for $100,000?" In Berlin's telling, Sandrich—"one of the most self-effacing guys in the world"—responded, "If we don't get Fred Astaire, we don't do the picture." That silenced the room, until Y. Frank Freeman, seeing his chance to trump the crafty DeSylva, leaped in: "Mark, if that's what *you* want, we'll get Fred Astaire."[4]

By March, everyone was fired up. In April, Berlin returned to Los Angeles with a conventional treatment. This time, Bing retires to a farm, which he turns into a musical inn during holidays. Fred, playing a Broadway hoofer at the outset of a movie career, stops at the farm en route to Hollywood to pick up show-business advice from Bing. Mary Martin ricochets between them as a secret heiress and an amateur singer performing in Bing's holiday shows.

Sandrich hired his cousin Zion Myers, who wrote *Skylark* and worked on the three Jack Benny pictures, to join with himself and Berlin at Arrowhead Springs in San Bernardino for an eleven-day conference. They emerged on April 28 with a new treatment and a declaration: "To start with, it is our aim to tell this picture in as new a way or form for the screen as possible."[5] Exercising his contractual control of casting, Berlin wrote Alice Faye, the queen of Twentieth Century–Fox musicals, into the treatment, replacing Martin as a shopgirl who answers an ad for a performer to work at the inn. Faye would be second-billed after Bing. Why Berlin and Sandrich entertained the idea, even in the rarefied ambience of Arrowhead, that Darryl Zanuck would loan out his top musical star is unknown, but the supposition of three major stars required an equitable division of songs. So Berlin created an emotionally climactic number for Alice, who was famous for her languid close-up ballads.

As Independence Day approaches, Bing sings to Alice a new song, "White Christmas," before performing "This Is a Great Country" for his July 4 customers. Fred arrives with a slam-bang idea for the next holiday: "The Wedding of Capital and Labor," with Fred as Capital, Alice as Labor, and Bing as the Board of Arbitration. A Hollywood mogul is present when this number is mounted, and he wants them to costar in a picture set in a studio replica of Holiday Inn. Bing declines, but Fred and Alice are swept into a montage of holiday songs, coming to ground at the premiere of their film in a Los Angeles theater on Christmas Eve. Sitting in the audience, Alice hears Bing's voice in her head and weeps. As she leaves the theater, the sun is shining. She hears a choir singing a verse that describes her feelings of dislocation in Beverly Hills. It is December

24; she is longing to be up north. She is dreaming of a "White Christmas." When the dream concludes, the dying notes mingle with the drone of an airplane and the tinkling of sleigh bells. We return to the inn as "Alice rushes in, covered with snow, wet and happy, and into his arms." The end.[6]

Clearly, they had a lot of work to do, though in all the drafts and correspondence, no one commented on the central silliness of the plot: How can an inn produce expensive musicals if it's open only on holidays? They compiled a list of writers who could work with Berlin in New York. Finding their first choice, Allan Scott (who wrote most of Astaire's RKO films), unavailable, they gambled on Elmer Rice, a playwright celebrated in the 1920s and early 1930s for navigating between expressionist parody and ethnic-slum realism. Rice's day had passed, but Berlin lunched with him shortly before the dramatist was scheduled to fly to California, and "he left me with the impression that he might have something to offer this set-up." Sandrich greeted Rice on his arrival and came away from their conversation "quite amazed at his understanding and sympathy for our story."[7]

The casting problem remained. Alice Faye was a pipe dream, and besides, Bing wanted Mary Martin for the love interest. It was because of him that Berlin, who was slow in cottoning to her, wrote Martin into his early treatment. This was a clash Bing could not win. DeSylva hardly needed to remind him that she was pregnant. Well, she wouldn't be pregnant when they went into production. Even so, DeSylva countered, she might not want to go from the maternity ward to a soundstage and they couldn't wait till the last minute to cast the female lead. Anyway, with two major stars on board, this was a chance to promote a couple of low-wage contract players. The press office let it be known that the studio interviewed hundreds of women for the picture. Some auditions and tests of actresses did take place (Dale Evans and Joan Leslie among them), but two players had the inside track. Sandrich wanted Virginia Dale for the pivotal role of Linda Mason. Having started in a music-hall act with her sister (the Paxton Sisters, each a beauty-contest winner), Virginia could sing and dance, and she had attracted notice for her appearance in *Las Vegas Nights*. Monta Bell had wanted her for *Birth of the Blues;* she wasn't hired, but she did appear in two of Sandrich's Jack Benny comedies.

That left the second female lead, Fred's fickle dance partner, who disappears for much of the film. Marjorie Reynolds did not sing or dance, though she had served time in a chorus line. But she was lovely and game and could lip-synch a voiceover vocalist (Martha Mears). She had paid her dues in dozens of programmers, mostly Westerns, during which she grew friendly with choreographer Danny Dare—the dance director on *Holiday Inn.* He told Reynolds to dye her brown hair blond and arranged a screen test that lasted a grueling eighteen hours. Impressed by her dauntless good humor, Sandrich cast her as Linda Mason, switching Virginia Dale to the lesser role. Berlin approved both women, as did Bing, whose attention was now devoted to leisure pursuits.

In August, the new season at Del Mar proved the most lucrative to date: the pari-mutuel numbers soared along with the attendance. Bing serenaded the first-day crowd of ten thousand with his track song, "Where the Turf Meets the Surf," before conducting an afternoon radio quiz on horse racing. Three favorites came in at the first meet. He played golf for charity and shared a box with Charlie Chaplin, Cary Grant, and Deanna Durbin at Wrigley Field for a baseball match that benefited Mount Sinai (the teams' captains were Martha Raye and Ann Sheridan). He appeared on air in the Treasury Department's *Millions for Defense* broadcast beside Paul Muni and Dorothy Maynor, a soprano who toured the world's great concert halls but was barred from American opera stages because of her color. A new list of outsize salaries surfaced, and Bing figured sixth among the Hollywood elite, after Gary Cooper (on top), James Cagney, John Ford, Hal Wallis, Edward G. Robinson, and Darryl Zanuck.[8]

ASCAP's strike showed symptoms of settlement or exhaustion. But just as those clouds seemed to break, the despotic head of the American Federation of Musicians, James Caesar Petrillo, excoriated record companies for cramping the income of concert musicians. One of his investigators declared, "It is necessary for us to evolve a plan for the possible discontinuance of the use of records on radio stations."[9] As a radio star, Bing saw the wisdom in that. As a recording star, he saw the graffiti on the wall: another strike! Most observers did not think it likely or possible. The nation faced greater perils, like the war in Europe. A musicians' strike and recording ban seemed too crazy even for Petrillo.

Bing had intended to make the South American trip with Lindsay Howard, the heir and sportsman (and Linny's namesake), with whom he partnered in Binglin Stock Farm in Moorpark and bought the La Portena Ranch in a province of Buenos Aires—home to Caballeriza Binglin Stock Farm. A ranking polo player, Howard frequently competed in Argentina, and he had already scouted and returned with notable horses, including Ligaroti, whose 1938 match race with Seabiscuit (owned by Howard's father) made national headlines. This trip, Howard had to cancel. Bing resolved to travel alone aboard the SS *Argentina*—the prize of FDR's Good Neighbor fleet—for a six-week vacation. He kept his departure a secret from practically everyone, including Paramount, recognizing that rumors of marital discord would follow. Thus far, the rumors remained sub-rosa, but a separation of six weeks would peel the petals. Dixie feared as much. The day before he departed from New York's Canal Street dock, she invited the *Los Angeles Herald-Express* columnist Harrison Carroll to the house in Rancho Santa Fe to laugh away the gossip.

Had he flown, she would have gone with him, she told Carroll, but the trip as planned included four weeks at sea, which was too long to be away from the children, and "I'd be sure to get seasick." She said she might work up her nerve to fly down and meet him but emphasized the fact that he "needed to rest, have a good time" and perhaps purchase horses. When Carroll asked the studio execs to comment, he got the impression that it was news to them. But they weren't concerned. His next picture, now called *Holiday Inn*, would not begin shooting until November.[10]

The outbound voyage, beginning August 29, lasted twelve days including a brief stop in Barbados. Bing sent five letters and two wirelesses to Dixie from the ship, all presumed lost today. Dixie returned to 10500 Camarillo Street to put the boys in school, and on September 7, three days before Bing landed in Brazil, she began writing him the first of four surviving letters, completing it the following morning. They bear out her insistence, conveyed to Carroll, that she was very much in love with her husband. Her references to Bing's letters and wires confirms him as a faithful correspondent, though surely not as emotional as Dixie. Still, no Coventry here, and nothing of the lingering breach Dixie predicted to Kitty in Sun Valley.

Sunday 7th
Bing Darling—

As usual this is about the third letter I've attempted and torn up but this one goes regardless.

We had a very gay weekend what with David and his clowning. We went to the track party. Pat put on the show as if he were broadcasting to the S.S. *Argentina*. Everyone really missed you. Sunday nite they started playing your records. That was the last straw. I don't know why but I miss you more this time than I ever have before. When I wake up at nite and realize how far away you are my heart goes right to me toes. You better have a good time 'cause this is the last time you go without me even if I have to walk around golf courses from morning 'til nite.

The house looks so pretty. I know you will love it. The bedroom isn't finished yet so Bess and I are living down in the guest room as I still don't feel settled.

Irma took the children yesterday and I fired Miss Waters (the old witch). She said she was leaving anyway. I have Georgie (the girl who has been with Bill's family all her life) taking care of the children until I can find someone. They all went to Pat Ross's for luncheon to-day and a picture show this afternoon so they're being entertained royally.

I went to the <u>baseball</u> game last nite with David [and] Elsie, Johnny and Bess and then we went to see Phil Silvers for a little while. To-nite they and Judy and Lin are all coming for dinner. Lin called and asked if he could come so I'll be nice to Judy if it kills me. They went down to the ranch yesterday. You probably already know that Preceptor did nothing. La Zonga ran second.

Monday—

You see what happens—Marge and Charles came right in the middle of my letter. Got all of yours this morning and was I happy. It just makes me more lonesome for you.

I'm glad you're getting a nice rest. I didn't realize you weren't
feeling well—you never let anyone know, you brat.

I'll write more often to make up for not having this at Rio.

I love you Darling with all my heart.

Dixie[11]

Arriving in Rio on September 10, he amused the press with his
informality, strolling down the gangway in a cowboy shirt and
smoking what one reporter called "an evil-looking pipe."[12] Bing
was also amused when the dynamic impresario Joaquim Rolla
tried to force him to accept a packet of American dollars. For the
United States, the Good Neighbor policy had specific aims in Brazil, chiefly to dissuade the dictator Getúlio Vargas from joining the
Axis and persuade him to consent to an American airbase in Natal.
Most Brazilians looked at the policy as a peculiar Hollywood game.
North Americans cheered Latino entertainers with flashy tags,
whether they actually came from South America (Carmen
Miranda, the Brazilian Bombshell) or not (Acquanetta, the Vene-
zuelan Volcano, was an American Indian born and raised in Wyoming), and South Americans received regular visits from celebrities
like Errol Flynn, Douglas Fairbanks Jr., Walt Disney, and Orson
Welles. Joachim Rolla, who owned seven casinos, including Corco-
vado's Cassino da Urca, where Miranda launched her career,
received advance notice from his government contacts when Hollywood royalty landed. He would not allow Bing to bypass the
Urca casino.

Bing declined the money, whereupon Rolla offered him a race-
horse, which Bing also declined, and then a sightseeing tour, which
Bing accepted, with the understanding that he was on vacation and
had no intention of working. By the end of the day, despite Rolla's
limited English and Bing's negligible Portuguese, they became
friendly. An observer noted that Crosby was deeply moved by the
beauty of Rio and agreed to make a brief appearance at the casino
when he returned to Rio from Buenos Aires. That night he visited
the rival Copacabana, where a flamboyant redheaded American
organist, Ethel Smith, enjoyed an extended engagement (a few
years later, she recorded saccharine numbers with Bing).[13] Two
days later, he re-embarked on the *Argentina* and continued on the

southwest leg to Santos, in São Paulo, and Montevideo, where he wired Dixie. She wrote back:

Tuesday Morn

Angel, just received your letter from Montevideo. Those clippings have me thrown—guess I will call Ramon.

The 'awfulest' things are happening to me. I have to go to the Pamona fair with Corrine and Jack and Lee and Lucy Batson to-nite. I think I run around with too young a crowd don't you. I'm supposed to play tennis with Don Budge and his wife this afternoon but will have to call it off to get my hair and nails done for the old folks. Nothing like making character. I also had an invite to Judy & Lin's tonight—Some popular.

Now I'm really mad. Bob just came down with a note that is so much better than mine. But I love you more than anyone else does anyhow.

Always

Dixie[14]

That afternoon, the ship reached Buenos Aires, where Bing spent seventeen days, beginning with a visit to a famous nightclub on Avenida Corrientes, Los Inmortales. Harrison Carroll, working from unknown sources, reported a fuss over his arrival, a reception said to be the biggest ever accorded a visiting celebrity. A holiday was declared in his honor; schools and shops were shuttered; a million people jammed the streets. "Bing, who dodges crowds and personal appearances in this country," Carroll wrote, made an automobile tour through the city so that fans could see him.[15] All ballyhoo. Bing waving to the throng? A *million* people? Yet much excitement did ensue and even Paramount executives claimed to be mystified by it since Bing didn't enjoy great box office in Buenos Aires. As *Variety* noted in its front-page story, tangos were "as far removed from Crosby's warbling as FDR from Adolf."[16] *Variety*, too, initially insisted that no Hollywood figure in years had scored such a "solid click" with Argentineans, but it followed up with a more realistic assessment. "Crosby down to vacash and look at horses refrained entirely from personal appearances."[17] To the consternation of local Paramount officials, he refused to attend an opera-house screening of *Road to Zanzibar*. He did, however, have a surprise in mind for which he needed to confer with his *KMH* writer Carroll Carroll.

<u>Thursday</u>
Sweetheart—

Your letters were so wonderful. I wish I could be like you (gee you're lucky) and write long letters.

It was so funny—I called Carroll Carroll to give him your phone number and Bo said he was talking to you. It makes it seem you're so near. If I could only give you one kiss I'd let you go back again.

I went to the Ice Follies with Alice and Hugh last nite. They were very good.

Don't laugh when you get Gary's letter—I had nothing to do with his line "Don't fall in love." He said he told you that to save you a "bump on the noggin" and to save my arm from using the rolling pin. You don't suppose he's been reading Jiggs and Maggie do you. Gee they're funny kids—they seem so much closer to me than ever before. Maybe I take them for granted when you're here and when you're gone they remind me of you.

Having read this one I'd like to tear it up but you said even hello and good-bye helped so here goes.

I love you—I love you—I love you—so there—
Dixie[18]

He visited the Binglin stables, a couple of hours from the city, staying at the ranch of his friend Juan Reynal. On Sunday, one of his best horses, the mare Blackie, won the Premio Selection at the Hipódromo in Palermo. Blackie had quite a career: twenty-three starts, twelve wins, six places, three shows. Bing's other discoveries included Don Bingo, who finished in the money in all but three of seventeen starts, triumphing in Belmont Park's 1943 Suburban Handicap. Bing's willingness to talk horses and his obvious knowledge enhanced his popularity in the country. An editorialist in the leading afternoon paper, *Critica,* observed to Bing that, having played host to a stream of commercial envoys, Argentineans found it a pleasure to (in *Variety*'s translation) "have a lyricist of finance such as you to teach us how to spend and throw away money."

He traveled six hundred miles inland to the cattle-raising province of Corrientes, where he and a couple of South American friends purchased (with Lin's approval) a fifty-thousand-acre cattle ranch and seven thousand head of cattle. Business out of the way, he put on his best good-neighbor hat and a specially tailored new suit (six fittings) for his last week in Buenos Aires. He and Dixie would be apart on September 29, their eleventh anniversary. Bing bought her an alligator handbag and a hand-carved mahogany footstool. She bought him a wedding ring. Bing phoned her the morning before their anniversary and asked her to write a letter now so that it would await him in Rio, a prelude to the long trip home.

> Sunday
> Angel—
>
> You wanted a note at Rio so here it is. I can't begin to tell you what's in my heart but I will when you get home. I was so glad you didn't laugh at me when I told you about the wedding ring. I don't care if you ever wear it as long as you carry it around. It was the only thing I could think of that you didn't have and besides I'm feeling very sentimental these days. I just received the most gorgeous flowers from Julie and an invitation from Mercer to go to Ciro's which I refused. I've decided it's no fun having an anniversary without you.
>
> I'm sorry our connection was so bad this morning but I love you with all my heart and you must know it.[19]

On the evening of October 2, Bing wowed Buenos Aires with his surprise: a thirty-minute *KMH*-style show for Radio El Mundo, which he emceed in Spanish. Kraft Argentina sponsored the broadcast and he donated his fee to a children's charity, Patronato Nacional de Infancia. The smart, funny program endeared him to the public. The script, worked out long distance with Carroll Carroll, required Bing to play straight man to Niní Marshall, the radio comedienne and singer who became one of Argentina's most beloved film stars, and to jive it up with Eduardo Armani's orchestra. Late the next evening, he boarded the SS *Brazil* for the seventeen-day return, with stops at Santos, Rio, and Trinidad. Dixie entertained the idea of flying to Rio and returning with him on the *Brazil* but decided instead to wait for him in New York.

This time when he arrived in Rio, he was greeted by Ed Sullivan, who just happened to be there and who later reported on an impromptu performance Bing gave for the Red Cross at Cassino da Urca. Bing sang one request after another, Sullivan wrote, and brought the house down when a photographer stepped into his light and set off a flash. "Without losing a note or the beat," he noted, Bing responded, "Come right in."[20] A Brazilian reporter remembered the evening enthusiastically but differently. He said Bing showed up unannounced at the benefit, which was promoted by Darci Vargas, the president's wife, to check out the club, not to perform. Carlos Machado, conducting the house band, introduced Bing and invited him up. He tried to demur but gave in and sang "Dinah." The overwhelming reaction pinned him to the stage, where he continued with "Somebody Loves Me." Then he came back to his table, smiling and a little bit tipsy.[21] Resuming the homeward journey, Bing performed solely for the ship's crew, unbeknownst to the passengers, who included a large delegation of deputies from the Argentine national congress.

Accompanied by Bill Sexton, Kitty's husband, Dixie flew to New York, planning a stay of eight days and hoping to "finally squelch the separation rumors."[22] When he docked on the afternoon of October 20, she was there to welcome him home, accompanied by reporters who took advantage of a rare opportunity to pepper him with questions. Asked what he did in South America, Bing said, "Not much," adding that São Paulo looked like Paris did before the invasion, though he had yet to see Europe. He explained that he left two horses behind, purchased to race in South America under Crosby colors (pale blue silks with yellow and red sleeves and a yellow cap). Before the two retired to their hotel, where Bing phoned Buenos Aires and Hollywood on horse business, Bing and Dixie went to the Pennsylvania Hotel's Café Rouge to hear Glenn Miller.[23]

He had maintained a cordial but distant relationship with Miller, whose martinet personality amounted to a reverse image of the Crosby persona. Glenn was all business and capable of blunt bigotry—he told one musician he preferred not to hire Jews or Italians because they were troublemakers—though he shared Bing's reverence for Louis Armstrong, whom he considered "the greatest thing that ever happened to music."[24] He readily acknowledged that a decisive factor in his (long and difficult) climb to the top was his transition to an orchestral style that embraced the baritone range Bing popularized, something he accomplished mostly by accenting trombones. They must have hit it off in New York, because Glenn wrote him a few weeks later, asking him to consider recording a song he partly owned, "Papa Niccolini"—"if you like it." Bing did not like it, but he came through for him the following June by endorsing Glenn's application for a U.S. Naval Reserve commission, writing with zestful support while also describing him as "adequately intelligent."[25]

The next day, he rehearsed two hours and appeared on *The Treasury Hour* with Secretary of the Navy Frank Knox, Carmen Miranda ("Bing! You sing so sweet!"), Noel Coward (patched in from London at the special request of FDR), the widow of John Philip Sousa, and a playlet by Herman Wouk on the formation of the U.S. Navy. Before the week was out, Bing took Dixie to see the Broadway hit *Lady in the Dark* and to a star-studded gala in celebration of the Ritz Brothers that didn't let out until five a.m.; lunched with a Paramount executive; recorded two dull songs completely new to him, one of which, "Shepherd Serenade," stayed high on the charts from Thanksgiving to Christmas; relaxed at the Rainbow Room till after midnight ("Bing Crosby, who doesn't give a durn," one columnist wrote, wore "a blue shirt, brown suit, and bald noggin"[26]); attended a reception for the Duke and Duchess of Windsor; shopped for Christmas presents; and spoke to interviewers with jaunty candor. He summarized his career as three films and forty records a year, and one broadcast and four rounds of golf a week. Concerning the last, he spoke of his tradition of buying the caddie a suit whenever he broke seventy. He took pride in his punctuality: "You have to train yourself to be on time. I lose most of my time, waiting for people, seems like." He admitted that his improvised quips with Hope were really a kind of "rehearsed ad-libbing."

And with all this activity, how did he find time for his children? "You don't need time for them," he said. "You can stand them about 30 minutes a day. Then you have to spend two hours putting the furniture back in place and repairing the broken lamps." He referred to the four boys as "toughies" and quoted Phil Silvers, who, after a rigorous family baseball match, labeled the Crosby boys the Gentile Marx Brothers. No one asked him or Dixie about the rumors of marital discontent.[27]

8

HAPPY HOLIDAY

Last the Musician, as he stood
Illumined by that fire of wood;
Fair-haired, blue-eyed, his aspect blithe.
　　　—Henry Wadsworth Longfellow,
　　　　　Tales of a Wayside Inn (1863)

Bing and Dixie left New York by train, transferred to the Santa Fe Super Chief in Chicago, and rolled into Pasadena on October 30. Dixie's parents brought the boys to greet them, but the gathering was short-lived, as Bing had to be at NBC Studio B in a couple of hours to rehearse his first show of the season, which would be followed by the evening broadcast. Adjustments in the *Kraft Music Hall*, argued about the previous year, began to take shape. Bob Burns, the Arkansas Traveler, left after five years to launch his own program. He was replaced by Jerry Lester, a thirtyish bada-bing veteran of nightclubs whose shtick included mugging, singing, dancing, impressions, and arthritic jokes spat out so quickly the pain had no time to set in. Lester was brought on as a "discovery" of J. Walter Thompson's John Reber, and audiences accepted him more readily than the show's writers did. Ed Helwick remembered him as "a nice guy and amusing but not of the caliber to be on a top show."[1] A few weeks later, they engaged a different type of performer, Victor Borge, the ingenious Danish comedian and pianist. A European concert star (under the name Børge Rosenbaum), he

had escaped the Nazis with empty pockets. Rudy Vallée phoned
KMH's producer Cal Kuhl and insisted, "You've just got to see this
man. You'll want to book him with Bing." When Kuhl asked why, if
he was so good, Rudy didn't book him, Vallée said, "We don't use
guests." Kuhl, with Carroll Carroll in tow, grudgingly went to see
Borge warm up Vallée's studio audience with a routine he called
"phonetic punctuation" and then signed him for the first week in
December.[2]

Bing's widely anticipated return to the air after thirteen weeks
coincided with the armistice worked out between ASCAP and the
networks. *KMH* would be one of the first programs to present
ASCAP music in eighteen months. This was evident in the program's opening notes with the restoration of Bing's theme song,
"Where the Blue of the Night Meets the Gold of the Day."

Otherwise, the program proved achingly familiar: "You Are My
Sunshine," "Ta-Ra-Ra-Boom-De-Ay," a Risë Stevens aria, and "The
Sweetheart of Sigma Chi," which *Variety* singled out for setting
"the kilocycles pulsating" in an otherwise withering review. Labored
gags and a shortage of Crosby songs failed to make much of the
ASCAP treaty. Connie Boswell sang with Bing on "Yes Indeed!"
but an announcement promoting her upcoming tour of theaters
generated rumors of her permanent departure. When that came to
pass, *KMH* held to its story of her hectic schedule until she refresh-
ingly set the newspapers straight. "I don't know why they put out
such stuff," she told a reporter. "To put it plainly, I was fired. They
wanted Mary Martin in my place, so they hired her."[3]

As Bing inspected the stables in South America, global tensions
had turned to unchecked barbarism pressing toward inconceivable
savagery. Few Americans knew of these developments or of the
slaughter already documented. Congressmen called the reports
exaggerated—Communist-inspired warmongering. A Senate commission accused Hollywood of advocating intervention. Better to
stay out of it. Hitler was protecting us against Bolshevism, argued
isolationists, who in August had come within one vote of terminating the draft. They never mentioned that Germany had invaded the
Soviet Union not only with its army but also with murder squads to
exterminate the surviving civilians as the army marched on. In
those weeks, Germany perfected its experiments with Zyklon-B at

Auschwitz and wiped out Kiev. In two days in the ravine at Babi Yar, nearly thirty-four thousand Jews—men, women, children, babes in arms, the elderly—were forced to undress in the icy cold and then shot. By then other ravines were turned into mass graves as hundreds of thousands died to settle old German and Soviet scores. The West slept on, while Himmler told associates: "I consider it wrong to make a great *Lamento* about it." Hitler, it was recalled, had remarked in Nuremberg in 1938, "I trust no mother will ever have cause to weep in consequence of any action of mine." As the Nazis laid siege to Moscow, Japan's prime minister Konoe proposed a peace initiative with the United States, after which he lost his office to General Tojo, who had a different idea. The day after Bing returned to *KMH,* a U-boat sank the U.S. naval destroyer *Reuben James,* drowning 115 men. The United States remained neutral.[4]

On that same day, Paramount Pictures debuted *Birth of the Blues* in Memphis over vigorous and—given the setting and plot of the film—reasonable objections from the mayor of New Orleans and governor of Louisiana, who felt betrayed. The mayor of Memphis, learning of their disrespect for his city, fought back. So contagious was the glory of war that two Southern municipalities contended for the honor of being known as the birthplace of Negro music. As the language grew increasingly bellicose ("disgust," "spurious," "with truth and justice on our side," "New Orleans Judas"), Y. Frank Freeman told the Louisianans that B. G. DeSylva had looked into the matter and chosen Memphis because of its association with W. C. Handy.[5]

Within a week, the picture opened nationwide, then settled into Radio City Music Hall as its Christmas show. Reviewers were generous. *Variety* called it "Bing Crosby's best filmusical to date"; Louella Parsons vibrated with joy ("an embarrassment of riches!"); and Howard Barnes of *Liberty* said it captured "Crosby at his very best." It was no different in New York. Kate Cameron of the *Daily News* warranted it would "chase away those early war blues." The *Times'* Bosley Crowther went native: "a film straight down the groove—a blend of jump-and-jive music that should make the hep cats howl with some sweet bits of romantic chaunting that should tickle the 'ickies,' too."[6] Bing turned up for the Mutual Broadcasting System's "Silver Anniversary of the Blues" with Mary, DeSylva, Rochester, Johnny Mercer, John Scott Trotter's Frying Pan Eight, and a singer named Betty Jane Rhodes, who happened to be married to Mutual's co-founder. Not a bluesman or blues woman in the bunch. The picture did good business, but not as good as Paramount anticipated, generating barely a sixth of *Road to Zanzibar*'s gross, the lowest for a Crosby picture in five years. Didn't matter; on November 18 Bing would begin work on *Holiday Inn*.

Two months earlier, as Bing checked into his hotel room in Buenos Aires, Fred Astaire started to rehearse. The Elmer Rice treatment had been touched up by several hands and neatly scripted by Claude Binyon, a respected Paramount veteran who started out at *Variety* (he is credited with the most famous headlines in that paper's history: "Wall Street Lays an Egg" and "Sticks Nix Hick Pix") and wrote Bing's *Sing You Sinners*, a film Sandrich admired. Binyon's screenplay triggered few warnings from the Breen office, which was mostly concerned that in his drunk-dancing scene, Astaire's character appear not too drunk, just "high," and insisted they revise the unseemly line "I love Jim, too, but after all, there are laws." The writers changed it to "I love Jim, too, but, after all, let's not get too chummy."[7]

Binyon devised screwball deceptions and misunderstandings to buy some time between the elaborate musical numbers, which required unswerving preparation, especially for a performer as scrupulous as Astaire. He began working with Danny Dare on September 18 and continued like a triathlon athlete every day but Sundays for fifty-two days *before* the production start-up. This did not include three days necessary to rehearse the "Firecracker Number," for which shooting would be halted in the final weeks, in February. Astaire rehearsed as many days as Sandrich was allowed to shoot the entire picture. After lengthy meetings at which every budgetary item was examined and contested, Sandrich agreed to reduce the production schedule from seventy-one days (ten of them reserved for the Labor Day number) to sixty-nine, then to fifty-eight (so long, Labor Day number). He accepted, reluctantly, the necessity of delegating exteriors to a second unit, which set up shop at the Village Inn in Monte Rio, in northern Sonoma County. The final timetable allowed fifty-three days of shooting, plus another five to rehearse and film "Say It with Firecrackers," for a total budget of $1,230,000—a bargain.

Fred and Bing got on famously despite what one reporter described as an obvious "study in contrast": "Astaire is the nervous worrying type and Crosby is calm and easy-going."[8] Crosby connived to make Astaire laugh and knock him off script, yet he revered his devotion, particularly the thirty-six or thirty-eight times (Sandrich estimated more than fifty) he did the firecracker dance. In this astonishing number, Fred complicated an intricate series of tap rhythms by lighting and tossing five hundred dollars' worth of firecrackers and setting off other small charges. Bing recalled:

> Two days it took him. Of course, he rehearses assiduously, even before the picture starts, but he's a perfectionist and he's never content. He always wants to do it once more, and says, "I think I can do it a little better." He has everybody exhausted, the camera-man as well as the extras working with him in a number, although he's doing all the work. They are just background, but they have to sit there under those lights. They're bushed but Fred is still going. He starts a picture at...a hundred and forty, a hundred and forty-two pounds. When he finished *Holiday Inn* he weighed a hundred and twenty-six pounds, and, as you know, he is about six feet tall. You could spit through him. He's just a shell. But he never gives up 'till he gets it the way he wants it, which is as close to perfection as human beings can get.... He just won't let anything slip.[9]

Fred was the ideal partner for Bing, who found him methodical, agreeable, no "big star show-boy or anything like that," with great comedic sense and no bad habits; he took a drink now and then and was crazy about golf and music and horses. He cheered Astaire's willingness to stand up and fight for an interpretation of a song, scene, or dance number. "That's the way you arrive at the right way to do things," he said. You "argue it out with somebody who has a good point of view [and] maybe you can reconcile your points of view. Fred will do that."[10]

For his part, Crosby liked to keep everyone a little off balance. They shot a scene in which Walter Abel, playing their agent, fires questions at Fred and Bing in order to get a name or description of a dancer (Marjorie Reynolds) whom Fred encountered drunk and is now determined to find. For this setup, Bing was not in the frame, but he stayed on the set to feed them his lines. His part would be filmed separately, as an insert, when Abel wheels around to where Bing is standing to ask him if he saw the mystery woman. His scripted response begins, "Who, me? Well, I wasn't watching very closely." But for the first take, when Abel turned to him, Bing said, "Well, I'll tell you, fellows, she was a kind of broken-down tomato with a face like a pan full of worms." Everyone laughed. The take was ruined, but the energy rocketed as they repeated it.[11] When Sandrich filmed the insert, Bing held his hands six inches apart, as though he were describing a tiny doll, babbling that she reminded him of a gal named Consuela Shlepkiss who used to hang out at a pinball parlor. That stayed in the picture.

Looking back after thirty years, the usually laconic Astaire recalled Bing as exceedingly attentive. "We got along very well indeed. He's a great man, you know, Bing is. He's sort of a very special person in the whole world, and it was a thrill to work with him. I'm very ready to say I used to get more laughs, too. He's funny. And he'd go out of his way to oblige me or try to see whether or not I was happy at his lot, and that always amused me and pleased me because I didn't really want any special treatment. But he used to always say, you know: Is that all right, do you like that, and so and so and so. And I'd say, oh yes, sure, fine, if it was. If it wasn't, I don't think I would have gone to him about it." Fred was so happy about his treatment at Paramount he worked two extra weeks free as a Christmas gift to the studio. Bing impressed Fred with the effort he put into their dance number "I'll Capture Your Heart Singing": "He rehearsed, he really rehearsed, and I don't think he rehearsed so much for almost anything that he did, just to get that darn dance number right." Fred noticed that Bing exercised to keep trim. "Of course, he has always been more or less of an athlete. He's a very good golf player, much better than I am. I played a lot of golf with him and we had a lot of fun. But to see him working on a dance step was amusing. And we had a couple of little routine bits there, comedy bits that were intricate, and he was going to get them and he got them. He knew what he was doing."[12]

Bing sensed that Walter Abel, an outstanding scene-stealer

especially adept at frazzled comedy, took too seriously the courtesy line between featured players and stars, a demarcation more evident in Hollywood than on Broadway. Most performers were wise to heed it, and Bing could be plenty standoffish. But he liked Abel, and in a scene when they had to race up a flight of stairs, Abel in front, Bing grabbed Abel's coat and, as they topped the stairs, poked his butt. Abel let out an *Ouch* that had to be cut from the soundtrack. Abel found the gesture playful and funny, yet out of character. Bing "liked to kid around with us, the cast and crew," he said, but "no matter how jolly or friendly he might seem, you knew there was that invisible line that you did not cross. I doubt anyone knew him really well."[13]

Two people, at least, resented not getting to know him. Walter Scharf, one of the uncredited orchestrators and composers of incidental music working under Robert Emmett Dolan (and subsequently an accomplished film scorer in his own right), was by nature a dyspeptic man who saw slights where none were intended. He remembered Crosby as "a cold cold man" who could do everything "so casually and so well." He thought it unforgivable that he left the studio at the end of the day without saying good night "to mere minions like me." Yet he warmed to his talent: "Once he heard a piece of music, within 15 minutes he knew it as well as if he had lived with it all his life." On *Holiday Inn*, by "the second or third take, he had perfection." Bing required the "right orchestrations and the correct sound equipment, to say nothing of the most accomplished musicians to back him. But he took instruction and direction when he needed it."[14]

Marjorie Reynolds harbored a grudge. She complained that Bing had wanted Mary Martin and consequently never accepted her. Yet she regarded *Holiday Inn* as the high point of her career and named her daughter Linda after the character she played, Linda Mason, and Bing approved her as his costar for the 1943 picture *Dixie* (a fictional portrait of the blackface minstrel Dan Emmett), her only other major musical. She may have felt self-conscious about the artifice involved in her performance in *Holiday Inn*. Not only was she not permitted to do her own singing, but Astaire requested a look-alike dancer, June Chapman, to double for her for sections of their numbers. The doubling is never apparent, but it explains abrupt long shots and changes in lighting as Fred and Marjorie dance into shadows that obscure their faces. According to Chapman's granddaughter, Fred gave June a diamond brooch to compensate for the absence of screen credit, but she preferred Bing, who "was quite the gentleman."[15]

He was not a gentleman to Marjorie on the day they filmed the scene in which she gets dunked in a creek. Shivering from the cold, she requested and received permission to dry off and relax in Bing's heated dressing room, as he was not working that day. He returned unexpectedly and asked her to leave. Most stars tend to be possessive about their dressing areas, but she took it as a personal rejection. She adored Astaire: "When the cameras rolled for our first dance together I was shaking, but he kept whispering encouragement like, you're beautiful, you're sensational." Bing offered no such chivalry. As usual, he didn't even offer a big movie kiss in their last scene, after he proposes marriage. Instead, in a gesture that is pure Crosby, he buses her on the cheek, clearly surprising her. "To me," she said, "he was very much a man's man and later when we did *Dixie* he still wasn't friendly."[16]

Only one other actor received credit in the opening titles: the ebullient, open-faced, incredibly busy Louise Beavers, who, along with Hattie McDaniel, met the unceasing demand for black maids. Beavers had already appeared in some one hundred and twenty movies. She could sing, shed tears on cue, and deliver deft comic zingers. Represented by Everett Crosby, who got her pay increased from five hundred dollars a week to seven hundred and fifty, Beavers brought both tears and a lighthearted sense of humor to one of the picture's most popular scenes: the minstrelsy number, for which Bing and Marjorie blacked up to join with Beavers and her character's two sons in a faux-spiritual homage to Lincoln that might have amused Jefferson Davis. The script rationalizes blackface as a ruse to disguise Marjorie, whom Bing is determined to keep hidden from Fred. This allows her to hide in plain sight (a device Berlin previously used in *Mammy*, his 1930 Al Jolson picture about a minstrel troupe) and enables him to propose marriage without sentimental or physical expression. "I broke in as a bootblack," he teases as he paints her face, and she, immobilized by the process, can only say, "You don't even give me a chance to say 'darling' and throw my arms around you."

The inclusion of such a number was never in doubt. Berlin loved minstrelsy and incorporated blackface whenever he could to furnish rhythmic pep, nostalgia, or sentiment. In one early treatment, he proposed "Abraham" as a showcase for Bing "to use his ability as a dialectician in the form of a colored preacher [for] a light humorous spiritual, singing the praises of the Great Emancipator."[17] Berlin and Sandrich considered the sequence racially sympathetic, and no one else questioned it either, certainly not the Breen office. Berlin's lyric humanized Abe as "a most respected gent" who brushed aside reports of General Grant's drunkenness ("Get all my gen'rals tight") and, above all, set "the darky free." Sandrich wanted to stage the scene in a black church, an idea that wasn't feasible due to budgetary restrictions. Instead, he had the inn's waiters and musicians black up too. Even so, they thought of themselves as upright, NAACP-supporting racial progressives whose acuity as showmen was validated by the critical and popular enthusiasm "Abraham" generated. How bewildered they would have been to learn that, before long, that scene would be censored, mocked, and condemned as unfit for general viewing. After the picture opened and Bing's recording of "Abraham" hit stores, *Time* reported, "Negro editors reach for their editorial shotgun," referring to an editorial in the *Baltimore Afro-American* protesting "the term 'd——y' [as] offensive to colored people." Berlin apologized immediately and ordered the word changed to *Negro* in all future editions of the sheet music. "I should never have released it had I known the epithet was objectionable," he told *Time*. Yet the editorial writer didn't protest the blackface, still practiced by comedians of both races. Bing would black up twice more during the war.[18]

As usual, Bing requested a bit part for Harry Barris, in this instance a gratuitous close-up and line of dialogue. Unusually, he asked that his brother's band be folded into the score, mixing the jazz ensemble with the Paramount string section to expand on the exciting dance-band sound Sy Oliver used so effectively in *Road to Zanzibar*. This was an important job for the Bob Crosby orchestra. The band doesn't appear on-screen beyond a long shot during "Freedom," but it is put to good use, revving up "I'll Capture Your Heart Singing," "You're Easy to Dance With," and the one imbecilic song in the score, "I Can't Tell a Lie"—in which Bob Crosby's drummer,

Ray Bauduc, in a George Washington wig, shares the screen with Bing. Despite Robert Emmett Dolan's overall command of the music department, Sandrich made the fundamental scoring decisions, like whether a song should have heavy or light strings, light brasses or none at all. He worked closely with Dolan to choose how many musicians were optimal for each number. In the post-scoring, he wanted thirty-two men; Dolan preferred more.

Bob Crosby's involvement proved especially significant for Paul Wetstein, a recent addition to Bob's writing staff who also worked with Tommy Dorsey and Dinah Shore and who, later, after he changed his name to Paul Weston, become well known for recording and television work. He was tasked with blending the Crosby band's arrangements (by Bob Haggart and Matty Matlock) with those of the studio writers, chiefly Herbert W. Spencer. As that work progressed, Dolan assigned him to all of Fred's dance numbers and duets with Bing, a heady experience for a tyro arranger new to movies. When the *Hollywood Reporter* indicated that Bing's arranger was "fixing" Berlin's music, Berlin flipped and Sandrich had to intervene. After the dustup, Bing thought Weston needed a morale boost and saw that he got it the following May at the Decca recording session for "I'll Capture Your Heart Singing." Paul rehearsed Bing, Fred, and Bob's band, then hollered to Victor Young in the control booth that they were ready. Weston recalled: "Victor said, 'No, you do it.' I said, 'Wait a minute, I'm not that much of a conductor.' He said, 'Well, you've been doing this thing, so do it.' So they turn on the red light and there I was conducting for Astaire and Crosby. I wasn't scared too much after that." Weston also worked on *Road to Morocco,* and in 1955, Bing hired him for his radio Christmas show. "The thing I remember most was we would start at eight thirty in the morning. And with Bing, at eight thirty, that baton better come down and start the band, because he's ready—always on time. And he wanted to get out of there as fast as he could. He'd never do things over because of singing out of tune or anything. He didn't make mistakes. The only reason he would do them over is if he didn't like the phrasing he used, or if something went wrong with the band."[19]

Bob Crosby's involvement with *Holiday Inn* also brought Frank Sinatra to the studio. He was back in town with Tommy Dorsey's band, this time getting the glossy MGM treatment in a movie called

Ship Ahoy. Yank Lawson, the trumpet soloist with Bob's band, mentioned to Frank he was at Paramount working on *Holiday Inn.* Whether or not Frank encountered Bing the previous year, he undoubtedly met him on this occasion. He asked Lawson if he could get him a pass to watch the filming. "Frank had never met Bing," Yank remembered. "He wanted to watch Bing work because Bing was his idol. [He] met me out at the Paramount lot and I took him in. He just loved it, watching Bing." A dialogue evidently ensued, because by the summer of 1942, Sinatra had determined to leave Dorsey, and he took to heart advice he said Bing had given him earlier that year. Recalling his own legal troubles after leaving Paul Whiteman and the Rhythm Boys, Bing cautioned Frank to pay whatever was necessary, no matter how costly in the short run, so that no one—not Dorsey and not the agencies—owned a percentage of him.[20]

Early in December, Bing filmed the scene in which his *Holiday Inn* character, Jim Hardy, another in his string of songwriters (as in *Birth of the Blues, Rhythm on the River,* and *The Star Maker,* with more to come), tries out his latest creation, "White Christmas," for Linda. This is a transitional moment for the Crosby persona; at ease with a pipe in a snug jacket over a striped shirt buttoned to the top, comfortable, sturdy, and safe—nothing in the particulars we have not seen before and often, yet subtly altered by a heightened and mature equanimity. The Crosby glow is emphasized by Sandrich's staging, which places him between the silently roaring fire and a huge Christmas tree. The plot of *Holiday Inn* calls for him and the other major characters to be brazenly devious, yet Crosby's conman routine as evident in recent pictures— superficial, matched by an almost adolescent self-regard—is gone. In this film and especially in this scene, he personifies a hearth to which anyone might long to return.

No one was thinking in those terms when the scene was shot, and few participants anticipated great things from the song he sang, according to accounts they maintained for decades to come. Yet the composer Walter Scharf recalled Berlin sneaking on the set during filming of the song and literally squatting behind a scenery flat, determined to see precisely how it would be presented. Berlin obfuscated his intent in writing the song and underplayed his expectations for it. He knew he was treading on dangerous ground, removing Christ from Christmas and advancing snow as the essential metaphor in a requiem of longing (redolent of Villon's "the snows of yesteryear"[21]), recasting Christmas as an American holiday for people of all faiths or no faith. In this secular carol, he took the opposite approach he had in "God Bless America," which challenged the national anthem by replacing martial fireworks with divine beneficence.

Initially, he covered his tracks with an introductory verse in which a denizen of Beverly Hills, lolling under palm trees and a golden sun, longs to be up north; as the verse shifts into the famous chorus, he—or she, as in the original story treatment, the song was intended as a reverie for Alice Faye—dreams of a snowy Christmas. Reviewers have proposed that the verse lampoons the well-to-do who pay lip service to the Christmas spirit while hoisting cocktails in Hollywood enclaves, but Berlin was most likely expressing his despair about the times he could not spend the holiday season with his family because he was working in the film colony. The idea for the song had been with Berlin for years, and he knew that the finished work was momentous. He told his assistant that "White Christmas" was the best song he had ever written, possibly the best song anyone had ever written. Yet not even he gauged its full potential, its emotional resonance. Berlin received little encouragement from Sandrich and Paramount executives who heard him audition the score in September (when Bing was in Buenos Aires). They shrugged. They figured the score's hit would be the Valentine's Day ballad, "Be Careful, It's My Heart."

Crosby admired it from the start, a sanction for which Berlin remained grateful, often repeating the story of the day he auditioned the songs to get Bing's okay. "I was nervous as a rabbit smelling stew. I sang several melodies, and Bing nodded quiet approval. But when I did 'White Christmas,' he came to life and said, 'Irving, you won't have to worry about that one.'" Bing recalled him sitting at his piano: "He had a lever you can change keys on and he had a little squeaky voice and you couldn't tell whether [the songs] were good or bad. I could hardly understand. That's why I flipped out. 'White Christmas' was so good, I couldn't miss on that."[22] Bing also decided from the first not to sing the Beverly Hills verse. A notorious worrier, Berlin dreaded a short life for "White Christmas" and conjured reasons to justify his doubts. Bob Crosby recalled him complaining that it would fail because it consisted of two sixteen-measure sections rather than the usual AABA format. (If he did say something like that, he could not have been serious; Berlin broke with conventional songwriting formats throughout his career in several of his biggest hits, including "Alexander's Ragtime Band" and "Cheek to Cheek.") Paramount intended to release the picture before Labor Day, which Berlin feared was too early for a Yuletide song. He also worried that the success of "Be Careful, It's My Heart" would dim the chances for another song in the same score. When Bing recorded "White Christmas" three months after the picture wrapped, Jack Kapp was so skeptical he considered issuing the song as the B-side of the mediocre "Let's Start the New Year Right." (He did release it as the B-side in England.) But nothing challenged Berlin's faith in the song more than Bing's debut of it on *Kraft Music Hall* on Christmas Day.

KMH struggled to regain its inspiration in the weeks after Bing's return. The pun-laden skits were wearing thin, Jerry Lester's humor didn't click, the guests were more varied than motivated (Michèle Morgan, Joe DiMaggio, Humphrey Bogart, Jinx Falkenburg, Ruth Hussey, Salvatore Baccaloni, Wingy Manone), and Bing's song selection, especially with the strike now settled, less than stellar. Cal Kuhl expected Victor Borge to infuse a jolt of energy into the December 4 broadcast. Cautious about signing a sophisticated performer with a foreign accent (a *Billboard* review warned that Borge's comedy, though "definitely worthwhile," was "rather intellectual, a bit on the screwball side"[23]), he secured his bet, presenting him as a guest on three consecutive shows—as though popular acclaim mandated return appearances. Borge was, in his way, as silly as Lester, but his way was original, cunning, and garbed in a tuxedo rather than baggy pants.

Carroll scheduled Victor after the midprogram station break, following a Crosby song, "Be Honest with Me." The rundown for the rest of the show, after Borge's spot, consisted of a commercial, another song, a guest spot with Carole Landis, another song, another commercial, the theme, and the sign-off. Carroll shortened Landis and deleted a Crosby chorus to give Borge a full twelve minutes. Bing introduced him as a man who, having warmed up Rudy Vallée's audience, was good enough for the old *Music Hall*. Carroll later wrote: "Victor came on and repeated the punctuation routine and got the same earthquakelike reaction. After 12 minutes, he was still going. We lost a commercial. He kept right on going. We lost a Crosby song. Then we lost a guest spot and another Crosby song and another commercial and the closing theme and we went off the air with people howling and applauding Borge." Reber called from New York and told the producers to "sign the guy for as long as possible."[24]

They were not expecting Reber's orchid in the studio that night. They had lost two of three commercials; unheard of, even "sacrilegious," according to Ed Helwick, who, along with the show's in-house producers, expected to be fired until Reber's ecstatic call put them at ease. What could they have done? The audience had applauded and guffawed nonstop, and Bing laughed as loud as anyone. "They lost a couple of minutes flogging cream cheese," Helwick recalled, "but Friday the whole radio audience was talking about *Kraft Music Hall* and the guy with the funny accent." In January, when Mary Martin came on board and Borge began to perform his weekly spot in his natural habitat, at the piano, the show found an ideal level with, in Helwick's view, "Bing at his all-time best both as singer and master of dialogue." They signed Borge to five years but reluctantly released him in fourteen months, when the show's format changed in 1943 to thirty minutes.[25]

On the day after Borge's coup, three versions of a short subject called "Angels of Mercy" were distributed by Paramount, MGM, and Twentieth Century–Fox. Bing sang Berlin's title song, for which royalties were assigned to the picture's subject, the Red Cross. Excepting Crosby's vocal, the films varied; each studio used its own stock footage.[26] That was on Friday, December 5.

Sunday in Los Angeles dawned bright and sunny with temperatures in the middle seventies. Toluca Lake residents raised their windows to catch a gentle breeze. Some returned from church in anticipation of a lazy day, tuning in afternoon broadcasts, including two from New York: Artur Rodziński conducting the Philharmonic (nonaggression at work: Shostakovich and Brahms), and the Dodgers crushing the Giants in football at the Polo Grounds. Announcers interrupted the programs with reports of a Japanese attack on the U.S. Pacific fleet. Many Americans wondered: *What, where, or who is Pearl Harbor?* The announcers spat out the headline and returned to the broadcasts in progress. But the reports kept coming.

Up and down the West Coast, including in Toluca Lake, where pedestrians were usually as rare as elk, people walked outside to commune with their neighbors, looking up or seaward, because they knew something about Hawaii and fully expected bombers or submarines to cover the 2,500 miles between them and the islands. "There was no cordiality," the celebrity photographer Gene Lester recalled, "everybody had worried looks on their faces."[27] That night, California, and especially Los Angeles and San Francisco, plunged into hysteria. Men with rifles and rocks shot or smashed marquees and shop lights, demanding blackouts; soldiers and police obeyed orders to lock down Japanese neighborhoods; crowds blocked streets and bridges. Fists and insults were hurled and rumors ran riot. By Monday, Roosevelt's Day of Infamy was confirmed as Churchill's final "climacteric," guaranteeing the salvation of Britain. America was in it now.

Kraft Music Hall enlisted directly. The December 11 broadcast opened with Irving Berlin's fund-raising ditty "Any Bonds Today." One skit featured actor Robert Coote, a flying officer of the Royal Canadian Air Force; another had Borge expounding on language inflation (for example, *wonderful* and *create* become *twoderful* and *crenine*); and a third found Veronica Lake joking about her peekaboo hairdo. However, the show's primary guest was Paul Robeson, and on Monday, Ed Helwick, who had been asked to write that segment, huddled with Cal Kuhl to discuss a delicate matter: How would Bing and Paul address each other? The question arose because after Robeson appeared on the show in February, Ed and Cal happened to flip through the pile of fan mail and found a letter that, in Helwick's recollection ("It left an indelible impression"), read: "The next time you have that black bastard on your show and he don't call Crosby Mr. Bing, we ain't gonna eat no more Kraft cheese." The letter was signed, "The employees of the Southwestern Gas and Electric Company, Shreveport, Louisiana."[28]

Cal buried the letter. It did not merit a response and there was no reason to bring it to the attention of Reber, let alone Kraft-Phenix or Bing. Neither did he want to chance a "boomerang in the South." He told Ed not to mention any names on the show—"Don't let Bing call Robeson Paul and don't let Robeson address Bing by name." Helwick was appalled. Crosby was "totally color-blind, about his clothing and when it came to booking guests." That was one of the things he admired about Bing. As for Robeson: "He was the most impressive man I ever met in my life. His voice came right out of the bowels of the earth." He obeyed Cal's instruction.[29] During the program, Bing introduced Robeson: "Equally at home in the Broadway theater, on a Hollywood soundstage, and particularly on the concert platform, Paul Robeson's presence in the old Kraft Music Hall this evening really makes it a Music Hall, for Paul Robeson is certainly one of the world's truly great artists." He sang two signature numbers, "Water Boy" and "Ol' Man River," and read the name-free patter as written (promoting Robeson's latest and final picture, *Tales of Manhattan*). Bing interpolated *Paul* in every line of his dialogue. For the finale, he brought him back to lead the cast ("We're all standing together," he announced) in "The Star Spangled Banner."[30]

The December 18 show opened with Bing's "Anchors Aweigh," a salute to the "intrepid" United States Navy, and included "Angels of Mercy," nostalgia, novelties, and comedy routines (Borge on Russian lit), closing with the national anthem and Bing's sign-off:

BING CROSBY: And Merry...no, no use saying merry Christmas now. We'll be around Christmas night and we'd like to have you join us.

KEN CARPENTER: I'm sure everyone will want to, Bing, when I remind them that you're singing "Adeste Fideles" and "Silent Night" as you do every Christmas time here in the old Kraft Music Hall.

BING CROSBY: Gotta adhere to a KMH Yuletide tradition of six years standing, Ken. Gonna try a new Irving Berlin song about Christmas, too.

Bing had asked Berlin's permission to premiere it on the Christmas show, the first song from *Holiday Inn* to get any kind of preview.

Irving agreed and returned to the bosom of his family in New York, where he listened, biting his nails. The show opened with "Adeste Fideles" and finished with "Silent Night." It included Berlin's celebrated World War I complaint "Oh! How I Hate to Get Up in the Morning" and Connie Boswell's long-forgotten song "When Christmas Is Gone" (her final performance on *KMH*). Toward the last third of the show, Bing debuted "White Christmas," backed by his resident vocal group, the Music Maids. The public's reaction recalled the curious incident of the dog in the night-time: there was no reaction—which, as Sherlock observed, was the curious incident. *Variety* recognized the appeal of "Any Bonds Today" and "Angels of Mercy," but failed to notice "White Christmas." So complete was the silence that, in later years, exculpatory theories were advanced: Bing could not have actually sung it that night and, if he did, he sang an earlier version. Seventy years later, a transcription disc turned up; Bing had, in fact, sung the same song he had already filmed for the movie. He sang it too slowly, with labored mordents. Perhaps that was the reason the nation's carolers did not take to it.

Bing spent the last afternoon of the year rehearsing that week's *Kraft Music Hall*. He and Dixie celebrated New Year's Eve at a party at Jack Benny's home.

Part Two

———

METAMORPHOSIS

9

KEEP AWAY FROM EUNUCHS

Nobody knows Bing Crosby like a book, for he is a man
of confusing contradictions and his personality is split
like the flared end of a rake.
                                    —H. Allen Smith (1942)[1]

New Year's Day was not a holiday for Bing. He did not get to sleep late or attend the Rose Bowl, which unfolded in North Carolina that year because government officials feared that ninety thousand spectators at the Pasadena stadium and ten times as many at the parade presented too tempting a target. (In an epic upset, the Oregon State Beavers defeated the Duke Blue Devils despite the absence of their star end, Jack Yoshihara, who was prohibited from leaving Oregon and who, after February's Executive Order 9066, spent the year in an Idaho internment camp.) Instead, at nine thirty a.m., Bing teed off at Lakeside for a Salvation Army benefit, inaugurating a day of celebrity golf with some three dozen participants, including Hope and Astaire. Bing played in a foursome with Jimmie Fidler, the much despised newspaper and radio gossip; Bud Oakley, a champ in the PGA Southern California section; and the not-yet-legendary Jimmy Demaret, who had lately won his first Masters. The match, mildly antic and cheered by buffs who paid a dollar to walk the course, portended things to come. Most of Bing's golf during the next four years would be charitable and public, necessitating a seven-day workweek.

Nor did he begin the year on the set of *Holiday Inn,* which continued to shoot into late February, because New Year's Day was Thursday, *KMH* day. After the golf match, he rehearsed *Kraft Music Hall* for four hours preceding the actual broadcast, when he introduced Mary Martin as the new cast member and they sang their first on-air duet, "Wait Till the Sun Shines, Nellie." "She is no Connie Boswell," complained a *Billboard* reviewer, who granted that *KMH* survives "talent changes" because "the show is completely dependent on Crosby."[2] Most listeners cheered Bing's number with Mary, which the pair reprised on four subsequent shows and recorded in March. Cal Kuhl graded the show "excellent" and told John Reber, "Mary Martin more than fulfilled our highest hopes and promises more than at first we thought."[3] Martin recalled her *KMH* year as an education in sangfroid. "Bing made me very comfortable because before I would sing a solo, we would do a duet together and that taught me not to be so nervous." Nothing fazed him. Once or twice he dropped his script and kept singing as he stooped to pick it up; he would sing with gum in his jaw. "I thought, you know, what is this man? He can do anything. I expected him to stand on his head and sing that way, too."[4] On that first show, Bing premiered a *Holiday Inn* song, "Let's Start the New Year Right." Berlin wrote it months before Pearl Harbor, but one phrase had now acquired a poignant double meaning: "When they dim the light, let's begin / Kissing the old year out."

Lights dimmed on both coasts, cutting the wattage on Broadway (the glow was bait for U-boats cruising ever westward) as well as on Sunset Boulevard. Regulations curtailed motoring on coastal roads and shielded streetlights to decrease upward rays. Dim-outs were increasingly enforced all year, sustaining the nationwide terror. An editorialist in San Francisco warned that compulsion might be necessary if persuasion failed to achieve absolute compliance. Sales of candles and flashlights soared. The Office of Civilian Defense issued a Q&A sheet.

Q. Our house is visible from the sea. Are any additional restrictions on lighting placed against us?

A. Yes. People living in the areas visible from the sea must not only shade those windows and doors visible from the sea, but they must not allow any light to shine upward from any window, skylight or lightwell, no matter what direction they face. Like everybody else, you must keep shades drawn as low as the bottom of the lowest light in the room.[5]

On the January 8 *KMH*, Bing sang "You're a Grand Old Flag"; urged listeners to buy defense bonds and stamps, as "we all know it will take a wad of moo to see this through"; and introduced a Marine Corps publicist assigned to the West Coast to explain what to do in the event of an invasion. Americans did not share in the devastation that cratered Europe and Asia—did not endure the dread of aerial bombings or the stench of massive civilian deaths or the chaos of dislocation—but their suspicions and fears were not entirely unfounded. A Japanese submarine had neared the coast of Oregon in December, sinking a tanker and disrupting transport. The news was far more alarming along the East Coast, where German U-boats sank hundreds of merchant ships during the first six months of 1942. Yet the only mainland raid came from the federal government in its roundup of Japanese American citizens. For most others, life's routines continued as usual as the meaning of sacrifice and duration began to sink in.

Johnny Burke's wife, Bessie, had twin girls in January. Bing stood godfather to Rory, and David Butler to Regan. After the christening the Crosby circle posed on the steps of St. Ambrose Church for a unique group portrait: the Crosbys, Burkes, Hopes, Dr. Arnold Stevens (who had suggested Dixie take brandy in her milk) and his wife, Jean, David and Elsie Butler, Barney Dean, Phil Silvers, John Scott Trotter, pianist Skitch Henderson, Pat O'Brien, and Sammy Cahn.[6] Yet even the most normal of events masked the shiver of uncertainty. The threat of danger produced a stimulating and not entirely disagreeable jolt, intensified by whining sirens and the new ritual of blacking out, which in some commercial areas meant the use of shellac or tar.

On the day the Japanese sub did its damage, newspapers carried the story of Goebbels's designation of the Japanese as racially pure, "yellow Aryans." Irving Berlin read that and sprang into song. He mailed Mark Sandrich a parody lyric, proposing a new holiday to be celebrated by his refrain "You may rest with ease / On our

Japanese knees / We're Aryans under the skin."[7] Levity aside, Berlin realized that Pearl Harbor obliged him to write another song for *Holiday Inn,* a wartime flag-waver. He initially intended to pair Astaire's "Say It with Firecrackers" in the Independence Day scene with Crosby singing "This Is a Great Country." But that song pandered rather emptily and they needed something pointed: a "Song of Freedom," which Bing premiered on a March of Dimes show aired by all the networks. Berlin made a counterintuitive decision in giving the song a swing rhythm, a far cry from the hymnlike "God Bless America." If this song ultimately lacked durable resonance, it did the job in *Holiday Inn,* backing a newsreel montage in what turned out to be the first musical sequence in a feature film to reflect America's declaration of war. And it pressed home the idea that only Bing ("Listen to this American troubadour / From the U.S.A.") could handle everyman patriotism without its curdling into rancid buttermilk, even while wearing an Uncle Sam hat — an attribute that inclined the GIs to pin their own handle on him: "Uncle Sam Without Whiskers."

Levity had its place, dampening fear. And entertainers had a calling: to establish a cozy unified home front, stirring up a lather that was part propaganda, part pep talk, part escapist reassurance, all scored to thumping can-do rhythms, sentimental values, and the nearly pious belief (sanctioned by the Production Code) in the warranties of melodrama: Johnny would be marching home in triumph to his faithful gal and proud folks. How successful was this pageant? Countless Americans who lived through the duration, when four hundred thousand Johnnies did not march home, revived it for decades, embracing it as validation of a golden era, the best years of their lives. The writer Carol Brightman later observed, "We are very likely the only people on earth whose vision of the good life is historically inseparable from an experience of war."[8]

But the terror abided, the news perpetually grim. In the first week of 1942, the Japanese army slaughtered the Philippine forces in Manila and continued to the Bataan Peninsula, where the fighting raged for months, ending in the most crushing surrender of an American army since the Civil War. Before January was done, the Dutch East Indies fell, then Kuala Lumpur, Burma, Malaya. (At the same time, the Final Solution was planned in the Wannsee villa near Berlin, but hardly anyone knew about that.) Amid this havoc, on January 16, the beloved picture star Carole Lombard died in a plane crash in Nevada on her way back from Indiana, where she had raised two million dollars in one evening promoting war savings bonds. Her death, at thirty-three, personalized the war, especially in Hollywood and not least for Bing, who had worked with her in 1934's *We're Not Dressing*, an important film for each of them. He cherished her inventive, profane wit. His portrait of her in *Call Me Lucky* is one of the longest tributes in the book, though limited to funny anecdotes and without mention of her death.

A few days before the plane crash, he told his accountant Todd Johnson and his lawyer John O'Melveny that he wanted to devote part of his time to "patriotic work" and wondered if he could get out of making his contracted three pictures for 1942. To the latter point, Johnson told Bing no, and O'Melveny followed with a letter arguing, with prickly impatience, that Bing was "almost compelled" to make three pictures because of the wartime economy and his free spending. "I think that we will all have to get ourselves on a different basis of living," he wrote, noting that he had had to dismiss a maid and a ranch hand. "We will all have to take care of ourselves without having the help we have had before" and economize to pay future taxes—something, he said reproachfully, Bing would find harder "because everything you do is done on a much larger scale than any of the rest of us. I think for the next couple of years you will probably have to make at least three pictures a year in order to save all the valuable assets we have built up over a period of years, and which you now own."[9]

Bing's appeal to patriotism didn't impress O'Melveny, who pointed out that even with the three pictures, Bing would have "approximately six months when you are not working, and many of us, including myself, are into all kinds of war jobs which we do overtime without having as much leisure as you have." O'Melveny, who apparently forgot the weekly radio hour and the recording schedule, closed by reminding Bing of the need to build up cash for his children, a subject he knew obsessed Bing despite all his talk of preparing them to make their own way in life. Though his eldest son was only nine, Bing had recently complained to O'Melveny that his will did not cover future grandchildren. O'Melveny answered that one's children usually accepted responsibility for one's grand-children, and besides, he could always amend the will.[10]

A coda arrived a few weeks later in Todd Johnson's report on Bing's taxes. For 1941, he and Dixie owed $164,291.86 in federal taxes and $41,034 in state taxes. The sting would have been a lot worse had Binglin stock farms not reported a loss of nearly $32,000, prompting Johnson to urge Bing to "close out this venture." The additional loss could then be claimed. More important, the divestment would greatly help him manage the escalating taxes due for 1942, which required everyone to cut down on living expenses.[11] When Bing's fat royalty check from Decca arrived at the office, O'Melveny, on his own initia-tive, bought Los Angeles City High School Bonds, as it is "a good thing to [put] something away from time to time."[12] Bing had no intention of parting with his horses, not yet, but he offered his own idea about "a good hedge," which involved more animal life. "I'm looking around for a good cattle ranch," he wrote Johnson, and he had his eye on a "fine buy" in Elko, Nevada.[13] He told Johnson to appoint the Citizens National Trust and Savings Bank as guardian to hold dividends for his sons. The war would not be his only preoccu-pation in coming years, but it would be the most demanding, remov-ing him from his family for long intervals. He hoped to make up for his absences with rigorous family summers at that ranch in Elko.

If Bing wasn't giving up Binglin, he had little choice about Del Mar. Shortly after he announced to stockholders, in his role as presi-dent of the Del Mar Turf Club, that 1941's dividends reflected the track's best season to date (his came to $125,000), the army requested and received his permission to adapt the grounds as a training camp for the Third Battalion, 184th Infantry. In addition to the track, Bing turned over his home in Rancho Santa Fe, including the tennis court, swimming pool, and his phonograph. The battalion moved out after a Christmas at which they were feted with dinners and gifts from the community. An officer wrote Bing, "No matter what the fortunes of war may bring to these men, the memory of Christmas week at Rancho Santa Fe will never be forgotten."[14]

O'Melveny underestimated Bing's seriousness about war work. Harrison Carroll reported that Bing "may be un-cooperative, as the lady reporters say," but when he entered the It Café one night and a handful of uniformed men cheered him, he took the stage and sang for thirty minutes.[15] One Sunday in January, Bing and other Paramount stars played softball to benefit the Red Cross. That same afternoon, he drove his sons to Mines Field in Inglewood to welcome a newly arrived air force tactical unit. He shared the stage with Johnny Burke and Jimmy Van Heusen (then in the throes of completing the *Road to Morocco* songs) and three-year-old Lindsay, who brought down the house singing "Popeye the Sailor Man" three times. Bing debuted songs from *Holiday Inn* and took an hour of requests. A reporter covering the event did not find Berlin's new songs memorable enough to mention.

Days later, General MacArthur, soon to flee the Philippines, radioed the White House that his men wanted to hear Crosby. A telegram from the office of William J. Donovan, the coordinator of information, advised Bing that MacArthur "specifically [asked] for you to broadcast to the men" in Bataan.[16] It had never been done before, but NBC transmitted a transcription disc of the January 29 *Kraft Music Hall* by shortwave to Luzon; it was the first radio program requested for and directed at the men on the front lines. Dedicating the broadcast to "the Philippine defenders," whom he was "honored to be able to get through to [with] a few tunes, a few wheezes, and maybe the general feeling of what's going on here in the States," Bing opened with "The Caissons Go Rolling Along," and sang another six songs, including "Blues in the Night" and, in a nod to FDR, "Home on the Range." A *Time* reporter attending the show described his "deceptively loafing air and unsinkable savvy" as he eased around the Hollywood studio wearing "a blue slack suit, looking, without his movie toupee, like a rapid-fire kewpie."[17] The broadcast triggered an avalanche of letters from recruits in training camps, many of them requesting that Bing appear on CBS's Saturday-night sensation *Your Hit Parade*. The demand grew so insistent that Kraft-Phenix yielded its exclusivity and allowed him to make one ballyhooed appearance on the rival network's program.

At the *Holiday Inn* set, Sandrich had to cadge balloons wherever he could find them for the New Year's scene; rubber rationing made them scarce. The costumer Edith Head complained that cloth rationing undermined her ability to design the seventy planned costume changes for the four stars. Worse, Paramount always purchased specially beaded garments from a family-run business in

Czechoslovakia; it was now unavailable, so her staff had to hurriedly master the craft of stringing beads. Bing was miffed to learn that the three days during which Sandrich had him pitching hay, painting a barn, currying horses, and milking cows would be compressed into a two-minute montage—deftly comical and scored with Bing's recording of Berlin's 1924 song "Lazy." Paramount grumbled when Sandrich constructed a Holiday Inn exterior for that same montage but amortized the cost by using it in René Clair's *I Married a Witch*. Between *Holiday Inn* scenes, Bing agreed to another studio task: an unbilled cameo in Bob Hope's *My Favorite Blonde*: Bing leans against a wall. Bob asks him for directions, walks off, and mutters, "Couldn't be." Intended as a one-off, it launched a cycle of Crosby walk-ons in Hope movies.[18]

Another dustup roiled the home front. The loud, abrasive James Caesar Petrillo personified everything people hated about union bosses: he was self-important, self-serving, and self-promoting. Petrillo wanted to be the American Federation of Musicians' John L. Lewis, but he lacked Lewis's tactical brilliance, his negotiating skills, and a righteous cause. To flex his muscles, Petrillo planned a strike of unparalleled magnitude against the recording industry and, by extension, the jukebox industry and all radio stations that played transcriptions or commercial discs. He needed a strike, not concessions, and accordingly borrowed a strategy from Hitler, who had needed a war with Poland, not appeasement. Hitler set a deadline for Poland to meet his terms without stipulating what those terms were and succeeded in confusing everyone as he mobilized his attack. Petrillo threatened a war on record companies unless they paid a percentage of profits to finance concerts or a pension fund or something. The industry figured he was posturing, as he never clarified his demands. Instead of seeking arbitration, he mailed carbon copies of a rubber-stamped threat, declaring a deadline of July 31. He initially agreed to exceptions, allowing musicians to record for military or home use. When informed that it wasn't legal for record companies to discriminate in selling their product—to soldiers and not civilians, or to civilians and not radio stations—he vowed total stoppage, which convinced executives that he could not be serious.[19]

But why take chances? Jack Kapp could not afford to. The other big labels had extensive libraries from which to reissue records made before a strike; they had classical music wings with perennial sellers. Decca, only eight years old, needed product. Kapp ordered a rigorous schedule for key artists, particularly Bing, who crammed five sessions into January alone, three on weekends and a dozen more before Petrillo's deadline. The tunes were a mixed lot of novelties, country songs, Hawaiian songs, and covers, and Bing often sounded drained and bored. Yet the first and only jazz date among them is effortlessly pleasing. Kapp teamed him with Woody Herman's Woodchoppers, a seven-piece band drawn from Herman's orchestra, which was then topping the charts with its only number one hit, "Blues in the Night." The arrangements echoed the polyphonic style of Bob Crosby's band and showcased the talented twenty-four-year-old trumpet player Cappy Lewis. Bing's swing is limber and understated on "I Want My Mama," adapted from the Brazilian "Mama Yo Quiero," absent lyrics in the Portuguese about breast-suckling. He sashays over the Carter Family classic "I'm Thinking Tonight of My Blue Eyes," and over Walt Yoder's pumping bass on the handclap arrangement of "Deep in the Heart of Texas," his most substantial hit for the next nine months; England's censors at the BBC found it so catchy that they banned it (along with dozens of other innocuous recordings) from broadcast for fear that factory hands would hurt themselves trying to clap along. A very good session, yet the next day he crooned four lackluster sides with Dick McIntyre and His Harmony Hawaiians.

A few days later, he returned to Decca with John Scott Trotter (for the first time in half a year) and recorded "Skylark," a new song by Johnny Mercer and Hoagy Carmichael that defined the breed of songwriting talent lacking during the ASCAP strike. The middle part is especially skilled, sweeping up and down through major and minor chords, supple as a jazz improvisation. Carmichael first conceived it for a never-mounted Broadway adaptation of Dorothy Baker's novel *Young Man with a Horn*.[20] He caught the wheeling rapture of Bix Beiderbecke with a melody perfectly complemented by Mercer's lyrics. So why is Bing's reading so tepid? Here was a great song that linked four men — Bing, Bix, Hoagy, and Johnny — whose love of jazz took them far beyond the worlds of their upbringing. Yet his affect is as flat as the tempo as he curls phrases with self-conscious mordents. (His rejected first take is more convincing for being less decorative.) Bing's recording was a hit, albeit the least successful of the four versions of "Skylark" that made the charts; Dinah Shore's held the lead. On the same date, he gave a lissome account of Mercer's "Mandy Is Two" and a pining one of the 1929 "Miss You," an exercise in blunt anxiety that had been revived for a B-musical (*Strictly in the Groove*). Issued as the B-side of his ensuing recording of "Blues in the Night," "Miss You" was the title Bing chose to promote on *KMH*, singing it five times on air and scoring a close second in sales to a version by the quick-rising Dinah Shore. The BBC prohibited the airing of Bing's "Miss You" on the grounds that its dreamy ardor might weaken public morale.

The gulf between Bing's records and his work in film and radio was rarely more evident than in this period. With only a day's rest, he returned to Decca on the last Monday and Tuesday in January, off from *Holiday Inn* while Astaire filmed the firecracker number. Monday's songs were lugubrious and soon forgotten. Tuesday's offered covers of three top hits (including "Blues in the Night" and Glenn Miller's "Moonlight Cocktail"); the singing is adequate while conveying little personal engagement, even on an essential wartime love ballad by Frank Loesser and Jule Styne, "I Don't Want to Walk Without You." Harry James scored a runaway triumph with this sentimental classic by combining schmaltzy trumpet and a finely judged chorus by his talented vocalist Helen Forrest. Bing's version ranked second among the several competing discs, but he must have regretted his awkward rests and emotional detachment because they are utterly absent in the stunning performance he gave the song a week later on *KMH*.

With seventeen tunes now in the bank, he avoided Decca for the next six weeks. He also avoided Paramount, figuring he ought to have the month of February off before getting back into harness for *Road to Morocco*. He asked O'Melveny to tell the studio that he would not be available for the new picture until March 1. O'Melveny made the call and told Bing Paramount seemed to find that acceptable. It wasn't. He was ordered to return on February 23 to rehearse the *Morocco* songs.[21]

To grab even three weeks, Bing notified Kraft, per his contract, that he would take off two weeks in February, without remuneration (he asked Mickey Rooney to fill in) to play golf for the Red Cross in Arizona and Texas. Before he left, a focal point in his sporting life ended with the sixth and best attended—two hundred and fifty participants, record-setting crowds—Bing Crosby National Pro-Am Tournament at Rancho Santa Fe. A casualty of wartime economy, the Crosby tournament would remain on hiatus until 1947, when it went north to Monterey. The sportswriter Darsie L. Darsie pointed out that the Crosby never covered its costs, nor was it expected to: "He simply wants to stage a grand golfing party for his golfing friends—and when he elected to put it on with all of the gate receipts going to charity, he clinched the good will of golf followers as well as the general public throughout the world."[22] Herb Polesie filmed the competition for a PGA short subject, "Don't Hook Now," a companion to the earlier "Swing with Bing." Partnered by Sam Snead in a foursome with Ben Hogan and Bob Hope, Bing came in seventh. At the army's request, he canceled the usual clambake.

Hope had expected to travel with him to help launch the Western Open Golf Championship in Phoenix but succumbed to tonsillitis, yet he ignored his doctor's advice in order to meet up with Bing for matches in Dallas, Houston, and San Antonio. Bob and the other celebrities flew from city to city; Bing, ever wary of the air, took the train. They usually ended the eighteenth greens with an impromptu entertainment. The crowds were as big as ten thousand, the largest gallery the Southwest had ever seen. In addition to raising money for the Red Cross, the players sold $20,000 in defense bonds and promoted the PGA War Relief Fund. On the eve before leaving Houston, they put on consecutive shows for servicemen at Camp Wallace and Ellington Field. When he could Bing played purely to compete. After a brief visit home, he entered the Invitational Match Play Tournament in Phoenix and won each round until the semifinals, which he lost on the twenty-first hole. That night he caught the last train to Hollywood, acceding to Paramount's demands with much anticipation.

The next morning, February 23, he reported to the studio to hear and run down the songs he would begin prerecording the next day. Despite the pressure to curtail his travels, Bing arrived at the rehearsal room keenly curious to encounter the first score written for him by Johnny Burke and Jimmy Van Heusen since *Road to*

Zanzibar. Victor Young conducted the studio orchestra for *Road to Morocco,* but for this rehearsal, Bing insisted on working solely with the pianist Charlie LaVere, from Trotter's *KMH* orchestra. They had created two songs for Bing and a duet for him and Bob. It was a savory, savory day. These were songs that fully vindicated his faith in the pairing of these gifted men. "Moonlight Becomes You" doesn't sound like a ballad that might have gone to anyone and just happened to go to Bing. It *is* Bing in its metaphorical caginess and nurturing range. According to a widely repeated story, Bing inadvertently gave them the title on the set as they waited for a cameraman to light Dorothy Lamour beneath a prop moon. "Pretty sharp, Dottie," Bing allegedly said, "moonlight becomes you." Burke and Van Heusen exchanged a glance and repaired to a piano. That did not actually happen, as they had yet to start shooting, but a twice-told fib may have the virtue of articulating an unspoken truth, in this instance, that "Moonlight Becomes You" captures Bing with every note, word, and rest. The melody begins with a descending sixth that practically coos *Cros-by* before moseying over half a dozen triplets in an airtight nuptial of music and images, not least the idea of moonlight as apparel timed to a conversational fillip ("you cer-tain-ly know the right thing to wear"). Van Heusen later marveled that the words and music "came almost simultaneously."[23] The upbeat songs functioned no less precisely. In "Ain't Got a Dime to My Name," Burke captures Bing's insouciance in the refrain "ho-hum." The delirious title song, "The Road to Morocco," expands on Bing's repartee with Bob Hope. Swinging, original, droll, it boasts one of the more memorable puns in popular music: "like *Webster's* dictionary, we're Morocco bound."

Burke submitted nearly a dozen verses for "The Road to Morocco" before satisfying Joe Breen, then wrote a few more to satisfy Jack Kapp, who thought the movie's meta-jokes would not work on Bing's solo record. The version heard in the picture sets the stage for a Hollywood travesty of Arabia; lines include, "Where we're goin', why we're goin', how can we be sure / I'll lay you eight to five that we'll meet Dorothy Lamour"; "We run into villains but we haven't any fears / Paramount will protect us 'cause we're signed for five more years"; and "I hear this country's where they do the dance of the seven veils / We'd tell you more but we would have the censors on our tails." They did; the censors made short work of such verses as "They say that little girls here marry much, much older men / It's just like Tennessee, except they wait until they're ten."[24] For Bing's Decca record, Burke wrote lyrics that shifted the milieu to Brooklyn: "Let's meet on the road to Morocco / Instead of the tunnel of love. / The desert night, the Arab tents, the harem atmosphere / It's the best attraction Coney Island has this year."[25]

The surest indication of Bing's delight in these songs is in the tracks he made for the film, performed with irresistible verve — the very quality so saliently missing from his recent Deccas. Burke and Van Heusen wrote four songs for *Morocco* (including a ballad for Lamour, "Constantly"). Putting aside "White Christmas" and perhaps "Be Careful, It's My Heart," did the great Berlin produce anything better or even as good for *Holiday Inn?*

Returning to *KMH,* Bing welcomed back Paul Robeson, and instead of vanishing during Robeson's numbers, he stood off to the side, arms crossed, and listened intently as the bass baritone sang "Balm in Gilead" and "It Ain't Necessarily So." Bing followed him to the microphone with "Miss You." That month he told the magazine *Music and Rhythm* that Robeson "thrills me right to my boots every time I hear him sing; he handles his voice as though he were playing a mighty organ." As usual, in 1942, Bing gave few interviews, but in March, he agreed to provide *Music and Rhythm* with an annotated list of his ten favorite singers, "in the degree to which they entertain *me*." He topped the list with Mildred Bailey, acknowledging that she launched his career but insisting his judgment was unbiased. He extolled her "impeccable" rhythm and intonation, her distinctiveness and sincerity — "she sings a ballad like it really mattered." The whole list emphasized his attentiveness to ballads. Number two was Bob Eberle ("best voice in the popular music field"); three was Connie Boswell; four, Ethel Waters ("she's given me more genuine kicks than any singer extant. Her comedy is delicious, and she can still swing one better than most"); five, Paul Robeson; six, Mary Martin; seven, Jack Teagarden; eight, Ray McKinley ("entertained me way back when he was drumming for Dorsey"); nine, Margaret Lenhart ("a new singer" with "perfect diction"); and ten, Frances Langford.[26]

Bing offered several such lists over the decades, always signifying the current state of pop and encouraging a politic reading between the lines. Bailey and Waters reflected his earliest influences; Boswell and Martin leveled the *KMH* controversy; Robeson and Langford were at the forefront of morale building for the men-at-arms; Teagarden and McKinley were old jazz friends; Eberle (the baritone with Jimmy Dorsey's band) represented younger fellas competing for Crosby's crown; and Lenhart, a radio singer whose career soon stalled, briefly became a Crosby protégée. Having met her through John Reber in New York, he was sufficiently impressed to consider her for the cast of *KMH* should Mary Martin turn down the offer. Bing's emphasis on ballads reflected his mood at the moment. Shortly after the war, answering a similar question, he emphasized jazz and blues. "My favorite male singer? It's Frank Sinatra [this when Sinatra's career had temporarily bottomed out]. Though sometimes it might be Perry Como. And let's not forget Jack Teagarden. And Louie [Armstrong], of course. I like the blues singer Eddie Vinson. And Johnny Mercer, he sings fine blues, about as well as anybody. A lot of people don't like the quality of his voice, but I like it. There's Mildred Bailey. Mildred, of course. She had a lot to do with my singing style; we sang so much together. She's so good. But, man, woman or child, the greatest singer of them all is Ella Fitzgerald."[27]

Ella would become a frequent guest on his radio shows; their buoyant duets were highlights. Yet Mildred held a unique place in his heart. In his last years, Bing typed out a series of notes and anecdotes for a proposed book, and he began with her: "If anyone can be said to have influenced my style of singing, it was this fine lady. She was far ahead of her time. She was also the sister of my friend Al Rinker, who with the irrepressible Harry Barris joined me in establishing the Rhythm Boys. I guess without those two stalwarts and my ever present cymbal, I never would have gotten started in show business."[28]

The morning after the broadcast with Robeson, *Road to Morocco*—a picture that Bing characterized as a Rover Boys story—went before the cameras. Radio taxed *Morocco*'s schedule, costing the production six days in April—three Thursdays for Bing's program and three Tuesdays for Bob's half-hour Pepsodent show. Yet high spirits on the *Morocco* set sparked the next *KMH* broadcast, which received a Reber orchid and "boffo" praise from Kuhl.[29] Bing continued to devote his weekends to charity golf and camp shows, golfing in Sacramento with Hope, Babe Ruth, and Governor Olson, and performing at the Mather and McClellan Air Force Bases. When Kapp wanted Bing, he had to schedule sessions at night. He was in demand as never before. David Butler, the director of *Morocco*, vainly hoped to minimalize interruptions by removing the one soundstage phone to an inconvenient distance.

Learning that producer Paul Jones had scheduled the next Road movie in Morocco, Luigi Luraschi warned him not to set the entire film in a harem. One harem scene would be acceptable, provided "1. That you do not refer to the girls in the harem as the Sultan's wives. You can call them the Sultan's slave girls or the Sultan's dancing girls. 2. That the comedy in the harem is not played for sex flavor. 3. That we keep away from eunuchs." He asked him to "please avoid Mohammedan customs of a religious flavor, as this would offend Mohammedans everywhere."[30] In those days, he did not fear Muslim threats; he feared Muslims boycotting the movie. Diplomatically, Morocco could be treated any which way. As a French protectorate, it belonged to Vichy, but sympathy for the Allies was as thick on the ground in Morocco as it was in France. An equivocal refrain is repeated throughout the film: "This is a strange country." They debated the title, however, for a different reason: A Paramount executive feared that audiences would think it was a war picture. Paul Jones countered that with Bing, Bob, and Dottie heading the cast in their third Road outing, audiences could figure out it wasn't. To be safe, Paramount copyrighted the alternative title, *Road to Bagdad*. In treatments and scripts ultimately credited to Don Hartman and Frank Butler, Bing and Bob were variously cast as reporters covering an uprising, racetrack touts in Rabat, or passengers on a freighter from South Africa or Norway. Eventually the writers bit the bullet and tossed logic to the winds.[31]

Road to Morocco is a sublimely harebrained comedy, widely regarded as the best in the series and certainly the most lucrative. If *Road to Zanzibar* consciously satirized jungle movies, *Morocco* had a purer goal: inanity for its own sake. Little is made of Arabian movie conventions as delineated in *The Thief of Bagdad* or *The*

Four Feathers; there is nothing of Marlene Dietrich pursuing a legionnaire over the dunes in *Morocco* or Rudolph Valentino smoldering in his tent as *The Sheik.*[32] This Arabia is a land of props, a pastiche of Middle Eastern set design, costumes, sexy women, music, daunting but easily foiled villains, talking camels, and Bing and Bob hoodwinking each other with adroit one-liners. *Road to Morocco* is racier than its predecessors. No longer yoked by their jealousy, Bing and Bob try to ditch each other so that the last man lounging in Lamour's arms can enjoy life as a pasha — "accent on the *pash,*" as Bob clarifies. Impotent buffoonery now gives way to leering desire. In a gag that inexplicably escaped the censors, Lamour avidly kisses Hope, both hands cradling his face, and his curled slipper unravels to a foot-long erection. Bing says, "Now kiss him on the nose. See if you can straighten that out." Bing easily flips her affections with a serenade, "Moonlight Becomes You." That much hasn't changed, though Hope, too, gets a souvenir in the form of a highly sexed handmaiden played by Dona Drake, the gorgeously dimpled, light-skinned African American actress and dancer who "passed" for white or Latina her entire career.[33]

Nor is *Morocco* content to break the fourth wall with an occasional wink. The wall is exploded like the freighter in the first shot — a standard opening for a war picture, as was the subsequent montage of the news being spread by foreign-language radio announcers, including Richard Loo, who pins to his lapel an I AM CHINESE button. No explanation is advanced as to how Bing and Bob, stowaways, survived or landed on a raft. Observing that cannibalism is de rigueur under the circumstances, Bing flips a coin, covers it, and asks Bob, "What's the date?" On shore, they mount a camel and sing "The Road to Morocco," the lyric foretelling the plot and the movie-ness of the venture, with Bing looking preternaturally calm as he fluffs the camel's tuft of hair and leans his cheek on his index finger. Escaping from a sheikh's caravan, which dumped them in the desert, bound hand and foot, Bob wonders if they ought to explain to the audience how they got loose. Nah, Bing tells him, they'd never believe us. A couple of Arabs roll cigarettes as Bing taps gunpowder on the fixings. Bob: "Say, what are you doing, making reefers?" Bing: "This'll give 'em that lift." Barney Dean conceived the closer, in which Bing disrupts Bob's overacting. Bob:

"You had to open your big mouth and ruin the only good scene I got in the picture. I might have won the Academy Award!" At times, it's like watching a movie watching itself.[34]

Buddy DeSylva involved himself each step of the way, deleting bad jokes and exposition and tightening bolts to produce a rigorous eighty-two minutes. "Keep this," he wrote in the margin of his script about the title song. Elsewhere, he annotated it for budgetary cuts, from shaving down the three hundred extras to skimping on the paper used for the scripts: "Due to the shortage of paper, all future scripts will have pages filled to capacity, thereby cutting down the length approximately 20%." He changed Marrakesh to the made-up Karameesh to forestall a potential libel action, shortened the jailbreak, excised a scene with a panther, and cut most of the lines scripted for two camels—a dated gag (Bing worked with a talking lion in a 1932 Mack Sennett short, *Dream House*) made palatable by the cartoon-voiceover specialist Sara Berner doing a mean Kate Hepburn.

David Butler's long association with Twentieth Century–Fox proved useful. In 1937, he built an Arabian marketplace on the Fox lot for an Eddie Cantor farce, *Ali Baba Goes to Town,* a set he now used for scenes in *Road to Morocco.* That connection enabled him to cast Fox contract actor Anthony Quinn as the sheikh who expects to marry Lamour after disposing of the two Americans. Quinn's stature had risen in the two years since *Road to Singapore,* to fourth billing. Butler outfitted him to enhance his resemblance to Valentino and gave him one piece of direction: Play it straight, as if you don't know you're in a comedy. Butler also found at Fox the Trinidadian Rita Christiani, who dances in the sheikh's tent. Admirers of avant-garde cinema remember her as the dancer in Maya Deren's short 1946 fantasy "Ritual in Transfigured Time."

Barney Dean devised the setup for the famous scene in which they find the camel that brings them out of the desert and into the story. Bing and Bob sit side by side, facing front, as the camel licks each of them in turn. Bing thinks Bob is kissing him and vice versa. It wasn't much of a joke and required double-printing the camel, but Butler agreed to try it out. An accident made the scene work. When the boys stood up to confront the camel, it sneezed in Bob's eye, propelling him out of camera range for a second before, blinded and in pain, he stumbled back into view. Without hesitation and before Butler stopped the action, Bing patted its flank and chortled, "Good girl, good girl." Butler kept it in the picture, a decision Hope accepted good-naturedly. But there was a second mishap that triggered hard feelings.

Butler arranged for a band of mounted Arabs to gallop down a tight passageway on the Fox set; he had rigged a loudspeaker so he could signal Bing and Bob when it was time to jump out of the way. He called "Action," and within seconds the riders were on the heels of the terrified actors, who leaped through the nearest openings. Butler blamed the episode on the lead horseman, the stuntman Kermit Maynard (brother of Ken): "I tried to time it, but I had no idea that this man would go so fast."[35] The actors blamed Butler. Bing recalled walking down the narrow street with Hope as the "tribe of Bedouins or whatever they were" attacked. The idea was that they see the marauders half a mile down and start walking fast, then faster, then break into a trot, and then run. "Dave wanted it to look real good so I started walking, then I started running, and I don't hear nothing yet and Hope cut out, dove into a doorway someplace. I didn't see him go, but I'm still running and I could feel these horses and I could hear them and their hot breath right on my neck. Dave never did holler *jump* and I finally jumped through a window and cut myself up and the horses just missed me by a whisker, I guess. And I pulled myself together, cut and bleeding, got up to the back of the set, and Dave said, 'Let's do it again. You jumped too soon. Ruined the scene.' Hope used to call him the Murderer because of the things he did to us."[36]

They did not do the scene again. Butler salvaged a shot of Crosby and Hope running and cut to the marketplace scene. A chill between actors and director briefly ensued. Butler readied a shot while the two stars conversed privately. When he called for quiet, they continued chatting. Butler swallowed his pride and stood there until they finished. Another time, Butler insisted Bing remove his fez and put on the wig. Bing refused and made light of the request, pontificating on head-covering customs in the Middle East. (DeSylva once promised to cast him as a rabbi so he could wear a hat in every scene. "That interested me," Bing said.) Butler argued with him as the crew waited. According to Hope, he summoned executive help: Y. Frank Freeman himself came to the set, chatted warmly with Bing, and left without saying a word to the director. They evidently patched things up before the two-month shoot ended. Yvonne De Carlo, who began her long career with a bit part in *Morocco,* recalled an abundance of "practical jokes and high jinks" that trounced "soundstage monotony." Three days after completion, Butler appeared as Bing's guest on *KMH.* Hope asked him to direct his next solo picture.[37]

One Friday night two weeks into filming *Road to Morocco,* Bing and Mary Martin met at Decca to record "Wait Till the Sun Shines, Nellie" (with pots-and-kettles drumming by Spike Jones) and "Lily of Laguna." Their success on radio prompted Paramount to option the title of a radio serial, *Manhattan at Midnight,* as a follow-up movie. That idea fell through, but Jack Kapp resolved to exploit their popularity with a disc that reflected wartime inflation. In the darkest days of the Depression, Decca revived a moribund business with low-price discs, thirty-five cents (three for a dollar in some areas), earning the hostility of his rivals until the profits rolled in. By 1941, sales exceeded 127 million discs, thanks to Crosby, big bands, 400,000 jukeboxes, and a broadening taste in songs, particularly the mainstreaming of country music and rhythm and blues. The future looked rock solid until war disrupted the flow of shellac from India and halted the manufacturing of electrical merchandise. Expenses escalated, but the key record labels had little room to maneuver, given rationing and price restrictions. In April, the War Production Board would cut the accessibility of shellac 70 percent, requiring plants to use a costlier plastic compound, polyvinyl chloride. On August 1, the Petrillo ban would force record companies to make do with stockpiles and reissues. Prohibited to raise the price of Decca's main line, with its distinctive blue label, Kapp shifted Crosby and other artists to his preexisting but largely dormant fifty-cent black label. The disc by Bing and Mary Martin was the first to signal that change. The price hike compensated for reduced sales and the higher cost of vinyl. After Bing finished shooting *Road to Morocco,* toward the end of April, and while Paramount prepared for the rollout of *Holiday Inn* in August, Kapp produced Decca's first black-label album: twelve holiday-related songs from the Berlin epic — in effect, the first "concept album" (although the phrase was not in use) by a mainstream singer, and a smash hit despite the price hike.[38]

10

CARAVAN

Sleep upon my shoulder as we creep
across the sands so I may keep
the memory of our Caravan
> —Irving Mills, "Caravan" (1937)[1]

Bing's war work meant longer absences from Camarillo Street. Between pictures, he hit the road, and friends wondered: Did Dixie's erratic behavior encourage his desire to travel or did his travel goad her erratic behavior? She told everyone how proud she was of his contributions to the war effort and pitched in on her own. Participating in the American Women's Voluntary Services, she opened the grounds of their home to the public for a United Nations bazaar and a tea to collect clothes. Dolores Hope poured the tea. Admission: one dollar or a bundle of clothes and fifty cents. Dixie captivated the military police battalion at Fort Ord in Monterey. They designated her captain of Company B and called themselves Dixie Lee's MPs. War inclined her toward a plainer look. She rinsed the blond from her hair, a vestige of her time as a starlet, in favor of natural brown tresses.

For Bing, natural meant losing the mucket. As much as he hated wearing it, he played the game (character actors can lose their hair; celluloid gods, never), as did photographers who wanted to remain in the studios' good graces. Most stars with vanishing hairlines rarely left the house without a rug. Bing preferred hats. If he wore neither a rug nor a hat on set or at rehearsal, press photographers—like their counterparts in the nation's capital did when the president appeared on crutches or in a wheelchair—lowered their cameras. The photographer Gene Lester had been warned about that before he relocated to Hollywood, so when *Radio Guide* assigned him to shoot a *KMH* rehearsal, he came prepared. Lester glued a patch of sheepskin to the top of a flashbulb and trimmed it neat with a part in the middle. "I'm sitting in the first row with my Speed Graphic, watching Bing rehearse without the hat or toup, so I took the flashbulb and put it into the reflector, got my camera ready, and Bing looks down from up on stage—he was three feet above me—and he points to his head. I said, 'Bing, you've got nothing to worry about, I use flashbulbs with hair on them,' and I show him. He broke out laughing, unbelievable! He says, 'Oh Jesus, do anything you wanna do.' That was my first time with Bing. After that, I got a lot of pictures of him without his toup."[2]

Bing rarely put it on when he entertained soldiers. Sometimes he wore a hat, but mostly he made a point of showing he was there not as a star, but as a regular guy—like them, except they risked their lives while he contributed songs and jokes. It was a question of respect. He thought it phony—unforgivable, really—to address these men who put everything on the line while sporting his fake pompadour: the mucket, scalp doily, bowser, divot. A lot of young men came from farms without electricity, without radios and phonographs, and didn't know who the hell he was. Bing understood that. He wanted them to discover him fresh. They wanted distraction, not a bill of goods, and he gave it to them. Soon his baldness became just another basis of *KMH* jokes. Bing Crosby: "Duke, am I to understand you consider me a longhair?" Duke Ellington: "Uh, yes." Bing Crosby: "Well, round again and case what used to be but ain't no more."[3]

Still, he maintained a distinction between Bing in the flesh and Bing on the silver screen. Hundreds of thousands of people saw him without the toupee at fund-raisers, camp shows, the Hollywood Canteen, racetracks, and when he lifted his hat to mop his brow on a golf course. Just not at the local Bijou. When newsreels reporting on the Crosby-Hope Lakeside Exhibition Golf Match made the rounds of theaters in early 1944, he found the images uncomplimentary because of his lack of makeup and hairpiece and telegraphed Frank Freeman: WOULD APPRECIATE IT IF YOU CAN DO SOMETHING AT THAT END TOWARD STOPPING THESE RELEASES OR AT LEAST EDITING OBJECTIONABLE FOOTAGE.[4]

Bing registered for conscription weeks after Pearl Harbor. In December 1942, the top age for the draft would be lowered from forty-five to thirty-eight, but before that, whether he signed in at thirty-nine (his real age) or thirty-eight (his professional age), he was eligible. Not that there was a chance of his being called; he was married with four small boys and color-blind. He had options. He could put in for the family exemption, like John Wayne, or the disability exemption, like Frank Sinatra, or arrange a photo-op enrollment, like Ronald Reagan. He might have tried to join the Marines for domestic duty, as Tyrone Power did. He obviously did not have the option of requesting a transfer for combat duty, unlike James Stewart, Robert Montgomery, Van Heflin, and Clark Gable—the widower of Carole Lombard, who requested dangerous assignments, as if he, too, wanted to die. Bing sought no publicity, uniform, or rank, but he made clear his willingness to serve in any capacity deemed useful for the war effort.

He could do nothing more important than promote (and buy; through O'Melveny, Bing pledged as much as one hundred thousand dollars) defense bonds. Thomas McInnerney at Kraft-Phenix assured him of that while congratulating him on the results of a new radio poll that gave top-place victories to Bing, Trotter, Victor Borge, and Ken Carpenter in their respective categories as singer, bandleader, comedian, and announcer. The government agreed. It had no interest in drafting Hollywood royalty except to raise morale and money. During the First World War, sales of Liberty Bonds froze until Charles Chaplin, Mary Pickford, Douglas Fairbanks, and other stars toured the country and helped promote them. Bonds were made to order for the movie colony. Gender was immaterial, as Lombard had proved. Merle Oberon, Dorothy Lamour, and Olivia de Havilland sold defense bonds as successfully as Cary Grant, James Cagney, and Laurel and Hardy. Bing sold more than anyone else. In March, he received a Distinguished Service Award from the Treasury Department. After a conference in Washington and a background check, Bing took an oath of office and accepted an appointment as "special consultant to the Secretary of War, assigned to the Special Service

Division"—a preliminary step that conferred "official status" on him while they figured out how best to use him in the future. Meanwhile, he took another road trip: the Victory Caravan.[5]

The Hollywood Victory Committee, created a few days after Pearl Harbor, aimed to realize the president's ambitions for the United Services Organization: using entertainment to inspire military morale. The various guilds formed subcommittees that invariably got mired in protracted late-night meetings. The actor Porter Hall predicted the epitaph for the actors' guild would be "Committeed to Death." Yet by the first anniversary of the HVC's founding, the guilds boasted a matchless record of achievement: more than 1,100 artists involved in 352 USO shows at training camps in the West and Southwest, 273 USO tours at camps throughout the country, shorter tours to Alaska and the Aleutians, Panama and the Caribbean, England and North Ireland, nearly 3,000 personal appearances at Treasury Department drives, plus hundreds of miscellaneous events and hundreds of radio broadcasts—6,828 individual appearances in all and more than a million miles traveled as of December 1942.[6]

The Victory Caravan was the most fabled of these events. As *Road to Morocco* completed shooting, the Army-Navy Relief Fund worked with the Hollywood Victory Committee to firm up plans for an unprecedented tour by rail. With the goal of raising money for families of men killed in battle, it brought together an outstanding array of stars, most of whom the fans never expected to see except on-screen. No one declined an invitation to join the Victory Caravan; as Hope later remarked, "Who in Hollywood had the guts to tell the IRS he was going to be out of town?" The adventure lasted three weeks, beginning with a four-day journey from Los Angeles to Washington, DC, where the tour kicked off at the White House with Mrs. Roosevelt's blessings, followed by a three-hour concert (no intermission) for thirty-four hundred patrons at Loew's Capitol Theatre. According to Bob Hope, Groucho Marx blanched when he saw the howling mob in DC and remarked: "If this is the American public, we ought to surrender right now."[7]

Pandemonium ensued at every stop as the Victory Caravan moved north through New York (no show there) to Boston, then through the Midwest and the Southwest, thirteen cities in all,[8] and then home to Glendale. Each arrival precipitated a street parade, usually with the stars assigned to individual automobiles, as hundreds of thousands of fans lined the avenues, after which the company could unwind in private at a hotel. The twenty-two performers who initially boarded the train (others joined them for specific concerts) included movie headliners, like Hope, James Cagney, Laurel and Hardy, Claudette Colbert, Cary Grant, Olivia de Havilland, Charles Boyer, Eleanor Powell, Merle Oberon, Joan Bennett, Groucho Marx, and Joan Blondell, as well as supporting players, comedians, and singers such as Bert Lahr, Risë Stevens, Frank McHugh, Desi Arnaz, Charlotte Greenwood, Frances Langford, and Jerry Colonna. The shows' skits were judiciously written, directed, and rehearsed to calm those performers who were lost without a script and to keep performances on a timetable that varied little from city to city. Mark Sandrich headed the production team, which included writers, hair and makeup stylists, carpenters and set painters, and eight starlets to sing, dance, and prettify the stage. Alfred Newman, the film composer and most admired of studio conductors, directed the music played by a core of ten musicians who traveled with the Victory Caravan and were augmented by local players in each city, creating orchestras as large as sixty pieces. Alfred's brother Irving served as the Victory Caravan's doctor, assisted by a couple of nurses.

Hope handled the emceeing, usually spelled by Cary Grant and occasionally by Pat O'Brien. Shows typically opened with the orchestra playing or Risë Stevens singing "The Star Spangled Banner" and closed with Cagney in a fully costumed medley from *Yankee Doodle Dandy*, which was scheduled to open in theaters shortly after the tour. Joan Blondell parodied a striptease act; Cary Grant traded repartee with Joan Bennett, Claudette Colbert, Bert Lahr, and Hope in various skits; Charles Boyer recited Daudet's "The Last Class"; Eleanor Powell tap-danced; Risë Stevens sang arias from *Samson and Delilah* and *The Chocolate Soldier*; Merle Oberon read a poem; Frank McHugh and Pat O'Brien performed a sketch about Corregidor; Frances Langford debuted the Jerome Kern song "Windmill under the Stars"; Groucho fast-talked de Havilland and led a choir through "Dr. Hackenbush."

The Santa Fe Railroad provided the Victory Caravan's train; it had two dining cars, a club car in which Newman rehearsed the music and Sandrich the acts, plus seven cars with sleepers and drawing rooms for the stars. The train conductor told one reporter, "It's like a front seat at all the motion picture theaters in the country at once."[9]

In DC, Gene Lester, the only photographer permitted to travel on the Victory Caravan, assembled most of the participants on the White House lawn for a group portrait with the First Lady. Bing was not among them, nor would he join the troupe during the first week, though his name was listed on all advertisements. The caravan had left Los Angeles on April 26 and arrived at the White House on Thursday, April 30. *Road to Morocco* was scheduled to finish shooting on April 25. Hope fulfilled his eight-week contract and, after a day's rest, flew into DC to meet the train. But Paramount extended Bing's contract to a ninth week, which was just as well, as he had to do *KMH* on April 30. He arranged to enter the tour in Chicago for the sixth concert and debuted at Chicago Stadium in the show's penultimate spot, right before *Yankee Doodle Dandy*. The program, which now included special guest appearances by Edward G. Robinson and Betty Grable, drew a capacity crowd of nearly twenty thousand and was billed as "$2,000,000 Worth of Stars!" and "Biggest All Star Show of All Time!"

In later years, Bing consigned his war work to cartons and file cabinets; most of it was in the form of countless letters from and to grieving parents and wives and soldiers. He rarely spoke or wrote of those activities. In *Call Me Lucky*, the Victory Caravan is given merely half a sentence, solely to set up an incidental anecdote; he described the Victory Caravan as nothing more than "a hegira cooked up by the Government to transport actors all over the United States in the interest of War Bond sales."[10] For James Cagney, however, that evening in Chicago "where Bing Crosby took over" amounted to a show-business tutorial, vividly recalled thirty years later:

> I had never worked with Bing before, and here was a great opportunity to see at first-hand the way this great performer did it. Bing had always been a remarkable fella to me, and I had always thought that everything he did was so relaxed and effortless. Not so. At our opening show... Bob Hope was doing his stuff and he said, "Well, I know you're waiting to hear the Groaner—," and the place went crazy. Bing walked out to a reception for which the adjective "triumphant" is inadequate.

He stood there in that very humble charming way of his, wearing a brass-buttoned blue coat, rust trousers, brown-and-white shoes, and a light green shirt that seemed to verify the legend that he's color blind. After the audience explosion died down, Bing said, "Whadda yez wanna hear?" and they exploded again until the stadium walls nearly buckled. After they subsided, he said, "Ya wanna leave it to me?" and they blew up again. Finally, he said, "Hit me, Al," and our orchestra conductor, Al Newman, started his boys off on "Blues in the Night." They had played only the first two bars when the audience went into rapturous applause once again. Bing finished that song, and never in my life have I heard anything like it. I got the traditional goose pimples just standing there, listening. He did another, same thing.

And if ever I wanted a demonstration of how it felt to live through that old vaudeville phrase, "What an act to follow!," this was it. I was next on the bill, waiting in the wings to do my little stint, "Yankee Doodle Dandy." Fortunately I had some good natural support in the form of my Civil War soldier's uniform, eight cute girls, plus eight American flags blowing in the wind. I danced my brains out, the girls waved the flag energetically, and the entire cast came out and joined in "The Star Spangled Banner," and that was, I can tell you, an experience.

But I've almost forgotten the point of this story, which is that when Bing came offstage, the perspiration on him was an absolute revelation to me. Here he had been to all appearances perfectly loose and relaxed, but not at all. He was giving everything he had in every note he sang, and the apparent effortlessness was a part of his very hard work.[11]

Bing would not have contested Cagney's point. He told a writer in 1942, "Few people outside of the theatrical profession realize what a tremendous task it is for an entertainer, accustomed only to a motion picture set, a recording studio, or a small broadcasting studio, to get up on a stage and face 10,000 sober faces staring at you from out of the darkness."[12] He had not appeared before a paying audience in a decade, not since the days when he broke the house records at the Paramount Theaters in New York, nor would he again until the last two years of his life. Like the stage actor who makes it in Hollywood and never returns to a Broadway theater except as a customer, he cloaked himself in the unassailable environs of media technology. No concerts, nightclubs, stadiums, or saloons. The studio audiences for *KMH* didn't count; they were bystanders and he played to the ether, not to them. Tremendous task or no, it was all right as long as no one bought a ticket expressly to see him. He was okay with the galleries on golf courses, the surprised onlookers at nightspots when he took requests, the crowds at benefits when he did his bit for the cause.

But he would not do a Bing Crosby show. He shrugged off the producers who wanted him to. How could he entertain an audience for a whole evening? What would he do without a script and other actors to play off? Just sing? In dodging impresarios, he dodged the public too. Barney Dean once said that when Bing traveled he packed his suitcase with clothes, a cap, and a ten-foot pole. Bing concurred. "Sometimes I'm afraid I'm a little mean to the fans. I don't want to be, but I can't help it. I guess I'm still self-conscious," he conceded in 1942. "While I don't mind signing a few autograph books, I get panicky if they start crowding in on me and, worst of all, I can't stand it if a fan starts getting gushy. If I see that coming, I duck!"[13]

Yet that year alone he performed before hundreds of thousands of soldiers and civilians. Numberless servicemen would recall meeting him, shaking his hand, getting an autograph or a pass to *KMH*. He was beset by gushing fans, unprotected by an entourage or a velvet rope. On the morning before his Chicago conquest, Bing, Bob, and two golf pros commenced a series of PGA-sponsored matches, followed by a nine-hole contest between the two stars — each increasing his renown as a comic of the links while maintaining his reputation as a solid amateur golfer. Bing won both events, which attracted thirty-five hundred spectators.

The quality and professionalism of the Victory Caravan shows surprised him. Heading for Chicago, he anticipated a jerry-built program with "mediocre material, rough edges, and a lot of bickering. Instead, I found a show that ran as smoothly as if it were being presented on ball-bearings, everyone having fun, everyone with first class material and playing to capacity business in the biggest theatre in town wherever we went."[14] From Chicago, the Victory Caravan traveled to St. Louis, where the Union Station platform was curtained off to allow the cast to sleep late. That afternoon at the Meadowbrook Country Club, Bing and his partner beat Hope and his partner. He also came out on top in their one-on-one match, during which a tragedy was narrowly avoided. On the eighth hole, Bob's ball hit a five-year-old girl. She wasn't seriously hurt, but a devastated Hope resolved to resign from the matches until Bing spoke to the gallery on the dangers of crowding the players, calming the crowd and Bob. That night the Victory Caravan played the Municipal Auditorium. At sunup, it continued to Minnesota, where it made two stops. In St. Paul, a 175-piece marching band roused the crowd, and then a string of politicians bored and dispersed it. In Minneapolis, they partied into the small hours. The next morning, a spry Bing phoned Bob from the Midland Hills Golf Club, where they had scheduled an exhibition match, waking him from a sound sleep. "My head was still ringing," Bob later recalled, "but I shot 35 on the front nine."[15]

Minneapolis turned out to be a highlight of the trip because Crosby and Hope, identifying a growing case of cabin fever among the voyagers, reserved two floors of the Nicollet Hotel so everyone could have a decent shower and comfortable bed. Bing knew the Nicollet from his days with the Rhythm Boys. Hope and his radio sidekick, Jerry Colonna, flew in from St. Louis to make the arrangements, which included armed security on both floors throughout the night. The break was ideally timed for the toughest day of the tour: a nearly four-hour matinee (after the Midland Hills match) at the St. Paul Auditorium, followed by an evening performance at the Minneapolis Auditorium. The luxurious stopover lifted the company's spirits.

On other nights, the celebrities repaired to their guarded sleeping cars, however late the hour. They were discouraged from seeking cozier accommodations in town; better to have a rendezvous on the train, where rumors could be contained. Sexual adventurism added to the mission's allure. No wives or husbands were allowed aboard, even if they were famous in their own right. Several participants were relieved at the chance to escape flagging marriages. The travelers were segregated by gender and placed on opposite ends of the train. Yet some men assumed that the starlets—among them such pinups-in-waiting as Marie McDonald, Frances Gifford, Juanita Stark, and Arleen Whelan—might serve as their private playmates. The committee addressed that issue in advance by appointing the Amazonian, high-kicking entertainer Charlotte Greenwood as den mother to the eight beauties, a duty she undertook while knitting a muffler with Defarge-ian devotion; Gene Lester said the scarf dragged on the floor six feet at journey's end.

It was a time when cheesecake was itself a kind of morale booster, a time when, as Evelyn Keyes wrote, actresses were told it was their "patriotic duty to answer the gallant servicemen" with "the nakedest [pictures] to encourage masturbation in the armed forces."[16] The most totemic pinup of the era was a curiously innocent shot of Betty Grable looking over her shoulder to hide the fact that she was pregnant, flaunting the most renowned backside in barracks history; the armed forces distributed five million tax-funded copies to servicemen. "Sexy, of course," the film historian James Harvey noted, "but evoking not so much the beach or the bedroom as the candy counter in the lobby."[17] Gene Lester earned a few bucks on the side photographing the starlets in their night-gowns or washing their hair for a risqué magazine called *Film Fun*. Its readers did not need much encouragement to fantasize about a caravan of attractive, temporarily unattached, and bigger-than-life idols of the silver screen in close quarters for three weeks.

The Hollywood guilds and the USO were determined to quash precisely those suspicions. Lester provided coverage for local papers as insurance against prying eyes in the drawing rooms, dressing rooms, and backstage areas. The idea was to avert speculation about the caravan as a party on wheels before it began. This was war work! Unable to develop pictures on board, Lester handed out extra nega-tives to the newspapers when the train pulled into a town—countless shots he never printed of stars embarking, disembarking, waving, and smiling. Salacious gossip circulated with much hilarity but never seeped into the press. The Victory Caravan kept its secrets. Only its denizens talked of how Olivia de Havilland missed the White House lawn photograph because of an impromptu tryst with John Huston, recently assigned to the Army Signal Corps, or that Charles Boyer was overheard by much of the company unsuccess-fully pleading with a starlet for sexual favors in his sleeper. Cagney told a friend that Merle Oberon bribed a porter to let her into his room, where she awaited him under the sheets. After the seduction went awry (he pounced, remembered his wife, withdrew), she turned to Bing, who took her to play golf; if there was anything more to it than that, no one said so. Claudette Colbert suspended the rules to smuggle aboard her husband, a navy doctor, for two days, at which point Groucho posted a note on her door: "Isn't this carrying naval relief too far?"[18] Bob Hope's indiscretions were known to all on board (one night he entertained two "cousins," flown in for his own relief), but the only resentment he caused stemmed from his insistence on carrying his own writing team to give him pertinent lines for each city. Fellow travelers complained after a *Variety* review referred to the mission as "Bob Hope's Victory Caravan."

Only one passenger sparked real enmity. Cuban-born Desi Arnaz, at that time a little-known musician who had appeared in a couple of films, boarded with his bongo drums while his uninvited wife, Lucille Ball, remained indignantly at home. In a sanitized retelling of the Victory Caravan, Hope described Pat O'Brien nearly decking Arnaz over his relentless drumming, but in reality the bongos had nothing to do with the fight. Arnaz attempted to personify the Good Neighbor policy by seducing every eligible woman on and off the caravan, offending other passengers who might have been as ardent but who practiced discretion. Audiences admired his enthusiastic drumming, dancing, and charm, but he did himself no favors as tales of his incessant lechery beat the train back to Los Angeles. Other participants provided more congenial memories: Laurel and Hardy performing riotous routines at every railway station and supplying every greenroom with a bottle of whiskey; Joan Bennett inadvertently walking into doors and microphones because she refused to wear her spectacles in public; Bing, Bob, Groucho, and Colonna singing barbershop harmony after hours in the club car.[19]

The night at the Nicollet cleared the air and permitted local newspapers to photograph the stars: Bing mugging with Colbert, Cary Grant unpacking, O'Brien in an old infantry uniform (courtesy of Warner Brothers) introducing Risë Stevens at Minneapolis Auditorium, Hope and Colonna entertaining at a high school, others smiling, holding court, queuing up at a movie theater. The three Minneapolis papers claimed to have taken thousands of pictures but developed relatively few. Crosby dominated all the reviews. A sharp critic at the *St. Paul Pioneer Press* identified the cunning in his presentation: "The audience took Crosby to its heart as a favorite prince no matter what he did. I have great admiration for his style in singing a song like 'Blues in the Night.' He has invented a way of doing this sort of thing that has perfect timing, neatness of touch, theatrical distinction. He has a pleasant urchin way of doing impudent imitations. He looks so innocent, so sleepy and is positively replete with guile."[20]

From there, they went to Des Moines and Dallas and, for the final official performance, to Houston, where the reviewer described most of the evening as "frivolous" until Bing revved up everybody with "Blues in the Night," mandating an encore. "After Crosby sang 'Miss You' and 'Sweet Leilani' the audience still clamored for more. He could stop their applause only by going into a comedy skit with Bob Hope, giving impressions of captains of industry."[21] Bing alternated with Bob as compere that evening. After the show, they left the Victory Caravan, as did de Havilland and Hope's radio companions Colonna and Langford, all of them heading east. While a few performers gathered in San Francisco for one last show, the rest traveled in exhausted triumph to the Glendale station, where they parted with tears, hugs, and promises to stay in touch. The next day, each player received a wire signed by Joan Blondell and Joan Bennett: ARE YOU GETTING MUCH?[22] The earliest reports credited the Victory Caravan with raising $600,000, based primarily on box-office receipts. The Army-Navy Relief Fund estimated that the tour had spurred tens of millions of Americans to buy war bonds, priced between $18.75 and $1,000, and computed the Victory Caravan's three-week take at just short of $1.1 billion.

As most members of the Victory Caravan went home, Bing headed for Memphis to stroll down Beale Street where W. C. Handy gave structure and copyrightable permanence to the blues; after that he went to Churchill Downs in Louisville to visit his horses, including Momentito, who had won a race at the nearby Keeneland track. Though favored to win again, the horse failed to place at Churchill Downs. The sportswriters who had recently joked about his late finishers now acknowledged Bing as a trailblazer—the first Hollywood star to seriously enter racing, a pioneer in importing South American thoroughbreds, one of the first to buy stock in Santa Anita and Hollywood Park, co-founder and presiding personage at Del Mar. His two strings of horses, those he owned himself and those he co-owned with Lin Howard, were faithfully followed. Dixie entered the sport, partnering with Lin's brother on a horse named Ras Taffari. Friends remembered her as a skilled horsewoman, riding her own pinto thoroughbred at the ranch. "And a beautiful sight it was," a friend wrote to Bing, "watching Dixie, Denny, Phil, Gary, Bing (Linny was too young) riding through the eucalyptus trees in full western attire on the rugged trails above the old Spanish ranch house."[23]

Bing's visit to Louisville increased his determination to breed prizewinning thoroughbreds in California. He admitted that the money he poured into racing outpaced his returns but remained optimistic. Horses from other West Coast stables had prevailed in the East, he pointed out; "We'll do it again, and I would sure love to be the man who does it." Toward that end, he took a firm hand in races he couldn't attend, sending a string of instructions, recommendations, and queries to Billy Post, his trainer in East Williston, New York. Don Bingo "takes a lot of the worst of it running against three-year-olds"; "If [Bingo the elder] can't get close, drop him down where he can win"; "If Maicena's that rank, it would be silly to lose the foal"; "Barracosa apparently has a little too much age to handle top mares anymore"; "Looks like running the mare in the Empire Stake was a good move. Picked up an easy thousand and she ran creditably." When he went out on extended army-camp tours, he sent Post his itinerary so he could reach him; "I believe it's best you wire me on the day before the race," Bing wrote. He stressed efficiency ("I sure need to win a good bet. I guess we all could stand it") and discretion ("Billy, if you wire me on a horse, don't mention names. Just 'good chance today' or 'fair chance today,' unless you run two and it's necessary to distinguish").[24]

After his day at the races and another spent trapshooting, Bing golfed in a foursome at Louisville's Audubon Country Club on behalf of Army and Navy Relief, losing before a crowd of fifteen hundred and raising a record amount for a local match, which he immediately increased by auctioning his clubs. His host, General Fred Miles, the head of Lafayette Oil and a prominent Kentucky horseman, paid $750 for the clubs and returned them to be auctioned again, adding another $250 to the pot. On a roll, Bing auctioned his golf balls, his scorecard, and a song, a number requested by and sung to the highest bidder. After deducting expenses, they divvied up $2,227.13 between the Navy Relief and the USO. That night at Fort Knox, he presented a show for servicemen but arrived late for a scheduled fifteen-minute interview on station WINN. He compensated by staying on air for ninety minutes, singing and kibitzing with Senator Happy Chandler and Lieutenant Governor Rodes Myers.

After the Victory Caravan ended, Bing didn't return home for two weeks. Bob Crosby nervously subbed for him twice at *KMH*, and Dixie's parents helped her with the four boys. As Bing's traveling increased, Dixie occasionally took them to stay with Evan and Nonie Wyatt in a house that Grandpa Wyatt had built with his own hands in the San Fernando Valley. Gary recalled him fondly as a "zealous socialist" who lived in book-lined rooms with his invalid wife and never punished him and his brothers except with occasional scowls. To Phillip, Gramps Wyatt resembled a cross between the Soviet prosecutor Andrey Vyshinsky and Colonel Sanders; he "would start with that communism stuff, and Dixie would call TWA and reserve a one-way ticket to Moscow for Evan E. Wyatt and then he would stop, because he knew Dixie did not bluff. She'd have made a terrible poker player."[25] Wyatt took them on a carousel and to the movies (*The Jungle Book*). Bing sent home presents and Dixie sat the boys down to write him letters. Gary wrote of catching trout at the boys' club and taking turns sleeping with their mother; Wyatt, he said, paid them for each A on their report cards. He also wrote that he was "being fair and will try to do better," suggesting Dixie's hand, as does his edited salutation. First Gary wrote "With regards," then crossed out "regards" and replaced it with "love."[26]

Returning to Hollywood, Bing had a light summer calendar. Other than a number to be shot in June for Paramount's patriotic and self-celebrating spectacle *Star Spangled Rhythm*, he had no film work scheduled until October. He had six *KMH* shows to do through June, followed by a three-month respite from radio. He used that time to make frequent guest shots on Armed Forces Radio Service (AFRS) programs like *Command Performance* and *Mail Call*; on bond-drive broadcasts sponsored by the Treasury Department; and on War Department one-offs like "Junk Will Win the War," a ditty commissioned for Bing urging the collection of scrap metal. He increased his USO appearances at training camps, mostly on the West Coast. The laziest man in Hollywood, as Paramount's publicists routinely characterized him, never let up. But the exertion strained his voice and dulled his reflexes, almost to the point of calamity in driving and fishing mishaps.[27]

Paramount selected Bing's next project early in the summer, buying an unpublished story called "Dixie" from William Rankin, a minor writer who had contributed to various movie treatments (Bing's *Pennies from Heaven*, Howard Hawks's *Only Angels Have Wings*). This time Rankin hit the jackpot, receiving $17,500 for his story and the research he assembled about the nineteenth-century minstrel Dan Emmett. After a preview of *Holiday Inn* earned a rave from *Variety*, the studio had no doubt that Berlin's musical would mint money and prepared *Dixie* as something of a reward for its top earner—the first Crosby film in his ten years at Paramount shot in Technicolor.

With the sword of Petrillo hanging over everyone's head, Bing owed considerable time to Decca. Jack Kapp played a dangerous game by waiting as long as he did to record the Berlin score, particularly considering the unevenness of the year's Crosby sessions. His most recent date, on a late afternoon in March, produced a doughy waltz and two routine Burke and Van Heusen songs, one of which, "Got the Moon in My Pocket," vainly strove for a pocketful-of-dreams outlook; Crosby never bothered to sing it on air. Now it was late May. The recording ban would go into effect August 1, and on August 4, Paramount would debut *Holiday Inn*; two months after that, *Road to Morocco* would compete with it in theaters. But back then, records could be made, pressed, and circulated within days, and there was something to be said for the immediacy of issuing them right away. Besides, Kapp required tests of the new vinyl compound for the *Holiday Inn* album (problems arose with the early pressings). He needed inventive arrangements to distinguish the Decca versions from those in the film, and he hoped that the seven-month lapse between the movie and the recording would goad Bing to fresh interpretations. He now required a week when Bing, Fred Astaire, Bob Crosby, and the other principals had free mornings—that's when Bing sounded best, from eight thirty to eleven thirty, after breakfast and before lunch.

Between May 25 and July 7, Kapp scheduled eight Crosby sessions that produced a hodgepodge of twenty-seven sides, among them a couple of contenders for the worst records Bing ever made and three chart-toppers, including "White Christmas," the bestselling recording of all time. Kapp's instincts were initially justified, as Bing, buoyed by his brother's band (with Buddy Morrow offering a Teagarden-style trombone solo), took "Lazy" for a stroll through the park, a superb performance. In later years, Bob Crosby acknowledged his brother's perspicacity in securing him for *Holiday Inn* at a time when rumors suggested bad feelings between them. They stilled gossip with their esprit at these sessions and Bing sounded rejuvenated. Paul Weston's arrangements jazzed up the movie versions, enlivening Berlin's trifle "I've Got Plenty to Be Thankful For" with a tempo boost and a Yank Lawson trumpet solo. Two days later, Fred Astaire recorded his solo numbers ("You're Easy to Dance With," "I Can't Tell a Lie") and the knotty "I'll Capture Your Heart Singing" with Bing and, in Virginia Dale's part, the radio singer Margaret Lenhart. Nimble as that trio was, with Astaire's tapping captured by a floor mike, the session reached its peak after everyone but Bing and eight members of Bob's band—the Bob Cats—went home, leaving them to frolic through "When My Dreamboat Comes Home" and Ernest Tubb's honky-tonk hit "Walking the Floor over You." These sides didn't make the hit parade, but jazz lovers cherished them as extremely welcome and increasingly rare paradigms of Crosby's subtle swing.

Two mornings after that session, May 29, Bing was back at Decca in the lap of John Scott Trotter's orchestra and the eight-person-strong Ken Darby Singers. Five months had passed since Bing sang "White Christmas" on *KMH* and seven since he'd filmed it for *Holiday Inn*. A few myths have hewed to the "White Christmas" session. One of them doggedly credits Kapp as producer, though most likely he wasn't present at all. Though he sometimes flew out for important sessions, he usually stayed in New York and delegated the responsibility to his West Coast producer A. J. Perry (the namesake of Bing's horse Decca Joe). Perry produced many Crosby records and was particularly proud of his participation in "White Christmas" and the "Silent Night" session that followed it.

Trotter claimed that Berlin fought with Kapp to retain the verse set in Beverly Hills. In Trotter's telling, Kapp told Berlin that it had nothing to do with Christmas. Something like this might have happened at some point, but it would have been long before the recording date. At the time he was asked to arrange the song, Ted Duncan had never even seen the verse, and his orchestration of the famous melody required the full three minutes of a 78 rpm disc. Not that Berlin had given up seeking "a new angle" for it. Six weeks after Bing recorded "White Christmas," Berlin wrote Sandrich that he would find a use for the verse after the picture opened.[28] Despite the "wonderful reaction to" the song, his publishing company warned him that without a verse the sheet music would be too skimpy to suit song pluggers, retailers, and customers. A colleague told him it would not sell anyway because no one but Crosby could sing the word *Christmases*. Trotter also originated the myth that Bing recorded "White Christmas" in eighteen minutes. Decca logbooks show the session ran two and a half hours and produced three songs, "Abraham," "Song of Freedom," and "White Christmas," which required the most time—three takes, possibly four.[29]

Ken Darby later claimed that everyone present knew it was an instant classic, but in fact, the doubters still outnumbered believers. According to Ted Duncan's son, Bing asked Duncan to amplify the song's drama beyond its stark presentation in the film. His solution was to assign the second chorus to Darby's singers, maintaining Bing's presence only in his contrapuntal whistling, until the closing measures when he returned to command the final phrases. This sage touch incarnated the song's potential as a secular carol. Duncan had three careers, first as a saxophonist, then as an orchestrator— including four years with Trotter and a busy stint at MGM—then as an inventor of toys marketed by Mattel and Ideal.[30] He arranged most of Bing's 1942 records but came into his own on the *Holiday Inn* numbers. His efficient scoring and sensitive tempo adjustments create an easygoing ambience. The illusion of spontaneity is upheld by the whistling, a contrast to the choir's formality. Yet even after the song was cut and delivered, Kapp remained uncertain. He made it the A-side in the United States and the B-side in Great Britain.

The "White Christmas" session took place on Friday. Then things went awry. Instead of resting his voice, Bing went on air Saturday night for an hour-long USO show. On Sunday night, Pat and Eloise O'Brien threw a Victory Caravan cocktail party at their home in Brentwood; the guest list exceeded fifty people and included everyone who had worked in front of or behind the curtains, plus spouses, though Dixie did not attend. Driving home from Brentwood, a few minutes after midnight, Bing crashed into a car stopped at the corner of Wilshire and Roxbury. He was taken to a Beverly Hills hospital, treated for bruised ribs and a cut lip, and sent home. After a few hours' sleep, he drove to Decca's Melrose Avenue studio for a recording session, looking slightly battered and nursing a head cold. This was the session reserved for recording the presumed hit "Be Careful, It's My Heart." All things considered, he did journeyman work, not up to snuff. Careful listeners could detect his struggle in the high notes, and 78s inspired careful listening. No one could fail to hear symptoms of congestion on "Easter Parade." Under normal circumstances, Joe Perry might have canceled the date and prevailed on Kapp to reschedule. But they had no time for that. The *Holiday Inn* album was in production, and Bing was slated for four more sessions with different personnel and instrumentation before Petrillo's deadline.

The album would have six discs—each available singly—plus an eight-page booklet with a summary of the film's storyline; biographical notes on Berlin, Bing, and Fred; and a discography of the nearly 160 versions of Berlin songs in Decca's catalog. Crosby's profile characterizes him as an embodiment of "Americana—hot dogs, the bleachers, ice cream, Thanksgiving and the Fourth." Nothing of Christmas or "White Christmas," though it does cite his broadcast to Bataan. Bing is said to be "reputedly a lazy guy...in a pleasant way, and *only* about work, which makes it perfectly all right." Kapp planned to release the album on June 30, five weeks before the New York premiere of *Holiday Inn* and nearly two months before its general release.[31]

In the next week, Bing recorded four emotionally muted religious or Christmas-oriented songs, including remakes of his 1935 bestsellers "Silent Night" and "Adeste Fideles." This pairing went gold faster than "White Christmas" did and remained his second most successful disc. Kapp first persuaded Bing to record "Silent Night" by suggesting he donate all royalties to charities, and the 1935 version became the industry's first annuity, successfully reissued each Christmas. In December 1941, it sold three hundred thousand copies and Bing donated his portion of the royalties (eight thousand dollars) toward financing army-camp shows. The 1942 version, released on the higher-priced black label, sold over a million copies but it was not his best work (he recorded it a third time, in 1947). The mordents are controlled, the low notes appealing, and the phrasing assured, but the upper range is enervated by a faint tremor that, as luck would have it, oddly heightens the piety of the performance.

Next on the agenda was the *Road to Morocco* score, which brought Vic Schoen into the fold. As musical director for the Andrews Sisters, Schoen had worked with Bing in New York when he and the sisters first recorded together. Jack's brother Dave Kapp produced those sessions and recommended Vic for the *Morocco* numbers—they needed something jazzier than Ted Duncan could provide. Schoen leaped at the chance, preparing himself for the assignment by attending the shooting of the film, where he made useful blocking suggestions for the musical numbers. Jack trusted him to select the musicians, and Vic knew Decca's guidelines well enough to keep the cost down and the melody out front. His writing, far hotter than the movie arrangements, snaps Bing into shape with a knockout intro of rising brasses on "The Road to Morocco" and a pulsating beat on "Ain't Got a Dime to My Name." He also arranged the novelty "Conchita, Marquita, Lolita, Pepita, Rosita, Juanita Lopez" for laughs it didn't get—Jack released it as the second-to-last blue-label Decca, backed with "The Old Oaken Bucket," which had been collecting dust for a year.

Surprisingly, the session's two *Morocco* songs sold poorly. Bing's solo version of the title number faded even as audiences flipped over the duet version in theaters, but the songs cemented his association with Schoen. Kapp realized his mistake in recording it as a Crosby solo and two years later hired Vic to arrange a remake using Hope and the movie lyrics, which sailed up the charts. For Vic, the first "Road to Morocco" session was made unforgettable by an unexpected visitor. Igor Stravinsky had settled in Hollywood a year before in a small house a few blocks from Melrose, and he occasionally visited the Decca offices. Schoen idolized him but did not know he was in the studio until he walked over and said, "You must know all the rules very well." Schoen, startled, asked, "Why would you say that?" Stravinsky said, "You've broken every one of them."

Vic later decided that the remark was a compliment, "because he was the greatest rule breaker in the world."[32]

At the last two sessions, Bing remained in good voice for "Moonlight Becomes You," recorded with Trotter and a Ted Duncan arrangement. But that was not the case for the dire songs that followed, which may be blamed on infantilizing patriotism—"My Great, Great Grandfather," "A Boy in Khaki, a Girl in Lace," "Hello Mom," the kind of rubbish Tin Pan Alley cranked out during the First World War. Kapp apparently recognized that these were not top-of-the-line war songs, as he used one to back the heartier "Bombardier Song" (Rodgers and Hart) and the others as the parting shot for his obsolete blue label. He foresaw a growing taste for songs that cheered fighting men, comforted their loved ones, saluted the flag, and made nostalgia palpable, but they would have to be better than these. Reviewers were kinder than customers, who could not be lured by mediocrity at a bargain price.

The "Hello Mom" session, a feeble kicker to a recording year that began with the sexy "I Want My Mama," indicates that the ban came none too soon for Bing. His voice was shot; tinny high notes, flagging midrange, wobbly intonation, whole notes out of the question. The backing was provided by a Decca standby, the popular pipe organist Eddie Dunstedter, now a captain in command of the (blaringly overmiked) West Coast U.S. Army Air Forces training center orchestra. Dunstedter composed "Hello Mom" to lyrics by his air force buddy Frank Loesser: "Sure Mom the food is mighty good / And lately we had a raise in pay / And the bonds that you're buying / That are keeping us flying / Makes the whole darn thing okay." Bing gave his share of the meager royalties to the air force. The first take, pitched unaccountably high, had him sounding like a teenager socked by testosterone. They brought down the key. Yet the rest was no better; a trite if tolerable rendition of vaudeville's serenade "By the Light of the Silvery Moon" and a Gershwin jewel, "But Not for Me," in which Bing's tones crack and trail off—never did the line "This is the time a fella needs a friend" sound more forlorn. Kapp didn't issue the last two in the United States; he did offer them to Indian Columbia, which distributed the disc only in West Bengal, near the international airport at Dum Dum.

11

FRIENDS

You must ask yourself:
where is it snowing?
—Louise Glück "Persephone
the Wanderer" (2006)

He needed downtime before the hullabaloo of the next five months, when *Holiday Inn* (August), *Road to Morocco* (November), and *Star Spangled Rhythm* (December) would break, along with "White Christmas" and "Moonlight Becomes You." The second half of 1942 brimmed with promise. As prologue, the SEC stated in June that, between his Paramount contract and Decca royalties alone, Bing Crosby had earned the highest salary of any Hollywood actor, second in the industry only to Louis B. Mayer. Yet the nearly metamorphic quality of his successes would fully exceed the dominion of money.[1]

Bing went fishing. On a July weekend, he and two close friends, Johnny Burke and Arnold (Steve) Stevens, a physician who liked to describe himself as the Crosby family's surgeon, drove six hours to the Mammoth Lakes district on the eastern ridges of the Sierra Nevada. The promise of glorious weather meant snow-coated peaks and upper trails and sun glinting on the network of four lakes rippling with brook, brown, and rainbow trout. Armed with fly-casting gear, baskets, and bourbon, they anticipated a merry stag respite from work, war, and family. Burke, more at home writing verse by his pool or hosting long riotously boozy parties than padding in the wild, tagged along as jester. The three had been tight since the late 1930s, after Johnny wrote the lyrics for *Pennies from Heaven* and Stevens, recently arrived in Los Angeles from the Mayo Clinic, set up his first office in the Crosby Building on Sunset Boulevard. Steve soon bonded with his landlord. He treated Bing's bursitis, removed Dixie's appendix, and made himself available to their sons, parents, and siblings while proving no less tenacious than Bing with a rod or hunting rifle.

At some point they hiked to elevated ground still caked in winter snow, intending to cast from the ledge of a high-angle gully. As they climbed the grade and gingerly stepped toward the overhang, Bing lost his balance on a patch of slush. Cumbered with his tackle, he skidded toward the twenty-foot drop. Burke froze. Steve sprang and grabbed him; the two men slid toward the ledge and only narrowly avoided disaster. It would've been an odd end for Crosby, a man so terrified of heights he flew only when necessary; whose client card at the Waldorf Astoria marked him for rooms no higher than the sixth floor. Had he died without witnesses, his carcass might have been as much a mystery as Hemingway's leopard: What in heaven's name was he doing up there? As for Stevens, he had a reputation for fast thinking and quick action, despite his customary state of inebriation. When his daughter Carole, born that year, learned the story, she was not surprised; he had caught her as she fell off a horse and saved her friend from drowning. "He was unflappable," she noted, "quick, brilliant, but always drunk."[2]

If a life can be measured, in part, by the duration of friendships, Bing's was perhaps better than average, though ultimately most of them fell away as the years went by, often because life wore down his companions. Thoreau cautions: "The only danger in friendship is that it will end." Throughout the 1940s and into the next decade, Burke and Stevens were especially close to him. Bob Hope was a professional friend and Barney Dean a loyal sidekick. Jimmy Van Heusen and John Trotter were matchless characters, the former a licensed pilot who could tell you the private numbers of madams on both coasts, and the latter an asexual gourmand. Louis Armstrong, Johnny Mercer, and Victor Young stood out among musical friends. Lin Howard, Dave Butler, and Pat O'Brien were racetrack friends.

Phil Silvers and the song plugger Jack Clark were poolside friends. Skitch Henderson was the protégé who made good (Bing gave Lyle Russell Cedric Henderson the nickname Skitch), and Jack Kapp was his mentor. There were a great many others in and out of the entertainment business, all of them men's men, oilmen, ranchers, jazz players, duck hunters, golfers, men who kept it light and funny. After the death of Bing's touring partner the great guitarist Eddie Lang in 1933, no one got too close; no one got all of him. Phil Harris, a particularly frequent companion after the war, told an outsider who remarked on their reputed intimacy, "If I knew Bing better than anyone, no one knew him."[3] Yet during the war, Steve Stevens and Johnny Burke had the inside track.

Pressured by the director Woody Van Dyke to enroll in his reserve unit, Stevens entered the navy a year before Pearl Harbor, little expecting to be called to active duty. He established a smart Beverly Hills practice for movie stars (Humphrey Bogart, Maureen O'Hara) and other well-off people. When the navy sent him to San Diego for a couple of weeks, a few influential clients pulled strings to get him returned to Beverly Hills. Fully uniformed, he saw patients in the morning and helped with recruiting at the Federal Building in the afternoon. He was eventually appointed chief of surgery at the naval hospital in Norman, Oklahoma. In his service dress blues and white officer's cap, Steve offered a snazzy front, and few would have suspected that normally he was as sartorially indifferent as Bing or that, despite a sterling reputation, he was mocked in the Crosby circle for vagueness about everything other than his patients. In phlegmatic contrast to the brash and jumpy Burke, he maintained a sober mien that never betrayed his drinking—at least in public. One night his wife, Jean, listened to him counsel a patient on the telephone. "When he hung up, I very meanly said to him, 'Do you really think you're capable of giving advice to people in the state you're in?' He said, 'No, but it helps them anyway.' I thought, *That's true, by God,* and we laughed."[4]

Jean Stevens did not like Burke, whom she found controlling. At the Burkes' pool, as she jotted down the guests' fast repartee for her own amusement, he pulled the notebook from her hands and bopped her on the head with it. "We strangely got along," she recalled, "but in a clashing kind of way." Jean and Steve married two months after she graduated from Stanford (the first woman to edit the university's daily paper) and three weeks after the night they met. They tied the knot in her hometown, Dallas, to escape Burke's determination to commandeer the wedding and turn it into a group jaunt to Las Vegas.[5] This was in 1939, two months after Burke married the stunning, deeply troubled Bessie Beatrice Patterson, formerly of Tucumcari, New Mexico, following a three-year courtship in which he coerced his fiancée to get an education. Bessie secured a Hollywood entrée by winning a national beauty contest as Miss College Humor, a promotional stunt for Crosby's 1933 movie of the same name. She was no more than fifteen at the time, as Paramount executives learned to their embarrassment.

Bing introduced Bessie to Burke in 1936, when she had aged sufficiently to receive her Miss College Humor prize (a walk-on in another Crosby picture, *Rhythm on the Range*). Smitten as he was, Burke, a highly literate University of Wisconsin graduate, thought Bessie, in Bing's politic phrase, "a little too homespun a gal"—he was "a little ashamed" of her uncultured persona, her, "shall we say, corny dialogue." He liked to tell people she did not have shoes when she came to Hollywood. Burke enrolled her at the University of Southern California, where she completed what was supposed to be a three-year course in half that time. She had help. Burke's friends, including Stevens, gathered in his large bachelor's apartment at all hours to write her papers and prepare her homework. It became a game for them, a competition, ensuring that Bessie got straight As, a feat she boasted about in later years to shame her less scholarly children. Johnny proposed to her as "a graduation gift." They bought a house near Bing and Dixie in Toluca Lake.[6]

Burke's patronizing way with Bessie was another thing that annoyed Jean, though Bessie did not offer her much in the way of personality: "There wasn't anything to get close to." Johnny endured his own heavy lifting. It was his second marriage, after a divorce that, as a Catholic, he was more distressed about than he could admit. After he bought his parents a home in the San Fernando Valley, his father, a construction contractor, hanged himself in their backyard. He had complained to several people that Johnny looked down at him, never inviting him to his parties. "And Johnny's whole life was one big party," Jean said. He hated to be alone, especially in the big Toluca Lake house. He fitted its front and back doors with removable doorknobs that disappeared when a party ramped into full swing, which meant the doors couldn't be opened. As the nondrinker in the group, Jean got chosen as the driver, but "we never got to drive anywhere because Johnny took the doorknobs off the doors and nobody could leave. People would say, 'Johnny, we've got to go home, we've got a home to go to, we've got a life,' but the doorknobs were gone."[7]

Crosby admired Burke's practical jokes and the planning that went into them, though he admitted they could get nasty. "The most heartless rib he ever pulled," he said, targeted Bessie soon after they married. Bing had signed a vocalist named Pat Friday to *Kraft Music Hall,* billing her as the Singing Co-ed.[8] They all went to Ciro's one night to support NBC's buildup for Friday. While dancing, Bessie said that she once knew a girl named Pat Friday. Burke said, "You did? Well, you win the contest." He told her that NBC had offered to pay $18.75 to anyone who knew a girl with that same name. This began a tease that went on for weeks. Bessie wrote to NBC and complained that she hadn't gotten a reply, whereupon Burke asked if she had enclosed a Campbell Soup label; she wrote again, only to learn that it had to be a label for gumbo, and so on. Months later, the two couples went bowling. "Bessie was a big powerful girl, beautiful, and real strong," Bing recalled, "and we were talking as we bowled about one thing and another and ribs, pulling ribs on people." Bessie lifted a ball and scoffed. "I can tell in a minute if anybody is ribbing me." As she swung back her arm, Johnny purred, "Did you ever hear of Pat Friday?" Bing said she pitched the ball so hard she "almost decapitated the pin boy," after which she retrieved her coat and stalked out.[9]

A few years later, in August of 1943, when Bing's standing with servicemen had soared, he invited a dozen fliers stationed in Monterey to spend a few days in Hollywood touring the studio, playing golf, attending broadcasts, a pool party, nightclubs (the Zebra Room, the Cocoanut Grove), and, on the last night, a "finale" at the apartment of someone named Harrison, for which Bing made sure they all had "dates." "Drinks were flowing and everything was great. They thought I was a great fellow to do this for them, but I was having as much fun as they were." Then Burke started wandering around among the fliers and making poker-faced comments like "You know, Bing does this for the publicity. Actually, he's quite a schmuck." He persisted in that vein "until they started swinging on him and he had me bail him out."[10]

Four of those fliers, from Squadron Thirty-Seven, wrote Bing a letter of fervent thanks, promising to send him "a Jap or two, and soon." Bing, who was then two weeks into filming *Going My Way*, responded with cheery irreverence: "[I] don't know when I've met a finer bunch of men, all so imbued with a single purpose—'pinning one on.'...I may tell you, however, that all my closeups the next day were shot through the white of an egg and had any members of the local Clergy chanced upon the set, my role of the Catholic Priest would have been in serious jeopardy." Bing invited them to "ring my office" when in town and signed off with "Your Pal."[11]

Burke pulled several stunts on Bob Hope, one hinging on the Lakeside Golf Club's unofficial refusal to admit Jews as members. Jimmie Kern, the well-liked, Fordham-educated attorney and erstwhile member of the Yacht Club Boys, found success in Hollywood as a screenwriter working with Dave Butler and wanted to join Lakeside. The procedure to join involved submitting an application that members could sponsor by signing an affidavit. They were talking in the locker room when Bob said, "Jimmie Kern will be in the club soon. I sponsored him when he filled out his application." Johnny exclaimed, "You know what you're doing?" He said that Kern was Jewish and that Bob would end up spending a "mint of money" to get out of the mess when the bid went before the board and everyone saw he was responsible for the "mistake." Hope protested; Kern couldn't be Jewish, he went to Fordham! He turned for support to Bing. "And I said, 'I don't know. Burke's known him for many years before I knew him. If Burke says he's Jewish, he must be Jewish.'" Hope called the president of the board, prepared to make an appearance. Burke had him "sweat it out for a miserable couple of weeks" before letting him off the hook.[12]

At one of Burke's 1942 parties, Bessie giggled at a Phil Silvers joke, which made Silvers coo, "Bessie with the smiling face." Van Heusen said, "Good title for a song," and turned to Burke, who, in Phil's telling, shrugged and said, "It's my day off. You two guys do it."

Silvers wrote the lyric and brought it to Burke, who revised it without credit. The song became an anthem for the Crosby circle of friends, sung for Bessie on her birthday and for other women on their birthdays—until June 1944, when Frank Sinatra's daughter Nancy turned four years old. This time the name change accompanied an alteration in the title, from *smiling* to *laughing*, perhaps in the hope that "Nancy (with the Laughing Face)" would be more age appropriate. The lyric had not been written for a child—"Keep Betty Grable, Lamour and Turner / She makes my heart a charcoal burner." Sinatra recorded it within the year, a signature hit forever associated with him. Before they locked "Nancy" into the title, Silvers and Van Heusen asked Burke for permission. Jean Stevens recalled, "It just killed him, Bessie's disapproval when he sold her song to Frank Sinatra. I felt more compassionate to Johnny Burke after that, because I realized he was hurting too." As late as 1956, at a party that Sinatra and Van Heusen threw in honor of Crosby at Van Heusen's Palm Springs home, Jean heard Sinatra say, "Johnny Burke wrote this for my daughter," and she said to herself, "Liar! liar! You know darn well you took it, that Johnny gave it up to you."[13]

It was perhaps an unconscious slip on Sinatra's part to credit the song to Burke instead of Silvers, who was terribly proud of it, or Van Heusen. Burke sacrificed more than the song to Sinatra. In the 1950s, his marriage ended after a long, painful decline. According to their daughter Rory (Bing's goddaughter), Bessie, who was believed to be mentally unbalanced, took dozens of lovers, including Sinatra and two pedophiles, one of them a priest. The marriage ended when Johnny realized that their youngest child was not his. By then, Bing had given him an ultimatum about his drinking and amphetamine addiction and had reluctantly broken with him. Van Heusen similarly complained he could no longer tolerate Johnny's excesses. Drinking also dissolved the Stevenses' marriage and hastened Dixie's death. Of the six friends, only Bing and Jean survived and flourished.[14]

Dixie was not present the day Phil Silvers coined the phrase "Bessie with the smiling face," but she attended another party that year at the Burkes involving Silvers. The living room had filled with actors, musicians, and other show-business people when Phil got up to do a routine he had devised in burlesque. (His career stalled in movies, with small roles as a waiter, an ice cream vendor, and a sidekick. Waiting for his break, he became a favorite among those in the know, and his party shtick helped get his name out.) In this evening's bit, later a staple of his television appearances, Phil would teach a stooge to sing "I Can't Get Started," by clutching his throat, slapping his cheeks, and pulling his lips every time the stooge tried to get a note out. The guests laughed uproariously until they became aware of a disturbance and turned to find Dixie almost incoherently needling Bing, snarling, "I'll get him," and making what Jean remembered as "jabbing and stabbing gestures." The room quieted down as two friends coaxed her out of the house and took her home. Visibly shaken, Bing stayed and urged the guests to continue with their party.[15]

Some took the fracas in stride; they had seen it before. Jean Stevens had not, and her husband explained that Dixie was a "periodic," given to episodes of drunken excesses broken by dry spells. Jean could hardly believe it. "Here was Dixie, a perfect lady, overly modest, you know she undressed in the closet and things like that, a beautiful, wonderful person, but then she would get drunk and be very foul-mouthed. Bing was always embarrassed by it." One afternoon, while Dixie's secretary Alice Ross was working in Dixie's study, Bing brought home a young athlete, a college star. When the two came in the door, Bing saw Dixie at the top of the staircase. He began introducing them: "This is my wife, Dixie; Dixie, this is—" She cut him off. "He looks like a sonofabitch to me." Jean, who heard of the incident from Ross, said, "It killed him. It was very hard; it would have been for any man."[16] These episodes alternated with the Crosbys' intermittent but widely reported public appearances during which Dixie exuded her usual charm and graciousness. On a lunch break while rehearsing *Kraft Music Hall,* Trudy Erwin, a member of the Music Maids who adored Bing and, in 1943, became a cast member in her own right, asked him, "'Can't you and Dixie get friendly again?' And he said, 'No, I don't think so. A person says many things in a lifetime and some of them you can't take back.' That was the most personal thing I think he ever said, and we never mentioned her again."[17]

Her friends remained loyal admirers. "We were birthday twins and very close," Jean said. "I was just enough younger that she felt like taking me under her wing and she was lovely to me. I was so fond of Dixie. And, oh, the presents! She gave me a nightgown and a pair of mules and they came in boxes, and she wrapped the boxes with bows and put bows on the bows." She was at her best when her confidante Kitty Sexton was around. "They were a riot, cute, so much fun. I only ever saw Kitty at Dixie's."[18]

Dixie's fastidious gift-wrapping amused her friends; she brought exquisitely packaged presents to baby showers, birthdays, Christmases, other occasions, and sometimes when there was no occasion. She had a room for her papers and ribbons and sat over her creations for hours, intent on every detail. When the Stevenses bought the five-thousand-acre cattle ranch adjoining the larger Crosby spread in Elko, Nevada, Dixie gave them "incredible pottery designed to resemble acorns and leaves," wrapped with such care they hesitated to open it.[19] Pauline Weislow, Dixie's friend from high school, saw it as a creative hobby, an antidote to her shyness: "She was a sweet and gentle person who tried to live up to being sophisticated, charming, and everything, and felt that she did not have it like Bing did, which was true. She was insecure, but she loved him, that's all I know."[20] Jean agreed: "Dixie would never give him cause to be *really* angry. Dixie was careful that way. She only got mad at me once, when I complained about my husband being all over me all the time. She said, 'How dare you complain when someone is affectionate to you. You don't know what it's like the other way.'"[21]

Dixie's instability surfaced in her treatment of the four boys. When she drank, Jean said, she was hard on them, calling them names, something Bing also did, especially targeting Gary and his weight problem. Yet when Dixie was on a tear, he would try to compensate with as much warmth as he could summon. Like Gary, Jean never saw Bing drunk: "He was always in control. But he was a cold person, like my father, with no way to show his affection at all, never hugging the children for fear of spoiling them, no public displays of affection. So Dixie—when she was sober—had to make up for *that*. She was demonstrative, loving and hugging. She was a mother, you know." Her volatility eventually curbed partying in their home; the Westwood Marching and Chowder Club tent shows in their backyard stopped (the war also played a part in ending such revelries). The parties moved to the Burkes' place, and Dixie often stayed home. "They used to say women drunks, respectable women anyway, hid in the house and men drunks went out in public to bars," Jean said. Gary ruefully noted, "You couldn't hide my mother. Thank God she didn't want to go out much. But you didn't hide her in the house."[22]

Some observers thought Bing's pastimes in this period included women, although more in the line of flings and one-nighters than romances. If this was so, he was very quiet about it; no one seems to have known for certain. A colleague who never saw him other than on a movie set assumed he played around. You could just tell, he reasoned; Bing seemed like the type. He conceded, however, that he never saw anything untoward. Nor could he recall gossip tying Crosby to any particular woman.[23] A neighborhood "friend" called him "a philandering sonofabitch" but admitted she didn't know for certain and that if Dixie had suspicions, she never spoke of them, at least until the final months of the war, when an affair he'd begun could not be ignored.[24]

Anyone close to Van Heusen had access to party girls—*chippies*, in the lingo of the day. The evening Bing arranged for the fliers to be equipped with "dates" implies his familiarity with that world. Professional companions were part of the Hollywood diet, a perquisite of male getaways and road trips, easily procurable through the studios, which relied on them in the hope of curtailing scandal. Even so, Bing's discretion seemed to make him almost unassailable. One friend, a radio actress, felt pretty sure that Bing sometimes attended Van Heusen's movable brothel of a home, but, now that you mention it, she could not be certain, though she remembered the hilarious time the boys got Desi Arnaz drunk and Jimmy sent him upstairs with a hooker, and while he was gone they stuffed the body of his guitar with fruit. The photographer Gene Lester figured Bing must have had "trysts" during the Victory Caravan, especially at the Nicollet, but he could not substantiate his surmise with specific observations or gossip, though he damn well knew of carryings-on by Bob Hope and others. That idea of everybody knowing everybody else's business irked Bing more than anyone's sexual peccadilloes. He did as he pleased, yet tactlessness—humiliating a wife, flaunting a mistress—offended him. Hope's careless behavior strained their friendship, as did Sinatra's a few years later. A reporter in 1943 asked him to identify the quality "most essential in a husband." He answered: "Faithfulness."[25]

Dolores Hope, as devout a Catholic as Bing, rationalized her husband's adultery by invoking scripture. "I think a man is primarily a polygamist. In the Bible, everybody had one or two or three or a dozen wives. The morality they live under now is a test for a man. But if a husband and wife accept what's going on, it's their business and nobody else's." In looking the other way, Dolores sustained a marriage of biblical proportions, sixty-nine years, one of the longest in show-business history. "All those guys had their flings and you hear rumblings, but I don't know if Bing had any. He didn't have one with me. I would have loved it. I'd *remember* that one. He was very, very attractive, his whole personality, everything about him, and funny. But the family never broke up. Bing was there and Dixie was there. He loved her and sometimes when you love each other too much, it is trouble. I think they loved each other that much."[26]

His obvious appeal, stature, and constant traveling gave him unlimited opportunity. Dixie's behavior may have given him motive. His private letters indicate nothing definite, though it is tempting to read romantic connotations into a particularly warm and revealing correspondence from a longtime cast member of *KMH*. Amorous undertones aside, her letters are treasurable for casting a light on backstage life in the swing era and showing the veneration of Crosby by vocalists who regarded him not only as a stylist but as the man who elevated pop singing to an art and made their careers possible.

The vocalist who became popular in 1942 as Trudy Erwin began life in 1918 as Virginia Erwin, and everyone close to her called her Jinny, with a J, before and after her professional name change. As teenagers, Jinny and her friend Dottie Messmer formed the nucleus of the harmonizing quintet called the Music Maids. She met Bing in 1937 as a freelance singer in the film *Double or Nothing*; while resting between takes on a cot, she felt the ding of a spitball, Bing's way of introducing himself. Two years later, the Music Maids' agent Larry Crosby asked them to cut an audition disc for an unidentified NBC show. Bing's innovative audio mixer Murdo MacKenzie recorded the disc, "Hawaiian War Chant." A week later, Larry booked them on Bing's program; a contract ensued. They started in early 1939 (Larry also landed them a role in Bing's *East Side of Heaven*) and stayed six seasons. Jinny, a lyric mezzo, sang lead with a somewhat anonymous polish and vocal mask. (Her technique and talent for mimicry ensured her work dubbing vocals for unmusical film stars like Lana Turner and Lucille Ball.) Three years into her stay with *KMH,* she considered going out on her own but did not see any way to make that possible. The Music Maids' Alice Ludes recalled her frustration at wanting to go solo and at the same time exuding an "energetic and playful" demeanor, keeping Bing laughing with her "impishness."[27]

Then she got a surprise call from Kay Kyser, a tremendously popular jester-bandleader. Kyser's radio hour, a mock quiz show called *College of Musical Knowledge,* established his persona, a mixture of Southern-fried corn ("C'mon, chillun, le's dance!") and a flouncy nervousness accentuated by his getup, a baggy graduation gown and mortarboard. He did more than anyone to advance the public's perception of musicians as idiots in funny hats, but he was a canny showman who made a fortune satisfying the lowest common denominator. From 1934 to 1941, one of his main assets was his girlfriend and vocalist Ginny Simms, whom he reasonably nicknamed Gorgeous. Working the lower sector of her soprano range, Simms conveyed a dark and dreamy longing on ballads, for which she earned high marks from musicians. Kyser presented her as his down-home gal, assigning her to sing inane novelties along with alluring ballads. It is not known why she suddenly quit the band in September 1941; she refused to marry him, or he refused to marry her, or she tired of the Kyser formula, or she had better offers. In any case, the split was bitter. In subsequent public encounters, they faked civility with frozen smiles.[28]

Suddenly shorthanded, Kyser sought a replacement. He turned to *Kraft Music Hall* and Jinny Erwin. As a friend of Bing's—they got along easily, worked with some of the same people (David Butler, Jimmie Kern, Burke, and Van Heusen), and shared a love of horses—he would never have raided *KMH* with a cold call. We don't know if Kay called Bing and asked for advice or permission or if Bing called Kay with a recommendation that would benefit two friends. Erwin, a bundle of energy, was just what Kyser wanted, a far cry from the statuesque Simms. She had a voice, personality, and looks—pretty, with a petite hourglass figure. Kyser would present her as his discovery, but he told her up-front that he intended to hire two or three women singers rather than create another standout like Simms. This diluted the offer, but Jinny took the news to Bing, the producer Cal Kuhl, and the Music Maids, who agreed that the opportunity was too good to refuse. Kyser stipulated that she must, of course, change her name; he selected Trudy, which she used professionally from then on.

At first Erwin enjoyed the attention and travel. She made friends with the band's veteran singers Harry Babbitt and Sully Mason, who shared her adulation of Bing and loved hearing her stories about working with him. But she never got on with the mandarin bandleader. After Pearl Harbor, she realized she had taken on a tougher gig than she anticipated. Kyser committed himself to the war effort. The traveling was relentless, the accommodations often primitive. "Hot and sticky places," she said. "One time we did thirty-one camps in thirty days, all across the United States—we didn't go overseas. That was really a rugged time. It was fun, but we worked really, really hard in some ungodly places."[29]

In March 1942, when Bing was shooting *Road to Morocco*, the Kyser band arrived in New York as part of the East Coast leg in a long tour. Jinny, feeling lonely and tired, missed Los Angeles; she missed *KMH*; she missed Murdo MacKenzie, with whom she was romantically involved; and she missed Bing. One Saturday afternoon, strolling up Lexington Avenue, she ran into a friend from home, Dinah Shore, who was headlining at the Waldorf Astoria. They made a date to meet that night in Dinah's room at the Waldorf after Jinny finished her last show.

Shore is well remembered today for her years in television, particularly a seven-season 1950s variety show, every episode of which she ended with an emphatic smooch. Her popularity first soared during the war, not least because she gave no quarter in her devotion to performing for servicemen. Her success stimulated a brief film career. She could not act and she photographed poorly, but on records and radio, her personality and Southern drawl gleamed. She placed three dozen records on the top rungs of the hit parade between 1940 and 1956. Born in rural Tennessee to the only Jewish family within miles, she had a honeyed contralto and easy rhythmic gait that led early observers to describe her as a blues singer (and to spread a persistent falsehood that she was "passing" for white). Small, plain-faced, toothy, and always sunny, she had the paradoxical good fortune to be rejected by almost every bandleader who let her audition. They wanted a prettier canary. Shore had no choice but to go solo, gaining an edge on singers, including Sinatra and now Erwin, who were contractually leashed to big bands. Her break came as a cast member on Eddie Cantor's show, which broadcast in the same building as *Kraft Music Hall*. "I'd go and sit up in the client box, way up in the top, and just watch and listen to Bing rehearse the show," she recalled. "And if they shut the sound off, I was just ready to die. Finally, one day somebody said, 'That's Dinah Shore up there'—I'd had a couple of hit records—and Bing came over and asked me to come down to the stage. I was blushing and shaking and said all the stupid things, but we got to be friends."[30]

Jinny and Dinah spent a long evening in Shore's room listening to Crosby records and writing him separate letters. The first one, from Jinny, is that of a friend, admirer, and former employee, little more. (The ellipses are Erwin's.)

3/28/42
Dear Bing,

Dinah and I are sitting here of a Saturday night playing your records and having ourselves a wonderful time....And I'm not getting any less homesick. Dinah really has a collection of your records and we're not missing a one.

I heard the show Thursday night and I almost called N.B.C. after you went off the air. I was going to ask Dottie [Messmer] to call down the hall and ask you to come say "hello" to me.

Right now we're listening to "Please" and it's been played so much the record's getting scratchy.

Gee I miss you, Bing....and by the way, how's your racing bike?

Last night after I went to bed, I listened to some of your records over my portable R.C.A. You sounded so wonderful.

I'd love to get a card or a note sometime. I'm at the Shelton, 49th and Lexington for the next two or three weeks.

I'll be listening
   love—
   "Jinny"[31]

Shore wrote a different kind of letter, that of a fan and a pal, with a reminder of the Thursday afternoons she had spent in the *KMH* client box.

3/28/42

Dear Bing –

We're sitting here currently knocking ourselves out listening to you—Gee! It makes even me homesick for California and everybody knows I'm a "strictly-from-Dixie-er"—I can imagine how Ginny [*sic*] feels.

I was lucky enough to bump into her this afternoon—it's about 2:00 a.m. now and we only stopped talking long enough for me to do a couple of shows downstairs. There are still a hundred things I want to know about everybody and everything. I really think it was downright inconsiderate of her to leave California so long ago and not know any more about those wonderful Thursday rehearsals than I do.

"What's New" is playing now, my-oh-my!!!

Please give my love to Larry [Crosby], Johnny & Bess, the twins [the Burkes and their twin daughters], Paul Wetstein, Skitch, and anybody else that looks familiar—I expect I'll be seeing all of you soon—come summertime.

Best Always—

Dinah[32]

Dinah's record collection merits comment. Many musicians lugged their favorite records on the road. The other musicians in the band or on the tour generally knew who was "carrying" and what they carried. This was no small thing. Records were transported in heavy boxes built to hold twenty-five or fifty 78 rpm discs, each weighing nearly half a pound, and every box was completely filled, to diminish chipping and outright breakage. A box of fifty records (two songs each), the equivalent of four compact discs or a quarter of 1 percent of the capacity of an iPod Classic, measured a foot high and six inches deep and weighed thirty pounds. Even with layers of protective wadding, the contents of the box were too fragile for it to be entrusted to porters and bellhops.

Bing responded quickly to Jinny's request for "a card or a note" with a letter that has not survived.[33] She was pleased to receive it, but he failed to satisfy her expectations, particularly with his use of the word *nostalgic* to characterize their relationship. Jarred by that word, Jinny filled eight pages of Shelton Hotel stationery, produc-

ing a more emotionally ambiguous letter and a record of an entertainer's life on the road. (The ellipses and dashes are hers.)

4/7/42
Tues. 12 midnight
Dear Bing,
 ...nostalgic eh?
 ...But you're quite right....Gee, I was glad to get your letter
and so help me, I bet I've read it ten times today. That doesn't
make sense does it? Considering everything...But as I've told you
before, I make myself awfully mad sometimes...

I'm glad you listen to the show—however, this blasted New
York makes me sound hoarse and I haven't thought I've sounded
very good....And as far as my ever getting a "break" as they say, I
doubt that very very much.

We open at the Meadowbrook in New Jersey May 1st and are
there 'til June 1st. Then home! I'd give anything to get on that
train for L.A. tonight. This traveling isn't all it's cracked up to be.

This last week-end, we played Lake-Hurst, Trenton, New
Haven, and last night Boston. What a grind—In Boston we did a
show and then a dance until 1 a.m......Saturday night we did three
stage shows plus 6 separate "cut-ins" on the two Lucky Strike
shows....We didn't get loaded into our bus to come back to N.Y. til
3:30 a.m. Just as we were pulling away from the "arena," we turned
on the radio and heard your record of "Miss You." There isn't
another thing in the world that could have sounded so good to
me....And of course, Sully was in seventh Heaven...

By the way, Bing—I've listened every week to your show and you
sound so wonderful. If the phone rings while you're on, I just refuse
to answer it. I think the show still "let's down" in spots—but everyone
seems to agree that you're always swell...I know it sounds silly as the
dickens but the most fun I have here is listening to you on Kraft.

Harry Babbitt and I and several of the others have been doing
quite a lot; we've been to see and hear Jimmy Dorsey twice and he
sounds fine—but not as good as he used to (my own opinion of
course)...and we went to Tommy Tucker's opening and that was
<u>dull</u>—and we've eaten dinner at some terrific places. I love the
Italian food at the "Red Devil" on 48th...Then we walk and go to
shows and swim here at the Hotel, and work a lot too I might add.

We're going to be in Chicago for a week or a little longer starting April 14th. We'll be at the Sherman—Clark & Randolph St...
Seven shows a day—how about that?

Roc Hillman's new tune "My Devotion" is wonderful for you,
Bing. I hope you do it sometime...Jimmy Dorsey is going to record
it, and so are we—Harry Babbitt's doing it. And by the way, Harry
really thinks you're the tops and he & I agree that no one will ever
be even half as good as you.....

I don't know what it is, but when you sing, I feel as if I'm right
there in the studio.

...And I can tell just how you look and how you're standing and
how your foot's beating rhythm.

...And I'd give my soul to be standing across the mike from you –

...But there I go again...darn it!!....

Last night when we finished the dance at the "Garden" in Boston, we all put our luggage on our car which was sided at the station, and then about fifteen of us walked to Ruby Foo's and had a
hilarious time over Egg Roll and fried rice and four or five other
Chinese dishes. We didn't get to sleep until about 5:30 a.m. But as
tired as we all were, it was sort of fun.

Well Bing, I guess it's about time I stop this "raving" and get
to bed.

Thanks again for writing and gee I'd love to hear from you
again.

...And incidentally, you know very well how I "feel about
  things"....

  Love—
  Jinny

  P.S.
  —will you be in Hollywood and on the show in June?
  —and when do you actually go on your vacation—and
  —are you ever coming to New York?
  XO[34]

Jinny did not have to give away her soul to stand across the mike
from Bing. She would get more of that than she'd dreamed of at the
end of the year. In the interim, they saw each other in August when
they participated in an all-star revue at Washington's National Theater for military and government brass. Bing served as the emcee for

a cast that included Ginny Simms, Dinah Shore, James Cagney, Hedy Lamarr, Abbott and Costello, Connie Boswell, and Larry Adler, among others. As the performers disembarked at Union Station early on Sunday morning, they were greeted by the Kyser band and a thousand fans. After the performance, which was sent overseas by shortwave via the newly launched (on May 26, 1942) Armed Forces Network, the National Press Club feted the performers. Impulsively swapping roles onstage, Bing interviewed the reporter Tom Stokes on his prizewinning exposé of corruption in Kentucky's WPA office.

The army demand for Bing and other performers permanently sabotaged the tyrannical rule of radio sponsors. Bing needed Kraft's permission to do a turn on *Your Hit Parade*, but Kraft had nothing to say about his AFRS work, little of which aired in the United States. When it did air domestically, it struck the radio audience as an extension of Crosby's own program. Bing turned *KMH* into what the Crosby researcher Mark Scrimger called a "traveling USO show," promoting war bonds, explaining, with the help of guest officials, rationing and other state and federal directives. Bing had more influence on the millions of families routinely huddled around their radios than anyone other than FDR. He was widely credited with putting over gas rationing with the public (though his racing partners groused that it hurt business at the track). After a program in which he inadvertently mentioned the wrong minimum age for enlistment, draft centers around the country had to turn away underage volunteers.[35] Much of his broadcasting involved shows created for the Treasury Department and other agencies that were aimed directly at the home front. With the slackening of *KMH's* control, Bing appeared on commercial series as well, like the popular *Lux Radio Theater* and the *Screen Guild Theater*, both on CBS. The shift from agency exclusivity to freelancing altered the balance of power.

The power of the AFRS rivaled that of any advertising agency after the army commissioned Thomas Lewis, an advertising executive and the husband of Loretta Young, as a major to head up the organization. Lewis immediately opened an AFRS office in Hollywood to be closer to the talent. Its most popular and meticulously produced series, *Command Performance*, came about when two men in the War Department's radio division—a writer, Glenn Wheaton, and a producer of *Quiz Kids*, Lou Cowan—suggested a program that encouraged GIs stationed around the world to write in and "command" what they wanted to hear, no matter how peculiar—a sigh from Carole Landis, the tap dancing of Ann Miller, the competing violins of Jascha Heifetz and Jack Benny, a hometown's street noise, or (radio was the magic kingdom of sound effects) Errol Flynn in the shower. No commercial entity could have mounted a weekly production of the caliber of *Command Performance,* heard exclusively (except for a few specials) overseas. Wheaton directed the show without budget limitations; in fact, he had no budget. No one was paid, not even the NBC and CBS networks for the use of their studios and crews.

In 1943, a resourceful tin-can station serving the army outpost in Sitka, Alaska, distributed a three-page questionnaire to get a sense of its audience. The 2,310 respondents rated seventy-four radio programs. The top five were news (1,074 votes), Bing Crosby (962), Bob Hope (952), the *Hit Parade* (896), and Jack Benny (874). Favorite male singers were Crosby (200), Sinatra (52), and Harry Babbitt (23); favorite females were Dinah Shore (200), Kate Smith (133), and Ginny Simms (88). The results of such polls differed from one area to another, but the top three—Crosby, Hope, Shore—represented a worldwide constituency reflected in their frequent AFRS appearances. Shore starred on *Command Performance* thirty-five times; Crosby was on thirty-one, and Hope twenty-nine. The initial *Command Performance* episodes were relayed by shortwave from New York to a handful of army stations. When the operation moved to Hollywood, the shows were scrupulously edited down to thirty-minute transcription discs that could be mailed anywhere. Each show opened to the strains of "Over There" as an announcer promised that *Command Performance USA* would be coming "this week and every week until it's over over there!" Bing noticed that these transcription discs sounded damned good and that the editing offered a useful curative for longueurs and mistakes. He kept that to himself for the duration. Afterwards, with the AFRS shows in mind, he would force radio to reassess its allegiance to live broadcasts.

For now, he merely increased his activities. Between the attack on Pearl Harbor and 1946, Crosby participated in at least 157 AFRS shows (*Command Performance, Mail Call, GI Journal, Song Sheet, Personal Album, Jubilee,* and dozens of stateside shows

promoting war bonds, spreading propaganda, and offering inspirational messages), in addition to the 135 *Kraft Music Hall* shows created in those years. His numbers are rivaled but not equaled by
those of Hope, Shore, or anyone else.[36]

Not all events were specifically war-related. The fifth annual
George Gershwin Memorial Concert, held at the Shrine Auditorium on June 18, 1942, reunited Bing with Paul Whiteman (conducting the Los Angeles Philharmonic alongside his own orchestra)
and initiated his working relationship with Dinah Shore. It took
place on a Thursday; one hour after he broadcast *KMH,* he was in
the wings of the Shrine, waiting to go on at eight fifteen for an
evening to benefit the Los Angeles Phil. Crosby sang "Maybe" and
"Somebody Loves Me" and joined with Dinah for a *Porgy and Bess*
medley. It was their first of many pairings between 1942 and 1975.
She never appeared on *KMH,* owing to her own radio contracts
(she performed on his postwar series for Philco, Chesterfield, and
General Electric), but after he brought her down from the *KMH*
client box, Bing lined Dinah up for concerts and a tour to benefit
the musicians' union. Much later he spoke enthusiastically about
her in a radio interview: "Marvelous girl, very infectious personality, hard worker, competent. I am very fond of Dinah."[37] Yet at the
Shrine, she felt far from competent. She was trembling as she
awaited her cue—until she observed the same phenomenon that
had startled James Cagney during the Victory Caravan:

I was a nervous wreck. I watched through the curtain as Bing was
singing and I saw his trouser leg shaking and I thought, "Oh, he's
nervous too!" That straightened me out in a hurry, because I didn't
think Bing could be nervous. But he was and he concealed it better than anybody I've ever seen. I never thought there was an
instance of uncertainty in his performances, in his confidence, in
himself, in any of those things. I never thought there could be. He
was Bing Crosby, one of a kind *ever,* and he was nervous like the
rest of us. He didn't do many personal appearances, but this was a
real apex in *my* career. [He] was a very generous performer, very
appreciative. If you said something funny, he loved it. I was doing
my portion of the program when we were doing those concerts and
in some of it I was self-deprecating, which is the best thing to do

when you're uncertain about how you'll be received. And this was Bing's audience basically and I got a lot of laughs. Bing came up and he said, "What is this? What are you doing?" with mock severity. And I explained, "I'm getting my share of laughs before you get out here with them." Because he got *all* the laughs....He was a funny man. Funny offstage, funny onstage. Everything he said had sophistication to it. He didn't waste words.[38]

Dinah made it into the Crosby club (invitations to the Johnny Burke parties and, later, those that Jimmy Van Heusen threw in Palm Springs), an indication of the chasteness, the safeness of their friendship. She thought one of the things Bing liked about her was their mutual interest in cooking. Curiously, having nicknamed her the Dixie Diva, he began calling her Dixie. He liked to visit the house she shared with three other women. "He'd go into the kitchen and say, 'I'm hungry, Dixie,' and he would do wonderful scrambled eggs and bacon. Nothing complex, but he liked to eat and he liked good food." She was even more pleased when she realized he respected her enough as a singer to "do licks and things like that....The things that he did with Armstrong were wonderfully jazz-inspired, and he paid me the compliment of singing the same way: freely." For the radio adaptation of *Holiday Inn* in January 1943, he arranged for Dinah to take over the Marjorie Reynolds part.[39]

Two days after the Gershwin event, on Saturday, June 20, Bing brought his nine-year-old son, Gary, to Paramount to shoot two scenes for *Star Spangled Rhythm*, the boy's first film appearance and an experience he remembered with grudging satisfaction: "[I] managed to stumble through them without embarrassing myself too badly." Midge and Herb Polesie recalled Gary "hamming it up" in his debut, to the enjoyment of everyone except his mother, who (sensibly, in the view of the Polesies) admonished him, "Remember, Gary, your name isn't Crosby. It's just Joe Doakes, and if you get anywhere in this business, you must get there on the strength of your own talent and not your father's."[40]

All the major studios produced spirited propaganda epics, and *Star Spangled Rhythm* was arguably the best, in part because it was the first and, except for Bing's finale, the least reverent. Set on the

Paramount lot with appearances by more than a hundred (mostly uncredited) contract players, it offers a clever if thin plotline involving two promising newcomers—brassy Betty Hutton, in her second feature, and timid Eddie Bracken—and the Broadway veteran Victor Moore as a gatekeeper pretending to be the studio boss. It makes balmy fun of the real bosses, with Walter Abel stealing scenes as producer "B. G. DeSoto" and a bit player, Edward Fielding, essaying a benevolent "Y. Frank Fremont." Asked for his opinion of *Reap the Wild Wind,* Moore tells the film's director-producer Cecil B. DeMille, "It stinks." With songs by Harold Arlen and Johnny Mercer and sketches by George Kaufman and the team of Norman Panama and Melvin Frank, it sprints to the finish: a pasteboard Mount Rushmore with Bing, hemmed in by a giant flapping flag to his right and George Washington's colossal nose to his left, singing "Old Glory."

Star Spangled Rhythm was one of the first pictures to consciously redress Hollywood's depiction of blacks. Two months before production, studio heads met with the NAACP's executive secretary Walter White and its counsel Wendell Willkie, the liberal Republican who lost to FDR in 1940. It was in America's interest, especially during a war involving Nazi and Japanese racial exceptionalism, to improve the job opportunities and portrayals of African Americans, routinely seen as slow-witted servants given disdainful names like Snowball, Shadrach, Geranium, and Wellington. Progress in this area was minimal during the war, especially considering the profusion of films with blackface routines, but the on-screen baby steps added up to a subtle paradigm shift—albeit one mindful of Southern box-office receipts. MGM evicted Tarzan, who found a new jungle at RKO, and put into production the all-black *Cabin in the Sky* (with the Hall Johnson Choir, whose pioneering founder wrote to its producer, "We love nothing better than to laugh at ourselves on the stage—when it is ourselves we are laughing at"). The *New York Times* found one "exceptional component" in John Huston's Warner Brothers psychodrama *In This Our Life* (1942): its "frank allusion to racial discrimination" and the depiction of the "educated and comprehending character," played by the African American actor Ernest Anderson.[41]

Star Spangled Rhythm approaches race three ways. It includes an all-black production number, "Sharp as a Tack," featuring the popular Eddie "Rochester" Anderson, who struts gloriously with the dancer Katherine Dunham, supported by a cast of some fifty extras. Among them were the future stars Woody Strode and Juanita Moore and the incomparable jazz satirist Slim Gaillard, who makes a show of *not* playing the (prerecorded) piano. That scene could be snipped by Southern distributors. But censors would think twice about cutting "Hit the Road to Dreamland," in which the Golden Gate Quartette serenades Dick Powell and Mary Martin, who chime in for a few measures. There is nothing the least bit servile about the virile members of the GGQ, yet their skirtlike aprons emasculate them all the same.

The censors could do nothing at all about the climactic number featuring Bing and an enthusiastic throng of all-American stereotypes: the twangy son of Georgia, the *dese*-and-*dose* guy from Brooklyn, a black choir droning a few bars of "Motherless Child." "Old Glory" isn't just a song, it's a dialogue between Bing and America, beginning with his meditation on the Pledge of Allegiance and building to a standard apple-pie-and-baseball litany as the crowd straightens out the one skeptic in its midst. Bing, in a double-breasted suit, is the perfect interlocutor, as well he should be—the sequence shamelessly echoes the 1939 cantata *Ballad for Americans*, by Earl Robinson and John La Touche, that Bing helped popularize. Bing's payoff line—"How about Washington? I mean all three: George, Martha, and Booker T."—may be small beer compared to the paradigm of *Ballad for Americans*, but it was a bracer for Paramount Pictures. Perhaps only Bing could have delivered that number.[42]

But it obliged him to forfeit a great Arlen/Mercer song, "That Old Black Magic," which went to the little-remembered Johnnie Johnston. Bing later expressed his regret at losing that number, which he put off recording until 1956. Johnston surely regretted his brazen behavior at the outset of what he assumed would be a stellar career. He told Buddy DeSylva that Paramount was not big enough for two crooners and it was time to let Bing go. Barney Dean liked to tell about a day when Johnston, better known for his trick shots as an inveterate golf hustler than his singing, approached Crosby at Lakeside, slapped him on the back, and said something like, "Nice to be in the stable with you, Bing, old boy." Bing walked off without a word.[43]

12

HOME FIRES

The meaning of Song goes deep....A kind of inarticulate unfathomable speech, which leads us to the edge of the Infinite, and lets us for moments gaze into that!
—Thomas Carlyle, *On Heroes, Hero-Worship, and the Heroic in History* (1841)

The transformation began June 25 as Bing did his last *Kraft Music Hall* of the spring 1942 season with guests Fred Astaire, Harry James, Bob Crosby, and Secretary of Agriculture Claude Wickard. "Bing was in especially fine fettle—also Mary," Cal Kuhl entered in his program report. Bing previewed three *Holiday Inn* songs: "Song of Freedom," "Be Careful, It's My Heart," and (in a duet with Astaire) "I'll Capture Your Heart Singing." Harry James played two instrumentals, including one that Bing liked to sing but never recorded, "Sleepy Lagoon." Crosby sang "Jingle, Jangle, Jingle," a faux–Western movie novelty with lyrics by Frank Loesser, partly as a kindness to Paramount's diligent music director Joe Lilley, who wrote the music—the only success he would ever have with a popular song. Bing never recorded it, but Kay Kyser did, and, coincidentally or not, after Bing sang "Jingle, Jangle, Jingle" three times in five weeks, Kyser's crafty version reached the top of the charts. Bing had been scheduled to complete the *KMH* season the following week, but he took early leave and turned the summer show over to his brother Bob.

Now he had a few weeks off except for the obligation to record the six aforementioned Decca sessions—from "Moonlight Becomes You" to "Hello Mom"—timed to beat out the Petrillo recording ban. Bing also took the opportunity to secure his family's future. Appointing John O'Melveny as the financial guardian to his sons, he established a $50,000 trust fund (about $740,000 in today's money) for each boy, to be paid when he turned twenty-one. Days later, he cooperated with the FBI in a situation regarding the arrest of a man who had tried to extort money from him and Harold Lloyd in letters that threatened their children. (The reprobate was sentenced to five years.) Bing chose Gary as his performing partner for a few army shows in Arizona and Texas, then he went with Burke and Stevens to fish in the High Sierras.

On August 4, a week or so after Bing had skidded toward the abyss, *Holiday Inn* debuted in New York. Paramount abandoned as unsuitable its plan for a gala Hollywood premiere, electing instead to present the picture at its Broadway theater as a (sold-out) benefit for the Navy Relief Society—top tickets went for $5.50 apiece. The lavish stage show featured the orchestras of Benny Goodman, Skinnay Ennis, Xavier Cugat, and Phil Harris; the Ink Spots; a dance team; and a comedian. Irving Berlin promised to take a bow but could not stay for the movie as he was appearing nightly a few blocks away in his Broadway triumph *This Is the Army*. A studio ad declared the evening a "dazzler" despite a dim-out of the marquee lights; a "super sendoff," Paramount crowed, "writ large in the history of movie World Premieres."[1]

Bing wasn't there; he was in Fort Lewis in Washington at the start of a two-week tour with USO camp show number 32, performing with Phil Silvers and Rags Ragland in the burlesque skit "Full Speed Ahead" and singing to Jimmy Van Heusen's piano accompaniment. Some afternoons, on his own or with Van Heusen, he visited local hospitals. Fort Lewis, where Colonel Dwight Eisenhower recently served as chief of staff, was twenty minutes south of Tacoma, Crosby's birthplace. A day or so into the tour, he went there to sing at the Liberty Center's noontime bond drive; that was followed by a golf match, the evening show at Fort Lewis, and an overnight stay at the Tacoma country club. A reporter at the Liberty Center observed Bing's feet doing "little dances" as "his hands toyed with the cord leading to the mike, twisting it into such knots the kilowatts could barely squeeze through." Silvers noticed a similar anxiety: "He wouldn't admit it, but he was a little afraid of working onstage. [There] was some subtle difference, in his mind, between entertaining a big live audience and amusing the unseen millions over the radio, even though he had an audience in the studio for the *Kraft Music Hall*."[2] He didn't sing anything from *Holiday Inn,* preferring the novelty "Conchita, Marquita, Lolita, Pepita, Rosita, Juanita Lopez" and those *KMH* songs he liked, "Sleepy Lagoon" and "Jingle, Jangle, Jingle," the last backed by a military band. Nervous or not, the reporter granted, "His feet shuffled and his winks kept the children, even the old ones, squirming with delight."[3]

As the tour continued to Seattle (where the cast did an open-air performance before fifteen thousand in Victory Square, raising ten million dollars, and a camp show at the naval air station), and then Wyoming and Colorado, Bing's jitters disappeared. They were never apparent offstage. Silvers accepted the responsibility of getting the show onstage and the team from town to town, but Bing "was absolutely in charge"—ever the imperturbable legend in his "relaxed, jovial, pipe-puffing way." With minutes to spare, Silvers and Ragland would plead with him to hurry to catch a train, and he'd sing, "Don't worry, Philly boy," and finish shaving. They never missed a train, nor did Bing complain or raise his voice. Calm followed in his wake. Once, a toddler got separated from her parents as Bing sang "Sweet Leilani." Phil carried her onto the stage and held her up for the parents to see, but he could not get her to stop crying. Bing stepped over to Phil, took the child in his arms, and sang to her. The wailing turned into a giggle, and the mother waited until he finished "Sweet Leilani" before claiming her baby.

Wherever they went, he rose with the sun and strolled through the area, exploring parks and squares. Townspeople occasionally did double takes, but he had a way of looking as though he belonged, and, as he wasn't wearing his toupee, they could not be certain. In Wyoming, he sat down on the grass, his back against a statue, drew on his pipe, and watched the clouds drift by. A cop marked him as a vagrant and rousted him. Bing insisted he phone Silvers. "The cop grumbled to me, 'If that's Bing Crosby, what in hell's name is he doing *there?*'" At one stop, two women who owned a record shop allowed Bing to borrow a jukebox stocked with Crosby records. When they came to retrieve it, Crosby—"stoned," in Phil's description, "but you'd never know it"—fixed them cocktails and invited them to board the train with the performers to the next stop. Silvers objected that they had no tickets, the train was full, and wartime conductors were notoriously inflexible. "Bing says, 'Don't worry, Philly boy. Everything's in order.' He sang me *and* the conductor into submission." Silvers and Rags attempted to emulate Bing's "admirable" habits and Bing grew so fond of working with them that he wanted only to do comedy. Silvers claimed he sometimes had to beg him to fit in a few songs.[4]

In Cheyenne, on August 11, Bing did an hour-long radio broadcast from the Plains Hotel, selling fifteen thousand dollars in bonds. That evening, the troupe put on two full shows at the Fort Warren Theater. Between the morning broadcast and the theater shows, Bing, Silvers, and Van Heusen went on a three-hour tour of the Quartermaster Replacement Training Center (QMRTC), finishing at Fort Warren's hospital with an impromptu performance. A reporter followed the afternoon jaunt, capturing Crosby in the process of remaking himself. No longer the friendly but remote personality bound up by technology, he now offered a sympathetic, unassuming presence, more older brother than paterfamilias (despite the bald head and dangling pipe, he was not yet forty)—interested and deliberate, unregimented and virtually unmarked by stardom.

These men stirred and inspired him. Bing was still young enough to share a pang of disconnection that troubled numberless civilian men who gawked at servicemen on recruitment lines and on trains, at bars and in stores, marching. So many uniforms, so many casualties—the papers ran daily lists, grouped according to where they fell in the theaters of war. They owed him nothing. He felt he owed them a great deal; as a citizen, of course, but also personally. A year ago he was in the grip of malaise, and these men had snapped him out of it. He found himself singing as in earlier days, with pleasure, for the fun of it, before the most appreciative audience in the world. He took uncharacteristic care in the way he dressed. The Wyoming reporter noted Bing's light gray "tropical trousers," his dark blue polo shirt with white stripes, his blue linen jacket, and the pipe, always there but never lit.

The QMRTC tour began at the motor maintenance school, where the visitors instantly established first-name familiarity. They were Bing, Phil, and Jimmy. They went through the large buildings, sitting in on a couple of classes. In one building, Bing walked to a group of black soldiers from the Fourth Regiment. He asked about the drill presses they operated and listened with evident interest as they explained how the machines worked. In another building, he exchanged quips with the men. "His casual, informal manner put the privates at ease," the reporter wrote, "every 'hello, Bing' was answered with a 'Well, how are you, glad to see you,' or some equally friendly greeting." Accompanied by officers, the visitors boarded jeeps and headed for the rifle range, where they watched classes in marksmanship, posed for amateur photographers, and signed autographs. Twice, Bing ran into privates he had known in civilian life, and "both times, he made them proud by warmly acknowledging the acquaintanceships." At the hospital's annex, to the cheers of the robed patients, Bing sang six songs, Phil told droll stories, and Jimmy played a piano medley.[5]

The trip continued to Colorado. Six thousand servicemen attended the shows at Camp Carson in Colorado Springs. More than ten thousand spectators trailed along at the exhibition golf matches at the Broadmoor Hotel and Denver's Cherry Hills, the latter involving a foursome with Bob Hope, succeeded by their one-on-one driving-range competition. A fan waved a copy of the six-disc *Holiday Inn* record album. Hope instantly confiscated it for auction, bringing in $250 (about $3,600 in today's money). They finished in Fort Riley, Kansas. A photograph taken at the twilight performance shows Crosby alone on a broad plank stage, wearing a sports coat and a fedora. Under lowering clouds, several rows of brass are seated near the platform; behind them, almost as far as the eye can see, thousands of soldiers sit on the ground, cross-legged or hugging their knees, and holding the hats on their heads to keep them from blowing away.

In 1942, Paramount inaugurated what it called a "special release," a platform method of film distribution that began with a festive premiere in one of its flagship theaters, followed by bookings in major cities in advance of the actual release date, when the film opened in all the theaters the studio controlled or corralled. The practice stimulated a word-of-mouth appetite and, within a few years, became the usual strategy for major productions. *Holiday Inn* was the third special release, after DeMille's *Reap the Wild Wind*, Paramount's top-grossing film of the year, and Bob Hope's *Louisiana Purchase*. As the picture opened nationally, sales of the Decca album mounted and the airwaves were inundated with the score. Bing, Fred, and Marjorie made promotional appearances and nearly nine hundred stations enacted scripted playlets in tribute to Berlin and to Bing's performance of "Song of Freedom."

As servicemen in the thousands cheered Crosby, filmgoers in the millions savored *Holiday Inn*. That the picture was a success surprised no one; the immensity of its success did. It was the first Crosby megahit, dwarfing past triumphs of the man already established as Hollywood's best-paid actor. *Road to Singapore* had been the top-grossing film of 1940; *Road to Zanzibar* increased its take by 20 percent. *Holiday Inn* doubled the receipts of *Zanzibar*, selling twenty-nine million tickets when the country's population was barely five times that—meaning lots of return customers. It was said to be the highest-grossing live-action musical (the top musical spot belonged to Disney's animated *Snow White and the Seven Dwarfs*) since the advent of talkies, though within months it would be overtaken by Warner Brothers' *Yankee Doodle Dandy* and Paramount's own *Star Spangled Rhythm*.

Not overtaken, however, was Bing's box-office ascension. Even James Cagney, who dazzled audiences and earned an Academy Award for his portrayal of George M. Cohan, would not be associated with a comparable box-office tally for a dozen years (when he played the second lead in *Mister Roberts*). Bing dominated the 1940s, starring in fourteen of the decade's top-grossing pictures. All but one of those upcoming films would exceed the grosses of *Holiday Inn,* and one, *The Bells of St. Mary's* (1945), easily doubled them. Despite all that he had been during Prohibition and the Depression and all he would be in the postwar era, the war and its immediate aftermath really were, professionally at least, the best years of his life.

Holiday Inn was the highest-grossing film Fred Astaire had made and would remain the second most lucrative musical of his career, bettered only by his second turn with Crosby, *Blue Skies* (1946). They are the only musicals in which Astaire loses the girl. If he resented the commercial boost Crosby gave him (as if he were Ginger to Bing's Fred), the lobby cards submitted after a sneak preview of *Holiday Inn* offered no balm. Bing emerged as the overwhelming favorite; Astaire and Marjorie Reynolds vied for a distant second place. Hardly anyone thought the film should be cut, though a few patrons expressed distaste for the fickle Lila, played by Virginia Dale. They named several songs as their favorites but, surprisingly, most preferred by a wide margin "White Christmas," the quietest and simplest number in the picture. What did they know?

Few reviewers mentioned "White Christmas," but many weighed in with a zestier choice for their favorite song: "Abraham," the big production number in blackface. *Variety* raved about the "ultra" production and Bing's incarnation of the American Troubadour, predicting that two new tunes, "Song of Freedom" and "Abraham," would take their places beside older Berlin classics: "With Louise Beavers as his housekeeper, and her two cullud kids, Shelby Bacon and Joan Arnold, for comedy assists, the Abraham Lincoln motif keys a corking 'Abraham' spiritual, which Crosby croons to wow effect." *Time* described it as "a solid swing spiritual for Lincoln's birthday," and the *New York Times* applauded Crosby's ability to "sell a blackface number." Only the *New York Herald Tribune*'s Kate Cameron predicted that "long before Dec. 25, the country will be playing, working and fighting" to "White Christmas."[6]

"Songs make history and history makes songs," Berlin remarked two months before *Holiday Inn* opened. "Music written under stress," he said, "in turn arouses similar emotions in those who hear it."[7] "White Christmas" fit the bill in all respects, but history thwarted "Abraham," a nifty lyric and arrangement undone by the gradual recognition that white actors (or, for that matter, black ones) masquerading as Negro caricatures no longer qualified as a cherished tradition in American comedy. It would have perplexed those who made *Holiday Inn* to learn that a song cheered by critics and audiences alike at the time would consign one of the most popular movies of its day to a period of limbo. Rather than ponder the world of their fathers, Americans shut their eyes or had them shut for them. By the 1980s, television stations cut out the offending scene; TCM, rather than censoring the film, took it out of the rotation. This was particularly unfair to Louise Beavers, who had advanced from a performer in an all-women minstrel troupe to become the cinema's most ubiquitous housekeeper. As Mamie, she is no Mammy but a confidante to Bing's reclusive and lovelorn Jim Hardy. In a scene that the film historian James Robert Parish described as "vital to the progression of ethnic minorities in American films," Hardy expresses "no flippancy or condescending attitude to 'compensate' for taking an employee's advice."[8]

All of Berlin's revue musicals, from *Alexander's Ragtime Band* to *This Is the Army* to the postwar *Annie Get Your Gun*, explore the same question: What does it mean to be American? *Holiday Inn* proposes the idea that the nation may be fiercely polarized by political and social issues, but one thing unites everyone in nonpartisan celebration: holidays. In choosing only eight, Berlin Americanized and secularized Christmas, Easter, and St. Valentine's Day, from which he deleted the saint. (In 1969 Pope Paul VI went him one better and deleted the holiday from the Roman calendar.) For the rest, he selected patriotic-historical days—Washington's and Lincoln's Birthdays, Independence Day, and Thanksgiving—as well as New Year's, a day of resolution after a night of carousing. In short, America as a sequence of family parties.

Holiday Inn is an odd film to generate reverent or nostalgic emotions. Despite its musical and comedic pleasures and its patriotism and fireside warmth, the story is a roundelay of impulsive betrayals performed by a not particularly likable cast of characters. Everyone abandons Bing except the maid. The principals are relentlessly self-centered, Fred in a callously aggressive way and Bing in a melancholic passive-aggressive way. Never does Bing kiss or touch Linda, preferring subterfuge to romance. Yet the audience enjoyed them all, confident that in the last reel Bing would not spend Christmas alone in his New England cabin. His mulish withdrawal, which seemed merely eccentric in *Rhythm on the River,* now resonated with families separated from sons and husbands who might never know another Christmas. The cabin, the hearth, the tree, the song, the intimate consoling baritone: the emotions of the moment were frozen in time.[9]

As August turned to September, "White Christmas" began to take hold, levitating beyond the film to have a life of its own. Weeks before the picture's New York premiere, Berlin decided to postpone publicizing it and bet everything on "Be Careful, It's My Heart," a surefire hit, he believed. "The music business has so changed," he wrote Mark Sandrich, "that it's possible to plug only one song at a time," especially, he added, given the scarcity of shellac. Besides, you could not promote a Christmas song in August.[10] Only after "Be Careful" topped the charts would he turn his attention to "Abraham"—"I think we have a much better chance with that swing tune than any other in the score."[11]

For a month or so, the Valentine's Day ballad looked like it might take off, but by Labor Day, sheet-music sales slackened. Berlin hardly had time to complain before receiving reports on "White Christmas" that flabbergasted him, though he initially pretended otherwise. On September 14, he wired Sandrich: AS I ANTICIPATED CHRISTMAS IS OUR NUMBER ONE SONG WITHOUT ANY PLUGS. IT IS OUT-SELLING CAREFUL AND LOOKS LIKE IT WILL BE THE BIGGEST HIT I HAVE HAD IN YEARS. WE ARE PLANNING TO MILK THIS SCORE AND KEEP ON IT FOR THE NEXT FOUR MONTHS.[12] Bing and Jack Kapp were less confident about promoting a Christmas song in autumn. A week after his USO tour, Bing took Dixie out for an evening at the Players, the VIP restaurant owned by Preston Sturges on Sunset Boulevard, and delighted patrons by singing most of the score. Yet when he returned to *KMH* on October 1, he sang only one Berlin number, "Be Careful, It's My Heart," listed that day by the Automatic Hostess Company, a Chicago-based music-distribution service, as the most played disc on American jukeboxes. The same broadcast proved significant for introducing the Charioteers, a black pop-gospel vocal group that would become a cherished *KMH* staple. Two days later, with no assistance from *KMH,* "White Christmas" arrived to stay.

Given the absence of plugs, noted by Berlin, the song's popularity caught everyone unawares. The business rarely worked like that; usually you begged and pleaded, bartered and bribed, pledged, wheedled, and collected debts to promote a song. "White Christmas" had none of that, but as soon as it cleared the decks on *Your Hit Parade,* Berlin and the others went to town. Bing sang it on the next *Kraft Music Hall,* October 8. He sang it for overseas troops on the short-lived AFRS series *Song Sheet* on October 19 (customarily for this series, he sang the song, then read the lyrics) and again three days later on *KMH* (the only *Holiday Inn* song on a program that debuted "Moonlight Becomes You," from the recently opened *Road to Morocco*); and yet again on November 14 for overseas troops on *Mail Call,* appearing with Astaire and Betty Rhodes to sing the *Holiday Inn* score. That week the jubilant Berlin wrote Sandrich: "You probably know that 'White Christmas' is the talk of the music business and looks like the biggest hit I have had since 'Always.' That is, I haven't had a song, including 'God Bless America,' that sold as many copies in so short a time. Last week, we sold over 92,000 copies and the week before 76,000 copies. The first mail today had orders for over 12,000 copies."[13]

Berlin referred to sheet-music sales, but by now Jack Kapp realized he had seriously underestimated the number of records he needed to press, especially as his office and Bing's were inundated with letters from military personnel requesting discs. In addition to the copies for sale, Bing directed thousands more be sent to ships and military installations around the world. Everett Crosby wrote to Jack explaining that their office could not handle the requests and asked him to mail the discs from his facility and send him the bill.[14] Despite the excitement, or because of it, Bing evidently harbored concerns about the secularity of "White Christmas." He sang it on the December 3 *KMH* and in a December 16 appearance on Lionel Barrymore's series *Mayor of the Town* but omitted it from his Christmas Eve program, which did feature "Adeste Fideles," "God Rest Ye Merry, Gentlemen," the Charioteers' "Sweet Little Jesus Boy," and "Silent Night." That was likely the last Christmas Eve that would pass without a Crosby rendition of "White Christmas."

At the end of October, "White Christmas" topped every sales chart; it would prevail as the number one record for nearly three months. Other than Bing's "Silent Night," it was the first recording to exceed the sales of Gene Austin's "My Blue Heaven," back in pre-Depression 1927. It was the first but not the last Crosby record to crown the Harlem Hit Parade. Berlin finally conceded that nobody wanted his Beverly Hills verse and ordered his company to excise the stanza, causing retailers to complain about the brevity of the sheet music until the demand by customers overwhelmed them. Kapp, seeing that the popularity of the single slowed sales of his *Holiday Inn* album, reformatted the latter with four instead of six discs, deleting "White Christmas" and three other songs. Writing Sandrich, Berlin marveled at the phenomenon: "The song seems to have a quality that can be applied to the world situation as it exists today. I understand many copies are being sent to the boys overseas, and it is just possible, while it isn't a war song, it can easily be associated with it."[15]

Unlike any war song ever written—and Berlin had written quite a few, heard nightly in *This Is the Army*—"White Christmas" didn't make anyone "want to go to war," as he put it in his first international hit, "Alexander's Ragtime Band" (1911). *Time* credited its unexpected success to the fact that "thousands of U.S. servicemen were facing snowless Christmases from North Africa to Guadalcanal."[16] Carl Sandberg wrote, "When we sing ['White Christmas'] we don't hate anybody....Way down under this latest hit of his Irving Berlin catches us where we love peace."[17] It sold six hundred thousand discs in the closing months of 1942 (Bing's royalties came to $298,946, $4.4 million in today's dollars) and two million as of 1944. Sales mounted year after year as it hit the number one spot again in 1945 and 1946, uniquely returning to the top thirty every year but one between its release and Christmas of 1962. By then, the record's sales exceeded twenty-five million, the bestselling record ever. In 2007, the *Guinness Book of Records* updated the number to fifty million, seventeen million more than Elton John's "Candle in the Wind," in second place, and twenty million more than Bing's "Silent Night," in third. Guinness numbers do not include Crosby LPs and CDs (his 1949 album *Merry Christmas* has never been out of print); their numbers registered only singles of his 1942 original and an almost indistinguishable 1947 remake.

In 1974, Bing recalled that it had been "kind of a wrench for me to sing it" with half the audience in tears. "It was wartime and so many people were away from home, away from their families, serving in the army, navy and air force and in faraway places. And a song like that is reminiscent of home and family, and that's why it had such an immediate and lasting impact, I believe."[18] The year after he made those remarks, the U.S. military command in Vietnam used "White Christmas" as code, broadcasting it to cue the evacuation of Saigon and the end of a war that produced little in the way of home-front sentiment. "White Christmas" launched an industry of holiday songs; seventy-five years later, the song and Crosby's recording remain as inseparable from the Christmas season as any traditional carol.

Bing's tenure as a top entertainer in music, movies, and radio never seemed more secure, but it was now inseparable from the need to boost the home front, a vocation that combined the things he liked best: entertaining the men in khaki and playing golf. Only one colleague—Bob Hope—handled this role as deftly as he, so like it or not, they were joined at the hip on- and offscreen. They didn't have to memorize lines or rehearse for golf tours, and the audiences inspired them, though they occasionally had to fend off spectators who ran across greens to demand autographs and avoid galleries of onlookers who crowded within the length of a club's swing. As business-savvy as Bing was, he liked to perform gratis; long after the war, he'd continue to reject offers to perform live for paying customers. Besides, everything he earned went to confiscatory taxes; the government asked wealthy citizens to live on a regulated budget (for Bing that meant $25,000; about $370,000 with twenty-first-century inflation), so he might as well give away his singing. Plus he liked to travel.

He liked it so well he once again focused on loosening the reins that held him in place. With the Petrillo recording ban in force as of August 1, he had no appointments at Decca, nor did he owe anything to Paramount until late October, when *Dixie* went into production. The tie that bound was radio, and shortly after returning from the August USO tour, he instructed Everett to inform Thomas McInnerney of his dissatisfaction with *KMH* and his longing to do something else. Nearly two years had passed since their previous conflict, and McInnerney was livid; he thought all the problems were resolved, that everything was running smoothly. He read into Everett's letter Bing's resolve to leave the air beyond AFRS broadcasts, and he yowled. Everett responded via a Western Union day letter:

Your letter of the 18th received and you apparently misunderstood the meaning of my letter. Bing does not want to leave the radio but feels there is nothing more he can do for the Kraft show and wants to go on some other program. These are the same feelings he had two years ago when you asked him to stay on for another year or so and that if he didn't feel any different then you would release him. He intends doing all that he can and more for the war effort. He has wired asking [me] to let him know whether you will release him or not as soon as possible. We can get no satisfaction whatever from the Thompson people. They told our Attorney that this was my doing and not Bings [sic] and were cheap enough to tell him that I only wanted to get my wife on a program with Bing.[19]

This curt, contradictory missive (McInnerney misunderstands yet Bing hopes for an immediate release) had no chance of severing Bing's contract. But it did succeed in softening the company's opposition to Bing's true objective: to do a more musical, less talky show that ran for only half an hour, like those of Bob Hope, Jack Benny, Eddie Cantor, Edgar Bergen, Ginny Simms, Kate Smith, Rudy Vallée, and just about every other top-rated radio star in 1942, including Fred Allen, who made the switch shortly before Bing. (The crack regarding Everett's wife, the twenty-four-year-old blond and bubbly opera singer Florence George, probably refers to his aggressive management style but overestimated his influence. Bing refused to book her after 1941, no matter what Everett wanted or who sponsored his show.) As Bing went on another tour, this time for the Treasury Department, Everett, Kraft, and NBC worked out the particulars for a revised program. By November, changes in cast and concept would prepare the audience for a streamlined *KMH,* set to debut in January 1943.

Radio wasn't alone in fretting over Bing's absence. As the year wound down, Paramount learned that it, too, had to compete with his war work. Dixie and the four boys already felt the pinch, sharing him with the world for longer stretches. For them, his absence had no financial ramifications; it represented the absence of a center that might have kept the family from spinning into dysfunction.

Bing recognized as much. Next year they would spend the summer at the ranch he had just bought in Elko; he would work his sons as he had been worked as a boy, with no special favors. In the interim, they had to accept wartime conditions like everyone else. Men were absent from millions of families; hundreds of thousands of them returned wounded or not at all. When the secretary of the treasury Henry Morgenthau Jr. asked him to do his patriotic duty on the manicured greens of the country's top golf courses, how dare he complain? As September was his last month free of *KMH*, he signed on to make the most of it.

On August 30, two weeks to the day after he returned from the USO tour with Phil Silvers, and as *Holiday Inn* and "White Christmas" infiltrated America's consciousness, Bing arrived on the south steps of the Treasury Building for a bond rally. After that, he traveled to New York and set out in the morning for Binghamton's IBM Country Club, where he played golf before three thousand spectators and improvised an auction on the first tee. The next day was similar, except that it brought him to Toledo's Inverness Country Club, followed by a show for recruits at Camp Perry. In Detroit, before a crowd of five thousand, he teamed with Jimmy Demaret (they lost to Byron Nelson and Chick Harbert) and sang, putter in hand, "Sleepy Lagoon," "Jingle, Jangle, Jingle," and "Home on the Range," then entertained seventy-five hundred soldiers at Selfridge Field. And so on: Chicago, Grand Rapids, Youngstown, Indianapolis, Cincinnati, Kansas City, Miami (Oklahoma), Tulsa (where he raised $315,125, his highest single-day haul, thanks to the auctioned wire recording of "San Antonio Rose"), Oklahoma City, and Houston. The PGA tournament manager estimated that in ten matches, Crosby averaged in the middle 70s, drew fifty thousand spectators, sold half a million dollars in bonds, and raised twenty-five thousand dollars for war relief. And that didn't take into account money generated by his appearances on local stations and at private functions, including a dinner that cost a thousand-dollar bond per ticket.

Everywhere he went, observers remarked on his energy and generosity—what a "regular fellow" he was, unspoiled by stardom, unattended by an entourage, unimpressed by the worshipping crowds. Had there ever been a star of such importance who wore his stardom, talent, fame, and wealth so lightly? Bing often part-

The Crosbys lived at 10500 Camarillo Street in the Toluca Lake district of North Hollywood from 1936 until a fire destroyed their home, which is depicted here on a bestselling postcard, in 1943. (*Gary Giddins Collection*)

Young lovebirds: Bing and Dixie in the early 1930s. (*HLC Properties, Ltd.*)

Bing and Bob Hope first shared a stage at the Capitol Theatre in 1933. (*Gary Giddins Collection*)

PHOTOPLAYS.

TODAY at the

CAPITOL

Broadway at 51st St.—Major Edward Bowes. Mng. Dir.

Broadway's great stage show plus the year's nerve-tingling sensation

The MASK of FU MANCHU

with

BORIS (Frankenstein) KARLOFF

KAREN MORLEY
MYRNA LOY
LEWIS STONE
JEAN HERSHOLT

IN PERSON

BING CROSBY

SINGING TO YOUR HEART

BOB HOPE

STAR OF "BALLYHOO"

CASS, MACK & OWEN

N.B.C.'s Favorites "RADIO RUBES"

BETTY JANE COOPER and LATHROP BROS.

and EXTRA ADDED ATTRACTION

ABE LYMAN

and His Famous CALIFORNIANS

A NEW Fu Manchu lives! Sax Rohmer has created a new and more sinister character, not to be confused with the Fu Manchu of other pictures!

This Oriental monster almost wrecked civilization with his love-drug.

A Metro-Goldwyn-Mayer Picture

Bing feeling no pain, ca. 1940.
(*HLC Properties, Ltd.*)

Dixie and the four boys in 1938.
Left to right: Phillip, Lindsay (on
Dixie's lap), Dennis, Gary. (*HLC
Properties, Ltd.*)

Bing and the boys, in their
St. John's Catholic Military
Academy sweaters. Left to
right: Gary, Dennis, Phillip,
Lindsay. (*HLC Properties,
Ltd.*)

Bing organized a birthday party for his costar Gloria Jean (née Schoonover) on the set of *If I Had My Way,* 1940. Back row: Gloria Jean's sister Sally; Lindsay; Bing; Dixie; director David Butler; Gloria Jean's parents, Ferman and Eleanor Schoonover; her sister Lois, Gloria Jean. Bottom row, left to right: Phillip (wearing baseball cap), Gary (in fedora), Dennis, Gloria Jean's sister Bonnie. (*Courtesy Gloria Jean Schoonover*)

The desire to preserve on film a performance by the blackface minstrel Eddie Leonard was one of the reasons Crosby and David Butler made *If I Had My Way.* (*Gary Giddins Collection*)

Bing's formidable mother, Catherine Crosby, on the porch of the Toluca Lake home she shared with his easygoing father, Harry. (*Pamela Crosby Brown Collection*)

Bing and Mary Martin between takes for *Rhythm on the River*, one of his most undervalued films, 1940. (*HLC Properties, Ltd.*)

Rhythm on the River consciously sought to assimilate Bing's work on *Kraft Music Hall*: John Scott Trotter, his bandleader (left), and Ken Carpenter, his announcer, frame Bing and Mary Martin, who would soon become a *KMH* regular. (*HLC Properties, Ltd.*)

Between Mary and Bing are Harry Barris, the former Rhythm Boy who showed up in many Crosby films (left), and the jazz trumpet player and vocalist Wingy Manone in *Rhythm on the River*. (*HLC Properties, Ltd.*)

In *Road to Zanzibar*, Bing lets Dorothy Lamour do the paddling while he sings "It's Always You," 1941. *(HLC Properties, Ltd.)*

The surprising jazziness of the opening music for *Road to Zanzibar* was triggered by Bing's fortuitous meeting with his old friend Tommy Dorsey, shown here with Bing broadcasting an episode of the Armed Forces Radio Service (AFRS) series *Mail Call*. Dorsey's superb arranger Sy Oliver is pictured below. *(HLC Properties, Ltd.; Gary Giddins Collection)*

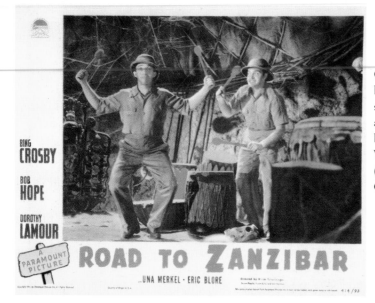

One of *Zanzibar*'s best-remembered scenes involves Bing and Bob Hope stumbling into a jungle Western Union. *(Gary Giddins Collection)*

Bing, the fabled jazzman Jack Teagarden (center), and the popular radio star Eddie "Rochester" Anderson confer in *Birth of the Blues*, 1941. *(HLC Properties, Ltd.)*

A lobby card for *Birth of the Blues* captures Bing characteristically not kissing Mary Martin, whose career he aggressively promoted. *(Gary Giddins Collection)*

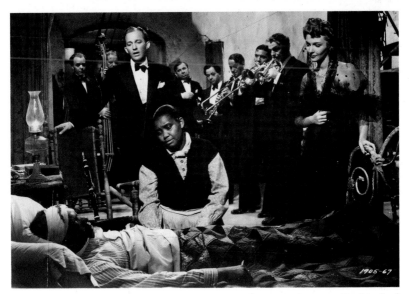

Ruby Elzy, who created the role of Serena in *Porgy and Bess* and who died at thirty-five, gave a haunting performance of "St. Louis Blues" in *Birth of the Blues*. She sits at the bedside of a beaten Eddie Anderson, surrounded by Bing, Mary, and the band, including Harry Barris with bass and Brian Donlevy with cornet. (*HLC Properties, Ltd.*)

Bing and Pat O'Brien, pictured on this flyer, were president and vice president of the Del Mar Turf Club, which they helped create in 1937 and which was turned into an aircraft plant employing 90 percent women for the duration of the war. (*Judy Schmid Collection*)

Two musical friends with beer: the jazz musician, memoirist, and club owner Eddie Condon (left), who recorded with Crosby in New York, and the songwriter and singer Johnny Mercer, whose career Crosby helped to launch and sustain. (*HLC Properties, Ltd.*)

Bing and the composer Jimmy Van Heusen work the land in Palm Springs, ca. 1950. (*HLC Properties, Ltd.*)

Bing called Johnny Burke, his troubled long-time lyricist, the Poet. Burke realized that Van Heusen would be an ideal partner and fought to get him. (*Courtesy Rory Burke*)

Most of Gary Crosby's favorite memories of visiting Paramount concerned the Road series; Bing was shooting *Road to Utopia* on this day. (*HLC Properties, Ltd.*)

Unlike his oldest brother, Linny Crosby retained good feelings about summers at the Elko ranch with his father. The two are pictured here ca. 1947. (*HLC Properties, Ltd.*)

After Bing completed work on *Rhythm on the River,* this rather grim family photograph (only Dennis appears to be having a good time) appeared in newspapers across the country, including Bing's hometown paper, the *Spokesman-Review,* which found it "interesting." Left to right: Lindsay, Bing, Dixie, Gary, Phillip, Dennis. (*Gary Giddins Collection*)

Bing at a *KMH* rehearsal in leafy shirt, with pipe in hand and hat on head and probably chewing gum, studying a lead sheet, likely boning up on the words, as he didn't read music. (*HLC Properties, Ltd.*)

The Music Maids began with *KMH* in 1939 and stayed for more than five years, during which Jinny Erwin (center) changed her name to Trudy and emerged as a solo cast member. She's pictured here with the other Music Maids. Left to right: Dottie Mesmer, Alice Ludes, Denny Wilson, Bobbie Canvin. (*Gary Giddins Collection*)

Orson Welles and Bing prepare for a broadcast of Oscar Wilde's "The Happy Prince," 1944. (*HLC Properties, Ltd.*)

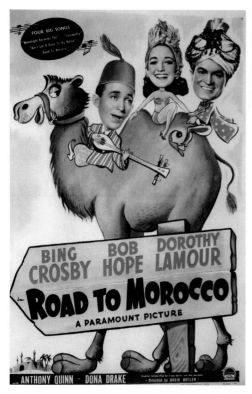

Road to Morocco, despite mishaps, was the most successful of the Road films and fulfilled the promise of the Johnny Burke–Jimmy Van Heusen songwriting team. (*Gary Giddins Collection*)

Crosby always got Lamour, but Hope finally found a woman, too, in *Morocco*: Dona Drake, the African American beauty who passed for white in a twenty-year film career. (*HLC Properties, Ltd.*)

Director Mark Sandrich assembled a cast of two megastars and two unknowns for Irving Berlin's *Holiday Inn,* the first musical to acknowledge America's declaration of war. Left to right: Bing, Virginia Dale, Sandrich, Marjorie Reynolds, and Fred Astaire. *(HLC Properties, Ltd.)*

Marjorie Reynolds is evidently overjoyed when Bing demonstrates his latest *Holiday Inn* number, "White Christmas." *(HLC Properties, Ltd.)*

One of the Barsa sisters poses in front of the Crosby Building at 9023 Sunset Boulevard. In addition to the owners (note Everett N. Crosby's managerial marquee on the third floor), it housed, among other renters, the ground-floor Finlandia Baths and the second-floor practice of Dr. Arnold Stevens. *(Pamela Crosby Brown Collection)*

Bing at Paramount with the *Racing Form* and three cronies: (left to right) his favorite wit Barney Dean and two devoted pals from Spokane, his lookalike stand-in, Leo Lynn, and Jimmy Cottrell, a former welterweight champ who worked as a studio prop man. (*HLC Properties, Ltd.*)

Frances Langford, always popular with the troops, was a regular on Bob Hope's immensely successful CBS radio show. Bing, displaying a characteristically ineffable tie, often traded radio guest shots with Bob. (*HLC Properties, Ltd.*)

After the recording ban ended in the fall of 1943, Jack Kapp traveled to Los Angeles for the reunion of Bing and the Andrews Sisters (left to right: LaVerne, Patty, Maxene) and flashed his signature poster of Pocahontas asking, "Where's the melody?" (*HLC Properties, Ltd.*)

"It's Been a Long, Long Time" remains one of Bing's most resonant recordings, stylishly accompanied by the innovative guitarist and musical tinkerer Les Paul and his trio, with rhythm guitarist Cal Gooden and bassist Clinton Nordquist, 1945. (*HLC Properties, Ltd.*)

Bing was never more at home than on his ranch in Elko, Nevada, here posing with Mary Barsa for her sister, Violet Barsa, 1950. (*Pamela Crosby Brown Collection*)

Bing confined most of his hunting to birds, and his companions in the field included Gary Cooper and Clark Gable, 1945. (*HLC Properties, Ltd.*)

One of the few times Bing allowed Hollywood to invade Elko was for a premiere (*Here Comes the Groom*, 1951) to benefit the local hospital. Wearing a denim tuxedo jacket made for him by Levi's, he is accompanied by his sons (left to right) Dennis, Lindsay, and Phillip. (*HLC Properties, Ltd.*)

During the war Crosby did most of his golfing at celebrity exhibition matches to raise money and sell war bonds. He's shown here with Frank Sinatra at the microphone, 1943. (*HLC Properties, Ltd.*)

While their representatives dickered to unite Crosby and Sinatra for the general public, the two singers often worked together for enlisted men on AFRS programs, as on a 1944 *Command Performance* with the indefatigable Dinah Shore (pianist unknown). (*HLC Properties, Ltd.*)

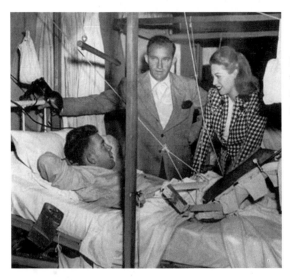

Bing and Dinah Shore visit a hospital ward in San Francisco, 1944. (*HLC Properties, Ltd.*)

Bing rehearsed an Armed Forces Radio Program in 1945 with the redoubtable Bette Davis, who along with John Garfield created the Hollywood Canteen, an essential stop for enlisted men. Officers and civilians were not allowed. (*HLC Properties, Ltd.*)

Bing, here backed by John Scott Trotter, was a favorite at the Hollywood Canteen, where the audiences were enthusiastic and, unlike the military itself (or this photograph), racially integrated, 1944. (*HLC Properties, Ltd.*)

The novelty song "Mairzy Doats" was a highlight of perhaps the best remembered (because it was filmed) performance that Bing and Bob gave before thousands of servicemen, Santa Ana, 1944. (*HLC Properties, Ltd.*)

Bleary-eyed but game, Bing was briefly feared missing after he made a two-hour side trip to sing for five thousand WAACs at Fort Oglethorpe in northern Georgia and hired a car for his next stop, Nashville, instead of using the train ticket reserved for him, 1943. (*HLC Properties, Ltd.*)

One of the sad ironies of the home front was the revival of blackface minstrelsy. Paramount did yeoman's research to get the superficial details right in *Dixie*. Bing, arms outstretched, stands in front. *(HLC Properties, Ltd.)*

Decca broke the recording ban by issuing "Sunday, Monday, or Always," the one enduring new song from *Dixie*, a cappella; crowning the charts for nearly five months, it brought Bing his sixth gold record. *(Judy Schmid Collection)*

The first of the all-star studio propaganda revues, *Star Spangled Rhythm* attempted to redress complaints of African American performers, as represented by the NAACP, in 1942. Perhaps only Bing could have delivered the climactic "Old Glory" bounded by the American flag and George Washington's profile. *(HLC Properties, Ltd.)*

nered with the recently installed PGA president Big Ed Dudley, who tutored him and Bob and would eventually do the same for President Eisenhower. Big Ed told a reporter in Grand Rapids, "I don't see how he holds up under the strain," after two policemen had had to flank him at every hole to keep autograph hunters away.[20] A mob of hundreds pressed in on him when he arrived at Union Station in Kansas City. Acknowledging his "devoted effort," Henry Morgenthau wrote him, "It was a strenuous assignment, and I know that it must have been tiring for you at times. Yet you showed untiring zeal and unflagging good humor throughout the tour, and your spirit was an example to the people who saw and heard you. I should like you to know that your work for us in September has been a real contribution toward the winning of the war and that all of us at the Treasury are deeply grateful."[21]

Life on the road was mostly agreeable to Bing. He met a wide variety of people, including the Oklahoma oilman George Coleman, perhaps his closest friend in the postwar decades.[22] It bumped up his energy, and he lost weight by eating large breakfasts and little else, though he gained it back by the time he started work on *Dixie*. The Red Cross National Sports Advisory Committee estimated that the thirty matches Bing played since January drew one hundred and fifty thousand spectators, with bond sales nearing the million-dollar mark.[23] Elmer Davis, the director of the Office of War Information, appointed Bing an OWI civilian consultant without compensation beyond reimbursed expenses and a ten-dollar per diem. In his acceptance letter, Bing wrote of his "great pride in being selected to assist in this work, and pray I may be of value to the effort." Yet he kept the OWI appointment to himself until it was broken as a story nine months later by a columnist. Bing began his "missionary work" lining up Edgar Bergen, Tommy Dorsey, Jimmy Dorsey, Kay Kyser, and Dinah Shore to appear beside him or alone at the naval hospitals in Mare Island, Oak Knoll, and Oakland.[24]

Publicly he appeared to glide through a charmed world. The latest Kraft mini-tempest played itself out quietly. Before the season began, Everett told the trades the show would favor music over comedy, though the only immediate change was the coming of the Charioteers. As he did with Victor Borge, Cal Kuhl signed them to two weeks as a test. But after they had the studio audience roaring over "Ride, Red, Ride," backed by their talented pianist Jimmy Sherman, Bing wanted them for the year. African American newspapers applauded the hiring and the group, which *New York Age* reported "captured the town's entertainment spotlight."[25] The Charioteers had started singing in 1930 as students at Wilberforce University. Bing liked working with them and they continued with the program until he left it in 1946. (Ironically, their Columbia Records contract prohibited them from recording with Crosby, though they did record with their label-mates Frank Sinatra and Mildred Bailey.) The contracts with Mary Martin and Borge came due in November and December. Mary had an appendectomy and left Hollywood for her true harbor of immortality—Broadway. Janet Blair took her place for five weeks (eight years later, she took over from Martin again for the national tour of *South Pacific*) until Trudy Erwin got the contract. Borge transferred his radio renown to concert halls. Bing elevated a short, stumpy comedy writer named Leo "Ukie" Sherin to be his on-air foil.

The week he returned to *KMH* coincided with the premiere of *Road to Morocco,* which opened with a higher gross than *Holiday Inn* and ultimately topped its receipts by nearly 6 percent—the most lucrative comedy since the advent of sound. "Let us be thankful that Paramount is still blessed with Bing Crosby and Bob Hope," the *New York Times* reflected, "and that it has set its cameras to tailing these two irrepressible wags on another fantastic excursion."[26] Crosby had two back-to-back movie sensations and number one records, as "Moonlight Becomes You" briefly edged "White Christmas" aside. The war itself seemed to take cues from him; shortly after Bing and Bob landed in Morocco, American forces arrived. General Patton, commanding thirty-five thousand men, pulled into Casablanca to launch Operation Torch, providing crucial support in the North African campaign that advanced the likelihood of an Allied victory in Europe while raising morale on the home front. Patton's men brought along a shoulder-mounted rocket launcher designed by an ordnance officer named Edward Uhl. He called it a bazooka, after the contraption that Bob Burns made famous on *KMH*. With the invasion providing millions of dollars in free publicity, Paramount rushed *Morocco* into wider release.

Bing took special interest in the invasion after the son of a Paramount grip mailed home the speech Patton delivered October 28 over the PA systems of the ships headed for Africa. The grip copied it for Bing. The address began with the general's congratulations to the men chosen to take Casablanca, continued with an estimation of the opposition he expected and a warning of the disgrace inherent in retreat or surrender, and finished with his blustery grandiloquence: "The eyes of the world are watching us; the heart of America beats for us; God is with us. On our victory depends the freedom or slavery of the human race. We shall surely win." Bing sent it to Carroll Carroll with a note: "Some epic phrases contained therein, it seemed to me."[27]

They decided to dramatize it on the December 17 *KMH*, hiring the actor Edgar Buchanan to play Patton and a sound-effects crew to simulate the noises of a ship at sea. Listeners did not know what to make of it (Kuhl thought it just "O.K."), but Bing was pleased when Corporal A. F. Morales of the 829th Signal Corps wrote him from "Somewhere in North Africa." Morales and eight other men had picked up the show on a portable radio; they heard Patton's words on board and were no less "thrilled" by the "duplicate," as it "brought home the fact that the people in America have by no means forgotten us here in North Africa. We sincerely hope that you can find time to answer this letter yourself." Bing wrote them that everyone at *KMH* got a "big jar" knowing that they approved their treatment of Patton's address: "We hang on the radio every day and fight for the papers telling of your progress in Tunisia. Those bums are getting a good practical view of what you fellows can do when you get operating. Maybe I can get down there to see you soon. Hope says he's got it fixed."[28]

A more lasting debut also occurred on the December 17 broadcast. Trudy Erwin, who in New York had despaired of ever getting a break, got two big ones in 1943 even as she grew increasingly disillusioned with the Kay Kyser gig. The bandleader teamed her and Harry Babbitt on a new song, "Who Wouldn't Love You," which shot to the top of the charts and earned Kyser his first certified gold record. Erwin received a flat fee of seventy-five dollars, but she now had a hit under her belt. Determined to leave Kyser and return to Los Angeles, she married Murdo MacKenzie, who was then stationed in

nearby Lancaster as a flight instructor in meteorology and naviga-
tion. (Their marriage lasted fifty-six years, until his death in 1999;
she died fourteen months later.) She soon received a call from Cal
Kuhl, who asked her to be a guest on *KMH* and perform "Who
Wouldn't Love You" as a duet with Bing, along with scripted patter.
She accepted happily, half resigned to resuming her place as a
Music Maid (now billed as the Music Maids and Hal, as the
arranger Hal Hopper had taken her place). She did not know it, but
the guest shot was her audition for the new half-hour *KMH*, debut-
ing in January. After the episode aired, they asked her back, not as
a Music Maid, but as Trudy Erwin, Bing's weekly vocal partner
with a yearlong contract. "Oh, I just loved that," she recalled. In
addition to her solo numbers, she and Bing played Trudy and Harry
in the popular "memory spot," a weekly routine in which they were
whisked back in time for a comedy sketch and vocal duet. Backstage she continued to be known as Jinny.[29]

Bing came home after the Treasury Department trip for two nights
before traveling to Sacramento to tee off for the Red Cross with
Hope and Babe Ruth. The resumption of *KMH* stabilized his schedule, but he couldn't sit still—a concert with Hope in San Francisco, a golf match with Hope in Oakland, a day at the races to blow
off steam. He had never felt so needed, professionally. At the same
time, he enjoyed a respite from a rocky domesticity, a respite that
wasn't available to Dixie. If his absences allowed her to escape his
disapproval—the silent, judgmental withdrawal to his study—his
returns provoked panicky anticipation. Dixie readied herself to look
and behave her best, but, in Gary's recollection, "her nerves were
so raw that the slightest wayward look or comment" triggered a
"black depression."[30] Bing's homecomings resembled the measured
stops of a tour; his departures sent her back to the bottle. When he
was around, they worked at maintaining a nimble banter. He tried
with mixed results to get her out of the house, to a nightclub or
restaurant, and she continued occasionally to do her bit for the war.
On a Sunday in October, she opened their home for a United
Nations bazaar on behalf of American Women's Voluntary Services. Bing spent that day on the links in Santa Ana with Hope,

Astaire, Randolph Scott, Oliver Hardy, Babe Didrikson Zaharias, and Sam Snead to benefit the Army Emergency Relief Fund.

The next morning he returned to Paramount to shoot *Dixie,* which had just completed a week of second-unit shooting in Sacramento. Studio complications delayed the start of principal photography at a cost of $10,700 in salaries. Buddy DeSylva and his producer Paul Jones, apprehensive about additional delays, attempted to control them in advance. Somehow the Broadway comedian Billy De Wolfe, making his film debut, managed to get a clause in his contract allowing him to leave one afternoon a week to appear on radio, though he had no offers to do so. Dorothy Lamour required two half days off in November, one to answer a live-on-the-air call from a Marine (the broadcast pretended she took the call at Paramount during a break from shooting *Dixie*), and one to rehearse a guest shot on *KMH.* Radio was closed to the other principal actors, Marjorie Reynolds, Raymond Walburn, Lynne Overman, and Eddie Foy. Bing could leave the studio on Thursdays, but not before noon. Because of wartime restrictions, they had to shoot several scenes at other studios—the opera-house scene at United Artists; the New York street scenes and interiors at Fox; the Maxwell Theater scenes at Vitagraph; the saloon, boat-landing, and Bijou Theater scenes at Columbia Ranch. Should Bing be broadcasting on one of those days, he would be permitted extra time to get to the NBC studio.

Problems began the first weekend. Bing took off Saturday to rest up for Sunday matches in San Francisco, promising the crew to be back first thing Monday. On behalf of the American Women's Voluntary Services, he and Hope played at Claremont Country Club and then, skipping lunch, at the Presidio Golf Club, where they fooled around for a Paramount newsreel (which has been excerpted in just about every documentary ever made about the home front). When he showed up late on Monday, he explained that he had missed his train. The director Eddie Sutherland spent Saturday and Monday morning doing "Thursday work," work that didn't require Bing and would ordinarily be done on *KMH* afternoons. But they wasted Monday afternoon, as Bing's scene wasn't sufficiently prepped without the morning rehearsal. On Tuesday, Bing arrived at eleven a.m., so Sutherland spent the first two hours completing more Thursday work. On Thursday, they expected to have him two hours in the morning, but he called in to say he would not be there, so they did Thursday work all day. An accountant sent a memo to DeSylva, Freeman, and other executives explaining that even if Crosby never again failed to arrive on time, they would still lose another half Thursday in wages because there was no more Thursday work to do. Thus his absence on three half days cost the production $14,050 (with inflation, $201,000).[31]

It isn't known if DeSylva addressed this issue; beyond a sick day on December 26, Bing does not appear to have missed another hour. But what recourse did Paramount have? Short of a sex scandal, the worst publicity that could befall the company would be reports of the studio disparaging its most beloved star for missing a few days because he was off entertaining our boys. Besides, all Hollywood would soon know what Paramount's executives already suspected: in the annual tally of earnings, their studio would sweep the industry for 1942. MGM had the top picture (and a rout at the Academy Awards) in *Mrs. Miniver.* But of the year's ten top-grossing films, five were from Paramount (*Reap the Wild Wind, Holiday Inn, Road to Morocco, Wake Island, Louisiana Purchase*), and they outearned the other five combined: MGM's *Miniver* and *Somewhere I'll Find You,* Twentieth Century–Fox's *The Black Swan* and *How Green Was My Valley,* and Warner Brothers' *Yankee Doodle Dandy.* Come December, Paramount would release *Star Spangled Rhythm,* which, though not a true Crosby picture, bannered Bing as its main attraction. With the exception of *For Whom the Bell Tolls,* it would be their most successful release for 1943. For the film's New York premiere at the Paramount Theater on December 30, the historic stage show presented the first solo concert by Frank Sinatra. Pandemonium! And a public relations coup for their picture. Were they prepared to pick a fight over $14,050? Did they carp even when it became evident that 1943 would be the first year in the decade since Paramount signed Bing that the studio would have only one new Crosby film to release? More likely, they popped champagne corks and chased starlets around desks, as in the old days when Paramount prided itself on its uninhibited revels. In 1934, the company had gone into receivership with an outstanding debt of ninety-five million dollars, largely due to an aggressive expansion in theaters and overseas facilities. They were now, despite the looming threat of antitrust legislation, driving the Hollywood economy. They had much to celebrate.

Little revelry brightened the days at 10500 Camarillo. As Bing toed the line for *Dixie,* his long hours at various studio lots, extended by leisurely games at Lakeside and his radio work, made him almost a ghost at home. Dixie sank into murkier seclusion. On the worst days, her de facto keeper Georgie Hardwicke barred her friends from the house; on better days, Dixie made an effort and entertained. Her friends discussed her drinking and reclusiveness with a tact and compassion sorely lacking in her family members. While the ever-loyal Kitty Sexton found Bing to be sympathetic, his parents mocked Dixie mercilessly, in private and in letters, offering him no consolation. They were embarrassed by her, offended. They continued to regard alcoholism as a moral failure. Incredibly, the most distressing response to her malady emerged from Dixie's adoring father, who had introduced her to show business via a singing contest when she was sixteen. Mr. Wyatt devised a solution, which he kept confidential by mailing a handwritten letter to Bing in care of his post office box at Del Mar.

11-29-42
Dear Bing,

I am convinced that there is just one thing to do with Dixie: Put her in a sanitarium legally, under restraint, until such time as she is able to control herself. I am quite positive there is no use to approach her in any other way.

If Dr. Stevens will testify for us in the action—and I believe, and hope, he will—I suggest, for your consideration, that you turn the case over to O'Melveny for immediate action (Incompetency). If it could be done without her knowledge it would be fine. Just let her get good and drunk some night and wake up next morning in a Sanitarium.

I'll testify, or do anything else you want me to, in the action. All I ask is your guarantee that you don't use the incompetency to take the children away from her, unless and until she is declared, by competent authority, to be permanently incompetent.

You have my authority (permission) to show this letter to
O'Melveny, or Dr. Stevens, or anyone else, in your opinion, essential to the action.

Very sincerely,

E. E. Wyatt[32]

Sanatoriums were the 1940s version of rehab, but getting her
"good and drunk," kidnapping her, and removing the children
should she be deemed "permanently incompetent"? There is no
indication that Crosby took seriously any part of the letter, nor that
he showed it to O'Melveny, Stevens, or anyone else. If Wyatt's sym-
pathies were clearly with Bing, his solution was painfully ludicrous.
Yet it goaded Bing into action. Within two days of receiving it, he
and Dixie invited one of her oldest friends, Pauline Weislow, to stay
as a houseguest through the holidays or as long as she liked. The
invitation reached Pauline at the right time; her husband was in
the air force, and she and her cocker spaniel were freezing in Chicago. Bing relieved Dixie of the burden of buying and wrapping
gifts, activities she ordinarily tackled with gusto, mailing a single-
sentence letter to everyone on their Christmas list: "In view of current conditions, we have decided to forego the customary practice
of exchanging Christmas gifts with our friends and relatives. The
time and money thus saved can be diverted to more important
activities." He signed the notes "Dixie & Bing" in his own hand
instead of routing them through the office where his secretary
reproduced his signature.[33]

They had a quiet month, Bing working but easing back on the
exhibition golf; no parties or late-night carousing, and he had dinner at home. The high quality of his work would seem to indicate a
state of calm or, more likely, a rigorous compartmentalizing. For he
performed exuberantly on *KMH*'s Christmas Eve program, which
Cal Kuhl reported was "great," especially the Charioteers ("really
great"). John Reber phoned to say he liked Janet Blair; Kuhl was
more impressed by the impeccable timing of Bing's "Silent Night,"
which ended mere seconds before the NBC chimes ding-dong-
dinged the show off the air.[34] Dixie, Pauline, and the boys listened
in the first-floor library, where they had decorated a mammoth
floor-to-ceiling Christmas tree with lights and other ornaments

scrupulously color-coordinated by Dixie. In a couple of hours, they would be able to tune in to more Bing.

After the broadcast, Bing, the Charioteers, Ken Carpenter, and Spike Jones, the *KMH* drummer since 1937 (and for just one week longer), drove to CBS to participate in the *Command Performance Christmas Special,* a major production emceed by Hope and announced by Carpenter. This was the series' forty-fourth program and the first heard in the United States. Alfred Newman conducted the Fox studio orchestra, and Charles Laughton delivered a recitation in an hour otherwise given to the comedians Jack Benny, Fred Allen, Edgar Bergen, and Red Skelton; bandleaders Kay Kyser and Spike Jones, whose current hit, "Der Fuehrer's Face," launched his career as leader of the City Slickers; and an array of vocalists with connections to Bing—Ethel Waters, Dinah Shore, Ginny Simms, and the Andrews Sisters. *Variety* singled out as particularly savory "the tonsil partnership of Bing Crosby and the Charioteers" on "Basin Street Blues."[35]

During the next few days, Bing lined up the Charioteers, the Music Maids, and Borge for a shortwave *Command Performance,* emceed by Kyser. In answer to a request from General Leo Walton, he made an unpublicized appearance at the Christmas show at the Santa Ana Air Force Training Center. On the last day of the year, he aired the final sixty-minute edition of *Kraft Music Hall,* an upbeat hour, quite unemotional, filled with comedy. Bing brought back Jerry Lester as well as Victor Borge, the effete English comic actor Richard Haydn, the five-alarm Betty Hutton, and the reliable Johnny Mercer. They kept it light until the final number, "Old Glory," a plug for *Star Spangled Rhythm.* Bing went home, dined, slept, and woke to a new year, 1943, and another early-morning Friday filming *Dixie* on the Paramount lot.[36]

On Sunday, January 3, 1943, Bing had a late-afternoon date to play golf with his friend Dick Gibson (a 1941 winner of the amateur International Team Championship of the Pacific) at Bel-Air Country Club. He told Dixie he wouldn't be home for dinner; he and Gibson would dine out. That evening at the Brown Derby, at around nine o'clock, they finished a round of cocktails and prepared to order food. The maître d' told Bing he had a phone call, Johnny

Burke. In Bing's telling, Johnny said, "There's nothing to be concerned about, everybody's safe, Dixie is all right and the kids, but your house burned down." Bing considered this a sorry rib, "a very bald approach for a guy who's supposed to be as clever at ramming in the needle as he was," and told him so before hanging up. Burke called back: "No, honest to God." He said the fire was out, but a few hundred people had filled the street as firemen fought it for more than an hour. They had tried to find him earlier, but no one thought of Bel-Air so they called Lakeside and other haunts before locating him at the Brown Derby. Dixie and the boys, plus Pauline Weislow, Georgie Hardwicke, and two Crosby servants, were two doors down the street at the home of the actor and radio announcer Bill Goodwin along with his wife, Philippa, and their two children.[37]

Bing liked to say he told Burke that as long as everything was under control, he might as well eat dinner before driving out to see "the smoking ruins." The news accounts of the time have him rushing to his car and speeding to Camarillo. Yet the newspapers got much of the rest of the story wrong, so perhaps he really did eat dinner before ambling to his car. Certainly, his behavior at the scene amply confirmed his *que será, será* composure. The firefighting, involving four (possibly five) brigades, had finished an hour or so before he pulled to the curb, but firemen continued wading through rubble, looking for live embers. Bing, sporting a fedora and long sideburns he had grown for *Dixie,* surveyed the mess and walked straight to the door. Half the house and roof were gone, though the outer walls and spiral staircase held. He started climbing the stairs. A firefighter tried to stop him. Bing said, "I'll be right down, hold everything," and kept on. The assistant chief and a few men trailed after Bing as he mounted the landing, kicking aside shattered furniture and debris, and made his way to a bedroom closet that contained a cabinet for his shoes—heels on rails, toes in slots, most of them charred. He unhesitatingly lifted out an unscathed black-and-white sports shoe and extracted from it a tightly wound roll of bills—two thousand dollars that he'd won at the track. After pocketing the cash, he thanked the firemen and went to join his family.[38]

The fire had started after the boys went upstairs to their bedrooms and Dixie and Pauline had set about dismantling the dehydrated Christmas tree. According to Pauline, they began to unhook the ornaments and decided to light the tree one last time. "The next thing we knew the tree was on fire and that started the house on fire. I lost my dog in that fire. I'll never forget it." She had safely carried her cocker spaniel, Timmy, from the house, but he ran back in and died of asphyxiation at the top of the staircase.[39] The battalion chief, Joseph Roeder, traced the blaze to a short circuit in the wiring of the bulbs at the bottom of the tree. It set off sparks that, as a morning paper reported, "turned the tinder tree into a torch,"[40] quickly consuming the room.

Dixie and Pauline ran upstairs, got the kids and the servants, and hurried them out the door. Chief Roeder, with expert accuracy, estimated the structural damage at $250,000. Insurance covered much of that and some personal losses, which included Dixie's wardrobe, furs, and jewelry; paintings and a highly prized $1,800 (about $30,000 today) crystal chandelier; furniture designed by Duncan Phyfe, Chippendale, and Hepplewhite; Georgian, Regency, and Victorian antiques; a band of china musical monkeys made in eighteenth-century Meissen; the boys' clothing and playthings. Most of Bing's possessions in his draperied and redwood-paneled "trophy room" were lost—books; racing, golf, and show-business awards; dozens of pipes in a 150-pipe rack given him by his brother Larry; an extensive collection of jazz, classical, and popular records, including a nearly complete set of his own 278 discs, now a mountain of melted shellac. Of twenty rooms, only the kitchen, living room, and servants' quarters escaped the fire, and those were ruined by water and smoke.

During the worst of it, after the boys were settled with the Goodwins, Dixie, wearing dark glasses and a robe over her clothing, huddled with Pauline on the lawn and watched, surrounded by police and strangers drawn by an explosion when flames shot through the second-story skylight. Some thought it an enemy attack. Bing's brothers Larry (who lived nearby) and Bob rushed over. With the blaze extinguished, they made a few runs into the shell to salvage what they could, mostly Bing's wardrobe, dozens of soaking-wet suits that they piled on a neighboring porch.

Now they were together at the Goodwin ranch house, stunned, exhausted, glum. It was late and they gratefully accepted Bill and

Philippa's invitation to stay overnight. The four boys and the Crosby staff had been given rooms. Most of the adults sat in the dining area and listlessly discussed the fire and the damages, whether or not they ought to rebuild and, if not, where they ought to live. A neighbor, Dave Shelley, strode into the room and said, "Hi, Bing. What's new?" Everyone fell apart laughing. The tension evaporated; a jolt of energy was restored by the kind of jest Bing savored. He later recalled, "Somebody got out a bottle of beer, we had a meal, and assumed a 'so what, it was only a house' attitude."[41] Shelley's feigned obliviousness endeared him to Bing, who regarded him as a natural wit and professional loafer. As the stepson of Buddy DeSylva, the silent backer and third-part owner of Capitol Records, Dave briefly held a few administrative titles at that company, though no one remembered him working. He drank prodigiously and maintained a chipper attitude while awaiting an inheritance that would obviate the need for even a pretense of working. Bing thought Shelley so funny he hired him as a guest on *KMH* in 1944, introducing him to listeners as a representative of the backbone of America, the small businessman. They did an eight-minute sketch with Shelley playing a song plugger who tries to convince Bing to record one of his songs, carrying an inside joke about as far as it could go.

The day after the fire, the family and Pauline moved into the Beverly Hills Hotel. Bing consulted real estate agents and other advisers and decided against rebuilding. Within ten days of the fire, he sold the property for $15,271 and put down an initial investment of $300,000 for a very different kind of estate in Holmby Hills, opposite the Los Angeles Country Club, just off the fourteenth fairway. He anticipated becoming a club member but confronted class lines that not even "Uncle Sam Without Whiskers" could cross. Expecting to move in in a few weeks, after installing essential furnishings, they briefly lived in an unoccupied home loaned to them by Marion Davies. Dixie's friends held a shower in Dolores Hope's home to help replenish her wardrobe. Over the years, Dixie had given Kitty Sexton, the godmother of her children, photographs of the boys, from their births through birthdays, all lost in the fire. "I'm going to burst into tears when I tell you this," Jean Stevens recalled when speaking of the shower to an interviewer, "but Kitty came through, giving all these pictures back to her. That was a heartbreaking thing." In the middle of the party, Dolores Hope, "who loves everybody and looks out for everybody," realized "here we were buying all these expensive things for Dixie, and Pauline is sitting there and her clothes burned up too. And somehow, Dolores rushed out or sent someone out, I don't know how she managed, but suddenly a box appeared from all of us for Pauline. Done so gracefully and cleverly. I was impressed."[42] Days later, Pauline returned to Chicago. "Pauline has been gone a couple weeks now and we all miss her very much," Bing wrote to her husband, Saul, stationed in San Francisco with the 424th Bomber Squadron. "She was a great help to us in our hour of travail and a tremendous favorite with the kids."[43]

Fans mailed him countless pipes to replace his rack, everything from corncobs to an expensive Dunhill. Bing set about restoring his record collection. Jack Kapp sent him everything he had in stock and ordered pressings of discontinued Deccas from the original masters. Milt Gabler, the proprietor of New York's Commodore Music Shop and later a producer for Bing and other Decca artists, mailed a gift of a hundred and fifty jazz discs. Louis Armstrong sent him a set of his own recordings. Unfortunately, Bing could not replace the transcription discs of his radio shows, made to order for him each week by NBC's radio-recording division. They were the only copies of those uncut hour-long *KMH* broadcasts ever made.[44]

On January 26 Bing made a long-planned guest appearance on Bob Hope's radio show. "What's cookin'?" Hope greeted him. Bing went off script: "A fine thing to ask a guy whose house has just burned down!"

In later years, the fire fanned malicious rumors: Dixie, drunk, accidentally started it, or Dixie, furious with Bing, deliberately started it. The gossip intensified after the war as the troubled Crosby marriage made occasional headlines, ultimately instigating a shameless film à clef, *Smash-Up: The Story of a Woman* (1947), a reverse *Star Is Born* (the wife gives up her career to make a star of her husband, whose coldness and infidelity drive her to drink and arson) with pretensions to *The Lost Weekend*. Pauline Weislow's testimony seems reliable, however; she did not recall Dixie expressing anger at Bing or anyone else, though she did remember Dixie occasionally berating herself over her addiction. The immediate postmortems proved surprisingly free of irony. Crosby—the voice of "White Christmas," which he introduced in front of a perfect pine tree in *Holiday Inn*—undone by a Christmas tree! Perhaps it was too obvious a point to belabor, though when did newspapers spurn the obvious?

Other ironies could not be known to the public. A few years earlier, the Fire-Gard Corporation of San Francisco submitted for patent a small (eight inches high) waterless fire extinguisher, provisionally called the Model X. The company sent a representative to the Crosby home to do a survey. He found the basement hazardous owing to a congestion of heaters that dried out the wood ceiling; a fire "might easily burn through the floor above long before any warning was given." He recommended, for "absolute protection," that Bing hang sixteen Model X units ($3.25 each), which, when brought to a certain temperature, flipped upside down like bats and released carbon tetrachloride. Bing installed fifty-four units. The receipt promised "great security to the remainder of the house."[45]

Paramount Pictures did not want people talking about the plot of the film Bing completed shortly after the fire—not at that point, anyway. Instead, the publicity department turned out reams of guff about the alleged high jinks on the set of *Dixie,* a picture that derives some of its humor and most of its plot from accidental fires—three of them. Bing's fictionalized Dan Emmett ignites two through carelessness, as he habitually leaves his lit pipe in flammable places. The first fire destroys the home of his fiancée (Marjorie Reynolds) and the second is in the theater where he enjoys a big opening night. The third fire, also in a theater, is caused when his other lover (Dorothy Lamour) burns but fails to completely douse a letter from the fiancée, starting a backstage blaze that forces Emmett to nervously step up the tempo of his lethal dirge "Dixie," going faster and faster as the fire is put out, until the audience members throw caution to the wind to sing along, thereby baptizing the Confederacy's anthem and ensuring a box-office windfall below the Mason-Dixon.

13

DIVERTISSEMENT

"Timberry won't be long," said Mr. Crummles. "He played the audience out tonight. He does a faithful black in the last piece, and it takes him a little longer to wash himself."

"A very unpleasant line of character, I should think?" said Nicholas.

"No, I don't know," replied Mr. Crummles; "it comes off easily enough, and there's only the face and neck. We had a first-tragedy man in our company once, who, when he played Othello, used to black himself all over. But that's feeling a part and going into it as if you meant it; it isn't usual; more's the pity."

—Charles Dickens, *Nicholas Nickleby* (1839)

Dixie opens with a lovely tableau, a master shot prudently posed and painted in saturated three-strip Technicolor. It's an unusual way to begin a film: An amorous ballad—Johnny Burke and Jimmy Van Heusen's "Sunday, Monday, or Always"—augurs a strained separation between Bing as the fabled minstrel man Dan Emmett and Marjorie Reynolds as his fiancée. The song, a meditation on long-distance ardor ("Oh, won't you tell me when / We will meet again / Sunday, Monday, or always"), struck a chord with the public, securing Bing his sixth gold record in spite of the American Federation of Musicians' recording ban, which Decca circumvented by limiting his accompaniment to a vocal choir. The film's director, Edward Sutherland, who steered Bing through two 1930s films, *Too Much Harmony* and *Mississippi*, was so pleased with the song and the shot, framed by the master cinematographer William C. Mellor, that he edited it merely to insert close-ups of Crosby, Reynolds, and a dog.

Reynolds resembles an inverted snow cone topped with a green hat, the white hoop of her skirt spreading into a mound that fills the lower-left quadrant of the screen. Crosby, just right of center, sings leaning against a tree with low-hanging leafy branches that frame the actors in an oval, their verdant richness matching that of the grassy ground. The sky is dark periwinkle, a tone complemented by Bing's silk tie and baby blues, with white near-luminescent streaks of brushstroke clouds. The only touch of red is Marjorie's lipstick. A river runs between sky and greenery. As the actors adhere as much as possible to the tableau vivant, the rippling water and leaves provide most of the movement. This opening song lasts seventy-eight seconds. Alas, the picture has eighty-five minutes to go.

Dixie is Crosby's most controversial picture today, rarely seen since the 1970s. Its historical interest, which now exceeds its entertainment value, is twofold. First, unlike most depictions of blackface in the movies, where the makeup is contained in a manner popularized by Al Jolson (black greasepaint, white mouth, short nappy wig), *Dixie* re-creates the true antebellum style with its monstrously ludicrous excesses, including an enormous tricornered wig. Second, the picture's box-office success reminds us that the affection for blackface minstrelsy held fast into the 1940s. The fact that its precision in costuming and makeup makes *Dixie* particularly objectionable today is an irony Paramount would not have appreciated. The studio's historical work did not end when it cut a deal for William Rankin's story and research. Paramount collated materials for over a year, from June 1942, four months before filming began, when Rankin signed on as consultant, to July 1943, a month *after* the picture opened, to prepare for press inquiries. The studio amassed a small library: volumes about Dan Emmett, white minstrels, black minstrels, the French Quarter in New Orleans, the Bowery, Ohio, entertainment and songwriting practices of 1830 to 1860, U.S. presidents of 1840 to 1850, apparel of 1840 to 1860; copies of *Harper's Weekly, Harper's Bazaar,* and *Punch*; Currier and Ives prints, drawings of Louisville houses, blueprints of docks, streets, theaters, bakeries; monographs on fire departments, the navigability of the Ohio River, the origin of friction matches, boiler rooms on paddle steamers, and the "general atmosphere of the period."[1]

This digging had little effect on the plot. Several hands worked on the script,[2] which was leavened with gags by Bing's comedy writers, chiefly the professional kibitzer Barney Dean, the only "writer" who attended the set every day. The result meshed reliable formulas from movies past, notably *Swing Time* and *Mississippi*: Dan Emmett, having inadvertently burned down his sweetheart's house, must leave town and earn a living before he can marry her. He falls in love with another woman only to discover that the gal he left behind has caught "the paralyzing sickness" and awaits him in a wheelchair. The opening song instantly disabuses us of the notion that Bing's Dan Emmett accurately portrays the Ohioan entertainer who innovated group minstrelsy on New York's Bowery, composing or adapting such national evergreens as "Old Dan Tucker," "Turkey in the Straw," "The Old Gray Mare," "The Blue Tail Fly," and "Dixie"—original title: "I Wish I Were in Dixie's Land."

By fluke or deliberately, *Dixie* is one of Crosby's more autobiographical pictures—in the enveloping title (Dan Emmett spends years working on the song "Dixie" until an accidental fire forces him to get it right); the withdrawn Southern gal trumping her Northern extrovert rival; the guilt-induced resolution of the romantic triangle; the theme of minstrelsy as vocation and longing; the melding of past and present; the triumph of the American style emerging from a black mask.

Dan Emmett, who died in 1904 at the age of eighty-eight, did not write or croon love songs in the manner of "Sunday, Monday, or Always," but he was an imposing figure and not entirely unlike Bing: a Yankee of Irish descent who championed cultural exchange with blacks and ridiculed class distinctions and pomposity. The marketing of *Dixie* triggered inquiries into the origin of his most celebrated song. Emmett wrote the lyrics to a melody he had learned in childhood, probably from his black neighbors the Snowden brothers, Ben and Lew, members of a family band. While appearing in Bryant's Minstrels in 1859, he introduced the melody as a banjo specialty.[3] Emmett bitterly resented the song's surprising success. In 1861, he vented his dismay to colleagues at a social gathering. A guest remarked on all the evenings he heard Confederate bands play "Dixie," which "they seemed to have adopted [as] their national air." Emmett "warmly" replied, "Yes: and if I had known to what use they were going to put my song, I will be damned if I'd have written it!"[4] An expert fifer, he exacted a modest revenge by writing the fife manual for the Union Army. Yet more than any other ante-bellum Northerner, Emmett devised and disseminated the rituals of minstrelsy and its egregious caricatures.

Since the 1960s, discussions of blackface minstrelsy have been dom-inated by two biases. The first is apologetic but unrepentant: It had become an American show-business tradition, practiced by black as well as white performers, divorced by time from the early racial dis-paragement so that the stereotyped characters represented human rather than ethnic manners, on the order of commedia dell'arte. "Man is least himself when he talks in his own person. Give him a mask," Oscar Wilde remarked, "and he will tell you the truth." The ingenious Bahamian American blackface comedian Bert Williams added to this dictum the echo of hard experience: "A black face, run-down shoes, and elbow-out make-up give me a place to hide. The real Bert Williams is crouched deep down inside the coon who sings the songs and tells the stories." Bob Hope, who also spoke from experi-ence, recalled how blacking up helped inexperienced performers overcome stage jitters by allowing them to hide behind its anonym-ity.[5] The second is unforgiving: Racism abides in the grotesquerie, and anyone who doubts its malice is invited to imagine a comical theater made up of false-nosed Hebrews or mustachioed Italian organ-grinders or pigtailed, opium-addicted Chinamen or pugna-ciously drunk Irishmen or miserly Scotchmen or grunting Indians or lazy Latinos or thieving Arabs or flighty women—all of which were quite familiar to minstrel and vaudeville audiences. Blackface endured after the other travesties faded. Even after blackface faded, the stereotypes remained, as African American actors played happy maids, obsequious porters, and genial imbeciles well into midcen-tury. If William Faulkner's fictional Colonel Sartoris "fathered the edict that no Negro woman should appear on the streets without an apron," Hollywood gave that decree the imprimatur of cultural law.[6]

Any discussion of minstrelsy that focuses on racial effrontery without acknowledging the enormous pleasure it gave to generations of Americans, blacks as well as whites, abolitionists as well as slave-holders, immigrants as well as natives, ignores the truth of its hold on the American imagination. Before the Civil War, countless Northern whites learned of "Negro life" by watching white men (always men) in lint wigs and overemphatic masks created by rubbing paste made of burnt cork and water onto the face, neck, wrists, and other exposed parts. After the war, black minstrel troupes rivaled and often bested the white ones by adapting the same format—costumes, makeup, songs, jokes—and adding the implicit promise of "authenticity." Blackface liberated an alter ego that was willing to be made fun of and to make fun of everything and everybody. Black vaudevillians continued to wear cork in the 1940s; for them and their audiences, it had historical and sentimental resonance, marking the passage from segregated circuits to the mainstream.

One striking example is *Stormy Weather*, the popular all-black musical film that opened a month after *Dixie*. Its scenario hangs on a slapdash survey of African American entertainment in the quarter century between 1918 (when the legendary bandleader James Reese Europe returned from the war) and a present-day show produced by the central male character, played by the equally legendary sixty-five-year-old Bill "Bojangles" Robinson and featuring Lena Horne, Cab Calloway, and the Nicholas Brothers. The film's token villain is portrayed as a product of the bad old days, a producer who costumes actors in African drag, Tarzan-style. Yet the only blackface routine in the picture is part of Robinson's modern-day show: the much imitated "indefinite talk" routine introduced by Miller and Lyles in 1910, here re-created by Flournoy Miller himself and Johnny Lee as the late Aubrey Lyles. They are introduced backstage as they are rubbing in the burnt cork. Every black filmgoer of a certain age knew Miller and Lyles's deathless routine.[7]

The summer of *Dixie* and *Stormy Weather* was the summer of the bloodiest race riots of the 1940s. The grip of Jim Crow was such that in order to maintain his Southern coalition, Roosevelt declined to tackle anti-lynch legislation or the miscegenation laws that outlasted those enacted by the Third Reich. His internment camps did nothing to quell epidemic xenophobia, which erupted that June in nightstick attacks on Latinos in the Los Angeles Zoot Suit Riots.

(The city's Mayor Bowron blamed the billy-clubbing on modishly dressed "juvenile delinquents," insisting that racism did not enter into it. Mrs. Roosevelt argued that racism was a factor. The *Los Angeles Times* called Mrs. Roosevelt a Communist.) The summer of 1943 also saw rioting in Detroit (the bloodiest of all, ignited when whites barred blacks from public housing); Beaumont, Texas; and Harlem. No one publicly ruminated on the juxtaposition of two articles in a July issue of *Life,* one hailing the opening of *Dixie,* another documenting the savagery in Detroit. Minstrelsy was said to offer continuity and heritage.[8]

Minstrelsy flourished in Hollywood, its acceptance too wide to generate criticism, never mind indignation. Between 1940 and 1946, Hollywood released more than sixty features and short films with at least one blackface routine, either a full-dress minstrel number or a mistaken-identity bit (soot on a white face betokens racial mutability). This was more than in the 1930s, when Jolson and Cantor heated up the box office. A fifth of these pictures, ranging from matinee Westerns to shorts by Our Gang and the Three Stooges, were directed chiefly at children. This does not include a raft of animations (Looney Tunes, *Dumbo*) with blackface gags or the dozens of films in which white actors portray American Indians, Asian detectives, and other persons of color.[9] After the debut of *Dixie,* the liberal *New York Post*'s Archer Winsten, who liked the movie (reviews were overwhelmingly positive), registered a rare complaint against minstrelsy as old-fashioned: "The minstrel show and its burnt cork humor are an outmoded form of entertainment. Improve it how you will, dress it up in the finest clothing, color and production, it still creaks."[10] Yet its popularity peaked *after* the war, when the return of eight million troops influenced the national taste. *The Jolson Story* (which opened in October 1946) ranked as the number one musical and number three film of 1947; the two top-grossing pictures of 1949 were *Jolson Sings Again* and *Pinky,* in which Jeanne Crain plays a black woman passing for white.

When Walter White and Wendell Willkie had met the reluctant studio moguls in 1942, the topic of minstrelsy wasn't even broached. If whites wanted to pretend they were black, let them. Blacks wanted to go beyond playing servants and idiots and demanded opportunities before and behind the camera. Bing understood this.

His apprenticeship had drawn its energy from integrated jam sessions, something he proudly recollected in later years: "Back then, there was a color line almost everywhere else, but not at those sessions. You could hear Bix and Louis Armstrong and Willie 'The Lion' Smith all mixed together. The jazz scene was way ahead of the rest of the country."[11] He fractured radio's color barrier, performing on air with black artists; put his money where his sentiments lay in defending the Scottsboro Boys; used his clout to give star billing to Armstrong in *Pennies from Heaven* (1936); presided over the first picture in which whites ask blacks for musical tutoring, *Birth of the Blues* (1941); aligned with Paul Robeson in popularizing the subsequently Red-baited *Ballad for Americans*. He represented a casual righteousness on the subject, never political or self-promoting, not as outspoken or vehement as he might have been, yet nonetheless forceful in what he did and did not do.

When he brought Armstrong to *Kraft Music Hall* in January 1938, the *Pittsburgh Courier*'s Sallye Bell editorialized her intention to start the year right by giving credit where it was due, beginning with Crosby "for his manner toward Louis (Satchmo) Armstrong.... If you heard the broadcast, you will recall that when Bing introduced Louis—rather when he announced him, for who needs an introduction to Ol' Satchmo?—there was not even the slightest shade of a difference in his manner as compared to when he announced Connie Boswell and the other guest artists." She noted Bing had called Armstrong the greatest trumpet player in the world (not the greatest colored trumpet player) and urged her readers to write to stations to encourage them to present "more of our Negro stars on these major programs."[12] In the weeks Bing filmed *Dixie*, he brought the Charioteers to *KMH* for what became the second-longest run (after Eddie "Rochester" Anderson's work on the Jack Benny show) by a Negro act on a "major" program in radio history.

Yet Crosby was a man of his time. Lena Horne recalled his live-and-let-live tolerance and how admired he was in Harlem before and after the war, but she also remembered his exasperation when, in 1947, she married his erstwhile accompanist and arranger Lennie Hayton. Hayton told her Bing tried to talk him out of it—interracial marriage was a bridge too far.[13] As for minstrelsy and blackface, they had been part of his life from the summer job

he took in a Spokane theater to watch Al Jolson play the black porter in *Sinbad* to the musicales staged at Gonzaga University to
Mack Sennett's "Dream House" to the Midgie Minstrels presented
in his backyard to *Holiday Inn, Dixie,* and, still to come, *Here Come
the Waves* (1944). This last film represents his final public bow in
cork, but early in 1946, he and several other Los Angeles members
of the Bohemian Club put on a minstrel show in its San Francisco
clubhouse. According to Bing's attorney John O'Melveny, the highlight was an astonishing blackface quartet made up of Crosby, John
Charles Thomas, Lauritz Melchior, and Dennis Day; during the
solo portion, Bing stole the show with "Swanee River."[14]

Unlike the old minstrels, those mentors who brightened his youth,
Crosby did not find an alter ego in blackface. Jolson is never more
galvanized than when blacked up; blackface releases Cantor's libido
as a wildly effeminate provocateur. But it hamstrings Crosby, restrain-
ing his natural charm—the alteration, no matter how much he cherished the idiom, is no deeper than the cork or his faux-Southern
diction. His one discernible model is the comical-gloomy Bert Williams of "Nobody" and similar numbers: sad of eye, put-upon,
bemused. Bing's musical innovations stemmed from his openness to
all he heard—Jolson's Broadway yawp and Armstrong's sublime
swing and John McCormack's nostalgic ballads. Those influences
and more melded in the style that individualized him. After the war,
such foundations became increasingly important to him. He regularly
booked Jolson and Armstrong (whom he alone called Lou) on his
radio show, though never for the same broadcast, using them as an
incentive to switch from one mode to the other, enjoying them equally.

Nothing is certain in movies, but everyone involved with *Dixie*
expected it to be, in the words of *Variety,* a "Technicolorful money-
getter, ideal for the summer [box office]."[15] *Dixie* fit perfectly into
Bing's recent career strategy. The consummate troubadour must domi-
nate the past as well as the present. This shrewd policy, developed over
several years, originally riled Bing, but he had long since come to
regard the rearview vista of Americana as a haven. Jack Kapp started
it by luring him away from jazz and the elitism of urban sophisticates,
remaking him as the everyman singer, a nonpareil conservator of
songs in the public domain. His picture career took a parallel path.

During the previous five years, he and Bob Hope radiated up-to-date impudence with their surreal road riffs set in mock locales. His other movies took him back in time to vaudeville in *The Star Maker* and *If I Had My Way,* the first stirrings of white jazz in *Birth of the Blues,* and the historical salutations of *Holiday Inn.* That alternation of irreverent comedy and unabashed nostalgia kept him on top while his contemporaries in movie musicals foundered or abandoned the idiom for dramatic roles. A new cycle of performers (Gene Kelly, Judy Garland, Frank Sinatra, Danny Kaye) pushed most of them aside; even Astaire stumbled in his pursuit of new partners and periodically announced his retirement. Yet Bing survived his predecessors, contemporaries, and others much younger than he, a roster that included Paramount's Maurice Chevalier, Mae West, and Marlene Dietrich, Warner's Al Jolson, Dick Powell, and Ruby Keeler, MGM's Eleanor Powell, Nelson Eddy, and Jeanette MacDonald, Fox's Alice Faye and Shirley Temple, Universal's Deanna Durbin, Goldwyn's Eddie Cantor, RKO's Ginger Rogers. They all moved onward or out. Crosby's best years as a musical star lay ahead.

Dixie seemed a natural after his Stephen Foster recordings; indeed, Sutherland had hoped to have him play Foster in 1937, but script problems delayed the production, and the release of *Swanee River* (1939, with Don Ameche as Foster and Jolson as E. P. Christy) scuttled the project.[16] Emmett was a logical second choice. Jolson's vainglorious style made audiences forget the cooler approach of minstrel men like Eddie Leonard and Bobby Newcomb, who, at thirteen, toured with the troupe that introduced "Dixie" to New Orleans in 1860. Newcomb wrote a pamphlet for novice minstrels in 1882, part of which reads like a harbinger of Crosby: "A man adopting the song and dance line should be of medium stature, clean cut limbs and good figure. [His] entrance upon the stage should be made with an easy kind of walk to the tune of the introductory music. Upon arranging himself before the footlights for the song, [he should not] assume a stereotyped attitude, but stand easy and graceful. Don't use the hands unless necessary...[sing] with as little exertion as possible."[17]

Bing tailored Dan Emmett to his persona as easily as he had with other characters, making him shyly amorous, resourceful, charming, absentminded—in this instance, with the result of unwittingly starting fires. A reviewer, recalling serial infernos in

Paramount's earlier color film *The Forest Rangers,* wondered if the characters' pyromania was the studio's way of showing skill with Technicolor. In truth, theater fires were a widely noted hazard in the nineteenth century; there were more than three dozen in New York City alone.[18] *Dixie* also fit in with Paramount's web of theater chains. Each of the five major studios (Paramount, MGM, Warner Brothers, Twentieth Century–Fox, and RKO) owned theaters in key markets, a decisive element in the monopolistic practice of vertical integration, which would eventually lead to the 1948 antitrust decision that doomed the studio system. Paramount controlled the largest number of theaters, particularly in the South, where it owned 1,450 outright and held interests in hundreds more. In 1926, it bought into the Wilby-Kincey syndicate, with over a hundred theaters concentrated in Alabama, Georgia, North Carolina, and South Carolina. It soon added other Southern holdings. Paramount could safely project a guaranteed audience for *Dixie.* After the June 23 New York premiere, the studio announced its strategy: "Flag-waving 4th of July Premieres in 20 Southern keys."[19]

Bing's participation proved lucrative, despite his missed hours in the first days of shooting, netting him more than $11,000 in overtime, beyond his per-picture rate—more than half the entire cast budget. Dorothy Lamour, who shared top billing with him, received $46,667; the comedians filling out the quartet of the Virginia Minstrels and their boardinghouse landlord (blustery Ray Walburn) earned between $10,000 and $15,000; Marjorie Reynolds received only $3,500. Though scheduled to wrap in early December, filming continued into 1943, with several instrumentals and choral numbers recorded as late as April, bringing the final budget to nearly $1.5 million. Bing worked himself into the role by following a strict diet. At first, he looked heavy and disconnected; as the shooting progressed, he grew trim and his performance more compelling.

As ever, Luigi Luraschi had to appease the censors. Despite the five-alarm blazes in theaters, industry policy prohibited any character in a movie crying, "Fire!" A scene involving a porcelain bedpan had to be cut. The blackface act had the line "You is a dumb black slob," which prompted a request: "I wonder if we could [drop] the use of the word black which used in this fashion by white people in make-up will be offensive to Negroes." The phrase "damned Yan-

kees" had to go, as did a farmer's daughter joke.[20] Joe Breen could
have saved the studio a headache had he been more sensitive to the
word *darkie*. As happened with *Holiday Inn*, the black press did not
protest the blackface routines, but they did take umbrage at that
"obnoxious" word, for which Paramount executives apologized while
noting that the film was a period piece and that *they* thought the
term one of "endearment and patronage."[21]

Dixie's problems exceed the unabashed re-creations of minstrelsy. The drama is slim and overwrought, the comedy fey and
self-important. It merrily revises history, reinventing Emmett's Virginia Minstrels, which, in their 1843 Bowery debut, introduced the
first group minstrel show (as opposed to blackface soloists and specialty acts). Other than Emmett, the original quartet consisted of
Dick Pelham, a New York dancer, singer, and tambourine player,
called Mr. Felham in *Dixie*, played by Eddie Foy Jr.; Billy Whitlock,
a New Yorker who got his start playing banjo in blackface in P. T.
Barnum's circuses, called Mr. Whitlock in *Dixie*, played by Lynne
Overman; and Emmett's first partner, Francis Brower of Baltimore,
who said he learned dance routines directly from blacks and established the castanet-like bones as a ritual instrument in minstrelsy.
In *Dixie*, he is called Mr. Bones, though the bones were eliminated,
as Billy De Wolfe could not get the hang of them. Crosby himself
devised the scene in which the Virginia Minstrels illustrate the
origin of the term *ham* to denote an actor; the quartet is shown
using the fat from a large ham to wipe off the cork.[22]

A genuinely moving moment in *Dixie* mirrors Crosby's stressful
life at home. Finding his fiancée stricken by polio, Dan puts aside
his intention to end their engagement and marries her. Filmgoers
could not know that Bing had asked his wife for a divorce and
changed his mind after acknowledging her alcoholism, but they
could hardly fail to be moved by the candor, guilt, and resolve with
which he played the scene. Yet one looks in vain for a 1943 newspaper or magazine story that exploits the punning potential of Dixie,
"Dixie," and *Dixie*.

A conceit running throughout wartime minstrel pictures is that
blackface is somehow inadvertent and only incidentally racial—a
convenience for overcoming obstacles. In *Holiday Inn*, blackface

conceals Reynolds from the talent-poaching Fred Astaire. In *Dixie,* the cork is applied to cover a couple of black eyes. African Americans do not figure in the birth of minstrelsy beyond an obligatory transference scene: as a Negro choir sings "Swing Low, Sweet Chariot" (stylishly arranged by Joe Lilley), Dan Emmett sings along as only Crosby can. The black folk gaze up at him in awe. The cultural historian Susan Gubar has described such customary tropes as "white people's efforts to repeat, rationalize, camouflage, confess, or repair the grievous injury inflicted on blacks." *Dixie* takes it another step, arguing for the minstrel show as an enduring source of pride. When Southern aristocrats protest its lack of dignity, Crosby's Emmett (much like his character in *Birth of the Blues*) responds that "our type of entertainment" is for everyone. A *New York Daily News* critic accordingly praised the picture for honoring "the only form of entertainment that might be called truly American."[23]

In *Dixie,* each aspect of minstrelsy is forged as a pragmatic necessity. Emmett wants only to sing and dance, but when he plummets into the orchestra pit (cue Harry Barris's customary walk-on), he saves the act by improvising a humorous dialect. Thus the end men are born. To drum up an audience, they invent the minstrel march and cakewalk. The landlord volunteers to act as an emcee — "Gentlemen," Mr. Interlocutor commands as if he had just thought of it, "be seated!" "Dixie" becomes the South's anthem because the theater is on fire and Emmett rushes the tempo, inciting the audience to sing along. They do — yee-hawing and tossing their hats in the air — as the camera zooms in for a closing shot of Dorothy Lamour, tears glistening, singing "Dixie" as though she were Yvonne leading "La Marseillaise" in *Casablanca.*

Indeed, the debut of *Casablanca* in January may explain why *Dixie's* score was revised as late as April. *Dixie* initially ended with a triumphant caroling of "Dixie" dissolving into a montage made up of stock shots and miniatures: the firing on Fort Sumter with "Dixie" on the soundtrack; Confederate soldiers marching while singing "Dixie"; soldiers at Bull Run charging while singing "Dixie"; a devastated countryside as Rebel soldiers "drag themselves homeward" to a dirge-like arrangement of "Dixie"; the White House steps where President Lincoln tells the band to play "Dixie."[24] But you cannot end a wartime picture with defeat, especially when the target audience is the defeated. *Dixie,* like *Casablanca,* ends with triumph and tears, signifying duty, resourcefulness, and sacrifice.

Coming after *Road to Morocco* and *Holiday Inn* and preceding *Going My Way* and *The Bells of St. Mary's* (and given its long banishment from the airwaves and home video), *Dixie* is often remembered as a flop. It was nothing of the kind, selling nearly twenty-three million tickets, grossing ten times as much as *Birth of the Blues.* "They're celebrating down on the Paramount plantation," the *Hollywood Reporter* wryly noted, "by minting juleps—and money."[25] For three months after the film rolled out, *Variety* tracked its progress with a seemingly limitless thesaurus to indicate "fat" business; it broke records in Cincinnati and Pittsburgh and proved "socko" in Indianapolis, "wham" in Providence, "plenty nifty" in Detroit, "big" in Buffalo, "sturdy" in Washington, "a sweet grosser" in L.A., "a wow" in Baltimore, "a smash" in Chicago, "torrid" in Seattle, "boffo" in Montreal, and "crack" in Portland while continuing to "pack 'em in" at theaters in New York. It ranks among the twelve most successful pictures in Crosby's filmography, nine of which were released between 1942 and 1947 and three in the 1950s. Pictures of Bing in polychrome minstrel regalia adorned magazine covers and sheet music, not least *Bing Crosby's Minstrel Song Folio,* filled with songs, jokes, and movie stills. He wore a coral-colored Uncle Sam hat decorated with high blue bow; a flying winged collar; and a striped satin swallowtail jacket with exaggerated lapels, often posing with a banjo, though never in blackface. Few male stars displaced beauty queens on the covers of fan magazines, but Bing did. *Dixie* opened in June, and Paramount's most profitable and prestigious release (in fact, the top-grossing picture of the year), *For Whom the Bell Tolls,* starring Gary Cooper and Ingrid Bergman, followed in July, yet *Screen Romance's* August cover allocated the latter a teaser line atop an otherwise full-bleed cover portrait of minstrel Crosby.

Meanwhile, the recording industry had its own Little Caesar gunning for it. If Jack Kapp had pressed James Petrillo's head in a shellac stamper, he would have sold a lot of copies. The recording ban had been on a year, and hardly anyone foresaw its long-term damage—the vanishing swatch of cultural history; the hastened passing of the big bands; the veiled advance of a music called modern jazz or bebop; the new songs that withered on the vine and the old singers who lost momentum. For the American Federation of Musicians, it backfired. Before the strike, most bestselling recording artists were orchestra leaders who featured singers; the dominant recording stars after the strike were singers who rarely identified their accompanists. Far from helping musicians, Petrillo's strikes (two shorter ones followed before the decade ended) sped their demise as the prevailing force in popular music. The record labels, recently returned from the dead, hibernated in impotent fury. Capitol Records and small labels without sustaining catalogs capitulated to the AFM, but the majors stood firm. Kapp was in a bind, his stockpile depleted, his great plans thwarted. *Dixie* premiered June 23 in New York and opened wide a week later. Everyone believed it had a potential hit in "Sunday, Monday, or Always," and he couldn't get a record out.

His biggest frustration, however, concerned a project that would be remembered as one of his greatest innovations. A new musical with the unlikely title *Oklahoma!*, the first collaboration by Richard Rodgers and Oscar Hammerstein II, burst like fireworks on Broadway. Instead of cherry-picking the best songs, assigning them to various artists—one version for the swing fans, another for the mainstream, one by this singer, another by that one—and hoping that a Decca cover or two would draw lightning, Kapp licensed the recording rights to the show itself, an unheard-of proposition in the United States. He would create an album of 78s that reproduced the score of a high-ticket New York attraction, employing the Broadway cast, chorus, orchestra, and conductor to perform the songs in their original (if necessarily abbreviated) arrangements. Yet he could not move forward; pit musicians would not cross Petrillo's picket line.

The U.S. military also resented the shutdown, as the stream of morale-boosting platters ebbed. Lieutenant Robert Vincent, an audio engineer in Special Services, devised a program to sidestep the strike, and the army allocated a million dollars to fund it. Thus was born the V-Disc, for which the most popular recording artists in the country waived fees and royalties, occasionally presenting unique ensembles and performances (often taken from rehearsals) and spoken introductions. The twelve-inch Vinylite "victory" discs played twice as long as ten-inch commercial discs, so that two and even three tracks could be banded on a side.[26] Petrillo approved the plan with the proviso that only military personnel could get access to them; the recording companies agreed once they were assured that V-Discs would be destroyed as army surplus after the war (a devastation carried out with brutal but, fortunately, not total efficiency). The first overseas shipment of 53,400 discs left RCA's Camden plant on October 1, 1943; some eight million followed before the program stopped in 1949. Crosby recorded about a hundred V-Disc titles, usually edited from radio broadcasts or dress rehearsals, including a few sing-along medleys, producing fifty-two discs.[27]

Without the army behind him, Kapp moved cautiously but decisively, with Crosby as his point man. Bing enrolled as a dues-paying member of Local 47, the Los Angeles musicians' union, as a drummer (vocalists did not pay dues to the AFM) and requested permission to record the two new songs from *Dixie* without using instrumentalists. Petrillo agreed on the condition that he not play drums. On July 2, ten days after *Dixie*'s debut, Kapp recorded Crosby for the first time in a year, backed by the Ken Darby Singers. After an introduction in which the a cappella choir sang the days of the week, Bing intoned "Sunday, Monday or Always"[28] with care and confidence in a nicely gauged but hardly inspired rendering, engorged by Darby's overripe arrangement. He proved less effective on the lackluster "If You Please." Implored by the Darby voices to "Sing a little song about it, Bing, if you please," he was merely obedient. It didn't matter.

Rushed to market, the disc took off like gangbusters, leaping to the top of the sales charts and parking there for two months. The welcome return of Bing's dulcet baritone and the unusual arrangements lifted "If You Please" into the top ten along with the million-selling A-side. Petrillo might have shrugged that one off. Then Frank Sinatra rather shamelessly recorded the same two songs in the same kind of arrangements, and his disc sold almost as well. And then Kapp recorded Dick Haymes in a voices-only version of "You'll Never Know" and reaped another gold record. Petrillo asked singers not to record anymore lest they incur the wrath of his musicians when they resumed work. The singers agreed to desist, but not before another pair of discs slipped into the commercial stream. In late August, forced to wait for *Oklahoma!*, Kapp had Bing warble its most acclaimed songs, "People Will Say We're in Love" and "Oh, What a Beautiful Mornin'," as duets with Trudy Erwin, backed by the maladroit Sportsmen Glee Club. Everything went wrong. Bing and Trudy connected charmingly on radio but were miles apart here, the lack of chemistry underscored by stubbornly lethargic tempos and indifferent interpretations. Again, Sinatra recorded the same songs the same way. Again, with Crosby slightly edging Sinatra, both sides of both discs ranked high on *Variety*'s jukebox chart (a dubious poll based on reports from "operators") and *Billboard*'s sales charts. Bing was not impressed. In his chatty reply to a soldier stationed in the South Pacific, he wrote that he was pleased if "the boys get some kick" from "my not very inspirational bleatings," but as the recording ban obliged him to make a few sides with vocal accompaniment, he cautioned: "They are not too good, as you can imagine."[29]

Rodgers and Hammerstein survived. Kapp's sovereignty did not. Within two weeks, Jack made his separate peace with Petrillo, agreeing to pay the AFM relief fund a quarter of a cent on each thirty-five-cent record, more for higher-priced discs. He was now in a rare mood, relieved, psyched, and beneficent. The other record labels would hold out for another year; Kapp got back to work. He asked Bing to his office and shocked him by solemnly explaining that he wanted to tear up their contract. Nearly speechless for once, Bing said, "If that's the way you want it, Jack." Jack tore it in half and brought out a new one to sign, this version with a ten-year guarantee at an improved royalty rate. A report Decca prepared on artist payouts for the Securities and Exchange Commission fully justified corporate largesse. Bing's 1942 royalties came to $298,946. Decca's second- and third-place earners that year, Jimmy Dorsey and the Andrews Sisters, earned $79,302 and $48,306. No one else broke $34,000.[30] Kapp now scheduled sessions to record *Oklahoma!*—a triumph that changed forever the relationship between recordings and theater. For Bing's return to "real" recording, Kapp planned to reunite him with the Andrews Sisters, who had not worked with Bing since a one-shot session in 1939. Jack traveled west and invited members of the press to be on hand for the much-awaited event, a session one headline writer proclaimed as "Bing First Over the Line."[31]

14

JUST AN OLD COWHAND

Men with graceful reflexes don't interrogate their opportunities.

—Denis Johnson, *Tree of Smoke* (2007)

"We are living in Beverly Hills now, since our North Hollywood home burned down. I like this area much better, and we were lucky to find a nice house, ready for occupancy," Bing Crosby wrote to a fan. Beverly Hills served as the postal address, but they actually occupied the more exclusive Holmby Hills zone, bounded by Beverly Hills to the east and Bel Air to the west and bifurcated by Sunset Boulevard. The house wasn't quite ready for more than a month. To his friend and associate Saul Weislow, Bing depicted "a fine house, much nicer than the old one, and when, if ever, we get it furnished, it should be quite a spot. The gentile Marx Brothers [his sons] love it and it's ideal for them." The eldest of those brothers, nine years old when they moved in, would later remember it as "the mausoleum" and "the castle of fear."[1]

The delays forced them to camp at several homes. Bing and Dixie spent a week with Bob and Dolores Hope in Toluca Lake while their sons boarded with Bing's parents. When the house was ready, they were thwarted by "no dearth of colorful incidents." A golf and bond-selling tour in Phoenix ended with Bing, hurrying to make the last train to Los Angeles, leaping from a moving automobile, slipping, and hitting the pavement hard. Before he could pull himself out of the way, the car rolled over his left lower leg. Refusing local medical aid, he was helped aboard the train by Johnny Burke and Jimmy Van Heusen, who cabled Arnold Stevens to meet them at the Los Angeles station. The x-rays revealed no damage beyond visible cuts and contusions, and Stevens counseled a week in bed and a pair of crutches. "[I] unwittingly thrust my leg under a Ford while Bond selling in Arizona," Bing wrote to Weislow. "There were no buyers under there, but the result is more painful than serious." He recovered without Dixie's care. That same week she began a "sojourn" in the hospital for "nerve and kidney trouble."[2]

A pictorial essay on the Crosby manse, published in the early 1950s and occasioned in part by rumors that the Crosbys might be separating, cautioned, "The pictures on these pages may surprise some readers. Unlike Bing's flamboyant wardrobe, his home is simple, unaffected and comfortable." Despite its aristocratic embellishments, the interiors created over several years by the designer George Hall in consultation with Dixie aimed for understatement and ease. The writer of the article, Marva Peterson, a frequent contributor to fan pulps who does not appear to have interviewed either of the Crosbys, encouraged her readers to adopt Dixie's decorating tips, such as concealing the television in a cabinet that matches the room's other antiques and setting off a winding staircase with circular carpeting. More ominously, she noted that Bing could take kidding about everything else, but not his home — "Even the script writers know that the house is forbidden gag territory." The house, she wrote, represented the Crosbys' last bid for privacy, "and very few people have actually been inside the place."[3]

Built on a six-acre knoll, it had seventeen rooms, including two libraries, but was never meant to be especially welcoming. The house at 594 South Mapleton Drive, unlike the Colonial on Camarillo Street, showed a NO TRESPASSING sign to passersby. Bing's public availability ended at the gate. Here he could let the persona slide and handle his business affairs, which had not slackened, particularly his racing interests; here he could enjoy his family or the solitude of his office. Bing and Dixie did less entertaining.

The Mapleton house had a short pedigree. A department-store magnate named Malcolm McNaghten commissioned the British-born architect Gordon B. Kaufmann to build his mansion. Kaufmann, who helped devise the Hoover Dam and created such enduring shrines as Greystone Mansion, the Los Angeles Times Building, and Santa Anita Park, completed it in 1932, conceiving the house (infamously demolished in the twenty-first century by the television producer Aaron Spelling) as a singular amalgam of compatible styles, chiefly Colonial, French, Spanish, and Moorish. Distinctive features included a protuberant circular stair tower, an airy portico with metal latticework running the length of the ground floor, traditional white clapboard on the second floor, and fortress-like walls made of thick stone blocks. Two large iron gates guarded the main entrance, one for driving in and one for driving out. The two gravel roads passed through an acre or so of shielding palm trees and shrubs—a small woodland of camouflage—before reaching the house. Phillip remembered with pleasure the front lawn, big enough to play football; the two courtyards, one as wide if not as long as a basketball court, equipped with backboards and hoops; and the garage that could house eight cars. Gary's memories might have been lifted from Shirley Jackson: "Big piece of property. It had those big stones, the way castles are made. There was an entrance on one street and an entrance on another street and two driveways that went up. All you saw in there was a forest, trees and bushes. You never saw the house and then—there it was! Big joint, scary as hell, forbidding-looking. When it rained on it, Jesus Christ, what a depressing-looking joint."[4]

Older visitors were bowled over by the place, which Edward R. Murrow toured on his 1954 celebrity chat show *Person to Person*. The butler Alan Fisher, who came to the house with his wife, Norma, in 1963, adored working at the chicest address in the film colony and particularly admired the formality. "Loved it. My wife loved it. A big formal dining room, and a formal little breakfast room, and a very formal drawing room....So much more upmarket than Bel Air or Beverly Hills." Yet in 1943, its celebrated tenant could not fight the battle of the Los Angeles Country Club's exclusionary practices: no Jews, no persons of color or visible ethnicity, no actors. A sportswriter once commented, "The smell of old money clings to [Los Angeles Country Club] like stale beer on a frat house carpet." Years later, Bing recalled: "I ran into Jack Benny one day and he said, 'Gee, it's pretty lucky for you, Bing, with that new house, you live right on the 14th fairway of L.A. Country Club, it must give you a nice opportunity to play.' 'Au contraire, Jack,' I replied, 'they don't allow actors to play there.' 'Huh,' Jack [said], 'How would you like to be an actor and a Jew?'"[5]

The house had a swimming pool, but before taking possession of the property Bing filled it in and paved it over with a black clay tennis court. A couple of years earlier, the two-year-old son of Anthony Quinn and Katherine DeMille had drowned in W. C. Fields's lily pond; more recently, a child drowned in a pool on Mapleton Drive. (Bing would fill in another pool when he moved his second family north to an estate in Hillsborough.) He explained his concern about inviting similar tragedy to his friends and associates but not to his sons, though they teased him about being too cheap to put in a pool. He would tell them, "Swim in Alan's pool." The boys regularly walked down Mapleton to Sunset Boulevard, where Alan Ladd and his wife, Sue Carol, lived in the third house past the crosswalk. They could always swim there. Recalling his parents' lifelong love of swimming, Gary theorized that he didn't build a pool—"There was plenty of room!"—in order to discourage visitors.[6] There is some truth in that. Bing needed a break from people.

In its *Dixie* review, *Variety* noted the adjustment in his persona: "Crosby now is as standard among the male singer toppers as the Four Freedoms, and today he shapes up more and more as the Will Rogers–type of solid American actor-citizen."[7]

In constant, unrelenting demand, Bing found it hard to say no. In addition to charity golf matches, shows at military camps, *KMH*, radio guest spots, AFRS and other transcription sessions, Decca recording dates, and film work (as other movie projects fell by the wayside, as of April, he was unusually concerned about setting up his next picture, this one involving priests in New York), he attended bond promotions or wrote spirited booster letters to be read in his absence; answered letters from soldiers or their bereaved relatives; and sang and washed dishes at the Hollywood Canteen. The man whose minders once fiercely guarded his image now signed off on his name being used as the punch line in movie gags for any studio from MGM to Monogram.[8]

The man who shunned for-profit concerts after his dazzling 1931–1932 run at New York's Paramount Theaters now volunteered himself to every cluster of uniforms in what amounted to an endless Victory Caravan of troop shows, benefits, and spontaneous drop-ins. The self-incarcerated prisoner of technology who persistently tried to bar audiences from his radio show now encouraged an avid, movable audience, mostly young and male. He appeared galvanized and avowedly humbled by the reaction. Servicemen around the country would long remember his greeting: "Hi, fellows, whaddya wanna hear?" Some recalled the pulp book of lyrics he carried in his hip pocket; responding to a request, he would pull it out and, to much laughter, pretend (though he wasn't always pretending) to sing from the cheat sheet. He remained just as forthcoming before civilians who bought bonds. At a Memphis golf course under cloudy skies, he told the audience of ten thousand to forget about the rain and sang for the better part of an hour—"Readily," noted a reporter, "with none of the pseudo-reluctance usually affected by the celebrity coaxed to perform at such gatherings. He didn't worry about keys either." He just hummed a note until the band, recruited from a local radio station, found common ground. Then he headed directly to Kennedy General Hospital to perform for wounded men, after which he boarded a train for Washington.[9]

The man who nursed a grudge against Paul Whiteman and appeared with him only at lavish fund-raising Gershwin concerts now agreed to his request to reunite the Rhythm Boys with Al Rinker and Harry Barris for NBC's Sunday-night summer show *Paul Whiteman Presents*. The trio did seven minutes of lame pun-filled repartee and a medley of "Mississippi Mud" ("darkies" still beating their feet) and "I Left My Sugar Standing in the Rain" in a sketch involving Bing's neighbor Bill Goodwin and Dinah Shore. After Al and Harry said they sang like Bing Crosby, Crosby said, "I sing like Dick Todd"—which was true, in that the once-popular Canadian baritone had unmistakably channeled Bing's sound and style in a successful series of Victor records. Bing's line was repeated by fans and comedians until Todd disappeared from memory. *Variety* called the broadcast "a treat of uncommon dimensions." *Time* gave it a full page, granting that some listeners might think the Rhythm Boys lean "slightly to the corn," but to those who had come of age with it, "the syncopated ditty, 'Mississippi Mud' seemed a solid perdurable part of U.S. musical history." In the show's second half, Crosby, Shore, and Whiteman's orchestra gave their all to a *Porgy and Bess* medley that required no apology.[10]

Bing asked that his fee be divided between Barris and Rinker. He had aided Harry for years by giving him cameos in his pictures, but he had hardly seen Rinker, a successful radio producer and occasional songwriter,[11] since the trio parted ways in 1931. He invited Al home for dinner that night. Bing's father made a great to-do over the Spokane school chum who had brought focus to Bing's musical ambitions while terminating his path to a law degree and who had initiated his road trip to fame and fortune in a rickety Model T. But Bing and Al had little in common beyond their memories and, except for a day of golf, made no attempt to revive the friendship.

The man who hated hospitals and had generally managed to avoid them in the years since Eddie Lang died now visited some of the most heartrending wards on the coast. During a tour of the U.S. Naval Hospital in Oakland, doctors discouraged Crosby from entering the room of one Marine who had lost a leg in a training accident and then toppled into a deep depression, refusing to speak or eat. Bing said he'd like to say hello if they had no objections. Noting a guitar in the room, he tried to engage the soldier in music talk, remarking that he always liked singing to a guitar. The Marine turned his face to the wall. Bing tried other gambits before leaving him with the suggestion that he might come back later to run down a few tunes. No response.

Bing and Hope played an exhibition match that afternoon in Oakland, and the Crosby savoir faire came through in the last nine. As he swung back his driver, an onlooker shouted, "Hey, Bing, how about a song?" Calmly lowering the club, Bing said he'd be glad to, and Hope would dance, too, if the fellow could collect the cost of a five-thousand-dollar bond from the crowd. The money was promptly secured, and fifteen minutes of song and dance ensued. Bing retrieved his driver and finished his game in the 70s. Afterward, he disappeared. A concerned escort found him in the despondent Marine's room, whooping "Deep in the Heart of Texas," backed by the patient's guitar. A reporter related this incident to illustrate the easy charm of "the greatest smoothie Hollywood has ever known." Bing didn't talk about it, but mindful of his OWI commitment, he convinced colleagues to visit Oakland, "where you'll really get applause you'll never forget, just the looks in those kids' eyes." He came back a few months later to produce and emcee a show in the hospital's amphitheater, after which he visited the wards to say hello to the men too wounded to attend. A twenty-one-year-old private first class suffering from a shell concussion credited his recovery to Dr. Crosby's medicine.[12]

The man who threatened to suspend his radio show because he could not function without the ASCAP catalog continued to embrace those allegedly "plebian" songs licensed through BMI. He struck gold at his heralded return to customary recording on Monday morning, September 27, 1943, reuniting with the Andrews Sisters — Patty, Maxene, and LaVerne — to cut two sides in an hour and a half, two more two days later, and two more on his own two days after that. Five of the six reached high on the charts and three topped a million sales. Bing's brothers Everett and Larry attended the first session along with Jack Kapp, who greeted press photographers and posed with his artists and a print of the cautionary poster that hung in Decca's New York studio — his younger brother Dave, while traveling through Virginia, had photographed the statue of Pocahontas, arms stretched out longingly, and added a cartoon bubble with Jack's interrogatory mantra "Where's the melody?" The poster would now adorn the Los Angeles facility. The vocal stars did not look like a match. The sisters, wearing heavy movie makeup, arrived at the eight a.m. session from the Universal studio where they were filming *Swingtime Johnny*; Bing strolled in after a round of golf. Yet the material was tailor-made for them, and within minutes of learning their parts in Vic Schoen's cunning arrangements, the four singers realized they had tripped into a charmed zone; they were focused and elated, whirling in lockstep, having such a good time.

Schoen's method of working compensated for the fact that neither Bing nor the Andrews Sisters could read music. Actually, LaVerne could, but that was no help to Maxene and the trio's soloist, Patty, so she didn't make a point of it. "I made them feel good about themselves," Schoen recalled, "because even though they couldn't read a note and couldn't improvise, I wrote them parts as though they were musicians, as though they could [take risks], you know. I wrote words under the music to cue them, and as time went on, I gave them more and more difficult things to do and they did them beautifully. In fact, after a while they took my difficult things and made them better." Crosby's natural facility for improvisation impressed Schoen particularly in the realm of harmonizing. "He had a wonderful, wonderful ear for that kind of stuff. It wasn't schooled, nor was it polished, nor was it always accurate, but it was always good." He knew the score cold after hearing the band run it down once; "he was that quick." Patty might go over the parts with him, but he usually had the lyrics in advance, allowing him time to work up alterations that sounded like ad libs and sometimes were. Patty figured he developed them in the car driving to the session — for example, the two bars in "Pistol Packin' Mama" when he interjects the line "Lay the thing down before it goes off and hurts somebody," which caught the sisters off guard and might have ruined a perfect take had they not felt too intimidated to laugh.[13]

Like Bob Wills's "San Antonio Rose," Al Dexter's "Pistol Packin' Mama" was released by the label Okeh Records months before Crosby's cover and netted each version a gold record. Dexter's rendition, inspired by the gun-toting wife of a Kentucky bootlegger, had been recorded in the spring of 1942, long before the Petrillo ban, and lain dormant for nearly fifteen months before Okeh put it out, sparking a national phenomenon that took Dexter from honky-tonks and square dances in East Texas to a posh nightclub on Broadway, a first for a "hillbilly" musician. It generated controversy when stations banned the song because of lines like "drinking beer in a cabaret and was I having fun" and "dancing with a blonde when my wife came in." He rerecorded it with emended lyrics and found himself with the hottest novelty song of the day, generating countless parodies and several adoptions, including versions by Sinatra and Glenn Miller. But Crosby and the Andrews Sisters took the first sip and walked off with the saloon.

Schoen said he hadn't heard of Dexter's record when Kapp assigned him the song and left him to his own devices as long as the band didn't exceed nine pieces. "That was Decca. All we could afford was nine bodies and I used them the best way I could. Those nine bodies became the established combination for Decca Records, and later Crosby used the same combination in his movies and on recordings."[14] His arrangement is a pastiche of jaunty details; he gussies up the material with a brassy intro and a repeated shave-and-a-haircut alarum, a tailgate trombone, a Dixieland interlude with a cowbell break, odd rests, a wholly original second theme, and a protracted, harmonized finish. Patty addresses her solo to Bing, who playfully enunciates *pistol* with a z. The recording served as a droll provocation in which war is reduced to hapless domestic tantrums. Retaining most of the original lyrics, Decca's disc was banned by a New York station because of the beer-drinking line and condemned by a newspaper editorialist in Alabama who deemed it "miserable caterwauling" and proposed a course in "compulsory musical appreciation" for the generation "forced to grow up believing that a juke box squalling, 'Put that pistol down, babe,' represents the ultimate in the tenderest and sweetest of the arts."[15] Most reviewers were dismissive, but *Billboard* defended it as a fitting alternative to the national anthem for occasions of "strictly informal intercourse with the enemy."[16] For formal intercourse, in preparation for the attack on the Solomon Islands, the U.S. Army Air Forces outfitted a B-25 bomber with a 75 mm field cannon that they called the Pistol Packin' Mama.

That belligerent record pulled off the first trifecta tabulated by *Billboard*'s three charts, simultaneously scoring first place on the country chart, second on the pop chart, and third on the rhythm and blues chart. In January 1944, the trade paper added its fourth chart, "Juke Box Folk Records," which in its inaugural appearance had Decca's "Pistol" at number one and Dexter's at number two. This despite Kapp's decision to release it in his high-priced (seventy-five cents) Personality series, passing on to consumers the double royalties he had to pay. The flip side, "Vict'ry Polka," a home-front hoedown that prophesies "a mighty cheer when the ration book is just a souvenir," proved a major hit in its own right, its jubilance embodied in a contrapuntal passage by Patty and Bing, who savors the bright morning luster of his voice, curling every upper mordent with the ambling gaiety of a boulevardier.

Kapp convened the same group on Wednesday to record a pair of seasonal numbers for the Christmas market, but he pulled a last-minute switch for one of the songs. On Tuesday afternoon, while Schoen and the Andrews Sisters were preparing a scene for *Swingtime Johnny*, Vic was called to the phone: "Dave Kapp said we want to do 'Jingle Bells' tomorrow. Tomorrow! So I made the arrangement later that day, and we stayed up most of the night and I taught it to them, and we recorded it the next day. Bing learned his part at the session. And again, it was a big one."[17] Perhaps they wanted to save on song royalties by raiding the public domain; Schoen could not remember what had been eliminated in favor of the caroling favorite, composed in the 1850s by James Pierpont (originally as a Thanksgiving song commemorating the sleigh races in Medford, Massachusetts). In any case, what fun he had, opening the arrangement with a raggy piano mimicking the sound of bells and providing the sisters with a countermelody and rhythm, including a scripted scat break. The pleasure Bing took in his own vocal production and in his chemistry with the Andrews Sisters was rarely more evident. The performance is taken up tempo, with a swinging instrumental passage centered on a brief clarinet solo by Jack Mayhew. Crosby, solidly in the moment, enters with rhythmic aplomb, gliding over the beat in a manner reminiscent of his 1939 alliance with the Music Maids "In My Merry Oldsmobile," but now driving an eight-cylinder sleigh. Kapp backed it up with the 1934 song "Santa Claus Is Coming to Town," another disarming number with festive singing and witty arrangement. Decca ultimately claimed sales of six million discs for "Jingle Bells."[18]

Despite those estimated sales, "Jingle Bells" was not Decca's most momentous Christmas release. Kapp assembled a third session that week, on Friday morning, this time for Bing and the John Scott Trotter orchestra, which had not recorded in sixteen months. The material consisted of two songs Bing had recently presented on *Kraft Music Hall* and a third, recorded by request, that he evidently never sang professionally. This last number, "Heaven Can Wait," was one of Jimmy Van Heusen's first successes (1939), with lyrics by Eddie DeLange. Early in the year, while golfing for bonds in Phoenix (the same trip on which he'd injured his leg), Bing made private transcription recordings by request for buyers of exceptionally large bonds. One woman requested "Heaven Can Wait," to be dedicated to her daughter and son-in-law, a corporal attending an officer candidate program at Fort Sill. Weeks later she learned that a technical problem at the radio station prevented the recording from being made; the station manager suggested she write "Bing Crosby himself." Her daughter did. Crosby arranged with producer Joe Perry to record the disc at the October 1 session. "Dear Mrs. Ross," he wrote her, "The recording, as mentioned in your letter of April 4, has just been completed. All copies are being shipped to you direct. Kindest regards. Sincerely, Bing Crosby." In making this particular disc, he had to learn a song that he never performed commercially on radio, record, or television. Other instances of his specially tailored recordings are known, but there is no documentation of all the circumstances or the number of them.[19]

The other recordings that day would be known by millions. "Poinciana," the 1936 adaptation of the Cuban folk song "La Canción del Árbol," received little attention before Bing took it up, despite Glenn Miller's version. Trotter delegated the arranging of it to Sam Freed, a violinist, who set the sixteen-bar verse to a firm bolero rhythm and modulated to a discreet rumba beat for the chorus. Bing spans the transition with a perfect whole note on the title's first syllable. Kapp smelled a hit and put it aside for a few months ("Poinciana" would top out at number three in March 1944); no reason to waste it as the B-side of the session's other song, which he knew would go the distance. "I'll Be Home for Christmas," one of the saddest of popular songs, was rescued from oblivion on a golf course. The lyricist Kim Gannon, desperate after several rebuffs, sang it to Bing between holes. Taken with the words and Walter Kent's music, Crosby agreed to record it. After he introduced it on the radio, however, a songwriter named Buck Ram claimed he had written a poem by that name when he was a lonely teenager and later showed it to Gannon and Kent, who were acquaintances of his. To settle the lawsuit, they added Ram's name to the copyright. Accompanied by Perry Botkin's guitar and an understated ensemble of strings, Bing's plaintive interpretation outdid "White Christmas" as the gloomiest recording of the war. The BBC banned it, arguing that a song in which a soldier promises to be home for the holiday ("you can count on me") but possibly only in his dreams would damage military morale.[20]

Kapp, who believed—and had statistics to prove—that he had his "thumb," as he said, on the pulse of American taste, expected it to have the opposite effect, cementing a mutually constructive morale between the military and the home front. He released it at the end of November, backed with Bing's patchy, dust-gathering 1941 rendition of "Danny Boy," and its popularity was instantaneous and long standing; it stayed on the charts for nearly three months. Three weeks later, he issued "Jingle Bells." The juxtaposition of the two discs and the ongoing success of "White Christmas" established Crosby as the Christmas crooner. From now on, he would be hustled by every songwriter who had a tune with a Yuletide twist. Ten recordings were designated as gold in 1943: the *Oklahoma!* cast album; one selection each by Al Dexter, fellow country singer Ted Daffan ("Born to Lose"), Jimmy Dorsey ("Bésame Mucho"), Dick Haymes ("You'll Never Know"), and Frank Sinatra (a rerelease of his 1939 number with Harry James "All or Nothing at All"); and four by Bing. In the order that they exceeded sales of a million, Bing emerged from the Petrillo strike with his fifth ("I'll Be Home for Christmas"), sixth ("Sunday, Monday, or Always"), seventh ("Pistol Packin' Mama"), and eighth ("Jingle Bells") gold records—two laments followed by two revels.

A funny thing happened at the "Jingle Bells" session—a breakdown take, the first of several that survive the twenty-three sessions (forty-seven tracks) that Bing and the Andrews Sisters recorded between 1943 and 1952. This take, unnecessary and inferior from the start, is signaled as such about two-thirds through, when Bing bursts into muddled laughter. The sisters instantly drop out and then start up again as soon as they realize that, in the peculiar tradition of Crosby breakdowns, the performance will carry through to the end. After he adds a dash of wry blasphemy ("Jingle bells, jingle bells, holy Jesus Christ"), everyone laughs. Perhaps the point of the take was to put any lingering sense of intimidation they felt to rest. Maxene thought so, later observing that although they entered the recording booth with anxieties, they left it in the certainty that they had made a friend. Trying to explain the process, she said, "Vic Schoen never had to write any harmonies. [We] didn't have to sing through our eyes because we couldn't read anything, so we sang how we felt." The sisters continued to hold Bing in awe.

"There was something about Crosby that was, uh"—Maxene flailed for a few beats—"that was true."[21]

"True" involved a shield of protective professionalism. However "wonderful," however much "fun, fun, fun"[22] he was to sing with, especially on those mornings when he arrived with his fedora pushed back on his head or the brim turned up all around, signaling a degree of receptivity unavailable when the brim shaded his brow, he was always, in Schoen's description, "first a businessman, there to work and no nonsense." He got along well with the sisters and was easygoing with the musicians ("lots of dialogue between Bing and the guys"), but they knew not to fool around. "Musicians can be slothful about time, wasting it, thinking they're into overtime. Not with him, never with him." He was "aloof and very cooperative" and "when he got his teeth into something good, he gave out, he really gave a lot. He came in so well prepared it was astonishing, beautifully prepared, always. It was almost always one take. Once in a while I'd ask for a second take, if I heard something in the background, and he'd say, 'We don't sell backgrounds.' I didn't like him that much because he was remote, you know. He didn't like me, but he respected me, that was key. He gave me a pipe every Christmas for years, one of those expensive jobs, because we both smoked pipes. He was generous in that respect. But he was a reclusive man—a loner and very private, not many parties in those years, not a lot of socializing. But we never had a problem. I wound up doing fifty-five sides with him."[23]

The man who ducked the press opened up a little. Though he managed to maintain a reputation for indifference (the Women's Press Club of Hollywood voted him one of the year's most uncooperative actors), he relaxed for writers he liked and trusted, and they in turn crowed over their prized access. Lincoln Barnett, a writer for *Life,* scored a lunch with Bing despite the warning of a Paramount publicist who called Crosby "the rare fish who does not like to be interviewed or photographed, who does not care if his name *never* gets in the papers." Barnett chatted while Bing grunted "punctuation marks," until for some reason Barnett mentioned Benjamin Franklin, which got Bing's attention. "Do you like Benjamin Franklin?" he asked. Barnett said he was his favorite character in American

history. Bing agreed and asked if he knew the biography by Bernard
Faÿ. Barnett said yes, he liked it, but Carl Van Doren's was the best
there was. Crosby said he meant to read it and made a note to
remind himself to get it. They shook hands and parted, Bing with a
memo, Barnett with the smarts to bring the book to Bing's Paramount dressing room that afternoon—a gift, he said, as Bing took
out his billfold. Bing suggested they lunch the next day, after which
he presented Barnett with a rare Prohibition-era quart of Kentucky
bourbon, bottled for the American Medicinal Spirits Company,
according to the label. They met several times and Barnett got
enough material for his lengthy *Life* essay "Bing, Inc.," which nonetheless paints a portrait similar to the ones rendered by every other
writer, with or without lunch: an entertainment titan with an irresponsible, hedonistic past and weird clothes; an ideal father of
"imperturbable composure" and the "inner relaxation of a completely successful man."[24]

Samuel Richard "Dick" Mook, a Memphis-born veteran of the
First World War, got much of his journalistic cred from a close
friendship with Spencer Tracy, whose ups and downs he chronicled.
Mook came to admire Bing after witnessing an incident involving
him in 1932, when Bing had few prospects beyond a one-picture
deal, for *The Big Broadcast*. On a night when Bing and Dixie dined
out, a press photographer requested a picture. Bing told him, "Sorry,
pal, we're not on parade tonight. We're out for a quiet evening and
not dressed to have pictures made." Mook hadn't heard that one
before, especially from a guy just getting his feet wet in Hollywood.
He wrote up his first Crosby interview later that week. As time
passed and Bing accrued several hit pictures, Mook told him he was
hurting himself by refusing interviews. Bing replied:

> I'll tell you, Dick, when someone I know well, like you, wants an
> interview it's O.K. I enjoy it. Or even if someone I don't know at all
> wants to see me and has something definite to talk about—
> something I *can* talk about—I still enjoy it. But most of them
> write to an editor and say, "How about a Bing Crosby story?" The
> editor may write back, "I'd like one." The writer comes to see me,
> takes up a couple of hours or so rambling around in hopes a story
> will come out of the interview. Most of the time they want to tell

you about themselves and when they've spent the afternoon with you when they've done all the talking. Then they want to come back for another session. If they do have something definite to talk about it is usually something very personal that I don't want to discuss. If *I* didn't happen to be hot they wouldn't be interested in me. *They* aren't hot so why should I have to listen to them....It's strictly a business proposition with both of us. They want to sell a story and I need the publicity. All right, they should get their story as soon as possible and let it end there.[25]

When Mook approached him after the Christmas-tree fire to discuss his private life, Bing laughed. What private life? "My private life is just like the private life of any other middle-class American family." That was a bit much for Mook. "If you're middle class, most of the rest of us must travel sub-steerage." But Bing insisted. "Middle-classism" wasn't defined by dollars but rather by opposition to aristocracy. An aristocrat was "to the manor born," "anyone else, no matter how well educated or wealthy, is middle-class. America is a democracy and with few exceptions, carefully listed in The Blue Book, there aren't any real aristocrats here." None of Dixie's or his ancestors had boarded the *Mayflower*. Before he got "lucky and hit the jackpot," every nickel "did double duty." They didn't dress for dinner or eat breakfast in bed. They didn't have a valet or a personal maid. "We're hopelessly middle class." But you just bought a three-hundred-thousand-dollar estate, Mook protested. "If I were a jillionaire, I would still be middle-class," Bing told him. Mook surrendered: "O.K., Babbit, you win."[26]

At which point Bing gamely raised the subjects Mook hoped to pursue: "You're going to ask me about those baby and divorce rumors that are constantly cropping up." Ah, well, yes. The pregnancy stories were news to Bing and Dixie, and the divorce scuttlebutt closed the circle that started the conversation: "Dixie is about as forthright and outspoken as a person can be. If we're in the midst of a tiff when guests arrive—and what married couple doesn't have them?—instead of putting up a solid front before outsiders," she spills the beans. Perhaps that's not a particularly polite thing to do, "but that's the way we are and there isn't much either of us can do about it"—proving again that "we're middle class, because your true aristocrat would never dream of exposing his private life to the scrutiny of an outsider." He averred that after ten years of marriage, he and Dixie would never separate. Mook was convinced. After all, he considered Bing and Dixie to be the most "honest, straightforward people I have ever known" and concluded that those who called Bing uncooperative made him "come pretty close to seeing red."[27]

The greatest smoothie Hollywood has ever known left unstated the Irish American self-reliance that anchored his posture as a barefoot boy during the war, when he continually encountered and wanted the respect of men who came from worlds of privation next to which Catholic, working-class, turn-of-the-century Spokane seemed literally middle class. He may also have felt obliged to clang the bell of democracy because H. Allen Smith had just published his bestselling book *Life in a Putty Knife Factory*, for which he unearthed a quashed 1933 CBS press book that had the idealistic young crooner styling himself as "pretty socialistic." Smith also described the Crosbys as having "traced their ancestry back to the Mayflower."[28] This hardly jibed with the tranquilly rugged persona of the Bing Crosby known throughout his career for songs such as "Brother, Can You Spare a Dime," "I've Got a Pocketful of Dreams," "I Found a Million Dollar Baby," "Ain't Got a Dime to My Name," "Busy Doing Nothing," and several more that, not unlike the pictures he made endorsing the simple, reclusive life of a strolling player, catboat pilot, jazzman, or priest, derided the values and morals of those who prized money, acquisitions, and pedigree above all else.

In his middle years, as a denizen of the most exclusive clubs and hotels on both sides of the Atlantic, Bing gave parity to his English ancestors, who had reached the New World a mere fifteen years after the *Mayflower*. Through his forebears' marriages, Bing himself entered the certified rolls of *Mayflower* descendants (a fillip omitted from *Call Me Lucky*). In researching the family's genealogy, brother Larry discovered two ancestral heralds, one Irish and the other English, and took pains to explain (for whose edification, we may wonder, as only the immediate family saw his handiwork) that coats of arms did not signify the aristocracy "but rather personal merit secured by the humblest as well as the highest." Bing wore the Irish shield on the breast pocket of his blazer and later acquired an English butler. Yet he never gave up the Jesuitical twists and turns with which he argued for his status as all-American Joe; a streak of barefoot boy persisted despite the isolating power of wealth and pomp. He continued to identify himself (at times apologetically) as a modestly talented, immoderately lucky guy—"distinctly one of the people," in the words of Mary Greene, another besotted writer he posed for in 1943. Even as he learned to venerate the service at Claridge's in London, he took perverse pride in getting himself expelled from that posh hotel in 1960 after he was caught aiming chip shots at a waist-high ashtray in the corridor. He switched to the quieter Stafford Hotel until Claridge's welcomed him back a decade or so later. Bing hired plenty of servants but no valet. His butler, Alan Fisher, complained that Mr. Crosby would not let him do a thing, not even carry his bags. He liked moneyed companions and detested fawning. He answered the letters of every stranger who wrote him but harbored sound suspicions of fans seeking friendship.[29]

Yet who didn't think of him as a friend? Who didn't think he knew Bing better than he ever could? Writing for a Catholic magazine, Mary Lanigan Healy postulated that this least naive of men conveyed "an almost naïve simplicity and unpretentiousness." His standing, she wrote, was "unique," because everyone liked him for reasons that were individual and personal. People needed him to be more than merely a crafted persona; they looked to him as an avatar of how Americans ought to live. Healy wondered how he achieved his "inner tranquility": "Dressed in noisy sports clothes, stretched out reading his favorite author, Dashiell Hammett, or leaning on a corral fence, eyeing a thoroughbred colt, or grinning companionably at his eldest, Gary, he is the epitome of contentment and serenity." After Crosby's death, Tony Bennett would ruminate, "You know, Bing invented suburbia. He taught everyone to relax."[30]

On January 25, even before he finalized the deal for the house on Mapleton Drive, Crosby closed on the property he had mentioned six months earlier to his skeptical accountant Todd Johnson. For nearly ten years, Elko, Nevada, would be his second home, a place to escape Hollywood, and not just for solitude, rest, and outdoor sports, though it afforded plenty of opportunities for riding, hunting, fishing, and carousing. Over the years, he emphasized three interlocking yet discrete motives for taking charge of and vastly enlarging a network of cattle ranches. Other film stars bought ranches, but few worked them, any more than they bred the horses they raced. Bing's buildup of acquisitions eventually produced a spread of baronial splendor. Not the least of his reasons was the lure of a Western modality that he merely skirted in his adolescence as a reluctant farmhand. He was the boss now, yet in speaking of his years in Elko—summers with his kids, autumns with friends, winters with the halest and heartiest of his comrades—his recollections drifted between the appeal of anonymity and the work ethic of his hardscrabble youth, when he rose before the sun to deliver papers, caddy, clean up a flophouse, mow lawns, pick fruit, serve Mass, and generally heed Seneca's counsel to ward off idleness with toil.

He had developed into a masterly rider, as easy on a horse as he was on a golf trail. But as a picture star, he remained physically and temperamentally unsuited for playing cowboys. He made one faux-Western, *Rhythm on the Range,* the 1936 dude-ranch-set romantic comedy in which he introduced the satirical, self-effacing song "I'm an Old Cowhand." Filmed in the High Sierras, that movie handed him one of his favorite roles and the inspiration that led directly to Elko. He would end his feature-film career with a conventional Western, playing the alcoholic doctor in the 1966 retelling of *Stagecoach.* If Westerns were beyond him, the West extended open arms. His daughter, Mary, born after he left Elko, speculated that despite his Gonzagan propriety, he was a "cowboy at heart" who required "a chunk of land somewhere in the middle of nowhere with cattle and horses on it." Before he cashed out of Elko, she pointed out, he bought the fifteen hundred acres of Rising River Ranch in Northern California; cattle branding and manure shoveling, she added, were "definitely part of our childhood."[31]

Teddy Roosevelt, Bing's professed hero in Paramount's 1932 public relations questionnaire, described "open-range ranching" as "perhaps the pleasantest, healthiest, and most exciting phase of

American existence."[32] Elko offered a closed-range version of that, in a "nowhere" in the middle of Nevada's Northeast Frontier. Carolyn Schneider, the daughter of Bing's beloved sister Mary Rose (the only sibling who ever visited the ranch), wrote of his morning ritual after the communal five-thirty breakfast. The first to leave the table, Uncle Bing chose a hunting rifle from the gun cabinet, saddled his horse, Doc, and rode for an hour joined only by his dog Bullet: horseflesh and solitude. He welcomed company when he welcomed company, drawing on a troupe composed of jesters (Johnny Burke, Barney Dean), racing associates (Lin Howard and his family), musicians (the clarinetist and songwriter Fud Livingston used it to dry out), and Hollywood royals (Gary Cooper, Clark Gable) who shared his devotion to fishing and hunting. One visit involved two golfing luminaries, Jimmy Demaret and Ben Hogan, who came up for two weeks of hunting. On their first day, as Bing told it, they drove up a mountain crest hoping to spot deer. "On the way back to the jeep, Jimmy, who was carrying a 30-30 carbine rifle, jumped a huge sage hen rooster. The rooster flew 50 or 60 yards in the air and Jimmy fired the 30-30 from the hip and hit the sage hen dead center. Guts and feathers flew all over. It was an incredible shot. It would have been a great shot with a shot gun, but with a 30-30 rifle and that sage hen flying fast as that bird was flying, it was almost impossible. We stood there for a full minute, speechless. Then Jimmy turned to Ben and said, 'Ben when you improve on that one, I'll shoot my next shot.' They were there two weeks after that [and] Jimmy didn't shoot again."[33]

A second motive, with which he justified the outlay to his lawyer, accountant, brothers, and Dixie, who accompanied him annually in the early years before developing an aversion to the journey and the destination, was his argument that the ranch was a lucrative business venture. Beyond the romance of the West, he observed, "looking at the proposition more cold-bloodedly, I think it's perhaps the best investment I ever made. We have been able to improve the ranch to the point where it is as fine an operation as there is up there for its size. It is not a vast place, although the acreage is considerable, because lots of that acreage is not usable. But it is a functional cow and calf operation, nothing fancy or dude-y about it, no swimming pool or anything like that."[34]

He began cautiously, but disastrously, with a decent-size place on the Humboldt River. Engorged by heavy rains, the river flooded him out before he had his bearings. Undeterred, he acquired the 8,700-acre Quarter Circle S in Independence Valley, which became the foundation for his serious involvement in the cattle business. At first, the area residents played down his arrival with agreeable disinterest. But after he'd made a couple of trips down Highway 225 to the town of Elko, with its population of a few thousand and its Crosbyan live-and-let-live attitude, Bing was roundly accepted as the man he wanted to be and not the famous personality everyone wanted a piece of. He found his place in "one of the last bastions of the old West."[35]

In *Call Me Lucky,* Bing describes Spokane as the place where his father found a new start in life because its people "don't care who you are, what you've been, or what your reputation was before they met you. It's how you handle yourself after you arrive there that counts." And yet the transcribed interviews that make up the bulk of his memoir show that he made that comment not about Spokane but about what most appealed to him in Elko. That new beginning he conjectured was for *him,* not his father. After nearly a decade in cattle country, he could declare with satisfaction that in those years he had never "been asked for an autograph by any residents of the county or asked to do benefit shows or contribute to any charity or in any way do anything but mind my own business. I think if I'm known at all up there, it would be simply as the fellow from California with a pretty nice cow-and-calf outfit up near Wild Horse." In truth, he had hardly settled in when Elko's postmaster wrote him, "I should very much like to sell you a bond—I'm not particular what denomination you purchase—anything from $25 to $1000 would be very satisfactory." She was certain his participation would stimulate sales of bonds to ranchers and stockmen. Bing authorized his ranch manager Johnny Eacret to buy $7,500 in war bonds. After the war, he accepted a lifelong designation as Elko's honorary mayor and participated in a few promotional ploys for the town, including using it for the world premiere of his 1951 picture *Here Comes the Groom,* an event covered on national radio, which raised $10,000 toward a new hospital. It was a neighborly thing to do, but it "kind of spoiled it for the future for me. Now they regard me in a little different light and I am not sure whether I am flattered by the change."[36]

The outfit continued to grow after the war, as Bing sold the Quarter Circle S and bought and consolidated several established ranches at North Fork, acquiring some twenty-five thousand acres plus a vast unusable expanse of national forest and thirty-five hundred head of Hereford cattle. He added ranches to the south, bringing with them valuable water rights—seven ranches in all, for which he built a reservoir, a hydroelectric plant, and, to accommodate visiting friends, the Stevens-Crosby airstrip, created with Arnold Stevens, after Steve and his wife, Jean, bought the ranch just north of Bing's central property. Local tax money helped finance the airfield in exchange for its use in the event of emergency or state-related landings. Crosby inherited and retained the name PX to denote his central ranch and the combined operation. He told Jean that "he did not want to put his name all over everything."[37] He kept the family names of the additions too: North Fork holdings that he took over from Newt Crumley, a legendary figure in the territory; the Truitt Ranch; the Johnson-Laing Ranch, and the rest, all indicated—along with the Stevens and PX ranches— on area maps of the 1950s. The Crosby name is absent except for the airstrip. He did, however, put his mark on the Herefords with his +B brand ("cross B"). He loved everything about his time in Elko County, not least the climate, which, despite brutal winters, he considered "ideal."

> It is five thousand feet at Elko, and about sixty-one hundred at our ranch. During the summer, of course, you can stand out barechested and feel the heat pretty good, but in the shade, even during the day—and of course, after five or six o'clock—it's pretty cool, even in July and August, and you need a jacket. You always sleep under blankets twelve months a year. A lovely part of the year is early fall, September and October. Cool clear days and frosty sparkling nights. The winters are real rough. They can get down to twenty-five or thirty degrees below and sometimes stay there for ten days or two weeks at a time. It is simply amazing what the white-faced cow can take in the way of cold. As long as you can get a little hay in their belly they can withstand the severest blast.

I recall last winter going out on horseback to look at some of the
heifers. It was about fifteen or sixteen below. Had on long under-
wear, all the jackets and scarves I could carry, and I had to come
back in after an hour or so. I was just congealed right to the bone.
These little heifers were kicking and playing down in the snow
drifts with a real blizzard beating on their backs.[38]

Bing left the running of the ranch and its three dozen or so
hands (depending on the season) to a foreman named Johnny
Eacret, who later did stunt doubling for him at Paramount, and his
wife, Doris Eacret, a licensed pilot and excellent shot. They took
care of the staffing, which in that first summer was almost as problematic as the flood; there was one young woman who disappeared
when her lover was around, a cook who did the same when he had
a snoot full and felt underappreciated, and a young friend who
came up to recover from her divorce and triggered the exodus of a
ranch hand's wife. Not the least of their responsibilities was minding the Crosby boys, a third motive for Bing's move into the West.
"Elko County [has] done a lot for me and I think it's done a lot more
for my kids," he said. Yet Elko proved to be a crucible for those kids,
defining the disparity between Bing's first and second tries at parenting. His daughter, Mary, born in 1959, acknowledged that it was
important to her father to have "a place where his kids could experience that sort of life"—on *working* ranches, she stressed, not
"McRanches." Mary and her two brothers enjoyed the experience.
Her four half brothers, she knew, were ambivalent, except for Gary,
who grew to hate it; they learned that the Western life was a hard
one but could not see why they had to keep learning it, summer
after laborious summer. Gary remembered it as another parental
test he was certain to fail and the one he found hardest to
forgive.[39]

Gary was ten, Phil and Denny were eight, and Linny was five the
first summer. Only Gary was old enough to join in the work. Seated
behind his desk and, in Gary's recollection, speaking "in that same
stern voice he used when I did something wrong," Bing explained
to Gary alone that the ranch was to be a character-building exercise, starting in June, after school let out. Gary convincingly conjured up the speech: "You're ten years old, Gary. It's time you

realized there's a lot more to life than Beverly Hills. You're going to have to work hard for a living when you grow up. There won't be any ne'er-do-wells in this family if I have anything to say about it. You're big enough to start now. I'm putting you to work this summer on the ranch. You'll be just another hand, treated the same as everyone else." After specifying some chores, assuring him that it would be good for him, teach him responsibility, make a man of him, he said it would be just the two of them, a proposition Gary did not welcome as a chance to bond.[40]

They drove, the two of them, seven hundred miles over two days, hardly speaking as Gary tuned in the radio to music that changed as the smog turned to dusty desert air, going from Crosby, Perry Como, and Frank Sinatra to people he had never heard of, country singers; Gary recalled Ernest Tubb and Hank Williams, but Williams would not record for another three years. That wasn't the only detail he misremembered. For one thing, the whole family did come up that summer of 1943, a few weeks later and for a shorter visit; also, he was not yet treated as "just another hand." He was treated as a boy and the boss's son, sleeping in the main house, not the bunkhouse (that came later), looked after by the Eacrets and the hands, attending local shows, making pets of animals, and learning to curry, saddle, and ride two horses for which he enthusiastically accepted responsibility. Looking back at Elko at age fifty, he insisted he "stayed hot and angry the entire ten years I was up there."[41] The letters he wrote during the first two or three summers there belie that, even as they verify the competitive unease between father and son that would swell and harden over the years at Elko.

They arrived midday. First stop was the general store, where Bing bought Gary shirts, jeans, and two cowboy hats, straw for work and felt for Sunday church. Early evening, they sat down to a dinner with the Eacrets and the ranch hands that exceeded his fantasies of cowboy life, though he claimed he was too afraid to indulge in the meal: steaks and chicken, biscuits, gravy, potatoes, corn on the cob, oversize bowls of vegetables, homemade bread and pies. Afterward, he watched his father with admiration and envy, for "as usual, he fit right in." Dressed in faded jeans and a plaid shirt, boots propped on the porch railing, he "seemed like just another good old boy who had been living that way all his life," while Gary spent his time "breaking in" his hats, kneading the brims so they would look just right.[42]

Gary was not wrong in assessing his father's objective. Bing believed in behavioral autocracy, where expectations are set and must be met, where obedience and achievement bring parental approval and a child's failure is taken personally, reflecting obstinacy and defiance that must be broken. He believed good parents molded their children like clay. Fretting, a decade later, over his and Dixie's failings, he referred to their boys as a kind of grist: "I am certainly not the best parent in the world, but I'm trying to be a good one [and] Dixie's doing the same. Maybe we've got the wrong approach. Maybe we're not good enough, I don't know. But we're doing the best we can with the material we've got to work with." Looking back at Elko, he approvingly paraphrased an essay by the doggedly anti-Communist general Albert Wedemeyer: "The great danger to the United States was not the threat of Communism from without, [but rather] our failure to develop resolute, self-reliant young men, young men with leadership, as we have done in the past generations." Bing continued at length in this vein: "What Wedemeyer had to say in my opinion made pretty good sense. A country is just as strong as its young people and if there is a proportion, an increasing proportion, of these young people who haven't got the leadership qualities [then] our country is in real danger." Kids today "have no particular goal, they just want to get through school the easiest way. They have no idea what they want to be."[43]

Bing spouted those complaints, as banal as they are eternal, in the period when he began to have second thoughts about the parental program. But in 1943, his determination to blot out the specter of "Hollywood kids," with their privileged sense of self-importance, chimed with the pragmatic need to compensate for Dixie's volatility and his own schedule, which kept him away for weeks at a time. The ranch would offset the hours filled in by nannies and grandparents—and not just the ranch. After the war he bought a vacation home at Hayden Lake, just over the Idaho line, a return to the stomping grounds of his youth, though there is little indication that he sentimentally explored them. Hayden Lake is seven miles north of Coeur d'Alene, from which Spokane lies thirty miles east on a road that passes through such memorable markers as Liberty Lake, where Gonzaga students swam and picnicked, and Dishman, where the Musicaladers (Bing on drums and singing through a megaphone) had their longest engagement. Secluded, ravishing, and socially centered on a country club, Hayden Lake served as a reward for the boys after six or seven weeks of humid labor. "The boys work fairly enthusiastically for the prescribed period," he said when they were teenagers, doing as "good a day's work as anybody on the payroll. They earn their money." So they could hardly wait to get to Hayden Lake, where they spent the second half of the summer waterskiing (Phil and Denny excelled at that), golfing, swimming, partying at the beach and at roasts and clambakes.[44] Hard work, hard play. Except that the play had restrictions too: inflexible curfews, rules of deportment. Phil, in his later years, repurchased the Hayden Lake house to relive those summers. This appalled Gary, who found it unsurprising that in the era when Phil returned to Hayden Lake, it had become a notorious coven of neo-Nazis and paranoid militias. As for Elko, it bewildered him that the twins and Linny "served out their time without complaining"; sometimes "they actually seemed to be having fun."[45]

Monday

Dear Folks,

I am having a wonderful time branding and wrangling calves, it is really fun. I named my calf that I am going to enter into the fair "The Major," and he is coming along fine. I have two horses of my own. Yesterday Dave and Warren, Pete and Connie's little boys came out and Dave is so cute, he says "poon" and "hork" for spoon and fork and when I held a knife up in front of him and asked him what it was he said "sive." I know that this will be good news to you dad there is a buck out in the willows and Johnny says he is a fine pointer with a spread of 3 ft. Good news huh. In the letter you sent me before the one you sent last time when you told me what kind of a dog I was going to get I almost jumped out of my shoes for I thought you said spit ball so that is what I am going to name him. Doris wants to know how many you are going to send up for me so she can make arrangements for them.

Love,

Gary[46]

Even though his early memories of the ranch were poisoned by the ritualized summers that followed, Gary had to admit that his initial fears were unwarranted. He saw little of the old man, who spent mornings hunting, fishing, and dictating letters, and when he did, there were no punishments or lectures. He complained that Bing's "great agate eyes" swept "across the terrain, noting each and every thing I was doing wrong," but allowed that "all he had to say to me" was "How's it going." Indeed, the experience sparked in him some of the very virtues Bing had hoped to instill, chiefly empathy for the way others lived. The men he worked with and listened to around campfires, the ones who cooked biscuits and used their saddles as pillows, filled him with wonder. Gary was touched by their resilience, the way they "sweated their butts off sixteen hours a day" and "could get joy out of a sunset or their coffee after dinner." They confused him, at first, when he wanted to talk about the cowboys he knew from Saturday matinees, and they wanted to hear about Bob Hope and curtly dismissed Hollywood cowboys as phonies—except for Roy Rogers and a couple of others who could sit a horse, like his dad, who was no phony. Crosby could do anything. That he had conquered every precinct of show business was a given; the daunting thing was that he was just as good at everything else he put his mind to, except for passing on his expertise to his son. Looking back, Gary came to mistrust every kindness, every pleasure. Yes, the flapjacks his first morning were ambrosial, but much good that was when he inhaled dust riding out on the horse reserved for him; yes, he had his own horse, but much good that did him after the haying started, a chore as monotonous as an industrial assembly line.[47]

Bing returned to Los Angeles at least once a week to cut records, to broadcast *KMH* or *Command Performance* and make guest appearances, to confer about the delays that pushed back the start date for *Going My Way*. Gary said Bing always left behind dos-and-don'ts lists to be enforced in his absence, but the Eacrets declined to act as his "wardens." Johnny mumbled little more than *Yep* and *Nope*, but Gary recognized the warmth in his eyes; "Doris stayed on my case a little, but she was no Georgie," and she didn't peach on him for sleeping late. He later conceded that he loved the Eacrets and the ranch hands, loved caring for the horses, loved waking at the crack of dawn to punch cattle—yet he also despised it because "I *had* to be there, because the old man just jammed it down my throat."[48]

In early August, Bing returned to Los Angeles to stay, as *Going My Way* began shooting midmonth. He wrote weekly letters to Gary and expected prompt replies. Bing's letters have not survived. Gary's have because his parents saved them. At the bottom of one letter in which Gary mocks Bing's work in judging the beauty contest at Elko's fair ("Dad, boy'o boy I never thought you were that bad of a judge. The girls all looked homely"), Bing penciled: "Dixie—save these for me. I talked to him on phone today. Your dad is going up Tuesday and will have him back on Saturday (11th). He's fine and claims his weight is okay."[49]

His weight. It had already begun—Bing's obsession with the only one of his sons who, like himself, visibly registered every mouthful. That Bing had worn a corset while shooting his 1930s films and fiercely dieted in preparation for his 1940s films brought nothing in the way of empathy. He remained certain that Gary's weight was a failure of character, reflecting somehow on himself, as he had been regarding Dixie's alcoholism. He tried a rough gamut of cures, from bribery to humiliation to punishment, which had no effect but to keep the two of them at loggerheads. He called his son Bucket Butt, Lardass, Chubby, and other names, often in the presence of others, who laughed at Father Crosby's wit; he tried carrot-and-stick negotiations; he scheduled appearances on the scales with a scorecard in hand and a number that had to be met by a certain day; it never let up. By seventh grade, Gary discovered speed and other appetite suppressants that were mood altering, dangerously addictive, and a curdling complement to the alcohol he consumed to dodge the pressure. No evidence exists in Bing's interviews or letters that he perceived incongruity in his failure to bring to his son the compassion, forbearance, and regard he brought to tens of thousands of uniformed sons he selflessly entertained. Unconditional love, or its expression, had no part to play in the moral science that was parenting.

Gary's letters were directed almost exclusively to his father. Whether he wrote *Dear Dad* or *Dear Folks* or *Dear Mommy and Dad*, his correspondence barely acknowledged his mother, a fact

Dixie could hardly fail to note. At one point she let her dismay be known. Doris took it upon herself to smooth the waters with one of her own amusingly chatty letters (written three days before Bing began to film *Going My Way*), offering a uniquely colorful account of life on the short-lived Humboldt River property.

Dear Folks,

We thought perhaps you would like to hear just how your man is getting along as I don't know just how newsy his letters are to you.

He felt very badly to think that he had hurt you, Dixie, and we know he just didn't think when he wrote. He usually gets his Dad's letter out and sits down and answers it, and in his mind is writing to you back in the one letter. He is a busy little bee, too, and is up at 6 o'clock, or before, every morning and doesn't get in until about 8 or 8:15 in the evening, By the time he takes his shower and gets to bed it's 8:30 or a quarter of 9:00. That leaves just Sunday to write—and how he hates to write letters. He is like Johnny. They are the "non-writingest" outfits!

I went in yesterday and made arrangements for Gary to join the 4-H Club, although they aren't supposed to take any new members after June 1st. Due to the Fair, etc., they have taken in a limited number of members since June 1st, however.

Do you remember the big 7 months old steer calf we always have talked about—the milk cow's calf? He is eligible in the single steer class (Hereford). We hope it is all right with you as he is so thrilled with the possibilities. He has to halter-break and feed the calf himself. Of course Johnny will help him with the halter-breaking. The calf is quite gentle but pretty husky.

Bessie has been gone since about the 25th of July. She was quite a bit of help at times but is just a youngster and couldn't seem to take any work seriously. During haying we are so busy that I didn't have time to check on her and things began to pile up to where it was a worry to us.

The week-end before we let her go, I let her have Saturday night and Sunday off as I knew the next week would be extremely heavy. Sunday night she didn't come home and didn't call Monday. They don't have a phone so I drove in to find her. I found her about one o'clock and she acted rather independently about it, but I let it pass and asked her to always call whenever she was detained so that we could plan accordingly.

That next afternoon I took Gary to the ice show—kid's day—and when I got home practically nothing had been done and she had several friends—including her boy friend—visiting with her. Oh-Me! When I had dinner almost prepared, in she came. We had a little talk and she felt she liked to have her friends visit her whenever it was convenient for them to come out—so Bessie doesn't live here anymore.[50] Isn't this boring to you? Please don't let Linny know as he liked Bessie so much—and we do, too—but I know things are done when I do them myself and can plan the day better.

Gary is so much help, too, as he keeps his room picked up, makes his bed, cleans up after his shower, and can help with little chores on this side of the river.

I just canned 24 quarts of peaches, 20 quarts of apricots, a few quarts of peas and rhubarb from the garden, and am waiting now for pears to come in full season. They will be grand this winter as there is a scarcity of any fruit or vegetables here in the winter time.

Everyone is so Fair conscious. Henry King and his orchestra and floor show—with Jane Pickens—will be here for a week during the Fair. We certainly wish you folks could get up here.[51]

It looks like the mowing will be finished about tomorrow and they will be baling and stacking for at least another week or ten days. It certainly seems good to see the end of haying season, too, and to see all that good baled hay on high ground. They are mowing and raking up by "Crosby Crossing" ('member) today.

Our cook went to town and got drunk Saturday night and refused to come back with the other men. So Johnny got up at 3:00 A.M. and went down to get him. He was feeling sorry for himself and said that the men didn't appreciate his cooking and guessed he would quit—Glory! Johnny talked to him until his patience gave out and paid him off and came home about 4:45. Sunday Mr. Chas. Howard asked us to have dinner with him (Peter, Lin's boy, spent Sunday with us) so we ran into the cook. He was sober but suffering from a terrific hangover and was beginning to realize what a spot he had put us in. He admitted he "blew his top"—and his roll—and wanted Johnny to re-hire him. I know Johnny could have shook his arm off (and then again cut his throat) but didn't let on and took him back. So now everything is quiet on the Humboldt front.

~~Well, it looks like I've written a novel~~—and no doubt a boring one at that—what with the help trouble you are experiencing. We hope it isn't too serious as it is aggravating as the very dickens. Ours here are nothing compared to some of the other outfits around here. It's murder.

Take an extra dip in the ocean and ride an extra wave in for us while you are at the beach, Dixie, while Johnny and Gary and I take on a little river swimming.

Sincerely,
Doris and Johnny
August 13, 1943[52]

On the morning of the day she took Gary to the ice show, he wrote two letters. The first, addressed *Dear Dad,* is, excepting an attempt at humor (a worker on the baler crew is named Orville and, no, it isn't Bob Hope, a reference to Hope's character in *Road to Morocco*), a justification for his not writing sooner; it had been 90 degrees in the shade yesterday and he was busy tying the bales. He stands up for himself in the postscript: "P.S. I don't like that dear Chubby. We get in from haying at 8:00 and go in the morning at 6:00. The reason I am not gone is because I am going to the Ice Show. Hope it is good." He addressed the second letter to *Dear Mommy and Daddy and Linny and Georgie,* but beyond the generic first sentence, he wrote playfully and exclusively to his kid brother: "How are you all? Linny the minute you left Doris brought in a little baby chicken that had hatched out that night. Oh, oh here he comes walking across the floor to where I am sitting. Then there is a little duck that is supposed to hatch out tomorrow but half the egg is broken and the mother won't keep him and you can see him. I haven't gone horseback riding since you left but yesterday I went into town. Oh here come that chicken again and I have to put him back. Excuse me! Whew! There! Well that's all I have to say and maybe next time I write I'll have more news. Love Gary."[53]

On the whole the summer went well enough that the prospect of returning was held out as a reward for good grades in school, a deal Doris reminded him of in a letter she wrote to Gary in October. She assured him that he was greatly missed and told him that they had finally gotten a milk cow that she trusted would have a calf like Gary's favorite, the Major. She enclosed faces and rattles that she and Gary had made from avocado pits, including one he put aside for Linny, and asked him to write back when he had the time.[54]

As she posted that letter, Bing was in the last month of shooting *Going My Way,* a picture about the conflict between two men of two different generations, each an ordained father. More inspired as an actor than ever before, Bing brought serene confidence to the part of the youthful, humbly unassailable Father O'Malley, whose liberality and compassion border on the superhuman, transforming the lives of everyone on whom his sagacious, enveloping eyes shine—in particular, the troubled children in his besieged Hell's Kitchen parish. He directs them on the right path, going his way, with music and baseball.

15

THE LEO McCAREY WAY

The Muse the bard inspires, exalts his mind;
The muse indulgent loves the harmonious kind.
— Homer, *The Odyssey,* translated by
Alexander Pope (1726)[1]

Leo McCarey had a way of owning a room. Of average height, standing just short of five ten, and at fighting weight, with polished black hair, hound-dog eyes, and a matinee-idol chin, he reminded some people—including Cary Grant—of Cary Grant. When he laughed, he pitched back his head, and his body shook. He had a contagious laugh that drew in people attuned to his blarney and mischief. Bing eulogized him "as a marvelous man to be around," claiming that he added risqué bits to the ends of the rushes he showed studio executives, who scrutinized them with steam coming out of their ears while "we'd listen to Leo crack up."[2]

He also had a sentimental, contemplative quality that surfaced when he sat at the piano, a standard piece of equipment on every McCarey soundstage. He would play and sing a rag, a pop song, or a ditty of his own—he composed countless songs, most unpublished or forgotten, and one minor hit—to create a mood as he kibitzed with his cast and considered what to shoot. As a director he banked on one strategy above all: improvisation. Actors might react with dread or anger when he told them to make up a line or an action as the cameras rolled, the lights blazed, and the crew looked on, fingers crossed. But in the end, they relished what they saw on-screen, marveled at what he got out of them. Leo made stars out of character actors and character actors out of stars.

He was generous with his money and time. Bing said he liked to probe "oddballs," people he met at bars or the track, for possible material. Leo saw life and his place in it as a sequence of anecdotes— vignettes he twisted, coddled, and improved for a laugh, whether to make a point or to hold his audience's attention, much as he did in his episodic films. Leo was venerated by his peers. Charles Laughton considered him "not only a great director, but in my opinion, the greatest comic mind now living." The French filmmaker Jean Renoir famously reflected, "McCarey really understands people— better perhaps than anyone else in Hollywood." Bernard Shaw is thought to have initiated an admiring correspondence with him. Ben Hecht likened him to an O'Casey character with "a comedy fuse sputtering in his soul."[3]

Yet mirthful embroidery often mingles with outright duplicity, and McCarey, a prodigious drinker and persistent philanderer, trafficked in both. Cynics wondered if his piano-playing mornings were meant to camouflage hangovers. His dalliances included leading ladies and hourly pros; if he fell off the radar long enough, his wife, Stella (they were married for forty-nine years, until his death), asked friends to find him and they usually knew where to look. He could be chary regarding on-screen credit. "He was funny, entertaining, cut your balls off if he had to," Dore Schary said in connection with a split story credit McCarey refused him.[4] Like Walt Disney and Frank Capra, Leo eventually commanded a possessory credit, his name above the title. Like them, too, he was a fantasist who subverted realism as he did truth to heighten the reasonableness of wish fulfilment. Like them again, he labored for the big studios but considered himself independent, an artist and not a factory worker turning out what he derisively referred to as "pattern pictures."[5]

He earned his measure of sovereignty, but a peculiar fate awaited Leo McCarey. The pictures he created with Bing Crosby, *Going My Way* and *The Bells of St. Mary's,* established him during the last years of the war as the world's most celebrated film director—in 1944, the Treasury Department identified him as the best-paid

man in America.[6] Up to that point, he had survived near-fatal accidents, illnesses, alcoholism, and artistic disappointments, and he
would face more of the same, along with the suicide of his younger
brother (comedy-short director Ray McCarey), an addiction to
painkillers, and a relentless examination by the IRS. Yet he could
not bear his nonpareil success, which slowed him down as much as
his aches and itches. His Academy Awards worried him and intimidated his muse. After the Crosby diptych, he invested his money
and time in ideas he could never launch; he mulled over concepts
too long between pictures, forfeited blithe spirits to crabby politics,
lost his mojo, reclaimed it in remaking an old hit, and then lost it
again for good. After the war he completed five features in seventeen years, in contrast to the nineteen features and hundreds of
shorts—among them the best of Laurel and Hardy, the team he
helped to create—in the not much longer period capped by *The
Bells of St. Mary's*. He endured his last seven years in silence, often
ailing, largely forgotten.[7]

"Many people helped shape my career," Crosby wrote in his 1969
McCarey eulogy, "but I would have to put Leo at the top of the list."
True, he was writing in response to a grief-laden moment and with
an equivocal rationale—"he was responsible for opening up a
whole new professional avenue to me."[8] Yet after Jack Kapp, who
died two decades earlier, McCarey might well have had the biggest
influence on Bing and his persona. Kapp steered him into his role
of troubadour for all seasons. The public image he created in film
and on radio in the first two decades of his career was, notwithstanding the guidance of advisers like the film director Frank Tuttle and
the radio writer Carroll Carroll, largely self-invented. Middle age presented the formidable challenge of extending that image without
slipping into self-parody or irrelevance. Bob Hope energized his
comedic skills but left the larger question unanswered: What might
"Bing Crosby" represent in the postwar era? He didn't need a palm
reader to see himself receding into a show-business conventional-
ism while the new generation, bolstered by Frank Sinatra, rhythm
and blues, and whatever musical and theatrical fashions might follow, sped ahead. That was unavoidable. The McCarey films slowed
the process, extending Bing's clout as a movie star a good fifteen

years while solidifying his unique and abiding stature. They enhanced his gravity.

McCarey showed him the way with a character that fused Bing's contrary qualities—his restrained warmth and casual diffidence, his erotic allure and glacial indifference. McCarey and Bing concocted a fantasy priest—a perfect, albeit celibate, man. The costume, a white collar and a straw boater, and the trappings, a crucifix and golf clubs, underscored the curious gloss of religious vocation and musical avocation. Liberated from romance, venality, and vainglory but not from intrigue and statecraft, Father O'Malley emerged as a superhuman fount of liberal wisdom, empathy, and action. As emblematic of the war years as Atticus Finch was to the civil rights era (and inspiring seminarians much as Atticus did law students), O'Malley represented a righteousness people could feel and believe in. This role of a lifetime ripened Bing, paving the road for the second half of his career. It proved to him, though he never quite admitted it—modesty forbade—that he really and truly could *act*.[9]

Father O'Malley arose from mutual interests of Bing and Leo. Never the closest of friends, they had known each other since Bing was a Rhythm Boy and a must-see at the Cocoanut Grove, and they got on well, sharing an entrenched Catholicism and a cultural leaning toward the Irish half of their mixed heritages (maternal Irish, paternal Anglo for Crosby; paternal Irish, maternal Franco for McCarey), a lifelong athleticism and sporting ardor, resolute if rocky marriages, and racial and social tolerance. They each had a college education that ended in law school, a taste for whiskey, a quick wit, a consuming love of music, and the capacity to laugh the laugh of Bacchus, which, Aristophanes tells us, ends in tears.

Their differences were no less telling and no less conducive to an inspired collaboration. To begin with, they hailed from opposite sides of the tracks.

Thomas Leo McCarey, named for his father, Tom, and his Pyrenees-raised mother, Leona, was born October 3, 1896, in Los Angeles, two years before his father made himself the first major boxing promoter in Southern California.[10] Leo adored his father, known in fight circles around the country as Uncle Tom McCarey. In the early 1900s, Tom knelt down for a photograph with Leo between his knees, the two of them circled by his fighters—a conspicuously mixed-race roster. In 1903, the *Los Angeles Times* reported that detractors accused him of running "a nigger club."[11] That was the year after McCarey spurred the career of the greatest fighter of the age by staging the match between Jack Johnson and Jack Jeffries, the brother of the heavyweight champion Jim Jeffries. Uncle Tom loved to tell how Johnson handed him a sealed envelope before the bout and, at the fifth-round bell, shouted at him to open it. "I did and on it was written, 'I'll stop Jeffries within fifty seconds after the fifth starts.' And when I looked up Jeffries was being counted out."[12] He promoted eight Johnson fights and was ringside in 1910 when Johnson got his turn at Jim Jeffries, the Great White Hope, who couldn't lay a glove on him. The *Los Angeles Herald* stated in 1908 that "the name of Uncle Tom McCarey" represented "honesty and integrity in the fight game."[13] When California passed a law in 1914 limiting fights to four rounds and purses to twenty-five dollars, Tom threw in the towel and opened a liquor store, where Leo worked after school. In either profession, Tom presided over a securely upper-middle-class home.

Frank Capra admired the elder McCarey's talent for showmanship. When he was a newsboy, on fight nights, he hustled his newspapers as near as possible to the Fight Pavilion, and he leaped into McCarey's crowd-pleasing and nose-bloodying Newsboys Shoe Contest, which awarded five dollars to the first boy who found his shoes in a mountain of them piled high in the ring. Charles Chaplin admired Tom's way of weaving a tall tale into comic gold. His most storied fight matched Mexican Joe Rivers and Ad Wolgast for the 1912 lightweight championship. It ended when the fighters hurled simultaneous knockout punches and both fell to the mat, dazed if not unconscious. Protests were lodged in vain against the referee who picked up Wolgast and held him up while counting out Mexican Joe. Chaplin staged that double whammy in *City Lights*. Leo spun variations on it in two-reel farces and in his 1936 boxing feature *The Milky Way,* made the year his father died.[14]

From his raven-haired mother, Leo got his looks as well as his determination to learn piano and write songs. When her husband died, she moved in with her son (a subject explored in McCarey's 1937 tour de force *Make Way for Tomorrow*). Leo's films are filled with parents and parental figures. His filial attachment suggests an emotionalism absent from Crosby's. Bing honored his forebears with unstinting Fourth Commandment dutifulness. Yet he showed a reserved respect toward his father. If Hollywood Harry, with his mandolin and easy manner, personified the "Bing Crosby" proto-type, Bing depicted him censoriously, in public and in private, as a too-carefree and irresponsible patriarch who failed to earn a proper living. Bing entrusted his father with small accounting chores at the office. Bing feared his mother, and perhaps worshipped her; he repeatedly attributed his successes to her piety. Like Leo, he took his mother into his home in her widowhood. But he displayed few indications, any more than his siblings did, of a demonstrative familial love—a remoteness he apparently inherited from her.

He was, however, a genuinely devout Catholic, unlike McCarey, whose devotion had a more romantic cast. Leo had a typical Irish Catholic boyhood. His paternal aunt Sister Mary Benedict of the Immaculate Heart Convent was the namesake of Leo's sister and daughter and the inspiration for the Ingrid Bergman character in *The Bells of St. Mary's*. Unlike his younger siblings, Leo did not go to a Catholic high school; instead, he went to Los Angeles High, where he met his future wife. He attended the University of South-ern California, where, at his father's insistence, he studied law. He remained a dependable Sunday Catholic, but religion played a more profound role in his pictures than in his life. His five Catholic mov-ies have deeper parallels with Graham Greene's five Catholic nov-els than with anything in American cinema of this era.[15] Yet one cannot imagine McCarey serving as a choirboy, mastering the Latin Mass, or regularly falling to his knees in prayer at home, activities that defined Crosby's very existence. He dabbled enthusias-tically in sports: boxing and rugby at USC, and later golf, tennis, and swimming, but pursued none with the zeal Bing brought to golf and horseracing. Boxing, in particular, turns up regularly in McCa-rey's films—conjoined with religion when Sister Benedict teaches a boy self-defense from a manual.

Tom McCarey figured law school would ensure Leo's way in the world. Bing gave up on the law and dropped out of school months before he would have received a degree. Leo studied hard, went the distance, and practiced unhappily for nearly a year. In 1918, after stepping into an elevator shaft (a mishap he would work and rework in two-reel comedies, memorably in Laurel and Hardy's "Double Whoopee"), spending his compensation on a barren copper mine, writing songs no one published, and losing the one or two cases he tried, he asked his friend and fellow pool-hall habitué David Butler if there was a way for him to get into pictures. Butler introduced him to Tod Browning, an ingenious if alcoholic director contracted to Universal, who hired him as a "script girl" and promoted him to assistant director for *The Virgin of Stamboul*.

In this he defied his father, who was dead set against Leo embarking on a risky career (unlike boxing or promotion). In 1920, four months after *The Virgin* was released, he again defied his parents. Figuring he had a future with Browning, he eloped with Stella Martin, his high-school girlfriend, two years his senior. In the 1940s, Leo described his wedding as conventional, noting that his father teased him about supporting a wife. But shortly before he died, he allowed, "I was secretly married and I wrote the priest a bad check, and I just vaguely remember the ceremony because I felt sorry for the little man when he went to the bank and tried to cash it."[16] Within three years, Universal fired Browning and his protégé. Still, Browning gave Leo a "priceless legacy": an A-to-Z education in filmmaking, a chance to direct a feature (the lost *Society Secrets*), and the valuable advice to create his own stories.[17] Later that year, 1923, he encountered Hal Roach, Mack Sennett's main rival in the field of knockabout short comedies, on the handball courts at the Los Angeles Athletic Club.

Born anew at Hal Roach Studios, McCarey found his métier in improvisation, presiding over widely imitated two-reel comedies with Charley Chase, an everyman character, and Max Davidson, a German-Jewish pantomimist. From the first, he called for a piano to be rolled onto the soundstage. During breaks, actors from his pictures and others on the lot converged to sing with him. "Some of the best material in Charley Chase's pictures came out of sessions with Leo McCarey fiddling around at a piano," Roach averred. "Sometimes it looked as though they were almost dreaming."[18] Oliver Hardy, a newcomer, appeared in one of the Chase shorts, and in 1927 Leo got the idea of pairing him with the brilliant gagman Stan Laurel. Leo helped fine-tune the duo into a consummate partnership, replacing the usual speed and disorder of silent comedies with simmering buildups, scrupulously developed manners, and tit-for-tat belligerence. Capra, also working on the Roach lot, recalled the "ease and speed with which this young genius cooked up laughs on the spot" for the new team.[19] Laurel and Hardy's pie-throwing epic "The Battle of the Century" opened on the last day of 1927. Four days earlier, knowing what he had and who was responsible, Roach promoted McCarey to studio vice president.

In all, McCarey supervised (rarely taking the director's credit) some three hundred short films for Roach[20] before moving on to feature filmmaking at Paramount in 1929. There he worked under one of his idols, Ernst Lubitsch, and earned the enmity of the studio head, B. P. Schulberg,[21] who fired him, a slight he never forgot. "It takes a lot to salve my pride," he later confided, boasting, "Every picture I make for Paramount costs them half a million more than it should."[22] Hired by Sam Goldwyn to direct Eddie Cantor and later rehired at Paramount by Adolph Zukor to direct the Marx Brothers and other great clowns, he proved he had mastered sound and feature films, blending spontaneity with acutely measured behavioral tics that delineated character. In the elaborate bullfighting climax for Cantor's *The Kid from Spain*, Leo combined shrewd editing, rear projection, undercranking, and slow motion—tricks he quickly discarded in favor of comic naturalism. When the Marxes demanded him for *Duck Soup*, he gave them their best showcase while deleting every signature element (piano and harp solos, juvenile love story, verbose gags) that might interfere with his pace; instead, he choreographed the sublime mirror sequence, in which the brothers pretend to be Groucho's reflection—an idea from the silent era that he honed to perfection. In *Six of a Kind*, he merged three established comedy pairs and captured W. C. Fields's incomparable Honest John pool-hall routine. In the Western-themed *Belle of the Nineties*, he had Mae West perform with Duke Ellington, which thoroughly vexed the censors.

The business changed in 1934, as Joseph Breen took charge of the Production Code Administration. That year Capra established a risqué new genre, the screwball comedy, with his canny burlesque *It Happened One Night*, performed by dramatic actors. McCarey had tried, in early sound films like the partially lost *Part Time Wife* and *Indiscreet*, to make nuanced comedies with emotional pivots in which the roles were played by character actors, rather than renowned clowns. He had never brought it off. But in 1935, inspired by Capra, he achieved a breakthrough directing the formidable Charles Laughton—known for portraying Nero, Henry VIII, and Dr. Moreau—in a piece that was already two decades out of date. As the butler turned Western capitalist in *Ruggles of Red Gap*, Laughton preened, posed, munched the scenery, and utterly charmed audiences. Today, we are perhaps less enchanted by his mugging than by two episodes invented at McCarey's piano. In one, Leila Hyams shows Roland Young how to play "Pretty Baby" on drums. In the other, a forlorn Laughton, seated in a saloon, quietly recites the Gettysburg Address. McCarey directed the first scene with a two-shot, giving his actors the space to work and his audience the space to laugh. He directed Lincoln's speech counterintuitively, showing his star hardly at all, favoring instead a montage of barroom listeners and encouraging filmgoers to respond with similar emotions.

After the enormous success of *Ruggles,* McCarey expected to produce his own pictures from original stories with top actors who could play comedy and drama. Yet his next job was an assignment to reverse the declining popularity of the silent-film comedian Harold Lloyd, who contractually demanded McCarey as director. Leo came through with *The Milky Way,* a crafty bundling of boxing, music, and wisecracks that lost money. Worse, a Hollywood dairy had provided gallons of milk as a promotional ploy, and Leo drank a bad batch and had to be rushed to the hospital. As he was recovering, his father died of a heart attack. McCarey vowed to do no more favors for producers and actors. He would create his own films his own way. *Make Way for Tomorrow* (1937), arguably the best picture made in Hollywood about old age, turned out to be Leo's act of defiance against the patriarch running Paramount. Adolph Zukor came to the set and begged for a happy ending in which the elderly couple is allowed to stay together. McCarey had the clout and contract to refuse and instead devised a sequence, at once deliciously witty and emotionally devastating, in which the aged pair, rejected by their children, experience a fantasy-perfect Manhattan evening vibrating with the kindness of strangers and then are forced to separate forever. An eloquent plea for the new program called Social Security, it was McCarey's most personal film and, as one pundit noted in 1944, "the favorite movie at the White House during Roosevelt's second term."[23] Audiences stayed away, and Zukor fired him. In 1941, Paramount's prodigious writer-director Preston Sturges made *Sullivan's Travels,* which lampoons a crack filmmaker who wreaks havoc by insisting on exploring social ills rather than generating laughs. Despite his long record of successes, McCarey would have to humble himself to return to the studio of Bing Crosby.

That he could return at all was made possible by Crosby's high regard for him and the regime change that installed Leo's friend Buddy DeSylva as chief of production. Crucially, he also regained his commercial stature with two ageless hits. In the wake of *Make Way for Tomorrow*'s failure, Leo agreed to another one-shot assignment. The disagreeable Harry Cohn had alienated his star director, Capra, and he lured McCarey to Columbia Pictures to remake a property so musty, he could do with it as he pleased. *The Awful Truth* began as a Broadway vehicle for Ina Claire in 1922 and was filmed unsuccessfully twice in the same decade. Keeping little more than the title, McCarey turned it into the definitive screwball comedy; he pinned it to the forbidden subject of adultery but evaded the censors with a calculated refusal to say whether the characters did or did not commit it. Irene Dunne, an intimate friend, knew McCarey's style. Cary Grant fought him at every step, horrified by Leo's practice of describing a scene in detail and then, instead of handing him a script, telling him to improvise it. When the dust cleared, Leo had helped to invent "Cary Grant"—the persona that brought Grant stardom after twenty-eight previous feature films. One need only compare a comedy he made earlier in the year, *Topper* (a Hal Roach film), in which he is bemused and stolid, with McCarey's film, in which he leaps out of the mise-en-scène with aggressive angularity and verbal authority, to appreciate the transformation. *The Awful Truth* earned Leo the Academy Award for Best Director in 1937. When Capra placed the statuette in his hands, Leo told the Biltmore Hotel gathering, "Thanks, but you gave it to me for the wrong picture."[24]

Cohn offered McCarey a lucrative contract at Columbia, which he rejected. Wanting independence, he signed a two-picture deal with RKO, where he was promised the opportunity to develop a production unit called Colony Pictures. RKO reneged on the deal, stalling with legal impediments while rushing *Love Affair* into production. Leo had other problems. After he submitted a draft of the script, the censors came down on him as never before. Joe Breen's office characterized it as a "low-toned story of gross sexual irregularities, without even a semblance of what we call 'compensating' moral values."[25] After multiple revisions, McCarey completed an unforgettable pipe organ of a movie, demonstrating a prodigious harmonization of farce, heartbreak, piety, and enough existentialist irony to gratify Saint Augustine or Jean-Paul Sartre. It furthered the careers of Charles Boyer and Irene Dunne—whose character twice asks Boyer's, "Going my way?"—and kept McCarey on top but with limits.

Love Affair was an international hit in the fall of 1939, and Leo had a sure winner set up for production in 1940 (another Grant and Dunne comedy of adultery and jealousy, *My Favorite Wife*). He proposed a third project to RKO's president, George Schaefer—the man who in three years would offer carte blanche to Orson Welles and lose his presidency for approving *Citizen Kane* and *The Magnificent Ambersons*. He was more circumspect with McCarey's idea, a film about Catholic priests in an urban church. He wired him his decision:

DEAR LEO: DELAYED ANSWERING YOUR WIRE UNTIL I COULD MAKE INQUIRIES AND GIVE YOU CONSENSUS OF OPINION AND MY OWN REACTION. INCLINED TO BELIEVE THAT BY THE TIME YOU GET THROUGH SKIRTING PROBLEM YOU HAVE WITH THE CHURCH, BEING CAREFUL TO AVOID ANYTHING OFFENSIVE OR PREJUDICIAL, YOU PROBABLY WOULD HAVE TO TAKE OUT MUCH OF THE REAL VALUE OF THE PLAY. AS YOU KNOW, WE ALWAYS HAVE TO BE CAREFUL OF THE USUAL CENSORSHIP PROBLEM BUT, WHEN ON TOP OF CENSORSHIP, YOU ALSO HAVE TO WATCH THE CHURCH PROBLEM, I AM VERY MUCH AFRAID YOU WOULD WIND UP BEHIND THE EIGHT BALL. THEREFORE I THINK IT WOULD BE TOO MUCH OF A GAMBLE. REGARDS.[26]

Two months after receiving that wire, Leo drove the writer Gene Fowler to his mountain lodge to work on adapting a play by Fowler and Ben Hecht. On an overcast evening ten days later, they sped home at ninety-five miles an hour, drunk and singing. At a cross-road in Azusa, Leo's Lincoln Zephyr rammed into a 1924 Packard sedan without working lights, knocking it on its side, though its only occupant was not seriously hurt. McCarey's car came to rest in an orange grove, the windshield shattered and the driver's side demolished. Fowler had bruises and gasoline burns on his body and face; he was taken to the hospital but was quickly released. McCarey barely survived. The accident report described multiple burns, gouge wounds, deep lacerations and contusions, broken bones, a possible skull fracture—the attending doctor "did not care to commit himself as to eventual outcome."[27]

Hospitalized for six months of operations (with more to follow), McCarey returned home dependent on painkillers. He produced *My Favorite Wife* in a wheelchair, having delegated the job of director to Garson Kanin. According to Crosby, Leo "never fully recovered, and though he never complained, I'm sure that he was frequently in pain."[28] Another setback followed: he made an agreement to direct a film for Howard Hughes that ended with a lawsuit (and $250,000 compensation to Hughes), forcing Leo's inactivity until RKO offered to pay off Hughes in return for another two-picture contract. The first of those films opened to disappointing business in late 1942. A romantic comedy with Cary Grant and Ginger Rogers, set against the Nazi conquest of Europe, it handed McCarey his first possessory credit, a mark of status unique to pictures: Leo McCarey's *Once Upon a Honeymoon*. He anticipated problems and held a preliminary screening for four "very representative Jews," including a rabbi and Jack Benny. They approved, yet McCarey ultimately regretted making it; "my public and I were not on the same wavelength." He complained that the studio ruined the comedy and added shots. The real problem was the unbalanced mingling of modes, including Nazi stock footage, Jewish refugees, American flag waving, romance on a train and an ocean liner, and protracted jokes about how to measure Rogers's breasts and kill a Nazi infiltrator played by Walter Slezak. McCarey's singular phrase is reworked as Rogers glumly asks Slezak, "Coming our way?"[29]

By January 1943, *Once Upon a Honeymoon* was playing in just one Los Angeles theater. McCarey needed a project and his freedom, and he became obsessed with the one idea that RKO had rejected—a film everyone tried to talk him out of. He had little more than a title, *The Padre,* but he used his position as studio director to commandeer a writer on RKO's payroll. Crosby also needed a new project, having nothing to follow *Dixie,* his only release in 1943. A few properties were floated and even touted in the trades: a musical, *All Around Town,* with which Paramount hoped to reunite Bing and Fred Astaire; *Stallion Road,* with Bing running a horse farm; *California,* with Bing joining the gold rush and crooning for statehood; an untitled story about training the naval auxiliary unit, Women Accepted for Volunteer Emergency Service, WAVES, which eventually got made as *Here Come the Waves.*[30]

Paramount insisted that a new Road picture go before the cameras before the end of the year and debated the locale as the world map became increasingly touchy. They briefly revived the title that had been switched to Morocco, *Road to Moscow,* and their writers began to hoard sledding and snow jokes. But the Soviet Union in 1943, engaged in the bloody Battle of Stalingrad with over two million casualties, more than half of them Russian, was hardly a destination for comedy. So they shifted the snow jokes to the Klondike, specifically Skagway, on the eastern panhandle of Alaska. As a title, *Road to the Klondike* was thought clumsy, *Road to Skagway* unappealing, and *Road to Alaska* only marginally more exciting than *Road to Ohio.* They settled on *Road to Utopia* and scheduled the shooting to begin December 3, 1943. That suited Bing, who had planned an extended spring vacation with Dixie for the period before he introduced Gary to Elko.

In the interim, two directors, friends of Bing and of each other, both approached him with genuinely stimulating ideas. Leo McCarey's went forward. David Butler's fell victim to his attempt to secretly sidestep Paramount. Butler had directed four successful Will Rogers pictures, including *A Connecticut Yankee,* which Bing would remake in 1949, and he now wanted to film Rogers's life story. He believed only Crosby could play the part. This was "the one great idea in my life,"[31] and he brought it to a producer at Warner Brothers, Mark Hellinger, for whom he had just completed an all-star home-front revue, *Thank Your Lucky Stars.* Butler and Hellinger planned to make it Bing's annual "independent" feature.

Bing had given up his free-agent clause in the three-year contract he signed with Paramount in 1941, but as he loved the idea—he asked Butler, "Do you think I can do it?"—they expected him to reinstate the clause in his new contract. They arranged covert meetings to create the makeup, padding Bing's cheeks with rubber sponges and building the facial structure to resemble Rogers; to select and rehearse a scene; and, finally, to shoot a screen test. The test, made at night at Warner with a crew Butler trusted to keep it secret, exceeded expectations. "Bing was great," Butler told a *Time* reporter after the project fell apart. "He chewed his glasses, looked over the rims, drawled just like Will." Somebody leaked the test to Harrison Carroll, who wrote in his column that Warner guarded the project "like a military secret" and that it would "electrify Hollywood because there hasn't been a breath of a hint that Crosby was being considered for the part."[32] It definitely electrified Y. Frank Freeman, who threatened to sue Harry Warner for daring to "make a secret test of our actor." Butler phoned Freeman and took responsibility, but Freeman shouted him down. "Boy," Butler later recalled, "I never heard such a thing as that before."[33]

There was no lawsuit and no Crosby picture, since Warner owned the rights to the Will Rogers story and Paramount owned the rights to Bing. But six months after the secret test, in September, the trades announced a new Crosby-Paramount contract. It called for seven pictures over three years, including just one outside film; in exchange for letting Paramount borrow McCarey (for *Going My Way*), RKO would get to borrow Crosby the following year. At this point, they had been filming the McCarey picture for weeks.

16

PADRES

My movie is born first in my head, dies on paper; is resuscitated by the living persons and real objects I use, which are killed on film but, placed in a certain order and projected on to a screen, come to life again like flowers in water.

—Robert Bresson, *Notes on the Cinematographer*
(1950s)[1]

"Someday," Leo told Bing, "I'm going to make a movie with you in it, and it won't be because of your vocal cords."[2]

They liked to tell of a running gag that began after they agreed to make a picture together. In Bing's telling, Leo promised, "Well now, I'll get an idea for you sometime and when I do I'll let you know." When they encountered each other, say on different fairways on the golf course, Bing would yell, "Now?" and Leo would "give me this slow, negative shake, 'No.'" This went on for a year. One day at a football game Leo answered with an affirmative "Now," and Bing invited him to the house on Sunday afternoon. They had a couple of drinks before Leo got down to business and said: "I want you to hear the idea I have for you and maybe you'll think it isn't now. You're going to play a hep priest."

"What's a hep priest?" I inquired. "A disc jockey at KFWB?" "No," he answered, "just a regular fellow, with a sense of humor. He achieves results, not with ponderous precepts, thunderous theology or frightening threats of Hellfire and damnation, but by making religion pleasant and attractive. Joyful." "I've known many such," I told him. "Well, you're going to be one," he said. And we parted on that note.[3]

Bing later recalled that, being "a great actor," Leo, who had nothing on paper, "told me a story that wasn't the story we used. But it was a hell of a story." Crosby gave him his handshake commitment. "I was sold. I said, 'By God, I'll be ready in the morning.'" But it wouldn't be so easy. On Crosby's side, there was a time-sensitive proviso. Given *Road to Utopia*'s December start-up and another Paramount production anticipated for early 1944, Leo needed to start shooting his hep priest in ninety days, otherwise he would have to postpone using Crosby for a year or more.[4] Hanging over McCarey's head was the $250,000 judgment awarded to Howard Hughes in their dispute. "We won't discuss Mr. Hughes professional probity here," Bing recounted to a friend. "He's a powerful man, and he <u>had</u> the judgment. Leo was blackballed in the industry until he paid it, and he didn't have it." RKO paid it, in return for a contract that kept McCarey on the hook. Bing assigned his brother Everett full-time to create a deal agreeable to the two studios, Paramount and RKO.[5]

Leo had no intention of postponing for another year. He had nursed and nurtured *The Padre*. "It possessed me," he said. "I had unwavering faith that it would make an outstanding motion picture." Before he ever approached Crosby, he considered producing it independently without major stars, and even "consulted" Johnny Mercer about playing the priest and composing the songs. This seems madness; Mercer showed in two 1935 features (he never appeared in another picture) that he could neither act nor attract moviegoers. Leo may have wanted Mercer mainly as a songwriter. He told Barry Fitzgerald, a well-regarded but underpaid character actor (his career had soared in the Sean O'Casey era of Dublin's Abbey Theatre, but he now treaded water in support of Tarzan and Deanna Durbin), not to accept commitments as Leo had a part for him that would make him a star. Knowing Mercer couldn't hold his own against Fitzgerald let alone carry a picture, he made a half-hearted pitch to James Cagney by way of his manager-brother

William, who said, essentially, not a chance. Only then did it "suddenly" occur to Leo that Crosby would be perfect in the part. "I was so enthused I set out to move heaven and earth to get him." At the end of McCarey's life, when Peter Bogdanovich asked him what "specifically" inclined him to cast Crosby, he answered succinctly, "He could do no wrong as an actor."[6]

With Bing and Fitzgerald lined up and some semblance of a story in mind, he brought the package, as he was obliged to do, to the new regime at RKO headed by Charles W. Koerner, who told McCarey "emphatically and at length that they wanted no part of a picture whose theme was so intimately related to a religious group."[7] The year 1943 proved to be spectacularly profitable for divine guidance, as two Catholic-themed epics went into production. But unlike *The Padre,* each of the pair was based on a bestseller that ensured audience interest and offered exoticism beyond that of an indigent American church. *The Song of Bernadette* depicted virginal Jennifer Jones in nineteenth-century France, and *The Keys of the Kingdom* dispatched Gregory Peck to evangelize the land of the Good Earth. McCarey had established the fact that a film about older people could not entice enough older people for it to break even. Why did he expect Catholics to queue up to see the world's most likable singer with his collar turned around? Koerner particularly opposed casting Crosby; he considered it too provocative to be anything other than "a bad commercial risk."[8]

Undeterred, McCarey moved ahead. As a writer who did not actually write, he enlisted (separately) two professionals who did: a journeyman screenwriter on RKO's payroll, Frank Cavett, and the incredibly popular Lutheran clergyman turned middle-aged novelist Lloyd C. Douglas, whose epic *The Robe,* a saga of early Christians, was then and would remain for years the nation's bestselling book. McCarey hired him and paid him out of pocket for seven weeks at $1,875 a week (a total of $13,125, an investment of about $184,000 in today's money), fed him story material, juggled ideas, and at length received from Douglas a fifty-six-page treatment. Cavett, also in collaboration with McCarey (but never with Douglas), developed a separate treatment and screenplay.

With an option on Fitzgerald, a Crosby handshake, and a vague story about a young Midwestern priest sent to New York's Hell's

Kitchen on a mission to save St. Dominic's Church but without informing or hurting the feelings of the aged priest in charge, McCarey took the package to Paramount and his pal Buddy DeSylva, who admired and believed in him. DeSylva may even have felt indebted to him; his 1922 song "Wishing," an indulgence in gross sentimentality, was not recorded until McCarey used it in *Love Affair*, after which it unexpectedly reaped a bonanza as the first number one hit by Glenn Miller. Still, *The Padre* was little more than a succession of anecdotes when Leo told Buddy what he had in mind. In Bing's words, Buddy "was willing to go along with it. Leo just told him I'd play [in it] and he…let Leo go to work." DeSylva could not, however, sanction a million-dollar budget; that was Y. Frank Freeman's jurisdiction. Buddy convinced Freeman and the New York office (Barney Balaban, Paramount's true ruler) to indulge the project, up to a point.[9]

McCarey intended to make *The Padre* as an independent film within the framework of Paramount Pictures (much as he had hoped to do with Colony Pictures at RKO). The new company was to be called Leo McCarey Productions. He authorized his agents to offer Freeman the story and screenplay along with his services as director and producer for $500,000. Freeman declined. He was unwilling to invest even $150,000, McCarey's standard rate for producing and directing. The two entered into personal negotiations. Since *The Padre* was not based on a bestselling book or successful stage play, the deal would hinge on the value of the story. Freeman showed him the grosses on Crosby's films. "No picture I had previously directed had come close to Bing Crosby grosses, so I had no confidence that my directorial efforts would justify the gamble," McCarey rationalized. "My confidence lay in the story." That confidence was well placed; the story and characters would enjoy a valuable afterlife through a sequel, publications, radio, and television. Freeman eventually offered him $80,000 "sure money" for the story ($50,000 to McCarey and $30,000 to allay his expenses for cowriters), with additional percentage payouts contingent on profits that Freeman cautioned were unlikely. Leo's salary to direct and produce was a mere $25,000; that price could increase from profits on distribution but not beyond the cap of $150,000, his standard fee. If McCarey accepted the offer, Freeman would accept his casting choices, though he reminded him that Bing's availability depended on Leo's having a shooting script in short order. Freeman also allowed him to hire Paramount's long-standing screenwriter Frank Butler, a veteran of seven Crosby films and McCarey's *The Milky Way* (they had also worked together for Hal Roach). But McCarey would have to pay Butler's salary out of his own pocket.[10]

McCarey and Freeman established their accord in the first week of March, yet Freeman postponed preparing a contract through spring, summer, and fall, forcing McCarey to begin shooting the film on faith. The contract ultimately set before him on September 8, twenty-three days into production, was not the agreement he had negotiated, one that compensated for his reduced salary by allowing him to establish an independent production arm. Freeman said that would set a bad precedent; other directors would demand the same thing. Instead, he was asked to sign the usual personal-service contract, stipulating withholding taxes and a provision that any residual fees would kick in if and when the studio recouped 1.6 times its costs. Leo had little choice; he could sign it and finish his picture or walk off the set and never again work in Hollywood.

By mid-April, Bing had spoken at length with Leo about *The Padre,* comparing notes on priests they had grown up with and agreeing on the casting of such mutual friends as William Frawley and Frank McHugh, though McCarey hadn't settled on the parts they would play. Bing arranged with *Kraft Music Hall* to take an early recess through mid-June rather than in July and August, when he would commute to Elko and embark on *The Padre*. He and Dixie needed some privacy. A month earlier he had hobbled about on a cane while she rested her nerves at Cedars of Lebanon. They planned to repair their marriage, visit family, and sell war bonds.

The radio show, a fast half-hour broadcast as of January, wobbled a bit in finding its new groove. Bing evidently enjoyed his latest comic foil, Leo "Ukie" Sherin, more than many in his audience did. Lacking the sophistication of Victor Borge, the mania of Jerry Lester, or the rustic resourcefulness of the ever popular Bob Burns, Sherin instead served as a stooge for Bing, whose barbs took an inadvertently derisive turn, as Ukie—a pleasantly self-effacing gag writer who earned his stage name playing ukulele and singing (off-key)—lacked the ability to keep up with the boss's timing and delivery.

The stature of Bing's guest stars declined, as the tighter schedule allowed for little more than a character actor or comedian to do a sketch and a military figure to salute the troops. Major film people were rarely invited to promote their latest, and aside from an occasional appearance by a singer like Ginny Simms, the program's regulars handled the music. In addition to the indefatigable John Scott Trotter and the bubbly Music Maids, who stayed on for a year after losing their arranger Hal Hopper to the draft, the Charioteers brought robustness to every broadcast, and Trudy Erwin relaxed into her role as Bing's vocal partner and sketch mate. Each week, they took a nostalgic turn as a romantic couple named Harry and Trudy, mooning over a bygone day before segueing into a "memory song." The show was slick (they rehearsed Wednesday nights and Thursdays until showtime) and sustained its high ratings. After the show, Bing often invited the cast to dine and dance down the block at the Palladium on Sunset. He seemed content presiding over an efficient, relaxed production. *Variety* declared him "right on the beam" and rated his show as "a sock half hour of diversified entertainment."[11]

On April 15, Bing broadcast his final *KMH* of the season; he announced his trip to Mexico and his spring stand-ins, two hugely popular radio couples: Fibber McGee and Molly, followed by Lum and Abner. Earlier that day, Bing had received a telegram at NBC from a Mrs. McClure in Colfax, Washington: IS IT POSSIBLE TO ANNOUNCE ON YOUR PROGRAM THAT CORPORAL TOMMY MCCLURE SERVING WITH MARINES IN SOUTH PACIFIC IS DADDY TO EIGHT POUND BOY BORN APRIL 12TH. BOTH DOING FINE. THEY LISTEN TO YOUR PROGRAM AND WE CANNOT WIRE HIM. Of course it was possible; he wasn't supposed to, for fear of endless requests, but Bing tendered his congratulations. That same day, Allied Headquarters in North Africa reported on the weekly broadcasts of a new program from Radio Berlin, *Home Sweet Home*, which interspersed Crosby records between "jibes at democracy, Jews and British communists." This was the first indication that the Nazis were exploiting Crosby's popularity in Germany for their own propaganda. Two days later, Bing and Dixie boarded a train for Mexico City. Harrison Carroll reported their leaving and confidently asserted that Bing would make no more pictures before *Road to Utopia*.[12]

Coincidentally, the train also carried Bob Hope, who was en route to Dallas. Hope tried in vain to get them to disembark with him for a show he was doing. Bing wanted time with Dixie, and for the better part of two weeks they went off the grid, disappearing from daily newspaper reports, press releases, and blind items. They arrived in Mexico City on April 21 and appeared together in an on-air benefit for the Mexican Red Cross; other than that, they kept to themselves. Meanwhile, Paramount began testing the waters for *The Padre* with vague announcements about Bing's next role as a songwriting priest. In early May, a day after resolving key issues with McCarey and RKO, the studio released a few details about the picture. Just how far McCarey remained from the eventual story may be fathomed from Hedda Hopper's breathless summary: "He writes them, then sings them. All the money goes into building a church. The character's sort of based on Father O'Connor of Brooklyn. Takes Bing into a world peace movement, which includes all races, and ends with Bing going off to war as a chaplain." The integrated peace movement sounds like something from two decades later; neither that nor the wartime chaplain exists in either the finished picture or in any prior drafts and treatments. McCarey improvised this placeholder strictly for Hedda.[13]

Bing resurfaced on May 2 to announce he had sold nine horses to two racing enthusiasts in Mexico City for thirteen thousand dollars and declare his intention to enter seven of his New York–stabled horses in the 1944 meeting at the recently completed Hipódromo de las Américas. Days later the Crosbys traveled to New Orleans, accompanied by a couple of friends and Barney Dean. It was Dixie's first return to the hometown of her adolescent years since 1929 and Bing's first visit ever. The next day, Bing met up again with Hope, playing in a benefit at the City Park golf course before a crowd of three thousand (Bing sang "Way Down Yonder in New Orleans" and auctioned his tie), the beginning of another war relief tour sponsored by the PGA; they also led a parade of ten thousand to City Park Stadium. Late that night, Bing and Dixie headed for Atlanta, where he continued his movable benefit with Hope on the links at Capital City Country Club. From there, without Hope or Dixie, he went to Chicago's Soldier Field for the third annual I Am an American Day (an audience of 130,000 got to see Bing, Dinah Shore, John Garfield, Paulette Goddard, and a navy band), after which he visited station WENR to serve as guest quizmaster for *Quiz Kids*. He donated this thousand-dollar fee to Mayor Edward Kelly—who had recently made news for banning Nelson Algren's *Never Come Morning* from the Chicago library—to support the city's servicemen's centers. Then he met up with Dixie in New York, where they watched races at Belmont and dined at the Stork Club, after which she returned to the house on Mapleton Drive. He went to Philadelphia to resume his contest with Hope.

Variety's May 5 article "Crosby, McCarey in 1-Pic Loan Deals at RKO, Par"[14] signaled a studio deal still being worked out: RKO would permit McCarey to direct a Crosby picture at Paramount, beginning immediately; Paramount would allow Crosby to make a picture at RKO, beginning January 2 or April 1, 1944. Even so, RKO demanded that McCarey repay $22,111.07, the salary he received while allegedly working on the second picture in his contract. He would also have to repay the salary earned by Frank Cavett for the time he worked on *The Padre* prior to RKO's rejection of it, a sum of $13,986.83, including $600 for wages paid to Cavett's secretary, nearly the same amount he paid Lloyd Douglas.[15]

The story Leo wanted to tell jelled slowly, forcing delays until July and then August. He later argued passionately that the finished film was his most personal, most autobiographical work and composed a memo listing the ways. The story involved a gang of toughs led by Tony Scaponi (played by Stanley Clements), which drew on mischief-making friends of Leo's youth. Bing and his friends had robbed a pie truck; Leo's pals rustled turkeys, just like the gang in the movie. Leo even had a witness to his criminal plunder, his old friend Fred Haney, the veteran third baseman who managed the St. Louis Browns for two seasons (1939 to 1941) and provided the Browns jacket Bing wears in the film. McCarey also claimed he was "closely associated with priests at all times" and had once envisioned becoming one, though he admitted he wasn't serious about it. Leo had no calling. But he had set out to compose edifying songs to uplift young parishioners while clarifying the Ten Commandments. He wanted to show that religion need not be gloomy. The Irish lullaby "Too-Ra-Loo-Ra-Loo-Ral," which his picture restored to prominence after three decades of neglect, commemorated his father, who sang it to him in his childhood.[16]

He said he modeled the Barry Fitzgerald character, Father Fitzgibbon, on Monsignor Nicholas Conneally, the pastor of St. Monica Church from 1926 until his death in 1949. McCarey got to know him when Conneally came seeking donations for a loud-speaker. McCarey handed him a check and asked how long he had been at the church. "Forty-five years. I built the church," Conneally said, gruffly asking in return, "Where have you been? I don't remember seeing you at Mass." Leo put the loudspeaker into the screenplay and shot a few scenes in the nave and church garden of St. Monica's.[17]

McCarey often said that he hated plots. The best scenes emerged from characters and the way they interacted. He prized spontaneity and encouraged surprise. But legally he could count on improvisa-tion only so far; his contract required a script well in advance of shooting.

He did not have much help from Lloyd C. Douglas, whose treat-ment, set in 1937, gets under way with twelve pages describing the spacious campus of St. Mary's in St. Louis, where Father O'Malley, while playing baseball with other curates, is tasked with saving New York City's St. Dominic's Church, located on Forty-Ninth Street between Ninth and Tenth Avenues. He must do this without hurting the feelings of the old pastor in charge. Douglas aimed to track "the moral rehabilitation of a tough neighborhood," as well as a battle of wills and strategies between "the Old Order and the New," each "devoted to their trusts," with O'Malley shouldering the responsibil-ity of keeping peace, "an irksome task demanding endless tact." His story has no stolen turkeys, no opera star, no marriage, no choir, no war, no fire, and no reunion between Father Fitzgibbon and his mother; it has no reconciliation between the priests, and no humor. It does have the basic setup of old and young priests, the broken window, the girl who wants to sing, and the sullen businessman, all of which originated with McCarey and Cavett. McCarey discarded Douglas's structure and social-science solemnity.[18]

Cavett's treatments and scripts, written between April and July, preceding and following Douglas, vary the location of the opening scene from New York to St. Louis to Pennsylvania. One script ends as O'Malley promises Fitzgibbon to look up his mother when he goes to Ireland. Another involves a Broadway entertainer named

Banjo Swartz and a tough *West Side Story*–type Tenth Avenue gang called the Pelicans. His final treatment begins unpromisingly with an Aesop-like moral: "There's an old adage which says that there is many a way to skin a cat, and in the course of this story we shall see the truth in it." It opens in a New York church in a "once rather exclusive residential section [that] has lost caste," as Fitzgibbon awaits the arrival of Father O'Malley. The St. Louis backstory scenes are gone, as is, innovatively, the preachiness.

Cavett took on the Production Code Administration with a satellite storyline that could never have been filmed. In this version, the girl who wants to sing, Carol, is a radio-contest winner who shows up in New York pregnant (as opposed to the picture's modestly talented runaway, willing to ply the streets to "get along"). A businessman supports her after she attempts suicide. His son is smitten with her despite her pregnancy, but he is drafted, at which point the baby's father shows up and marries her, learning at the wedding of her pregnancy and his paternity. Breen never read any of that. Cavett's writing has little of the anecdotal impulsiveness that defines a McCarey script, but it does have story points that would make their way, thoroughly reconstructed, into the final film. One is O'Malley's reunion with an old friend, a nightclub singer called Miss Betty, whose startled reaction to his collar is meant to indicate their amorous past. This was the state of the script in late June, weeks before they were scheduled to begin shooting.[19]

Meanwhile Bing and Bob continued the May tour, selling war bonds on golf courses and local radio shows, at municipal halls and department stores, anywhere city officials could arrange for them to go, and in addition they kept entertaining troops and visiting hospitals. Hope traveled by plane, Bing mostly by train. In Memphis, Bing enjoyed a storied golf match. He was teamed with the illustrious Byron Nelson, at the height of his powers, against his mentor Ed Dudley and the local favorite, Jake Fondren, before a crowd of ten thousand. He had played other matches Nelson was in but usually on the opposing and losing team. This triumph must have boosted his spirits, as he sang for forty-five minutes on the last hole, backed by a radio-station orchestra, and then a cappella at Kennedy General Hospital before catching the 8:14 to the capital.

Appearing in Washington, DC, with Babe Ruth and Kate Smith, he stirred a crowd of twenty-nine thousand at a game between the Senators and the Norfolk naval station. At the seventh-inning stretch, he sang "Dinah," "As Time Goes By," and, seven months before the holiday, "White Christmas."[20]

That week the armed forces announced the conversion of Del Mar Turf Club to a plant manufacturing aircraft with an unparalleled employment proviso of 90 percent women. Women rarely made up more than 40 percent of the workers at other plants, and most would be pushed out of the labor force after the war, but the tide was turning and the cultural memory of Rosie the Riveter, who ruled Del Mar, helped to turn it. Crosby was doubly pleased that the nearby track would serve the war effort. His financial interest in racing proscribed his investing in other sports, and he had begun to rethink his commitment to it.[21] He didn't need a franchise to race. On a break from the tour, he attended New York's Belmont Park to watch Don Bingo, a four-year-old bred at his Argentina farm, win the Glorifier Handicap with a $3,000 purse. Four days later, while he and Hope played an exhibition match in Atlanta (selling more than $300,000 in war bonds), Don Bingo took the Suburban Handicap, earning Crosby $27,600 at twelve-to-one odds and setting the world's record for generating bets, nearly $2.7 million. The jockey, Joe Renick, auctioned Binglin's blue and gold silks to a Wall Street broker for $200,000 in bonds. Hope declared a cease-fire on Crosby-horse jokes.[22]

Bing's sporting successes notwithstanding, his hosts noted signs of exhaustion when Crosby arrived alone in Birmingham to present a plaque to an aircraft plant. Yet when a planned exhibition match fell through, he agreed to ride two hours to Fort Oglethorpe in the northernmost part of Georgia to sing to five thousand members of the Women's Army Auxiliary Corps, backed by a local pianist. Afterward, he posed for pictures, bleary-eyed but laughing. He wrote to a WAAC sergeant, "It was a thrilling thing to stand in front of those fine young women and feel that I was their friend, and that they enjoyed my music." It made no sense to return to Birmingham to board the train for Nashville, so he hired a car for a twenty-minute ride to the Read House in Chattanooga, where he spent the night. One of his Nashville hosts panicked and called the city's major hotels in search of him. At noon, an army car brought

Bing to Nashville's Hermitage Hotel. He tipped the driver fifty dollars and called Dixie to tell her he was all right. Two hours later he played the Belle Meade course teamed with Ed Dudley, losing to Byron Nelson and Adrian McManus, after which he appeared in a show that raised an astonishing $514,000. Bob Rule reported in the *Nashville Banner,* "Immediately, when he walked out on the platform and took over the microphone, he captivated the crowd." And yet "Nashville people didn't see him even close to his best. The man is dead tired. He has been doing this for weeks and weeks, and he's actually numb from the constant strain. He has few moments he can call his own." Rule predicted that Crosby "will come out of this war one of America's heroes."[23] That night Bing and Ed Dudley took the train to Chicago, where he checked into the Drake Hotel and hastily sent a telegram to his brother Everett asking him to contact J. Walter Thompson's New York office with a request to extend his so-called vacation by an additional week, postponing his return to the show until June 17. He asked to be advised of the response at once. Instead, Everett contacted Thompson's chief executive in Los Angeles, Willard Lochridge, who told him to have Bing phone him. At 6:14 the next morning, Bing wired Ev: IF I WANTED TO DEAL WITH LOCKRIDGE [*sic*] I WOULDN'T HAVE WIRED YOU PLEASE HANDLE IMMEDIATELY AND ADVICE [*sic*]. BING.[24]

Permission was granted, and after a few days of decompression, he traveled to Colorado Springs, where he and Dudley and a few pros played golf for a week at the Broadmoor without the attention of a gallery yet made news anyway when he "achieved his lowest score in several summers of play" at the resort: 73. That day at his office on Sunset Boulevard, a short legal notice arrived from J. Walter Thompson informing him that their 1937 contract, amended in 1938 and twice in 1940, provided Thompson with an option for his services on the Kraft show for 1944, and "we are taking up said option." Something else happened that day, unknown to Bing, that would soon jolt his personal life: Buddy DeSylva announced he was importing from Broadway, at a record salary for a newcomer, the former model Joan Caulfield, recently voted most promising actress by the New York Drama Critics. He named three pictures he had in mind for her, including a role opposite Crosby in *The Padre.* Louella Parsons commented, "If she gets a chance to emote opposite Bing her fame would be assured." On June 13, a well-rested Bing returned to Hollywood, signed and mailed the carbons extending his obligation to *KMH,* then drove Gary up to Elko; four days later, he resumed his program.[25]

McCarey had no script for Crosby but assured him it would be ready in July, the original deadline to secure Bing's services. Working with Cavett, he made headway in story and music. He decided to make the nightclub singer an opera star, though he continued to call her Betty, and offered the role to Grace Moore, the Metropolitan Opera soprano who had made several pictures in the 1930s. She wired him: THE FACT THAT I CAN HAVE NO SCRIPT PUTS MY LIFE IN YOUR HANDS WHICH I AM WILLING TO DO FOR I KNOW YOU WILL DO A GREAT PICTURE. But they could not reach an agreement. Leo then turned to an up-and-coming Met diva, fifteen years younger than Moore, who had starred in one picture, a travesty of *The Chocolate Soldier,* that so soured her on Hollywood she went on suspension to get out of her MGM contract. Leo would have to be at his diplomatic best to get Risë Stevens.[26]

She was in rehearsal at the Met when McCarey phoned her from Los Angeles. He said he would be in New York and asked her to lunch. Her imagination, speeding with possibilities, failed to prepare her for the proposition he put before her when they met in a Manhattan restaurant. Would she be interested in making a picture with Bing Crosby? Why me? she asked. Leo said he had approached Lily Pons and Grace Moore, but they had declined to sing with a crooner and turned him down. That *might* have been the case with Pons; Moore's telegram indicates otherwise. But he evidently expected their names, exalted company, to beguile her. Stevens was not easily beguiled, though she did venerate Crosby: "I'm a typical American, you know. I mean, I grew up in the Jazz Age and I adored Bing for many years, going way, way back. I just loved the quality of his voice and I just liked *him*—the absolute control he had, the sureness, the professionalism." Risë told Leo she was interested but would not do anything without consulting her husband and manager, Walter Surovy, recently drafted and stationed in Sacramento. Leo said, Let's call him right now. He beckoned a waiter to bring a phone. Surovy told her, "Sign anything, just do the film." He asked to speak to Leo and suggested to him that he write a preliminary offer, no money, on a napkin. Leo took out his pen. "I signed it," Risë recalled. "It was a cloth napkin." Surovy ultimately negotiated her two thousand dollars a week for ten weeks (a significant fee; by contrast, Barry Fitzgerald received twelve hundred and fifty dollars a week). On June 23, Risë wired Leo: DELIGHTED WITH OPPORTUNITY OF WORKING WITH YOU AND BING. LOOK FORWARD SEEING YOU BOTH NEXT MONTH IN HOLLYWOOD. KINDEST REGARDS. He gave her a start date of July 26. He did not give her a script.[27]

Crosby desperately wanted to make this picture; he had never displayed deeper commitment to any project. He loved the character and the story, such as it was, and he wanted to work with Leo McCarey, who understood the Bing persona as well as anyone and who could channel it in a new direction. Not everyone at the studio shared his enthusiasm. If the film failed, audiences might never forgive his hubris in playing at religion. McCarey later told of a Paramount executive who came to his office, asked how much he had invested in his priest movie, and offered to cover his outlay and add a generous bonus if he would pull the plug.[28] But McCarey evidently did not know of an attempt to peel him off the project. Given Bing's obstinacy and DeSylva's support, Paramount was stuck with the picture, but why did it need Leo? Thirty years later, Crosby told Risë Stevens that he had been summoned to a meeting where it was suggested that the studio buy the story and turn it over to a more efficient staff director. Bing replied, "I don't do it without Leo McCarey," and walked out. But he admitted to Risë that he was so unnerved by the hostility that he made a pact with Leo: From start date to wrap, neither of them would take a drink until after work, and even then no more than a couple. As far as she could see, they kept to it.[29]

Leo continued talking his way into a script, incorporating bits of everything he had done, from slapstick gags he created for Laurel and Hardy to the collegial friendship of *The Kid from Spain* to the sexual ambiguities of *The Awful Truth* to the struggle of age and youth in *Make Way for Tomorrow* to the boys' choir and chapel of *Love Affair*. He would later remark of *Going My Way* and *The Bells of St. Mary's*, "You could say they constitute my whole career." He added, "They weren't really religious films—there was a lot of humor—and there was nothing at all pious in them."[30]

He used paradigms, parallels, and reverses. The pilgrim-in-a-strange-land motif is echoed throughout the story—in the young Midwestern priest in New York, in the aging curmudgeon in the land of the young, in the impasse for both men in the wake of a fire that destroys the church, and finally in the ninety-year-old Irish-woman inching down the aisle of the miraculously revived church. Sketches, dramatic and comical, are built around unlikely pairings: O'Malley and Fitzgibbon, O'Malley and the wiseacre Father O'Dowd (Frank McHugh), O'Malley and his old girlfriend Jenny Tuffel, who later changes her name to Genevieve Linden (Risë Stevens's character's name had gone from Miss Betty to a variant of Jenny Lind), and so on, scene after scene. Another McCarey trope is to pin emotional pivots to clothing; Fitzgibbon's stunned first look at O'Malley in his sweatshirt is echoed by Jenny's astonishment at seeing his clerical collar, which is echoed by the mortgage broker Mr. Haines (Gene Lockhart) discovering his son's air corps uniform. As the characters became more distinct, their stories took form as a quintet of parallel relationships, discrete but connected, dramatically organized as in musical counterpoint. Each was a kind of love story in which love had to be taken on faith and fought for: the thorny attachment between O'Malley and Fitzgibbon, the new affair between the would-be singer Carol and Mr. Haines's son Ted, the old affair between O'Malley and Jenny, the assimilation of the kids into the church community, and Mr. Haines's transition from self-interest to selflessness.

Leo thought in terms of emotional texture, combining comedy and pathos, a melding innovated and perfected by Chaplin in *The Kid* and *City Lights*. In the sound era, no one did it better than McCarey—not even Chaplin. The trick was to ask of the audience two physical reactions, laughter and tears, without abusing its patience or its willingness to suspend disbelief. He believed in the power of film to elevate, enrich, and unite. He believed in the healing force of music—music more than prayer. Leo asked Johnny Burke and Jimmy Van Heusen, who wrote the picture's new songs, to convey his idea of music that taught biblical lessons. He sought to inspire them by playing his own song with the uncatchy title of

"Rhythm in the Catechism." They were baffled until Burke overheard a clash between Bing and Gary that ended when Bing dismissively said, "You wanna be a mule, okay, be a mule." Originally, "Swinging on a Star" was entitled "The Mule," which is how it is referred to in the film. The Burke/Van Heusen songs are as close as the picture gets to sermonizing.[31]

McCarey was scheduled to begin shooting on July 16, a date that aligned with the ninety-day window Crosby had given him and the contracts with Risë Stevens and others. But Leo's preferred screenwriter, Frank Butler, promised by Freeman, had not yet been made available. It is unclear why, as Butler didn't sign any films produced in this period. Yet Paramount tried to convince Leo to accept other writers, ranging from the future master of noir A. I. Bezzerides (Warner Brothers would not loan him) to the author of *Goodbye, Mr. Chips*, James Hilton (his price was too high). Insisting on Butler, McCarey finagled another two-week extension. Thus July 16 became not the starting date of the picture's shooting but of his collaboration with Butler.[32]

During the waiting period, the great art directors Hans Dreier and William Flannery assembled the studio's New York stage, dressed by Steve Seymour. Location shoots were arranged at the Riviera Country Club (after Lakeside turned them down), St. Monica Church, and the Shrine Auditorium's stage (doubling for the Metropolitan Opera House) and parking lot. Edith Head designed the costumes, including the ones used in Risë's big number from *Carmen*. Based on the Douglas and Cavett treatments, a preliminary and prescient budget estimated the cost as $1,050,000 for a forty-eight-day shooting schedule; that included the cast allowance of $261,500 and a set that would take $77,900 to build.

McCarey delegated his assistant director Alvin Ganzer to "audition" the Robert Mitchell Boychoir at Choir House, its home in St. Brendan's Church. Mitchell, one of Hollywood's fascinating eccentrics, began his long career in 1924, at the age of twelve, as an organist accompanying silent movies. Ten years later, he introduced the Mitchell Singing Boys at St. Brendan's and made it an institution, the group appearing in dozens of movies (including *Love Affair*), on the radio, and eventually on television. He directed it for sixty-six years, until 2000, and played at silent-movie festivals until his death, at ninety-six, in 2009. He also played piano in speakeasies, saloons, and churches throughout Los Angeles and at Dodger Stadium. McCarey's concern was that Mitchell's boys might look too young to play the boys in the mob led by Tony Scaponi. He needed to be certain that the voices would be believable and that he could combine Mitchell's boys with lip-synching actors in the choir's on-screen appearances. Ganzer assured him it would work on all points.

Leo also had to come up with a title. No one much liked *The Padre*. In mid-June, he received a memo with eighteen alternative titles, among them *Let Freedom Sing, Paradise Street, The Singing Padre, Right Guy, Saints and Sinners, Music Hath Charms, He Shall Have Music,* and *The O'Malley Way.* A month later, the picture was still referred to as *The Padre,* but Leo now had the title he wanted: *Going My Way.* In later years, he told reporters that he got the idea when he picked up a hitchhiking sailor who said those very words; he did not mention that characters in the previous two pictures he had directed also said them. On July 14, Paramount's New York office launched a search on the title's availability. It was deemed free and clear, as was the name of St. Dominic's Church, as long as it was not situated in Greenwich Village. On July 28, Paramount authorized the official title, *Going My Way,* and asked McCarey to commission a song of that name for "advertising and exploitation purposes."[33]

The movie was now set to begin shooting on August 2. Leo pleaded for two more weeks. Bing drove down from Elko to sort it out. McCarey allayed his concerns; Frank Butler was on hand and they were working around the clock, making tremendous progress. This would be the last delay. As ever, Bing had a full plate. In addition to his weekly program, there were guest appearances on the radio: a tribute to the Merchant Marine on CBS's *Camel Comedy Caravan;* a concert at the Santa Ana air base broadcast on Mutual's *Soldiers with Wings; Command Performances;* the Rhythm Boys' reunion on Paul Whiteman's show. He recorded the poststrike Decca sessions with and without instruments and the Andrews Sisters. He participated in an all-star Hollywood Bowl evening to benefit a Build the Cruiser campaign. Bing authorized William Meiklejohn, Paramount's chief casting director, to grant Leo an extension through August 16. But Bing was not the only concern. Meiklejohn notified Leo that, given the latest postponement, James Brown would no longer be available to play the broker's son. But he spoke glowingly of a recent graduate of Oregon State named Jean Hetherington and suggested Leo see her screen test for the part of Carol. Leo did, and thinking he had a romantic team in the making, he hired her—she changed her name to Jean Heather—and managed to keep James Brown. Risë Stevens also rankled at the delay, having canceled concerts for late July; they would have to put her on salary as of the original start date. Freeman warned McCarey that the August 16 deadline was ironclad.[34]

Surprisingly, while casting and departmental contracts had been signed and the sets constructed, the picture did not as yet have a director of photography. On August 4, the head of the camera division submitted to Leo a list of ten candidates that included such fabled veterans as Karl Struss, Karl Freund, Lee Garmes, and Arthur C. Miller. Struss was the obvious choice; he had shot nine of Bing's films, more than anyone else, as well as McCarey's *Belle of the Nineties*. But Leo chose the one novice on the list: thirty-seven-year-old Lionel Lindon. He had worked at Paramount as a camera operator and assistant for over a decade and had recently completed his first picture as a cinematographer, a minor Bob Hope vehicle. Known as a hard drinker and a fast, first-rate technician, "Curly" Lindon proved himself on *Going My Way*, which would be the first of six pictures with Crosby, the first of three for which he was nominated for an Oscar, and a portal to such distinguished work as *I Want to Live, Too Late Blues, The Manchurian Candidate*, and more than three dozen episodes of *Alfred Hitchcock Presents*. The first shot of St. Dominic's Church, nestled among the featureless buildings of a New York street, has the darkly gleaming resonance of a great photograph, which is what it is. It sets the stage for a movie that looks as distinct as it plays.[35]

In later years, when he was more concerned with appeasing the tax collector than entertaining journalists, McCarey complained of having had to rush everything to meet the August 16 target; he insisted he should have had at least three months with Frank Butler, who commonly spent three to six months on a script. And yet, the month they worked together was among the most exhilarating of

Leo's career. Butler, born and educated in Oxford, England, began as a stage actor. Shortly after coming to the United States, he signed with Famous Players–Lasky (the predecessor of Paramount Pictures), and by 1923, he was happily ensconced at Hal Roach Studios. He appeared in more than thirty shorts before 1927, at which point he began writing full-time. He was a talented gagman who could think visually, and he understood structure as well as anyone in the business. Butler's lengthy gabfests with Leo, recorded by secretaries, followed by solitary hours of writing brought the script's disparate elements into focus, shaping the final film, particularly the first half. A few scenes are in different order—he begins with Father O'Malley finding his way on the streets of New York rather than with the broker haranguing Father Fitzgibbon for his mortgage payments. Relationships are underdeveloped, significant scenes are absent or framed as pale setups of what they would become, and much of the dialogue reads like placeholders for better dialogue to come.[36]

Indeed, the written screenplay *never* got beyond the incomplete stage. McCarey later estimated that "at least twenty-five percent of the picture was not in the original script." Crosby tripled that estimate. The truth lies somewhere in between, as the opposing recollections reflect the perspectives of a director who, resenting the rush, grumbled about "having to write both on the set and every night" and an actor who found McCarey's extempore demands wonderfully bracing. The studio's departmental rules required the director to produce script pages daily. Leo complied; he just didn't use those pages. It was "tough on the actors who had already learned the lines he had sent to the story department," Bing recalled, "but it didn't bother me because I never learned by heart until I came to work."[37]

Still, Butler made it possible to have a representative script within three weeks of his arrival. Though his loan-out to McCarey terminated five days after shooting began, he remained attached to the film for another two weeks, and the additional salary of $3,700 was not charged to McCarey. As William Dozier, the head of the writing department, explained to Leo, it was the studio's reward "for his zeal and enthusiasm in connection with his services for you."[38] Those long-awaited pages went to all the executives, including Luigi Luraschi, the studio's indefatigable liaison with Joe Breen's office at the Motion Picture Association of America.

On August 12, Breen assured Luraschi that "this basic story, as far as it goes, appears to be acceptable" under the Production Code. But he was far from enthusiastic. He advised "considerable revamping against the possibility" of giving offense and was particularly upset that the three priests' "conduct and language" lacked dignity: "Father Timony [later renamed Father O'Dowd] at times appears to be definitely obnoxious."[39]

He found much of the dialogue "questionable." For example, "On page 22, in response to the aged priest's question, 'How did you [O'Dowd] ever come to be a priest?'—Father O'Malley replies, 'We blind-folded him and he thought he was joining the Elks.' Such a speech would, of course, give serious offense to Catholics everywhere." McCarey cut the line, but for a different reason—Luraschi told him it would be resented by the Elks. He worried about scenes involving the opera singer and suggested that whenever she appeared with Father O'Malley, "she have a companion with her, another lady possibly, who could be established as her secretary or maid." And he wanted the church on board: "As I presumed to suggest to Mr. McCarey yesterday, we strongly urge and recommend that you get in touch with Father Devlin (telephone number Crestview 6-3726), who is the technical adviser appointed by Archbishop Cantwell for consultation with studios on all motion pictures having any bearing on Catholic matters."[40] Luraschi checked everything censorable with Breen, including lyrics to "Silent Night" and "Three Blind Mice." He also checked copyrights and names. The script has O'Malley wearing a Mickey Mouse sweatshirt; if Leo wanted to promote an animated character, it had to be one owned by Paramount, say Popeye or Superman. (They chose a St. Louis Browns sweatshirt and added the three monkeys who see, hear, and speak no evil on the back.) As the Bach/Gounod "Ave Maria" was controlled by Heugel of Paris, they would have to use Schubert's 1825 "Ave Maria," and since both versions were banned for ritual use by the Catholic Church, they could not be performed in the church proper. (McCarey sequestered Schubert in the church basement.) Frank McHugh could not play "Father Timony" as there was a real priest of that name in New York City. (They renamed the character Father Timothy O'Dowd.) A reference to *Police Gazette* had to be dropped, as did a reference to the Bijou Theater, as New

York actually had one. A request to depict the Metropolitan Opera House awaited a reply.[41]

Leo and Bing figured it would be wise to heed Breen's recommendation and call Father John Devlin, the curate assigned to handle cinematic matters by the formidable Archbishop John Joseph Cantwell, who had played a decisive role in establishing the Production Code. He had been so offended by Cecil B. DeMille's *The Sign of the Cross* that he went to Washington in 1933 and ranted about the plethora of Jewish studio executives. He soon amended his accusation to focus on screenwriters, three-quarters of whom were pagans "who care nothing for decency, good taste, or refinement [and live] lives of infidelity and worse."[42] That year he had chosen as his man in Hollywood Father Devlin, and Devlin took the job very seriously, evaluating dozens of scripts each year, accepting as payment voluntary contributions of as little as fifty dollars. Leo asked Luraschi about how to approach Devlin, and Luraschi said that the way to get him as an adviser was to contribute to his parish the amount an ordinary technical adviser would receive. Frank Freeman said the decision was up to Leo, since Leo would bear the cost. McCarey gave twenty-five hundred dollars to Devlin, who personally attended the shooting or sent an assistant in his place every day. A smart move it was; in addition to offering astute suggestions, Devlin served as a shield against criticism. When the auxiliary bishop of Los Angeles wrote Breen of rumors he had heard concerning the picture's "sex angle," Breen himself wrote that Father Devlin was on the case and therefore "the finished picture will contain nothing that is offensive. Of this you may be certain."[43]

With no more delays possible, at dawn on August 16, a sizzling Monday, crewmen, costumers, makeup artists, and hairdressers began gathering on a soundstage at Paramount Pictures to make *Going My Way,* the modestly budgeted black-and-white picture that several executives who were supposed to have a say in these things wished would go away. At nine o'clock, Bing and the other actors arrived and were enthusiastically welcomed by Leo, who turned to his piano while the cast got pastries and coffee and then circled the upright to learn who was going where.

17

SWINGING ON A STAR

ESTRAGON: *When you think of the beauty of the way.*
[Pause.]
  And the goodness of the wayfarers. [Pause.]
    —Samuel Beckett, *Waiting for Godot* (1953)

Bing made certain that the *Going My Way* budget included a hundred and fifty dollars a week for his sidekick Barney Dean. Barney is not known to have come up with any lines; on a film directed by a man who prized ensemble improvisation, Dean's vaudeville chortles—those rehearsed ad libs of the Road pictures—were not solicited and probably wouldn't have been appreciated. Instead, he earned his keep as a gopher or, as one reporter styled him, a "pet bull pup," cheerfully furnishing Bing with the morning *Times*, the *Herald*, the *Daily Racing Form*, and anything else his master required, including a partner to toss a ball or share hot dogs for dinner. Barney told a *Time* researcher that the sight of Father O'Malley in clerical robes studying the *DRF* and placing bets with his attendant bookie drew visitors from everywhere on the Paramount lot. This sounds like a Barney Dean put-on, an iteration of the jocularity Bing's circle spun around him.[1]

Risë Stevens saw something else that, like several of his leading ladies, she initially misjudged as formality. She came to appreciate his aloofness as an aspect of his preparation; he connected with other actors, even close friends like Frank McHugh and William

Frawley, in character. "I come from opera and I know about rehearsal and work and preparation," she noted, "but I never saw anyone with a work ethic like Bing, so focused on his part. It surprised me. He was either in character or silent, by himself, very shy." At first, at day's end, he would leave the set and studio right away—no socializing or postmortems—and invariably arrive early the next morning. As the shoot progressed, he might stay late to have a drink with Leo or chat. "He was absolutely charming," Risë said, "but very direct. Everything was work, very concentrated on the work, even at the prerecordings. He was meticulous about everything, involved in everything."[2]

He looked unusually fit. The exhausting regimen of bond-selling followed by weeks of ranching and riding at Elko combined to give him a trim, youthful glow. As ever, his *Going My Way* hairpieces were made by the House of Westmore, but this time he requested a modification, a wig to distinguish O'Malley from the familiar Crosby characters. They came up with a credible wig, wavy, combed to the side, reducing the usual pompadour flip. It did the job but served so clearly as gilding for this specific character that Bing could never use it again. With *The Bells of St. Mary's,* in 1945, he switched to Max Factor's wigmaker Bob Roberts, who devised a compromise look. Bing stayed Roberts's client for the rest of his life.

McCarey's method of shooting kept Crosby on his toes. It demanded more concentration than memorizing a script. Over the years, Leo's actors related similar anecdotes attesting to the mood on his sets. George Burns wrote of W. C. Fields sitting by himself in a corner, learning his lines during the filming of *Six of a Kind;* he had given up learning them at home the night before after he realized they changed every day. Ralph Bellamy groused that on *The Awful Truth,* nobody except McCarey knew what was going on. On *The Milky Way,* McCarey acted out for Adolphe Menjou a long, illogical speech he wanted him to deliver in his big scene with Harold Lloyd. After he "did it for me with all the gestures," Menjou wrote, McCarey asked, "Why not adlib it," as it's all "hocus pocus" anyway? "Maybe," Leo joked, "we've discovered a new technique.... The McCarey system, the ultimate in the true art of making motion pictures." Menjou summed it up: "He was kidding about the new technique [but] he wasn't kidding about adlibbing the scene."[3]

McCarey's manipulation of actors mirrored an important theme in *Going My Way,* as the priests are constantly manipulating one another with white lies and ruses. O'Malley's mission is to take charge without letting Father Fitzgibbon realize it. O'Malley and Father O'Dowd think nothing of fibbing about Fitzgibbon's golf stroke or of getting music publishers to enact a charade to make the old man think he'd raised enough money for overdue mortgage payments with his preaching. The moneylender Mr. Haines attempts to con the church, which instead cons him. His son is manipulated by his mistress; the son and mistress are manipulated into marriage by the title song. Above them all, an unseen bishop pulls the strings that gets the story going and brings it to a close. Father O'Malley's abracadabra is achieved through unalloyed charm. He can read most people well enough to get them to do his bidding— which pretty much describes how McCarey directed. Bing recalled, "He let you do about what you wanted to do and read the lines about the way you wanted to read them or thought they should be read. But he'd never let anything go by that was slipshod or wrong. In other words, he strove to achieve natural delivery of dialogue rather than over-direct, as some fellows do, and he must have felt that this picture had a chance if the performances [were played in a] natural, normal, homey way, rather than making the characters pious or sanctimonious."[4]

Bing found the whole thing "just an enjoyable chore." He liked everyone in the cast and behind the camera. On a Friday in October, between the day's shooting and his evening recording of a *GI Journal,* he sang the Bridal Chorus from *Lohengrin,* accompanied by Leo's piano, as Risë's stand-in Irene Crosby (no relation) got married on the set. He appeared content, approachable. All was well. Yet McCarey's way required blind trust.[5]

I don't think he had a story when we started, [just] a few ordinary scenes that established the locale, established the character. And after we got into the meat of the yarn, why, Leo had a funny schedule he operated on. We'd come in about nine just as we were at home—nobody'd bother to make up—and have coffee and doughnuts, and Leo would be playing the piano. He'd play and maybe we'd go over and sing a little barbershop. And then he'd think a little and wander around, might even walk down the street and come back. About eleven o'clock he'd say, "Let's get in the set, let me see what you've learned." So we'd do the scene we'd learned, three or four people, and he'd say, "We're not going to do that at all. Now you all go to lunch, go to Lucy's [a favorite café] if you want. Take a two-hour lunch and I'll get something whipped up and that's what we'll shoot after lunch." And we would come back and he had something all ready, and it'd be altogether different, might even change the whole direction the story was taking and we'd shoot that. He shoots most of his shots full figure, and if we got it right he'd say, "Print that one." We'd say, "What, no close-ups?" and he'd say, "It looked good to me right from that angle, so that's what we'll play." And that's the way it did play.[6]

This routine, which according to Crosby happened more days than not, rocked the shooting schedule, causing McCarey to fall behind and then lurch ahead. Somehow the shooting schedule hewed to the allotted number of days and the budget. The picture developed episodically, reflecting the director's and the actors' increasing confidence in their material, a process that necessitated alterations both large and incidental.

Leo lamented the passing of traditions and individuals but welcomed the new order that he was certain would follow the war. His film had to mesh sadness and hope, loss and courage. From the time filming began, he mapped St. Dominic's and its neighborhood as a closed society, a curbed microcosm centered on a strangely spectral church (O'Malley can't find it at first), situated in the present to illumine a typical American community. In *As You Like It*, Jaques declares that all men and women are merely players enacting seven ages. As pieces of the puzzle fell into place, McCarey decided to present the whole Shakespearean tableau, all seven ages: the mewling infant (Carol and Ted's baby); the whining schoolboy (the members of Tony's gang); the sighing lover and his mistress (Ted and Carol); the grown-up soldier, jealous in honor and seeking reputation (O'Malley and Genevieve); the middle-aged "justice" of round belly and eyes severe (Haines Sr. and the superstitious atheist Mr. Belknap); the slippered pantaloon, spectacles on nose and pouch at side (Fitzgibbon); and in the "last scene of all," the second childhood (Fitzgibbon cradled in his mother's arms), all the world a church in Hell's Kitchen.

Ultimately McCarey had to eliminate the first age. The advancement of the story conspired to delete Carol's baby, for which the budget stipulated two hundred dollars to hire an infant for two weeks. As a result, the film has a disquieting aspect that was largely ignored by audiences fastening on the teat of its wholesome premise. An unmistakable precariousness hangs over the bunker-like claustrophobia of the closing scene. The players huddle in a church recently cleared of wreckage, destroyed by an inexplicable blaze, itself a reflection (underscored by the use of stock footage) of contemporary newsreels showing churches and other buildings similarly ravaged. There is no new life to celebrate and the life they cling to is as fragile as Fitzgibbon's ninety-year-old mother. Ted is home from the service, injured not in a battle but in a stupid mishap, and certain to be recalled if the war doesn't end soon; he relies on his wife, who refuses to reconcile with her parents. Tony's gang sticks with the limited prospect of the church choir. Jenny will return alone to the opera and Chuck to the-bishop-knows-where. It is Christmas, and St. Dominic's makeshift family is united in its makeshift nave. Yet if the bright, comical optimism of the movie's early scenes, embodied in O'Malley's jaunty appeal, has darkened, a communal bond—demonstrably absent on O'Malley's arrival—is now manifest.

Some of McCarey's best ideas were conjured in response to circumstances.[7] He requested a copy of a New York State sheriff's foreclosure notice, planning to shoot a close-up of it taped to the church door. On the day filming began, Luigi Luraschi informed him that no such thing would ever happen; all property in a Catholic diocese is owned by the bishop and is passed from one bishop to the next.[8] This meant that a crucial element of the story had no basis in reality. McCarey registered the information and kept it to himself until October, when he found a fix for it and worked it into one of the last scenes he shot, which became the first scene in the film. After apprising Fitzgibbon of his debt, Haines and his son Ted (Gene Lockhart and Jim Brown) exit the church.

TED: Dad! You can't foreclose. Why, it just isn't being done. I've
   read up on it, and there's never been a Catholic Church fore-
   closure in the history of New York.
HAINES: Well, there's always a first time, isn't there?
TED: Don't you think you're being a little harsh with him?
HAINES: You've got to be. Son, never loan money to a church.
   As soon as you close in on them, everybody thinks you're a
   heel.
TED: Well, aren't you?
HAINES: Yes.[9]

The next sequence introduces Father O'Malley, who is heard
("Good morning!") before he is seen. The film cuts to a bright,
sunny day, and there he is, in a dark suit and straw boater. McCarey's framing and Lionel Lindon's meticulous lighting draw attention to the rakish angle of his hat and his life-size shadow, doubling
him on a brick wall. As he walks up the street and into a stickball
game, a sailor ambling by situates the film in the present. In later
years, Bing remarked on the several priests at Gonzaga who influenced his portrayal. Yet one knows instantly that never in the world
has there been a priest like this or an actor like this to incarnate
him. O'Malley is the apotheosis of all the virtues of the Crosby
persona with none of the defects.

In past roles, he flouted authority; now he personifies it. In earlier
roles he cherished the fantasy of a quiet isolation; now he is pledged
to the human condition. Gone are the pouts, the neediness, the flippancy and cockiness, the insecurity and erotic yearning, the want,
the need, the ambition — though not the impulse to perform, which
he does throughout the picture as singer, pianist, songwriter, straight
man, the choreographer of other people's lives, and the church's
savior. He is a benevolent *übermensch*, an infinitely resourceful
Saint Fixit. You want miracles? O'Malley converts street toughs into
choirboys, a cynical runaway into a loving wife, a shylock into a
philanthropist, a petulant old cleric into Mother's baby boy.

Yet McCarey completes the introduction of O'Malley with a
humiliation he initially devised for Laurel and Hardy in the 1928
two-reeler "We Faw Down." Grouchy Mr. Belknap throws a baseball that busted his window under a car. O'Malley sighs, says, "You

even throw like an atheist," and goes to retrieve it. Kneeling with his rear in the air, he is drenched by a street sprinkler. According to Risë Stevens, the only consistent prodding in McCarey's direction of Crosby was to discourage him from acting too priestly. "No, Bing," he would say, "I want the real you as the priest."[10]

Going My Way pivots on the interplay between O'Malley and Fitzgibbon, between what James Agee characterized as the "wise young priest whose arresting resemblance to Bing Crosby never obscures his essential power" and "the quintessence of the pathos, dignity, and ludicrousness [of] old age" incarnated by Barry Fitzgerald, together invoking "just about the last word in teamwork." The teamwork evolved as the wily Fitzgerald added jabbering bits of business to his part, not least a finicky, abstracted way of walking. Sometimes the two actors competed for the camera, as when Crosby follows the older man to the vestibule and nimbly leaps over a bush. (In a later scene, Fitzgerald comically mimes his desire to copycat the leap.) But one could no more compete with Fitzgerald than with a gurgling baby or a chimp, and Crosby relished the growing of Fitzgerald's role. Stevens recalled Bing as "very much involved" in Barry's performance, enjoying his every turn and often going stock-still so as not to distract from Barry's line readings.[11]

"It was remarkable working with him," Fitzgerald observed. "He'd look at his lines and somehow *absorb* them instead of learning them. Then he'd say them as they should have been said: naturally. He has a great gift, that man. People say that he's just himself. He is. But that's a special thing. It's no accident. It involves a keen sense of timing, an ear for sounds, relaxation, and common sense. [His] acting talents have been vastly underestimated." Fitzgerald was fifty-six but playing a much older man. McCarey directed him with what Stevens called "little nuances," encouraging his Irishness to flow.[12] O'Malley's progressive infantilization of Fitzgibbon— embarrassing him as an accessory after the fact to the turkey thieves, triggering his truancy and apprehension by a policeman (Fitzgibbon: "There's no reward, you know"), singing him to sleep with an Irish lullaby, reuniting him with his mother—is countered by their increasing playfulness, which involves the third priest, Frank McHugh's impudently funny Father O'Dowd. Most of this was unplanned, beginning with a golf sequence in which Fitzgibbon is brought along as a "kibitzer." "Can you do that every time?" he asks O'Malley after a masterly shot. O'Malley responds as if he were musing in a *Kraft Music Hall* sketch: "Oh, I've been known to miss, Father—you know, a strong crosswind or something."

That scene is paired with another that has virtually no dialogue. It originated after McCarey noticed an ongoing checkers match between electricians during breaks. In one game, an observer silently coached an inferior player to victory. Leo borrowed the board, set up the checkers in a church interior, and positioned the actors in a triangle with the camera as the fourth wall; Fitzgibbon is on the left, O'Malley on the right. O'Dowd, dead center, subtly sends signals to the older man. But O'Malley prevails and O'Dowd departs with the counsel "Let that be a lesson to you, Father. Don't trust anyone." "We ad-libbed that right on the set under his direction," Bing marveled. "Played it once and 'Cut!'"[13]

Going My Way is an innovative musical with eight numbers (nine if you include Burke and Van Heusen's uncredited "Hail Alma Mater," twice sung by O'Malley and O'Dowd), three of them reprised at length. In this purportedly religious film, singing supplants prayer, and the problems of the parish are answered by song. All the music stems directly from the plot, a novelty in the 1940s. Its functionality is underscored by the absence of references to the songs in Robert Emmett Dolan's background score or during the opening credits. Each number advances and parallels the plot.

The new material, except for "Swinging on a Star," had little life beyond the film. Indeed, the film treated the two other new songs with bemused condescension, something that infuriated their begetters. Burke and Van Heusen labored manfully in tailoring three songs to the requirements of a director who wanted them to double as homilies. Yet one is burlesqued and another is rejected by a music-publishing company bearing their names. McCarey knew what he was doing. "The Day After Forever" is a lackluster ballad that the picture connects to Jean Heather's Carol, who cranks it up with semaphore and flirty eye-rolling, to which Bing reacts with bemused double takes.[14] Bing sings a chorus to demonstrate his advice to Carol that she think about the words and scrub the histrionics, but even he can't do much with it. His subsequent Decca recording, weighed down by a lethargic Trotter arrangement, is one of his lesser efforts in that period.

Taking the songs in the order they are heard, the next three are traditional. "Three Blind Mice" is used as the warm-up number to get the choir going while irking Father Fitzgibbon, and "Silent Night," beautifully sung, shows the progress they have made, as does "Ave Maria," performed by Bing, Risë, and the Robert Mitchell choir.

Stevens remembered "Ave Maria" as a tune Bing wanted in the score. They had planned to add "Adeste Fideles," but as both of those nonliturgical melodies would have had to be remanded to the basement, they dropped the second (and resurrected it for *The Bells of St. Mary's*). As if to stress the covert status of "Ave Maria," O'Malley conducts it from the piano in his nifty St. Louis Browns jacket. Squaring an inside joke, O'Dowd chatters during the scene about the idiocy of the latest pop songs, notably the enduring strippers' anthem "I Lost My Sugar in Salt Lake City," which enjoyed great popularity while they were filming, thanks to Mae Johnson's rendition in *Stormy Weather* and a hit record by Johnny Mercer. "Ave Maria" introduces Mitchell's integrated boys' choir. McCarey pans over their faces, and the African American member stands beside Risë Stevens, sharing her shot. The frequent appearance of a solitary black face in postwar pictures and television shows would later be decried, aptly, as tokenism. Yet the practice signified a critical baby step toward African Americans' fuller representation, especially in the way McCarey pulled it off, here and four years earlier in *Love Affair*. Southern distributors could not edit out the Negro boy without deleting a star. Later in the film, when Bing and the choir launch into "Swinging on a Star," that boy is placed at O'Malley's side and gets a solo. Again, he cannot be removed without maiming the number. These deceptively innocuous scenes were among the few racially integrated musical numbers produced by a major Hollywood studio up to that time.[15]

The "Ave Maria" sequence ends with the humbling news that Chuck's song "Going My Way" has been rejected by a publisher as schmaltz. O'Malley's fleeting look of disappointment and anger represents the only instance when his shield of confidence falters.

The film's title song isn't one of Burke and Van Heusen's best, but it is nonetheless well crafted and alluring in its own way. Burke's lyrics—in the manner of "Swinging on a Star" and at least two dozen other songs, from "Pennies from Heaven" and "The Moon Got in My Eyes" to "Here's That Rainy Day" and "Misty"—aim skyward, albeit with a candied mysticism that leads from Rainbowville to Dreamer's Highway. Van Heusen's legato melody is memorable if rhythmically static, particularly the bridge, with its fixed quarter notes and a moseying, downward cadence from B-flat to F. On his dutiful Decca recording of it, Bing anchors the rhythm by doubling a quarter note (the word *full* in the phrase "just a basket full of").[16] In the film, he sings it at the piano in Carol's apartment after an informal autobiographical discourse about his days leading a jazz band and his belief that religion doesn't have to be all Sturm und Drang. As O'Malley takes his leave, Carol and Ted remain leaning against the piano, mellowed out. They will marry. Ted will enlist.

The second performance of "Going My Way" is a big production number staged at the opera house showcasing Risë Stevens, an orchestra conducted by the amusing Fortunio Bonanova (playing one Tomaso Bozanni), and thirty or so voices (the numbers vary on the call sheets, but they appear to include twenty-five boys from the Mitchell choir and several unseen women). Their sole audience is the music-publishing firm of Dolan, Lilley, Burke, and Van Heusen. (In real life, the cost of this audition would have amounted to a substantial gift from the Met's diva and its unionized musicians.) Everyone is confident that the publishers will buy the song for an advance against royalties to lessen the church's debt. The real Burke and Van Heusen also thought it would be a hit, and so at first did McCarey. His original notion was to have the publishers go whole hog for it; in one version of the script, they like it so much they try to get O'Malley to work for them. McCarey even depicted it as a hit to an executive at the Metropolitan Opera.[17]

Shortly after signing Risë Stevens, Leo learned that the Met had refused permission to use its name in the picture, let alone allow the studio to build a simulacrum of its stage. Risë, however, argued the point with the company's longtime assistant general manager Edward Ziegler. During the second week of shooting, she told Leo of some softening in Ziegler's position. He rushed out a straight wire:

I JUST TALKED TO MISS STEVENS AND SHE INFORMS ME THAT YOU
WERE KIND ENOUGH TO RECONSIDER YOUR DECISION. I AM THE DIREC-
TOR OF THE PICTURE AND I WANT TO ASSURE YOU THAT I HAVE A
DEGREE OF INTEGRITY AND I INTEND TO TELL A STORY OF GREAT
BEAUTY ABOUT THE CATHOLIC CHURCH. THEY HEARTILY APPROVE OF
MY STORY AND ARE COOPERATING WITH ME IN EVERY WAY IN THE
TELLING OF IT. I FEEL CERTAIN THAT THE SCENE SUBMITTED TO YOU
WAS POORLY PRESENTED AND CRUDELY WRITTEN.... THROUGH THEIR
JOINT EFFORTS THE SONG IS ACCEPTED AND THE YOUNG PRIEST IS
ENABLED TO PAY OFF THE CHURCH DEBT.... RATHER THAN BEING
DEROGATORY TO THE METROPOLITAN OPERA COMPANY I FEEL THE
AUDIENCE WILL BE IMPRESSED BY THEIR GENEROUS AND CHARITABLE
GESTURE. I AM HOPING YOUR RECONSIDERATION WILL BE FAVORABLE.
SINCERELY LEO MCCAREY[18]

That and an additional payment to the Met of one thousand dollars did the trick. But on the day this scene was shot, Leo changed
his mind, deciding he wanted another checkers-like reversal. He
filmed the performance with all due reverence, focusing on Stevens's glistening eyes and commitment to the song, but then he
inserted cutaways to the music publishers, who listen with reluc-
tance, all but squirming and looking as if someone had made a rude
noise. Max Dolan (William Frawley) tells O'Malley it's a great song,
too good for them, not the kind of song "a guy would—pardon me,
Father—that a gentleman would croon to his babe." O'Dowd
gripes, "If that isn't good, I'll go into the real estate business," possibly unaware that the movie's plot has effectively put them all in
real estate. When the publishers leave the theater, Maestro Bozanni
asks the choir to sing another song, just for fun. One of the boys
suggests "The Mule."

The film's three remaining songs helped to cement *Going My
Way* as a cherished home-front event in the penultimate year of the
war and for some time to come.

"Swinging on a Star" is a masterly example of pop songwriting,
amalgamating sophisticated harmonies and folk-song simplicity. If
Burke's lyrics are clever, Van Heusen's music is ingenious, linking
two complementary melodies—a wistful, swinging eight-bar verse
and a comically hoedown-style twelve-bar refrain, the latter skipping along in easy-to-sing eighth notes. It was an instant sensation,

sustained by Bing's rhythmically stepped-up recording; his ninth gold disc, cresting the charts for seven months, staying nine weeks at number one. For the Decca session, Bing replaced Robert Mitchell's boys with a young quartet he encountered on the AFRS series *Mail Call.* The Williams Brothers (including sixteen-year-old Andy Williams) came cheap, at twenty-five dollars apiece, but Bing, who didn't pay costs, most likely chose them for their more limber, modern harmonies. The admirable arrangement, credited to Trotter, though he may have farmed it out to a jazzier mind, employs the "White Christmas" template of giving more room to the choir than to the soloist, thereby emphasizing its singalong quality. This factor and its scholastic theme ("And by the way, if you hate to go to school / You may grow up to be a mule") won the hearts of countless elementary-school teachers. The song remained a part of public-school curricula for two decades, sung in classrooms and at assemblies. In addition to rescuing St. Dominic's, the song salved the vanity of Burke and Van Heusen by winning them the Academy Award for Best Song. Van Heusen referred to it as a high point of his career. His widow had the title chiseled on his tombstone.[19]

"Too-Ra-Loo-Ra-Loo-Ral (That's an Irish Lullaby)," a bonanza on the stage and on records for Chauncey Olcott in 1913, was scarcely remembered when McCarey revived it in *Going My Way,* and most people who knew it assumed it to be an old Irish song. In fact, it was composed, words and music, by the Detroit-based songwriter James Royce Shannon. In the picture, it represents the essential selflessness of O'Malley. He sings it by request to the ailing Fitzgibbon and exits St. Dominic's and the film as the choir reprises it to cue the reunion of Fitzgibbon and his mother. For some filmgoers, Crosby's rendition is the highlight of the picture, too genuine to feel mawkish. A mortified, ailing Fitzgibbon has returned to his church in police custody. Put to bed by O'Malley, the old man suggests "a wee drop of the craiture" and directs Chuck to a bottle of Bushmills hidden behind *The Life of General Grant.* They talk of their mothers. O'Malley's died when he was a child. Fitzgibbon has not seen his in forty-five years, but every Christmas she sends him a bottle in a wooden music box that plays "Too-Ra-Loo-Ra-Loo-Ral." They toast their mothers, and O'Malley, seated beside the bed and accompanied by the tinkling chimes, sings Fitzgibbon to sleep. It is hard to imagine two other actors in that era confidently reversing gender and ageist norms to enact, in essence, mother and child.

The Bushmills was a mildly irreverent touch for the time. In 1950 the director Mervyn LeRoy visited the Vatican for an audience with Pope Pius XII. The pope asked him if he remembered *Going My Way*. LeRoy said, "Of course. One of my friends, Leo McCarey, made it." Pius told him, "I have a print of it. Don't you love that scene where the priest takes a little drink?"[20] Jack Kapp had reservations about the tune. When Crosby recorded the three Burke–Van Heusen songs, "Too-Ra-Loo-Ra-Loo-Ral" didn't make the schedule. (Kapp backed "The Day After Forever" with another current Burke–Van Heusen number, "It Could Happen to You.") Nor did he record it at Bing's next session or at the three after that. He finally recorded it in July, five months later, by which time fans clamored for it. Bing's expressive, richly intoned performance, accompanied by a Trotter arrangement that mimics chimes before bringing in strings and woodwinds, shot to the top of playlists. In keeping up with orders, the stamper was damaged. To ensure continuous sales, they recorded a nearly identical version a year later. Hardly anyone could tell the difference, and between the two, Bing received his tenth gold disc.

The Irish-lullaby scene dissolves to an exterior shot of Broadway on a wintry afternoon, the time of year when New York gets dark early. O'Malley is buttoned up in an overcoat and wearing a black fedora. Having taken the neighborhood boys to a Hopalong Cassidy double feature (their turf is peculiarly bereft of girls), he gives them bus fare for the half-mile ride home. He prefers to walk back so he can contemplate Sunday's sermon. Passing by a stage door on Thirty-Ninth Street, he is hailed by an old friend he has not seen since St. Louis—Jenny Tuffel, whose musical abilities he encouraged. She has since reinvented herself as Genevieve Linden. Hurrying him through an animated crane shot across the backstage area of the Metropolitan Opera House (re-created at the Shrine Auditorium), she explains that she is rehearsing *Carmen*. "Believe it or not," she exults, placing a rose between her teeth, "I'm Carmen." That surprises him. He surprises her in the picture's nerviest moment, the revelation that Chuck and Jenny were lovers.

McCarey had rehearsed Stevens in her dressing room, emphasizing a "real love interest there. He was very specific about the way he wanted me to play it." They hadn't let Bing in on it until the afternoon they shot the scene, when he could see for himself. It was the first time she witnessed Bing's trepidation. Joseph Breen insisted on others being present in their scenes to undermine any suggestion that O'Malley had not always been celibate. But the whole point about O'Malley is that, like Augustine, he has experienced life, made a choice, a sacrifice, found freedom in conversion and does not look back. McCarey covered his flanks with *two* chaperones: Jenny dresses behind a screen attended by her helper Effie; O'Malley removes his overcoat in the presence of the conductor Bozanni. McCarey shot the scene late in the day, after Father Devlin's departure. Leo would later chide every prelate and censor who complained of a sexual implication that they were reading something into a perfectly innocent scene—it was their problem, not his.[21]

In the scene, she reviews her grievance with Chuck while getting into costume: "I don't know why I'm even talking to you." His letters, which awaited her at every stop on a hectic musical tour, meant the world to her: "The moon was so bright" in Lucerne, she says, "that I read your letter on the way home and I answered it that night." Bozanni enters the outer area and Jenny, behind the screen, calls out, "Meet Chuck O'Malley. He's a very old friend of mine." Bozanni, sotto voce, says: "Father *Chuck?*" O'Malley responds: "Oh, she always calls me that." Jenny prattles on obliviously about the letters until they all realize that his last letter never reached her, at which point she steps out from the partition and sees his white collar. McCarey then called for her close-up.

McCarey had prepped her to register "total surprise" with notes of confusion, admiration, regret, and nostalgia. When she recoups, Jenny says, "Father Chuck! It'll take me a little while to get used to that."

Bing protested. They'd never get away with a scene depicting a priest and his ex-lover. The Catholic Church wouldn't stand for it, nor would Breen, nor his public. Besides, they were all aware of the steady griping from Paramount executives who believed it would be financially sounder to eat the costs of the picture and bury it than release it to a mudslide of derision that would damage Bing's value to the studio. Leo sent him home with the promise that he would privately show him the edited scene, and if he still objected, the close-up would go. Leo later told Stevens that after Bing saw it, he leaned over and said, "You are absolutely right, Leo. It makes the scene."[22]

Yet Crosby continued to worry. McCarey arranged for a preliminary screening of the completed film. All the members of the cast sat together, except for Bing (who sat alone), Barry (who sat alone), and Risë (who sat with her husband). The honored guest for the unveiling was Archbishop John Joseph Cantwell, who sat with a few of his priests. Midway through the picture, Cantwell raised his hand and asked if they would stop for a moment. The clergy left the screening room as the lights went on. Bing stood up and Risë saw panic in his eyes: "That expression on his face, I could see it written all over him: *This is not a good omen, he doesn't like it.*" In ten minutes, Cantwell returned and apologized for the interruption; he had needed the toilet. Risë thought Bing still looked unconvinced. But after it was over, she recalled, Cantwell "went to everyone, congratulated *everyone*. Said to Bing, 'You are wonderful, everything that is beautiful is in this picture.' And he went on and on and on." Still, over the next few weeks, Risë and her husband continued to hear rumors that "Paramount would shelve it."[23]

No one at the preliminary screenings or after objected to the fact that the picture cut directly from the dressing room to one of the most sexually willful arias ever written: "L'amour est un oiseau rebelle," better known as the Habanera. Risë Stevens became so firmly established as the Met's definitive postwar Carmen that numberless moviegoers have assumed that her bravura performance in *Going My Way* exploited her fame in the role. The reverse was true; the Habanera launched her campaign of several years to convince a reluctant Metropolitan Opera to allow her to develop the part. In 1938, she sang it in a German-language production in Prague and then put it aside until 1943, when she sang it at the Cincinnati Zoo Opera and realized she wasn't ready. When McCarey asked her to suggest operas for the movie, she compiled a list, starting with *Carmen*, and "to my great surprise they chose it." They filmed the Habanera and the first-act finale but dropped the latter.[24]

Stevens had qualms about the way McCarey directed her. She disliked the bleached look of her makeup, resented having to dye her hair blond (to heighten the contrast with the black wig she wears as Carmen), and thought the rose-between-her-teeth gesture trite. She took up knitting to endure the long setups and did as she was told. When the lights were finally on her, she triumphed, seductively threading her way through a throng of soldiers and townspeople. The number was elaborately staged with flats, a chorus, and a "technical advisor" (Italian director Armando Agnini) borrowed from the San Francisco Opera. Paramount executives raved over the footage and sought to clear worldwide rights for *Carmen*. They were rebuffed in markets where it remained protected, and so another aria was quickly filmed for foreign prints, Mařenka's third-act aria from Smetana's *The Bartered Bride* (shot at Paramount with little preparation), which is what most of the world saw her perform instead of the Habanera.[25]

Because of *Going My Way,* Chesterfield hired her for print ads costumed as Carmen. She was thus famous as Carmen before she ever played it in a major house. In 1945, the Met gave her the chance in a production that had remained unaltered since Geraldine Farrar introduced that staging in 1908. Stevens ruefully recalled her interpretation as having the "trace of a well-bred sorority girl," but Columbia Records hustled her into a studio to record excerpts. Not until 1951 did the Met commission Tyrone Guthrie to tailor the bawdier, landmark staging that established her as the voracious, flesh-baring Carmen that one reviewer described as "pure alley cat. A creature earthy and unwashed." Over the next decade, she sang the opera 124 times.[26]

Postproduction, including retakes for Stevens and others, continued into January, as did the debate over releasing it at all. They ignored the whispers and focused on the mundanity of issues like credits. First, they had to deal with the screenwriters. William Dozier, who supervised the studio's writing department, asked McCarey to help sort out the contenders. They eliminated Lloyd Douglas and assigned a sole screenplay credit to Frank Butler and a shared story credit to Frank Cavett and McCarey. Cavett responded with a model of tactful dissent. He had no desire to "minimize the good and hard work that has gone into the script since I left it," but "a substantial number" of his scenes (specified) remained in the script, and though many had been revised, "they represent a sizable and basic contribution." He was troubled because "the industry makes writing credits a matter of economics." As for how he thought the credits should read, Cavett wrote, "I am willing to leave it up to Leo." McCarey must have been delighted to promote Cavett to a shared screenplay credit, thereby keeping the story credit to himself.[27]

Years later, McCarey griped that Paramount denied him his proper billing; the credit ought to have read "Leo McCarey's *Going My Way*." Given the grandeur of the credit he received, his longing for an apostrophe-*s* seems incredibly petty. Paramount gave him precisely what it had promised him contractually: "Corporation agrees to announce 'A LEO MCCAREY PRODUCTION' either above or below the title of photoplay, as we elect, but on the same frame on which the title shall appear, in size of type not less than 60 percent of the largest size of type appearing on said main title." Some people might doubt the hand behind Genesis, but no one seeing the picture would doubt the hand behind *Going My Way*. In addition to taking 60 percent of the title card and 9 percent of the story credit, he closed the credits with a 75 percent producer-director card.[28]

Bing's credit sized out at 50 percent, at his insistence. Paramount hoped, given all that was at stake and how much the project meant to him, that he would relent on the Crosby clause and permit the studio to award him star billing, "above or below the title, as we elect." The studio realized it had no chance of billing him as the sole star on a card of his own, but it hoped he might agree to have his name at 75 percent and the other actors sharing his card at 40 percent. A handwritten edict from his office eliminated that option: "Bing does not want star billing. Definitely." Crosby suggested a simple five-name card; for example, "With Bing Crosby, Barry Fitzgerald, Frank McHugh, Risë Stevens, Jean Heather." That raised another issue. The studio wanted to maximize the exploitation of Stevens but feared that billing her—or, for that matter, Jean Heather—as his costar might imply the leading-lady status of a typical Crosby romance. They settled on three actor cards with five names on the first (Crosby, Fitzgerald, McHugh, Brown, Lockhart) and the second (headed by Heather) and just one on the third (Stevens); it read "Risë Stevens, Famous Contralto of Metropolitan Opera Association." No one ever explained to Stevens, one of the most celebrated mezzo-sopranos of her time—and promoted as such by the Met—how she came to be tagged as a famous contralto. "I don't know where they got that," she said, adding that there weren't a lot of great contralto parts in opera.[29]

Actors' credits often signified nothing more than their standing at the studio and how much contractual clout they had. Porter Hall was in only one scene, but he was a top-flight character actor (and a leader of the Actors Guild, and famously religious) and he always got a credit. Stanley Clements had a major role as Tony Scaponi, but he was seventeen years old at the time, with barely two years of small parts under his belt, so he got no credit. The uncredited cast member who collected the most fan mail was the extraordinary Adeline De Walt Reynolds. Born during the Civil War, she graduated from the University of California at age seventy; she began her film career eight years later and sustained it until her death in 1960 at age ninety-eight. She played Fitzgibbon's mother, who was brought to this country by O'Malley as a parting gift. McCarey liked to tell how he sought the oldest woman in Los Angeles, ran all over looking for her, and corralled her for the final walk-on—as if Reynolds were not a dues-paying Actors Guild member who could be seen in theaters dying of a bat bite in *Son of Dracula* even as they were filming *Going My Way*. She signed on for two days' work, commencing October 19, at her weekly rate of $350.[30] James Agee considered her scene an "unusually valid and powerful tear-jerking climax," a judgment that must have pleased McCarey, who, like Chaplin, sealed his comedy with tears.[31]

On October 22, they called it a wrap and shut down the set.

The two and a half months spent filming *Going My Way,* intense as they were, hardly exhausted all of Bing's time. In addition to his weekly radio shows, each adding a day to his guarantee period for the picture, he continued war work. A *Command Performance* he emceed on a Saturday in August presented his first duet with the twenty-one-year-old Judy Garland ("People Will Say We're in Love"); she could hardly contain her excitement. They had never spoken beyond a passing hello. She told a writer, "I haven't looked forward to anything so much for a long time—to me, Crosby is the Master." The writer asked if he was better than Sinatra. "You can't compare the two," she said. "Bing is an institution. Sinatra is a fine singer—maybe he's even wonderful, but he's just beginning."[32] In 1950, Bing would rescue her faltering career, hiring her as a regular on his Chesterfield radio show shortly after she recovered from a breakdown at an East Hampton getaway in Sinatra's arms.

Bing took charge of the series *GI Journal* for September and early October, serving as emcee and key performer, usually recording it on Friday evenings with a rotating cast that included Eddie "Rochester" Anderson, Linda Darnell, Mel Blanc, and Jimmy Durante. Each show began with roaring presses and an announcer proclaiming, "The *GI Journal* goes to press!" The standard twenty-four-page script, loose enough to permit ad libs, featured parody skits suggested by GIs and closed with a Crosby ballad. He continued to make unpublicized appearances at army camps and publicized ones at country-club fund-raisers.

He was available for anything as long as it did not interfere with his film work. When the navy named a Liberty ship the SS *Nathaniel Crosby,* after his grandfather, the Worcester captain who rounded Cape Horn in 1849 and went on to help found Portland and pioneer the China trade, he sent his mother to Oregon to accept the honor. Bing himself was the source of a nickname for a B-24 bomber—Crosby's Curse—that was assigned to the Ninetieth Bombardment Group of the Fifth Air Force. Transported to Australia, it flew extensive missions over New Guinea and, according to one report, downed twelve Japanese Zeros in a single engagement. Nose art—sexy, mordant designs painted on aircraft fuselage—reached its pinnacle during World War II and usually featured pinups: Memphis Belle, Tondelayo, Idaliza, the pendulous breasts of Over Loaded. The nose art for Crosby's Curse was elaborate, combining a musical staff, stars, an almost naked woman pointing at a knotted sash around her waist captioned *C.O.D. Knot for Tojo,* the legend *Crosby's Curse,* and a scoreboard with bombs to indicate the missions flown and the planes downed. Captain William Henry, a Crosby's Curse pilot, visited Los Angeles with his Australian wife to present Bing with the bomber's logbook and spent Christmas Day at the Crosby home.[33]

Henry Morgenthau wrote him to say that the Treasury Department needed his help to launch a campaign for the Third War

Loan, the most ambitious ever mounted. The goal was fifteen billion dollars, to be generated by a Hollywood Cavalcade tour of thirteen cities. To meet it, they had to convince nearly one in three Americans to purchase a hundred-dollar war bond. Asked to wire his response "if possible today," Bing sent his regrets; he was shooting *Going My Way* and could not leave Los Angeles. He volunteered to appear on the all-star opening broadcast publicizing the campaign, which would be heard on all four networks, and sing the drive's theme song, "Get on the Road to Victory," just before James Cagney introduced Morgenthau and President Roosevelt. He stumped for bonds on *Treasury Star Parade* and other broadcasts generated by the Treasury Department, which called his services "invaluable," as the drive exceeded its goal by 25 percent.

An army war-bond officer asked him to participate in a program aimed at military personnel in the South Pacific meant to encourage soldiers to invest "some of their free cash" in bonds. He asked Bing to record a greeting and sign a photograph for auction. Bing expressed ambivalence: "At first blush my feelings were Whoinell am I to tell the boys who are carrying the ball they should also pay for tickets?" But he supported "future security" and agreed. The officer made a widely distributed poster with the "Whoinell" line reproduced in block capitals followed by the advice (not written by Crosby, though the implication is that it was) that "future security investment is solid jive, men."[34]

A seaman mailed Crosby a song he had written. Bing thanked him, recorded the song on a test disc, and broadcast it (a Bing demo) over shortwave for the composer to hear. He sent a 16 mm projector in response to a request from one outfit. A stranger appeal came from two aerographer's mates attached to the naval air station at Pasco who anticipated hand-to-hand combat in their assignment to the South Pacific. They hoped to prepare by procuring daggers, stilettos, or knives with eight- and ten-inch blades. Having struck out elsewhere, they turned to Bing "as a last resort," suggesting that he might be able to obtain them at a nominal fee through the studio property department and could forward them COD. Crosby checked up on the mates at their base and after "hard trials and great tribulations" obtained two commando knives from a contact in Mexico, which he sent "unsharpened." It was relatively easy for him to have Decca send fifty thousand records to barracks and troopships. He received a ream of thank-you letters from crewmen. In the margin of one containing some five hundred words of gratitude, he penciled, "Apparently—this is a good move."[35]

To raise money for the National Tuberculosis Association, he filmed a short at Paramount that was paid for by the studio and distributed gratis to fourteen thousand theaters. He appeared on the season opener of Bob Hope's Pepsodent show, singing and playing in a skit. Hope devoted much of his humor to Sinatra, observing he wouldn't be so skinny "when he gets that job on the Kraft program and can eat all the cheese he wants." Bing made a transcription and appeared in a trailer to promote Canada's Fifth Victory Loan. That country's minister of finance, James Lorimer Ilsley, told the press he asked only two stars to participate, Crosby and the Canadian-born Mary Pickford, because they "are the screen actors most in the hearts of the Canadian people." J. J. Fitzgibbons, the chairman of Paramount's Canadian division, called it "the biggest and best three minute selling job ever produced in a motion picture."[36]

During these months, Bing returned to recording. The jollity of "Jingle Bells" and the candor of "I'll Be Home for Christmas" might, each in its own way, reflect the fulfillment he experienced on the movie set. In the early weeks of shooting, Dixie relieved him of family distractions by taking the boys on an extended vacation to Malibu. But in the six weeks between the completion of *Going My Way* and the start of *Road to Utopia*, his home life was troubling. The end of the year mirrored its beginning with another fire, this one originating in a forest on the outskirts of Rancho Santa Fe. It destroyed six homes completely and seriously damaged one hundred and fifteen properties, including the Crosbys'. Two weeks later, Dixie checked into St. John's Hospital in Santa Monica for her nerves.[37]

The more he had on his plate, the more he added. But now, in the lull between the cassock of *Going My Way* and the flannels required for the new Road trip, he decompressed at his ranch, reading the script and growing a beard. He later said he had been advised that *Road to Utopia* would begin filming with scenes in which he and Bob were hirsute. Crosby took off five weeks from *Kraft Music Hall*, October 28 through November 25, 1943; his replacements included

Bob Crosby and, in a dominating guest-star appearance, Hope, repaying Kraft for Bing's recent visit to the Pepsodent show. A few columnists had Bing visiting army camps or embarking on a tour during these weeks, but they were just guessing. Beyond a couple of sightings — one public, one private — he vanished into the wilds of Elko, where reporters had no dominion. The public event, a golf match with Hope for which Lamour pretended to caddy, raised funds on behalf of the Citizens Committee for the Army and Navy. The private event allowed him to repeat his role as wedding singer, serenading Julia Quigley, the bride of his longtime stand-in and driver Leo Lynn.

He returned to *KMH* on December 2, the evening before filming started on *Utopia,* wearing the beard, which generated sarcasm, as he complained that he now had to shave because the filming schedule had changed. In truth, the beard had nothing to do with the movie beyond generating publicity for it; in a comedy, particularly the kind of burlesque cooked up for Bing and Bob, no natural growth could compete with whiskers made by the House of Westmore. Perhaps the real meaning of the beard lay in its symbolic value as a token of Bing's six-week retreat from work and his family.

Yet no sooner was he back in harness to Kraft and Paramount than he began filling up his off-hours and planning war-related getaways. Hope had returned from an immensely successful USO tour abroad, the first such tour of the European theater, eleven weeks long and involving two hundred and fifty shows in England, North Africa, and Sicily. It was an extraordinary feat and it earned him *Time's* cover and universal praise, including John Steinbeck's. In his much quoted account of the entertainers' visit to a paraplegic ward, he described how Frances Langford had broken into tears, and Hope, sizing up the situation, had walked briskly past her and said to the men, "Please don't get up." Hope and his small troupe of players, Steinbeck wrote, "must come into this quiet, inward, lonesome place, and gently pull the minds outward and catch the interest, and finally bring laughter up and out of the black water." He concluded, "There is a man for you — there is really a man." Additional USO tours were revving up, and Crosby wanted to steer one scheduled for the Southwest Pacific area, centered on Australia. But Paramount demanded he go directly from *Utopia* into another picture, *Here Come the Waves*, and those plans were suspended until August 1944, after D-day.[38]

Once put into motion, Crosby, like Hope, could not be still. They were men who dodged idle time as they did introspection, working and playing relentlessly. With *Utopia* occupying most days, Bing redoubled broadcasting and trouping. In December his Hooper rating for *KMH* increased dramatically, to 25.8, making it the third-most-listened-to program on the air, after Hope's Pepsodent show and *Fibber McGee and Molly*. After a *KMH* with Phil Silvers and Joan Davis, he went to the Palladium, where an audience of ninety-five hundred gathered to hear an orchestra made up of the leaders of prominent bands to raise money for disabled and hospitalized servicemen. That week he recorded a *Command Performance*, a *Lux Radio Theater* adaptation of *Dixie* (introduced by Cecil DeMille as if it were a history lesson), an episode of *Soldiers with Wings*, and a one-shot called *Sailor's Christmas Party*. On Christmas Day, Bing and Hope starred on the two-hour *Elgin Watch Show* on CBS with Jack Benny, Judy Garland, and the Charioteers, Bing closing with "White Christmas." But Bing wanted to travel, to stand before the troops, to get into the heat of it. He figured he would have a month between pictures, which was not enough time for a trip overseas, but how about improvising a USO tour of Alaska?

He was motivated to go to Alaska less by the locale of his current picture than by his friendship with the young radio writer Ed Helwick, stationed in Nome, with whom he maintained a correspondence that allowed him to quietly bitch about *KMH*, which, he said, "goes on interminably." Despite ratings that indicated tens of thousands of new listeners, *KMH* had lost the favor of older ones, whose complaints Crosby took to heart. "You could give your fans a break," one wrote to him, by getting "good guests or better still none at all. We can take Crosby neat when it's only a half hour at best." He knew he needed fresh writing. Genuinely funny people— Rags Ragland, Oscar Levant, Lucille Ball, and especially Phil Silvers—zinged the show to life; skits with Ukie and familiar cronies thudded. He had two writers in mind, both in the military: Bill Morrow, a longtime writer for Jack Benny and a Crosby confidant, and Ed Helwick.[39]

Ed was at a top secret base of the Air Transport Command, where hundreds of Russian pilots picked up nine billion dollars in aircraft, supplies, and medicine, ferried to Nome by American pilots, to fight the Battle of Stalingrad. Bing got letters to him at the undisclosed location by routing them through a postmaster in Minneapolis. Telling Helwick of *Road to Utopia,* he rather innocently suggested he might premiere it for Ed's outfit, a gift likely to play havoc with the base's secret status. He sent him a carton of records and a transcription disc of sound effects so that Helwick could create radio skits on the base. After a *KMH* broadcast in mid-December, Bing asked his audience to stick around for a special thirty-minute Christmas show, organized by Crosby and Carroll, and recorded on disc solely for the men in Helwick's outpost. No one but those men and the studio audience ever heard it. Ed recalled, "We played it twenty-four hours, around the clock, on Christmas Day. A gracious effort that I doubt anyone else knew about."[40]

Bing wrote him, "I've been doing a few shows for Colonel [Tom] Lewis—*G.I. Journal, Mail Call* and *Command.* Do you dig them up there?" Yet he also expressed guilt about not doing more. Hollywood was launching "quite a series of Overseas troupes," and where was he in all this? "I'd sure like to make one, but I'm damned if I can find the time." He continued, a bit defensively, "Actually, I believe visiting the Hospitals here and entertaining is about as important a thing as can be done. They don't get much of a tumble." He detailed his idea of doing shows in Alaska. "I don't think he realized how far it was away," Helwick recalled. "He did realize, though, that you could only get to Nome by boat or by plane and you could not drive up there and there was no train because the town of Nome was on the tundra. So Bing was planning on chartering a Navy boat to go up and do a show for my men." Two weeks into the new year, Bing wrote to Phil Silvers, then making waves at a New York nightclub with his partner Rags Ragland, and invited him along: "What would you think of slipping up to Alaska (by boat of course), with a tomato and a guitar player for about a month? Probably leave in late February. Let me know about this as soon as you can. They really need something up there."[41]

It didn't happen. Nor did Helwick return to radio beyond a brief stint in New York in the late 1940s. He visited Crosby on the set of

Blue Skies in 1945, and Bing offered him a place on his first post-war radio series—an invitation he did not extend to Carroll Carroll, who nursed a grievance about it for the rest of his days. But Ed didn't want a career in radio, nor did he want to have to choose between his loyalty to Bing, whom he adored, and J. Walter Thompson, which had given him his first job and assigned him to *KMH*. He opted instead for a life in education, teaching high-school social studies in Culver City. He won a Fulbright Scholarship in 1957 and was selected as California's Teacher of the Year in 1974, seven years before he retired.

A transcribed radio show was only one of Bing's plans for the peace. He also wanted to create an independent production company. This proved, in the short run, to be one of his few professional mistakes and perhaps the costliest. He was warned. Frank Freeman told him he would lose a lot of money. Everett huffed and puffed and wrote to Bing's formidable lawyer and fixer John O'Melveny, who in turn cautioned Bing. The idea began, unsurprisingly, on the fairways with Bing and two of his friends. The trio, who made a regular thing of it, consisted of Bing, the prolific screenwriter James Edward Grant (who went on to write a dozen pictures for John Wayne), and a mysterious if not shady would-be producer named Frank Mastroly (who had never achieved a screen credit, though he had been kicking around the business for years). In his letter to O'Melveny, Everett declared him "thoroughly incompetent." O'Melveny bluntly advised Bing: "Of course what you are supposed to do under the terms of the contract is to guarantee the completion bond and if it is not completed you are going to be out about $100,000 and you can't afford to lose that. You have saved up and put away about all the money you are going to until after the war [and] to take a loss of that kind, or even risk it, seems very foolish. If the picture makes money it will do you no good because you will have to pay it out in taxes and it seems to me that you are again doing something to accommodate friends who want to make money out of using your credit and good name."[42]

Bing could not be dissuaded, and thus Bing Crosby Productions, which eventually enjoyed a huge success on television (*Ben Casey*, *Hogan's Heroes*), launched itself with *The Great John L.*, a biopic of John L. Sullivan, boxing's first heavyweight champion, starring a forgotten bit player named Greg McClure. It was directed, not without some flair, by Crosby's old confederate Frank Tuttle, who had initiated Bing's feature-film career with *The Big Broadcast* and now needed the work. The production went forward in 1944, doubled its original budget to nearly one million dollars, and debuted a year later. The columnist Florabel Muir wrote of it, "Bing's bankroll was nicked to the extent of $125,000, a pretty superficial nick. In fact, the major casualty seems to have been a frolicsome threesome that is no more. They do not speak now as they pass by." After the war, he stubbornly produced, on his own, another feature with more embarrassing results.[43]

Crosby also looked beyond the war in terms of his sports affiliations. On the first day of shooting *Utopia,* in partnership with a Marine Corps captain and a Chicago-based businessman, he applied to the Los Angeles Coliseum for a franchise to produce football games on Sunday. The idea was to match West Coast and East Coast teams, taking advantage of the fact that in the postwar era, transcontinental flight times would be reduced to eight hours. He had little chance of getting started, given the coliseum's ban on professional grid games, and he was not allowed to buy into league sports because of his involvement with racing. After the National Football League postponed looking at his application until after the war, a sportswriter noted the irony that Crosby, "a model American citizen," could not own a baseball or football franchise because he was "mixed up in the horse racing business," while the owner of the New York Giants, Tim Mara, was a "reformed bookmaker" who had made his fortune gambling. He predicted that after the war, Crosby would "be postponed again then and probably indefinitely." Bing quietly considered selling his holdings in Del Mar, a retreat made easier by his turf club's wartime suspension.[44]

On the first Saturday in December, Crosby learned from the trades that his new recording of "I'll Be Home for Christmas" debuted high on the charts, but a reissue of his year-old "White Christmas" did too, just a few numbers below it. Though hardly noted at the time, this was a historic event for the record industry, the beginning of a Christmas tradition that appears to be everlasting. The immensely successful rerelease of Bing's 1935 recording of "Silent Night" in 1941 prompted Decca and Bing to record a new version of the song to take advantage of the superior technology while demonstrating that the Christmas season might be as receptive to the annual recirculation of beloved records as it was to caroling. But "Silent Night" *is* a carol, which was why Crosby pledged its royalties to charity. "White Christmas" was a brand-new song written for a Hollywood movie by the Jewish patriarch of Tin Pan Alley. It had enjoyed epochal sales a year earlier. How many would sell now? And if successful, would its sales cut into profits for "I'll Be Home for Christmas"? Jack Kapp gambled that a concurrent release of the two discs would boost each other. Once again, he was right; the new one went gold, and the older one implanted itself as a perennial, establishing Crosby as the ritual voice of Christmas.

That status was made especially clear on Christmas Eve. It was a Friday, a whirlwind of a day for Bing, as he performed or traveled between venues from 1:00 p.m. until well after midnight. First he appeared on a two-hour CBS revue involving Hope, Jack Benny, Judy Garland, Lena Horne, and Carmen Miranda, then he spent a few hours rehearsing for the Christmas Day program to be broadcast the following afternoon by the Elgin Watch company, and after that he sang at an "at home" party for soldiers and sailors at the Masquers Club, an exclusive lodge created in 1925 by New York actors who had settled permanently in Hollywood. At seven o'clock, he returned to CBS as a guest on *Christmas Eve on the Fronts,* broadcast on all the networks, singing "God Rest Ye Merry, Gentlemen" and "O Come, All Ye Faithful" during a warm-up for Roosevelt's address to the American forces via pickups in Algiers, Naples, New Delhi, Tarawa, Cairo, Guadalcanal, New Guinea, and half a dozen other locales, including a battleship and an aircraft carrier.

The buoyant power of FDR's charm, despite his failing health, boosted American confidence in an imminent victory, though he himself was uncertain about the imminence. He had recently returned from a grueling monthlong trip, meeting with Churchill in Cairo before the two of them met with Stalin in Tehran, where Roosevelt promised the Soviet leader a second front with a channel crossing (Operation Overlord) no later than May. Pressed by Stalin to name the commanding officer of the operation, the president surprised everyone by selecting Dwight Eisenhower instead of George Marshall—a decision the *New York Times* thought would remain inexplicable until "the publication of somebody's memoirs." Stalin promised to turn his army toward Japan when Europe was settled; Roosevelt and Churchill promised to be flexible about Poland's postwar borders. While few military strategists could envision an Axis victory, much remained uncertain. Britain's RAF suffered monthly decimations; the Italian campaign had stagnated; the fear that Stalin would make peace with Germany, a nation it had more reason than any other to abominate, remained potent; and the channel invasion could prove disastrous. Of the slaughter of European Jewry, discounted by the State Department, most Americans remained ignorant. Few outside the Third Reich knew that three weeks before the Tehran meeting, eighteen thousand prisoners were mowed down by machine guns in Majdanek, or that thousands were gassed every few hours at Auschwitz. The propaganda aimed at Americans by the White House, the Treasury Department, and Hollywood worked its magic. A citizenry swaddled in entertainment looked upward and beyond. No one incarnated the bliss of pulling together more than Bing Crosby.[45]

Late that Christmas Eve, Bing rounded up Jimmy Van Heusen, to accompany him on piano, and his four boys and visited the Hollywood Canteen. Four decades later, Bette Davis recalled the occasion: "One Christmas Eve, Bing Crosby came through the kitchen door with his four little boys. He said, 'Thought maybe we could help out tonight,' and he got on that stage with those four little boys. Everything those men were fighting for were those four little boys! He sang carols for an hour and a half! Oh God!" He sang fourteen songs, including an impulsive duet with a sailor, and finished with "White Christmas." Six hundred servicemen, black and white (officers weren't admitted, and the canteen was not segregated, unlike the Warner Brothers movie made about it or, for that matter, the armed forces), sat on the floor or at tables ringing the room and listened to an unassuming man who could not have looked less like a motion-picture star, balding, ordinary, informally dressed. They gave him what one observer reported was the longest ovation in the canteen's four-year existence. Afterward, Crosby and

Van Heusen dropped the four boys at home and visited three different army camps, where they entertained the troops until the early light.[46]

Two nights before the new year, Decca scheduled its first Crosby session since the one that had produced "I'll Be Home for Christmas" three months earlier. It began with two languidly paced first-rate songs: Burke and Van Heusen's "It Could Happen to You" (written for the film musical *And the Angels Sing,* starring Dorothy Lamour and Betty Hutton) and Kurt Weill and Maxwell Anderson's reverie "September Song" (from the 1938 Broadway hit *Knicker-bocker Holiday*). Both would endure as standards, no thanks to Bing, who failed to customize either. Beyond a few uneasy high notes, he does nothing wrong; he is deliberate and tender. But this is Bing minding his manners, bending to the laborious strings of John Scott Trotter.

The third and final number sounds as if it flew in from another session, certainly another temperament. Gordon Jenkins, an arranger and conductor working with Dick Haymes, had tossed off "San Fernando Valley" for the Roy Rogers picture of that name, and no one expected much to come of it. The song plugger Sam Weiss, an old friend of Bing's and someone whose taste he trusted (and who had recently partnered with Doc Sexton, the veterinarian husband of Kitty Sexton, in founding a music publishing firm), called Bing a week before the session to play it for him. Bing's immediate response was "Hey! That's it." In the cowboy picture, the title represents an idyllic destination, out "California way," in "cow country," "where the West begins." Crosby's performance shapes it into something more. When Tony Bennett made the droll observation that Bing invented suburbia, he wasn't being entirely fanciful. Crosby's nuanced interpretation established "San Fernando Valley" as the first canticle to urban flight. Its quietly certain rhythm rolls on like a wagon train that tens of thousands of servicemen wanted to join, a journey to a real and accessible place where one "could settle down and never more roam / And make the San Fernando Valley my home." Nearly sixty-five years later, a Los Angeles reporter wrote of Crosby's record, "It seemed as if the chamber of commerce ordered up a new civic anthem to sell wood-frame houses in America's suburb."[47]

If "It Could Happen to You" represented the bland cookie-cutter

Bing, "San Fernando Valley" reminded everyone of what he could do when he had a beat to focus him. It underscored his uniqueness. No one else could have made that record, not even Sinatra, who continued to regularly cover him but, having treated the song as a flavorless romp on *Your Hit Parade,* declined to record it.

Trotter begins with a short swing riff, clarinet in front, and stays out of Bing's way, weighing his six wind instruments against his twelve-man string section, particularly in the instrumental interlude. The song is composed long form, at sixty-four bars, which adds to its steady, wheeling character. Crosby steers the lyrics as if he were the most carefree man on earth, applying well-placed mordents, embellishing the melody, emphasizing consonants, recomposing the final sixteen bars, and finishing with a climactic whole note. He makes it sound so damned easy, as if anyone could do it.

In March Bing's record began a five-month stay on the charts, five weeks in the top slot. It sold well over a million copies, though Kapp did not put it up for gold recognition; Bing, unusually, complained to him that Decca wasn't promoting it enough. The record was clearly important to him. But like "White Christmas," it needed no nudging. In his later years, Bing recalled that only "White Christmas" drew more requests than "San Fernando Valley" at the 1944 camp shows he played in the United States and on tour abroad. He performed it seven times on *KMH,* once in a duet with Roy Rogers. At least one of those performances, from the February 24, 1944, show, is superior to the recording. The tempo is brighter, the arrangement is improved (with the Music Maids replacing the instrumental passage), and Bing cuts a rug.[48]

During those same months, men in executive suites on both coasts argued about the advisability of distributing *Going My Way* despite DeSylva's support, Crosby's clout, and the archbishop's benediction. A January preview augured great success; another one in February imperiled its release.

18

PUT IT THERE, PAL

Long ago I was a king
Now I do this kind of thing
On the wing, on the wing!
Bing!

　　　　　—James Joyce, *Ulysses* (1922)

"Our fortunes seem to be improving with 1944," Bing wrote to Phil Silvers early in the new year. He was referring to a run of luck in wagering. With Barney Dean in tow, he had earned "quite a chunk" at the Rose Bowl, taking the underdog USC Trojans in a straight-up bet at sixteen-to-five odds; they demolished the Washington Huskies, 29–0. Through his bookie, he put over "a big parlay" at Miami's Tropical Park. At the Los Angeles Open, he "bought" golfer Johnny Bulla in the Calcutta Pool for seven hundred dollars; Bulla didn't win, but he brought Bing a return of forty-four hundred dollars. On the third weekend of January, he went to San Francisco with Bob Hope's usual troupe, which included the comedian Jerry Colonna, the guitarist Tony Romano, and the ever-present Barney Dean, to launch a fourth war bond drive. "A smashing success, of course," following a blowout party the previous evening. "We're adored there, as you well know. Details when I see you. For now be assured it was a standout." Best of all, Paramount held a sneak preview for *Going My Way*: "Everybody is greatly excited over the reaction it evoked. ~~Looks like a sure hit.~~ It's 13,000 feet and they don't want to cut a thing."[1]

He was less confident about his day job, *Road to Utopia*, which had been proceeding in fits and starts since the first day of filming, December 3. Hollywood columnists who witnessed an instance or two of on-set hilarity spewed the usual guff about the joys of Road-tripping. But interruptions, mishaps, and second-guessing plagued the production. Scheduled to wrap at the end of January, it continued with reshoots, add-ons, and reedits through the middle of March. The trades reported that it might be the last Road picture because Paramount chafed at putting two highly paid box-office favorites in one film. The investment was substantial, given Bing's guaranteed $175,000 and Bob's new rate of $100,000, achieved after he threatened a walkout. Yet receipts from the Roads exceeded anything Bob did alone and most of what Bing did alone. They were as sure a bet as anything in Hollywood could be—a license to mint money. A reporter with a long memory compared splitting up Bing and Bob to Connie Mack wrecking the Philadelphia Athletics, once the winningest club in baseball, purportedly to give other teams a chance.[2]

The studio was not unaided in signaling a breakup. The stars were also ready to call it a day; in fact, they insisted it was their idea, though they buried the separation in bad jokes. Bing: "The real reason is that I had been given to understand that Dorothy would wear a sarong in all our pictures. Comes this *Road to Utopia* and what does she wear? She wears boots and a fur coat...I can't stand Dorothy in boots and a fur coat." Hope said he lost money on the Road movies because "Crosby pouts if I don't bet on his horses," and Lamour expressed relief that she would no longer have to kiss them both in the same picture. When Paramount finally released *Utopia*, two years after it was completed, it ranked as the fourth-highest grosser of 1946, leading to another road (*Rio*), followed a few years later by another (*Bali*), and, after several more years, another (*Hong Kong*). A proposed septuagenarian junket was shut down by Bing's death.

Still, above-the-line budgetary concerns were real enough and contributed to the promotion of first-timers to direct and write *Uto-*

pia. Burke and Van Heusen, Robert Emmett Dolan, Joe Lilley, and cinematographer Lionel Lindon were ported over from *Going My Way.* But they needed a new director, since Victor Schertzinger, who did the first two Roads, had died, and David Butler, who did the third and best, *Morocco,* was unwelcome at Paramount after the Will Rogers screen-test imbroglio. (In this same period, Butler guided Hope through two Samuel Goldwyn pictures, *They Got Me Covered* and the very successful *The Princess and the Pirate,* which outperformed and outclassed Bob's recent Paramount work.) *Utopia* had been assigned to Sidney Lanfield, but despite his long hit-and-miss (*My Favorite Blonde* and *Let's Face It,* respectively) association with Hope, neither of the stars thought him right for it. Buddy DeSylva selected Hal Walker, who had worked for a decade at Paramount as an assistant and second-unit director on comedies, including *Zanzibar* and *Morocco.* Bing unhesitatingly approved. Hope, too, liked Walker, who had gone to New York to direct revised scenes for *Let's Face It* as Bob waited for orders to embark on his overseas army tour for the USO. Hope had an edge over Bing with the new writers as well; Norman Panama and Melvin Frank had worked on his radio show and devised the story for *My Favorite Blonde* (1942), his most recent Paramount hit without Bing.[3]

Panama and Frank, school chums and ardent liberal reformers, both of whom had left the University of Chicago with the aim of writing socially conscious plays in New York, discovered, under Hope's tutelage, their true talents in comedy. They enjoyed a long and fruitful tenure in Hollywood, writing (and eventually producing and directing) such enduring hits as *Monsieur Beaucaire,* Hope's favorite among his own films; *Mr. Blandings Builds His Dream House,* the Cary Grant and Myrna Loy satire of the fad for country living; Bing's indelible *White Christmas;* and the merry Danny Kaye parody *The Court Jester,* for which they devised the immortal line "The pellet with the poison's in the vessel with the pestle." *Road to Utopia,* their first completed screenplay as a duo, eventually earned them an Academy Award nomination. In Panama's 2003 *New York Times* obituary, the film is described as "a deconstructionist classic from an era before the term had been coined." The script did not come easy.[4]

*   *   *

Panama recalled that they had to alter their story to appease the male leads but could not remember their specific complaints. In truth, the producers were the ones with serious objections, as they thought the treatments and scripts submitted by the writers were either too intricate or not intricate enough. From the beginning, their story involved the Klondike, a lost gold mine, an extended flashback, and a contrivance in which Hope's character (named, with typical flaccidity, Chester Hooten) suffers from amnesia that Crosby's character (manfully named Duke Johnson) tries to cure while both men vie for Lamour's character (delectably named Sal Van Hoyden). At one point the story was so convoluted that the producer Paul Jones attempted to make sense of it by telling it to Jack McGowan, a Broadway librettist who collaborated in the 1920s with DeSylva and was now attached to Paramount's writing department. McGowan typed up the yarn as rendered by Jones and noted that it had strong possibilities: "A story of the gold rush is necessarily pretty cut and dried stuff, and it needs some trick—a farcical trick—such as amnesia to take it out of the horse opera flavor." After more revisions, however, Panama and Frank sacrificed the amnesia angle. (They revived it in 1962 for their reunion with Bing and Bob in *The Road to Hong Kong*.[5])

In October, an unsigned memo to Buddy DeSylva, presumably from Paul Jones, implored him to assign Frank Butler to the picture "to follow up [the] writers, sequence by sequence, with me" and also suggested that "Mr. DeSylva or I tell story to Mr. Crosby, since the script will not be finished for some time." They did not recruit Frank Butler, nor did they hire the popular magazine humorist H. Allen Smith, who one columnist reported had been engaged for the "mysterious chore" of contributing special material to *Utopia*. But in March, days after completing production, Paul Jones hired the humorist turned actor Robert Benchley to appear intermittently on-screen and comment facetiously on the action. It took Benchley three days before the camera. A few months earlier, in December, Benchley had signed a yearlong contract with Paramount to work solely as a character actor, admitting, "I don't think I write funny anymore. I've run out of ideas." That self-assessment is sadly borne out in *Utopia,* where his jovial befuddlement merely curbs the pace. He died before the film's release.[6]

For their part, Panama and Frank had been forced to toss several Hollywood name-drop jokes, which would have required written permissions from the actors named, as well as a wisecrack about "Mohammedans at prayer," which Luigi Luraschi cautioned would bring the State Department "on our necks." Bing finally received a workable if not quite finished script at Elko on November 26, one week before shooting began. One can understand Jones's concern. For all the one-liners, the film has a surfeit of dogsled chases and a chilly core, caused by the compromised romantic angle, which one of the weaker Crosby love songs, "Welcome to My Dream," fails to thaw.[7]

Determined to do something different, Panama and Frank wrote the only Road picture that began in the present and unfolded in the past (the 1890s), making the film a feature-length flashback. As the picture is filled with allusions to Sinatra, bobby-soxers, cheese and toothpaste sponsors, the Paramount logo, a sarong, vaudeville, and the stars' recent pictures, along with lines spoken directly to the camera, talking animals (again), and an actor in tails who walks through a scene as a shortcut to another soundstage, this Road is as careless of time as it is of geography. The fourth wall had cracked before Benchley arrived to shatter it; after Hope kisses Lamour, he turns to the camera and announces, "As far as I'm concerned, this picture is over now." Panama and Frank additionally upended the formula by discarding the patty-cake routine and letting Hope get the girl—this time with a subversively sexual connotation. Buddy DeSylva claimed to have written the infamous closing line, which he guaranteed would get past the Breen office. Panama and Frank devised the situation leading up to it, but DeSylva's kicker enabled them to use it. As Duke Johnson, presumed dead these many years, completes his tale (the long flashback), his old friends Chester and Sal introduce him to their son, Junior, who is also played by Bing. An embarrassed Duke ahems as Chester turns to the camera and blushingly explains, "We adopted him."

A reviewer in *Film Daily* wrote that "the surprise finish" would "throw audiences into hysterics." It did just that. They roared at the line, much as they would in 1959 to the kicker in Billy Wilder's *Some Like It Hot,* and for a similar reason. In that film, Joe E. Brown, upon learning that his girlfriend is a man in drag (Jack Lemmon), tells him, "Nobody's perfect," as though homosexuality, as opposed to cross-dressing, were a casual option, ha-ha, when it was still relatively unmentionable. *Utopia* brings extramarital sex out of the shadows, where the Production Code had often treated it as a capital offense. It undermined the chasteness of the Road pictures and other male-bonding comedies in which sexual humor was confined to saucy quips, leers, and kissing interruptus. Junior was proof that consummation actually went on between dissolves. Incredibly, DeSylva won the day by arguing that his adoption line proved the absence of anything morally untoward, the implication being that Duke had long ago married and, for reasons unknown, placed his son in an orphanage. The studio asked columnists to avoid giving away the ending.[8]

That was good enough for Joe Breen, if not for the dismayed Larry Crosby, who wrote to Breen on Bing's stationery: "Is it possible your office will permit release of 'Road to Utopia' with a finish including the 'bastard son'? If you do, it will have the worst possible effect against Hollywood, and motion pictures generally." Breen responded drily: "It seems to me, if you don't mind my saying so, if you have any serious concern regarding the scene that you mention in 'Road to Utopia,' it might be well for you to first register your protest with the gentleman whose name appears in the upper left hand corner of your stationery. If you will do this and let me know what his reaction is to your protest, I shall be glad to go into the matter again with you." Breen did not tell Larry that directly after receiving his letter, he asked Luraschi, in vain, to excise Bing's abashed cough.[9]

The filming began with something less than the usual joie de vivre. Hope was distracted. He had returned from Europe "changed," "hooked on fear, the real thing," sobered and serious, but nonetheless determined to wrest control of his film career from Paramount.[10] His lawyer advised him to create a production company to share in the profits, but when Hope raised the idea with Frank Freeman, he got the same rebuff as Leo McCarey had. Bob refused to sign on for another film and held up production on *Utopia* by coming down with the flu, an ailment that was probably legit but looked suspicious. It may explain his listlessness in the "Goodtime Charlie" vaudeville duet, which Crosby—energized, focused, funny (and well rehearsed by the choreographer Danny Dare)—steals from under his nose. Two days after they shot it, Hope took sick leave and the production shut down. He remained indifferent upon returning to work, as did Bing. A couple of visiting columnists noted that Bing was less interested in discussing the picture than in discussing his coup in arranging a screen test for the legendary athlete Jim Thorpe. "There's a story for you," he said. Thorpe got an uncredited, unidentifiable walk-on as a shipboard passenger.[11]

Hal Walker was no disciplinarian—not that he could have done much to rein in his actors. As Mel Frank once remarked, "They were enormous stars. It's impossible to imagine the prestige of these people." Crosby later crowed, "If I had a big golf game, I'd say, 'can't you do something with Lamour, or with Bob?' And he'd do the same. If there was an important race at Santa Anita, we'd take the afternoon off and go to the races and let them shoot something with some of the other people. You could just about do as you pleased." Lamour recalled that on the day she was to perform her big number in the film, "Personality," they arrived hours late; she had spent the day leaning on a slant board to avoid wrinkling her gown. Gary Cooper dropped by and told her not to stand for their behavior. They apologized and Lamour forgave them. They had a good excuse, she thought, a charity golf match (although no charity matches were scheduled that week), and they never "pulled another stunt like that ever again."[12]

Just how indifferent to the film were they? It's difficult to know, given the overall polish of their performances; in several colloquies, their timing is as good as ever or better. Yet there is no question that the mood varied greatly from the long lunches and leisurely inventions on the set of *Going My Way* and the sustained antics of the earlier Roads. The front office kept tabs on them, noting occasions of tardiness as filming picked up in January and February. On January 13, they arrived five minutes late for their 8:00 a.m. call but were not actually on the set as of 8:40. On January 31, they returned from lunch a half an hour late because of a charity luncheon at the café. On other days, Crosby was fifty-eight minutes late or seventy minutes. Kid stuff, it seems. But by then shooting had been halted for reasons that had little to do with Bing or Bob; equipment had to be transferred to other locations, mild illnesses other than Hope's had to be looked after, and soldiers stopped by to see the fun, causing delays while the stars welcomed them. Bing brought his four sons to the set on at least two occasions (Dixie, said to be ailing, never appeared), and their "impish" behavior disconcerted him; for the second visit they were attired to be photographed, but no pictures were taken and Frank Freeman, of all people, came to the set to play with them "in a dusty corner." In his letter to Phil Silvers a week or so after the flu derailed Hope, Bing gives in to impatient sarcasm: "'Road' continues with the usual interruptions. We work about three days a week—grand business this is becoming." He writes of "doing countless Army transcriptions, etc.," and his plans to get to the Santa Ana air base "around" February 15. He invited Silvers to join him.[13]

Bing did make it to Santa Ana on the evening of February 15 to emcee an alfresco show for the enlisted men with Hope, Frances Langford, Jerry Colonna, Vera Vague (a recurring character on Hope's show, played by Barbara Jo Allen), the Charioteers, and John Scott Trotter conducting an orchestra of servicemen. The event marked the base's second anniversary and brought out the best in everyone. Thousands of men sat in the meadow, ringed by folding chairs for their wives, children, and friends, against a backdrop of snowcapped mountains fusing into the darkening sky. Two minutes of film footage survive, and they include the most frequently excerpted clip in documentaries about entertainers on the home front: Crosby (hatless, wigless) and Hope sing and caper to the inane, immensely popular novelty song "Mairzy Doats." Brief as it is, the clip captures the vitality and good humor they could spark before a field of delighted servicemen.

The men raucously cheered amateur performers that Bing brought to the stage, including the defense worker who played a homemade musical contraption with a tire pump, a virtuoso bicyclist, trained bulldogs, and eight women dancing in sarongs. The high point was Crosby's collaboration with the Charioteers on songs that they seemed to be winging. "Lay it in there, Will," he encouraged the group's high-note man, Wilfred Williams (who could sing F above high C), and "Who starts this," and "If anyone remembers the next line, remind me." They were accompanied by the group's swinging pianist, Jimmy Sherman.

It was a Tuesday evening, so after the two-hour open-air performance, the stars repaired to Theater Three at the Santa Ana Classification Center to broadcast Bob's Pepsodent show. Each enlisted man and officer had to buy a war bond and donate a pint of blood to gain admittance. The base radio engineer asked Hope to tell the audience not to whistle, and no one did. Stan Kenton conducted his orchestra as Bing sang the 1930 evergreen "My Ideal," which he had recently begun singing on *KMH* (but would not record until 1955), a mellow moonlight ballad to wrap the long day.[14]

Phil Silvers returned from New York days later and Bing booked him on the February 24 *KMH,* now in its third week with a new cast member replacing the expecting Trudy Erwin. There were several contestants for the job. The veteran agent Cork O'Keefe, who had helped launch Crosby's career, offered him Eugenie Baird, the singer with the Casa Loma Orchestra (a Decca band), whose dark-lidded eyes, pillowy lips, and hourglass body turned sober men into Tex Avery wolves. Cork sent Crosby her latest Casa Loma recording, "Don't Take Your Love from Me," and four eight-by-ten head-and-shoulders-and-cleavage portraits that were too steamy for publication. O'Keefe confidently described these pictures as "the clinchers. This gal really has it." Come November, free of her Casa Loma contract, she would have the job.[15]

Meantime, *KMH* wisely recruited twenty-two-year-old transplanted Iowan Marilyn Maxwell—a girl-next-door type, if your neighborhood was MGM, which had her under contract. Spirited, uncomplicated, and blindingly blond, she was so charming and well liked that columnists shielded her through successive, widely known affairs with two married men, Sinatra and Hope. Crosby found her a joy to be around, and they worked well together. Marilyn could carry a tune and excelled in their scripted sketches, especially the memory songs, which helped bolster the show's ratings. At Crosby's urging, she fully embraced the regimen of AFRS broadcasts, appearing with and without him on *Command Performance.*

Someone else joined the show at the same time, though listeners would not have known it. Trotter recruited a new trumpet player for the orchestra, someone to whom he could delegate arrangements. Billy May would go on to play an effective role in Crosby's later work and a pivotal one in Sinatra's. By chance, Nelson Riddle, the innovative orchestrator who helped to transform Sinatra's style in the 1950s, also came into the Crosby orbit in 1944. Tommy Dorsey introduced him to Bing after Bing commented on a Dorsey chart he liked; Bing gave Nelson a card with Trotter's phone number and invited him to call. Riddle arranged a few Crosby recordings (including the minor 1947 hit "That's How Much I Love You," an Eddy Arnold country novelty enhanced by a Riddle bass line, voices, and winds), and ghosted arrangements for Trotter over a period of three years. Thus two decisive musical figures of the 1950s, who spruced up not only Sinatra's records but those of Nat King Cole, Ella Fitzgerald, Rosemary Clooney, and Peggy Lee, served all but anonymous apprenticeships with Crosby, whose recording career too often lacked the skills of great orchestrators.[16]

Bing may have gotten another idea from Dorsey, though nothing came of it. In April, he hired a teacher to coach him in correctly singing the Yiddish lyrics of Peretz Sandler's 1919 "Eli, Eli," a song that had found traction in vaudeville, folk, ecclesiastical, and classical music. Dorsey recorded a dramatic instrumental arrangement (as did Harry James, but only for a V-Disc). Bing told a reporter that royalties from the record would go to Jewish causes. But he never recorded it. The subject stayed on his mind. One project he discussed with McCarey as their follow-up film sounds like a barroom joke: a Catholic, a Jew, and a Protestant go to war and become buddies. The film would intercut their respective returns to peacetime America. In 1946, Bing selected as his second independent production the 1920s Broadway phenomenon *Abie's Irish Rose*. This mawkish farrago about a Jewish Romeo and a Catholic Juliet was outdated when it was new, and despite its revival in the 1940s as a radio series, the Crosby production received so thorough a lambasting that he permanently withdrew it from release. It also ended his career as a film producer.[17]

Bing's transcription work continued apace, usually after a day of *Utopia* or the *KMH* show; *Mail Call, GI Journal,* and a historic broadcast on Monday, January 10, when Bing became the first white performer to guest-star on the usually segregated *Jubilee*. This exceptional show represented the Negro wing of the Armed Forces Radio Service and proved immensely influential in mainstreaming performers as diverse as Count Basie, Lena Horne, Art Tatum, Lead Belly, and Charlie Parker. With the emcee Ernie Whitman presiding, Bing crossed the racial gulf singing Phil Moore's "Shoo Shoo Baby" and left the door open for other whites to follow, which they did. Among them were Jack Benny, Johnny Mercer, George Burns and Gracie Allen, Tommy Dorsey, Peggy Lee, Dick Haymes, and Kitty Kallen, drawing larger audiences to an otherwise black variety show.

Bing's weekends were occupied by war-related golf tournaments, including the much ballyhooed two-day pro-am benefit at Lakeside in the last days of January, with an auction that yielded another perpetually played film clip. This time Bing and Hope ("Bob, why do you suppose this Sinatra's so skinny?" "I don't know, Bing. Maybe when he was a baby his mother tied his bow tie too tight." "Yeah, Bob, but not tight enough") were outdone by a much anticipated, albeit strictly for-laughs duet by Bing and Frank: "People Will Say We're in Love." It was paid for by a twenty-thousand-dollar bid from Kay Kyser. The two baritones' seconds wrangled for months to bring them together on commercial radio, while *Command Performance* ordered up an encore of the same duet within three days and united them again in June for a whole show of skits and parody songs. Until November, no one could see them or hear them share a song without first walking nine holes or joining the army.

A Paramount secretary assigned to Crosby for the duration of *Utopia* later remarked on studio scuttlebutt to the effect that Bing did all he could to smooth Sinatra's entry into Hollywood. He (and Hope) definitely smoothed his way into Lakeside; beyond that, Bing was undoubtedly welcoming but hardly vital to Frank's success. A day or so after their duet on the links, Frank called Bing to take him up on an invitation to visit the set at Paramount. As word got around that he was on the way, the *Utopia* crew prepared a prank. The moment Bing brought Frank to the soundstage, they screamed and fell to the floor in swoons. Bing, as surprised as

Sinatra, cracked up until he saw Sinatra's embarrassment, then he marched into the muddle of bodies and, stifling his laughter, said, "What are you doing? That isn't right. Get up, get up!"[18]

Road to Utopia brought its stars to a location site in June Lake, California, close to the Nevada border, where the men suffered a couple of accidents. They were not seriously hurt when they slipped on an icy ledge, though according to Hope they were perilously close to a fifty-foot cliff. But during a mountain-climbing scene, Hope, higher on the rope, lost his hold and fell on Crosby (the fall is in the picture), necessitating a brief hospitalization for both men. Hal Walker worked with doubles the rest of the week and Crosby endured back problems the rest of his life. The soundstage was covered with gypsum and cornflakes to simulate snow, and they did their stuff against rear-projection footage provided by a second unit. A couple of off-camera grips made their sled wobble. Then there was the mythical killer bear.

This story, which is now retailed in dozens of books and on thousands of websites, including the Internet Movie Database, first appeared in 1954 when Bob Hope (and Pete Martin, who one year earlier co-authored Bing's *Call Me Lucky*) published his most serious go at a memoir: *Have Tux, Will Travel*. The passage is quite brief, given the elaborations that followed.

> In *The Road to Utopia*, a bear was supposed to sniff Bing and me while we were sleeping in a cabin. I gave my reluctant consent. I didn't like that bear's personality or the way he sniffed. My instinct was right. We made our shot on Wednesday. The next day the bear tore off his trainer's arm.[19]

It never happened; Hope libeled the bear while misidentifying its gender and altering the name of the film (adding *The*). By the 1970s, the tale had been told so often that Bing's authorized biographer incorporated an expanded version from an interview with Hope, even though Bing never mentioned such an incident. Dorothy Lamour's as-told-to helper also used it, and so did a raft of Hope biographers, always with the same specifics: the bear went berserk the next day and tore off the trainer's arm.[20] Hope probably came to believe it. Asked in a 1993 interview if the trainer had died, he said, "That's right. Yes, he was killed." What happened to the bear? "I don't remember. They shipped it right away. I don't know what the hell happened." The trainer, Stanley Beebe, and the bear, the 250-pound Brooklyn-born Rosie, were profiled in *Life* magazine and worked together into the 1960s, appearing on radio and television, apparently unaware of all the fuss.[21]

The mood picked up as filming proceeded. The difference in teamwork between "Goodtime Charlie," the first musical number they shot, and the effortless "Put It There, Pal," the last, postponed until February, is palpable. Crosby was pleased that the snowy setting allowed him to wear a hat in almost every scene; he wore the fake beard more often than his wig. Both men were relieved that the bear was mostly played by Charlie Gemora, who also played the wrestling gorilla in *Zanzibar*. As Hope grew more involved, his and Bing's interactions reached peak precision, and Bob got to deliver one of his best-ever lines, written by Mel Frank. Duke and Chester saunter into a saloon, pretending to be ruthless killers. "What'll you have?" says the villain (Douglass Dumbrille, also returning to the series after *Zanzibar*). Duke orders "a couple of fingers of rotgut." Chester says he'd like lemonade and then, prodded to remember he's supposed to be a tough guy, scowls and adds, "In a dirty glass." As one chronicler of the home front, Roy Hoopes, later reminisced, "Soon, in bars all over the country, young men—including yours truly—were ordering drinks 'in a dirty glass.'" Hope cherished the line as "a standout, it really caught on."[22]

Utopia's assistant director, Alvin Ganzer, hired a young woman named Hazel Sharp as a studio secretary for the duration of the film but had little work for her to do. She had previously applied to be Bing's secretary, but though he quizzed her on her secretarial skills, nothing came of it. Then one day he saw her on the set and after some small talk, he asked her, "Do you still want to work for me? Be in my dressing room at eleven in the morning." He had a small desk stacked with about two feet of personal mail that had been filtered and sent over from the Crosby office building, which he told her never to touch: "I know exactly where everything is." Then he started to dictate, pausing only to ask her, "How fast can you take it?" "Just as fast as you want, Mr. Crosby," she said. She later recalled, "He was such a kind man, one of the few men I ever met in Hollywood who didn't even try to make a pass, never once. The only person I've taken dictation from faster was David O. Selznick. Bing used very good English and he loved big words and never hesitated." For the next few months, she was a fly on the wall with a steel-trap memory.[23]

At Christmastime, a priest invited Crosby to sing at Midnight Mass. "Bing thought about it a lot and wrote back that he was deeply honored but that Christmas Mass was such a solemn occasion and since he was thought of as a crooner he would only detract from its significance." Hazel wanted to get him a Christmas present and good liquor was hard to find ("Everybody was drinking Southern Comfort"). But she knew a friend who knew a friend and managed to get a bottle of Canadian Club. She wrapped it in white tissue with a ribbon, and after the set cleared and everyone prepared to go home, she went to Bing's dressing room with the bottle hidden behind her back. "Bing asked, 'What you got there, Haze?' I said, 'Well,' and stopped when I saw that one side of his dressing room was loaded, floor to ceiling, with cases of bourbon. I said, 'Well, I brought you a bottle of Canadian Club, but it doesn't look like you need it.' He grinned and said, 'Aw, Haze, I got that for the cast and the crew. And it ain't Canadian Club, Haze, *it ain't Canadian Club.*'"

The worst mood she ever saw him in came after he received a letter that "hit him where he lived." The crew of a B-17 bomber named after the Mercer-Carmichael song "Skylark" had sent him lyrics they wrote that were more in line with their work. Bing wrote back that he liked the lyrics fine and would get together with Johnny Mercer to record them on a disc and send it to them. A couple of weeks later he received a letter from the squadron commander: the Skylark and its entire crew had been shot down. They had found Bing's letter among the pilot's effects, and the commander wanted him to know that there was no point in making the recording. "Bing dictated a brief response and told me, 'That will be all for today.' He was really upset."[24]

Sometimes Hazel entered the dressing room and saw small white envelopes had been slipped under the door; she would place them unopened on his desk. She didn't know what they were until she had lunch with a woman from the mail room who asked her if Bing had gotten her payment. She said Bing loaned her money and she was paying it back in installments, although he kept telling her she did not need to pay him back. "It turned out Bing loaned lots of money to various lesser employees and they didn't have to pay it back at all, but most of them, I guess, wanted to. As far as I could see everybody adored him. I used to wonder if he even knew he was Bing Crosby, he was so unassuming, so self-unimportant. He didn't take himself seriously, didn't believe his publicity. But he didn't let anyone tell him what to do." A studio publicist gave him a hard time because he was photographed at the Santa Anita racetrack without his toupee. "He said he would do as he wanted away from the studio and that was that. He wore hats a lot and his yellow tie—oh, that idiot yellow tie. He hated ties and when he had to wear one it was always the same tie. He was color-blind so he probably didn't know it was yellow."[25]

The film's shooting, which she attended almost every day, could be chaotic, especially for "the poor script girl," who had to note every change, every ad lib. "She had to work like a slave to put in what they said instead of what they were supposed to say and at the end of the day she had a script that was a mess." Hazel thought they were merciless to Lamour. Dorothy once made the mistake of saying she would like to be an opera singer. From then on, every time she got anywhere in their vicinity, Bing and Bob broke out into some operatic number. Hazel left the film set a few days early to get married (her second marriage). "Bing called Bob and Dottie over and said he wanted to give me a picture of them to take with me because I was to be married. Well, it was well known that Dottie was trying to get pregnant so Bob looked at me and said, 'You're getting married?' I said, 'Yes.' He said, 'Well, Dottie better take you over in a corner and show you the motions.' Bing said, 'Whaddya mean? Haze has a little two-year-old girl.'" "Bob looked at me and said, 'You've got a two-year-old girl?' I said, 'Yes,' and he said 'Well, you better take Dottie in a corner and show her the motions.'"[26]

Jack Kapp scheduled Bing's first Decca session of the year, to record "Going My Way" and "Swinging on a Star," for February 7, and the second one four days later, in a rush to record a new song that was not really new although it had slipped from people's memory. Sammy Fain and Irving Kahal wrote "I'll Be Seeing You" for a 1938 Broadway show (*Right This Way*) that tanked in ten days. It isn't known if Kapp found it for the mononymous singer Hildegarde, who performed in cabarets in arm-length gloves and billed herself as the Incomparable Hildegarde, or if, as she claimed, the songwriters asked her to be the first to record it. Her story is improbable; Frank Sinatra recorded it as early as 1940, at his second session with Tommy Dorsey. However, even the *Billboard* writer thought it a new song when he reviewed Hildegarde's version, which he indicated might be most pleasing for "the after-dark set at the smarter saloons."[27]

Kapp knew it would be a hit for Crosby, and before he released Hildegarde's recording, he sent Bing a test pressing so he could learn it and try it out on *Kraft Music Hall*. Expecting to take dictation, Hazel Sharp walked into his dressing room as he played the test, singing along, which was his preferred method of learning a song. During the lines about "the wishing well," he frowned and said, "She's wrong, she's wrong. Listen to it. Isn't she wrong?" Hazel had never heard the song and didn't know. "You're no help," he muttered.[28]

He continued playing it because he planned to sing it that evening, January 13, on *KMH*. Hazel said she had never been to a radio station to watch a show. He asked, "Would you like to go? I'll leave a ticket for you at NBC." She went and took a seat down front, uncertain if he knew she was present. During "I'll Be Seeing You," when he got to the problematical phrase (measures 15 and 16), he looked straight at her with a smile and winked. Apparently, Hildegarde's version jarred him because she had added the conjunction *and* between the phrases "the chestnut trees" and "the wishing well." She did so for decades, although, as Bing suspected, it is not in the sheet music. He deleted the conjunction and the lugubrious verse.

"I'll Be Seeing You" emerged as one of the great standards of the Second World War, a totemic song of longing and remembrance, frequently recorded (magnificently by Billie Holiday in April 1944) and performed for years as a way of evoking the era. Yet only two versions qualified as hits: a daringly upbeat dance-band version by

Tommy Dorsey (vocal by Sinatra), which reached number four, and Bing's, which charted for six months, four weeks as the nation's number one record, soon to be supplanted by "Swinging on a Star." The song cleaved to him; servicemen requested it everywhere. He sang it seven times on *KMH* between January and July; it tied "San Fernando Valley" and was topped only by "Swinging on a Star" as his most performed song that season. Yet it is one of Crosby's more enervating records from the mid-1940s, often cited as an example of his sporadic vocal slump, his voice weakened, his attention blurred. He had to schedule two sessions just to get a releasable take, one on February 11 (when he didn't do Cole Porter's "Night and Day" any favors either) and one a week later. In the opening phrase, he degrades the world *old* (in "the old familiar places") from a dotted quarter to half that, as if he had run out of breath after three bars; he strains at high notes; he pauses, often and oddly, as Trotter's strings grind intrusively. Maybe his failings made the performance more human, almost tremulous.[29]

Bing had struck a chord with the song, and he kept striking it to promote bonds. He sang it on the air the week after D-day, and as the strings continued and before the studio audience could think to applaud, he read a short prepared statement: "'I'll Be Seeing You,' that's the dream of every infantryman holding his little piece of ground because he knows the battle line is only as strong as its weakest link and he's not going to be that link. I say 'every infantry-man' because we have finally gotten around to recognizing and giving a little credit to the foot-slogging soldier without whom wars can't be won. Your infantry man is the first guy to set foot on a beach and he's the last guy to get leave and the very last guy to get a string of ribbons for his tunic. Today was Infantry Day and there's no better way to observe it than by adding your best and biggest buy to the Fifth War Loan. Every bond you buy is a vote of confidence and another weapon in the hands of the men who are fighting to defend our happy future. Good night."[30]

Several slow ballads, among them classics by Cole Porter, Jerome Kern, and Bing's own team of Burke and Van Heusen, would defy him in the course of this year and the next; sluggish tempos, blasé phrasing, notes bitten off or not quite reached—all of this very unlike Crosby, occasionally to the point where one might wonder why they were released. But then one considers the windfall of "I'll Be Seeing You," recorded the same day as a *KMH* broadcast. The curious thing about this session, however, is how good he is on the other numbers, each more rhythmic, verbally inventive, and Crosby-esque than "I'll Be Seeing You." Decca delayed Johnny Mercer and Harry Warren's "On the Atchison, Topeka and the Santa Fe," richly orchestrated by Billy May, until 1945, when the impending release of *The Harvey Girls* helped several versions scale the charts, Bing's second in sales only to Mercer's. On "Amor, Amor," a big Crosby hit in the summer of 1944, he crests the Latin beat without hesitation. The most likable performance of the session is on a 1927 Harry Warren melody, "One Sweet Letter from You," sung at a snug tempo that encourages him to glide like a soft shoe with a vibrant Bob Goldrich trumpet improvisation to confirm the mood. Maybe the title and subject were too touchy to be treated with effortless detachment in 1944, when letters often delivered death or desertion. Decca buried it until 1949, when its release caused not a ripple.

In the last week of February, they filmed the wraparound scenes, in which Bing, Bob, and Dottie are depicted in their seventies, courtesy of Wally Westmore. Hope hated the aluminum paint in his hair, but Crosby got to wear a robust gray wig and a mustache modeled after Frank Morgan's and thought he looked quite handsome "in a lascivious, degenerate sort of way."[31] A few under-the-wire additions, including a scene in which the men hallucinate Lamour in a sarong, were shot in March, and then it was over, except for the Benchley filler. Bing headed for Elko.

He now had two movies on the shelf awaiting release, and seven weeks on his hands before he had to report for duty on *Here Come the Waves*. He spent much of this time producing and casting *The Great John L.*, reports of which greatly exceeded the spotty hype for *Going My Way*, an indication of ongoing irresolution behind the Paramount arch. Now that he was between pictures, he made occasional visits to the Hollywood Canteen, the converted barn of a nightclub at 1451 Cahuenga Boulevard where enlisted men and, less conspicuously, women could congregate free of charge to eat, drink, dance, mingle with stars, and cheer the big-name, half-prepared and half-impromptu forty-five-minute shows, usually two a night. No one could elevate that audience like Crosby, who came by on Sunday, April 9, to take a turn in the Easter show.

The Hollywood Canteen is little honored today, in part because of the acrid taste left by the Warner Brothers picture of the same name, released in December 1944. A typical musical revue brought low by its depiction of American soldiers as movie-addicted bumpkins who cower before Barbara Stanwyck and hanker for Eddie Cantor's autograph, it compelled several enlisted men to write a letter to Warner to express their outrage. They labeled the movie an insult to "the intelligence and acumen of every member of the armed services." Pity, because the Hollywood Canteen embodied a visionary act of generosity and courage.[32]

In its three years of existence, from October 1942 to November 1945, it provided an oasis for three million servicemen, on average twenty thousand a week. John Garfield, who would be exiled from Hollywood by the postwar blacklist, pushed the idea after he visited Broadway's Stage Door Canteen, the free nightclub for servicemen that opened in March 1942. Bette Davis shared his enthusiasm and agreed to chair the effort. Together they got the Hollywood guilds and unions to support them. Davis proved valiant. When the Hollywood Victory Committee (of the Screen Actors Guild), chaired by James Cagney, reneged on its promises and told Davis she could no longer call members without going through the committee, she delivered an ultimatum: Either they would reinstate permission by morning or she would close the Hollywood Canteen and explain why to the forty-two cooperating guilds and the press. She stormed out of the meeting before Cagney or anyone else could respond. At six a.m. the next day, the committee rescinded its interdiction.

The Hollywood Canteen operated six nights a week from seven o'clock to midnight and on Sundays from two to eight p.m. It had a staff of thousands of volunteer workers and hostesses, but entertainers routinely helped in the kitchen, poured coffee, dished up pie, sat at tables to chat with soldiers, and partnered with them on the dance floor (and sometimes off the dance floor, though perhaps not as often as proliferating rumors would have it). No money changed hands and no officers or civilians unaffiliated with the entertainment world were admitted. Most remarkably, at a time when the armed forces enforced segregation, and Hollywood night-clubs, bars, and restaurants habitually rebuffed blacks, the Holly-wood Canteen did not discriminate between races at the door or try to separate them inside any more than it tried to separate the enter-tainers onstage. It recruited black as well as white hostesses. Warned that Southern whites might start trouble if a black soldier danced with a white woman, Davis developed a contingency plan: at the first sign of tension, the orchestra would strike up "The Star Spangled Banner." According to her, the canteen had to resort to the national anthem only twice in three years.

Practically every major star, supporting player, bandleader, singer, comedian, radio personality, studio musician, and wannabe starlet found time for the Hollywood Canteen. Did Davis write personally to thank them all? She wrote at least five thank-you letters to Crosby in 1943 and 1944. He was usually expected at Christmas, but he sometimes came by without warning on other days. One of the things that impressed him and other performers was the num-ber of soldiers who did not know or especially care who they were. The draft reached areas that had no electricity or indoor plumbing, let alone radio and movie theaters. A private from Greenfield Cen-ter, a tiny hamlet in upstate New York, recalled his experience at the canteen.

> I'd just come out of the country and we were training in the desert in Arizona. But then I went home on furlough, and met [the woman who became] my wife, and she got to talking about Bing Crosby. Well, I didn't know Bing Crosby from Johnny Crooks but she said if you see or hear or get anywhere near Bing Crosby, ask him to sing a song for me, "Night and Day." I went back after a couple of weeks and, first thing, I had to make a trip from the desert into Pomona, and I had to wait for a return trip-load for the army. So we asked a few fellas, "What do you do when you're sit-ting around here?" They all said go to the Hollywood Canteen. I did go and as I came through the door a guy took my arm and said, "We need some help behind this food bar here." I said, "Yeah, sure, I'll help you, whatever I can do." So while I was helping load the counter with stuff, a guy came in and tapped me on the shoul-

der and said, "Hey, I'm supposed to be doing this, if you want to let me in." Okay, so I did, and I didn't pay attention to him. And after I was there for a minute or two more, the first guy says, "Do you know who the guy is that tapped you on your shoulder?" I said, "No. I don't know who you are really." He said, "Well, I'm Roddy McDowall and I'm a movie actor." See, I'd just come out of the country and we had no radio, no telephone, nothing. He said, "That's Bing Crosby." I said, "Oh, so that's Bing Crosby, huh." And I turned around and I said, "Hello, I'm Tom Smith and I understand you're Bing Crosby," and he says, "That's right, I am." I said, "I didn't know who you were. I'm sorry." He said, "That's all right. There are a lot of kids coming in from the country who don't know who anybody is because they don't have radio." But anyway it was simple as that. So I said, "I have a friend at home that asked me if I ever saw you to ask you to sing 'Night and Day.'" And he did. He went on the radio, maybe three or four weeks later, and said, "A soldier over here would like to have this song sung for his sweetheart." I just took it for granted he was just another guy, but he wasn't just another guy. He was a special guy. He was some man, some performer.[33]

Nearly six weeks after the screening that cheered Bing ("They don't want to cut a thing"), on February 25, Paramount showed exhibitors *Going My Way* along with four other features scheduled to be released in the spring. On March 22, *Variety* implied that as a result of the trade show, the Crosby film had been withdrawn from the schedule and bound over for a September opening. That one notice spurred Crosby and DeSylva into action, and within days the withdrawal was countermanded and Paramount announced a new release date, which just happened to be Bing's (true) forty-first birthday, May 3, 1944. It would debut in a single theater, the New York Paramount. The advance work could, at long last, begin.[34]

Suddenly, the hills were alive with *Going My Way*. Bing had just signed an unparalleled contract with Paramount—ten years, taking him through 1954, during which time he was expected to star in twenty-three pictures. He would have the final say on director, leading lady, story, script, and songs and publishers of songs; and he would hold an option to do one outside movie a year. He personally contacted Louella Parsons, who, fast off the mark and six weeks before the premiere, wrote that a little bird had told her that Bing's momentous new Paramount deal, "with nary an option to worry him or them," reflected the studio's high hopes for the forthcoming picture "in which Bing looks so young and so attractive and sings so well he will be an academy nominee." Not to be outdone, Hedda Hopper, who predicted the contract "would raise hell in our town," declared Bing "an American institution" and observed rather haplessly, "He doesn't act in *Going My Way,* but the picture's so good he needn't have done a song in it. At least, that's what Barry Fitzgerald, from the Abbey Theater, tells me." A *Variety* reviewer screened it and approved but saw no reason to have palpitations; Crosby had a "tailor-made role" in a "top-notch entertainment [with] wide audience appeal." As the release date neared, an unimpressed columnist named Jimmy Starr warned that Crosby was "throwing the dice for a big gamble when he plays a serious role without benefit of a 60-piece orchestra or a bevy of tightly dressed gals."[35]

Bing attempted to take charge of the rollout the one way he could, by presenting the movie's songs on *Kraft Music Hall.* A radio-news editor alerted her readers that on the April 13 show, "The Charioteers will sing 'Swing [*sic*] on a Star' from *Going My Way,* a Crosby picture."[36]

Of course it was Crosby who sang it that night, backed by the Charioteers *and* the Music Maids. He also had a brainstorm and, with Leo McCarey and Buddy DeSylva, he arranged for one of the strangest premieres in cinema history—indeed, as McCarey described it, it was "65 world premieres." They dispatched 16 mm prints of *Going My Way* to sixty-five battle stations, from the Aleutian Islands to Sicily, to be screened on the evening of April 27. That night Ken Carpenter announced the Fighting Front Premiere on *KMH.* "Marvelous," Marilyn Maxwell gushed. "Just think, soldiers all over the world will see that picture before we do." And they would talk and write home about it. At the end of the broadcast, Crosby said he was certain that the soldiers, sailors, Marines, and Coast Guardsmen who saw "Barry Fitzgerald's new Paramount Picture *Going My Way* [on] battle fronts this evening," would agree that Barry "gives an Academy Award performance."

Mail poured in. A sergeant wrote to McCarey, "Sometimes in

the routine of training, in the worst heat of battle, we lose sight of the things for which we are fighting. It is a strange, unpatriotic feeling—you're just tired and dirty and don't give a damn. 'Going My Way' refreshed my memory...I can't give you a medal. I can only express, in my own humble way, my appreciation for your great contribution to a world at war." A chaplain wrote, "Never will I forget the reactions of all these men here as they heard [Crosby] sing 'Ave Maria' with the backing of the crowd of boys." *Billboard* reported that the great comic-strip artist Milton Caniff would devote a Sunday installment of *Terry and the Pirates* to dramatize "the motion picture industry's 16mm gift films for servicemen in combat areas." The first nine panels, set in and around an American base in an Indian jungle, convey covert preparations. The tenth and last panel solves the mystery, depicting silhouetted soldiers arrayed before a makeshift outdoor screen illuminating the uncaptioned faces of Crosby and Fitzgerald.[37]

On the morning of May 3, a Wednesday, Bing returned to Decca's Melrose Avenue studio to commune with John Scott Trotter and loiter through four superior ballads. He gave his all to the first, Kern's "Long Ago and Far Away," and was rewarded with good reviews and sales, though his vibrato wobbles and, perhaps for the first time, his signature mordents sound ostentatious and overbaked, as if warbled by a Crosby mimic. His dilatory readings of "Like Someone in Love," "Begin the Beguine," and "Dearly Beloved" indicate the need for more rest. He would not record again for nearly two months.

By the time Bing left the Decca session, *Going My Way* was packing in audiences at the 3,663-seat Paramount Theater, where the doors opened at eight a.m. and the first show began half an hour later, a show that included the sugary Charlie Spivak orchestra, the inventive tap dancers Tip, Tap, and Toe, and a short-lived comedy team called the Wesson Brothers. The whole shebang repeated through the day, ending with a midnight screening. As usual during the war, there was no nighttime opening premiere with kliegs and stars. Yet compared to the ad campaign that Warner Brothers lavished on *The Adventures of Mark Twain* (launched the same day eight blocks north at the Hollywood Theater) and

MGM's for *Gaslight* (launched the next day a block south at the Capitol Theatre), Paramount's print ads were noticeably modest, if exclamatory: BING IN HIS GREATEST ROLE!—AS THE SINGING PADRE OF THE TOUGHEST PARISH IN NEW YORK. Fitzgerald was billed second, his name in a smaller font than Crosby's and the "famous contralto" Risë Stevens's, and he was omitted entirely from the three-story color mural overhanging the Paramount marquee. They added a new credit, absent from the film, to ads and trailers: *B. G. DeSylva, executive producer.* The morning after the premiere, Paramount's head of publicity in New York wired the coast: opening day did "the biggest non-holiday business in the history of the house." He forwarded a sheaf of clippings.[38]

The reviews in New York were stunning across the board. Reviewers expressed amazement that Crosby gave such a genuine performance, a true characterization that might even get him an Academy Award nomination. One marveled that McCarey had somehow created "one of the funniest comedies of this year and one of the tenderest" (the *Sun*). James Agee, in *Time,* said that *Going My Way* was "one of the year's top surprises," and that it "points the way to the great films which will be possible when Hollywood becomes aware of the richness and delight of human character for its own sake."[39]

Word of mouth underscored the fact that Bing played a *character.* He had starred in twenty-seven feature films before *Going My Way,* but who had ever heard of Fred Danvers, Eddie Bronson, Bill Williams, Stephen Jones, Paul Jones, Jim Hardy, or any of the other interchangeable Anglo-Saxon names that doubled Bing Crosby? Now he had an alter ego. Like Edward G. Robinson's Little Caesar or Gary Cooper's Sergeant York, Crosby was bound to Father O'Malley, a name to be remembered, a fabrication that magnified the actor rather than the persona. The studio's ads grew in size and boldness: "Now he's got a story as great as his voice!"

At the end of the first week, receipts totaled $103,000 (*Gaslight* ran second, with an impressive $78,000, while *Mark Twain* lagged with $26,000). By the end of its record-breaking ten-week run at the Paramount Theater—the second picture ever to be held over that long—it had raked in $847,000 from 1,010,000 customers at an average ticket price of eighty-three cents, high even for a Broadway movie house. The only other picture held over that long had also been a new Paramount release, *Lady in the Dark*, which opened in February and enjoyed its prolonged run because receipts continued to be respectable and Paramount had nothing big enough to replace it with. In contrast, the *New York Times* reported, the "Crosby picture retained consistently high figures from week to week" and was pulled only because of the backlog of new films the theater was committed to exhibit.[40]

The rollout was just getting started. It would roll on like a snowball, the momentum accelerated by "Swinging on a Star," far and away the country's most popular song. Shortly after the film's debut, *Box Office Digest* devoted most of an issue to *Going My Way*. The magazine analyzed box-office receipts by measuring each theater's ticket sales for a particular movie against its average business (which provided the 100 percent yardstick). Until more accurate methods came along, this paradigm was considered reliable, as were the trade paper's ballpark predictions. *Box Office Digest* predicted 165 percent for *Going My Way*'s first week (that is, the theater would sell 65 percent more tickets than it typically did), which proved low. *Box Office Digest* upped its estimate to 180 percent. Eventually, it reported *Going My Way*'s national commerce at a colossal 264 percent.[41]

It would not premiere in Los Angeles until August 16, by which time it had played all over the country, but only in major cities that defined a first-run release, theaters where tickets tended to range between twenty-five and fifty-five cents. Similar-sounding trade-paper headlines followed: "Crosby 'Way' Eyes Record 25G, Cincy," "Pitt Goes Bing's 'Way,' Smash 40G," "'Way' Wows Indpls." After eight weeks at the Chicago Theater (where no picture had been held more than four weeks), it continued to pull in a "terrific" $55,000. A Texas correspondent wrote, "There's never been anything like 'Going My Way' in the history of Dallas show business." One in Philadelphia wrote, "As the lights faded out, the throng at the Mastbaum rose en masse and roared its applause to the Leo McCarey masterpiece—and then went forth as individual evangels spreading their acclaim of the newcomer." In Spokane, Crosby's hometown, it played four weeks, the first picture "ever to attract more than 100,000 admissions"; the previous record holder, *Snow*

White, drew 75,000. The manager of Spokane's Evergreen Theater was unhappy when the film closed, noting, "We would keep it going if we could hang onto the film any longer"—a complaint echoed by theater owners around the country.[42]

"The principal battleground of this war," the poet Archibald MacLeish avowed in 1942 as he assumed directorship of what would become the Office of War Information, "is not the South Pacific. It is not the Middle East. It is not England, or Norway, or the Russian Steppes. It is American opinion." Whether or not a nation is in the line of fire, a unified home front is essential to winning a war; its people, as General Eisenhower wrote, "occupy a strategic place." The successful home front is a kind of organism, economical and emotional. When it ceases to function, the strongest armies and the political resolve behind them are undermined and depleted. America learned that during Vietnam. The anger and perplexity expressed by members of the generation who lived through the Second World War toward young men who avoided the draft reflected in part their nostalgia for the near-perfect home front that had steadied nerves in the years 1942 to 1945. They remembered, or believed they did, a national coziness, all citizens united by the sacraments of popular culture, recollections so powerful that they all but superseded memories of anguish and death, internment camps and homespun bigotry, shortages and rationing, mistrust and loneliness, savagery and vengeance, the newspaper casualty lists, and even a guilty indifference. The home front keeps the assembly lines running, and civilians forgo their own desires to meet military needs. It collects supplies, sustains unbowed morale, and honors those who do the fighting. Entertainment, in this equation, is no mere diversion but a necessity, the oil that keeps the gears turning. And when the rest of the era is dimmed, it lingers on and praises those who were there.[43]

Countless war adventures, service comedies, and other kinds of propaganda movies rolled off the studio assembly lines, but few epitomized the emotions that the French film writer Jacques Lourcelles would later attribute to *Going My Way:* "Kindness as permanent catharsis, as providential remedy to all the physical and moral ills of humanity."[44]

O'Malley's priestly liberalism intensified in importance as victory loomed, in particular after D-day and Roosevelt's spellbinding D-day speech. FDR's extraordinary use of radio had paralleled Crosby's since 1932, when those men of very different backgrounds with almost contradictory oratorical gifts represented the triumph of the American vernacular over the highfalutin pretensions embraced by the networks. On the evening of D-day, the president, with less than a year to live and in racking pain, commandeered the networks to deliver a consummate performance as preacher-in-chief, inviting the country "to join with me in prayer." In rhythmical entreaties, he asked the Almighty to guide "our sons" toward the liberation of Europe. His ten-minute incantation drew one hundred million listeners, more than 72 percent of the entire population— the most expansive hearth in American history.[45]

In July, on the basis of four months of receipts, Paramount's vice president in charge of distribution, Charles M. Reagan, went on record to say, "It is clearly apparent that it [will] be the biggest grosser ever released by Paramount." In August, two weeks after *Going My Way* opened in Los Angeles, the *Hollywood Reporter* calculated that in the early first-run phase alone, the picture had set more than 2,420 theater records, smashing "every conceivable theater record to date." Before the year was up, Frank Freeman wrote to Leo McCarey's Rainbow Productions that his "conservative estimate" of the picture's North American grosses, calculated in September at $5 million, was far too conservative. It would easily exceed $6 million, and he was certain that 1946 would increase the American and Canadian totals by no less than $1.5 million. He told McCarey that Paramount intended to withdraw the picture from release after it had played "all possible theaters" on the first-run engagement. They would wait a few months before giving it a "so-called second release," which he predicted would add $2 million, maybe $2.5 million, for a total of $10 million ($138 million in today's money)—and that was exclusive of grosses from the rest of the world. Not foreseeing the film's sweep of the 1945 Academy Awards or the imminent march of returning servicemen in 1945 and 1946, he continued to underestimate the picture's returns; the first-run receipts alone approached $8 million.[46]

*   *   *

Crosby kept his head down during these months, never giving in to the exhilaration that enveloped the studio, declining interviews and even the kind of jocular comment that publicists could dress up as a story or at least an item. Colleagues invited to studio screenings before the picture hit Los Angeles wrote him personal notes like ordinary fans, among them people he hardly knew or had not seen in years: Fredric March, Jack Warner, Cecil B. DeMille, Loretta Young, Barbara Stanwyck, Pat O'Brien, Kate Smith, Congressman Jerry Voorhis, Mary Martin, Louella Parsons, and Hedda Hopper, a rare professional outpouring. Hope and Lamour tried to crack wise in their notes to him (Dorothy: "You are great, fatso, great!"), but they put it in writing, as did his current costar Betty Hutton: "Yours is one of the great performances! Believe me, I know what Mark Sandrich meant when he said I would be happy for the chance of working with you...Bing, you're terrific!"[47]

He took his sons to Elko but worked most of the summer with Hutton on *Here Come the Waves,* his third picture in nine months. He continued with broadcasts and transcriptions, army camps and hospitals, golfing, and fund-raisers. He served as emcee for the July 4 Military Musical Spectacle at the Hollywood Bowl and sang the Brahms "Lullaby," "Going My Way," and "Long Ago and Far Away," on a mostly classical music program—Mendelssohn meets Wagner—featuring the AAF Symphony Orchestra and Chorus, Metropolitan Opera tenor James Melton, and pop singers Ginny Simms and Ella Mae Morse. Bing tried unsuccessfully to purchase the film rights to *Oklahoma!* He petitioned Governor Earl Warren to look into the reason racing had restarted at Bay Meadows and Hollywood Park but not at Del Mar; upon learning that B-17 bombers were still being manufactured near track grounds, he agreed to delay a reopening until after the war. Bing and McCarey discussed ideas for the picture they owed RKO. And, taking advantage of the proximity of Decca to Paramount, Crosby resumed a full recording schedule, usually in the morning and at least once at night: eight sessions, twenty-two sides, between June 30 and July 31.

These recordings were a mixed lot, absurdly so, among them two gold records, a few enchanting sides of the sort only Bing could do, several tiresome slogs, and a baffling descent into unrelieved bathos. The series kicked off with the first of two reunions with the Andrews Sisters and their musical director Vic Schoen, and it was just the ticket: a revivalist brew, a cure for tired blood. If Bing's loyalty to John Scott Trotter resulted in a decade of far too many featureless arrangements, Schoen offered an antidote. He belonged to the Andrews Sisters, but his canniest work was elicited at meetings with Crosby, where the tempos were customarily up and the levity freestyle.

The first two songs initiated two Crosby collaborations. Joe Bushkin, the wired, fast-talking, Bronx-born jazz pianist who built a profuse and swinging style on the framework of Teddy Wilson (and played respectable trumpet after his idol Louis Armstrong), spent two years with Tommy Dorsey's band, during which he wrote a signature hit for Sinatra, "Oh! Look at Me Now," before being drafted. The song he provided Bing and the Andrews Sisters was not as musically rewarding, but it fit the moment perfectly. The Crosby-Andrews recording "(There'll Be a) Hot Time in the Town of Berlin (When the Yanks Go Marching In)" was the number one record for six weeks in the fall and the first to put in words what everyone was thinking—the war was practically over. The Americans had liberated France and were heading east, taking "a hike / to Hitler's Reich" to "change that 'heil' / to 'gimme some skin.'" The performance and the harmonizing are loose, impulsive, and happy. Bushkin, who later married an heiress and lived the life of a country squire, enjoyed commercial success in 1955 with a mood-music album (*Midnight Rhapsody*). He accompanied Bing on the concert tours of his last years. Joe lived to eighty-seven despite, or because of, a fixation on pills (he traveled with a pharmaceutical suitcase) that inclined him to occasionally rush the tempo. Bing liked him so much that he secretly kept another pianist on call in case the rushing got out of hand; it never did.

The second and more enduring number, "Is You Is or Is You Ain't My Baby," charted for three months, reaching number two, and gave Crosby a model jazz vehicle while launching a brief but important association with Louis Jordan and His Tympany Five, the hottest band Decca had signed in years. Jordan, the father of rhythm and blues, altered the musical terrain of the 1940s and after, not least because he broke the stranglehold of big bands with innovative combos that set the table for postwar jazz and pop music. Born in Arkansas, he started out at fourteen as clarinetist with his father's Rabbit Foot Minstrels, then moved north and earned a chair as saxophonist and singer with Harlem's beloved bandleader and thunderous drummer Chick Webb, King of the Savoy. Webb, however, kept Jordan in the shadows to feature his other singer, Ella Fitzgerald. Jordan left to create his own unit. In late 1942, he was a force on the race charts,[48] which tracked recordings aimed at the African American audience. By 1944, his popularity demonstrated major crossover potential, and his manager resolved to move him from Decca's blue-label Sepia series to its premium black-label pop line.

Jordan's music mixed boogie-woogie and shuffle rhythms, glaring saxophones, electric guitar, Hammond organ, pithy jazz solos, outrageous humor, and sunny vocals on witty and often trenchant songs that white bands were eager to cover. His music reflected the everyday life of black communities, which he sometimes mocked and always celebrated. His songs chronicle sexual and marital mores, weekend parties, the draft, slang, travel, and the church. The white world hardly existed in these songs, which reminded everyone that African Americans had a life, a culture, not just a grievance. Jordan's manager offered Bing "Is You Is," introduced by Jordan in the Universal film *Follow the Boys,* hoping that the man who had pioneered alliances with the Mills Brothers, Duke Ellington, Louis Armstrong, and, each Thursday evening, the Charioteers would record with the Tympany Five.[49]

It worked. Schoen's arrangement begins with a biting trumpet intro by Charles Griffard, which sets up Bing's immaculate rendering of the slow, snake-charmer verse, shared with Patty Andrews and her sisters. A bold brass fanfare takes them into the swing chorus, floated by John Cyr's rumbling drums, as Bing bends notes and lights up phrases with smooth mordents. This is primo Crosby, and it remained so when he adapted Schoen's arrangement to sing it with the Charioteers on *KMH.* With recordings like "Pistol Packin' Mama," "The New San Antonio Rose," and "Is You Is or Is You Ain't My Baby" in mind, the writer and professor of ethnic studies George Lipsitz incisively noted, "Of all the popular singers, Crosby best preserved the properties of the songs he expropriated, and his records did help to prepare a mass audience for the country and blues artists who would soon enjoy great success among the pop audience."[50]

The next few sessions are head-scratchers. How could he deliver so lovely a reading of the strangely deferred "Too-Ra-Loo-Ra-Loo-Ral" and allow the marvelous ballad "I'll Remember April" to drift mechanically downriver? Why rerecord "Let Me Call You Sweetheart," which he had rendered definitively at his very first Decca session, in 1934? Can collegial bonds justify "Moonlight on a White Picket Fence," the second collaboration by Trotter and Carroll and entirely without virtues? He also did a favor for Meredith Willson, then a major with the AFRS, by introducing "Iowa," high corn to celebrate the Corn State's centennial, issued with a directive that it would be used for that purpose only and would never be rereleased. He offered a sleepy competence to a few Burke and Van Heusen songs, including the *Utopia* ballads. Oddest of all is the reunion with his old friend the composer Victor Young, organist Ethel Smith (the dishy redhead he met in Rio in 1941), and the Ken Darby Singers, which produced a slumberous favor for Jack Kapp's brother Dave, the lyricist for "Just a Prayer Away" ("There's a happy land somewhere and it's just a prayer away"), coarsened by the bogus sentiment that the genuine sentiment of *Going My Way* shames. Bing may have taken the piety of the impossible flip side, "My Mother's Waltz," as a challenge, because he sings the hell out of it before organ and choir restore its brimstone misery. "Just a Prayer Away" charted ten weeks, peaking at number four.

At the next session, he bounced back for perhaps the most charming of the Andrews Sisters dates. They recorded Cole Porter's cowboy manifesto "Don't Fence Me In," adapted from a poem by a mining engineer named Robert Fletcher, and Manuel Esperon's "The Three Caballeros," composed for the 1941 Mexican film *¡Ay, Jalisco, no te rajes!* and outfitted with audacious English lyrics by Ray Gilbert. Both songs would make their respective American movie debuts in December, the first in *Hollywood Canteen* (performed by Roy Rogers) and the second in Walt Disney's improbably wanton *The Three Caballeros*. Schoen's arrangements encourage the vocalists to be rigorously casual, impeccably serendipitous, particularly "Caballeros," rife with whimsical sampling, including a brass obbligato of "Hail, Hail, the Gang's All Here." Bing entered the studio not having seen or heard Porter's song. Half an hour later, loping on his cayuse, he made it sound as though Porter had had him in mind all along. It brought Crosby his eleventh gold record, the Andrews Sisters their fifth, and their work together its second.

Bing had no warning, let alone preparation, for the recordings he made the following evening. He and Dixie were hosting a party when a Decca producer called to say he had Louis Jordan at the studio. Bing and Jordan had discussed doing a session but with Jordan on the road, their schedules had never chimed, and now that Bing was planning a USO tour of Europe, they were loath to miss the opportunity. According to Jordan, "He said, 'I'll come in tonight' and he just came down. Nothing was pre-planned and when Bing walked in they said, 'Here's the music.'"[51] Today, one listens to the two numbers they recorded with pleasure and unease. Meeting for the first time, they interact like old friends, especially on the second tune, "Your Socks Don't Match" (previously recorded with unexpected delicacy by Fats Waller), where they verbally joust and Jordan telegraphs his delight in an ebullient solo on the alto saxophone. Another memorable moment occurs on "My Baby Said Yes," where Jordon plays gruff tenor saxophone and responds heartily to Bing's encouraging comment "Come on, Lou." Still, and as ever, when things go Southern, Bing can't help but resort to his minstrel voice, which is more pronounced on the rejected takes than those released. No one minded at the time, least of all Jordan, whose standing at Decca and beyond rose immediately. Sales were modest (the record got to number fourteen), but as Jordan's biographer noted, the "one coupling gained an enormous amount of air plays" and broadened his audience. For Bing, it added another category to his checklist of idioms: rhythm and blues.[52]

Bing's imminent and long-delayed USO trip became official when he went to New York, provided satisfactory proof that he had been immunized against smallpox, cholera, yellow fever, and typhus, and received embarkation approval. The War Department issued "Invitational Travel Orders" ten days before, on August 3, with the destination withheld; having requested the South Pacific, Bing assumed that's where he was headed. The manifest identified Bing and a supporting troupe: Harry Lillis Crosby Jr., the musicians Earl James Baxter and John Calvin (Buck) Harris, and the entertainers Darlene Cecily Watts (Darlene Garner), Joseph Franklin Wardell (Joe DeRita), and Jeanette Elizabeth Wineman Brown (Jeanne Darrell). They would travel by sea from either Brooklyn or Boston with baggage totaling not more than one hundred and seventy-five pounds. The group prepared to spend the interim testing out its material in San Francisco. On August 16, one year after *Going My Way* began production and on the same day it premiered in Los Angeles, the Crosby group signed up with Overseas Unit No. 329 at the Brooklyn Port of Embarkation and put on an extemporized show surrounded by the port's cheering workers. They still had another day to wait. Bing stayed at the Waldorf Astoria, as usual, and dined at the Stork Club with the stunning model Anita Colby. A note came for him at the hotel from the visiting chairman of the Democratic National Committee, Robert Hannegan, who had accompanied the saloonkeeper Toots Shor to see *Going My Way*. "It was a marvelous picture," he wrote, "and you were great, but, I just can't believe it—that you are a Republican, for the Father O'Malley I saw last night certainly was a Democrat."[53]

Part Three

———

DER BINGLE

19

HEER SHPREEKHT BING CROS-BY

No war is ever really over until the last veteran is dead.
—Robert Kotlowitz, *Before Their Time* (1999)[1]

Bing's niece Carolyn later recalled that her aunt Dixie greatly fretted over her husband's departure, fearing for his safety traveling to and through a continent combusting with war. Dixie had reason. Travel mishaps don't exempt celebrities, as Carole Lombard's death in a plane crash as she was returning from an Indiana fund-raiser in 1942 reminded everyone. A plane carrying Leslie Howard had been shot out of the sky. In 1943, a Pan American Clipper had crashed near Lisbon, killing USO performers, reporters, and businessmen. Among the twenty-four killed was the Broadway star Tamara Drasin, who costarred with Bob Hope in *Roberta,* the 1933 musical that made him famous. Several others were severely injured, notably the radio singer Jane Froman, whose heroic recuperation was dramatized by Hollywood in the 1952 tearjerker *With a Song in My Heart.* At least three dozen USO performers died of war-related causes before war's end, including Glenn Miller. The acrophobic Crosby stuck to land and sea except for his unavoidable channel crossings, but travel was risky and discomfiting at any level.[2]

The majestic *Île de France* had been through its own hell since it first departed Le Havre for New York in 1927, an art deco monument to a kind of luxury soon to be rendered obsolete. On September 3, 1939, the day France and Great Britain declared war on Germany, it left home for good, under blackout conditions and convoyed by two British destroyers, the dining area fitted with bunks to billet hundreds of extra passengers. The ship eluded U-boats and mines to be laid up in Staten Island until Britain appropriated it to transport tanks, bombers, and other matériel. While docked in South Africa, all remnants of splendor—carpets, paneling, mirrors, chandeliers, bathroom installations—were dumped in favor of barbed wire as it was converted first into a floating POW camp and then into a troopship. In January 1944, the Île de France commenced a series of weeklong crossings from New York to Greenock, Scotland. It had plied that route seven months when Bing and his unit discreetly boarded on August 17.

In the morning the ship's daily mimeographed newssheet, Stand-By, verified the rumor sweeping from deck to deck: "Bing Crosby's on Board!" After breakfast, the first in a series of shows—three or four a day, each running a little longer than an hour—took place in B Deck's mess hall. Showtimes were announced over the PA, and only personnel quartered in the specified parts of the ship were admitted, to avoid congestion and guarantee everyone a chance to see Bing.[3]

Designed for no more than fifteen hundred passengers, the Île de France carried twelve thousand GIs and Canadian-trained RAF pilots, all packed, Crosby said, "like bride's spoons." They shared quarters that peacetime travelers would not have recognized. The two adjacent cabins with private bathrooms that a family might once have reserved were turned into a single room bunking twenty junior officers. They slept or reclined in their bunks in eight-hour shifts. "Then," Bing recalled, "you'd have to get up, go on deck or sit out in the hall, and amuse yourself however you could while someone else used your bunk." At any hour, day or night, men sprawled on the decks trying to catch a little shut-eye. They lined up for meals twice a day, a long but efficient process that served each man, a shipmate drily noted, "in precisely four and a half seconds." Crosby was invited to have three meals a day with the ship's officers in their wardroom, but he declined and lined up to eat with the troops

in the mess. He availed himself of one privilege, the officers' cocktail hour, yet always left in time for the eleven p.m. Coast Guard
gunners' change of watch for which he provided songs as requested,
invariably wearing a white Dixie cup sailor cap. According to
Stand-By, his singing was contagious; a medic diagnosed numberless "G.I. throats [with] Croonitis."[4]

Crosby had a cubicle barely large enough for a bed with a door
that opened onto the quarters of a group of paratroopers, "a really
tough-looking bunch with crew-cuts, most of them all scarred up,
wore polished high boots, got into fights nearly every day; two or
three climbed up in the crow nest and wouldn't come down; they
were in the brig a good deal of the time." One guy, a "big Boston
Irishman," truculently demanded a song. Crosby blew him off a
couple of times, but he was relentless, and after a few days at sea,
Bing and his guitarist gave him a private rendering of "Sweet
Leilani." He wasn't impressed. This is the kind of story Bing frequently told on himself: unemotional, mildly mortifying, not terribly amusing, and a reliable substitute for the unbearably affecting
incidents that genuinely humbled him.[5]

Bing evidently spent much of his time alone writhing with nau-
sea. He "worked harder than anybody," according to the ship's
chronicler, although he was "miserably, agonizingly seasick through
most of the crossing; nevertheless he insisted on putting on four
one-hour shows a day so that all the troops could be entertained,
2500 at a time—a grueling schedule for any entertainer, even one
who could keep his lunch down, which Crosby could not, as a rule."
To *Stand-By,* Bing insisted he had not suffered a moment of mal de
mer. The *Île de France* shows served as rehearsals for the seventy-
five-minute shows he and his troupe gave in the UK and France.[6]

The United Services Organization originated as a compromise
between the armed forces, which sought to control every aspect of
military life, including recreation, and Roosevelt's determination to
preserve civilian authority. It empowered the army and navy to req-
uisition entertainers through an independent subsidiary called
USO–Camp Shows, the biggest booking agency ever devised. The
details were managed by a veteran William Morris agent, Abe Lastfogel, as it was understood that auditioning, casting, scoring, and

rehearsing shows while balancing the artists' schedules to the satisfaction of the studios and the unions required a measure of skill and diplomacy beyond the capacity of the military. By the end of 1945, Lastfogel had produced, depending on sources, 273,599 or 428,521 live shows, reaching 171,717,205 or 212,974,401 service personnel. It remains the most extensive tactical feat in showbusiness history. The cost—budgeted at $10,765,000 in 1941 and exceeding eighteen times that as of 1945—was borne almost entirely by the home front.[7]

The USO–Camp Shows produced four discrete circuits, or tours, three of them domestic: the Victory Circuit, the Blue Circuit, and the Hospital Circuit. The Victory Circuit delivered major stars and large supporting ensembles to army posts and naval stations with troop populations exceeding fifteen hundred. The majority of USO performers were not stars of any kind; they were nightclub or ex-vaudeville performers, glad to be wanted and nominally paid for their work, and they toured the Blue Circuit in groups of five, known as tabloid units, entertaining audiences as small as fifteen and as great as fifteen hundred. The Hospital Circuit debuted in 1944 and formalized celebrity visits to wards. The most storied, reported-on, filmed, and later televised tours were on the Foxhole Circuit, which went overseas in small packets with a big star for each one to carry the weight.[8]

Crosby's five-person crew exemplified Foxhole efficiency. It included the veteran burlesque comedian Joe DeRita (who finished his career as a member of the Three Stooges); two talented and, more important, fetching women: Jeanne Darrell, a recent addition to the Music Maids and the only one to pose for a pinup, and Darlene Garner, a blond tap dancer and singer whose specialties included Duke Ellington's "Don't Get Around Much Anymore," which she dramatized with overhead kicks and somersaults; Earl Baxter, an accordionist known for his work with the short-lived nightclub act the Quintones; and Buck Harris, a guitarist about whom nothing is known.

They were outfitted in USO fatigues, plain, deep-pocketed, loose-fitting khakis with optional patches or pins that bore little resemblance beyond the color to military uniforms. (Bing sometimes opened his jacket to reveal the yellow tie that had dismayed

Hazel Sharp and that was often mentioned in reports and subsequent letters. The manager of a British radio station wrote him, "Even that wild tie you were wearing seemed to symbolize the very essence of freedom and self-expression."[9]) If they were captured, they did not want to be mistaken for combatants, and the fatigues, along with USO cards, were meant to prove they were civilians.

Darrell had sailed twice before. DeRita had recommended Baxter and Harris after a tour of the Solomon Islands, where the three men "got their USO baptism under fire."[10]

Bing brought five typed pages of jokes, topical one-liners, gags about Sinatra ("I'm not Frank Sinatra's father! All my kids are grown up!"), Bob Hope ("Paramount just let Hope work for another studio. It's part of the Lend-Louse Bill"), women ("I don't know why guys are crazy about sweater girls. That's one mystery I'd like to unravel"), and home ("Everyone back there is geared for war. The hens are even eating talcum so they can lay powdered eggs"). He memorized and added to them. He scribbled pages of gags on stationery embossed with the logos of Paramount Pictures and San Francisco's Palace Hotel—random notes, mnemonic reminders.[11]

Before leaving for New York, the troupe spent a week in San Francisco arranging and refining it all. On a Saturday afternoon at Oak Knoll, the amphitheater of the Naval Hospital in Oakland, they went on for hours, using all the material they had for an audience extending as far back as the eye could see, dozens of men in wheelchairs in front, and behind and around them thousands upon thousands of men and women. One of the favorite bits of the touring show was introduced here. Slim, seductive Jeanne Darrell, in a tight, white knee-length dress with a high neck, full sleeves, and a center pleat in the skirt, and black open-toe pumps with ankle straps, summoned a GI to the stage and emoted "All of Me" up close and sealed with a smooch. Crosby, infallibly debonair, rarely left the stage. Afterward, they condensed the show for two of Oak Knoll's hospital wards and then did it again thirty miles inland at the Shoemaker Naval Hospital. Days later they repeated the show for the Naval Station at Treasure Island.[12] Bing assumed they were headed for the South Pacific ("the quinine circuit"[13]), and said as much to a few friends, including the writer Bill Morrow, who advised him to look up a few people when he got to Oahu. Bing was genuinely surprised when he got a call in his hotel room telling him to report to New York. In a reasonably truthful comedy sketch about the USO tour, broadcast the following year, he said, "It was really something to know we were going to have a small role in Ike Eisenhower's big show."[14]

Bing tried out a few opening lines in San Francisco before finding the right tone, which was usually something along the lines of "It's a pleasure to be hitting the road somewhere without Hope. We just finished a picture called *Road to Utopia* and I want to tell you, he was a problem, he's aging. I won't say what part of him was dragging, but it's the cleanest road picture we ever made."[15] The week on the *Île de France* gave them time to work out various bits and find new ones. They were forging a show that combined rehearsed showmanship with extempore fraternization. Bing joked about army food, his four sons, life on the home front. When a plane flew overhead he would say, "For a moment I thought it was the stork again," and the men always laughed. A reporter for the *Stars and Stripes* noted that "soldiers who proffer pictures of their wives are countered with photos of Crosby's wife, the former Dixie Lee, and his four sons."[16]

In the weeks before Overseas Unit No. 329 boarded the *Île de France*, the Allies recaptured Myitkyina and liberated Florence, Rennes, and Guam. As the ship crossed the Atlantic, the D-day divisions pushed toward Germany, the Japanese retreated from India, Romania's King Michael took his country out of the Axis, and President Roosevelt urged delegates visiting the capital for the Dumbarton Oaks Conference to create a postwar peacekeeping union of nations. The day the *Île de France* anchored at Greenock, the Nazis surrendered Paris, and for the first time in four years, the French tricolor flew atop the Eiffel Tower.

On the evening of August 25, after eight days at sea, Bing and his troupe disembarked at Greenock and drove an hour to Glasgow's central station to catch the overnight train to London. A crowd gathered and badgered Bing for a song. He sang "Where the Blue of the Night" and then turned the tables on the Scots and urged them to sing the lively chorus of "I Belong to Glasgow"; they did, and he energetically harmonized along with them. Sixty-five years later, John Burney, a veteran reporter for the *Daily Telegraph*, told of approaching Crosby in his carriage and requesting an interview. He was fifteen at the time, a copy boy for the *Glasgow Daily Record* in short trousers. Crosby "took a long puff on his pipe" as he considered the request and then said, "Fire away, Mr. Burney." Bing's departure from the same station two months later would be far more tumultuous.[17]

In London, he checked into Claridge's and attended a breakfast in honor of Colonel "Jock" Lawrence, formerly a Hollywood publicist, now attached to Eisenhower's headquarters as chief public relations officer for the European theater of operations. Among those present were a few of the most influential figures in wartime broadcasting. Edward Kirby had made his mark on the American home front as radio's unpaid adviser to Secretary of War Henry L. Stimson. In the year before Pearl Harbor, he effectively argued to protect radio's independence from the tacit federal threat of expropriation. After Pearl Harbor, he and the producer Louis Cowan developed *The Army Hour,* which documented the war's progress through field reports (devotedly followed by Americans via 115 stations on Sunday afternoons), and the jewel in the AFRS crown, *Command Performance.* In 1944, Ed Kirby, now a colonel, joined Eisenhower's staff as the head of SHAEF (Supreme Headquarters Allied Expeditionary Force) Broadcasting Services, directing coverage of D-day and its aftermath. His primary objective was to create an inter-Allied radio service in collaboration with the BBC that would be supervised by the tough and resourceful BBC executive Maurice Gorham.[18] Over fervent SHAEF protests, Gorham insisted that the joint effort, which also included the Canadian Broadcasting Company, be called simply the Allied Expeditionary Force Program (AEFP) of the BBC. This seems not unreasonable, as the BBC provided offices, studios, most of the personnel, a transmitter, and the frequency for broadcasting to France at its Portland Place facilities. The Americans provided half the programming; the BBC provided the rest with assists from Canada. Even so, Gorham faced a daunting task in filling a seventeen-hour broadcasting day. He created successful shows around the orchestras of George Melachrino and Robert Farnon but achieved his greatest triumph in

~~launching its principal star,~~ Glenn Miller, selected by Kirby to lead the U.S. Army Air Force Orchestra and consequently summoned to London as a "top priority" by General Eisenhower.[19] Gorham's work was greatly assisted by another fabled figure in BBC history, Cecil Madden, remembered today as its first television producer (a post assigned to him in 1936). As AEFP's head of production, Madden had dibs on USO performers.

A few days before Crosby arrived in London, Gorham sent a memo to Kirby and Madden with suggestions on how to make the best use of him. These included three programs for AEFP beamed to the troops working their way toward Germany, one of which was a prerecording of *Variety Bandbox* at the Queensberry All-Services Club, and two domestic broadcasts that were canceled for lack of time.[20] "I should also, of course," Gorham wrote, "like all possible broadcasts of recordings of Bing entertaining troops in France, and I hope that by the time he gets there we shall have better facilities for getting these."[21] Alas, they did not. At the time the memo was sent, Crosby was crossing the Atlantic and nothing could be decided until his arrival. Knowing there would be a rush for Bing's services, Madden buttonholed him that first morning at Claridge's and asked him to appear on *Variety Bandbox* the next evening. Bing readily agreed. He also accepted an invitation to play golf before the show, the only opportunity he would have this trip.

And now, with a few hours to himself, he wandered through Mayfair to Marble Arch and into Hyde Park. The sky was congested with barrage balloons to obstruct the German V-1 buzz bombs (a week later, the city would be targeted by the more pernicious, because silent, V-2 rockets). People swept rubble into the skeletons of blasted buildings and into empty lots where even the skeletons of the buildings were gone. Sandbags lay everywhere, and netting protected passersby from falling bricks. The curbs shone with white painted squares for safety during blackouts. Military vehicles rumbled heavily through the streets. Still, London remained London on this brilliant summery day, and Bing had never seen it. He told friends in all seriousness that he wanted to write a book about it.[22] He even stopped at a stationer's to buy a pocket-size Alwych address book, its soft black "all-weather" cover stamped ENGLAND with the date 1943–44 and a Base Air Depot insignia, its fifty-eight leaves alphabetically tabbed. He used the first few pages to jot down names, addresses, reminders, appointment notes, but within a week it turned into his diary, his handwriting shrinking as his entries intensified in dedication and detail. This was evidently the only journal he ever kept.

He walked to the American army headquarters, where men of every rank pressed him for autographs. Later in the afternoon, hoping to locate Glenn Miller, Bing ran into Jack Russin, playing the piano in a rehearsal room. He asked, "Where's Glenn?" One of four alternating pianists in Miller's Allied Expeditionary Force (AEF) Orchestra and the brother of the well-known tenor saxophonist Babe Russin, an old acquaintance of Bing's, Jack started to explain that Captain Miller was performing in Plymouth. He got only as far as "Captain," because Bing repeated the word with a question mark. "Yeah," Russin said. "You gotta call him Captain, Mr. Crosby." (Russin had forgotten that a few days earlier Miller had been promoted to major.) Crosby said, "Call me Bing," and asked him if he would like to "run out some tunes, because I'm supposed to do something with an orchestra tomorrow"—the *Bandbox* show. They went to work and Bing drafted him as his accompanist.[23]

The next day, Sunday, August 27, Bing played on two golf courses in Surrey—Wentworth Club in the morning and Sunningdale in the afternoon—then returned to the hotel to change his clothes and await his next ride while a crowd gathered at Claridge's hoping to catch sight of him.[24] That crowd was nothing compared to the one that, despite a piercing air-raid warning, awaited his arrival at Soho's Queensberry All-Services Club, the home of *Variety Bandbox* and other programs. Cecil Madden remembered Crosby blanching as the fans encircled the army Packard. Military police created a cordon between the car and the stage entrance, and Bing darted through. A full house of four thousand crammed the theater for the six p.m. show. Those unable to gain admission hovered outside until after it ended.

The Queensberry All-Services Club occupied what had been the Prince Edward Theater and, for a short while, the London Casino dance hall; a 1941 air attack damaged the building and shattered all its windows. The club now catered exclusively to servicemen who dropped by to relax or attend the recording of AEFP radio shows.

Most programs were transcribed a week in advance of airing to avoid transmitting the sounds of buzz bombs, which, in addition to distressing overseas troops, would have informed the Germans that they had the correct range. The hour-long *Variety Bandbox,* broadcast Sunday afternoons, was among the most popular programs of the era.

The show's producer, Stephen Williams, took Bing aside to tell him that the evening's compere, presently on stage doing his act, was one of Britain's best-known radio stars, Tommy Handley. Crosby asked if he was the chap with the famous catchphrases. As Williams talked, Bing wrote down a few notes. Handley suddenly announced, "Now I've got a very pleasant surprise for you." Crosby, anticipating his cue, shuffled out before Handley could complete the introduction. The audience rose in thundering applause. As Williams recalled it, "They shouted and shouted and shouted, and nobody announced him. I mean, he just—there he was. They all recognized him at once." The ovation, edited for broadcast, is said to have lasted three minutes.[25]

As the shouting diminished, Handley asked Bing if he had any gum, chum. He did. The crowd roared. Handley presented him with a gift, a pipe he had bought that afternoon when told that Bing would be on the show. "Well, I am delighted to meet you, Bing. Welcome to London. My name's Tommy, so you won't call me Bob, I hope." "Certainly not, Bob." "Well, thank you for being so frank, Sinatra." And so forth, Bing saying he was "eternally grateful that I was afforded the chance" to sing for the Tommies and Yanks as they pushed ahead on the road to victory. As Handley left the stage, Crosby turned to the pianist. "So, Private First Class Jack Russin, if you'll join me."[26] He sang "San Fernando Valley," "Long Ago and Far Away," and, giving fair warning that he wasn't sure of the lyrics ("Go ahead, Jack, I don't know if I remember all of it, but we'll struggle along"), a requested "Moonlight Becomes You," ad-libbing through flubs that generated appreciative laughter. Invited to have the last word, Bing wished good luck to the boys in France, India, the Middle East, Italy, Africa, and the Pacific. *Variety Bandbox* ended, but Bing kept going. "After an interval," *Melody Maker* recounted, "Bing sportingly came back and gave the boys and girls of the forces half an hour's entertainment—and believe me that really WAS something."[27]

While Bing was on stage during the *Bandbox* segment, Cecil Madden phoned Anne Shelton, the beloved teenage singer who toured camp bases with such success that the BBC gave her a show of her own, *Calling Malta*. He told her to get a cab immediately ("We're waiting") because "Bing Crosby wants to meet you." She arrived to find him in the dressing room, a cup of tea in hand. "I couldn't see anything except those two big blue eyes," she recalled. "He said, 'Hiya, doll.' He was charming, he really was. He said, 'I'd like you to sing with me.' Well, I mean, you know, this was ridiculous. I was coming up for my sixteenth birthday." Her knees shook as he suggested a duet on "Easter Parade" (without rehearsal) and a "little gag."[28]

Before the gag, he took the stage for a monologue, warmed up and fearless. Mentally rifling through the pages of one-liners and shtick he had carried across the Atlantic, he gave one of the brightest monologues of his career. The jokes creaked but his timing restored them to health; he ginned up the laughs with each line. "It's a great pleasure to be here in civilian clothes," he began, and then took off:

> Actually it's a tremendous pleasure to be on the road to someplace— any road to any place—without Bob Hope. I finally got rid of him. I must tell you, and this is not to be booted about, this is off the record, but I must tell you in all confidence that Mr. Hope is starting to fall apart at the seams. He's getting a little old, a little tired. He's getting a little slouchy in the pouch, shall we say, a little slaggy in the bag, that boy. He's not a young man anymore, and we have to husband his resources very carefully. For instance, we just did a picture called the *Road to Utopia* and I won't tell you what part of him was dragging but it's the cleanest road picture we ever made. Really is clean. After we finished that picture, Paramount studios loaned Mr. Hope. They loaned him to the Sam Goldwyn studios to do a picture over there. Sort of a Lend-Louse Bill, I think it was. At the completion of that picture Mr. Hope went out to the South Pacific. Son of a gun will go anywhere to get free mailing privileges.[29]

He continued riffing on Hope for a while, then segued to Betty Grable and Harry James ("She married that cornet player...but I understand, after the war they're going to kill all the buglers anyhow"), then his horses. He brought out Joe DeRita ("I carry him so I'll look thin") for ten minutes of creaky vaudeville, much of the humor directed at Sinatra, dreadful stuff, and the audience could not get enough. With barely a pause, he brought out his guest: "I've never heard her sing, but she comes to me highly recommended, and they tell me she's a big favorite in England, sort of the Dinah Shore of this area. We didn't have a chance to rehearse anything but I'd like to hear her sing a song and I'm sure you would too, so I'll just stand by. Give a big warm welcome to Miss Anne Shelton." She sang her trademark number, "I'll Get By."

He set up the gag right away. "Isn't it nice to be here, Anne? Are you glad to see me?" Anne: "Oh, we're really thrilled, Bing. But I wish they'd have sent Charles Boyer." She mused on Boyer's romantic allure: "He looks deep into your eyes and flutters those long eyelashes." Bing: "What do you want, love or air-conditioning?" Big laugh. He continued: "He's a fair boy, he's coming along, but I have a few maneuvers, a few mild operations I don't think he knows anything about." For instance? He bets Anne two bob he can kiss her without touching her. She takes the bet. He kisses her. She protests that he touched her. He gives her two bob. Recounting the evening thirty years later, Anne said, "I still have that two shillings in a little plastic case."[30]

He suggested they take a whack at a duet and started on "Easter Parade" in the wrong key, amid much laughter. He asked Russin to give him the right note. Instead, Anne told him the correct key and as he looked at her, she added a *bu-bu-bu-boo*, convulsing the house. He closed the show with "White Christmas." By this time, Bing occupied an empire beyond entertainment, as suggested by the *Melody Maker* reporter who admitted that objectivity was not possible: "I'd like to place on record at once," he opened his review, "that all of us who have met and seen him agree that a more charming, sociable, kindly, and genial guy you could never wish to meet."[31]

After the show, the Scottish peer Lord Queensberry invited Crosby and company for dinner at the poshest and most storied restaurant in Soho, Kettner's, just half a block from the theater. In later years, Bing became a regular, but on this night, given the blackout, a fog, and the unshakable crowd, getting there was a trial. He stumbled along the street with the actor Broderick Crawford, then serving as a staff sergeant and announcer for Glenn Miller shows. "[Brod and I] were just kind of following the curb and we fell in the gutter a couple of times. Of course we'd had a few belts at the bottle. Finally, we got to the restaurant and quite a crowd gathered, and they kept calling for a song."[32]

Queensberry's table was on the second floor and the windows were blacked out, but as the two men disappeared into the building, the crowd chanted, "We want Bing." A couple of air-raid wardens emphasized the danger and illegality of the gathering and asked Bing to do something. Kettner's turned off its second-story lights as Bing opened the window, put his legs out, and sat on the sill. He offered to sing a song if the throng would head off to someplace safe afterward. The crowd quieted. Bing sang "Pennies from Heaven," facing his audience in a blackness broken only by the flashlights that employees shone on his face. When he recounted the story later, he emphasized the speedy dispersion: "I thought it was a form of criticism the way they took off."[33]

In his memoir, Colonel Ed Kirby compared Crosby's arrival in England to that of Uncle Sam: "Nothing short of a procession for the King, or an open car parade by the Prime Minister, Eisenhower, or Montgomery evoked such wildly shouting throngs." He described thousands of people queuing at the Queensberry All-Services Club at dawn on the day Bing appeared, thousands more standing outside his hotel to catch a glimpse as he boarded the vehicle that brought him to Soho, and "five thousand people, jammed together, a nice, juicy human target for Jerry," shouting in the dark in front of Kettner's.[34] The adulation was real, but so was an antipathy between the two cultures that it helped to mask.

In Kirby's view, Bing's voice symbolized for the Brits "the friendly, genial Americans who were now fighting by their side," and there is little doubt that such symbolism played a role in his visit. Both sides desperately sought to veil and counter the top-down hostility between their armies, from General Montgomery's envious disparagement of the supreme commander to resentment in the ranks against the Yanks ("overpaid, oversexed, and over here") and their hosts ("underpaid, undersexed, and under Eisenhower"). "Before the war," George Orwell observed, "there was no popular anti-American feeling in this country. It all dates from the arrival of the American troops, and it is made vastly worse by the tacit agreement never to discuss it in print." With Crosby's appearance, the need for that discussion, which the USO had no desire to encourage, effectively vanished. *Melody Maker* cheered: "Bing had brought a breath of peace-time atmosphere, a reminder that there are other things in the world to get excited about than battles. And that evening did more for transatlantic relationships than a hundred speeches."[35]

On Monday, August 28, Crosby appeared with Broderick Crawford on a live broadcast for the BBC's Allied Expeditionary Force Program *Mark Up the Map,* a daily posting for the troops on where the fronts were located and which territories had been captured or liberated. Kirby suggested he sing "Going My Way" and let combat divisions know he would soon be visiting them. From the moment he arrived at the BBC, work skidded to a standstill. Maurice Gorham spirited him to the sanctuary of his office. "Before he left," Gorham recalled, "I asked him just to walk through our AEFP offices and say Hello to the girls, and he did. On the way out he was attacked by other BBC staff in search of autographs, and he remarked how nice it was that none of our girls who had met him had asked for one." Gorham described him as the "calm spot in the center of the whirlwind." Bing granted most requests, including some Gorham thought "anybody would have known better than to ask," not least the appeal for him to sing an a cappella version of "Going My Way" on a show about troop movements.[36]

The next day Bing and Jack Russin spent several hours in a studio in Bedford, fifty-eight miles north of London, recording songs later integrated into SHAEF broadcasts. After lunch, he entertained the service command of the recently established Eighth Air Force at Milton Ernest Hall, a palatial country manor built in the 1850s that was served by a private landing strip and rumored, because of intense security, to house top secret transmitters, covert operations, and cabinet-level meetings. Glenn Miller was boarding there, but, owing to rotten weather, he would not return from Plymouth until the next day. Bing stayed the night and greeted Miller's plane when it rolled in. He spent that morning with Russin,

recording more discs for future radio use, and the afternoon recording with Miller for an episode of the latter's series *A Soldier and a
Song.*

Bing returned to London and that evening appeared on a live
BBC broadcast at the Paris Cinema accompanied by George Melachrino's plush orchestra, which boasted nearly as many players as a
symphony. After the war, Melachrino achieved immense success
with a viscous style of mood music characterized by "tumbling
strings," but he was an accomplished and respected musician, never
more so than as musical director of the Army Radio Unit, particularly on the evening he backed Crosby. His wife and two sons,
twelve and fifteen, had recently been killed by a buzz bomb that
also destroyed his home. Few expected him to appear with Crosby,
but he did, for a prim recital introduced by Captain Franklin Engelmann, at the start of a long career in broadcasting. Melachrino
acknowledged both sides of the Atlantic with tributes to Duke
Ellington and Spike Hughes and debuted his own arrangement of
"Sweet and Lovely." Engelmann brought Crosby to the microphone
three times, observing that his first selection, "I'll Be Seeing You,"
would shortly "be coming true for a great many of you," as Bing
indeed planned to cross the channel. Melachrino sent a short note
to Bing's hotel, apologizing if he had seemed distracted and for failing to acknowledge Bing's on-air greeting: "So may I say now,
Thank you, Bing, & safe journeys wherever you go." That night
Crosby met Miller for dinner at Kettner's.[37]

On Thursday, August 31, Harry Lillis Crosby, who got his lifetime
moniker at the age of six, inadvertently paved the way for a varia-
tion on it, one that would also stick. What turned out to be a long
day began with several hours of transcription recordings requested
by an alphabet soup of wartime broadcasting, including the BBC,
CBC, AFN (Armed Forces Network), ONI (Office of Naval Intelligence), and the OWI's recently established ABSIE (American
Broadcasting Station in Europe). A mine of propaganda as well as
coded messages and speeches by exiled leaders Charles de Gaulle
and Jan Masaryk, ABSIE operated for a little more than fourteen
months, April 30, 1944, to July 4, 1945. It provided an average of

forty-two hours of weekly programming to Germany and occupied territories in half a dozen languages and at medium-wave and shortwave frequencies to thwart Nazi jamming. It was considered a major success. A survey conducted in Allied-occupied Germany showed that 50 to 60 percent of Germans had listened, at grave personal risk, to Allied broadcasts, and a third of them had tuned in to ABSIE.[38]

ABSIE's Wardour Street studio could not accommodate a band, but it had a piano and it aimed for a coup in having Bing record three fifteen-minute installments for the broadcast, speaking and singing in German and French, backed by Russin. They had done very little with live entertainers and nothing like this (weeks later, ABSIE got Dinah Shore to do the same, also backed by Russin). Robert Musel, a writer for United Press and *Variety*, covered the session: "While Hitler is fooling around with buzz-bombs and pick-a-pack planes, we're hurling a real secret weapon at Germany. Der Bingle is what the Germans call it." In truth, the Germans did not call it anything yet because the shows would not be beamed to them until September. But Musel's term echoed throughout Europe and the United States, and Bing was soon Der Bingle to servicemen everywhere. OWI's chief of radio news wrote to his superior, "The Bingle story certainly made a big hit." Musel, he said, claimed it had gotten the biggest play of any United Press feature story in the previous two months.[39]

An ABSIE producer named Oliver Nicoll typed out and handed to Bing a paragraph in German that began *Hallo, Deutsche Soldaten. Hier spricht Bing Crosby: Ich komme soeben aus Amerika.* Translated in full, it read: "Hello, German soldiers. This is Bing Crosby speaking. I have just come from America, the country where nobody needs to be afraid of a Gestapo, where every man enjoys the same liberty to say and write whatever he wishes. I come from the land of Lincoln, where there is no master, no slave. I hope that our liberties and rights shall soon return again to your country. For this, we Americans are fighting! But I am not here to preach to you, I am here to sing a few songs." Bing penciled in a couple of pronunciation reminders, but it didn't help. He knew no German and there was no time for someone to coach him word by word. Nicoll retyped it phonetically, using uppercase letters to indicate accents, even for Bing's name. According to Kirby, Bing studied the phonetic version and within fifteen minutes recited it in what sounded like casual, acceptable German.[40]

> Hahl-LOH, DOIT-Sheh Zohl-DAH-ten!
> Heer Shpreekht Bing CROS-by.
> Eekh KOHM-meh zoh-AYBEHN.... Ouse Ah-MEH-ree-kah.[41]

The same was done with the songs. The recording of his convincingly Germanic-sounding "Going My Way" survives. The other titles have not come to light, though Musel reported that one song, taken from a Crosby film, had special lyrics inviting German listeners to return from Hitlerland to the free world. Musel also reported that Bing sang a song in French for the benefit of captured French laborers. In fact, he sang two songs in French for the OWI French broadcast *Parade of Stars*. Bing had numberless German fans, among them vocalists who emulated his style. Goebbels sought to exploit his popularity by sponsoring a swing band featuring an English-speaking Nazi crooner, Karl Schwedler, whose covers used special lyrics. (Schwedler's "I've Got a Pocketful of Dreams" offers this verse: "Gonna save the world for Wall Street / Gonna fight for Russia too / I'm fighting for democracy / I'm fighting for the Jew / Lucky, lucky me / I can live in luxury / 'Cause I've got a pocketful of schemes.") Crosby later remarked that the broadcasts were an "answer to the type the Berlin bastards and Tokyo Rose send out."[42] Those transmissions may or may not have affected DOIT-Sheh Zohl-DAH-ten, but rumors of their existence roused Allied infantrymen, who thought the idea pretty funny, and perhaps that was the real point.

In the late afternoon, Bing returned to the Paris Cinema to rehearse for Glenn Miller's most widely listened-to program, *American Band of the AEF*, broadcast live every Thursday night at eight thirty. Musicians playing in Miller's Allied Expeditionary Force Orchestra and his other overseas ensembles were, with few exceptions, new to his brand of steely discipline. Most of his regular stateside musicians had declined to sign up, convinced that Captain Miller would be even more autocratic than Civilian Glenn. Crosby, who invariably addressed him by his rank in public but was known to parody his mandarin vanity in private, recognized a chill in the air two days before in Bedford and had resolved to defrost it that day.

Following the rehearsal, they had a dinner break, and Bing brought libations to grease the wheels. The trumpet player Bernie Privin recalled the scene to Miller's friend and biographer George T. Simon: "Glenn came in and immediately said, 'Okay, fellers, let's go.' But Bing stepped in and said, 'Hey, wait a minute. This is a freebee for the guys, isn't it?' And he brought out bottles of Scotch and whiskey for all of us. I got to tell you, that day we recorded some of the best stuff the band ever played!" Privin definitely did; his bell-ringing half chorus on the Jerry Gray swinger "Here We Go Again" gets the broadcast off to a roaring start. In Bing's telling, he had already begun passing around the booze when Glenn arrived and expressed his disapproval. "But I said this is a freebee for the guys. That seemed to calm him down." Cecil Madden recalled Miller as being nervous during the rehearsal, especially after they ran down Gray's arrangement of "Poinciana" without Crosby's vocal. "He was really quite shaky and said they must run through it again [with the vocal]. Bing absolutely refused. He said, 'What, and make all these boys tired? Glenn, dear boy, just wave your baton and I promise I'll come in.' Of course, he did it perfectly."[43]

The show went smoothly in its grimly scripted way, with Crosby and the major trading sober compliments, primarily to let the men in France know, once again, that Bing really would be going over there. He sang "Long Ago and Far Away," "Amor, Amor," "Swinging on a Star," and "Poinciana," and he sang well. But the amber that sparked Bernie Privin didn't do as much for Bing and the bandleader. How did Bing really feel about Glenn? After the program, Bing took off what George T. Simon described as his "beautiful hand-painted tie" and gave it to Miller, first writing on it that his AEF band was "the greatest thing since the invention of cup mutes"—a double-edged compliment at best, but proof in Simon's mind that "Bing was completely knocked out by the band." Cecil Madden also remembered Bing's "very bright hand-painted ties. They showed naughty girls on them. I said you can't wear them over here. He began to laugh, and then took them off." Glenn accepted the gift but continued to wear his khaki military tie.[44]

Bing had a second onstage encounter that evening with a performer of a different kind and temperament. The occasion was the opening night in Piccadilly Circus of London's Stage Door Canteen, where Dorothy Dickson and Beatrice Lillie had assembled a momentous bill of English and American stars. Gorham was determined to have Bing participate. Churchill's war secretary Anthony Eden launched the festivities, scheduled to begin at nine fifteen. The performers included Jack Buchanan, Fred and Adele Astaire, and the RAF Squadronaires. One member of the last noted, "Everybody wanted to be there at the opening because Bing Crosby was there.... He was as bald as bald could be." He was hardly that, but the natural look continued to impress.[45]

Jack Buchanan, the revered Scottish song-and-dance man, never quite clicked with Americans, perhaps because his eternally gay gentility played as a bit too gay and in the wrong sense for a leading man. A top box-office attraction in British cinema of the 1930s, he is most remembered today for one superb performance near the end of his career, playing opposite Fred Astaire in Vincente Minnelli's 1953 musical film *The Band Wagon*. Buchanan had made a sensational Broadway debut back in 1924 with Bea Lillie and Gertrude Lawrence in *Charlot's Revue*, which warranted a 1926 production at the El Capitan Theater in Hollywood. Crosby and his partner Al Rinker, then struggling vaudevillians, were invited to perform at the celebrity-studded opening-night party. After Bing sang "Montmartre Rose," Buchanan, Lillie, and Lawrence leaped from their seats and showered him with praise, the first he had ever received from professionals remotely of their station. Bing cast Lillie in his 1938 film *Doctor Rhythm*, but he had not seen Buchanan in eighteen years.

After Eden's speech to the "noisy, milling crowd,"[46] Dorothy Dickson introduced Bing, who sang "San Fernando Valley," but it was Buchanan, arriving slightly late, who brought order to the event, singing, dancing, and telling stories to an enthusiastic if obstreperous audience. He brought Astaire (also sans toupee and even balder than Crosby) to the stage and they performed a number together, something Astaire later said they had wanted to do for years. Yet the moment that crystallized the evening for W. J. MacQueen-Pope, the prolific chronicler of England's theater, occurred when Buchanan brought Bing back to the stage. After he sang "Amor, Amor," Crosby bantered with Buchanan at length, riffing on the quickly prepared scripts in hand.

> JACK: Bing, it's good to see you again.
> BING: Are we on the air? Watch your language.
> JACK: I think so. I haven't seen you since we were both in Hollywood, you know, about three years before the war.
> BING: Which war? I don't think we better tell. But no kidding, you look grand, Jack. You haven't changed a bit.
> JACK: Oh, you haven't changed much either.
> BING: If you're referring to my suit, it's a lie.
> JACK: Never you mind, Bing. Well, I like it. Never mind what people say. You go on wearing it.
> BING: This suit was made by the best tailor in California.
> JACK: Yeah? Where were you at the time, Bing?

They continued in that vein, yet MacQueen-Pope nostalgically recalled it as a meeting of titans: "Bing was as good as Jack in his own way. He, too, sang to them, yarned to them, cracked jokes; he signed autographs, he was pushed about as Jack had been and enjoyed it, just as Jack did. Then the two of them went on the stage together and for half an hour they wisecracked at each other, right 'off the cuff' and totally unrehearsed...two really great artists working together, each supreme in his own line, each perfectly confident of himself, giving and taking gags, never trying to crab each other, an example of professionalism at its very best. It will live in the memory of all who saw it." Many did see it, at least in part; it was filmed by newsreel cameras, and selected footage was distributed in Europe through Pathé News and, two weeks later, in the United States by Paramount News. AEFP aired it repeatedly.[47]

The most emotionally strenuous day of Bing's British tour began several hours after the canteen show when he and his USO troupe boarded the night train to Preston, 230 miles north, in Lancashire.

Cars brought them to the nearby rural village of Warton on the northwest coast. It was now September 1, the war's fifth anniversary, though no one thought to commemorate that miserable occasion, made all but unendurable at Warton (an air force modification center) and its neighboring community of Freckleton. A ghastly accident had occurred on August 23: two American bombers—B-24 Liberators—took off on a test flight from the Warton Aerodrome, then known as BAD 2 (Base Air Depot No. 2). They were recalled because of dire weather, but one pilot ignored the urgency of the command and flew too close to the ground into a fiercely blackening storm. The plane lost a wing, and the fuselage smashed through Freckleton like a locomotive, razing three houses, the Sad Sack Snack Bar (where fourteen servicemen died), and the Infants' Wing of the stone cottage–like Holy Trinity School. Sixty-one people were killed in all; thirty-eight were children between the ages of five and seven.[48]

Five children were carried to the base hospital at Warton. One died the following day and another, the last casualty, died shortly after Bing's visit. The other bodies, many burned beyond recognition, lay under linen sheets awaiting identification and were eventually buried in a mass grave. Several had been relocated to Freckleton to escape the German air attacks on London. Incredibly, Freckleton grieved alone; military censors curbed coverage and no accounts reached the London newspapers. Crosby was told on arrival of the incident and of the four children in the base hospital and he asked to visit them.[49]

But first, Bing's troupe had a ten a.m. show for which several thousand BAD 2 fliers and other personnel crowded into hangars 6 and 7. Weeks before the disaster, Glenn Miller gave an acclaimed performance at Warton on a stage built outside a hangar, but no performer had come by since then to alleviate the despair that threatened to envelop the place. Bing's company was received rapturously, and they did another show at two p.m. Jeanne Darrell called to the stage a preselected soldier and wrapped her arms around him during "All of Me"; DeRita rat-a-tat-tatted his double entendres. Bing's songs included "Sweet Leilani," "Easter Parade," "If I Had My Way," and his revised lyrics for "Swinging on a Star," in which Johnny Burke's animals are replaced by a sergeant, a bugler, and a cook:

> *A sarge is a character with stripes on his sleeve*
> *A guy that you'd never call naïve*
> *When he gives orders he will rave and rant*
> *You try to understand him, but you can't*
> *And if you dare ask the sergeant what he means*
> *Next day you're cleaning out latrines.*

Between shows, he visited the burn ward to see the four children, two nearly completely hidden by bandages. The three who survived faced years of pain and reconstructive surgeries. Bing, for once, lost it. Ruby Whittle was five years old at the time, but six decades later she remembered how he had sat on her bed holding the fingertips of her otherwise bandaged hand and asking if she would like him to sing. She knew two songs that her mother liked, "White Christmas" and "Don't Fence Me In." But "the sight of us lying there was too much for him. He couldn't sing a note."[50] He stood and walked into the hall and steeled himself, then returned to the doorway and sang both songs standing there. "It's a strange memory to have, but a good one," Ruby said, "because he was a very nice man and he was genuinely saddened by what he heard of the disaster and seeing anyone who had survived."[51] He visited adult survivors as well. A member of the RAF, who had suffered extreme burns at the Sad Sack, recalled the surprise of seeing him at his bedside determined to lift his spirits.[52]

In the late afternoon, the Crosby troupe drove fifty miles south to Burtonwood, a U.S. Army Air Forces servicing center (and Europe's largest wartime airfield), to give two more shows to audiences of ten thousand, one at five o'clock in an open field and one at nine o'clock in a hangar. They slept over in Burtonwood and then spent a rainy weekend driving south, first east, then west, stopping at camps en route to London. At two p.m. the next day, they entertained men of the U.S. 482nd Bomb Group at Alconbury in Cambridgeshire ("wonderful audience," Bing noted for the first but by no means the last time. "Met missions just returning from strike on bomb sites—great success"[53]). He ran into friends of Hope, Cagney, and the comic actor Billy Gilbert, who put them up for the night. They entertained the Eighth Air Force's Seventy-Eighth Fighter Group in Duxford, Cambridge, in a light rain, but "nobody left"; at nine thirty, heavier rains forced them to work in a hangar for the 381st Bomb Group in Ridgewell, Essex. According to a diarist of the 381st, "Some 600 wounded from neighboring hospitals were guests of the Group for the occasion. They were literally hanging from the rafters (not the wounded) when Crosby opened the show. It was the most successful entertainment ever offered on the base."[54]

One GI recalled rain pelting the hangar and seeping through the roof when Bing arrived at the door wearing a hat and a trench coat, his blue eyes surprising those who knew him only from monochrome movies and his easy manner and willingness to converse drawing everyone to him; the "pounding rain" against the hangar roof and sides "did not deter him from performing," nor did the absence of stage facilities. At one point, as his two musicians played, "Bing climbed to a spot reached by some fliers to gain a better visual vantage point. There surrounded by these 'hot-shot' pilots, Bing sang his heart out.... He sang as though he had been on an outing with a bunch of guys." After the show—he closed with "White Christmas," bringing an unavoidable solemnity to the occasion—the enlisted men and the nurses mobbed him to get a closer look or an autograph or to shake his hand; whatever it was, "patiently, unruffled, Bing complied."[55]

The chaplain for the 381st Bomb Group, Lieutenant Colonel James Good Brown (who chronicled the entire history of the group and lived to be a hundred and five), introduced himself to Bing: "I had quite a conversation with Crosby before the show began as he was waiting for the men to get the stage arranged in the proper manner. He thoroughly enjoys going around to the war camps and bases. To him, it is both fun and a patriotic duty. He feels that it is the way he can do his part in this war. Neither did I hesitate to tell him I thought he was doing as much good for the men as the chaplain. To this he remarked, 'Not quite as much good as you chaplains are doing.'"[56]

After the show, the station held a tea dance, complete with a beauty queen, to celebrate the anniversary of the Red Cross Club.

The performers stayed the night in Ridgewell and drove the next day to Hitcham to present the show to the 353rd Fighter Group, another audience of ten thousand. Bing ran into several boys from Los Angeles and Spokane as well as Irving Draper, of Yakima, who had played basketball at Gonzaga University in 1919 when Bing was also a student. The commanding officer at Hitcham, a Colonel Moody of San Francisco, gave them dinner and lodgings, and in the morning a staff car returned them to London in "beautiful weather," taking them through "heavily blitzed areas it will take years to restore." The next day Bing, his troupe, and Fred Astaire boarded a plane at Heston and flew to Cherbourg. They were headed for the front, and the crossing wasn't too bad at all.

20

SOMEWHERE IN FRANCE

*In war all you have to do is not worry and know how to
read a map and give co-ordinates.*

— Ernest Hemingway, letter to
Marlene Dietrich (1952)[1]

The German army did such a thorough job of demolishing the port
of Cherbourg before surrendering to the Allies on June 29, 1944,
that Hitler presented the Knight's Cross to the *Konteradmiral* in
charge. On Monday, September 4, the damage remained startling.
The USO's C-47 orbited the harbor on a nearly cloudless day, permitting Crosby and the other passengers a clear view of the devastation, images that would soon become all too familiar. "Lots of
scuttled vessels," he wrote in his notebook. "Town well blasted.
Members of French citizenry returning from safety of the country,
wandering around the ruins of their homes."[2]

It isn't possible to map every stop on his itinerary, which included
as many as five shows a day, most of them last-minute setups. Crosby's diary, its very existence virtually unknown for seven decades,
is our most detailed source, but even he did not always know where
he was. The performers would board for a few days in a town and
take off each morning in jeeps to as many places as they could
reach before nightfall and the blackout. Bing claimed that Astaire
advised him to keep an eye out for telephone wires and not to go
past them for fear of driving into an area still in enemy hands, a

lesson he understood when his driver got lost and did just that. Sometimes they pulled over and put on a show simply because they happened upon a potential audience.

In advance of the Normandy invasion, the American army picked up on a British innovation, fabric maps intended for "escape and evasion." They manufactured several tons of them, titled "Zones of France, Second Edition," printed on silk or rayon, which could be folded and hidden away or worn as a neckerchief and opened without fear of making a sound. These strikingly lovely maps, the colors—greens, oranges, yellows, fuchsias, against a powder-blue sea—richly reproduced on the translucent cloth, were distributed chiefly to pilots and other fliers. Crosby brought back a few, probably given to him as souvenirs, as his job did not call for map reading, a lucky thing, given his convoluted travels. Three weeks into Bing's twenty-six-day sojourn in France, the *Stars and Stripes* estimated that he had covered more than fifteen hundred miles.[3]

Before Bing and Fred split up—Crosby to the Third Army (under Patton) and Astaire to the First (under Bradley)—they improvised a few shows as a team. Fred, suffering from back trouble, found that jeep travel provided an osteopathic cure, despite the chaos on the ground as Red Ball Express supply trucks commandeered the road and forced the players aside during their drive down the Cotentin Peninsula in Normandy. They did their first unrehearsed show shortly after landing, twelve miles south of Cherbourg, at a COMMZ (communications zone) close to Valognes for several thousand men brought in from nearby areas and assembled in a large field. The war memoirist Forrest C. Pogue took notes: "The show was largely spontaneous and filled with the type of ad-libbing for which Crosby is famous. The two men appeared without their wigs and proved to be extremely bald, a fact that served as the basis for many of their jokes. Astaire showed his age when, after some of his more exacting dance routines, he had to struggle against the speechlessness brought on by his exertion. Although the two men appeared without makeup, special microphones, and the like, they were an uproarious success."[4]

Pogue doesn't say if Crosby was made aware of the "bad feelings" that erupted between enlisted men and officers after the show when the latter group, tired of waiting for the buses arranged exclusively for them, took the enlisted men's trucks, forcing them to hike back to camp. But Bing made it clear in a day or two that the shows were intended primarily for enlisted men and that he would not tolerate the sight of officers sitting up front; his material, after all, was directed at the enlisted men and the grunts, the Willies and Joes. Nearly a decade later, he rhapsodized: "I can never forget my amazement at seeing young men snatched out of civilian life, many of them irresponsible, pleasure-seeking youngsters, thrown into the most rugged assignment in the world and delivering and doing a great job, applying seriousness and ability to the fearsome task which is war." Nothing in his life, he insisted, gave him as much "pride and satisfaction" as making those "guys happy for a few moments at a time they sorely needed [it]."[5]

As they continued southward, going through Sainte-Marie-du-Mont, an air base for the huge P-47 Thunderbolt, where they performed for wounded men at a field hospital, to Saint-Lô, they could see the "success of the Allied drive" and its terrible price: "Devastation on all sides. Roads, rail installations blasted. Heavily fortified German line absolutely leveled flat. Formerly a town of 60,000 souls, now not a wall standing. A few sad-eyed French people wandering about, poking in the ruins of their homes. A sight which must be seen to be believed." Bing learned about friendly fire at Saint-Lô, a university town that the Allies had taken twice and lost twice; saturation bombing by the U.S. Air Force inadvertently took the lives of more than eight hundred American soldiers on the ground. Still, he was told, the shelling of Saint-Lô had hastened "the crackup" of the Wehrmacht. Wherever the troupe traveled, Bing saw "the same condition prevalent" in "practically every spot where the Germans could take a foothold." They drove from Alençon to Le Mans, thirty or so miles, seeing scorched Axis vehicles everywhere. The jeeps periodically pulled over to make way for the huge convoys heading for Paris with food, fuel oil, high-octane gasoline, equipment. Children lined the road displaying V-for-victory fingers and "waving with broad smiles." They approached the annihilated Le Mans airport weeks after the Germans had fled, leaving behind tons of equipment. They went to bed after an early dinner and rose with the rooster's crow to visit the prison camp at Nonant-le-Pin, an hour away. Used successively by the English, Germans, and Americans, it now held "16,000 prisoners of all descriptions, most of them just in from fronts. Some English speaking, with Oxford accents." They returned to Le Mans to do a late-morning show for eighteen hundred wounded men at the Nineteenth General Hospital.

They did an early-afternoon show for P-47 fliers and Army Signal Corps personnel. The position was heavily mined and the players and the troops were restricted to cleared areas. Even so, bomb blasts "punctuated" the shows as demolition squads blew up mines, duds, booby traps. Astaire, who would pick up his own accompanist in Paris, did his stuff with Crosby's two musicians. Bing's format remained pretty much the same, though the jokes changed and he altered the song list to accommodate requests. He sang, on average, eight songs per show and kept it light, even trying to convince the men that they didn't really want him to close with "White Christmas" but with something jolly. Not a chance; they demanded the right to shed a few tears. If he opened the show with it to get it out of the way, he would just have to sing it twice, and he never sang it "without a wrench." "I could never get out of it anyplace we worked," he said.[6]

> We generally tried to do three shows a day and in between visit the local field hospital or any other place there were wounded men being cared for. I guess we were four or five weeks completing the tour but it seemed like about four or five days. So much excitement, always on the move, meeting friends here and there, seeing the welcome written on the faces of the men you entertained. They were so glad to see anybody from home, particularly the girls, who were part of the ruggedness of the trip, the mud and equipment we had to ride in. [Yet they] always managed to put on a good-looking gown for each show and keep their hair done up real pretty. I think they had the toughest job of all, the girls, changing clothes four or five times a day. Many times using the back of the truck for a dressing room, a tent or whatever could be found to be suitable. They never complained, they were wonderful sports.[7]

A medic with the Third Army wrote to a friend at home: "He took us right back to college with 'Sweet Leilani' and when he sang 'Easter Parade' there were oh's and ah's. But when he sang 'White Christmas' there wasn't a sound, not even breathing, and suddenly no one was looking at Crosby, but just at the ground and making a little wish. There was no applause following it, just a ghastly silence, which is the noisiest thing I have ever lived thru. Even Crosby had no answer or explanation; he must have known what was going on. And so back to our tents, but the men are smiling now. If Crosby can come up to the front just to sing when he doesn't have to then I can get out there and work and get this thing done—which is what every man who heard him this aft is saying."[8]

The troupers packed up the jeeps and turned eastward, "following the path of the armed forces," which would eventually lead them to and beyond Paris. They drove through Chartres to Étampes; the roadside had "slit trenches dug every 50 yards for miles by French labor under German control, for drivers to take cover when strafed (if they had time)." Cheering French citizens lined up on the highway. The U.S. Army Services of Supply had chosen Étampes, the former headquarters of the Luftwaffe, as the advance section for a communication zone. The troupe spent three nights there in "Göring's nest," evacuated by the Germans five days before.

Bing transcribed the field-hospital show for eventual broadcast in the United States. He interviewed patients (some "just got in from [the] front this morning"), nurses, and staff.[9] They did another show in a tent for those who could leave their beds, by which time it was "raining like hell [with] C-47s coming and going incessantly with wounded." That night, they did the fifth show of the day, for a gathering of five thousand; it was the last show with Astaire, who would join the First Army come morning. They shared 10-in-1 rations ("not too bad") but had a difficult time getting back to Göring's nest due to a bad storm. The car, its headlights prohibited by the blackout, advanced slowly until two army nurses found the gate. Their elegant billet had no lights, no hot water, and no dinner except for K rations. Bing had a drink with Major J. H. Dingle of the Medical Corps ("a friend of Hope's, nice guy") and had his vanity wounded by two French waitresses who had not seen any entertainment in five years yet did not care for his show beyond the music; they knew of Astaire and Rogers from their mothers, "but nobody knows me at all." Bing slept in his first real bed since they had landed three days before.

In Fontainebleau, they performed on a dormant golf course for the Ninth Replacement Depot, attracting an audience of seventy-five hundred, including many casualties and transients going to the front or coming back as well as "counts, countesses, and assorted Marquis resident in the vicinity, which is loaded with castles and chateaux." Bing ran into a golf pro who had played the U.S. Open in 1931, the one "at Inverness which [Billy] Burke won." Motoring through town, they "cased" the summer palace and then turned south to do shows at Augerville-la-Rivière and Loiret, where they performed for the Seventeenth Replacement Depot, under the command of Colonel Leslie Brown, "a big bottle man." Brown welcomed Bing to his stately château (recently a Gestapo headquarters), served him an excellent dinner topped off with Johnnie Walker Gold, and gave him his field jacket as a gift. This was the same Colonel Brown who, that very month, had given orders that a pianist named Dave Brubeck could not be sent to the front, as he was needed to lead the depot's band. Brubeck credited Brown with saving his life.[10] After dinner Bing did a show for ten thousand men in a lovely glade and for a brief spell, the war "seemed far away."

The next morning, walking to the officers' mess, he passed a heavily bombed area that German prisoners, under American guard, were sweeping clear of debris while French citizens "stood by in high glee." He observed that the French had little to eat and that they eagerly traded their watches and other personal items to GIs in exchange for chocolate bars. He wandered through the medieval architecture that had survived the bombing and lamented the damage done to the cathedral of St. Giles, the "walls still standing but no roof...a once beautiful edifice almost a ruin." Standing there, he heard "a bell tinkling the offertory of the Mass" and climbed over the rubble to enter the church.

> There, at a small side altar a priest was celebrating Mass for about 50 people, with the wind whistling thru the gaping holes in the wall and the paneless great windows. After Mass one of the women who spoke English stopped me and being baffled by my uniform (U.S.O.) asked me if I was a chaplain. I told her I was a chanteur or artiste, but no light of recognition appeared in her eyes. I asked her if the French were bitter about the bombing and over the unfortunate killing of many of her friends and relatives in the

area. "Oh no, M'sieu," she replied. "Many Boche go too." This seems pretty generally the French attitude. Anything that brings relief from the five years they have been thru can be endured.

At eleven a.m., the troupers drove an hour east to Melun, the last major stop before they turned north to Paris. They stopped to watch "500 American bombers glittering in the brilliant sunlite" on their way to hit the Siegfried Line. To cross the Seine into Melun they traversed a pontoon bridge built to replace the one knocked out by the Germans. They lunched with the Third Replacement Depot in the woods and did a two o'clock show for eight thousand men. During their performance, an Allied bomber flew overhead at a thousand feet "with one motor shot out and two great holes in the wing." Yet it seemed able to get home and received the afternoon's biggest hand.

Bing's shows were not publicized and quite often the men had little advance notice of a performance. A combat soldier wrote home from "Somewhere in France," September 1944:

> Dearest Peg...Tis rumored that Bing Crosby is to be here this afternoon. You know he is touring the ETO and it isn't unusual for him to be in a place like this. If I am able to, I am going to take some pictures, and try to get him in it, to show you later. As you move around, there are more things to see and pictures to take. At present we are 150 miles from war front.
>
> Just went down to see Bing Crosby and his show. Took my camera with me and had quite a time taking pictures. There was a huge mob all around, and I thought I would get some close-ups. I walked to the left side of the stage and got some good views, if they turn out OK.
>
> Bing was dressed in G.I. clothes and looked much as he does on the screen, except that he is older and balder. He asked me to send him some of the pictures, showing you that being away from the camera makes him like anyone else. Also took some of the cast, a couple of girls and three men. I need to take care to keep the pictures safe, don't want to take a chance in losing them.[11]

Another show was scheduled for the Third Depot at six forty-five, and Bing spent the intervening hours visiting the Eighth Field Hospital, where a barber named Van Cleave gave him a haircut, and soldiers introduced themselves as friends of friends who knew or had worked with Bing. The second show attracted a "wonderful audience" of ten thousand. In the morning, they left Étampes and Göring's nest. This time when they crossed the pontoons on the Seine, they headed for Paris, driving past leveled airports and mangled rail installations. They noticed signs of food shortages, men, women, and children looking hungry and lost. Still, it was brilliantly sunny that Saturday morning as they entered the City of Light and learned that Parisians were "still hysterically glad to see Americans."

This was to be a fleeting visit; a longer stay in Paris would come later. "Terrible confusion still reigns," he wrote. "Nobody knows where he's going. Everybody lost—no food or power." After a brief excursion down the Champs-Élysées to the Arc de Triomphe, the performers left and drove an hour east to Meaux, finding the spectacular pastoral countryside blighted by "burnt and blasted vehicles where air force caught fleeing Germans." Again, "happy if hungry people" waved them on. A Colonel Ficke greeted them with a fine lunch, including good wines, assembled from captured German stores. The First Division of the First Army quartered in Meaux and awaited orders to join the Third Division, which had taken Liège in Belgium forty-eight hours earlier; days later, they would combine forces and break through the Siegfried Line at Aachen. Meanwhile, the orders to move up to the front were delayed a day, and the soldiers were astonished to learn that Bing Crosby was among them and about to put on a show.

A combat soldier wrote home from "Somewhere in France," September 1944:

> To my darling angel, my precious wife: So much has happened during the past few days I hardly know where to start.... The 1stD was the first to enter Germany in the last war and we were on our way to do it again when things were postponed for twenty four hours and they were the best twenty four hours I have had overseas. First I got a letter from you #462, it was very short, a two day letter on one page. I was a little disappointed but nevertheless glad to get it, for to even hear from you is a Godsend regardless of how

short your letter may be. Thanks for the prints darling. They didn't come out too bad for an amateur, do you think? Secondly, we all got clean clothes, washed, shaved etc. Thirdly, we had a little food to go with our bread and pickles which has been about our main dish for a week now, but I like the bread... Fourthly I managed to read a Tree Grows in Brooklyn and it was excellent, it's been so long since I had the time to read that I really appreciated it. Fifthly and best of all who should come and see us but Bing Crosby. He stayed with us for several hours and we enjoyed every minute of it. He did so much for the morale of everyone that I can't begin to tell you how appreciative we all were. What a guy, a regular guy, a real pal, he was almost like a ray of sunshine and everyone talked late into the night last night about Bing, his humor, his singing and his reality. He sings so wonderfully, so easily and I could hardly keep from crying when he sang, for he brought home right to your heart and I could see you in all your loveliness in each word, in each note. He sang "Amour-Amour," I think that's how you spell it, then "The Blue of the Night," "The Last Time I Saw Paris," "Swinging on a Star" and "San Fernando Valley." He told a lot of good jokes and humor. He had an old burlesque man with him as a side kick and he was a riot. He also had two girls, both could sing swell and they did. One of them called a soldier to her and she put his arms about her waist and her arms about his neck and she sang "All of Me." I was about four feet away from them for I was taking pictures and I had the closest spot and the soldier was just shaking, he couldn't control himself. She would pull him closer as she sang and [when] she was finished she gave him a big tight kiss and he almost fainted. He could hardly walk, as if he had lived a dream. Then the Red Cross served hot coffee and doughnuts, and our band played and what music, it just leaped and jumped and you could hear their happiness in their music....We were remembered and it was because Bing wanted it that way. The dangers of snipers, of the front lines meant nothing to him or his group. It is the first we have ever had like that right in the lines, and now we are ready to go.[12]

Colonel Ficke loaded up the Crosby car with German canned goods, cognac, wine, tobacco, French bread, and cheese, and they drove a good ninety miles to the heavily bombed Châlons-sur-Marne (now Châlons-en-Champagne) and nearby L'Épine, where they joined at last with the Third Army, billeted in the forest. The

Special Services officer showed them more than five hundred cases of captured liquor and wines and food. They were also welcomed by Dinah Shore, with whom they did a show at Châlons, on the open flatbed of a USO truck. Bing wrote that it "went very well."

A United Press reporter described the scene: "Three hundred GI's stood in a sort of congealed mass of tin hats around a large gray truck. Behind it was a line of pine trees and behind them convoys pounded up and down a dusky road. Remnants of the sunset were blotted out by rain squalls bearing down from the west and a few fitful drops were whipped across the field by a sharp wind." After the magician Harry Mendoza and then Joe DeRita did their turns, the key attraction took the stage: Dinah Shore, "a girl with bright hair and a big smile, dressed in a thin white shirtwaist and a flaring blue skirt," and Bing, "a little guy bundled into an army issue coat, pants and heavy shoes, with a yearning look." They sang "Easter Parade," clowning and "barbershopping it a little," but when someone requested "White Christmas," Crosby sang it straight and "the GIs were quiet." They cheered at the finale and Dinah shouted back, "Thanks for the use of your pasture." Most of the audience pulled out immediately in trucks, while a USO crew rolled up its portable stage for "another performance somewhere along the windy front."[13]

On the way back they did another show in the dark for an anti-aircraft battery. That night they met General Hugh Gaffney of the Fourth Armored Division and General George Patton, whom Bing characterized as "a colorful character, little depressed over stalemate at the Moselle, where high cliffs and river have halted our advance." Bing ran into his old friend from vaudeville days Bill Hearst, the man who had once brought him to a three-day bacchanal at his father's castle in San Simeon. Bill was now making his bones as a war correspondent, tagging along on a bombing sortie. During the troupe's dodgy drive back to the billet in the blackout, the Special Services men were plastered, despite several alerts they'd gotten to expect German raids. They "slept cold as the devil" when they did sleep. In the small hours, a German recon plane dropped a flare "looking for Patton's Hdqs."

*   *   *

Letter of commendation, Signal Security Division, Somewhere in France:

> Today, while out on the road I happened to see the Bing Crosby, Dinah Shore show which is touring these parts. I'm from a Gun battery, and my men man the equipment 24 hours a day which means it's hard to leave our area, so I requested the impossible and asked Mr. Crosby to come to us. They had just done a show and it was accompanied by a light cold rain as evening crept slowly in, so my request was more than difficult to fulfill.... By the time the show ended it was dark, but they still came. Our unit is located in a lonely field and walking thru it in the dark was magnificent— but singing a few songs and making all the boys forget for a few minutes that they were away from home, and they'd been sleeping in holes for almost three months or more with a belly full of K rations—that part I just can't find words for that could properly convey that certain grin, that ear to ear smile and that wonderful light that those two put in their eyes again. They entertained in a hole which is protection for one of the instruments. Instead of stage settings, the hole was covered with sand bags, rifles and military gear. The stage was bad—there was almost no light, save for a glow from one of the instruments, the night was cold and they were tired, but the audience was the happiest bunch of guys that ever listened to a person sing. It's not correct, I know, but from us, to them, thru you—thanks a hell of a lot.[14]

Sunday began with morning Mass, "sun streaming through the panes," and as many as a thousand in attendance. They performed somewhere west of Châlons for the 103rd Field Hospital, followed by a nighttime concert before four thousand men of the Third Army Division in a "beautiful woodland setting." A young soldier, formerly a member of the vocal group Six Hits and a Miss, did a number. During the show a B-17 limped home from a raid on Stuttgart, badly shot up. The crew bailed out safely right over the camp.

Much of the days were taken up mingling with the men and hearing repeated and sometimes unnerving rumors, like the reports, which turned out to be true, that the Germans had retaken Nancy, stalling the Allied advance. "This is an eager army," Bing wrote, "itching to pour thru to Germany. All, to a man, are staunch in their loyalty and devotion to Patton. He apparently takes good care of them and gets them every privilege and comfort he can procure. They seem to have carte blanche in regard to captured German food, liquor and equipment and they're having a field day. Behave themselves pretty well with French property and civilians. Every kid in this area has giant fur coats, Parkas, guns, select sardines, pate de foie gras, champagne, Noilly Prat, wine, cognac—Martell's, Hennessy, Courvoisier—all courtesy of the fleeing Wehmacht."

They continued southeast toward Commercy, then stopped midway, not far from Saint-Dizier, formerly a Luftwaffe airfield, recently cleared by the air force. Bing lunched with Colonel Alfred de Lorimer, an alumnus of Gonzaga, one of Everett Crosby's pals in the class of 1915 and a cavalry veteran of the First World War who played professional polo for sixteen years. Shortly after they parted, seven hundred and fifty Germans entered the town, thinking it was under their command, and were "very warmly received"; the survivors were marched to a prison camp.

Commercy, barely an hour west of the battle at Nancy, was the troupe's headquarters for the next few days, and from it they toured units of the Third Army's forward echelon. They were in an area where pro-German sentiment ran high because (Crosby heard) "of the border proximity and high percentage of German blood." They gave the first show of the day for the Twelfth Corps in the town of Foug, about six miles east of Toul and the Moselle River, in a warehouse packed with hundreds of "war-weary men from advance elements, really terribly glad to see anyone."

Crosby was much taken with the redoubtable if often neglected Major General Manton Eddy, the commander of the Twelfth Corps, who had figured prominently in the victory at Cherbourg and who, come December, would hold the southern front in the Battle of the Bulge. Eddy explained to Bing the current map. Bing wrote little about his shows beyond the size and enthusiasm of the audiences, but he studiously noted problems facing the Allied campaign, such as the gasoline shortages that had halted their advance at Commercy and given the regrouped Wehrmacht the chance to make a stand at the Moselle River near Nancy. The USO players again dined on German stores and drove back to Commercy in the black-out as columns of troops marched in the other direction, to the front six miles east. The performers got to bed at eleven but were awakened abruptly at five thirty a.m. by "all the ack-ack [antiair-craft artillery] in town" as soldiers chased off German recon planes taking pictures: "I did a levitation act over my bed for 4 minutes," Bing wrote.

The shows and Crosby's eagerness to perform grew as he became more involved with the men and better understood the specifics of what they faced. This was a different order of men than those he had entertained in the States, those insufficiently trained and untested recruits who lacked the one component Eisenhower declared essential in a fighting man: unreasoning hatred of the enemy. The men in France were no older than those he had encountered at home, but they were transformed. They had spilled blood; they had seen communities devastated and civilians slaugh-tered and children go hungry. They could scarcely imagine the horrors to come in the Ardennes or the gust of hell that would greet those who liberated extermination camps. But they were now warriors, and their company deeply affected Crosby. He marveled at one unit's "very sharp outfits," its "fitness and military decorum, more than is ordinarily apparent." The night's show for these men was "a fairly spectacular sight," played out against intervals of artil-lery fire.

The stage was set up on an enormous German trailer, the floor a bed of tightly stacked K rations covered with a dance mat. Looking out at the men, Bing saw soldiers on tanks, armored cars, and half-tracks, soldiers hanging from trees. It was the first show these men had seen since landing, and their gratitude shook the ground and extended past the performance. Assembled officers of the two divisions honored the troupers with a grand dinner and unlimited cognac and champagne. The artists and the officers sang "gang songs" and exchanged toast after toast. Within twelve hours, this divi-sion, the Thirty-Fifth Infantry, also known as the Santa Fe, would smash the resistance at the Moselle River and capture Nancy.

As the performers returned to Commercy, Bing noticed that the caravan took a different route. Their chaperon, Major Wayne

"Goose" Gander, told him that a town they passed through on the way down, Maxey-sur-Vaise, now teemed with German patrols and stragglers fleeing north from the rout at Dijon. The ack-ack started up as they retired for the night and continued every few minutes, driving off reconnaissance planes. One plane came in as low as a thousand feet: "Everything in the area opened up on him and the walls of our joint shook with the blasts. He apparently came in under their fire because he got away—ack-ack falling on roofs for 5 minutes, it seemed."

They heard the good news the next day, Wednesday, September 13: "We have Nancy almost encircled and several units across the Moselle." Crosby strolled to the Red Cross Clubmobile and "ate a ton of their good donuts," fooled around with some of the children who liked to follow him and other Yanks about (they sang "Alouette"). That day, replicating his experience as a five-a-day vaudevillian, he presented three consecutive shows at the Rex, the only cinema in Commercy and the first theater he had seen the inside of since alighting in France. These shows were for men trucked in specially from contiguous antiaircraft and supply outfits. Despite continuous hours spent on the stage, the performers felt the luxury of a genuine playhouse offered recompense: "Boys packed in like sardines, very appreciative, and show was much better in theater on regular stage with footlites, wings, curtains, etc." The owner of the Rex told Bing that the Nazis had not let him screen an American picture in five years and that for every two films he did project, one had to be German. Colonel de Lorimer invited Bing's troupe to his home for supper—pâté, cheese, Piper-Heidsieck—courtesy of the previous resident, Field Marshal Günther von Kluge, who had killed himself after the botched attempt to assassinate Hitler. Bing's letters home to his family have not come to light, though Hollywood columnists occasionally reported on them. In one from London, he wrote of a "Nazi robot bomb"; in another, he alerted Dixie and the boys to listen to a broadcast. Louella Parsons learned that, "with his usual loquaciousness, Bing Crosby writes his family 'Feeling okay'—and that's all." But Carroll Carroll kept one that indicated Bing's desire to compose his own *Innocents Abroad*. Given their chilled relationship, this may have been Bing's way of side-stepping Carroll's offer to collaborate on a book.

> Somewhere in France
> (Almost in Germany)
> Sept 14—44
> Dear Carroll,
>   Very exciting time ici, and should I have the temerity to write a tome it would have to be in a serious vein. The only ameliorating circumstance is that the Krauts, in their headlong flight before Patton, left many interesting and appetizing items, and G.I. Joe is eating and drinking quite well—and nobody deserves it more. Boy what a job they've done. They're wonderful. Regards to all,
>   Bing[15]

Intent on learning more about the work of the Third Army, Bing took scrupulous notes about Patton's "daring gamble" after the breakthrough at Saint-Lô when, at the risk of annihilation, he drove his army through the seventeen-mile gap he had opened between Avranches and Mortain, circled below Paris to take Orléans and Troyes, then sped north to Reims and due east to the Moselle, moving an entire army two thousand miles in seventeen days with a "speed and mobility [that] surely stunned the German strategists into impotency." Crosby found the whole thing, the leadership and coordination, staggering, especially the problems of supply: "For instance 318,000 gals of gas is needed to run the outfit one day."

Not much glory was to be seen in the aftermath of the successful attack at the Moselle River, only a diorama of the wounded. "We really had it today," he wrote on the evening of the fourteenth. They began the morning visiting the men of the rear echelon of the Twelfth Corps, then drove five miles to the Thirty-Ninth Evacuation Hospital at Sorcy-Saint-Martin, where they walked the wards in an effort to hearten or console those in from the front, mostly men from the Thirty-Fifth Infantry hit in the river crossing. They put on a show outside for the ambulatory men and the staff. After lunch, they did the same at the 106th Evac, twenty miles away at Bulligny, where they watched as around four hundred and fifty more men were brought in, their clothes bloodied and their wounds hurriedly dressed, all groaning in pain, waiting for operational priority. The subsequent show brought a thousand men to the field, anyone who could get there. From Bulligny, they drove half an hour north along the Moselle River toward Dieulouard, where they found that the 404th Artillery had moved closer to the river to shell the enemy on the other side. A Messerschmitt came over them, but antiaircraft fire diverted it before it strafed. They set up the six p.m. show three miles west of Dieulouard at the presumably safer commune of Griscourt, but they were still only a couple of thousand yards from the enemy. The several hundred artillerymen who gathered to watch the show were "visibly amazed to see us way up in that area. Guns were shooting from behind us and on all sides during the show, providing material for many conscious but more unconscious ad-libs." A Piper L-4 Grasshopper landed on the field, and the pilot taxied right up to listen. Crosby thought it was their best show thus far.

Afterward they watched, mesmerized, as shells were dropped on German positions, and Bing could not help but admire the gutsy German resilience: "Though flanked on both sides and behind Nancy by powerful armored columns, pounded steadily from the air and by our artillery, they show no signs of weakening." Walking back to the cars, he admired a different kind of resilience: "I saw a small boy in a red jacket, cycling uphill with a violin on his back. I asked him where he was going, and he replied, 'To take my violin lesson.' This between gun bursts." The ride back to Commercy was "disquieting." The driver warned them of German patrols in the area and of stragglers hiding in the woods and then lost his way in the blackout.

France 1944

Dear Leo, I figured you might like to know that "Going My Way" is, by the testimony of the qualified, the #1 morale builder as the E.T.O. Projectionists, Special Services men, chaplains, U.S.O. officers and just plain G.I.s elaborate in this vein, almost to the point of embarrassment. Many have told me it's the only picture they have been induced to repeat for the same audience as many as three times. Leo it's really phenomenal. Have had many interesting and exciting experiences, and have been up close enough to nicotine my celanese[16] several times. Someone with your active imagination would have a fertile field here, where the fantastic is commonplace. The Americans are kicking hell out of the Hun. Every day I see and hear of things that make a fellow proud of these guys. One German captain told me he'd fought on every front and the Americans were the most murderous men he'd encountered. The Krauts in their haste left tons of food and thousands of cases of choice liquors. Free for all to apply to their own use. Need I say more?

Bing[17]

On Saturday morning they moved to their next home base, Vézelise, forty miles southeast of Commercy and closer to the front. To get there, they followed the same route taken two days earlier by the Thirty-Fifth Infantry Division in flanking Nancy from the south, a road now cratered with shell holes and cluttered with the debris of blistered trees. The troupers' new landlord, a brewer named Moreau, had arranged for them to use his loading platform as a stage, and as the forward echelon of the Thirty-Fifth approached Lunéville, two thousand men of the rear echelon gathered at the brewery dock to see the Crosby show. A sergeant asked Bing to autograph a snapshot of his son, who had caddied for Bing at Santa Anita.

Bing's troupe drove to the command post of the forward echelon to lunch with Major General Paul Baade, arriving only fifteen minutes after a counterattack was repulsed. Crosby did not say where this was, but he gave coordinates ("about 6 miles south of Nancy and eight miles east") that suggest the area of Saint-Nicolas-de-Port. The firefight continued throughout the afternoon show. A French newspaper photograph, published a year later and captioned "Bing Crosby entertains the Santa Fe at Nancy," shows him in fatigues and a helmet, with his guitarist and accordionist, singing on a flatbed truck overhung with a tarpaulin to protect him from the rain. They are encircled on that damp, dim day by men hugging their knees. A colonel later recalled, "We set up our tents on the heights. The town was so small that there were not many distractions for us. We spent our days in the camp. This is where Bing Crosby gave us a show. It rained all the time, and the day he arrived we spent the morning waiting for him. His show was very beautiful, exactly as it was in movies. [He] ate with us when he was not outside." Bing's accounts of the nearby fighting now had the confidence of a veteran correspondent's:

> Yesterday one of our Battalions crossed the canal at this point [and] was isolated by Germans and badly hacked up before withdrawing. Today another battalion feinted as if to cross and go up hill toward Lunéville road, when about 800 Germans came down the hill with 20 tanks to smash them. An L-4 exposed their movement for C.P. and within 7 minutes they were hit by 77-105s and 1.55s in timed fire. With the L-4 still radioing their position they continued to pound the remnants of the German column—12 tanks were burning and about 100 Germans were left to flee up the hill where they dug in. This activity was going on as we arrived. We were 1800 yds from the action. It continued thruout show with batteries leaving to replace other men to allow them to come and see the show.

Bing and Joe DeRita worked out a mind-reading act that was drawn partly from the one in the not-yet-released *Road to Utopia*. They were doing the act when an announcement ordered the immediate deployment of a section of men. DeRita cracked to Swami Bing, "You didn't know about *that*," and the crowd roared—"the best audience we ever worked for," Bing wrote. A colonel told him it was the first time he had laughed in two months. Baade thanked the players, assuring them that the army would soon clear "all resistance short of the Siegfried Line." The champagne flowed; toasts were made. Major General Baade ruminated about the "breathtaking complacency of French civilians during various actions. Shells falling all around but they go about their daily tasks as tho nothing was happening," which led Bing to reflect: "Quite a few killed and I've seen many badly hurt in evac hospitals, including children, but they never change....Children are unswervingly devoted to the G.I. They even think I'm one and every time I go on the street they cling to my clothes and kiss my hand. The little girls are particularly sweet, and warm-hearted."[18]

At Sunday Mass, in an old and "lovely" cathedral, the priest himself took up the collection. Heavy rain forced Bing to cancel the show but gave him hours to visit wards at the 110th Evacuation Hospital. Several dozen men lay on stretchers on the ground waiting for treatment. "Saw one boy we entertained at 17th replacement depot last Monday—now back from front with shattered leg." Another boy who had been a singer with Alvino Rey's band had been shot in the face and brutally stitched up. Despite the weather, the group drove down to the commune of Vittel expecting to do a show and spend the night, but midway they were rerouted to Neufchâteau; the Germans had retaken Vittel. "This front is so fluid," Bing wrote, "and the armored units have bypassed so much ground that many pockets of resistance are left, which boil over again a few days later."

Back at Vézelise and the handsome quarters provided by the brewer Moreau, they walked to evening mess. Bing recognized several boys who had traveled with them on the *Île de France* now waiting in trucks to leave for the forward echelon, ten miles away. "It's a dirty, rainy nite and some of them looked pretty blue and apprehensive. We did what we could to cheer them up, and they went off to fight." He saw "steady streams of prisoners." One convoy consisted of sixteen trucks, each with fifty prisoners. On occasion, prisoners were allowed to see Crosby's show. Asked later if he converted any, he said, "I probably widened the breach."[19] The rain and cold did not let up that night, but Moreau provided a "wonderful bed" and Bing had his best night's sleep since coming to France.

On September 18, the war came to Crosby's front door. The day began typically with a drive, twenty miles directly south of Vézelise to Mirecourt to perform for the Seventy-Ninth Infantry Division, which had never seen an overseas USO show. Over the past five days, two regiments of the Seventy-Ninth had formed a circular pocket and trapped some five hundred Germans; they tried to break out at Ramecourt, less than two minutes west of Mirecourt, and "were destroyed to the last man." Bing was told that because of the size of the regiments, he would be presenting two shows, one at two p.m. for the 313th Regiment in an open field north of Mirecourt, and one in the evening for the 314th Regiment eight miles east at Charmes. For the first show, fifty-five hundred men turned out and, as the Seventy-Ninth's historian wrote, "for more than an hour the battle-weary doughboys had the opportunity to forget the war." Bing, however, felt "uneasy with such a large concentration so close to [the] combat zone." The troops built a performance platform in the center of the field and placed antiaircraft guns and guards in key positions "to safeguard the USO troupe [in] the event of a surprise attack." The show went off without a hitch, interrupted only by artillery fire in the distance.[20]

The situation at Charmes, a commune bisected by the Moselle River, was far more tenuous. The army had secured the city a week earlier but rumors of a counteroffensive kept the battalions of the 314th Regiment on full alert even as the 313th and 315th Regiments arrived to reinforce their hold. The battle at Charmes had cost the Germans an airplane-engine factory with an inventory of hundreds of motors and heavy antiaircraft weaponry. They wanted it back. Two days before Crosby's show, eight miles away, the Americans had repulsed a German offensive with four tanks. Now the cavalry sighted a German infantry column a mile long with fifteen tanks moving in from Gerbéviller, about eighteen miles east. This was the situation as the division, thousands of men, gathered in the airplane factory before a stage erected earlier in the day. The show got off to a good start; "Swinging on a Star" brought down the house. Within twenty minutes, the regiments were put on alert. One soldier came onstage and explained to Crosby that the Germans had sprung a surprise counterattack as the loudspeaker erupted with orders for combat teams to return to their units, one at a time. "I'd do a song and they'd call out: 'Company F meet outside.' I'd do another song and Company E would be called. Pretty soon I was left singing to a Corporal's Guard." Bing spoke briefly to the men as they left. It was "unfortunate," he wrote in his journal, "as it was a good audience." A *New York Times* headline read "Bing Crosby Left Alone as Troops Run to Battle." Two weeks later, Decca Records bought a "Welcome Home, Bing!" page in *Variety*; it showed the *Times* story with a Milt Caniff–style illustration of Crosby, dressed in a garish blazer and a fedora, singing on a plank stage as helmeted soldiers run in the opposite direction. A banner reads "The only time an audience walked out on Bing Crosby."[21]

*   *   *

A veteran wrote from North Carolina sixty-five years later, in December 2009:

> Sir,
>
> I served in Europe in W.W. II, with the 79th Infantry Division, 313 Regiment 3rd Battalion Compy M 1st Platoon. A heavy machine guns platoon. We went up front, had broke through the German line, meeting no resistance. I was surprised when they told us Mr. Bing Crosby was over a hill we had captured, he being so close to the front lines. He giving a show for us, we went to see and hear him. As we gathered, leaving up front for the officers, Mr. Crosby came out on the stage. He said men come up front. I do my show for you the men. I don't reserve any space for officers, they are guests. He is the only one that reserves up front center stage for the men. [He said] I don't wish you to applaud after a song. It is you doing a job for me. He sang some songs. White Christmas was the best for us. The girls with him came out and sang and did their acting. Then Mr. Crosby came out and sang a song. Then a G.I. came on the stage and talked to Mr. Crosby. We could tell something was wrong. The G.I. left the stage. Mr. Crosby said men I have been told to tell you to return to your unit quickly. There is a unit of Germans headed this way. He said he was sorry they didn't get to do the show all the way. But God be with you. We went back to our unit. We stayed in the same place and captured a full German division the next day. That's why I was so surprised when they told us that Mr. Bing Crosby was there to entertain us. So close to the front lines.
>
> I wish I could have written to Mr. Crosby and told him how much it meant to me for his group coming that close to the front line to entertain us.
>
> Please excuse the misspelling and blunders. I was up front 248 days. Was wounded 3 times, injured 8 times, in a jeep wreck. Bad nerve condition, shake a lot, lost hearing. I am 85 years 7 months old. I do the best I can with what I have left. I wish to get the mailing address [for BingCrosby. com]. I don't have a com. I can't tell you the joy Mr. Crosby gave to me by coming and singing. He has always been my favorite singer. No one as good.[22]

The players set out early the next day, stopping at Frenelle-la-Grande to perform "under leaden skies, which was a good thing because

Jerry planes [flew] over twice during show and the overcast saved us from possible strafing." While Bing was visiting the Fifty-Fourth Field Hospital, a soldier whose arms and legs had been splintered by a mortar shell regained consciousness. He later recalled, "There was a guy walking around with fatigues on, tapping guys on the shoulder and asking, 'How you doin' soldier?' and I look around and it's Bing Crosby." The soldier told him how strange it was to see him in such circumstances. Crosby said, "It's no big deal—what you guys are doing is." With the harrowing increase in casualties, Crosby wondered if they would continue to find "sizable audiences."[23]

Finding audiences proved to be less problematic than getting to them. They had late starts, waiting for vehicles that had been sent to the wrong town. When they finally left, it wasn't unusual for the driver to lose his way. Still, they made it out every day, playing for five thousand men in a field near Bayon and twelve thousand (their largest audience to date) in the airplane factory at Charmes, "best show yet, I believe."[24] After a Lucullan dinner with the Fifteenth Corps, presided over by the self-proclaimed Kraut killer General Wade Haislip (who took Lunéville a few days later), they had a stressful ride home in the blackout. But Monsieur Moreau greeted them at the brewery. It was his son's birthday and the players' last night there. They serenaded the boy and his family, and for their valedictory breakfast Moreau insisted they accept his last dozen eggs. "He didn't have to bend my arm," Crosby wrote.

They were now set to move sixty miles north to the Metz area of Alsace-Lorraine, a dangerously unstable province (taken, lost, retaken), haunted by armed stragglers and not easy to find. Their hapless driver drove them to Verdun, an hour west of their target area. The sun set during the show and they finished in the dark. They spent the night in an old French barracks and in the morning drove closer to Metz to perform for the Second Battalion, four thousand strong. Piper Cub pilots in the audience were called away during the show. One of them told Bing they were going to work on a fort a mile and a half over the hill; he said that his outfit "had 60% casualties in the Metz show."

The battle for Metz held back the Allies for three months, allowing the Germans time to mount a surprise attack in the Ardennes

Bing's embellishments, if that's what they were, launched a cycle of retellings, evolving like an urban myth, invariably linking a censorious Patton to a blithe Crosby. In the typical version, Patton is enraged about Bing's disappearance, and when Bing finally shows up in the evening, Patton bellows, "Do you know you were in German territory?" to which Bing coolly responds, "Well, we had it this morning." No one claims to have witnessed it. Patton was not in Onville that day, and Crosby's absence involved minutes, not hours. More credibly, it is said that Patton was annoyed by headlines like "Bing 'Captures' a German Town" simply because he was easily annoyed. Perhaps the story lasted because it afforded the raconteur the pleasure of pitching his voice half an octave lower to mimic the vaguely insolent Der Bingle; perhaps Patton was grafted to it as the obvious fall guy, the man who, in another tale—also widespread, also unlikely—threatened to court-martial Bing for wearing his soft fatigue cap rather than a helmet.[28]

Of course, Bing did meet Patton, and on one occasion during the Metz leg, from a distance, he heard him address a replacement depot: "There were about twelve or sixteen thousand men there. I was standing way at the back and there were about a dozen army nurses standing there too. He talked real high, like Jack Dempsey, you know, and he says, 'Now, you boys have been well prepared, are beautifully trained, and you're going up to the front lines tomorrow. There is nothing more we can do for you. It's up to you now. You got to be alert. If you fall asleep some Kraut is liable to sneak up behind and hit you over the head with a sock of shit.' You should have seen those nurses laugh."[29] Crosby never mentioned Patton in connection with the Vandelainville detour, and two weeks after Bing left France, Patton wrote to him in care of his London hotel and expressed only "regret that I did not have time to see more of you personally. I trust that the next time we meet, either in Germany or Japan, you will give me the opportunity of a longer visit. With warm personal regards and thanks for the inspiration which you and your team gave to the soldiers, I am, Most sincerely, G. S. Patton, Jr."[30]

The Onville show, which got under way as soon as Bing arrived, was in a memorable setting: a ravine with the stage at the bottom and three thousand men arrayed on the surrounding hillsides. It rained and poured and you could not take two steps in any direction without sinking into mud, but the audience loved every minute, as did the players. The mud became a problem when they were ready to leave; the cars needed planks and muscles to get free of the mire, which made them late for their performance for an artillery group waiting east of Doncourt-lès-Conflans, eighteen hundred yards from German positions. Trying to get warm before the performance, Bing accidentally set the tent on fire. Then the amplification system broke down and they did the show without it. It "went alright though," with "about 4,500 in this audience. Very rough characters indeed." The scuttlebutt indicated that the plan was to isolate Metz (given the dismal weather) while continuing operations in the north and south. "Guns were firing all the time we were in that area and shells were whistling over us. As we drove out a couple big babies went right over the car."

They finally left Metz and drove thirty-five miles west to Verdun to entertain the U.S. Army Air Forces, the last major stop before they could decompress in the qualified comfort of Paris. They approached Verdun on a wet and gloomy morning and took a tour of one of the bloodiest battlegrounds of the First World War and of human history, a battle that had resulted in a million or so casualties and left the fields haunted by carnage and surrounded by cemeteries. The rain worsened and made the first show "tough duty." Afterward, they drove several miles to visit the wards of the Twelfth Evacuation Hospital, now "sunk in mud," but with hard roads to facilitate its twenty-four-hour receiving section. Patients were given penicillin and moved out, usually within forty-eight hours. The staff tried to make the hospital pleasant, screening movies, playing records over the public address system, offering concerts by the Third Army Band. Crosby visited there for over an hour; the show drew ten thousand soldiers and medical staffers attached to the Twelfth Army Group.[31] In Verdun the troupers were invited to General Bradley's headquarters, where they drank good scotch and got a lesson in reading the war map from three of the eminent generals in that arena: Bradley, Raymond Moses, and Terry Allen. A month earlier, Bradley had suffered a wound to his authority and his pride when he overruled Patton and ordered troops to withdraw at Argentan, unintentionally allowing the encircled German forces to escape the Falaise Pocket, a battlefield Eisenhower later wrote could be described only by Dante.[32] Bing encountered the unbowed popular image of Omar Bradley and was duly impressed: "This is a charming man, beloved by all his officers and men, and a tremendously able tactician. He's not too optimistic on early war's end and spoke regretfully of the probable necessity of a winter campaign. Says Hitler's oil is low. But our problem of supply is also a serious situation."

The generals and their staffs attended Crosby's evening performance at the Verdun Theater. "It was great luck to work in a theater again." The players were elated at the reception. But the elation vanished when they left the stage and found that looters—widespread looting had been a sorry fact since the invasion of Normandy—had targeted Der Bingle's company. Persons unknown had made off with their trunk, containing their equipment, gowns, music, instruments. They felt "great sorrow at this," but later that night military police recovered the trunk, which was found on a roadside in the hands of four inebriated soldiers; "Summary court for them," Bing logged. In the morning downpour, they visited the military building that housed the Thirty-Fourth Evacuation Hospital and were pleased to walk through wards with a roof. The staff of the hospital felt the same way. The Thirty-Fourth Evac had traveled six hundred miles since it had landed in Cherbourg in July, and Verdun provided an opportunity for personnel to work in brick-and-mortar structures rather than in tents and use the high-quality medical equipment abandoned by the Germans. The Thirty-Fourth Evac stayed there two and a half months, remaining until it could safely reconstitute itself at Metz.[33]

The Crosby troupe now headed for Paris, a hundred and seventy miles away, in a blinding rain that pursued them all the way to their hotel door. The particular road they traveled, Crosby surmised, must have been favored by the fleeing Wehrmacht too, because "thousands of vehicles blasted by our air force littered the fields." They checked into the city and were directed to a "nice hotel"—the palatial Hôtel Ritz, no less, recently relinquished by Hermann Göring—that had no heat or hot water. Despite the Liberation, Paris seemed glum and depleted, given the abysmal weather, the

sacking of shops, the exhaustion of war, and the absence of ameni-
ties. "I went into Cartier's to buy some presents for Dixie," he told a
reporter:

> The manager said, "I would have to charge you more than any-
> thing is worth. I prefer to keep your friendship. Don't buy now.
> Please come back again." In Schiaparelli's and Paquin's there was
> nothing to sell, except a few handkerchiefs. I bought Dixie a few.
> I had plenty of presents for Gary, Phillip, Dennis, and Lindsay.
> Every G.I. over there is so big-hearted and so appreciative that he
> wants to give you his souvenirs. I came back with German iron
> crosses, money, and a captured German Luger.[34]

The desolate mood extended to a couple of old friends, George
Stevens and Bill Mellor. Stevens, one of Hollywood's finest directors of comedy and light fare (Bing counted *Vivacious Lady* among
his favorite pictures), had recently followed John Huston, William
Wyler, John Ford, Frank Capra, and other less renowned directors
into the armed forces to document aspects of war. He had landed
in Normandy to cover D-day, and within a year, he would be the
first American filmmaker to shoot concentration-camp footage (at
Dachau). Stevens's work figured as evidence at the Nuremberg
trials. After the war, he eschewed comedy for a quarter of a century, forging a reputation as an independent producer, directing
infrequent pictures that explored good and evil (*A Place in the Sun,
Shane, The Diary of Anne Frank*). William C. Mellor, a cinematographer with the army's photographic unit, shot most of Stevens's
postwar work. Before the war, he worked at Paramount, where he
shot four of Bing's films (*Road to Singapore, Road to Morocco, Birth
of the Blues, Dixie*); he would later photograph Crosby's last independent feature (the well-meant but incredibly misguided hash of
ethnic banalities *Abie's Irish Rose*) and his first television special.[35]
The "great job" Mellor and Stevens had done "covering this
whole thing since D-Day pictorially," Crosby observed, had worn
them down and they appeared "a little lonesome." Resolving to
restore their spirits, he accompanied them to the "good army mess"
at the Ritz, and they rounded up Bill Hearst and embarked on a
"big" night that "warmed [them] up." It was the first of several

charmed days and big nights that took the edge off the past few weeks and reunited Bing with friends, including Fred Astaire, also at the Ritz.[36]

The tour and its drudgeries were basically over, but the shows were not. He did two memorable ones for the Ninth Air Force on his first Parisian morning, in nearby Versailles, with Astaire and Dinah Shore. They performed before fervent audiences of twelve thousand, which Shore thought to be the "crowning achievement" of her USO adventure.[37] It was a memorable day for Bing too, in part because Eisenhower invited him to an elaborate lunch at his Versailles headquarters, as he had done with Astaire. Bing initially ignored the invitation, which arrived at his hotel in the form of a memo from Ike's aide Colonel Galt. He figured the general was just being polite and should not feel obliged "to entertain any itinerant minstrel just to be nice." But he checked with Hearst, who told him, "No, he really wants to see you. You ought to do it." Hearst added, "If you go out there and Eisenhower asks if there is anything he can do for you, for God's sake, get an automobile for a couple of days." Paris cramped their mobility. Beyond army vehicles, cars were scarce and gas unobtainable, and the Métro was under repair; civilians without bicycles could get only as far as their legs took them. Crosby recalled military drivers chaining jeeps to hydrants or chaining a vehicle's front wheel to the steering wheel and removing the carburetor, "otherwise the jeep vanished."[38]

After the two shows, Crosby lunched with Eisenhower, who "proved to be a most agreeable and entertaining guy with a great personality." Over coffee and digestifs, Bing, Ike, and two staff members sang barbershop-quartet arrangements of old songs; the general sang baritone, but strictly harmony, leaving the lead to his guest, who noted in his journal that "he moved plenty of channels to try and lengthen our stay so we could do a show for him but it couldn't be done. All he wants in life he says is some hominy grits, which I'll surely send him." Bing took out his tiny black address book and uncharacteristically asked Eisenhower to autograph it.[39]

I was ready to leave and he says, "Anything I can do for you?" And I said, "Yes, you could let me have an automobile if you've got one handy for a couple of days." I told him I wanted to go down to

Fontainebleau to see some friends of ours from California who'd
got stranded over [here] and have been down there since the war
began. "In fact," I said, "I wanted to have them come up to the
show," which we were doing at Chantilly on the next night. That
was true. I thought that would be a good use for a car and a good
excuse to give Eisenhower. So he said, "Well, take my car and the
driver." I said, "Well, when do you want it back?" He said, "When
you're through with it." That was about Wednesday and I think he
got it back on about Saturday.[40]

It was indeed Wednesday and the general got his car back on
Friday, along with his wartime and sometimes postwar driver, Sergeant Leonard Dry. Hearst was delighted, as this was the first time
he had had personal transportation since coming to Paris. They
made another large night of it, exploring nightclubs and theaters,
including several in the Place Pigalle. Crosby later felt a bit sheep-
ish about having Eisenhower's car, boldly decorated with five stars,
parked "in front of some funny places, a lot of Frenchmen standing around watching it." But Dry, who knew the city well, didn't
mind at all, as Bing insisted he come along with them at every
stop—"He had a great time." Bing suspected that Eisenhower had
known all about it when, three years later at a celebrity golf tournament in the capital, they met again and "he looked at me slyly
and asked with a smile, 'Are they taking good care of your transportation here?'"[41]

The next day Sergeant Dry drove Bing to Fontainebleau, where
he was eager to see one of Dixie's and his oldest friends, someone
they knew from their courtship days at the Ambassador Hotel in
1930. His post-Whiteman career had begun there when the Rhythm
Boys appeared with Gus Arnheim's band in the hotel's nightclub,
the Cocoanut Grove, and Bing, virtually unknown beyond the
world of jazz and dance bands, made history crooning, swinging,
enunciating, and establishing the stage microphone as a musical
instrument. In 1940, a photograph of this old friend had appeared
in American newspapers, captioned "Missing in France. Unheard
from since the German capture and bombardment of Le Touquet,
Mrs. Paul de Ricou, the former Louise Miller Winnett of Beverly
Hills, Cal., and her two children are being sought. She is the wife

of the noted French tennis star." Louise had regularly accompanied Dixie to the Cocoanut Grove and grown close to both of them. She later married the Davis Cup player Paul Barrelet de Ricou. Once Louise and the children were safely located, they could not leave France or German custody. "They had it pretty rough for four or five years," Crosby recalled. Their reunion was intensely emotional.

That night he asked Dry to pick up Paul and Louise in Fontaine-bleau and bring them to Chantilly, about thirty miles north of central Paris, where he did two shows, one at the Chantilly Racecourse. The combined audience for both shows, made up mostly of the Ninth Air Force and the Army Signal Corps, was estimated at fifteen thousand. Paul and Louise were taken to the first row at the track, and Bing, in a rare display of outright sentiment and surely to the mystification of much of the audience, sang songs from the Cocoanut Grove era, 1930 and 1931, many of them largely forgotten: "I Surrender, Dear," "Just One More Chance," "It Must Be True," "So the Bluebirds and the Blackbirds Got Together," and an obscurity he recorded as a duet with their mutual friend Loyce Whiteman, "Ho Hum!" "Everything that was peculiar to that period," he told Pete Martin. Crosby made a point during the tour of taking requests, some of them obscure, but this recital was a one-shot feat of memory and skill, requiring him to recollect the songs and teach them to his accompanists. It worked: "The tears were rolling down her face, and down my face. A pretty lugubrious performance."[42] He wrote in his journal, "Louise was so thrilled she shook for hours. First American friends she'd seen in 6 yrs. Has had many terrifying experiences but is a fine game gal. Very happy with Paul, who did great pre-invasion job. Never saw anyone so grateful for the few little things we did for them — cigarettes etc."

After the de Ricous returned home, Bing enjoyed another "big nite," his last in France, with Hearst and a small group that included Major John Hoover, a young pilot with the Seventh Photographic Reconnaissance Group whose low-altitude flying and picture-taking on D-day and in the days that followed earned him the Distinguished Service Cross. Hoover accompanied Bing's troupe to London, where it would perform for his division. The flight was uneventful: "1 hr & 20 min. Very smooth crossing, low ceiling over

England." Bing checked into the Mayfair Hotel and took his first hot bath in...well, he wasn't sure how long, "since Vézelise, I guess."

He went out to dinner with Glenn Miller and Jack Harding, the manager of the Queensberry All-Services Club, and ended up at the home of Jack Hylton, the bandleader, pianist, and, later, in the 1950s, prominent theatrical producer. He sold millions of records before the war and was often regarded as the British Paul Whiteman, though his greatest influence on European jazz resulted from his powers as an impresario — he arranged for the first continental visits of Duke Ellington and Coleman Hawkins, with whom he famously toured and recorded. Though married, Hylton carried on a widely known affair with the singer Pat Taylor, whose sister Rene Taylor, also a singer, visited that evening and impressed Bing enough for him to record her name alone (without comment) in his journal. He spent the night at Hylton's.

The next day, his last full day in London, Bing and company capped their tour with a concert for Johnny Hoover's Seventh Photographic Reconnaissance Group at Mount Farm airfield, in Oxfordshire, fifty miles west of London. Elliott Roosevelt, the president's profligate son and a U.S. Army Air Forces commander who leveraged his name for rank and pulled rank when it was handy, welcomed them to what Crosby considered a fitting summit for the tour, a show before a large, wonderfully enthusiastic crowd. Roosevelt was nothing if not resolute in his carousing and he helped to supervise festivities, which began with a boozy lunch and lasted through the night and the next day. The hilarity began with Hoover, Colonel Clarence "Shoopy" Shoop (the pilot who flew D-day's first photographic mission over Omaha Beach), and two hard-drinking associates from San Antonio. Bing had met one of them, Pleas McNeel, a photo reconnaissance innovator who had a powerful tenor voice and did not have to be pressured to sing, at the bar of the Broadmoor Hotel in Colorado Springs a few years earlier. Pleas (short for *pleasant*) had served with Roosevelt in North Africa; when Elliott transferred to London, Pleas wrote the order that shipped him as well.[43]

As night fell they made the rounds of London with a group that waxed until it was near forty strong. Roosevelt, Bing observed, "broke the world's record for consecutive nip-ups and also broke Claridge's up pretty good." After a dinner party at the Ambassador, the group gathered at the Milroy Club, an exclusive terminus for high society operated by John Mills, a hulking bear of a man who claimed to have served in the Polish army and was said to have made his fortune in the black market. Marlene Dietrich joined the party and sang a few songs. They all went to Mills's home for cocktails till dawn and then enjoyed "more of same" in the suite of Bill Hearst's wife, Lorelle, a socialite and correspondent stationed in London.

Bing was probably bleary-eyed when he boarded the train for Glasgow with his USO team and Fred Astaire. Bing and Fred had both asked to return by sea and discovered in London that they were booked on the same *Queen Mary* voyage. Neither of them was prepared for the reception in Scotland. In his 1959 memoir, Astaire glossed over it with three words, preceded and followed by ellipses: "Glasgow fan mob." In his journal, Bing wrote: "Several small riots developed in Depot over Fred and I. They see very few picture people around here I guess." He had more fun with it in his memoir: "I can only conclude that the last American actor seen there before Fred and I hit the town was Tom Mix or John Bunny. It seemed to us that people came out of the braces and glens who hadn't been in Glasgow for years."[44]

But it wasn't a joke at the time, and Bing later shuddered when he spoke of it. He claimed that the police estimated some thirty-five thousand people descended on the Glasgow depot, "pushing and crowding and milling, so we went in the baggage room and they locked us in there and got some police to protect us until the train could leave." The mob cried out for a song and dance, but there was no room, nor were the stars inclined to be showmen on demand for civilians. "The train was now made up and ready to go, but we couldn't do anything, we couldn't get out of the baggage room to get through this crowd. A few policemen showed up and they were waving their nightsticks, but it didn't make any difference." The crowd "kept surging around the baggage room, thousands of them, and we looked out the window once in a while and then went under the table for a while and this went on, I guess, for a half hour or forty-five minutes and we got to be pretty desperate because we had to make that train." Finally the station master strode down the ramp—dressed in "striped trousers and frock coat and wing collar and ascot scarf and a tall silk hat"—and shouted, "Stand clear!" The crowd "fell back like a wave," and the official escorted them the quarter mile to their compartment. For the rest of his life, when the subject of unruly fans came up, Bing would say, "Well, you know, during the war when Fred Astaire and I were up in Scotland, they had to put us in a baggage room and surround us with police to keep from, well, they just wanted to tear our clothes off and everything else."[45]

At Greenock, they went through customs and boarded the *Queen Mary*, where Bing soon learned that his luggage could not be found. (It turned up in the hold several hours later.) Bing and Fred played poker with the sportswriter Paul Gallico and, along with Bing's USO group, put on a few shows in what Astaire described as "a special setup in the main dining hall" as well as in the "hospital sections for the many returning wounded." Astaire recalled the ship as overloaded with exhausted men sleeping in corridors and stairwells; he remembered it making "several deviations to avoid submarines." Bing, in contrast, noted that the passenger list of six thousand amounted to but a third of the number it had carried when it traveled in the other direction, and he did not comment on submarines. Having used up the last pages of his address book, he wrote a final entry on the back of the officers' menu for October 8, 1944—a menu offering items such as sheep's head broth, silverside of corned beef, darne of salmon mousseline, calf's head grand-mere, and fedora pudding.

Queen Mary Trip—Not too crowded—good food. Paul Gallico, Constance Cummings aboard, others. 600 wounded. Bomber crews with Missions Completed. R.A.F. and Ferry pilots aiming to pick up more equipment. Also Aussie and New Zealand fliers. Quite a few civilians, English and American, and six congressmen, about 6000 in all. Only needed two shows and couple visits to wards to cover trip. Great names for Bombers, Superstitious Aloysius, Heaven Can Wait, etc. Everybody out on deck early in the morning to catch first sight of land. Some of them away for 3 yrs, a few with English brides and children. Such wounded as could walk hanging on rail straining for a sight of skyline. A chorus of "Home Sweet Home" could break everybody up right in here. Cursory survey reveals first item men are going for is chocolate ice cream soda.

In the February 5, 1945, *Cavalcade of America* show, "The Road to Berlin," featuring Crosby and his USO unit in a comical, superficial re-creation of the tour, the closing scenes dramatized three points from this entry: the emotional crowding on the decks to see the Statue of Liberty, a chorus by Bing of "Home Sweet Home" (which he may or may not have sung on board), and the desire for ice cream sodas.

21

A LITTLE TOUCH OF HARRY IN THE DAY

*He is that amazing product of the Far West—the Cos-
mopolitan American. He is also that odd American
freak, a gifted artist without temperament, with all the
normal instincts and the average reactions, the reasonably good citizen, the* homme moyen sensuel.

—Gilbert Seldes (1944)[1]

Bing startled May Mann, a young Hollywood magazine writer, with
his willingness to be interviewed. "Fire away!" he instructed.
"Crosby was a changed man when he walked into the conference
room at NBC," she reported. "He was voluble. He wanted to talk.
He didn't doze off in the middle of the interview. Even Hope would
have had a high time getting a word in edgewise. Sounds
unbelievable—I know!" Louella Parsons and her staff were stunned:
"I didn't believe that Bing Crosby meant it when he said he would
see me at 9:30 in the morning at my house for an interview. But I
did him wrong. I thought he was the Bing of old and that he would
forget all about it, but, sure enough, right on the dot, in came Bing,
and the whole household went to pieces." Her maid trembled as she
announced him; her secretary asked Parsons if she could deliver a
message during the interview "so I can just look at him." Louella
could not get over how "sweet and unassuming" he was—

particularly now, when, "make no mistake about it, he stands alone as the most important star, male or female, on the screen today."[2]

Despite his sudden cooperation with the press, Crosby remained icily submerged, hidden from all but his closest intimates and in some instances from them as well. As far as the public could see, he had returned from Europe the same old Bing, only more so, and his hardly surprising need to talk reflected some of the urgency of he only who escaped alone to tell thee. Entertaining the troops was only the first leg of the Foxhole Circuit; the second leg involved bearing witness.

For the most part he handled it superbly, but there were difficulties. After arriving in New York on October 8, he phoned the wives and parents of men who had asked him to and whose numbers he had entered in his address book. He also discharged a duty that, he averred, hundreds of "very concerned fellas imposed on me": he asked Walter Winchell to stop referring to the Thirty-Fifth Division of Patton's army as Hollywood Commandos, "a sobriquet which they claimed you hung on them for their antics on Southern maneuvers." They "more than redeemed themselves" at the Moselle and in Metz, Bing wrote the columnist, and they deserved a new name. Crosby would soon find himself the subject of the infantry's touchiness.[3]

Four days after disembarking from the *Queen Mary*, he held a press conference at the Waldorf Astoria in an eighteenth-floor room that was bare but for a table, a baby grand, and rows of folding chairs, mostly unoccupied. Civilian and uniformed cameramen set up their equipment in the back, and a young soldier up front turned on floodlights; reporters trickled in, blinking at the glare. At the appointed time, ten forty-five, an officer escorted Crosby in. As he walked "jauntily" past the unattended chairs, he cracked, "Looks like the size of the audience of Hope's last picture." The photographers had at him first. He removed a slouch hat, revealing his thinning hair, which initially stymied the well-trained journalists until they realized he did not mind them shooting his natural look. Evenly taking the measure of everyone in the room, Crosby put an unlighted pipe in his mouth and signaled his readiness.[4]

One photographer attempted to hand him a Nazi flag—red with a black swastika—which Crosby refused. "Oh, no, you won't get me with that." But he agreed to sit at the piano in a German helmet pretending to sing and play or smoke his pipe, cheerfully bantering with the picture takers. "Give us a good one now," "Just look as if you're singing," they shouted. "You want expression? I don't do that type of work," Crosby said, then he mashed a chord and crooned, "La-da-dee." "Do that again"; "Look this way." There was much laughter as writers entered and stood behind the photographers, and after dozens of bulbs popped, Bing asked, "Enough?" in a manner that answered itself. The photographers backed off and the writers took their seats, filling them all, while others leaned against the walls. Bing lit his pipe. He was tanned, slightly gaunt; his gray jacket and taupe slacks hung a bit loose and everyone noticed it. A reporter said he looked thin—how was the food? Bing said he had lost ten pounds; the food was simple but okay. A woman in back asked him to speak up. "Oh, you want the *Hope* delivery," he said, clearing his throat. What had the GIs asked to hear? Mostly old songs, "because I'm an old guy." He paused to let out a smoky cloud and spoke seriously of his futile resistance to "White Christmas." The last thing he wanted was to generate tears in men who were "sitting in the mud and sweating it out, sometimes for three years," but they always requested it.[5]

Crosby's relaxed temperament held the press corps spellbound. The stories that generated most of the headlines over the next few days concerned his inadvertent drive into occupied territory during the Metz campaign, and the show where his audience ran off to stop a counterattack. Those endlessly syndicated stories generated a skeptical letter from members of the Medical Detachment of the 351st Infantry, writing from "Somewhere in Italy," who doubted his proximity to the front and his account of units pulling out of a show to fight; fairy tales, they groused, that hurt the "morale of men dying for their country." The medics breached the fortress of Crosby's reserve, prompting the rarest kind of retort in his voluminous wartime correspondence: a boast. "I did shows <u>closer</u> than 1000 yards from the front—and <u>several</u> times men were called from performances to duty, contrary to what your experience has indicated as probable. Since returning home I've done everything possible to convince folks that this war is just plain 'hell' for you fellows." He signed off, "Always your friend."[6]

Everyone at the Waldorf press conference was happy. Later that afternoon, Maxwell Fox, the publicity director for USO–Camp Shows, wrote Crosby a note of congratulations for "creating the most enjoyable press conference yet conducted under our auspices." Some of the writers "remarked that 'it was more like a party than an interview.' Perhaps you noticed that several of the cameramen hung around to hear most of your story—thus breaking all precedence. They usually whizz out as if they had been given hot-feet." Fox thanked him for his "ready and intelligent cooperation," his punctuality, his "friendly and accommodating attitude to all and sundry."[7] Still, a few issues emerged, one merely annoying, another embarrassing, and a third farcical.

The first was political. The Hollywood for Dewey Committee included Crosby's name in circulars supporting the Republican presidential candidate Thomas Dewey. It is unlikely that Crosby would have signed on, particularly after his escapade abroad and for a candidate far less agreeable than FDR's 1940 opponent, Wendell Willkie, even had he been asked. But he was not asked, and when he learned about it from journalists he explicitly disavowed backing Dewey. "I had nothing to do with it," he said. "I don't know anything about politics." The *New York Post*'s gossip columnist Earl Wilson pressed him about it one night at the Stork Club. Crosby "stood up courteously when I talked to him," Wilson wrote, and said, "I'm not for Dewey." When Wilson continued to push, Crosby protested, "I'm a nobody man. I don't think we should have an election with the war on. It's a hokey, expensive thing. First we ought to get the boys home. When you do a show for a boy one day, and see him come back the next day with a leg off, that's how you feel." Then you're for Roosevelt? Wilson asked. "I don't think I'm even registered." He sighed and changed the subject. On November 7, Roosevelt won in a landslide, despite his failing health; six weeks later, Germany launched its desperate offensive in the Ardennes, the bloody Battle of the Bulge. Roosevelt lived to see the Germans routed at the end of January, but he died in April, a month before the surrender.[8]

The second issue sounded innocent enough at first. Explaining the need for entertainment, he told the press corps that morale was highest at the front: "They dress and look better, their salutes are

sharper, they're more businesslike." Consequently, he said, entertainers were appreciated more behind the lines, especially in hospitals where "they have nothing to do but look at each other and wait
for the beckoning finger to get to the front." These remarks were
pounced upon by Bill Mauldin, the favorite cartoonist of dogfaces
everywhere, in *Stars and Stripes*:

> When Bing Crosby returned to America after his visit to the
> French front, he told reporters, according to one news dispatch,
> that entertainment is needed most by the dispirited troops of the
> rear echelon rather than by the front-line soldiers. Up there, it
> seemed to him, "morale is sky-high, clothes are cleaner and salutes
> really snap." The dogfaces who read that dispatch in the foxholes
> didn't know what front Bing was talking about.
>
> Please, God, don't let anybody become a lecturer on front-line
> conditions until he has spent at least a year talking to the combat
> men. Many of us over here have been trying to find out about the
> front for several years and we feel like anything but experts.[9]

The fuss never made it into the mainstream press. As he left New
York on a westbound train, Bing had no reason to suspect that plenty
of front-line infantrymen were peeved. He did not find out until a
few dozen of them wrote say-it-ain't-so-Bing letters, taking umbrage
at the idea that they did not need entertainment or that they gave a
damn about sharp saluting and orderly dress. Considering all the
Willies and Joes he fraternized with overseas, it is hard to know
what Bing had meant. The editor of a newssheet put out by the
Ninth Army's Forty-Seventh Infantry sent him an issue of *Raiders of
the 9th* featuring a drawing of two grizzled dogfaces reading "Bars
and Gripes" in battle. As bombs explode over their heads, one
shouts, "Hey! Didja read what Bing said 'bout us guys?" The editor
wrote him, "Our lads are real combat soldiers, Bing, not rear-echelon
Commandos, so it kind of hurt when the statement you made
regarding the greater need for entertainment by the rear groups
than for the lads who are really sweating out this war became
known. Sincerely hope you were misquoted or something."[10] Crosby,
who wrote back to every military correspondent, thanked him for
the *Raider* and offered his standard response in the matter:

It has always been my conviction that actors returning from Overseas should keep their kissers closed. Partly because the short time any of us spends in theaters of wars doesn't qualify us to speak authoritatively on anything, and partly because it seems very hammy to me for actors to be taking bows for doing so little.

However, the public clamor for news about you guys is so insistent that a press conference is inevitable and unavoidable.

All I can say in defense of the item you take exception to is that I was <u>flagrantly misquoted.</u>

He signed off with "Always your friend."[11]

The grievances weighed on him enough to color a concurrent farce that involved General Eisenhower's yen for hominy grits. With time to kill on the train, Bing wrote to Eisenhower that he had carried out the "grits detail" in New York, placing orders with two suppliers. He added:

> The press has cornered me on several occasions, and wherever possible, I've tried to confine my remarks to the concerns expressed in the [European theater of operations] over the growing complacency at home. This I will accent on the radio and whatever outlets are available, and if my small voice and those of my friends has any persuasive powers, we may keep some of them on the ball around here.
>
> I'm grateful to the Army for affording me the richest experience of my life. The courage, resourcefulness, and general all-round class of our men is something every American should be proud of, and the privilege of watching them at work is something I'll never forget. They are wonderful.
>
> Thanks for the lunch and the use of your car. Your driver is a nice guy, and very capable. If I can do anything for you over here—command me.[12]

He neglected to say that several hours after the press conference, he was patched by wire into the *Kraft Music Hall* for a homecoming show (with Bob Hope as guest and George Murphy as substitute host) and mentioned the supreme commander's request. "Dear Bing," Eisenhower wrote. "Had I had the slightest idea that you were going to say anything on your radio program about my liking for hominy grits I would have kept still in all the languages I know.

My secretary tells me that already she has a couple dozen letters saying the hominy grits are on the way."

"Dear General Eisenhower," Bing replied. "I am sorry if my little slip on the radio caused you to be deluged with shipments of grits. At any rate, you are now 'loaded' with this delectable commodity, and should have enough to supply Supreme Headquarters with ease." He added, "I have learned since coming home that returning actors have to be awfully careful what they say on the radio, or for the press." He closed: "We are working hard now on the Sixth War Loan, and hope the results will convince the men over there there's no letup in support from the people at home."[13]

The morning after the *KMH* transmission, with packed bags and train tickets in hand, Bing stopped at Decca to record two songs from a new Broadway show, *Bloomer Girl*, set during the Civil War. Its libretto concerned suffragettes and slavery, but the good intentions of the songs (by Harold Arlen and Yip Harburg, the lyricist behind Crosby's 1932 classic "Brother, Can You Spare a Dime") are undone by rank folksiness that Crosby's skill, including a nicely slurred low note à la Paul Robeson, could not alleviate. He then boarded the train for Chicago, where he transferred to a streamliner called the City of San Francisco, aiming to visit Elko and Idaho before heading to Mapleton Drive. In Coeur d'Alene, he hunted pheasant, grew a beard, and told a reporter looking for an election quote that he would cancel Bob Hope's ballot by voting for "the other guy."[14]

However chagrined he might have felt about his comments on morale, Bing was determined to lead a second overseas tour to the South Pacific after completing a couple of films and other professional obligations. In the spring, his brother Bob had reported to the Camp Pendleton marine base. Given the rank of second lieutenant, Bob was posted to the Pacific War Zone as band director of the Fifth Marine Division. While Bob worked on getting Bing a commission through the navy (which resented the army's control of transportation for entertainment units), Paramount's Henry Ginsberg, the vice president who had replaced Buddy DeSylva as head of production that fall, worked to clear Bing's schedule for 1945.

In the interim, the world was shocked to learn of Glenn Miller's disappearance over the English Channel as he was flying to Paris on December 15. Bing wrote to Jack Harding of the Queensberry All-Services Club, "Terribly sorry to hear the news about Miller. We all pray he'll turn up a prisoner, at least." Two weeks later Harding told him that the military was certain Miller was dead; his plane did not crash-land on the Continent and he could not have been taken or survived. Harding collected fifty thousand signatures of servicemen and -women to be bound in a testimonial volume and asked if Bing would present it to Miller's widow. Crosby penciled on his letter, "Understand Miller has been reported a prisoner of war" and held off on responding. Two months later, he wrote Harding, "It now appears all hope for the life of Glenn Miller must be abandoned and I know that all of you over there share with us in America the irreparable loss we have sustained. He was a great man in this business, always did an outstanding job, and was a good friend to all." Bing said he "should be much pleased to attend to the matter of the testimonial volume" and planned to visit England as "circumstances permit." Privately, he redoubled his efforts to tour the Pacific. After several delays and at the insistence of Admiral Nimitz, who demanded that at least two shows a month be transported and controlled by the navy, Crosby was scheduled to depart on a combat ship to Guam in September 1945 — a plan happily scuttled when Japan surrendered on August 15.[15]

As 1944 wound to its end, he maintained his compliant attitude with the press. He leavened his narrative with cracks about Hope and told of exploits in which he was at loose ends, the lost pilgrim, the abandoned showman, even an unknown showman: "France didn't know me," he liked to say, because they had not seen an American movie in four years. Yet he avoided cant. W. H. Mooring, a Los Angeles–based correspondent for the English fan magazine *Picturegoer*, wrote: "His references to the British and French people had about them none of that patronizing ring which so often arouses my ire when stars 'give forth' about the heroism of . . . towns that have 'caught it.'" He admired the way Crosby, "too polite to disparage anyone," answered with humor while deflecting daft requests to compare French and American women; when a reporter persisted in that vein, asking if women mobbed him in Paris, Crosby said, "They didn't know me from Adam, and wouldn't have even if I'd had my toupee on, but they'd sure have mobbed me if I'd been a beefsteak!" When another reporter made light of V-1 rockets, asking if he had ducked, his description "brought them to silence for a full minute." Bing observed, "If one fell here, this whole building would be gone and for two blocks all around houses would be de-roofed, trees uprooted, lamp posts shattered." Mooring figured "he had done more to convey to Americans an accurate picture of Europe at war than anyone else I'd ever listened to, not excluding my friends who've come through places like Coventry."[16]

Still, when the press used up his amusing stories, they turned to emotional ones, laying on the pathos. The Associated Press syndicated Crosby's purported description of returning home on the *Queen Mary:* "As she steamed into the upper bay of New York, 1,000 American soldiers, all of them casualties and many without hands, arms or legs, begged to be brought topside to the forward deck. These boys hungered for a sight of their homeland and the Statue of Liberty, the epitome of all they had been fighting for, all they had sacrificed. I cried unashamedly along with them as the Manhattan skyline came into view and we passed Bedloe's Island where the Statue of Liberty stands. A fellow from San Diego who had lost both legs was near me as we sailed by. 'She's a great old girl,' he murmured in a choked voice. 'She was worth every bit of it.'" Did Crosby really say any of that? Did he mention the upper bay and Bedloe's Island and cry unashamedly? In the countless newspapers that ran the item, he did. But if so, he said it just the once; nothing like it exists in his correspondence or memoirs. However, news editors never worried overmuch about accurately quoting film stars.[17]

Cranky letters counted for a small percentage of his correspondence, those hundreds, possibly thousands of letters that reached him between fall 1944 and fall 1945. The majority of them came from bereaved parents, wives, siblings, or friends who in their grief found reason to write to *him*, the minstrel, the crooner. He unfailingly responded. The letters were markedly consistent. They often began with an avowal that this was the writer's first fan letter or that he or she wasn't really a fan but had to write him anyway; some apologized for the informality of addressing him as Bing and explained that he was regarded as a member of the family. They often closed with blessings for Dixie and the boys. A very few requested a signed photograph, but not as many as those that were seeking information: "Dear Sir, On October 9, the War Department reported my son missing in action in France. In his last letter to us, he said, 'Last night (September 8, 1944) I heard Bing Crosby sing.' I am wondering if at this late date censorship rules would permit, and if you would kindly give us, the location in France where you sang on the evening of September 8, 1944. If you can do this, it would bring a measure of satisfaction to his mother and me to know at least where in France our son was located." Others thanked him for the pleasure he had brought a loved one in France or elsewhere through his radio, records, and films. Most saw no light between the public Bing and the private Bing, if there was a private one. In Bing they trusted; given his ubiquitous appearances in all media, his devotion to golf and horses, his endlessly publicized handful of a family, how could he have found the time to be anything other but what he seemed?

Then there were his replies. All his life Bing fancied himself a writer in hiding, one who would one day find the time to test himself. He was proud of his vocabulary, of his ability to turn a phrase. But his linguistic talent was almost entirely verbal. Sitting before a blank page, he lacked every writerly attribute: insight, candor, observation, discernment, delineation, style, diligence, purpose. After the success in 1953 of *Call Me Lucky*, he made an attempt to compose portraits of the people in his life and produced a folder of lifeless sketches, each friend a character, each character the butt of an anecdote, all rendered featureless and dusty. Crosby himself is entirely absent, wiped out by a relentless modesty or dread of exposure. He was more successful in later years composing doggerel rife with inside jokes, set to music and recorded by Bing for various traveling companions.[18] But even this verse, amusing as it was to those who appreciated the allusions, lacked the wickedly funny rhymes he made up on the spot when a record session (for example, the 1939 "Wrap Your Troubles in Dreams"[19]) went awry, and it had none of the jazzy, conversational parlance and wit with which he narrated his life story to Pete Martin, a venture that required surprisingly little rewriting.

One passage in *Lucky* was not spoken. When they came to the USO excursion, Bing told Martin he would type a few pages of notes to get it right. The passage began with agonizing rectitude—"Sometimes, I have been asked what has been the most satisfying, rewarding experience in my career or my life"—and lightened up only to reduce the experience to yarns in which Crosby was the goat. Realizing that his gravity and flippancy shortchanged the experience, he offered his old wartime journal to Martin and encouraged him to use it any way he liked: "It may not even be a daily accounting, Pete. It might skip days. I don't know. But it tells about a lot of different groups, army groups that I visited and a lot of places. There are some little stories in there, things that happened to us. I think maybe if you read it over and pick out what you want maybe I can help you with it." Martin used none of it, nor did he query him about his correspondence.[20]

Yet in his private letters, particularly those driven by the war, Bing produced a body of writing with impressive confidence—brief, tone-perfect replies to those myriad letters from civilians, servicemen, friends, barely remembered acquaintances, officials ranging from government big shots to country-club treasurers, and the clergy. Here his diligence proved inexorable, as he spent a few hours daily in his home office penciling his responses on the bottoms of letters and attached sheets. If the letters were long, he underscored (often in red) the phrases that required or engendered specific responses. Each day's pile was picked up by a messenger from the Crosby Building on Sunset Boulevard so that his secretary Betty Eastman could type and mail them. The originals were returned when a new batch was collected and deposited in Bing's filing cabinets, desk drawers, and storage boxes. Notes of condolence, thanks, or mere acknowledgment hardly constitute an art form, but they are hard to do—greeting-card companies thrive on the millions who can't find the words. Most celebrities treat them as an obligation best delegated to an assistant. Crosby's responses were notable for a dearth of erasures and cross-outs. They are not drafts; Betty Eastman typed them faithfully. In 1947, he exchanged his pencil for a new innovation, the Dictabelt, and recorded his letters on thin, flexible vinyl loops to be transcribed. These belts were no less remarkable for an absence of revisions, do-overs, and silences. His authorial poise, boosted by equable, unsentimental frankness, was ideally suited to wartime missives.

Dear Mrs. T, I appreciate very much receiving excerpts from your son's letter concerning our appearance in England. I remember particularly the occasion, because of the sound system breaking down when the show was about two-thirds over, and we were forced to entertain to small groups of a few hundred or so, without benefit of mechanical support. That was at a place called Burtonwood, and they were a wonderful audience, in spite of the mishap....Dear Mrs. M, I share your sorrow on the loss of your son-in-law. It is particularly poignant to me, because we sailed on the same boat, the "Ile de France," which arrived in Glasgow on the 25th of August. Quite a number of men on the boat were encountered in France, some of them in the front lines, but I do not recall Lieutenant H. from your description. You were very kind to make such generous comment on my program and pictures....Dear Miss R, The incident you refer to occurred at a town called Charmes. The town had been in our hands about twenty-four hours and during the show a counterattack developed somewhere on the outskirts. Some of the units were summoned from the show to repulse this counter-attack. I hope your cousin turns up as a prisoner of war, and I will be praying for his early return to this country and to his family....Dear Lieutenant, If you are successful in bringing "Big Bing" home from over Berlin, I may give you the permanent job of bringing me home from the Palladium every Saturday night. Sometimes the going's a little rough and a good navigator would come in handy.[21]...Dear Mr. B, I regret very much to learn that your son has been reported missing in France. I have checked over what notes I made on my trip overseas, and to the best of my recollection it appears we entertained for your son's group at a Replacement Depot near Melun, France. We did three shows that day, all in the field, under perfect weather conditions and for a very responsive audience. He was doubtless sent to the front within the next day or so. Sorry this information is of such general character, but it is all I can provide....Dear Miss H, I wish I could tell you something specifically personal about your brother, but I honestly can't. We were kept so busy at all times, there was practically no opportunity to get to know the boys. I met him on a Paris street in September—about the 26th. Why he was there, I don't know—nor have I information on the other boys in the picture. To you and your family I extend my sincerest sympathy in your great loss.... Dear Corporal, You are very nice to send me the snapshots. I don't know where Einvaux is, but it seems to me it was somewhere near Commercy. We played in so many orchards that I am a little confused as to which was which. You really go back a bit on my career, don't you? I think the Brooklyn Paramount was a good thirteen years ago. Why didn't you tell me all this when we met in France? I would have bought you a couple drinks in an effort to keep you on my list of fans, which is rapidly dwindling with the advent of all these new boys. There isn't much I can do about it professionally because they all sing a little better than I do.[22]

Understated strength was inseparable from emotional reticence in his letters, as it was in his music. Yet in the context of the times, that combination wielded tremendous authority, as characterized in a letter to Crosby from a transport commander stationed in Antwerp. He wrote of that "quality in your voice which strikes to the bottom of the hearts of men. I have watched it happen, often, not just in the rare case but in many many thousands of men—sitting silent, retrospective, thoughts flying back to home and loved ones." He emphasized the singer's "power to soften the heart of the man who so shortly after goes back to shoot down his brother man," saying it was a determinant in helping to keep "our boys from turning into the beasts they are asked to be." This, he said, was "something big, something too big not to have you know and understand"—the "power of music, put into humble, throbbing words, as these fellows want it, need it, bow to it."[23]

This strikes a surprising, counterintuitive note. Despite the tears generated by Christmas anthems, Crosby is rarely singled out for the emotional tenor of his music. Emotion, verging on vulnerability, is a quality we associate with Billie Holiday and Frank Sinatra. Bing expressed inborn virility, secure and stoic; he did not invite listeners to inspect his insecurities. Dinah Shore caught the distinction between him and Sinatra: "Bing never pressed. He was always in tune. His phrasing was basically very good jazz phrasing, and yet he could sing a ballad. I don't know if he could make me weep like

Frank could make me weep. Ballad singers like Frank, you empathize with them and your heart breaks 'cause you're experiencing their heartbreak. Bing didn't do that to you. He had simplicity. It definitely had style, but there was no affectation. When he talked, it seemed like something he thought of at the moment, totally inspired, and he would get that quality in his singing—totally off the cuff and inspired. Bing was great. [But] he wouldn't let you see that deeply into his soul. Frank let you see an awful lot."[24]

Crosby's reserve was at the core of his success with the troops, on the air, at army camps, and in the fields of Europe. To sing to men separated from families and lovers and often starved of sexual companionship, he had to create a particular kind of bond, a zone of emotional safety. A zone has boundaries. Crosby's USO repertory faithfully stipulated what they were. For once, his customary aversion to I-love-you songs flattered the occasion; restraint carried more weight than amorous histrionics. He did not tour with any conventional love songs of the kind tendered by a guy to his gal, the kind that Sinatra successfully recorded in 1944. Such songs—"I Fall in Love Too Easily," "A Lovely Way to Spend an Evening," "Night and Day," "Nancy," "Saturday Night"—are aimed at women, not masses of lonely men, and could serve only to remind them of what they were missing. Bing sold millions of records of love songs—"Sunday, Monday, or Always," "I Love You," "People Will Say We're in Love," "Miss You," "Moonlight Becomes You"—and yet he left them at home. The only love songs he carried to war worked on parallel levels of nostalgia ("I'll Be Seeing You," "Easter Parade") and exotica ("Sweet Leilani," "Amor, Amor"), which he interspersed with the rhythmic humors of "San Fernando Valley" and "Swinging on a Star." He nurtured the emotions of male bonding, something evident even to his eleven-year-old son, Gary, who, when asked by a *New York Times* writer what he and his brothers thought of Sinatra, answered, "He's good. But the way we feel about it [he] sings for girls. But Pop, now, he's got a voice that men like." A few months earlier, one of Crosby's childhood idols, John McCormack, wrote in the same vein to a reporter: "Some of our favorite records here [Dublin] are those of my old friend Bing Crosby, who incidentally in his own line is by far the finest artist of all. His work is <u>clean</u> and <u>manly</u> like himself."[25]

*   *   *

Scribes nurtured the transformation of Crosby into living folklore. People had been telling Bing he was a great man for a long time and he invariably acted as if it were news to him, and not news he wanted to seriously consider. In 1944, the language inflation reached density usually reserved for eulogies, complete with a pious strain befitting the transformative *Going My Way*. Several months before the film opened, Gilbert Seldes, savant of popular culture, chronicler of *The Seven Lively Arts,* published his *Esquire* ode "The Incomparable Bing" and redrew the parameters of the conversation. Crosby, he argued, was "somehow a great man," although he gave the impression of "the amateur and the dilettante." He was the "Cosmopolitan American," the artist without temperament, *l'homme moyen sensuel,* the musical master of taste, intelligence, and tact in whose work one cannot "spot 'art' [or] pomposity or prestige." Like certain executives at Paramount, Seldes admitted he was "terrified" that this paragon of naturalness would shortly be seen playing a young priest, for Bing "shines through every effort to make him an actor." He hoped to be "reassured" by the new movie. After twenty years of Crosby, he found himself "untired; so is the rest of his radio, motion-picture, and record public." Seldes closed with cymbals clashing, selecting him as the "single talent" that best personifies "the kind of thing America can produce," the "kind of thing America cares for."[26]

In October, as Bing sailed home, *Metronome* devoted its entire issue to "Der Bingle," because "he has stepped far beyond the limited sphere of a singer of popular songs and become, as Will Rogers before him, a part of American life, an astonishingly successful symbol of the good man." Carroll Carroll, in an appreciation written for the reissue of Bing's early 1930s Brunswick recordings, expanded the historical allusions while willfully conflating art with the opium of the people: Bing belonged in a lineage with Will Rogers, George M. Cohan, Mark Twain, and "other earlier characters who didn't need a Gallup Poll to tell them what the people wanted because none of them ever forgot that he was one of the people." Since Crosby had averaged a new record every other week for the past ten years, selling in excess of seventy-five million records in the not quite two decades he'd been at it and thoroughly dominating radio play, "day in & day out, from coast to coast," *Time* calculated that his voice had been heard by more people than anyone else's in history.[27]

He figured large in the wartime equivalent of urban myths, some of which began with an element of truth that got stretched into gossamer and some that were quite preposterous. Some were syndicated in newspapers, others relegated to Chinese whispers. A soldier in New Guinea claimed he had been spared the bite of a four-foot-long death adder—its tail coiled and head raised, ready to strike—because a nearby radio had suddenly begun to play a Crosby recording, hypnotizing the snake long enough for him to borrow a machete and whack it in two. A wounded POW in Stalag IX-B, Bad Orb, Germany, dispirited, weak with hunger, hobbled suicidally to the camp's main gate when the camp speakers erupted with Bing singing "Blue Skies." His spirits rose in response to this "mystical or paranormal experience meant for me" and he "resolved then and there at the front gate to overcome any obstacles and make it back to the United States." A veteran of the Battle of the Bulge recalled hearing of a skirmish that came to a halt as both sides paused to listen to a broadcast of Bing's "Silent Night." A radioman posted in Manila who was interned with his wife for seventeen months in the Santa Tomas concentration camp after the fall of Bataan reported a "Recalled to Life" experience. On July 4, someone slipped Bing's version of *Ballad for Americans* on a camp phonograph; it imbued "Americans in distress with the feeling of home and the renewed determination to hang on."[28]

By December, the endless reiteration of his war stories, the handful of complaints, and his return to work helped to restore his public taciturnity but did nothing to slow his war work. After a full day at the U.S. Naval Hospital in San Diego performing with Bob Hope's radio cast and speaking personally (a reporter noted) with every man in the disabled and bedridden unit, he reconvened his USO team for a show at Hoff General Hospital, in Santa Barbara. That same week, he aired his Kraft program, recorded a Christmas show for the AFRS, played exhibition golf matches with Hope in Long Beach and Sam Snead in Santa Maria, and appeared on two *Command Performances* and a special broadcast for the WAVES. On Christmas Eve, he emceed the *Philco Hall of Fame,* performing with his USO team and the Paul Whiteman orchestra and reading Oscar Wilde's "The Happy Prince" with Orson Welles. When he arrived home, Bette Davis called to say a celebrity had reneged on a promise to star at the Hollywood Canteen's Christmas Eve show and the place was packed. Crosby drove his sons to Cahuenga Boulevard; after he and the boys exhausted their repertory of carols, Bing took requests for two hours. And so it went, a broadcast or appearance or exhibition match nearly every day until late February 1945, when he and McCarey finally went to work on a new project.[29]

The year closed with a plethora of plaques and prizes that culminated the following March when *Going My Way* swept the Academy Awards. Crosby did not figure in all the early awards for the film. Leo McCarey and the picture were cited by the New York Film Critics and the Golden Globes, which parted company in the acting category, choosing, respectively, Barry Fitzgerald and Alexander Knox (for *Wilson*). Fans protested the Crosby shutout, but he won everything else; nearly a dozen annual polls — *Film Daily, Redbook, Radio Daily, Look, Photoplay* — named him the top male star, singer, or entertainer of the year. The short-lived Interracial Film and Radio Guild, founded in 1944 to combat racial stereotypes and promote better roles for Negro actors, gave its IFRG Unity Award to Bing for "outstanding contributions to Interracial Harmony through the medium of radio." *Down Beat*'s readers voted him best male singer. *Billboard* calculated that he had had fifteen charted hits during the year, not including the reissue of "White Christmas," which surpassed two million in sales, and an unparalleled seven had reached number one.[30] The New York Newspaper Guild's Page One Awards honored him and twenty-three other newsmakers at its Madison Square Garden ball, among them Eisenhower, Eleanor Roosevelt, Ernie Pyle (posthumously), Bill Mauldin, Frank Capra, and Hank Greenberg. The one-shot GI Oscars, selected by soldiers in eight theaters of war and presented at the Walter Reed Hospital by recovering men, honored Crosby for "his rare ability in creating and delivering weapons designed to eliminate the mental heaviness attendant upon GIs." The most curious accolade came from the India Film Journalists' Association, Mysore City, in its first

22

DIAL O FOR O'MALLEY

What a gush of euphony voluminously wells!
How it swells!
How it dwells
On the Future!
          —Edgar Allan Poe, "The Bells" (1849)

While Bing traveled abroad in fatigues, Leo McCarey experienced the dread and elation that come with the fusion of deadline pressure and the knowledge that the whole world is at your door, waiting for the next offering. After several months of rumination, he gave into the demand for more Father O'Malley. During and after the filming of *The Bells of St. Mary's*, he would say, at different times, that his decision was made for him by boys overseas who wrote three hundred thousand letters asking for another *Going My Way*, or that he bit the bullet because of one letter from a naval chaplain named Father Pat Duffy. Duffy's letter exists, unlike the pleas of the three hundred thousand. The chaplain was stationed somewhere in the Pacific (in Duffy's words, "a stinking island on the equator...a veritable purgatory"), and he argued that McCarey had only touched on the mysteries of priestly vocation and ought to do more: "Are you now going to sit on your fanny and rest on your laurels, and revert to human love when you can translate the supernatural to them as very few can? You see, I am not asking you, Leo, I am showing you your duty."[1]

Duffy's letter made for a good story and alibi, but it was mailed in late September 1944, two weeks *after* Louella Parsons reported McCarey's resolve to "go into competition with himself" by dispatching the writer Ketti Frings to Notre Dame to gather data for his next RKO picture, *The Bells of St. Mary's*, in which Crosby would star when he returned from Europe. He would not use Barry Fitzgerald—"wouldn't be fair to Paramount"—but someday, Leo said, he would reteam the two men for a sequel. This was his way of making fully clear the real point of his newsflash, that *Bells* was another religious-themed picture but not, not, *not* a sequel.[2]

He had his reasons for insisting that the new picture did not take up where the previous one left off, but his secrecy irked Parsons. It was not until five months later, when the picture was about to start shooting and she interviewed its other star, Ingrid Bergman, that she learned of Father Chuck's return. Parsons noted that Bergman was "such a fine person—a credit to the motion picture industry" and that "if we had more women like Ingrid Bergman we'd have fewer divorces in Hollywood or in any other town," but she grumpily shared Leo's misdirection with her readers: "I had understood [the films] were not related, inasmuch as one was made for Paramount and the other is for RKO." McCarey had not been completely disingenuous. The film's few indications of chronology point to *Bells* as a prequel; its O'Malley is far more tentative than the supremely confident super-priest of *Going My Way*, its setting is the Midwest (O'Malley's home ground), and the war is all but invisible.[3]

McCarey had neither a story nor a cast when he gave the scoop to Parsons, but from the beginning he had in mind a character based upon his late aunt Sister Mary Benedict, and he was determined to do anything necessary to get Bergman, the most acclaimed actress of the decade, to play her. As Bergman's contract was owned by David O. Selznick, he had to do quite a lot in addition to paying an outsize ransom. Selznick hated sequels. He mulishly refused to loan her out for a picture that, as it was certain to fall short of its predecessor, could only weaken her luster and value. His serial demands included a year of rent-free space on the RKO lot and rights to three RKO pictures he had produced in the 1930s (*Little Women, A Bill of Divorcement,* and *Animal Kingdom*), confident that McCarey could not oblige him even if he wanted to. But Leo cleared every hurdle. The total value he paid Selznick in cash and properties came to $410,000.[4]

Leo needed *Bells* to be a commercial hit. His dream of an independent production company depended on it. Ten days before Crosby boarded the *Île de France*, McCarey incorporated Rainbow Productions with five other investors: Crosby, Buddy DeSylva, David Butler, Hal Roach Jr., and Bob Hope, who proved problematic—he was on suspension at Paramount and difficult to reach. Going over Selznick's head, Leo told the general idea of the picture directly to Bergman, who quickly accepted; Bing and McCarey were on her short list of people she wanted to work with, and Sister Benedict promised a delicious change after a spate of dramas in which she played women of dubious virtue. She threatened to move back to Sweden if Selznick did not allow her to do it, and he believed her. When Selznick asked her how she would emote while Crosby was singing, she responded, "I shall register radiance, adoration, perhaps perplexity."[5]

"I wrote a check to Ingrid Bergman the other day and my hand shook," Leo told a reporter. In truth, he wrote a check to Selznick for $175,000, of which Bergman received $50,000 and never complained. Even so, Selznick issued a press release that diminished the McCarey picture by mentioning it as one of two religious films on Bergman's schedule; the second would be an account of Mary Magdalene called *The Scarlet Lily* (it was never made, as Selznick could persuade neither Bergman nor the retired Greta Garbo to sign on to it).

McCarey had his leading lady and a sturdy $1.4 million budget (it would grow), nearly a third of which went to pay for his two stars. To guarantee completion, he agreed to sell his interest in *Going My Way* to Rainbow Productions for $1 million, payable in installments. The valuation was suggested by Frank Freeman, whose counsel McCarey had sought.[6] To craft a screenplay, he once again pursued a bestselling novelist associated with religious themes, this time A. J. Cronin (*The Keys of the Kingdom*), who declined. He then turned to the veteran screenwriter Dudley Nichols, renowned for nearly a dozen pictures with John Ford and other classics by Fritz Lang and Howard Hawks, now riding high after adapting and politically eviscerating *For Whom the Bell Tolls,* a box-office bonanza. The new year approached, and the picture obviously would not be ready to shoot on its announced February 15 starting date.[7]

Crosby shrugged off the usual delays. He probably looked forward to working at RKO as a respite from the unexpected turmoil at his own studio. He provided a flip rundown of the situation to Harry Ray, the respected if often uncredited makeup artist (Kim Novak in *Vertigo,* Jack Lemmon in *Some Like It Hot*), who before joining the navy had helped create the Paramount looks of Crosby, Hope, and Lamour. According to Bing, Ray had helped him overcome his aversion to cake makeup, which made his skin itch.[8]

> There have been many switches at Paramount since last you stole money there. The current boss of the joint is Ginsberg; Frank Freeman, according to Barney Dean, is going into vaudeville with his dogs. I guess you have heard that Hope is currently on suspension, and there's no immediate prospect of his difficulties being straightened out. I have just finished pulling him through a picture for Goldwyn, called *The Princess and the Pirate,* but I can't keep doing this forever, so he is fighting for only two pictures a year at Paramount instead of the four he contracted for. I imagine by the first of the year some sort of a compromise will have been worked out.[9]

Hope had triggered his suspension by refusing to show up to shoot a film. As well as wanting to reduce his picture count (he had signed to make three films per year, not four, plus an annual cameo), he wanted a salary increase and the right to launch a production company in the manner of Crosby. It took seven months, but he prevailed; Paramount could not withstand the bad publicity, which suggested that its greed interfered with Hope's war work. This was especially true after he received a life membership in the Academy of Motion Picture Arts and Sciences at the March Oscar ceremony dominated by *Going My Way.* (He said, "Now I know how President Roosevelt feels.")

The more remarkable story involved a change at the top, but that

attraction—after *Lady in the Dark* and *Going My Way*—to complete a nine-week run.[13]

Bob Hope's refusal to appear in the picture prompted the studio to assure the press that it had no such problems with Crosby, whose ten-year contract was the talk of the industry. Why, he even remained on the set until eleven thirty one evening to complete his number, saving the studio heavy overrun charges, and after that, when he dined at the Brown Derby, he picked up the tab for a couple of sailors. Compared to Hope, Crosby suddenly sported a company man's halo.[14]

Bing did not appear physically in *Out of This World*, which completed shooting shortly before *Duffy's Tavern*, but its one-joke script revolves around his voice, which magically drifts from the unlikely maw of Eddie Bracken. Both pictures were directed by Hal Walker, who made nine hits in seven years (including *Road to Utopia* and four Dean Martin and Jerry Lewis comedies) yet disappeared from the business in the 1950s, as did several actors he favored. Each studio had its share of performers who were popular in the 1940s but could not sustain screen stardom through the next decade. Paramount's troops included Bracken, Betty Hutton, Sonny Tufts, Veronica Lake, Diana Lynn, and such ancillary cutups as Cass Daley, Billy De Wolfe, and Olga San Juan. All the above appeared in *Duffy's Tavern* and four starred in *Out of This World*, movies that preserve the fickle tastes of wartime and have all but disappeared from modern memory.

Bracken, a stage veteran since the age of nine, became a star working with Hutton in *Star Spangled Rhythm* and *The Miracle of Morgan's Creek*. Permanently typed as a shy nebbish with a faltering adolescent voice, he disliked the script for *Out of This World* but agreed to do it, thinking it would boost him into musicals. He balked when he learned that Buddy Clark was set to dub his vocals. DeSylva insisted that the role demanded a crooner like Crosby or Sinatra, as their stardom inspired the plot, which involved women paid to swoon. Bracken told him to get Crosby or Sinatra; that, at least, would be funny. Frank Freeman, not a funny man, threatened him with suspension and a suit to recover three hundred thousand dollars in preproduction costs.

Bracken, who had a good rapport with Bing,[15] phoned him at home and said, "Would you listen five minutes to a very sad story and then make up your mind if you want to do something for me?" Crosby heard him out and said it was a cute idea and that Buddy should call him. DeSylva refused to waste time calling Bing, as he would never do it. Hal Walker made the call, mentioning an idea he had for a gag involving Bing's sons. Each would get a line: "Where have I heard that voice before"; "I was just thinking that"; "Aw, shucks, I'd rather hear that bow-tie guy sing anytime"; "You'd better not let Mother hear you say that." Bing agreed to record the score's three new songs by Harold Arlen and Johnny Mercer without payment, but he wanted $12,500 for each of the boys to be held in a college trust fund. Everyone was thrilled. The picture was a hit. DeSylva and Walker claimed credit for the cute idea, which they promoted: "The voice is Bing's... the tie belongs to the other guy...and it'll send you *Out of This World*." In the closing scene, Bracken interrupts his lip-synching and turns to the camera to say, "Thanks, Bing."[16]

The film would ultimately vanish, but the title song survived as a standard and produced Crosby's finest recording since his return, a richly stentorian, note-perfect rendition of a difficult, harmonically and melodically eerie seventy-two-measure melody, suitably fitted with fairy-tale lyrics about an armored knight, an enchanting Lorelei, a long and lonely nighttime, and eternity. The rhythm, alternating triplets and whole notes, takes on a dancing intensity in the second half, underscored by Trotter's pizzicato strings. Despite the picture's success, the recording evidently alienated listeners, a rare instance of Crosby going beyond their comfort zone. Over the years, singers and instrumentalists continued to tackle "Out of This World," none more imaginatively than John Coltrane, who fashioned its curious modality into a jazz classic, and none more precisely than Crosby, who honored it exactly as written.

Meanwhile, two of his efforts preceding the overseas tour reached theaters. In November, Samuel Goldwyn, distributing through RKO, released Hope's first color film, *The Princess and the Pirate,* which ends with Crosby's most roguish cameo. In the film's final seconds, Virginia Mayo appears to run toward Bob but then hurries by him and into the arms of Bing. He looks up at Hope and says, "Stick around, son, something older may show up for you." A couple of men from a naval training corps in Seattle wrote Crosby that they sat through two showings, but the laughter was so loud they couldn't hear his lines. Crosby sent them the last pages of the shooting script. After Hope wails about knocking his brains out for nine reels only to lose the girl to a "bit player from Paramount," Bing says, "Hush—go sell your rack-shellac [toothpaste]."[17] Sinatra's swooners triggered more laughs in the one Crosby vehicle to open that season, *Here Come the Waves,* filmed in the spring and released in December to surprisingly charitable reviews and solid returns. The director Mark Sandrich had vowed after *Holiday Inn* that he would make only war-related pictures for the duration, and he kept his word. This film was conceived in part to recruit women into the armed forces, and it was leavened with a little sex, a dash of satire, and sufficient idiocy—confused identities, imagined slights—to offend the intellects of Abbott and Costello. Those who feared that Crosby might fade into ecclesiastical dramaturgy were reassured; those who required a dose of blackface minstrelsy were gratified; and those who trembled before Betty Hutton's frothy volatility would find comfort in her nearly sedate twin, an alter ego made possible by special effects. Hutton was said to average eight hairdos a day, as she switched from her blond curls to her twin's auburn wig. Crew members appreciated Sandrich's ability to oversee her in two roles when, as the assistant director recalled, "she was always a handful in one."[18]

Here Come the Waves is a doltish film, but it looks great, thanks to the glistening cinematography of Charles Lang, and it gave Bing a chance to finally claim the song he had failed to get in *Star Spangled Rhythm,* "That Old Black Magic." In the movie, he croons it while drolly clutching a microphone as young women sigh and one is carried off on a gurney. Except for that scene and a set decorated by the peerless cartoonist Milt Gross, the best footage is made up of second-unit montages, shot at New York's Hunter College and in San Diego, of WAVES smartly marching in geometrical waves.

That the picture's feminist themes survive the romantic hysteria, of which the swooning is only a forewarning, may be credited to the fortitude of Lieutenant Commander (later Captain) Louise K. Wilde, known to her friends as Billie. Appointed as a representative of the Women's Reserve to ensure that the picture earned for the

WAVES the kind of respect that Sandrich's *So Proudly We Hail* achieved for army nurses, she dug in her heels at conferences and in correspondence to argue her concerns. Wilde agreed to a few compromises—the uniforms were authentic, despite Edith Head's sexy adjustments; hairstyles were short, if not quite regulation. But she persevered in her commitment to having the WAVES portrayed as serious women doing serious work.[19] Following a military screening, Wilde wrote Sandrich that everyone loved it, particularly the song "Ac-Cent-Tchu-Ate the Positive"—the blackface number performed by Crosby and Sonny Tufts. Conceived as a faux sermon, it is easily the best new song in the picture and the only one of five by Arlen and Mercer to endure as a standard. Some reviewers who singled it out (one wrote that its "maddeningly catchy" melody would endear it forever to "the hepcats") were too inured to minstrelsy to even mention that component. Nor did anyone mind the dialect-filled recordings of it by Crosby and the Andrews Sisters and by Mercer, which took turns as the bestselling discs in the nation. Today this scene seems more painful than the "historical" minstrelsy of *Dixie* for being set in the present day.[20]

The historian Paul Fussell observed, "Understanding the past requires pretending that you don't know the present." *Here Come the Waves* meant something in its day—grosses were huge, and it pleased people like James Agee, who dismissed it as "almost totally negligible" yet acknowledged he "would enjoy Crosby even if he did not amusingly kid Sinatra, and probably if he did nothing but walk across a shot." Most reviewers shared the enthusiasm of the *New York Times*'s Bosley Crowther, who described "attractive vistas and several gaily amusing jolts." Of all Crosby vehicles, this one has perhaps aged the least well.[21]

Crosby's home life was far more discontented than life at Paramount and would continue to deteriorate throughout the upcoming new year. Dixie's drinking and reclusiveness had begun to tell in the infrequent photographs she tolerated. This lovely, adored young woman—who eight years later, three days short of her forty-first birthday, would succumb to ovarian cancer—was a mere thirty-three, but her eyes were tired and heavy-lidded, her complexion wan, her smile pinched. She made a tenacious effort to socialize at the end of the year, going with Bing to Jack Benny and Mary Livingstone's black-tie bash on New Year's Eve and to Bob and Dolores Hope's lavish party (guest list of three hundred) the next afternoon. Later, her friends said the holiday festivities wore her down. She collapsed on January 9. Bing phoned her doctor, Jud Hummer, who insisted that she be taken to St. Vincent's Hospital. Bing accompanied his unconscious wife in the ambulance and sat by her side all afternoon. Before leaving, he told reporters, "She's going to be all right." Larry Crosby initially told reporters she had a bad cold. Hospital staff diagnosed a respiratory infection, possibly pneumonia, and admitted she was comatose; they put her in an oxygen tent.[22]

The papers covered her confinement for five days despite a lack of updates. The hospital would not commit itself beyond "incipient" pneumonia, with a remedy of an oxygen tent and penicillin. Dr. Hummer refused interviews. She remained in the hospital for nearly two weeks. When she was out of danger, Larry said, "Dixie was quite a sick girl for a while. She was unconscious the first couple of days, but we now are confident she's going to pull through." A relieved and shaken Bing credited her recovery to the miracle of penicillin. The scuttlebutt attributed her hospitalization to drugs and booze or an accidental (or not) overdose of sleeping pills.

Dixie managed to stay out of the public eye for nearly three months, until the day of the Academy Awards. These were the months in which almost every film fan magazine and several mainstream publications ran stories on the four boys and their entry into the movie business. These pieces were never entirely about the boys and their predictably cheeky cracks about Pop. Rather, they provided a new avenue to the ever-fascinating patriarch, the "No. 1 Pop" (*Movie Stars Parade*), the leader of the "Crosby Quintette" (*Modern Screen*), or the head of the "Crosby Team" (*New York Times*), the man who in June would be selected by the National Father's Day Committee as top Screen Father of 1945. The teaser to a Dick Mook article put the case boldly: "Best way to know Bing is to spend time with the Crosby kids."[23]

Bing seemed amenable to presiding over these interviews. Dixie rarely showed up; the *Times* portrait noted that she was still in the hospital recovering from pneumonia. He liked showing the boys off, especially in their spiffy school uniforms. All four were enrolled at St. John's Catholic Military Academy in the San Fernando Valley, an hour's drive from their house. Looking back, Gary could never decide if going to military school was a good thing or a bad one. On the one hand, he said, "We always had to have that discipline over our heads at all hours of the day and night. I mean, if Dad wasn't there to do it we had to go to Catholic school. If that wasn't enough we had to go to Catholic military school." On the other, it offered him "an escape route to freedom" through sports. At four ten and 107 pounds and heading into his teens, he played second-string guard on the middleweight football team. "For two hours a day, I could break loose from all that [discipline]. I could put on a uniform and kick ass and hit and run and learn things that were important and enjoyable." But he soon connected with a coterie of drinkers. His grades fell. According to Phillip, who likewise recalled the sports and not the academics, Gary began to swan around with attitude. They both recalled battling their way through recess periods because they were sons of a movie star—"Honest fights," Phillip clarified, "no kneeing or kicking, nothing like that. Then we got bored. Me and Denny were tough little kids."[24]

The brothers were toughest on one another. Jack Haley Jr. attended St. John's in the same years, in the grade between Gary and the twins. His mother drove him to school and picked him up every day, as Dixie or the family chauffeur did for the Crosby boys. Jack grew friendly with Gary and one afternoon he asked his mother if he could sometimes go back with the Crosbys; they could easily drop him off at his house on their way home. As the Haley station wagon pulled onto the freeway directly behind the Crosby station wagon, she said she would think about it. After a short while they saw the boys embroiled in a terrific fight in the backseat. "One of them kicked out the rear window. My mother said, 'You're not going home with the Crosby boys.'"[25]

Louella Parsons asked Bing how he kept the boys in line. He readily answered, "Good old spanking routine. There isn't a week goes by that one of 'em doesn't get a good spanking, but I leave their upbringing mostly to their mother." Later she reflected, "He's a far stricter father than the average and the kids hop when he says something. But in his seemingly careless way he's crazy about them. He can't stand the idea of the children not being well mannered when there the cathedral menacingly months later in Val Lewton's Boris Karloff period piece *Bedlam*) and industrial modernism. Other than McCarey, the man who had the greatest influence on the look and visual mood of the film was the much-married (seven wives), short-lived (he died of heart failure at sixty) cinematographer George Barnes. A veteran of the movie business and the mentor to Greg Toland, who honed deep-focus photography, Barnes was an innovator of photographic expressiveness and focused panning. He was equally stylish in both monochrome (*Jane Eyre, Spellbound, Force of Evil*) and color (*The Spanish Main, Samson and Delilah*, the awesomely prismatic *The War of the Worlds*). Barnes brought to *Bells* a sunny clarity, in contrast to Lionel Lindon's darker scheme in *Going My Way*, suitable to the story's lighter nature and the relatively artless, more youthful-looking O'Malley. With the special-effects expert Vernon Walker, Barnes created dissolves and other optical effects, such as when Benedict and Bogardus (the businessman played by Henry Travers) imagine what they would do with St. Mary's property. But the film's best special effects are what Barnes achieved in lighting extraordinary faces, particularly the sustained elegiac close-up of Bergman's final supplication. Crosby recognized Barnes as a stylish alternative to Lindon and used him repeatedly, more than any other cinematographer after Karl Struss in the 1930s. Of eighteen films he made in the decade beginning with *Going My Way*, fourteen were shot by Barnes or Lindon.

On Valentine's Day, Leo McCarey finally had a detailed, working script. Its cover page has no ascription of authorship but gives fair warning of what it is in two parentheticals: *Rough Draft* and *Being Used as Final*. Paramount—or any studio, for that matter—would have insisted on something more definitive before sanctioning a start-up, but this was a Rainbow Productions film, and the great improviser had no need to pretend that the 131-page screenplay was much more than a general game plan. In the course of shooting, scenes would be shifted, dropped, invented; the dialogue endlessly revised, often radically. The most famous scene in the film—a Nativity play performed by first- and second-graders—runs five and a half minutes but is keyed in the script by merely a one-sentence prompt: "He [O'Malley] witnesses a play, written by children, which is so simple and beautiful that he realizes it is far more effective than any plan he might have had for a Christmas celebration."

This scene is unlike anything else in American movies. When it came time to shoot, McCarey worked only with young Bobby Dolan, asking him to teach the story to the other children. "You're Joseph," McCarey explained, "and this little girl is Mary, and you want to get a room in Bethlehem. What would you say?" "I'd go up to the hotel and say, 'Knock, knock. I'm Joseph and this is Mary and we want a room.'" Leo told him to say it just that way: "I'll fix it so the second hotel you try will let you in." They discussed a carol to end the scene and Bobby suggested "Happy Birthday." McCarey told him to rehearse the play with the kids and left the set. But George Barnes filmed everything with two or three cameras as McCarey peeked through a window. There were interruptions for bathroom breaks, but they nailed it in a day. Later McCarey inserted the reaction shots of Crosby and Bergman. The footage delighted everyone except the head of RKO, Charles Koerner, who feared it would offend Catholics. He leaked a print to the Hearst estate. "When word came from San Simeon, that citadel of good taste, that the Nativity sequence was offensive," McCarey recalled, "the head of the studio decided to leave it out." Leo screened it for a bishop, who loved the scene. He launched a campaign of letters and telegrams to restore it and won the day.[30]

A week after the film started shooting, Joe Breen belatedly read the draft screenplay and groused about a major element. Much of the plot revolves around the problematic girl Patsy and her unmarried parents. Breen had no objection to the father who had abandoned his pregnant fiancée thirteen years earlier. But he was appalled that the mother is "hardly more than a prostitute and the girl herself is an illegitimate child." He found particularly offensive the implication that O'Malley, in marrying the couple, condoned "the acts of the erring woman." McCarey brushed him off with a reminder that the script was a draft.[31]

Even so, he did little to soften the situation. McCarey's original draft reads, "She eloped with Patsy's father when she was young, but they were never married and...her life became a succession of men." Martha Sleeper plays the mother with remarkable naturalness, rivaling that of Crosby, who hears her out and, as the novelist Mary Gordon wrote in an appraisal of the O'Malley pictures,

Costumed for a vaudeville number with Bob Hope in *Road to Utopia*, **Bing** heads for the soundstage accompanied by his sons: Lindsay (front) with (left to right) Gary, Dennis, and Phillip. (*HLC Properties, Ltd.*)

Dixie reverted to her natural hair color when the military police battalion at Ford Ord in Monterey designated her captain of Company B. Photograph by Emmett D. Griggs. (*HLC Properties, Ltd.*)

Bing invariably got a big laugh when, in response to the line "A voice like Sinatra's comes along once in a lifetime," he deadpanned, "Why did it have to be my lifetime?" (*HLC Properties, Ltd.*)

Hope and Crosby competed for wisecracks and often succeeded in cracking each other up, as at this *Kraft Music Hall* broadcast. (*HLC Properties, Ltd.*)

James Cagney (right), 1943, was surprised to learn during the Victory Caravan that Bing's "apparent effortlessness was a part of his very hard work." (*HLC Properties, Ltd.*)

An audience of twenty thousand launched the 1944 Fifth War Loan at the Hollywood Bowl, a night of mostly classical music, though you wouldn't know it from the program cover. Clockwise from top left: Ginny Simms, Bing, Ella Mae Morse, James Melton. (*Gary Giddins Collection*)

Frank Sinatra and Bing Crosby sing "People Will Say We're in Love," as Bob Hope looks on, 1944. (*HLC Properties, Ltd.*)

Barney Dean, Crosby's ubiquitous (Jewish) jester, posed with him for a gag photo at the start of *Going My Way,* 1943. Photograph by John Miehle. (*HLC Properties, Ltd.*)

Director Leo McCarey, arms outstretched at the top of the stairs, prepares for the entrance of Bing's Chuck O'Malley (in straw boater at the bottom of the stairs), in *Going My Way.* (*HLC Properties, Ltd.*)

On a break from shooting *Going My Way,* Bing demonstrates his dexterity on the bicycle he invariably used to get around the Paramount lot, 1943. (*HLC Properties, Ltd.*)

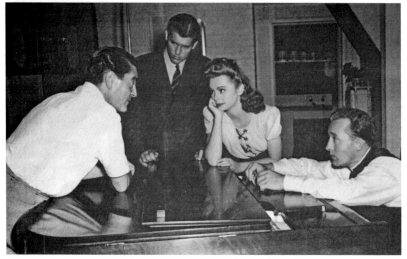

Leo McCarey directs the scene in which Father O'Malley sings "Going My Way" after recalling his days with a jazz ensemble. Left to right: McCarey, Jim Brown, Jean Heather, Bing, 1943. (*HLC Properties, Ltd.*)

"Believe it or not," the former Jenny Tuffel tells her long-ago beau from St. Louis, Chuck O'Malley, "I'm Carmen." Bing Crosby and Risë Stevens rehearsing for *Going My Way,* 1943. (*HLC Properties, Ltd.*)

Barry Fitzgerald and Bing in *Going My Way*. Alexander Knox, who competed with them for the year's acting honors, later predicted that those who saw the film would "carry with them for the rest of their lives some vivid recollection of Mr. Fitzgerald." (*HLC Properties, Ltd.*)

Bing at the piano leads the boys' choir in *Going My Way*'s "Swinging on a Star." Their audience includes (left to right) Fortunio Bonanova, Risë Stevens, and Frank McHugh. (*HLC Properties, Ltd.*)

Among the awards collected by *Going My Way* were Gold Medal loving cups presented by the English magazine *Picturegoer*. Left to right: Leo McCarey, Barry Fitzgerald, Bing, and producer Hal Wallis (who won for *Watch on the Rhine*). Photograph by Bill Dudas. (*HLC Properties, Ltd.*)

March 15, 1945, Dixie and Bing arrive at Grauman's Chinese Theatre for the seventeenth presentation of the Academy Awards. (*HLC Properties, Ltd.*)

Inside Grauman's, the Crosbys' neighbor Alan Ladd looks on with a smile as Dixie and Bing peruse the Academy Awards program. (*HLC Properties, Ltd.*)

Afterward, Barry Fitzgerald, Ingrid Bergman (named best actress for *Gaslight*), and Bing pose for newspapers with their temporary plaster Oscars. (*HLC Properties, Ltd.*)

The gold dust twins go incognito: Bob Hope and Bing in the *Road to Utopia*, completed in 1944 and released in 1946. (*HLC Properties, Ltd.*)

A lesson in tactful publicity: the discerning use of the words "magic," "artistry," and "genius." (*Judy Schmid Collection*)

Ingrid Bergman's Sister Mary Benedict and Bing's Father O'Malley offered different approaches to surrogate parenting in *The Bells of St. Mary's*, 1945. (*HLC Properties, Ltd.*)

It's a wrap for *The Bells of St. Mary's.* Left to right: Leo McCarey, Bing, Ingrid Bergman, and Barney Dean (behind Bergman's left shoulder). (*HLC Properties, Ltd.*)

Bing helped out his friend Eddie Bracken by dubbing the vocals for his comedy about an unlikely crooner in *Out of This World,* 1945. (*HLC Properties, Ltd.*)

Bing takes up ironing in *Here Come the Waves,* 1944. The spirited cartoonist Milt Gross drew the backdrop. (*HLC Properties, Ltd.*)

Fred Astaire has designs on Joan Caulfield, who has eyes for Bing Crosby, in Irving Berlin's surprisingly gloomy 1946 blockbuster, *Blue Skies*. (*HLC Properties, Ltd.*)

Bing insisted on casting Joan Caulfield in *Blue Skies*, and she held her own though she had no training as a musical performer. (*HLC Properties, Ltd.*)

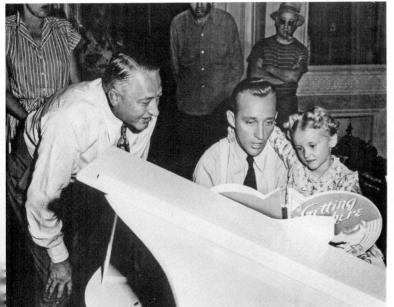

The director Stuart Heisler rehearses Bing and Karolyn Grimes in the Irving Berlin song that seemed to describe the *Blue Skies* script, "(Running Around in Circles) Getting Nowhere." (*HLC Properties, Ltd.*)

Joan Caulfield brought out a romantic quality in Bing, rarely seen before *Blue Skies*. (*HLC Properties, Ltd.*)

Overseas Unit No. 329 on the Foxhole Circuit, 1944. Left to right: comedian Joe DeRita, accordionist Earl Baxter, singer Jeanne Darrell, Bing, guitarist Buck Harris, and dancer and singer Darlene Garner. (*HLC Properties, Ltd.*)

Heer shpreekht Bing Crosby at a microphone in London's American Broadcasting Station in Europe (ABSIE), singing phonetically transcribed German, backed by pianist Jack Russin. (*HLC Properties, Ltd.*)

On August 31, 1944, Bing participated in two much-heralded evening shows, a broadcast with Glenn Miller (left) on the bandleader's *American Band of the AEF,* and the opening night of London's Stage Door Canteen. (*HLC Properties, Ltd.*)

Bing played only two golf courses during his European tour, both on the same day and both in Surrey, preceding his evening show at the Queensberry All-Services Club. (*HLC Properties, Ltd.*)

Bing entertained thousands of fliers in a Burtonwood hangar on the day after his harrowing visit to the burn ward to sing to four preschoolers who barely survived the Freckleton disaster. (*HLC Properties, Ltd.*)

Bing and Dinah Shore, whose paths occasionally crossed during the USO tours, visited with General George S. Patton during the ongoing Metz campaign. (*HLC Properties, Ltd.*)

Bing and Dinah trade lines in Châlons, performing on the open flatbed of a USO truck. (*HLC Properties, Ltd.*)

Bing and Joe DeRita relaxing between shows, and (below) with Darlene Garner on a stage created out of K-ration crates and a dance mat. Photograph by the Army Signal Corps. (*HLC Properties, Ltd.*)

Bing and Fred Astaire arrived in Cherbourg together and improvised several shows before Bing was directed to Patton's Third Army and Fred to Bradley's First. They sailed home together on the *Queen Mary*. (*HLC Properties, Ltd.*)

Bing, seen here in Melun, soon became inured to jeep travel, even when inadvertently driving into German-held territory: "Well," he would later insist, "we had it for two minutes." (*HLC Properties, Ltd.*)

During a downpour near Nancy, Crosby and his accompanists (Earl Baxter and Buck Harris) sing under a protective tarpaulin erected by men of the Thirty-Fifth Infantry Division, also known as the Santa Fe, three miles from the front. (*HLC Properties, Ltd.*)

Returning to England, Bing enjoyed a night of R & R with a party that continuously waxed in number, eventually including Marlene Dietrich. Left to right: Earl Baxter, Buck Harris, Colonel Clarence Shoop, Elliott Roosevelt (FDR's carousing son), and Bing. (*HLC Properties, Ltd.*)

Bing's return to New York was made official with his October 12, 1944, press conference at the Waldorf Astoria. He refused to pose with a Nazi flag but agreed to sit at the piano and don a German helmet. (*HLC Properties, Ltd.*)

Bing was shooting *Blue Skies* when pandemonium broke out: Japan had surrendered. The crowd of Paramount workers shouted his name, and a siege ladder appeared so that Crosby could X out the third malignant helmet, representing Tojo. (*HLC Properties, Ltd.*)

Bing spent the last month of 1945 and the first of 1946 in New York, shadowed by Mary (left) and Violet Barsa, sisters who often wore matching outfits in reverse color schemes. Bing and the Barsas became lifelong friends. (*Pamela Crosby Brown Collection*)

Bing was careful not to be photographed with Joan Caulfield in New York but was happy to pose with other friends, including actress Nanette Fabray, with whom he danced at the Stork Club (left), and singer Patrice Munsel, backstage at the Metropolitan Opera on her opening night as Gounod's Juliet. (*Courtesy Nanette Fabray; HLC Properties, Ltd.*)

Bing spent several evenings at New York's sundry nightclubs, especially the Stork, where he evidently drank Cokes with the eminent Manhattan chronicler Damon Runyon (left) and the singer who preceded Crosby as a national radio star, Morton Downey. (*HLC Properties, Ltd.*)

Although Crosby made front-page news as part owner of the Pittsburgh Pirates, he stayed loyal to his alma mater, for which he suited up with his sons in 1950. Left to right: Lindsay, Bing, Gary, Dennis, and Phillip. (*HLC Properties, Ltd.*)

Dixie accompanied Bing (and Barney Dean, sitting behind her) to the track at Santa Anita in 1945. Despite increasing rumors of "strained relations," they remained together. (*HLC Properties, Ltd.*)

"doesn't bat an eye or suggest that she find another line of work." Her character is plausibly what the Jean Heather figure in *Going My Way* might have become without O'Malley's intervention. McCarey's only concessions to Breen were deleting a scene in which the couple secretly goes off to marry and the last two words of Patsy's line "Is it my real daddy this time?" As the father, William Gargan helped appease the censor with sustained sheepishness called for in the script, especially when his piano backs O'Malley's stately rendition (better than Bing's ensuing record) of "In the Land of Beginning Again."[32]

One of the picture's best-remembered scenes involves Sister Benedict teaching a boy to box after he turns the other cheek and is bloodied for it. O'Malley sides with the victor—it's a man's world, he says. "How," Sister asks, "are they doing, Father?" Still, she shops for a boxing manual. The written template for the next scene has her instructing the boy in bobbing, weaving, and footwork and climaxes with her entreaties for him to throw a punch: "Don't worry, I won't be there"—an old joke (used in *The Milky Way*), though not with a nun taking it on the chin. McCarey insisted she play the scene without rehearsal.[33]

They shot it a few times with two cameras, one stationary and one mobile. The finished scene is five minutes long with no editing in the first eighty-six seconds and very little after that. This episode in particular moved Bergman to praise McCarey as the kind of director who can "give you marvelous ideas that you've never thought of." McCarey called her "my springboard." Unfortunately, he had another springboard, one he was loath to credit. He had found the idea for the scene in *Story* magazine: "Fight for Sister Joe" by Richard Coleman. To avoid a charge of plagiarism, he paid a thousand dollars to use it, with the proviso that Coleman receive no screen credit. Still, McCarey kept telling people that the sequence was strictly autobiographical, inspired by the time his Ursuline aunt taught him to box.[34]

One of the indelible lines of 1940s cinema, uttered by O'Malley first in a convocation speech and later in the closing scene, is not in the film's screenplay. In the convocation speech, it goes: "If any of you are ever in trouble, no matter what, just dial O for O'Malley."

Although *The Bells of St. Mary's* takes place in a school, not a church, a signal plot contrivance echoes *Going My Way*: a crusty old businessman wants to turn St. Mary's into a parking lot for his new office building across the way. Sister Benedict expects to pray him into a different frame of mind that will incline him to donate the office building and adjoining land to the school. Throughout the picture, the *in loco* parents O'Malley and Sister Benedict compete in the rearing of children—or, as Dudley Nichols put it in his treatment, "The mother and the father try to outwit each other in how the family should be trained." O'Malley is a liberal dad who casually declares a holiday (in violation of state law); argues against failing a child who apparently cannot do the classwork; defends the manly art of self-defense; and keys the gruff businessman's change of heart with a rather underhanded psychological trick involving his health, thereby sidestepping the need for prayer. Benedict is a no-nonsense if improbably radiant matriarch (would that we were all perpetually framed by George Barnes's lighting) accustomed to having her way who believes that bending the rules renders them useless. Each is at times right without either being wrong. In *The Fall*, Camus describes charm as "a way of getting the answer yes without having asked any clear question." Crosby/O'Malley and Bergman/Benedict have such charm in spades.[35]

Until, that is, O'Malley learns that Benedict is ill and must be moved to a dry climate. In a failure of nerve (and a deus ex machina) inconceivable for the O'Malley of *Going My Way*, he accedes to the doctor's medically unsound insistence that she not be told she is ill or why she is to be transferred from St. Mary's to a place where she will not be allowed to work with children. She believes O'Malley is exercising the bullying prerogatives of male power, and he almost allows her to leave St. Mary's believing that.[36]

The last page of the script reads:

FATHER O'MALLEY: Wait! Wait, Sister! Driver! I can't let you go this way! There's something wrong with you, but it's not that serious! Sister, although I've never wanted to, it seems like ever since I came here I've been holding out on you. Remember when you said I had a dishonest face?

SISTER BENEDICT: But you know I didn't mean it.

FATHER O'MALLEY: Oh! But you had a point there!

SISTER BENEDICT: But strangely enough, Father, if I did, that expression is lacking now.

FATHER O'MALLEY: I've been holding out on you again. Doctor McKay told me what he didn't tell you—that you have a touch of tuberculosis. That's why—Arizona. He said you shouldn't be around children for a little while.

SISTER BENEDICT: Thank you, Father, thank you! I'll get well very quickly now!

FATHER O'MALLEY: You can go now, driver! That's all!

The grotesque number of exclamation points alone signifies melodramatic drivel. Here's how the actors, fully conversant with their roles under McCarey's confident direction, play the last scene in the film. Other than O'Malley's call to the departing sister, everything is understated, economical, quietly intimate:

FATHER O'MALLEY: Sister Benedict! I can't let you go like this. You know when Doctor McKay said you were perfect he was right, for that's what you are. But he didn't mean physically. Because, Sister, you have a touch of tuberculosis. Doctor McKay felt that you shouldn't know about this, but I've...

SISTER BENEDICT: Thank you, Father. Thank you. You've made me very happy. I'll get well quickly now.

FATHER O'MALLEY: Of course you will, Sister. If you ever need anything, no matter where you are...

SISTER BENEDICT: Yes. I know. I just dial O for O'Malley.

FATHER O'MALLEY: Right.

Not a dry eye in the house. No one did endings better than McCarey, and this one is in the pantheon with *Make Way for Tomorrow, The Awful Truth, Love Affair,* and *Going My Way.* It is perhaps more resonant than the last, which unites an elderly man and his mother in the chill of winter. Here we have the parting (probably for good, not unlike the elderly couple in *Make Way for Tomorrow*) of a man and woman in the spring of their lives, sharing a chaste love and understanding that will bind them always.[37]

*   *   *

The filming went smoothly. Visitors to the set shook their heads in admiration of McCarey's insouciant piano-playing intervals and sudden inspirations that appeared to alter the story entirely. "Neither precedent nor occult science," a feature writer observed, "could predict the play of his imagination from one scene to the next." That there may have been tension offscreen is suggested by McCarey's two run-ins with the police, both allegedly fueled by alcohol, one triggered when he drove down an up-ramp and lost control of his car. Yet to the end of his days he recalled the filming as an oasis of unspotted pleasure: "God had his arm around me."[38]

Bergman, accustomed to costars and directors falling in love with her, was stymied by Crosby, who did not respond to whatever romantic intimations she may have dangled. Years later, returning to America after a seven-year exile mandated by national outrage at her adulterous affair with Roberto Rossellini (Colorado senator Ed Johnson thundered in the language of Salem, "Out of the ashes of Ingrid Bergman will arise a better Hollywood!"), she blamed her shyness for her failure to enter the private lives of her leading men: "Bing Crosby, for example, was one of the most charming, most relaxed persons I have ever worked with, but I never knew him or his wife or his children." This was disingenuous; stars meeting on a soundstage rarely socialized with each other's families, and her love affairs with Gary Cooper and Victor Fleming indicated she had no interest in doing so. She elaborated in a memoir she published after Crosby's death: "He was very polite and nice, and couldn't have been more pleasant," but he was always "chattering away and protect[ed]" by his "gagmen." She turned instead to McCarey, with whom she did develop a lasting friendship. During her banishment, he tried to launch a film about Adam and Eve for her.[39]

Crosby had fond memories of working with her. His sense of the dynamics on set differs from hers. "A great sense of humor, that Bergman," he told Pete Martin in the time of her exile. "[She was] very fond of Leo and one of the hardest-working women I've ever seen. She'd be the first on the set and the last one to leave. She would talk every scene over with Leo after we got through working." Her fondness for a hearty repast reminded him of the intoxicated afternoons working with Marion Davies on *Going Hollywood* in 1933. "She had a bungalow with a kitchen in it and she had her cook come over and cook a smorgasbord with aquavit. Swedish liquor can be pretty filling and, of course, it was so delicious it was hard to turn down. On days she served the smorgasbord there wasn't much work done that afternoon. It was siesta time. We were grateful to her for going to all the trouble to make our noon hours a little different."[40]

A quarter of a century later, Bing conceded, "I was in awe of that lady before I worked with her and even during the period we worked together, because of her great ability. She's a marvelous lady— great ability to communicate." She had the most "composure" of any actor he knew: "We were making a scene in the picture, she was at the blackboard, talking to her class, standing at the blackboard and drawing things, and one of those big lights fell from quite a height. I guess it weighed several hundred pounds, and it came right down, just grazed her and hit the floor with a terrible crash. She didn't move a muscle, didn't bat an eye, just moved aside to let them clear away the debris and went right back into the scene. Most leading ladies would have gone home for the weekend, I'm sure, been in a state of shock. She never moved a muscle. Shows you how disciplined she is."[41]

Personal taste and awe aside, Crosby had four strong motives for keeping their relationship professional. First, there was his conviction that you save everything for the screen, backed by his working method of a decade. Second, there was the sensitive subject of the picture, which could easily be dismantled through offscreen rumor or on-screen innuendo. "We had mail from people who took exception to the position that these two people were put into," he explained. "I think Leo handled it very delicately and was careful all through the shooting of the picture that no such innuendo would be perceptible." Third, his longtime friend Gary Cooper had made no secret of his love affair with Bergman during *For Whom the Bell Tolls* or his anguish when she ended it. Fourth, Crosby had met another woman on the lot who looked remarkably like the young Dixie Lee, and he was smitten. Hardly anyone knew how smitten yet, but he pressed for her to play opposite him in the film he was scheduled to make with Mark Sandrich and Irving Berlin directly after *Bells*—though he uncharacteristically waived his right to approve the leading lady beyond consultation ("the final decision of [the studio] shall be binding on you")—despite the fact that the part required a dancer, and Joan Caulfield could not dance.[42]

On March 4, the first Sunday during the shooting of *The Bells of St. Mary's,* Mark Sandrich died, at the age of forty-four, and his sudden death shook Hollywood and particularly Paramount. He suffered a massive heart attack, not in the pressure dome of prepro-duction but at home, playing gin rummy with his wife. A greatly liked man and a much-admired director and producer, he had until recently served as fourth president of the Directors Guild. At the time of his death, he was working on two projects: producing the Academy Awards show, which would be presented in his honor eleven days later, and preparing the most expensive picture on Par-amount's upcoming schedule, the three-million-dollar Technicolor extravaganza *Blue Skies,* featuring Berlin's vast songbook and Crosby. This time Bing would share billing not with Fred Astaire but with two performers unknown to moviegoers: the nightclub dancer Paul Draper, for whom Sandrich had argued mightily, and Caulfield, the Broadway ingenue eager to escape her current status of starlet. That project was now in abeyance.

On March 15, McCarey closed the set early. It was Thursday, so Crosby was rehearsing the *Kraft Music Hall* airing that evening, after which he and Leo and Ingrid and everyone else of note in Hollywood would be at Grauman's Chinese Theatre at eight sharp for the seventeenth annual presentation of the Academy Awards. *Going My Way* had garnered nine nominations—in all the major categories except for actresses—and everyone expected it to tri-umph despite a relentless campaign by Darryl Zanuck for his dra-matically inert fiasco *Wilson.*[43] The only contest for which *Going My Way* was not considered a shoo-in was best actor. Barry Fitzger-ald was uniquely nominated in both the lead actor and supporting actor categories, and he had a grip on the town's sympathy; weeks before, he had been acquitted of vehicular manslaughter at a trial in which the judge lambasted the district attorney for pursuing the charge. Some observers thought that even if he won the supporting

actor Oscar, he and Crosby might split the best actor votes, allowing *Wilson*'s Alexander Knox to slip through.

But as eight o'clock approached, even Crosby felt confident. He
left *KMH* after the broadcast in a good mood. The show's music
had been mostly upbeat; Bing sang six songs, and other numbers
featured Artie Shaw's Gramercy Five, the Charioteers, and Eugenie
Baird. He drove home to change and pick up Dixie, who was making her first public appearance in three months. "I had heard there
was some chance that I'd get an award," he recalled. "I never took
it too seriously, but down towards the last it looked like I had a real
good chance, and I took it seriously enough to put on a dinner
jacket, which indicates that I really felt it was going to be in there
for me." In fact, he dressed to the nines: brown double-breasted
suit over a light blue shirt and a busily striped tie with a scarf hanging casually from his overcoat pocket, a pipe in his hand, and his
fedora pulled down over his left eye. He held the arm of a radiant
Dixie, beautifully made up with her hair styled in blond waves and
wearing a full-length mink and white gloves, an orchid at her
shoulder. The crowd of five thousand fans jamming Hollywood
Boulevard — the biggest turnout for the event since Pearl Harbor —
went wild when they arrived.[44]

Another two thousand people filled Grauman's. Thanks to Sandrich's innovations, this event launched features that have remained
standard fare for every Oscar night since. For the first time, a "cin-
ematage" — a montage of clips from each of the nominated films —
was presented, as was an elaborate musicale featuring the Andrews
Sisters and Danny Kaye, though it occurred to no one to have them
perform the nominated songs. The musical interlude served as an
intermission between the technical honors and the starrier awards,
introduced by Bob Hope and broadcast in their entirety on the
inconsequential Blue Network (which would soon be renamed ABC
and become a major player with the acquisition of Crosby's radio
show). Given that the broadcast was live, Hope was told to discourage anyone who embarked on a long speech. No one did.

Going My Way won every category except cinematography and
editing. "Swinging on a Star" was the first of fourteen nominations
for Jimmy Van Heusen and the first of four wins. Leo McCarey
made Oscar history as the first recipient of two awards in the same

evening, for director and original story, while his writers Frank Butler and Frank Cavett won for the screenplay. Barry Fitzgerald received the biggest hand of the evening, accompanied by whispers of surprise that he didn't look nearly as old as Father Fitzgibbon. Still, the main "hunk of sentiment" focused on the best actor category. Never one to concede nervousness, Bing remembered that Gary Cooper opened the envelope and "gave a look down at me with a sly smile and I knew what was coming. A great warm feeling came over me and I stumbled up on the stage in a kind of vacuum. I don't even remember what I said." No one saw him stumble, and his remarks were graceful and brief: "This is really a land of opportunity when Leo McCarey can take a broken-down crooner like me and lead him by the hand so he can wind up with a piece of happy crockery like this statue. Now if he'd find me a horse to win the Kentucky Derby, it would be the greatest parlay in history." The pundits noted, with admiration or astonishment, that he appeared without "his movie toupee," while "getting balder by the moment." "He was that way about the whole thing," Harrison Carroll later noted, "the same old easygoing Bing."[45]

The lead actress category came next. Bergman won for *Gaslight*. She had lost to Jennifer Jones the previous year, and now Jones handed her the statuette with a line probably written by Jones's lover and soon-to-be-husband, David O. Selznick: "Your artistry has won our votes and your graciousness has won our hearts." Bergman told the audience, "I'm deeply grateful for this award and I'm particularly glad to get it at this time, because I am working on a picture with Mr. Crosby and Mr. McCarey at present and I'm afraid that if I went on the set tomorrow without an award, nobody would speak to me." *Going My Way* won for best picture. Buddy DeSylva accepted the award, and although Buddy no longer presided over Paramount, Hope, still on suspension, convulsed the house by falling to his knees to plead for forgiveness and polish DeSylva's shoes.

Going My Way delivered to Paramount its first prize for best picture since *Wings*, in 1927, the ritual's inaugural year. The film's seven Oscars represented a transitional moment in the academy's history, between pictures concerned with the war (*Mrs. Miniver*, *Casablanca*) and those delineating domestic ills (*The Lost Week-*

end, The Best Years of Our Lives, Gentleman's Agreement). Going My Way made America feel proud, and *The Bells of St. Mary's* would sustain the high in that brief window before peacetime paranoia rattled Hollywood's cage and sped up a noirish cinematic underclass. The real rival to *Going My Way* was not *Wilson* but *Double Indemnity,* Billy Wilder's brilliant, bark-peeling nightmare of adultery and murder. Wilder resented McCarey's win but faced an implacable trend. Even the star of *Double Indemnity,* Barbara Stanwyck, nominated for best actress, praised the victorious film: "I have seen *Going My Way* three times and I love it," she said, lauding its influence on religion and sending effusive congratulations to Crosby. Wilder would go on to direct *The Lost Weekend,* for which he won his first Oscar, and follow it with *The Emperor Waltz,* a vehicle conceived for Crosby.[46]

The winners reacted variously to their prizes. McCarey was the least happy. He now had three golden men looking over his shoulder, and they interfered with his concentration; periodically, he would ask his secretary to remove them from his office so he could think. Alcohol, painkillers, and pain undoubtedly contributed to the decline in his output, but there is the ring of truth also in Edgar G. Ulmer's comment that success made him afraid to fail. For Bergman, the prize capped her triumph over the commercial film business, and when she later landed in a few flops, it may have helped steel her resolve to look beyond Hollywood. For Crosby, it had a minimal effect. He wanted to make good pictures but continued working along his customary path. Over the next twelve years, there would be a few disappointments but no categorical flops; of his fifteen most profitable pictures, nine—*The Bells of St. Mary's, Road to Utopia* (as yet unreleased), *Blue Skies, Road to Rio, Welcome Stranger, The Emperor Waltz, White Christmas, The Country Girl,* and *High Society*—lay ahead, as did two more best actor nominations. When asked about his Oscar, he invariably gave the credit to McCarey or to the dearth of good actors, as so many were serving in the military, or to the industry's gratitude for his war work; he found it difficult if not impossible to concede that he had given a distinguished performance.

He did not allow the statuette to cast a shadow. Years later he told a friend that his sons had made a mock trophy for him in case he lost. Yet having won, he promptly put the crockery in its place. "It really is true, really is," Gary Crosby recalled of that evening. "He took the damn thing and used it as a doorstop, the door to the library. We came down the next morning and it was sitting in front of the door, and it sat there as long as we lived in that house."[47]

Each of the recipients received a letter from the executive secretary of the academy assuring them that "as soon as the required materials are no longer on the war priority list," they would all get genuine gold-plated statuettes to replace the plaster placeholders presented at the ceremony. Barry Fitzgerald learned how fragile the temporary one was when he swung his putter in his living room and accidentally decapitated it. He had to pay ten dollars for a plaster replacement.[48]

23

NOTHING BUT
BLUEBIRDS

This we prescribe, though no physician;
Deep malice makes too deep incision;
Forget, forgive; conclude and be agreed;
Our doctors say this is no month to bleed.
—William Shakespeare, *Richard II* (1597)

Bing Crosby's professional streak of luck appeared to be unbreakable in the final year of the war, despite a few hiccups. Newspapers and magazines had but to print hints of his upcoming projects to ensure pandemic enthusiasm. *The Bells of St. Mary's* had a niche all its own, building on a year of fealty to Father O'Malley and the curiosity about how he would relate to the sexiest Scandinavian import since Garbo. Photographs of the year's key Oscar winners interspersed with hack reportage about the happy hours they shared on an RKO soundstage saturated print media, compounding anticipation. The war was a long way from home and, beyond rationing and victory gardens (twenty million in 1945), had a diminishing sway over Americans—except for those who received dreaded visits from grim envoys of the armed forces. Like bygone promises of prosperity, peace was said to be around the corner. It was in the air, a vague perfume to disguise the odor of enervated patriotism and anxiety encumbering the new world a-coming, in the African

American journalist Roi Ottley's race-centric but in every way pertinent phrase.[1]

The shooting schedule for *Bells,* February through May, played
out against events that culminated in Germany's unconditional
surrender and hastened the subsequent capitulation in the East. As
Father O'Malley and Sister Benedict civilly dueled for parental
authority, headlines were bloody but heartening. The Allies captured Bastogne. The Japanese retreated from Burma. The Americans landed on Luzon and bombarded Iwo Jima. Hitler went into
seclusion. The Red Army entered Warsaw, East Prussia, and Auschwitz and headed for Berlin. The front page was an atlas: Manila,
Yalta, Dresden, Corregidor. Americans raised a flag on Mount
Suribachi, took the bridge at Remagen, and firebombed Tokyo.
They crossed the Rhine together with the British and liberated
Buchenwald, and the Brits liberated Bergen-Belsen. Roosevelt died
on April 12 in Warm Springs at age sixty-three. Hitler shot himself
in his bunker on April 30 at age fifty-six. Seven days later, Germany
folded. The proclamation of victory in Europe resounded throughout the West on Tuesday, May 8, a week before the picture wrapped.

The cast knew they had a remarkable film on their hands. Bing
confided to a friend that it was stronger than its predecessor and he
was stronger in it.[2] Leo's confidence led him to use a silent-comedy
device that usually did not work in talkies. In 1943, RKO had
enjoyed a tremendous surprise hit with *Cat People,* a stylish horror
film produced through a B unit created by the highly inventive Val
Lewton. It grossed thirty times its budget, and was practically all
that the RKO executives talked about, vaunting it as a riposte to the
flamboyant, recently ousted Orson Welles. McCarey thought it
would be amusing to introduce O'Malley to the sisters with a cat-in-
the-hat gag—he hesitantly speaks a few words to the seated nuns,
unaware that they are giggling at the cat on the mantelpiece behind
him, capering with his signature straw boater. The joke relies on a
convention of silent comedy, which maintains that characters cannot hear what they cannot see. In this instance, moviegoers have to
believe that the cat's shenanigans are as quiet as the grave and that
for some time, O'Malley does not notice the nuns staring at something behind him. Yet the scene works to defuse the tension inherent in his arrival and establishes a disarmingly mirthful tone.

*   *   *

With *Bells* in the can (except for a reshoot and dubbing, postponed until September) and *Blue Skies* busy being born again with a new producer, director, and writer, Bing revved himself up for another demanding excursion, mid-May through mid-June, of fund-raising, golf, and hospitals, the first half side by side with Bob Hope. In the brief interim before the tour, Bing attended to his usual schedule of broadcasting for Kraft, the AFRS (*Command Performance, GI Journal*), and specials, including a patch-in for *The Road Ahead*, produced at Bethesda naval base, and a VE Day *Chapel of the Air,* where he spoke of his family's devotion to the Rosary and his desire for his sons to inherit a love of God and country.

The May 17 *KMH* show was characteristically robust, with the Charioteers, featured vocalist Eugenie Baird, and two guests: the jazz pianist Eddie Heywood and the near-mythic opera singer Florence Quartararo, a Crosby discovery who began her brief career that spring, at age twenty-three, with four bookings on the program under the name Florence Alba. No one, not even Kraft executives who privately felt the sting of Bing's discontent, expected this show to be his last (beyond a few legally mandated returns), given that he was under a contract aimed to keep him in place through 1950. Indeed, *Variety,* which had broken the story on page 1 a day earlier ("Crosby Off KMH Reported—Again"), did not take seriously its own scoop, dismissing it as "a fairly perennial affair—those late-spring and early-summer rumors that Crosby wants to scram out of radio." Insiders said that this time he really meant it and confidently predicted he would get his way, though they didn't know what that way would be. Bing wasn't talking yet. Not until the end of August, after Willard Lochridge, the vice president of J. Walter Thompson, traveled from Chicago to Los Angeles for a two-day showdown with Bing and his attorney did the trades realize the immensity of Crosby's intentions: he aimed to abolish the ban, rigidly enforced by NBC and CBS, against recorded network programs and challenge, almost as a side issue, the legality of ten-year contracts.[8]

Meantime, the tour animated by the Seventh War Loan drive opened with a concert at Hollywood's Wiltern Theater followed by a road trip with Hope that began in Chicago and continued to

Cleveland, South Bend (at a two-hour bond show at Notre Dame Stadium for an audience of fifty thousand, Crosby cautioned those who swooned and squealed, "Please! I'm an old man!"), Indianapolis, Omaha, Topeka, and Kansas City. In Kansas City, they turned eighteen holes into a strolling vaudeville act with dancing, yodeling, insults, skipped holes, and a thumbed ride with a motorcycle cop from one hole to the next. At the Municipal Auditorium that night, Hope emceed the Seventh War Loan rally, with Crosby as the unbilled guest (he did four songs, including his current hit, "Ac-Cent-Tchu-Ate the Positive," and "imitations" he and Bob had devised at the Capitol Theatre back in 1932). The show raised nearly $2.7 million in war bonds.[9]

Then they split up, Bing leaving in the wee hours for St. Louis, then going by train to New York. There he connected with another line for Montreal, where for two days he alternated between golf and impromptu concerts. He returned to the United States, arriving in Boston at daybreak for a marathon schedule that a reporter who kept up with him called "grueling." It began at eight a.m. in Quincy, where Crosby helped launch the cruiser USS *Oregon City*; it finished twelve hours later in Framingham at Cushing General Hospital, where he appeared so energized, joking and singing for paralyzed soldiers, that only admonitions from medical personnel regarding the patients' bedtime could stop him. Between those episodes, he entertained for half an hour on the Boston Common, accompanied by a hotel guitarist, for an audience of well over thirty thousand (one paper estimated twice that), selling $80,000 in bonds and auctioning his tie for $2,500. A performance at Commonwealth Country Club preceded an exhibition match in which he beat two champions (Jesse Guilford, Fred Wright) and Governor Tobin. By the reporter's count, Crosby signed 1,754 autographs and skipped dinner to get to the hospital. He took a night train to Washington, DC.[10]

The big event in DC was the GI Oscars, a ninety-minute open-air ceremony at Walter Reed Hospital. An audience of ten thousand cheered as men recovering from serious wounds gave out the prizes to Crosby, McCarey, Rita Hayworth, Jennifer Jones, and Eddie Bracken. Sergeant Lou Norulak, who had left both of his legs on a field in Europe, handed Crosby his award and thanked him for his sincerity and morale-building. Bing swallowed hard and sang "Sentimental Journey" and "Don't Fence Me In." Emotions were impossible to control two days later when, after taking a day off to watch the Senators beat the Yankees 5 to 3 at Yankee Stadium, he walked the wards at Valley Forge General Hospital and Philadelphia Naval Hospital. A nurse on staff at the latter recalled an amputee asking Bing to sing his mother's favorite song, "Too-Ra-Loo-Ra-Loo-Ral," adding that he had not yet told her about losing his left leg. The nurse said Bing "sort of gulped" and acknowledged the soldier's bravery before singing the request. "[We] were surprised when Bing left the room without saying a word after singing the song. I went into the hallway and saw Bing leaning up against the wall in tears. I got him a glass of water, and after a few minutes he went right back to entertaining the boys."[11] The train west stopped at Salt Lake City, where he teamed again with Hope for a few events. It was the last great tour of the war, adding significantly to the Associated Press's 1946 estimation that as "one of Hollywood's most indefatigable workers during World War II," Crosby traveled more than fifty thousand miles entertaining troops.[12]

In Los Angeles he resumed his film work, reading the script for *Blue Skies*, scheduled to begin shooting in a few weeks. He recorded three sessions at Decca, waxing a coolly amorous masterpiece central to his legacy, "It's Been a Long, Long Time"—the most resonant coming-home song since Johnny marched back from the Civil War. He returned to a chaotic domestic life and an intensifying romance.[13]

It was probably Ginsberg's predecessor Buddy DeSylva who introduced Joan Caulfield to Bing in the late summer of 1944. At that time, Crosby was filming *Here Come the Waves* and getting ready for his European USO tour, and Caulfield was preparing to go before the cameras as the third lead in *Miss Susie Slagle's*. DeSylva signed her in 1943, but after the flurry of press releases, he had played it down until she finished her obligation to Broadway's *Kiss and Tell* (her younger sister Betty took over her role). Joan and her mother were now settled in Hollywood and ready to begin work. According to Caulfield, an executive, presumably DeSylva— in any case, someone important enough to welcome her to the studio—mentioned that Bing was working that day; would she like to watch him on the set? She later told her neighbor Iris Flores Schirmer, a socialite formerly married to the chairman of the music publishing firm and Joan's periodic business partner, that as she and her mother stood to the side, watching the scene, she caught Bing's eye. In Schirmer's words, "He took one look and fell madly in love with her."[14]

This sounds very Harlequin romance, yet two months abroad did not weaken Bing's fixation. It was said that as Thanksgiving approached, he showed up at the Caulfields' door bearing a "raw turkey."[15] *Miss Susie Slagle's* completed shooting in November 1944 but was not released until March 1946; Caulfield's only other work was a starlet cameo in *Duffy's Tavern*. In short, she was celebrated in New York and utterly unknown in Hollywood. Nevertheless, Crosby requested her for the Irving Berlin film. Usually, he simply approved his leading lady. This time he chose her, though Sandrich undoubtedly shared his enthusiasm. According to Berlin's daughter, Mark considered Joan his "protégé [*sic*]."[16]

As 1945 dawned, the *New York Herald Tribune* proudly reported that the porcelain-skinned beauty who charmed Broadway as the bubbly teenager Corliss Archer in *Kiss and Tell* had just landed a contract with Paramount Pictures (actually signed some eighteen months earlier) and, what's more, would test for a role as Bing Crosby's costar in *Blue Skies*. Caulfield, a scion of privilege and parochial schools, dropped out of Columbia University when her modeling career took off. *Life* put her on its cover in May 1942, dressed in a turn-of-the-century frock, as a "dead-ringer" for Fluffy Ruffles, a once trendy 1907 comic-strip heroine who popularized ruffled blouses and pleated skirts and came to personify young women determined to be taken seriously in the workforce. Like Fluffy, Joan was thought pushy and naive by some. She had obtained her first small stage part after barging into the producer George Abbott's office waving that issue of *Life*. She impulsively spent her Paramount advance on a mink coat, though she was too self-conscious to wear it. Responding to persistent comments on her looks, she memorably observed, "Actually, I'm not beautiful. I just *look* beautiful in pictures."[17]

Sandrich, whom she likely encountered on the day she visited the *Here Come the Waves* set, asked to see the *Miss Susie Slagle's* dailies and arranged for Caulfield to take dancing lessons with the Paramount dance coach Josephine Earl. But he hedged his bets, auditioning others, even assuming the expense of shooting a test with the dancer Miriam Nelson, who worked on *Here Come the Waves* (on-screen as a chorus girl and offscreen dubbing Betty Hutton's taps) and *Duffy's Tavern* (her only featured number on camera is a duet with tap dancer Johnny Coy). Nelson wanted the role not least for the chance to work with Bing again.

> He loved all the chorus people because [they] are the most fun. They don't have the pressure of the acting job on their backs. So he would hang out [on *Here Come the Waves*] with all the dancers, male and female, and we got to know him by sitting around talking to him. A very bright man; he could talk on so many subjects and would always relate to people, always be right in there asking the right questions or saying the right things. With me he talked dancing. When Josephine Earl and her husband went on vacation, she asked if I would house-sit their lovely house in Laurel Canyon for a couple of weeks. They had a big pool and a rolling backyard, and she said I should have a party. So my mother and I moved in, and I invited a lot of the dancers on the picture, and Bing heard us talking and said, "What party? You haven't asked me yet." I said, "You mean you'd like to come?" I was so surprised to have him come to my party, but he and his friend Barney Dean were the first to arrive and they brought a bunch of bottles of scotch and had the best time. We were having a barbecue and he just got right in to help with everything. I always thought he was just a great down-to-earth person who liked to laugh.[18]

When Nelson read in the trades that Caulfield had gotten the part (no one called to tell her), she was mystified that they hired a nondancer until she heard the rumors about Joan and Bing. For the better part of a year, the rumors were closely held, whispered and uncertain. Bing and Joan took every precaution to keep their friendship under the radar — never socializing in public, never going anywhere as a couple, not even to lunch if Bing could help it. His home life deteriorated as Dixie's alcoholism dominated her every day, and she grew increasingly morose and erratic. He, too, took to having a drink or two at the end of the workday.

In April, Jack Kapp came to Los Angeles to supervise recordings. Bing had had one too many after completing a day on *The Bells of St. Mary's*. Feeling no pain, he strolled across the street to the Decca studio for a six thirty p.m. recording session. After two attempts at "Ave Maria," Kapp told him, "No, Bing, you're not going to make it. We'll schedule it another time." Flushed and indifferent, Bing sat down, and Gene Lester, who photographed the session, pointed out a hole in the crotch of his pants. "Oh, Jesus," Crosby said. "Hey, but that makes it convenient, doesn't it?" Lester took a picture of him fingering the hole. Minutes later, he told Lester he had a date at Paramount and asked if he would like to come along, adding, "I'm sure she can get a friend." Lester thanked him but begged off as a newly married man who didn't want to "start screwing up." "Yeah, wait a couple of years," Bing told him. Lester knew Crosby was seeing Caulfield and figured he wanted a beard, particularly one with a camera, as "it would look like they're out working." Days later Joan and Bing did work together on a *Lux Radio Theater* adaptation of Bing's 1938 picture *Sing You Sinners*, with Joan capably handling a supporting role. That was also the day Germany surrendered; the show's guest producer, Mitchell Leisen, promised listeners to stop the play in the event of a news bulletin from Europe.[19]

There were not many ways for them to be alone. Joan rarely went anywhere without her protective, devoutly Catholic mother. Her younger sister Betty, who remained in New York with their father, wondered how and even if they managed it: "I guess they were just very circumspect. There certainly was not a blatant incident. My mother was personally with Joan all the time and there was no opportunity for them to go off together. When they came to New York, he stayed at the Waldorf and Joan stayed with us at our apartment. Bing always had an entourage, a couple of friends. My mother and father would not have stood for it." Yet the family warmly accepted Bing into the fold, knowing he and their daughter were in love. Eventually they came to believe that everyone who saw *Blue Skies* knew it too.[20]

*   *   *

A fan magazine reported that the twenty-two-year-old ingenue "beat her brains—and her feet—out in learning to dance so that she might have a chance at the dancing role opposite Paul Draper in the forthcoming *Blue Skies*." She worked "ferociously" to meet the challenge, studying three hours each morning with Josephine Earl. Some said she also enrolled at an outside dance school at her own expense. Yet it soon became apparent that she was making little headway, despite assurances from the ever-flexible Louella Parsons, who wrote that "pretty little Joan Caulfield...dances but beautifully." She did photograph beautifully, and she performed professionally, displaying a talent for light comedy. But dancing was beyond her, and Draper, who began rehearsals in December 1944, fumed that he had finally gotten a break in Hollywood with a woman he had to "carry" through their number.[21]

This was not Draper's first chance in movies. In late 1935, Warner Brothers brought him to town for a featured role opposite Ruby Keeler in *Colleen*. During shooting, the then-twenty-six-year-old dancer gave a sensational show at the Century Club, where Bing and Dixie cheered him on and joined with him on the floor. It is not hard to see why Warner let him go after that film. Although tall, genteel, obviously sure on his feet, he lacked charisma, drama, wit; when he held his arms at chest level, they inadvertently seemed to flap—more seagull than seducer. But that isn't how audiences saw him over the next ten years; he developed into a prominent concert draw, a consummate dancer of undeniable originality who combined intricate tap rhythms with balletic refinement. Sandrich went to New York to convince Draper he could hold his own in a major musical with Crosby. He convinced Paramount that Draper's popularity would transfer to film. He convinced himself that he could help Draper overcome his speech problem—he stuttered. Sandrich had made stars of Astaire and Rogers. He knew what he was doing.[22]

He did not have to convince Bing, who looked forward to working with Draper as long as the equation included Caulfield. Under Sandrich's guidance, it would be an efficient, pleasurable shoot and when it was over he would be finished with his obligations to Paramount for the year, free to get back in fatigues and tour the South Pacific.

Things did not turn out that way.[23]

*   *   *

Paramount put Berlin's musical back on track by replacing Sandrich's associate producer Joe Sistrom with the eager Sol C. Siegel,
whom Bing had encountered during his days recording for Brunswick in the early 1930s. Siegel had made his way to Hollywood not
long after Crosby debuted at Paramount and initially turned out
matinee Westerns for Republic. He signed with Paramount in
1940, but despite his copious output, he had never been associated
with a major film. *Blue Skies* catapulted him to a higher bracket
and a dynamic career at Paramount, Twentieth Century–Fox, and
MGM.[24]

Stuart Heisler seemed a strange choice to direct a big-budget
Technicolor musical, but Paramount felt he had earned the plum
assignment. He belonged to a generation of filmmakers who had
scraped their way up from the bottom, in his case from extra, prop
man, and dogsbody to an editor with an enviable reputation
achieved over fifteen years. He began directing at the age of forty,
and by 1945, his laurels included an elegant adaptation of Dashiell
Hammett's *The Glass Key* and a well-regarded recruitment film
called *The Negro Soldier*. His work gravitated toward the American underbelly (alcoholism, crime, corruption, nativism, suicide,
the disabled), though he also directed two successful children's
movies, one early in his career, *The Biscuit Eater*, and one toward
the end, *The Lone Ranger* (with a plot about white men maligning
American Indians). He never made another musical, but he followed *Blue Skies* with a picture about an alcoholic singer whose
career plunges as her crooning husband's soars. Its producer Walter Wanger "vehemently" denied that *Smash-Up: The Story of a
Woman* drew from the life of Dixie Lee. The film combined *A Star
Is Born* and *The Lost Weekend,* but those in the know recognized
Dixie in the character's insecurities, shyness, and jealousy and her
inadvertent arson; in addition, there was a physical similarity
between Susan Hayward, its star, and Dixie. Bing saw the parallels, and he mulled over a lawsuit until his attorney John O'Melveny
counseled that, absent the millions in publicity generated by legal
action, the picture would pass unnoticed. Bing had reason to dis-
trust the director.[25]

No sooner had Heisler come on board than Draper began complaining about Caulfield, with whom he was paired in the film's first production number; it involved a Ziegfeld-style staircase and Berlin's perpetual runway anthem for the Ziegfeld Follies, "A Pretty Girl Is Like a Melody." As the start date was delayed from June to July, rumors of dissent mounted. Paramount parried them with a story about the finicky director shooting dozens of Technicolor tests "just to find the right kind of flooring" for that scene. Heisler, however, quietly dismissed Caulfield without consulting Crosby and called for auditions. Crosby, no less quietly, insisted on her reinstatement. None of this alleviated Draper's stammer. According to Berlin's daughter, it announced itself as soon as the camera turned and he had to speak Caulfield's character's name, which came out "M-M-M-M-Mary."[26]

Draper lasted nearly three weeks, though there was no getting around his affliction or Crosby's exasperation. Heisler also lost patience with him, while the studio was kicking itself for listening to Sandrich rather than investing in the surefire reteaming of Crosby and Astaire. In Caulfield's recollection, the shooting was tense, as "scenes weren't flowing, and that is putting it mildly." One day Bing said, "That's it," excused himself, and "the next thing I know Fred Astaire is going to be on the set Monday morning. And he was." The turnabout was not quite that quick, but it was mighty quick, because Fred readily accepted the call.[27]

Contemplating retirement, Astaire wanted to leave the business on a high note, and a Crosby picture virtually guaranteed that. His most recent effort, *The Sky's the Limit*, had come out two years before and it made money but received oddly lackluster reviews and abruptly disappeared. Astaire signed with MGM and made two expensive pictures that the studio delayed releasing: *Ziegfeld Follies*, an all-star pastiche for which he received top billing, though only through alphabetical serendipity, and *Yolanda and the Thief*, a fantasy loathed by MGM executives who correctly predicted it would never recoup its costs. Offended and frustrated, Astaire demanded to be loaned out to Paramount. Draper's dismissal was hushed up for a week as the contracts were negotiated.[28] The one drawback for Crosby was that the delay made his trip to the South

Pacific impossible, as he explained in a letter to the Navy's Entertainment Branch, omitting his own agency in the casting change:

> As I anticipated, and as is often the case with these ponderous productions, "BLUE SKIES" has encountered several serious setbacks. For instance, after three weeks work with Paul Draper he was found unsuitable, removed from the cast and all the work in which he figured must be done over with Fred Astaire who was engaged to supplant him.
>
> I have been going over the schedule thoroughly with the Director, and it appears impossible, even if no more trouble occurs, to finish me in the picture before the end of September. As I am due back on the air in October, a South Pacific tour can hardly be arranged.[29]

He expressed his regrets and promised to call immediately if circumstances altered "the current outlook." Given the situation, Bing's willingness to leave the country might well have waned, though a few weeks earlier—on the day before *Blue Skies* (and Paul Draper) went before the camera—he told a reporter he intended to head for the Pacific in late summer, after he finished filming.[30] But circumstances *had* changed, and they had nothing to do with *Blue Skies*. On the same Tuesday morning Bing wrote to the naval liaison, Americans learned that the world had entered the atomic age. On Monday, August 6, at 8:15 a.m. in Japan (which was Sunday, August 5, 4:15 p.m. in Los Angeles), a B-29 named the *Enola Gay* dropped an atomic bomb called Little Boy on Hiroshima. Three days later, another B-29, *Bockscar,* dropped a more potent atomic weapon called Fat Man on Nagasaki. The Empire of Japan surrendered on Tuesday, August 14.

That morning Crosby filmed the scene in *Blue Skies* where Joan Caulfield, her face positively shining with impeccably Technicolored makeup, gives birth to their daughter. Word of the surrender animated the lot and soon penetrated the soundstages, and everyone, enchanted by excitement and wanting to be together, made for the central square, where a billboard featured the caricatured helmets of Hitler, Mussolini, and Tojo, the first two x-ed out. Someone yelled, "Crosby!"—a cry picked up by others. As the crowd chanted his name, a siege ladder was wheeled to Hideki Tojo's headwear and a bucket of black paint passed to Bing, who climbed up the rungs. "With two sweeps of the brush," the Canadian broadcaster Gord Atkinson (a visiting serviceman at the time) remembered, "Bing placed an 'X' over the image of Tojo, and the crowd let out with a loud cheer—and took off in every direction to celebrate."[31]

Colonel Tom Lewis, the head of Armed Forces Radio Service, recruited Bing to act as compere on a *Command Performance Victory Extra* to be transcribed at seven thirty p.m. at the CBS Radio Playhouse on North Vine and aired the following day. Dozens of stars who had appeared on *Command Performance* and *Mail Call* were hurriedly invited to appear. To be certain of an all-star lineup, the AFRS team assembled discs from previous programs. The result is a remarkable mélange of music, speeches, jokes, invocations, and fleeting hellos (audio autographs). The original program was said to be two hours; one hundred minutes of it survive. At such a moment, a bit of grandiloquence could hardly be avoided; opening and closing prayers plummily intoned by Ronald Colman and Orson Welles, respectively, enveloped other actors, who puffed themselves up for the occasion—even Cary Grant was self-conscious and stiff. Crosby, who sang three songs in terrific voice, traded quips with Frank Sinatra and handled the introductions, providing a necessary note of average-Joe understatement in stark contrast to the mannered oratory of such actors as Edward G. Robinson, Loretta Young, and Robert Montgomery.

The show begins as the announcer, Ken Carpenter, proclaims the *Victory Extra* to prerecorded shouts, applause, and the strains of "Over There." Crosby introduces himself: "What can you say at a time like this? You can't throw your skimmer in the air. That's for a run-of-the-mill holiday. I guess all anybody can do is thank God it's over."

A recording of Risë Stevens singing "Ave Maria" is cued. Bing explains that the show will offer a "scrapbook" of AFRS memories: "Though our deep-down feeling is one of humility, we're going to include some of the laughs and some of the songs that might have helped out in the dark days." These memories, which were new to stateside listeners, predominate until guests start arriving and reading their scripted bits. A disc of Dinah Shore singing "I'll Walk Alone" is followed by an excerpt from a post-D-day broadcast

involving Bette Davis and Jimmy Durante. With no discernible
shift between discs and live performance, the stars parade by, from
Marlene Dietrich and Burgess Meredith paying tribute to the correspondent Ernie Pyle, recently killed in Okinawa, to celebrity
readings from the speeches of FDR and generals, to hallmark songs
by Lena Horne, Danny Kaye, and Carmen Miranda. It is a wonder-
ment how efficiently all the parts are integrated, so meticulously
edited with stock cheers and laughter that it is difficult to know
who is in the studio, on disc, or on the phone. Given the radio revolution Crosby soon initiated, this gala, transcribed on "the first day
of world peace" (in Carpenter's phrase), surely confirmed Bing's
belief that prerecorded shows were the wave of the future.[32]

Fred Astaire's association with Irving Berlin produced several of
the cinema's most glorious moments. He inspired Berlin to write
songs with tricky rhythms to suit his own terpsichorean ambitions
and gave them definitively sly and elegant vocal interpretations. He
had appeared in four Berlin films in ten years, all directed by Sandrich: three with Ginger Rogers (*Top Hat, Follow the Fleet,* and
Carefree) and *Holiday Inn. Blue Skies,* announced as his cinematic
swan song, was the fifth, followed two years later by his last Berlin
film, *Easter Parade,* which he also vowed would be his final film (it
wasn't). Although he claimed to have nothing but fond memories of
working with "Cros," it must have galled Astaire a bit to ride his
coattails to another megahit in which he loses the woman of his
dreams, and this despite a quarter century of humbling entreaties;
his ability to dance after drunkenly tumbling from a theatrical platform (a quite unnecessary plot device); and an equal share of screen
time.[33]

He more than compensated with his dance sequences. "Puttin'
On the Ritz" was a career high point and possibly the most dazzling
solo dance ever choreographed for a movie. His primary partner
is a cane that he jabs, swings, discards, retrieves (hidden spring
traps in the floor make it shoot up into his waiting hand), while
process photography provides him with a chorus of Astaire iterations. This he offhandedly described in his memoir as "one of my
most useful trick solos," conceding elsewhere that it required "five
weeks of back-breaking physical work." He reserved that effort for

the end of the shoot, when the other performers were mostly done. His first days, however, were taken up with the Ziegfeld number; the set was built, the costumes fitted, and all was ready. Astaire gallantly recalled his dance with "the beauteous" Caulfield as turning out "well." But Hermes Pan, his longtime dance director, described Astaire's response after their rehearsal as far from sanguine. Pan told a friend, the costumer Donfeld, that Fred politely excused himself, sought out the producer, and told him, "You will have to replace the leading lady because I can't do a thing with her." Sol Siegel told him that that was impossible; she was Bing's girlfriend. "Hermes laughed so hard when he told me this," Donfeld recalled, "because Astaire was the sweetest, gentlest man, and he screamed, '*What?*' Hermes said it was the only time he saw Fred call for something and not get it."[34]

The problem with *Blues Skies* is not Caulfield, who handled her largely decorative role with aplomb and, as her parents were not alone in noticing, generated moments in the picture's superior first act of sensual chemistry with Bing, something no other leading lady succeeded in doing. She was scheduled for just the one dance number, in which she was charmingly sheltered by Astaire and relieved of the chancier staircase moves.[35] For her two vocal numbers, she credibly lip-synched recordings by Betty Russell. Her performance delivered what was required. The problem with the film is the bizarre script.

Berlin devised the basic idea: A romantic triangle unwinding over nearly three decades, beginning in 1919 at the Ziegfeld Follies, with two dozen Berlin songs emerging in approximately the year of their composition. Crosby's character, tagged, with typical Anglo banality, Johnny Adams, creates and neurotically sells a succession of nightclubs, courting unpredictability along with an excuse to sing current Berlin songs, sometimes with a composure bordering on indifference. His rival, also named with *Mayflower* piety, is Jed Potter, a stage star and ladies' man without a lady. We are in the land of Irving, where time and loss are inextricable. Johnny's serial inns allow the story to travel through the years and across locales, but the reduction of womanhood to a single chorus girl of acceptable ethnic stock, Mary O'Hara, triggers ominous instability.

To keep the pot boiling, Johnny and Mary marry, quarrel, breed, quarrel, divorce, and then reunite thanks to a broadcast by Jed, who turned to radio after his drunken fall and who, apparently and despite his rakish affect, entered middle age as chaste as he is chastened. None of the characters are admirable, yet Johnny turns out to be particularly unpleasant after a mostly enchanting courtship in which Crosby displays his delectable poise, wit, and sky-blue eyes (dotingly photographed by Charles Lang). The look he and Caulfield exchange brings to mind a line from Jack Trevor Story's novel *The Trouble with Harry*: "It was the look of an adult man to an adult woman in an adult world." The look is short-lived. Audiences were familiar with the Crosby character who longed to be free of ambition, untrammeled by responsibility, relieved of fame, and left alone to croon in the moonlight. But this time his willfulness has an irrational, callous element. The presence of a child, the adorable daughter he casually abandons except for a lullaby neatly crooned on the fly (he is always good with child performers), poisons his Huck Finn autonomy. The secret wound, the thing Hemingway characters sublimate by fishing, is expressed in petulance. The lullaby Bing sings to the little girl, composed specifically for *Blue Skies*, embodies the gloomy theme of the whole film; it's called "(Running Around in Circles) Getting Nowhere." The final rapprochement is a gimmick, not a resolution.[36]

This was the film returning GIs could not get enough of. No one appeared to notice, let alone mind, the failings of the story, which was accepted as an uninspired but tolerable hanger for the trove of great Berlin songs, the free and easy warbling of Crosby, and the dazzling footwork of Astaire. Arthur Sheekman, the veteran comedy writer principally associated with the Marx Brothers, signed on to write the screenplay. In June, he had his first hit (Danny Kaye's *Wonder Man*) in nine years, most of which had been spent in New York attempting to write for Broadway. Sheekman added two melting-pot sidekicks, played by Billy De Wolfe and Olga San Juan. The latter was promoted by Paramount as the Puerto Rican Pepperpot, though she was advised against flaunting "sexual inference" in "You'd Be Surprised," a song that is all sexual flaunting. She was similarly forbidden from saying, let alone making, "her seat wave" in "Heat Wave"; the altered lyrics gave her waving feet. This was to be expected, but a more general ambient censorship also asserted itself in the film. The dogface's anthem of gleeful revenge "I've Got My Captain Working for Me Now" is purged of glee. The passing years leap over the Depression. The war is now the stardust memory of a song, as Bing sings (for the five thousandth time, he estimated) "White Christmas." A reporter asked Sheekman about the plot. The man whom Groucho once called the fastest wit in the West answered, "It's very sad. You'll cry your eyes out when you see the picture." The reporter observed, "The whimsical Mr. Sheekman secretly hopes it will be funny." That secret was well kept.[37]

Reporters often visited the set. One asked Astaire what he thought of Gene Kelly, and Crosby interjected, "I know exactly how he feels. It seems that everyone has their Sinatra. So what?" He invited his young radio friend Ed Helwick, on leave from his base in Alaska, to a leisurely lunch, fetched him a chair on the set ("he plopped it down just out of camera range"), and explained lip-synching, which he was about to do. When Ed remarked on Sinatra, Bing said that Perry Como was the more formidable rival. Bob Hope came by a few times. He and Bing occupied themselves with chip shots and putting and invited Astaire, Caulfield, and others to join in. A few weeks before *Blue Skies* wrapped, Hope's *Monsieur Beaucaire* went before the cameras; it costarred Caulfield, who had to troop from one set to the other. "This is awful," Bob remarked for publication. "After those love scenes with Crosby, she's sound asleep." Bing renewed his acquaintance with the composer Sy Oliver, who attended one of the prerecord sessions to juice up the arrangement for "Everybody Step," making it—as he did the title sequence in *Road to Zanzibar*—one of the liveliest moments in the film. Buddy DeSylva made a surprise visit, his first to the studio since illness had sidetracked him. Seeing him enter the soundstage, Bing prompted an ovation by cast and crew.[38]

Bing checked into a hospital shortly after he completed his work on the picture. He had taken a couple of days off for back pain in late August, but his medical friend Arnold Stevens told him it was more serious than that—he had gallstones—and arranged a week for him in St. John's, ostensibly for a thorough checkup and badly needed rest. Before checking in, Bing managed a day of retakes with Joan Carroll for *The Bells of St. Mary's*; worked all night with Hope, at the navy's request, on a short movie to dissuade men from jumping ship (desertion had escalated now the war was over); sang a *Porgy and Bess* medley with Dinah Shore and Frank Sinatra at a Hollywood Bowl benefit; transcribed three AFRS broadcasts, including a *Command Performance Christmas Show*; and, between August 29 and September 14, recorded *six* Decca sessions—fatigue is occasionally evident. He took painkillers. Yet Mel Tormé, whose vocal group the Mel-Tones backed Crosby at one session ("Day by Day," "Prove It by the Things You Do"), noticed no stress. Apprehensive at first, the group was relieved when Bing arrived at the studio "grinning, relaxed, and friendly," treating them like "old friends, making, not forcing, suggestions," encouraging Tormé in his solo passages. The columnist Florabel Muir, however, wrote that he suffered physical torment on the navy film and underwent surgery the next morning.[39]

Several people, including Dixie, attested to the torment, but the surgery was averted until early 1951, when the flare-ups were unendurable and life-threatening. Crosby's abhorrence of surgery—on one occasion in the late 1940s, he stopped an anesthesiologist at the last minute and removed himself from the operating table and hospital—originated with the traumatic death of Eddie Lang, the guitarist and bosom friend who died unnecessarily at the age of thirty from an inept tonsillectomy.[40] Secluded at St. John's Hospital, Crosby instructed his office to publicize his cancellation of screen and broadcast engagements for the rest of the year, fueling speculation about his ailment, until Larry Crosby announced that the trouble was combined gallstone infection and arthritis—nothing dangerous and no need for surgery. Bing, he said, planned to recuperate at the Nevada ranch while his family remained in Los Angeles.[41]

Crosby stayed at the ranch through much of October and November, rarely idle. "Save for a couple of short snow flurries we are having a beautiful Indian Summer here," Bing wrote to his brother Ted, "sunshiny days" and freezing nights. "The deer are plentiful, very fat and highly edible this year. If the game warden ever came by I fear he'd hit us with the book. But after all, we must protect our range." When Gary Cooper visited, they crossed into Idaho to hunt pheasant near Ketchum. A few days later, Florabel Muir reported that Joan Caulfield and her mother visited the ranch to have "a look at the great outdoors," while Crosby "recuperates." Four days after that, Muir noted that Caulfield would be spending the Christmas holidays in New York. Crosby, too, would be in New York, the first time he had spent Christmas apart from his family. In the interim, he pulled strings that helped to redefine his presence in the new world.[42]

For one thing, he took on the responsibility of chairing the fundraising campaign for the widely admired if controversial Australian nurse Sister Kenny, who had arrived in the United States championing a treatment of polio involving muscle exercises and heated wrappings. The appellative Sister, signifying senior nurse in Australia, led many Americans to assume she was a nun, a confusion she passively exploited while gaining support from the Catholic Church, an affiliation she virtually sealed with Crosby's recruitment in July 1945. Despite her claims to the contrary, Elizabeth Kenny held no medical or nursing certification, but she was hardly a fraud. Her methods, though obviated in regard to polio following the widespread use of the Salk vaccine, are credited with breaking ground in physiotherapy. Yet she effectively turned a war against polio into a war between politically linked philanthropies.

The March of Dimes, founded by President Roosevelt as the National Foundation for Infantile Paralysis to battle polio, used Democratic celebrities—notably Eddie Cantor, who coined the name—to raise funds. The Kenny Foundation drew upon Republican celebrities and institutions. The ensuing battle in the medical community and the press had as much to do with a competition to raise money as it did with divergent therapies. Coins dropped in Sister Kenny's seven-inch yellow-and-orange Sock Polio canisters were coins diverted from the March of Dimes. Her canisters and posters, distributed nationwide, displayed a jaunty Bing Crosby asking, "Will you go my way...all the way in the fight against Infantile Paralysis?" and a looming, half-naked little girl taking a hesitant step on a tabletop as Kenny stands below her, right arm forcefully raised, eyes filled with godly determination, a miracle worker commanding her charge to walk.

Crosby, no ideologue, volunteered to help in the fight against a terrible disease without hewing to a party line. He had made at least three broadcasts on behalf of March of Dimes from 1942 to 1945, and in the midst of chairing the Kenny drive, he made a point of visiting a child in an iron lung, the kind of treatment Elizabeth Kenny vigorously contested. Her Sock Polio campaign of November 22 through December 8 aimed to raise five million dollars. It raised, unsurprisingly, a tenth of that. The public's joy of giving had diminished after years of pleas to buy bonds, conserve rations, and donate time, goods, and spirit. At the ranch, Bing worked out the details of his participation, which included writing letters, lining up public appearances, and selecting state chairmen for the drive. The Kenny Foundation's advertising agency arranged for the Mutual Network to air a thirty-minute fund-raiser, *That They Might Walk,* in New York in December. Bing had been scheduled to sing, but the agency now asked him to emcee the show. He agreed, declining reimbursement for expenses, possibly grateful for a credible reason to justify a stay of two months in New York.[43]

From the ranch, Crosby negotiated the divestment of his racing interests. The postwar world would find his sons transforming into young men; Gary was twelve years old. Although Bing loved racing and breeding horses, the track did not provide the right example for the boys. Also, Bing paid more into it than he got out at a time when taxes were crushing him. His every effort to buy into a family-oriented sport had met with condescension; it was as if he had threatened to install pari-mutuel windows at the Rose Bowl. Kenesaw Mountain Landis, the commissioner of baseball since 1920, maintained an ad hominem opposition to Crosby that he took to his grave in 1944. In the more reasonable environment that followed his passing, Bing joined with a conglomerate to buy the Cleveland Indians, but his group was outbid by another, which included Bob Hope. He tried again when the Pittsburgh Pirates went on the block, this time successfully, though he still had to lose the track before negotiations went forward.[44]

Del Mar was an extremely attractive acquisition when Bing put his shares on the market that November. The meeting in July, the track's first since 1941, set an opening-day record with 8,823 spectators. With the better part of a week reserved to benefit war relief, the publicity was exemplary, and to top it off, municipal powers offered the Turf Club a ten-year lease to compensate for the wartime closure. Crosby transferred his stock in April 1946. In August, the Dreyfuss family, which had owned the Pirates since the year 1900, sold the team to a consortium of four for $2.25 million; Crosby paid $215,000 for a 14 percent stake. He grew to treasure his participation, particularly in 1960 when the team won its first World Series since 1925 in a rousing seven-game contest against the Yankees that was capped by Bill Mazeroski's walk-off homer. Baseball's pooh-bahs did not at all mind the publicity bonanza that came with thumbing a ride on the Crosby-Hope vaudeville tour. "Crosby can't hurt the Pirates. They're already dead," Bob said. "He'll probably use Frank Sinatra as a bat." Bing retorted, "I don't think Bob Hope's Indians will ever play the Pirates. After all, we throw overhand in this league."[45]

The sale of Del Mar harbored a hidden cost—a family rift that tore at Bing Crosby and his siblings and imbued their fearsome mother, Catherine, with an unforgiving, unreasoning enmity toward her third-oldest son, Ted. The primary trigger was financial: a certificate for one hundred shares of Del Mar stock made out to Ted in exchange for his $10,000 promissory note ($124,000 in today's money). Two lateral events, involving a book and a broken marriage, heightened the tension.

During Ted's years at Gonzaga, he endeavored to make his name as a writer. He worked hard, turning out stories of adventurous young men of spotless moral standing, and got nowhere, while his young brother could thumb his nose at the muse and still seduce her. At the same time, their mother made no secret as to her favorite. In one college story, Ted borrowed Bing's initials to name his despicable villain. Genial, upstanding Ted took a wife, Hazel Nieman, in 1924 and a job at Washington Water Power Company, where he rose to the vice presidency of public relations; his 1930s chronicle of the company is still cited on historical websites. As Bing's fame soared, Ted briefly worked to generate publicity for him, and in 1937, with editorial help from Larry (who shared

authorship) and covert input from Bing, he wrote the dialogue-
heavy faux biography *Bing*—part ballyhoo, part *Boy's Own* saga,
and in every respect a fiasco.[46]

In 1944, Bing asked Larry to find something for Ted in "any of
your undertakings." Larry positioned him at the Del Mar defense
plant with the understanding that he would segue into the Turf Club
when racing resumed. Bing approved the stock transaction with the
understanding that Ted would not take possession of the shares until
he had paid the note. Ted moved to California with the understanding that he would be named the assistant general manager in charge
of public relations. Ultimately, none of these understandings had
been understood. Ted's arrival was resented by the men running the
plant, especially after Ted let it be known that he suspected dubious
financial dealings. With Bing now intent on unloading his shares,
including those assigned to Ted (the new baseball commissioner,
Happy Chandler, asked about those shares at the hearing before
approving the Pirates sale), Ted would have no job. Angry at his
treatment, Ted lit a fuse when he saw the stock certificate made out
to him on his father's desk and walked off with it.[47]

At the same time, Ted's reentry into the family fold revived his
literary ambitions. He signed a contract with World Publishing to
revise and update his 1937 book as *The Story of Bing Crosby* and
asked Bing to write a foreword. "I haven't sent you the foreword you
requested for two reasons," Bing wrote from the ranch.

> First: I haven't been able to think of anything suitable or in
> good taste. Second: I think I should see what you have done with
> the material and find out what your publishing arrangements are
> before writing anything. I'm leaving here on the 21st for New York,
> and I'll be at the Waldorf from November 24. I suggest you phone
> me before the end of the month, and you can run up here. We can
> discuss these matters. Naturally, I want to help you in any way I
> can, but, as you know, someday I want to write some sort of an
> autobiography, and I've discussed this many times with Simon,
> Schuster and others. I don't want anything to prejudice this pro-
> posed book.[48]

Adding to the turbulence in Ted's life was the dissolution of his
marriage. He had fallen for a younger (by sixteen years) woman,

Margaret Mattes, who worked for him at Washington Water Power and who followed him to Washington, DC, when he left Del Mar to work as publicity director for an electrical company. When he divorced Hazel to marry Margaret, Bing commiserated: "I'm sorry to hear of your domestic estrangement. I'm in something of a spot myself, but there seems to be nothing I can do about it. I don't know whether we Crosbys expect too much or give too little." A year earlier, their father, Harry, had anticipated the imminent failure of Bing's marriage. He wrote to Ted, "Bing sent Gary up to the ranch at Elko Nev for the summer, Dixie and the rest of the kids have gone down to the beach house at Malibu for the summer. She is not acting any better, and we look for a breakup this fall." In late 1945, as the dispute between Bing and Ted intensified, their mischievously garrulous sister Mary Rose took Ted's side, referring to Bing as "the Grand Lama" and reporting to Ted that Dixie was "throwing the bourbon down faster than ever." Referring to her and Bob Crosby's wife, June, Mary Rose asked Ted, "How did those guys ever marry those dames in the first place and why are they staying married to them? It is too much for my feeble brain to try and fathom."[49]

Ted could have told her why. The price he paid for divorcing his wife was a lifelong excommunication by his mother. Ted's siblings Everett, Mary Rose, and Bob had previously divorced (Mary Rose twice) and remarried, and Larry would do so in 1947. But they had married non-Catholics; the imperious Catherine Crosby could accept those divorces. Ted and Hazel had married in the Catholic Church. He had committed a mortal sin. Howard Crosby, one of Ted's two sons with Margaret, asserted, "There is no question that my grandmother was furious about the divorce from Hazel, and she ordered the rest of the family to cut off my dad." They didn't all comply, but Bing did, for nearly twenty years, though he helped out Hazel with an annual check for a decade. His anger festered around the stock incident, which detonated publicly in 1946.[50]

Bing demanded the return of the certificate, promising to pay Ted back from the expected capital gains. Ted refused, arguing that the shares had greatly increased in value and insisting he would make good on his note. As pressure on him mounted, Ted wired Larry that he would not be intimidated by his "client," whom he compared to a Shakespearean tyrant ("Upon what meat doth this our Caesar feed that he is grown so great?"), and would resist his "persecution" and publish his book as planned. To which Larry replied with bemused impatience: "Just received your ridiculous wire, and I'll be damned if I can understand what's happened to you!" Of Ted's characterizations, he wrote, "Bing is not a client of mine. He is, first, my brother; second, my benefactor; and third, my employer." Misreading the literary allusion, he asked, "Where, in your studies at Gonzaga, did you learn that Shakespeare was a moralist, or Julius Caesar a fine guy?" Ultimately, he warned that John O'Melveny, the trustee for Bing's children, "who are really the owners of the stock," would sue him. He did sue, demanding an injunction; Ted countersued, demanding damages. The papers were full of it until the brothers settled. Ted returned to Spokane and Washington Water Power.[51]

Bing did not write the foreword to the book; Bob Hope did. It sold 24,936 copies in the six months after publication, netting Ted $450.22 in royalties on top of a $2,000 advance. Ted never spoke to his mother after 1946. In 1950, as his father lay dying, he asked for Ted; Catherine forbade her children to call him. Mary Rose broke ranks, but it was too late.[52]

Bing weighed his next steps as a filmmaker. The hottest show on Broadway, Mary Chase's *Harvey,* won the Pulitzer Prize and would pack the Forty-Eighth Street Theater until 1949, the fifth-longest-running show in Broadway history to that time. Paramount offered to buy it for Bing, and Crosby declined, he told a friend, because he didn't want his kids to see him playing a heavy drinker. (Bing, who began at Paramount playing an alcoholic radio singer in *The Big Broadcast,* would not repeat the mistake when offered alcoholic roles in *The Country Girl* and the remake of *Stagecoach,* not to mention the sober but homicidal small town doctor in the 1971 television movie *Dr. Cook's Garden.*) He wisely passed on John Wildberg's *Memphis Bound,* an all-black adaptation of Gilbert and Sullivan's *HMS Pinafore* that had starred Bill Robinson on Broadway. Paramount expected to reunite him with Barry Fitzgerald in a film of Stephen Vincent Benét's leprechaun story "O'Halloran's Luck" and to create a vehicle to pair him with the Cuban bandleader Xavier Cugat, neither of which came to pass.[53]

Yet despite the middling response to his production company's boxing drama *The Great John L.*, Bing persevered in producing a film of the third-longest-running play in Broadway history, Anne Nichols's *Abie's Irish Rose*, which weathered bad reviews and widespread disdain between 1922 and 1927 and inspired Lorenz Hart's couplet (in "Manhattan"): "Our future babies we'll take to *Abie's Irish Rose* / I hope they'll live to see it close." Bing might well have consulted with Irving Berlin, who kept ethnicity under the radar; Johnny Adams and Jed Potter indeed! Yet when Bing announced his intention of reviving a mixed-marriage comedy involving stereotyped Irish Catholics and Jews, it was considered a stroke of genius, a commercial sure thing, a totem of peace and understanding.

"If I ever heard a 'natural' it's Bing Crosby producing *Abie's Irish Rose* for his independent set-up," Louella Parsons fluttered. "Can't you just see Bing in the center of this Irish-Jewish love story?" But Bing had no intention of appearing in it, and in fact, the idea to do it probably originated with the director Eddie Sutherland. Just as Crosby helped out Frank Tuttle, his friend and favorite director of the 1930s, by hiring him for *The Great John L.*, he now offered to back the once-prolific comedy specialist who had guided him through *Too Much Harmony, Mississippi,* and *Dixie*—the last being the epitome of an ethnically awkward motion picture. Neither director reaped much from Crosby productions. Tuttle would be undone by the 1947 invasion of the House Un-American Activities Committee, and the protests and boycotts that greeted *Abie's* put paid to Sutherland's Hollywood career. Today, the film stands as a fascinating curio, chiefly as a merger of thespian styles. The cast includes J. M. Kerrigan, formerly of the Abbey Theatre, who worked with Yeats and Synge; Michael Chekhov, the nephew of Anton and favorite protégé of Stanislavsky; George E. Stone, born Gerschon Lichtenstein in Lodz, typecast as a punk gangster in some one hundred and fifty films but rarely as a Jewish one; Emory Parnell, a veteran vaudevillian; and the twenty-four-year-old Joanne Dru, born Joan Letitia LaCock in West Virginia, making her film debut. Certain of universal acceptance, Crosby, Sutherland, and Anne Nichols, who adapted her play, boasted they would dub it in a dozen languages. Now it is almost impossible to see except by appointment at the Library of Congress.[54]

*　　*　　*

On November 21, Bing left his ranch for a sleeper on the Super Chief to Chicago, where he picked up the connection to New York, in all a three-day journey. Arriving in Manhattan on Saturday, he checked into room 667 at the Waldorf Astoria, his home for the next ten weeks. If he thought he was escaping prying eyes, he was mistaken. His stay was scrupulously documented by two young fans, sisters, who followed him daily and kept a diary.

24

A LONG, LONG TIME

And now it has passed us the sound of their war
Resembles the sound of Niagara
Heard from afar in the still of the night.
—Christopher Logue, *War Music* (1994)[1]

Crosby refers to them as his "omnipresent twin-girl fans" in *Call Me Lucky*, "likely to pop up anywhere." He would be golfing in the capital and find them walking the links, or he would appear in Chicago and see them looking back at him from the crowd. Mostly they stalked him near their home ground in New York City, following him to and from his hotel, theaters, restaurants, even church; Bing saw them in a pew as he exited a confessional, shook his head, and walked quickly to the street. "I don't suppose we should use their names," he cautioned Pete Martin, "they come from a pretty nice family and I don't think the family would appreciate it if this got around."[2]

They must be twenty-two or twenty-three years of age now [October 1952]. But when I first picked up their trail they were about sixteen or seventeen. And for a couple of years, when I'd be around New York, they'd just peek around the corner of a building and that's as close as they would come. When they saw that they were detected, they'd giggle and run. They got a little closer as the years rolled on and finally one day I grabbed them both and bought them hot dogs at Howard Johnson and found out who they were. They were nicely dressed children, very well-mannered, very pleasant.... One day I was sitting on the front porch of the ranch. Elko is sixty miles beyond the ranch and there's no way to get there, no train or bus or anything, just car. And here trudging down the road comes my dear little friends from New York. They had hitchhiked out from Elko. So I brought them some tea and a sandwich out on the veranda and they went on down to the main road again and got a ride back to Elko, got on the train, and went back to New York.[3]

Shortly after *Lucky* came out and a month before he began work on the 1954 Irving Berlin picture *White Christmas,* he wrote to them, wondering if they had "noticed the episode in the book which concerned you and your visit to Nevada. I was fearful that you might be offended by it although no offence was intended—I thought it was rather a cute item and I was sure the way it was handled you would be unidentifiable." Fifty years later, the older sister, Violet, said she and Mary were relieved that he had shielded them and did not mind his changes to the story; "I mean, we never hitchhiked." One of Bing's friends, the writer Bill Morrow, had driven them from Elko to the ranch that day for lunch. The sitdown at Howard Johnson's took place three weeks, not years, into their stakeout.[4]

The Barsa girls came from a well-to-do, proper Catholic family who lived in Pelham, New York, just north of the Bronx. Their grandparents were successful Lebanese immigrants, and their parents treasured their social standing; Mr. Barsa was a Knight of Malta and they sent their daughter Violet to the Convent of the Sacred Heart alongside Kennedys and Skakels. Still, the sisters had no fear of offending their tolerant family. They did worry about Bing uncovering Violet's secret: she had begun her adventures in high school by trailing Fred Astaire, then switched her allegiance to Frank Sinatra until Mary argued that she preferred Bing. After Bing caught them out and proved to be kind and genuinely interested in them, they focused exclusively on him, and they became friends until his death, corresponding and exchanging gifts; he was godfather to Violet's firstborn. But they worried that one day Fred,

Frank, and Bing would meet and turn to the subject of fans, and as the veil fell from their eyes, they would think the sisters fickle. Crosby admired how "they [got] around." He had no idea how well.[5]

Nor did he have a clue as to their ages. The Barsa "twins" were born eight years apart, and in 1945, Violet was twenty-seven and Mary nineteen. They dressed "young" and in complementary outfits; if one had a dress with a blue design on a pink field, the other's dress had the same design in pink on a blue field. They wore matching beaver coats and hairdos. Bing often confused them with each other, as it is easy to do looking at their photographic scrapbooks, which record visits to Crosby homes when the Crosbys were away. They charmed Bing's chauffeur and other servants into posing with them on the grounds, looked into windows, exploring the garage. They became friendly with a chambermaid named Betty at the Waldorf, who allowed them into his room, and they were not above "dipping our fingers into the refuse basket into which she had just emptied his loaded paper basket." They found letters addressed to him that in time a biographer might find illuminating. In 1964, when Violet saw the Peter Sellers comedy *The World of Henry Orient,* about two schoolgirls who follow a concert pianist around Manhattan and inadvertently out his adulterous affairs, she said, "It's just like us!" But Violet and Mary believed their observations proved the opposite—that Bing and Joan Caulfield were not lovers—because as far as they could see, Bing kissed her good night and returned to his hotel alone.[6]

Yet the secret diary Mary Claire Barsa kept of their encounters with Bing, written between December of 1945 and June of 1950 and given the dreamy title "Moments of Bliss," shows that, purposely or not, he regularly eluded their surveillance. Nor did they realize that while Bing Crosby kept a suite at the Waldorf Astoria, a certain Harry Lillis may have had a hotel room elsewhere. He told the friend who made both reservations for him, "That's where I'll be living, because Celebrity Services and Paramount Pictures will know I'm at the Waldorf, and every sonofabitch in town will be calling me there."[7]

Crosby lived in New York for two full months. He did eight recording sessions and appeared as a guest or emcee on five radio broadcasts.

He went to the theater and the opera and nightclubs. He palled around with friends and took long, focused solo walks, two miles at a time, outpacing autograph hunters and usually avoiding recognition. He attended parties and benefits. He cultivated the quietly persistent sisters who were everywhere he turned. He was content, charming, social, and gay. He was miserable, angry, alone, and frustrated. His life was roiled by complications.

As the world celebrated peace or revved itself up for the new struggle with former allies, Crosby declared war on Kraft, J. Walter Thompson, NBC, and the habitual way radio governed itself. He had attempted something on this order five years earlier but did not then know how to articulate or cure his vexation. The war forced him to lie low while showing him the way forward. The Armed Forces Radio Service, with its constant production of transcription discs, proved that recorded programs were just as effective as live broadcasts, and maybe more, given the technical options of editing and rerecording. Prerecording would enable him to create a tighter, better show, and it would be strike-proof. After two years of the Petrillo ban, he proposed an idea new to broadcasting: reruns. When the head of the American Federation of Musicians called another strike (and James Caesar Petrillo did, twice), radio would be ready with a stockpile of programs. Petrillo shared the networks' disdain for recorded music, so, like it or not, Crosby was also warring with the union. The payoff, however, would be worth it: freedom from a sponsor's schedule and a network's studio. He could record a show when and where he liked. As *Billboard* demonstrated in an issue allocated to Crosby's insurrection, which it declared the most important event in show business since the advent of talking pictures, the majority of radio stars wanted to switch to prerecorded programming. But none wanted to publicly take sides until they saw how Bing's offensive played out.[8]

Crosby was confident; he expected to win in the courtroom, if it came to that, if Kraft displayed what John O'Melveny referred to as a "sinister attitude." The lawyer assured him: "If we have to have a lawsuit, we will have to have it. I feel quite certain we can win it, although it may keep you off the air for a while. That doesn't mean a great deal during these high tax days and I am sure by the time income taxes come down, you will be in good shape to go back on the air." In 1944, Olivia de Havilland triumphed over Warner Brothers after the studio tried to extend her seven-year contract, a move that a judge characterized as peonage. No judge would rule for a ten-year contract. Bing had equal confidence in his audience. Listeners, he believed, would not care if radio transmissions were live or channeled through a stylus.[9]

Another complication, also long-standing and put on hold by the war, undermined his confidence and, worse, the control he exercised in most facets of his life. The deterioration of his troubled marriage—which five years earlier narrowly averted dissolution, only to flatline into a routine of her drinking and his absences—afflicted him in ways he could acknowledge only in the confessional, if then, or in correspondence with a priest to whom he could concede that he loved Dixie but hated what she had become. (The Barsa girls observed that he spoke proudly of his sons, whose pictures he displayed, but never mentioned Dixie or, for that matter, explained why he was apart from his family on Christmas.) Crosby's marital crisis posed a threat to the public's conception of him and to his own moral code, exacerbated by issues of contrition, mortal sin, and a mother as unforgiving as the Catholic Church. In 1940, there had been no other woman vying for his attention. Now he had the attentiveness of Joan Caulfield and the harbor of her cultivated family. After two months at the ranch, he planned another two in New York; four months away from home, longer than his USO tours. Joan and her mother were arriving in New York the second week in December, after a vacation in Pebble Beach, so he had a few weeks to brood over his situation.

The public saw no brooding. In fact, it saw very little of Crosby during his first weeks in town, as he kept to himself and at a distance from the press. The Women's Press Club of Hollywood, which had routinely listed him as one of the town's most disobliging players and then gaped in surprise at his accessibility after the European adventure, announced open nominations for its Golden Apple and Crab Apple awards—Hollywood's most and least cooperative stars, respectively. Anyone could be nominated except Bing, whom the club designated as a problem child and in a class by himself. (A year later, in December 1946, after the votes were tabulated, Crosby challenged that characterization by showing up at the club's gala in a Santa Claus suit and beard, dispensing gifts. "I guess I made friends with them," he recalled, "at least for the time being."[10])

The press generally treated him as a virtually unassailable institution. *Newsweek* greeted the new year of 1946 with an astute cover story headlined "Going His Way Is a Nation's Habit After Twenty Years of Crosby Song." Had it really been twenty years since Bing and his friend Al Rinker drove their Model T down the coast from Spokane to Los Angeles in the vague hope that Al's sister, Mildred Bailey, might find work for their voice-and-piano act? To some, it seemed a lot longer. A whole generation had come of age when one singer all but dominated American popular music; it embraced Sinatra, in part, as a generational signifier, much as its children would embrace Elvis.

The magazine's story opens with Bob Hope: "Don't worry about Bing. He is the man who made Sinatra's mother swoon. And, in 1960, he'll be the man who will make Sinatra's daughter swoon." Even the editors of weekly news journals took sides, and the article relegated Sinatra—the Voice—to a "triumphant reign of adolescent hysteria," while shoring up Crosby's "incredible record" with bullet points: in recent months, he had earned an "astonishing" $400,000 in Decca royalties; won the Oscar for best actor; topped the major radio polls as the number one male vocalist, even though he had appeared on radio only five months in 1945; was ranked top box-office star for the second consecutive year; and, most impressively, won the GI poll tabulated by *Yank* (which ceased publication in December) as "the person who had done most for the morale of overseas servicemen."[11]

Newsweek might have added that among several other accolades collected in 1945, he prevailed as *Down Beat*'s best male singer; achieved two tributes in *Look,* "Entertainer of the Year" in February, and winner of its "Film Achievement Award" in December; and was widely and rightly cited as a shoo-in for a precedent-setting Oscar nomination that would make him the first actor nominated twice for playing the same role.[12] Crosby continued to collect polls, prizes, and princely sums throughout the 1940s, his steady glide receiving an unwanted boost when Sinatra crashed in 1948 and scraped bottom for the better part of five years. The Voice was undermined by bad press (front-page marital woes, a battery charge), bad musical and film choices, and the antipathy of returning GIs— the very men who later rallied behind his 1950s makeover. Sinatra embodied no less than Crosby a home-front phenomenon, a residual of the war. But Crosby bonded with fighting men while Sinatra, classified 4-F because of a perforated eardrum and chronic mastoiditis, sang love songs to the women left behind. A *Stars and Stripes* columnist jeered, "Mice make women faint, too." In his history of midcentury America, William Manchester observed that Sinatra complained about accommodations in Italy after making his one USO tour, *after* VE Day, and concluded, "It is not too much to say that by the end of the war Sinatra had become the most hated man in the Army, Navy, Air Corps, and Marine Corps."[13]

The return of those forces encompassed a vast migration. More than twelve million service personnel returned home, nearly three-quarters of them from overseas. The Hollywood studios greeted them with the promise that in the cozy darkness of neighborhood theaters, they would be able to stop time or roll it back. In Darwin Teilhet's *The Fear Makers,* one of the first of countless novels about returning GIs, the central character's amnesia is cured when he watches Hope and Crosby on the big screen. He laughs at the farce, until it "unexpectedly caught me. I said it out loud. I said, 'Look! It's Bing Crosby,' as if I wanted to tell the entire theater." The film reboots his memory, giving him "hope for the first time."[14] The studios were rewarded beyond their dreams. Unparalleled ticket sales in 1946—the last year when pictures were the national pastime, a benign addiction, cheap, ubiquitous, year-round—deluded them into feeling invincible. Movies trounced radio, the Depression, and war. Who was to say they would not prevail over television, the demise of studio-owned theatrical chains, and peace? Bing's unflagging succession of hits in the postwar years represented a bulwark of stability and reassurance. The admiration he had banked in wartime returned untold dividends in a devotion that superseded the box office.

In 1908, Bing's hometown paper, the *Spokesman-Review,* caught the spirit of the times with a poll of intellectuals and educators

asked to name the five greatest living Americans. The list was
headed by President Theodore Roosevelt and weighted with scien-
tists, businessmen, and fighters for unions and Negro rights. Four
decades later, a national poll aimed to identify living persons most
admired by Americans. Those near the top included the president
(Truman), two generals (Eisenhower and MacArthur), an entertainer (Bob Hope), and the pope (Pius XII), but all of those men
trailed Jackie Robinson, who came in second to Bing Crosby.[15]

In 1945, five days after Bing arrived in New York, a literary club
called the Banshees hosted a glittering dinner with a thousand
guests in the Waldorf's grand ballroom to celebrate George Mc-
Manus and the thirty-third anniversary of his comic strip *Bringing
Up Father* (Jiggs and Maggie). Crosby headed the roster of speakers
and performers and developed an instant rapport with another
entertainer, the droll and talented twenty-five-year-old stage star
Nanette Fabray, who had recently taken over the lead role (replacing Celeste Holm) of Evelina in *Bloomer Girl*. She mentioned to
him that her roommate was Edith Fellows, the actress playing the
title role in another musical, *Marinka,* who at the age of thirteen
had starred with Bing in *Pennies from Heaven*. He took them both
to dinner, and Fabray became his dance companion at the Stork
Club and El Morocco.[16]

"He was a good dancer and a nice friend," Fabray recalled, "and
we had a lot of laughs, but we never dated, if you know what I mean.
He liked me because I was no threat to him—he had his life and I
was seeing Leo Durocher—and I made him laugh. He loved that."
He phoned her one Sunday, waking her up, as she always slept late
after doing two shows on Saturday. He told her he had been to
church and she said, "Well, then, I will genuflect in the direction of
the Waldorf." He laughed. "He must have laughed for five minutes.
If he felt comfortable with you, you could do anything, say anything, and he just loved that kind of thing."[17]

The second act of *Bloomer Girl* has a scene where people leave a
church, stroll around the stage, and sing "Sunday in Cicero Falls."
Fabray suggested that Bing come to the Shubert Theater, dress up
as the preacher, and walk through that scene with a Bible in hand,
his head shaded by a large-brimmed hat, to see if anyone recog-

nized him. "Yes!" he said. "I'll do it!" He bought a row of seats and invited friends to the show. At the intermission, he went backstage and was starting to get into costume when a representative of Actors' Equity, the actors' union, stopped him; he was not a member and could not go onstage. "Bing said, 'I'll join now, right now, I want to do it,' but they wouldn't budge, and he went back to his seat. He was so disappointed."[18]

The day after the Banshees' banquet, Bing went to Philadelphia for the opening night of the musical *Nellie Bly,* a starry occasion, as its producer and primary sponsor Eddie Cantor filled the theater with such celebrities as Sinatra, Claudette Colbert, and George Raft. He didn't have to pull strings with Crosby, who had an emotional (and possibly financial) stake in the show. Johnny Burke and Jimmy Van Heusen wrote the score, Joe Lilley supervised the music, and Marilyn Maxwell—Bing's *KMH* partner and Sinatra's paramour—played the intrepid reporter determined to circumnavigate the globe in fewer than eighty days. Maxwell never made it out of Philadelphia. By the time the show, which featured the popular stage team of Victor Moore and William Gaxton, moved to Boston (Crosby went there too), she was replaced by Joy Hodges, who brought the role to Broadway, where crushing reviews ended the excursion after sixteen performances.

Set in 1889 and 1890, *Nellie Bly* relied on the abiding fashion for Americana that boosted the only-yesterday indulgences in minstrelsy, nineteenth-century melodramas, and costume musicals like *Bloomer Girl* and the as-yet-unreleased *Blue Skies.* Nostalgia haunted the repertoire of Bing's recent recordings, and, after Crosby won his fight and returned to the air with a prerecorded program and a new sponsor on another network, it would lead to his gleeful embrace of his childhood idol Al Jolson. *The Jolson Story* (1947) and *Jolson Sings Again* crystallized the national attachment to blackface and—in the blacklisting of the actor who played Jolson, Larry Parks—its increasing paranoia. But Bing's nostalgia for his roots also led to his escalating return to jazz and its makers. He attended the christening of Eddie Condon's daughter (one of Bing's twenty-eight godchildren) and dropped in at Zucca's, a West Forty-Eighth Street restaurant that occupied the premises of Billy La

Hiff's Tavern, the speakeasy where he and Bix Beiderbecke had frequently toasted Prohibition.[19]

He indulged his love of opera, working and socializing with Patrice Munsel, with whom he had two ties beyond music. She had lived in Spokane until age fifteen, when her mother brought her to New York to study with a vocal coach—at which time she became a close friend of Joan and Betty Caulfield. At twenty, Munsel was now in her third season at the Met, starring as Gounod's Juliet and Donizetti's Lucia. An Associated Press photographer snapped Bing backstage with her on opening night of *Romeo and Juliet,* Bing in tuxedo, sans hairpiece, miming piano accompaniment for Munsel. Two nights later, she joined Jimmy Dorsey's band and vocalist Dee Parker for Bing's Sister Kenny broadcast, *That They Might Walk,* on the Mutual Network. She sang a Verdi aria, accompanied by Sylvan Levin's chamber ensemble. Bing, backed by Dorsey, his first *KMH* bandleader, threw his "heart as well as his best showmanship into a well-paced half-hour" (*Variety*). The next night at eleven thirty, he reunited with his first major employer, Paul Whiteman, for a half-hour Victory Loan show on ABC; two nights after that, he participated with Munsel, Sinatra, Judy Garland, Dinah Shore, Nelson Eddy, Earl Wrightson, and others in a tribute to the late Jerome Kern, aired on ABC and CBS.[20]

His conspicuous absence from NBC and *KMH* was noted, but no one appeared to understand what was driving the split. *Billboard* declared it a sure bet that Bing would not return to Kraft, pointing to his certainty that the cheesemaker would lose in court, thanks to the seven-year limit on contracts under California law and the fact that Kraft had extended its deal with the actor Frank Morgan, the "substitute" host of *Kraft Music Hall.* Crosby was seen "huddling" with the advertising executive Vic Hunter, of the agency Foote, Cone and Belding, and local radio men wagered on which of FC and B's clients would get to "grab the tab"; competitors included American Tobacco, Sunkist Orange, Armour and Company, Safeway Stores, and General Motors. *Billboard* predicted GM would win but warned that Kraft would not surrender Der Bingle without exhausting every legal option. Hunter, who also stayed at the Waldorf, clung to Crosby's side, and before the dust settled he accompanied him to Elko, Sun Valley, and Jasper Park. Their friendship apparently did not survive Crosby's eventual choice of Philco, a sponsor unaffiliated with FC and B.[21]

On December 6, *The Bells of St. Mary's* opened at Radio City Music Hall, though Bing postponed seeing it for three weeks, when he went alone on a Sunday afternoon. Reviews were enthusiastic, if restrained by familiarity. James Agee praised its "leisure and spaciousness," its "delight in character and atmosphere," its "use of scenes inserted not to advance the story but for their own intrinsic charm," as well as that cat "fouled up in Fr. Crosby's famous straw hat." But he did not think Ingrid Bergman's sex appeal could compare to that of Barry Fitzgerald,[22] resented Hollywood's growing approval of "the romantic-commercial values of celibacy," and feared that O'Malley might carry on as long as Andy Hardy. The public had no doubts; *Bells* dominated the box office throughout 1946, taking in $8 million on its first release. Four films tied for second place, at $5 million each: *Blue Skies, Road to Utopia,* and the suspense stories *Leave Her to Heaven* and *Spellbound.* When Bing finally saw *Bells,* he was particularly amused by the Nativity play, which had been filmed in his absence: "One day, Leo McCarey called Bergman and me and told us to come to the studio," he explained. "He told us what was supposed to be going on and when we were supposed to clap and laugh. But we never saw the play."[23]

On December 8, Crosby's recording of "It's Been a Long, Long Time," which already topped *Variety's* computation of "best sellers on coin machines," hit *Billboard's* more decisive number one spot. It would coast in that vicinity for four months, competing neck and neck with a more dramatic version by Harry James that featured Kitty Kallen and included the verse, strings, a Willie Smith alto-saxophone solo, and a brassy reprise. By contrast, the Crosby performance—voice, solo guitar, rhythm guitar, and bass—was a study in emotional composure, forever lyrical and as informal as a cider party before a winter fire. It expressed the unspoken temper of the day and demonstrated the convalescence of Crosby's voice, coming after a string of recordings that had inclined a few longtime fans, notably the critic George Frazier, to consign him to memory lane. "Crosby sounds tired, disinterested, and incidentally, badly advised not to rest his caravan," Frazier wrote of recordings made before and after "It's Been a Long, Long Time." He incurred the wrath of loyalists, but he had a point. Bing needed to record fewer and better songs.[24]

If the sessions that Decca crammed into Crosby's New York stay were meant to provide Bing with new associates—not least a new producer in Milt Gabler, Jack Kapp's junior by a decade and the brains behind one of the great jazz independents, Commodore Records[25]—the efforts paid off handsomely with another gold record. But the overall workload mirrored a patchy year. In 1945, he recorded more sides (fifty-eight) than in any year other than 1940 (sixty), along with a record number of rejects. He would later have far more prolific years (seventy-nine sides in 1947) but never again fire quite as many blanks. Bing's voice is often arid and hollow. The upper mordents flutter effortlessly, but the phrasing is mechanical and the repertory is maddening. Dreadful new songs, several of them novelties, prefigure all too accurately the anodyne era of "(How Much Is) That Doggie in the Window," when a producer like Mitch Miller could force Frank Sinatra to yelp on "Mama Will Bark" in a duet with the tone-deaf, comically busty Dagmar.

No one could resurrect the deadwood of "I'd Rather Be Me," "Early American," "Yah-Ta-Ta, Yah-Ta-Ta," "Connecticut" (neither Rome nor Paris can challenge the maleness of its men, the slickness of its chicks), "Why Do I Like You" (pressed in a limited edition of one thousand and sold at five dollars apiece to aid St. John's Hospital), and a trio of Meredith Willson numbers written for the cherished AFRS broadcast *Dick Tracy in B-Flat,* which could not be commercially broadcast for civilians: "Whose Dream Are You," "Good, Good, Good," and "Happy, Happy, Happy Wedding Day." The Tracy hour was a *Command Performance* spectacular, with more high-priced talent than a commercial network could afford. Crosby played Tracy; Dinah Shore, Tess Trueheart; Frank Sinatra, Shaky; Bob Hope, Flat Top; Judy Garland, Snowflake; Jimmy Durante, Mole; the Andrews Sisters, the Summer Sisters; and on and on—peers at play. It triumphed across the seas, on disc, an orgy of artlessness that continues to sparkle plenty. But the songs didn't travel well. The excessively happy wedding-day number was too much for Kapp, who, despite the incredible success of discs teaming Crosby and the Andrews Sisters, declined to release it.[26]

Bing had a few good songs that were done in by unpreparedness or dreary arrangements. One can imagine, as John Scott Trotter's plucked strings sugarcoat "Just One of Those Things," Sarah Vaughan parodying them, Louis Armstrong ignoring them, or Frank Sinatra slamming the door on his way out. Bing is genially submissive, bending to their whimsy as he overthinks the lyrics and misses the song. A session with Xavier Cugat produced four numbers, including the agreeably performed but neglected "Hasta Mañana." Their double-sided hit, Augustin Lara's "You Belong to My Heart" and Ary Barroso's "Baia," both adapted with brio in Disney's *The Three Caballeros,* is languorous and dull. Kapp requested many primordial songs and pointless remakes—"I Love You Truly," "Just Awearyin' for You," "Home Sweet Home," versions of "Temptation" and "Ol' Man River"—that kindled memories of Bing's indelible originals, substantiating George Frazier's scorn. On almost every session, he strains for the high notes. His intonation wobbles. Les Paul remembered Meredith Willson nervously asking him to nudge Bing to do a second take of one of his songs because of a weak closer. Bing said, "That's all right, let 'em see that I'm human." Yet he agreed to a second take, to no better effect.[27]

After the inebriated "Ave Maria" farce, he avoided recording for two months, traveling with Hope on the Seventh War Loan drive, then going back to Hollywood to begin *Blue Skies.* His return to Decca marked an unmistakable vocal restoration. Aside from the trite Dick Tracy tunes, he and the Andrews Sisters rallied on "Along the Navajo Trail," invigorated by a swinging Vic Schoen arrangement, yielding a number one hit. Kapp continued to feed him retreads, but he handled them with élan. A sensitive rendering of the 1875 ballad "I'll Take You Home Again, Kathleen" sold modestly but showed legs; John Ford built a scene around the song in *Rio Grande* (1950), and it entered the repertories of such performers as Elvis Presley and Johnny Cash. Milt Gabler speculated that Kapp wanted a new recording of Bing's theme, recorded at Brunswick in 1931 with guitarist Eddie Lang, just to have one on Decca; the 1945 "Where the Blue of the Night," with guitarist Perry Botkin, is achingly slow and utterly controlled, with no hint of hollowness or shaky intonation. He returns to "Ave Maria," in resounding Latin, and imbues it with a chest-thumping excitement. Undaunted by Carmen Cavallaro's lounge piano, he croons "I Can't Begin to Tell You" as though he does not know or could not care less that it's a nothing song, borrowed from *The Dolly Sisters*. He probably sang it as a favor to his old friend James Monaco (the composer replaced by Jimmy Van Heusen), who died six weeks after the session. Nominated for an Oscar, it lost to another song Bing helped popularize, "On the Atchison, Topeka, and the Santa Fe," but it brought Crosby his twelfth gold record and the Monaco estate handsome royalties.

The most enduring record was "It's Been a Long, Long Time." The lyricist Sammy Cahn had been writing with Jule Styne since shortly after Pearl Harbor, and they perfected the wartime ballad with "I'll Walk Alone," "I've Heard That Song Before," "I Guess I'll Hang My Tears Out to Dry," "Saturday Night (Is the Loneliest Night of the Week)," and more. Their first coming-home song was "The Vict'ry Polka" in 1943, wishful thinking and a big hit for Bing and the Andrews Sisters. According to Cahn, after VE Day he said to Styne, "What do you think of this for a title? 'Kiss me once and kiss me twice and kiss me once again, it's been a long, long time.'" Cahn later realized, "When I gave him the title, I gave him half the song, because it's a sixteen-bar song, half a normal song, but it sounds like a full thirty-two-bar song." Their publisher Buddy Morris gave it to the song plugger Sam Weiss, who handed it directly to Bing, who chose to record it with Les Paul's guitar instead of an orchestra. Bing saw immediately that the lyric worked equally well as the entreaty of Odysseus to Penelope or Penelope to Odysseus.[28]

It was a turning point for Paul, who idolized Crosby and had wanted to work with him for years. Just out of the army and engaged in booking musicians and other artists for AFRS shows, he approached him with puppy eyes, self-assurance, and undoubted brilliance, and they hit it off. Although he and his sidemen (rhythm guitarist Cal Gooden and bassist Clinton Nordquist) were paid scale and no royalties, Bing gave him an equal presence on the recording, playing continuous obbligato and a full-chorus solo, handled superbly, every phrase spare and melodic; jazz for people who think they don't like jazz. Paul's first signature performance on record secured him a place in the higher echelon of Hollywood players. Crosby featured him regularly on radio. Fascinated by his electronic tinkering with instruments and audio fidelity, Bing offered to finance him in creating his own recording studio. Paul demurred at the time, but a few years later, Bing's resolve to perfect prerecorded radio led him to the forefront of a new invention and a new industry: the introduction of magnetic recording tape and tape-based recording. Bing presented one of the first Ampex reel-to-reel machines to come off the assembly line to Les, who cottoned to its potential for overdubbing. The history of popular music owes much to the offhand sorcery of "It's Been a Long, Long Time."

It also made Bing more receptive to working with small jazz combos, taking a suave approach laid well behind the beat, casual almost to the point of insolence. He found a terrific partner in the shrewdly facile pianist Eddie Heywood, whose six-piece band scored a gold record in 1944 with "Begin the Beguine." As a pianist, Heywood cradled Billie Holiday on several of her finest recordings (mostly on Milt Gabler's Commodore) and gave Coleman Hawkins a run for his money on their celebrated roust of "The Man I Love"; as an arranger, he could make four winds sound like a larger band. They did three sessions, and if, at times, Bing seems to contemplate how still the eye of the hurricane ought to be, they embraced fully at the last session on those old paradigms "Who's Sorry Now" and "I Found a New Baby." Kapp took out an ad in *Variety* in Heywood's name: "Thanks, Bing, for letting me cut those Decca records with you. They tell me 'Who's Sorry Now' is selling like ceiling price nylons."[29]

Even so, Crosby struggled vocally. The flip side of "It's Been a Long, Long Time," Willson's "Whose Dream Are You," is a throwaway with faded top notes. In a series of yearning sessions with Jimmy Dorsey, he lets himself loose on "Give Me the Simple Life" and comes off as stale and overemphatic on "Sweet Lorraine."

Crosby's most peculiar recording in 1945 was the four-sided adaptation of Oscar Wilde's story "The Happy Prince," narrated and directed by Orson Welles and held together by the static, shimmering background music of Bernard Herrmann (seven winds, nine strings, harp, rhythm, conducted by Victor Young). Happily, the prince is not required to sing in this glum, doomed narrative, whose themes — divine justice, life after death — suited the aftermath of a shattering war. Welles first presented the story on his program in 1941; three years later, he enticed Crosby to play the prince on *Philco Hall of Fame*, garnering enough attention to warrant the recording. Welles, typically the sonorous bass in any setting, reads with a high, dentalized fussiness that cedes the resonant lower register to Crosby. They begin awkwardly but build convincingly. Welles later considered a movie adaptation and claimed that Decca postponed the release "because neither of us would take first billing. In the end, they had to toss a coin just to get the thing out." It seems unlikely that Jack Kapp hesitated about giving first billing to the most popular recording artist on earth.[30]

The New York sessions produced more of the same, good and bad. Kapp drowned Crosby in strings and organ to channel the turn of the century with "The Sweetest Story Ever Told" and the sentimental Ethelbert Nevin lullaby "Mighty Lak' a Rose," which enjoyed a revival in the 1940s, recorded by John McCormack and Paul Robeson and sung by Bing without the dialect or much enthusiasm. Two days later Milt Gabler teamed him with the arranger Bob Haggart, who more than anyone else crafted the Dixie-swing sound of Bob Crosby's band. Bing sprang to life. The repertory remained graybeard, but it was all Irish knockabout, and Haggart's charged ensemble inspired him, as did the challenge of the rapid-fire lyrics of "Dear Old Donegal" and "McNamara's Band." The latter had been recorded unsuccessfully for Decca by a vocal trio called the Jesters, who returned to sing backup.

"Bing knew me through Eddie Condon," Gabler recalled. "They were very good friends. And Jack knew I was a Crosby fan from when I was a dealer, so he called me up to his office on the sixteenth floor—you had to walk a flight because the elevator stopped at fifteen—and there's Bing and he says, 'Hello, Curly.' I was pretty bald. His songs were generally chosen by Jack, but I liked Irish humor and I thought it would be great if we could do the song with the Jesters and Bing as a Crosby record. Crosby, of course, loved the material. He was always early. I'd walk in and he'd be sitting on a folding chair, reading the *Times*." Haggart remembered arriving at 8:45 for the 9:00 a.m. session, and Bing was waiting there, "rarin' to go and anxious to get it over with. Usually, one take was plenty for him. He was really very pleasant and very cool." Haggart's resourceful arrangement assigned the bass part to bassoon and emphasized the martial air with piccolo obbligato to the trumpet lead. "McNamara's Band" brought Bing his thirteenth gold record.[31]

A middling session the following week with Tutti Camarata was salvaged by a disarmingly even-tempered reading of Jerome Kern's demanding "Till the Clouds Roll By," ending on a Jolsonesque high-flier. He returned to Bob Haggart for a more conventional jazz date ("Sioux City Sue"), featuring Yank Lawson's trumpet and Bud Freeman's tenor sax. On December 31, he finished 1945 with more Kern and Camarata, three songs, including three stentorian takes of "Ol' Man River," his pitch wavering, his dynamics self-conscious. In describing his approach to phrasing, Crosby wrote, "Anything natural is more listenable." Henry Pleasants aptly rephrased that to suggest "he grew as a singer the less he tried to *sing*." Paying homage to Kern, an imposing monument of American melody, Bing tried awfully hard. Back in 1928, buoyed by Bill Challis's bespoke arrangement, he tossed "Ol' Man River" around like juggling pins, an effusion of derring-do, the cry of a new music, Melville's "real juice of sound." Small wonder Louis Armstrong recognized in him a kindred spirit.[32]

In January Crosby settled comfortably in a communion with Eddie Condon's pre-swing traditionalists, always a snug fit for him. Condon had just opened his eponymous Greenwich Village nightclub (it stayed alive, despite a couple of moves, through 1967), keeping Crosby up late and wobbly on more than one occasion. Kapp reserved Decca's Studio A from three till six p.m. Bing arrived fifteen minutes late and Condon rushed in thirty minutes after that, complaining about the dearth of taxis. No matter; within ninety minutes, they had three exemplary numbers. When the first take of "Blue (and Broken Hearted)" broke down, Bing kicked aside a sound absorber meant to isolate him from the instrumentalists and turned in a performance tinged with germane sadness, serenely at odds with Condon's quasi-Dixieland cheer. They had an embarrassment of pianists, one for each number: Condon's regular, Gene Schroeder; Joe Sullivan, who had bonded with Bing in a definitive 1934 recording of "Someday Sweetheart"; and Joe Bushkin, who would lead Bing's touring quartet in the 1970s. Sullivan rocked

"After You've Gone," which was slightly raucous for Kapp, who asked Wild Bill Davison to tone down his trumpet growls. Crosby chided Kapp, "You go back to the board of directors if you make one more remark. I've flown these boys in at great expense. Eddie flew in without a plane." The tumult proceeded, but Bing rode his own wave, always the eye of the hurricane. When Bushkin botched his entrance on "Personality," the number Dorothy Lamour sings in *Road to Utopia,* Bing told him to "take off the boxing gloves," and kept going. Kapp deleted the flub for the hit 78, but it was restored on subsequent releases.[33]

As if on cue, two luckless sessions ensued, including what had seemed to be a promising encounter with Lionel Hampton. On "Pinetop's Boogie Woogie," Hampton plays two-finger piano while Bing exhorts him with barrelhouse patter marinated in ersatz Southern inflections, no singing. He does sing one of Hampton's trademark numbers, "On the Sunny Side of the Street," but misses each and every high note, finding his comfort zone only on the bridge and in a chorus of chatter as Lionel blithely tweaks him about his vast wealth. That evening Crosby went to the Adelphi Theater for the opening of *Nellie Bly,* and the next morning he was back in the studio with an ensemble led by Jay Blackton, who switched from opera to Broadway after Rodgers and Hammerstein asked him to conduct the orchestra for *Oklahoma!* Bing hoped to boost Burke and Van Heusen's show by recording two of the songs (one is aptly called "Just My Luck"), but he is as flat and affectless as the material. Even Berlin's new song "They Say It's Wonderful," one of fifteen versions recorded in anticipation of the upcoming *Annie Get Your Gun,* is mechanical. It charted anyway.

"Moments of Bliss," by Mary Claire Barsa, Sunday, December 9, 1945:

> That afternoon over CBS there was a Jerome Kern memorial program on which many important stars appeared. Violet and I tried our best to get in (we even tried to bribe the worker in the boiler room to let us through) but to no avail. So we listened to the program over a Sinatra fan's portable radio. While there we met a Crosby fan who told us that Bing's room number was 667 of which

we made a mental note. When the broadcast was over we stood with all the other fans who hadn't gotten into the broadcast and all of a sudden a cab drove down the street and they all jumped on it screaming with surprise. In the cab was Bing, smoking a pipe. He looked quite pleased and kept saying "Be careful," for they were jumping all over the cab. They were so numerous that the cab had to stay for a few minutes on the street corner while the kids got out of the way.

When Bing had driven away, Violet, Ruth (a Sinatra fan), and I walked to the Waldorf and proceeded to go to room 667. When we arrived there we saw Bing's keys in the door and we were about to ring the bell when a chambermaid came along and asked us what we wanted. We said we were looking for room 600 and after she had shown us the way, she said "I thought you were looking for Bing Crosby!" We admitted we were and she told us to come back to room 667 via the fire escape and that she would meet us there. She did and went into the room and told Bing that three nice girls were outside, who wanted his autograph. He told her he would be out in a few minutes after he had finished calling. When he finally did come out we all became panic stricken and without saying a word, backed up against the wall. Finally I summoned up all my courage and said "Mr. Crosby, do you think we could have an auto-graphed picture?"

To which he replied, "I don't know why not." And with those words he put on the lights and walked to his desk. "Come in," he said three times before we budged. Then he said "What's your name?" (We told him our names.) "What school do you go to?" Being the only one who went to school, I said, "New Rochelle College." "You're sisters, aren't you?" he remarked and then looking at Violet and I who were dressed alike head to toe, he pointed to us and said, "You two are the sisters!"

Walking them to the elevator, he asked which was the older, and before they could answer, he pointed to Violet and said, "You are!" He asked their "nationality" (they said Syrian), and if they had sib-lings (two married brothers), and seemed annoyed when Violet asked if he had brought his kids to New York. He answered disin-genuously, "Sure, they've often been here." He chatted with the elevator girl and excused himself. That night Bing and the radio actor John Conte went to the Monte Carlo on Fifty-Fourth Street, two blocks West of El Morocco and around the corner from the Stork Club. The city's most exclusive nightclubs were close to each other and to the Waldorf. It happened that the Caulfield family also lived in that area, at 17 West Fifty-Fourth Street, something Violet and Mary Barsa quickly learned. Joan returned to New York that week. Meantime, Violet realized that Bing had inscribed his photograph to Vi, a name she hated. She left a note requesting a do-over.

"Moments of Bliss," by Mary Claire Barsa, Thursday, December 13, 1945:

> Violet and I sat in the Waldorf lobby and around 7 p.m. out walked Bing. I was delighted to see him and when I am delighted I grin and when I grin I look like a hyena. Bing saw us and probably wondered what I was laughing at. He turned around and glared at us when he got to the other end of the lobby. We were petrified. When we sufficiently recovered we followed him out the front door and saw him getting into a taxi and then we lost him.
>
> We then met a little autograph hound by the name of Al who after much coaxing went up to the doorman at 17 West 54th Street who told him that Bing had gone to the opera with a girl. So there we went. By some stroke of luck the ticket taker let us in for $2 and we were able to stand near where Bing was sitting with Joan Caulfield. During the intermission another lady took them backstage to see Ezio Pinza who was singing that night in *Don Giovanni*. When they came back for the second act Bing said to Joan, "My goodness, next thing we know we'll be on the stage!" During the opera Bing saw us and we covered our faces with our bunny fur mittens which matched the bunny fur ear muffs we were wearing throughout the opera everytime he looked over. Bing and Joan left early and the two of them walked outside in the snow looking for a taxi. Bing was whistling. They got in a cab on the corner of the block and we lost them.

A Crosby photograph arrived in Pelham the next morning with the inscription: "To Violet with sincere apologies for calling you Vi, Bing." That evening Bing and Vic Hunter, the advertising man who hoped Bing would choose one of his clients as a sponsor, walked to the Plaza Theater on Fifty-Eighth Street to see the new Danny

Kaye picture, *Wonder Man.* They sat in the loge and the sisters sat behind them and thought it obvious that Bing didn't find it funny. He laughed but once. The next night, he left the hotel at 6:20 p.m., but they could not follow, as Violet was in the ladies' room. They thought he might go to a show and gambled on the season's big hit, *Carousel,* at the Majestic Theater. They stood in the Majestic's doorway until eight thirty, when a taxi dropped off Bing, Vic, Joan, and "another sophisticated blonde woman (they were both in evening dresses)": Joan's sister, Betty. During the intermission, Bing stood in the lobby smoking a pipe and signing a few autographs. "He seemed to be looking at us for all his worth," Mary recorded. "Joan Caulfield came over about the end of the intermission—Bing looked at her and she blushed crimson." After the show they walked a block arm in arm and as they got into a taxi, "two girls asked Bing for an autograph but he refused angrily and said 'No!' "[34]

Crosby spent the better part of his days on the phone or reading and dictating telegrams from his suite at the Waldorf. Everett remembered the qualified results of Bing's air war in 1940, when his brother let down his hair in a meeting with Thomas H. McInnerney, the man who built Kraft-Phenix into a major industry. McInnerney, whose Murray Hill office was just blocks from the Waldorf, now sought a meeting at Crosby's convenience, and Everett aimed to bolster Bing's resolve with a telegram: REMEMBER LAST TIME YOU TALKED WITH HIM YOU SAID AFTERWARD HE WAS A HARD MAN TO TURN DOWN SO BE CAREFUL THIS TIME AND DON'T FALL FOR ANY NEW DEALS. JUST KEEP ON TELLING HIM THE SAME THING WE SAID IN THE LETTER OF WHICH WE SENT YOU A COPY BECAUSE THEY THINK YOU WILL EVENTUALLY GIVE IN AND RETURN. PARTICULARLY AFTER YOU'VE HAD YOUR VACATION YOU'D PROBABLY FEEL BETTER ABOUT THE WHOLE THING. BUT ONCE THEY ARE SATISFIED THAT YOU ARE THROUGH EVERYTHING WILL BE ALL RIGHT. Crosby wanted no meetings. He wanted no more Kraft, just a clean break and a new start. Five years earlier, McInnerney assured him that if he really wanted to leave the show, he would let him, but he hoped he would stick for a couple of years. Reminded of that in late 1944, McInnerney told Everett he did not believe Bing was serious. He still didn't believe it.[35]

John O'Melveny pelted Bing with wires advocating compromise: I CANNOT URGE YOU ENOUGH TO SETTLE WITH KRAFT IF YOU CAN DO SO

BY GIVING THEM TWO OR EVEN THREE MONTHS MORE OF BROADCASTS
AND GETTING COMPLETE RELEASE. THE OTHER SPONSORS CAN MAKE A
BETTER DEAL WITH YOU IF YOU CAN START IN FALL ON NEW PROGRAM.
IT WILL GIVE US MORE TIME TO LOOK OVER NEW DEALS AND WORK
THEM OUT AND IT WOULD RELIEVE US FROM ANXIETY OF PROTRACTED
LITIGATION. *KMH* expected Crosby back at its microphone on January 3. That was out of the question. Bing would return only to fulfill a deal guaranteeing his release. O'Melveny did not think the January 3 mandate required a formal reply, but he advised Crosby:
IF THE RELEASE IS NOT GIVEN AND YOU DO NOT INTEND TO APPEAR ON
THAT DATE YOU SHOULD TELL EVERETT TO NOTIFY THEM OF THE FACT.
OTHERWISE THEY MAY USE THIS IN CONNECTION WITH A CLAIM OF
DAMAGES AGAINST YOU LATER. O'Melveny offered to set Bing up with
a Manhattan lawyer for advice, but Bing would not consult a sub.
O'Melveny and Everett agreed to arrive in New York on January 2.
Accordingly, Bing did not notify *KMH* of his refusal to appear on
the January 3 program until the last minute.[36]

Aside from a visit to Bellevue to cheer up a twelve-year-old boy
in an iron lung and a cocktail party that he and Vic Hunter threw
at the Stork Club in honor of Barney Dean, Bing kept a low profile
for several days. The *Times* ran an odd story announcing that his
next picture would be *Coming Through the Rye,* "a semi-biographical
story of Robert Burns" — odd because it wasn't remotely true (*Welcome Stranger* was up next, and Crosby never considered the Burns
project). Other than that, the Barsa sisters heard and saw so little
of Bing, they figured he had left town.[37]

"Moments of Bliss," by Mary Claire Barsa, Sunday, December 22,
1945:

> So you can imagine our surprise when we woke that morning and
> read that he was going to appear on the *Atlantic Spotlight Broadcast* at 11:30 am. We called [the radio actress] Pat Kelley and she
> was able to get us in. He sang "White Christmas," "It's Been a
> Long, Long Time," and "Santa Claus is coming to Town" with
> Cornelia Otis Skinner and Roland Young. When the broadcast
> was over Pat Kelley told us that she had overheard that he was
> going to catch a plane after the broadcast and that a cab was going

to be waiting for him at the 6th Ave. entrance. We went there, and in a few minutes out he walked with two radio executives. He saw us, waved, and said, "Hello there!" He then got into the cab, smiled, and waved again at me—I waved back. We couldn't get a cab to follow him so we lost him and took it for granted that he had flown back to Hollywood.

Crosby emceed the *Atlantic Spotlight Broadcast,* a pre-Christmas show that patched in the BBC announcer Leslie Mitchell. Before he went on the air, Bing was trailed not by the girls but by a radio reporter for the *New York Times,* who asked him to "review a few matters that have engaged the attention of the listener and more than one radio executive." His article itemized the matters and Bing's responses:

Item: Mr. Crosby does not expect to be on the air regularly until spring at the earliest and possibly not until next season depending upon when he completes a deal to his liking.

Item: Mr. Crosby describes as "all finished" his relations with the Kraft Music Hall, his sponsor of late years. He says he and the sponsor are still "friendly"—it has been reported that the Music Hall intends to hold him to a contract—and that he may do "one or two" guest appearances for the M.H.

Item: Though "the networks don't like the idea," Mr. Crosby wants to do future programs by means of transcriptions, making three or four in advance so that he "can get away a little bit." The record of the Armed Forces Radio Network in use of transcriptions, he believes, proves the disks are the coming thing, chiefly because with them it is possible to edit, change or revise a program before it finally hits the air.

Item: Mr. Crosby vigorously disapproves of "Till the End of Time," one of the hit tunes of the moment. "They shouldn't make a soggy ballad of a Chopin military work written in tempestuous times," he explained.[38]

The third item should have been the lede. Except for a couple of lines in an October issue of *Newsweek,* the threat of canned radio had hardly been noted by the press. *Newsweek* reported, "NBC does not permit the use of transcriptions on anything but news programs," as if that settled the matter. But two weeks after the *Times* story, a Hollywood columnist identified prerecording as the key to "the Kraft-Crosby battle." He, too, assumed that fighting a network on an issue intrinsic to the medium was at best quixotic. The one letter the *Times* published as a rejoinder to its items took issue with Crosby's disparagement of the million-selling Perry Como record "Till the End of Time."[39]

Crosby did not fly back to Hollywood. He went to see Francis Spellman, the imperious archbishop of New York, who weeks later would be formally appointed cardinal. Ravenous for power and publicity, fiercely opposed to Communism, ecumenicism, liberalism, and free speech, Spellman was the antipode of Father O'Malley. But Crosby was looking for succor. He had told Joan that he was seriously thinking about divorce, and the visit to Spellman was seen by her family as evidence of his intentions. If he expected an ecclesiastical solution, he was disappointed. In the account he gave of the meeting, as remembered by Betty Caulfield, "Cardinal Spellman said, 'Bing, you are Father O'Malley and under no circumstances can Father O'Malley get a divorce.'" Betty added, "I think that was the beginning of the end for Joan and Bing."[40]

As rumors about the affair spread, Crosby found himself pressured from four sources beyond the Caulfields, a continent away: his home, the press, his mother, and a priest who was one of his oldest friends. Most painful was Dixie's hurt and outrage. In Bing's absence, she took it out on her eldest son. "Joan Caulfield, your father's with Joan Caulfield," Gary recalled her saying. "I know who he's with. He was with her this night and that night, they went here and they went there, and then she'd cry and drink." Shirley Mitchell, a radio and voiceover actor, felt responsible for Dixie's agony after she confirmed rumors of the affair. "Caulfield told everybody. She was very proud of it, I guess. So she told our hairdresser at Max Factor, Marie, who told me. Unfortunately, one night I was staying with Dixie and Dixie knew! She knew about Caulfield, and I said, 'Yes, it's true, Marie told me.' I never should have said that. A year later, Bing and I were working on the Bob Hope show and I walked over to him, very friendly, and he was so cold, as only Bing could

Besides, "the vast majority of people cannot distinguish between legal separation and divorce with intent to re-marry." Presuming on an old friendship, and perhaps the verities of B-feature melodramas, he went on to argue that any woman in pursuit of Bing must be covetous of his fame and wealth, a "terrific combination" that "naturally makes you highly attractive to the women of Hollywood, et al." Corkery thought Bing "too smart to be taken in," but these women would "give anything—and I mean anything, to get their hooks in you," and "in a home circumstance like yours, a man is pretty vulnerable in these matters."[45]

He advocated a solution similar to the one suggested by Dixie's father, although without the kidnapping factor, and apparently in line with Spellman's plan, which Crosby wanted no part of: "Bing, don't you think you should insist that Dixie go somewhere and try at least to overcome her truly sad condition. I am afraid she can never do it alone—or probably won't—on her own volition. This may be a strange thing to say Bing—but unless a radical change is made very soon, I don't think Dixie can last very long." He concluded, "Hang on, Bing. Somehow things will clear up and God will bless you, if you take this cross and bear it manfully, until such a time as He, in His Providence, sees fit to lift the burden from your shoulders." Crosby responded immediately, in longhand, one patriarch to another, relating some of his encounter with a prince of the church.

Tuesday Feb 5th '46
Dear Frank,
 Mother called me just before I left New York and told me there was some chance your Los Angeles visit might be extended a day or so. I was hopeful of finding you here upon my arrival, but I can well appreciate that more important and vital affairs called you to Spokane. I'm glad you took appointments to meet my wife and children, even if the visit had its unpleasant aspects. She was once a wonderful girl, and basically, is still a highly moral person. Unfortunately this appetite is a little too strong for her and has produced a split personality. The history of her case, of course, would take much more time than I would care to devote to it in a letter, and when you return in April (as you indicate you intend) I can supply the dreary details. I have no definite plans. This kind

of a situation defeats planning. All I really know is that it's impossible for me to do the amount of work my responsibilities require me to do, and abide this kind of a life at home. I saw Cardinal Spellman in New York, and he told me the most important thing was to put her in a sanitarium at once. That the children should not be daily witnesses to what generally transpires. But she would have to be placed there by force, and being a very proud person, I am sure would not long survive such a move. Or if she survived, past experience hardly provides hope that she would be cured. Since returning home, I've taken one step. I have told her that unless she improves I shall have to arrange a legal separation, and her partial custody of the children will depend on her ability to take care of them properly. This has frightened her some, and some improvement can be noted. The local newshawks have long heard the rumblings and smell a story—as a result every step must be carefully taken, and every precaution employed. I propose to go along on this line a few weeks and see what develops. I don't start a picture for about a month, and am thus able to spend a great deal of time at home, which is a good thing, even if sometimes unpleasant.

It's constantly amazing to me what a tough time these Crosby boys have with their wives. I guess our mother, by her example, led us to expect too much. I know I spoiled Dixie for the first eight years of our marriage. She had too much leisure, too much money, and lacked the background or experience to handle it. I'll look forward to your visit in April.

—Your friend,

Bing[46]

Spellman may have had doubts about Crosby's fortitude. According to Arnold Stevens, the cardinal wrote to Leo McCarey to emphasize "the great calamity to the church and family life everywhere" in the event of divorce.[47] For his part, Bing was underestimating Dixie if he thought his threats of separation would mute her anger, a factor ignored in his comments on her behavior and her appetites. In March, Dixie asked their lawyer to institute a suit for divorce, demanding full custody of the boys and a property settlement. Dissatisfied with his response, she threatened to hire another lawyer. "She may be just threatening," Bing's mother wrote Corkery, verging on hysteria, reluctant to use Dixie's or Bing's name.

"She is in very poor health and taking no care of herself and I think it strange that her doctor and her father and husband do not do the only thing left for her own good and safety—otherwise the disgrace will be greater and the children's lives will be in my incompetent hands. As for him, he has started work on a picture and with his broadcast is working very hard and looking badly and very thin. [Dr. Stevens] tells me that he is under a tremendous mental strain."[48]

He kept the strain under wraps. Crosby no sooner returned to Los Angeles (in late January) than he wrote the producer Sol Siegel a witty, eight-point letter with "my highly inexpert opinions" about the treatment of *Welcome Stranger*, due to start filming in March. Point six: "I am wondering if the Trudy Mason part is big enough for us to get a girl of some stature. I make this suggestion in full appreciation of the fact that a picture involving Barry Fitzgerald and myself doesn't permit much footage for a female role." Point seven: "I am wondering if a warmer and more romantic feeling between Trudy and Roy wouldn't help to accent the importance of their romantic break when it occurs." Three weeks later, Louella Parsons reported Trudy Mason would be played by Joan Caulfield.[49]

Betty Caulfield was right. Spellman marked the beginning of the end for Bing and Joan, though they continued seeing each other for nearly two years. Their friendship was quietly shaken in October 1946, a few days before *Blue Skies* bowed in theaters, when *Life* put the two of them on its cover, although it dismissed the movie as "only half good" and had previously put Crosby (with Hope) on the cover in February, thus violating its tradition of one cover per person per year. The reason was obvious to anyone who passed a newsstand. They had a stunning photograph: Bing and Joan seated on a stoop, eyes locked, she smiling radiantly in profile and holding a script, he full-face with pipe and looking sexily arch. It was surely aboveboard, two actors at a rehearsal, and yet strangely dissident: "the look of an adult man to an adult woman in an adult world." Betty Caulfield ruefully cited it as "a declaration of love on the cover of *Life* for everyone to see. And poor Dixie—my heart went out to her when she saw that picture." In 1948, after it was over, Joan's mother took her on an ocean liner to England. Patricia Neal was aboard, nursing her own wounds following a romance with Gary Cooper. "I liked Joan," she wrote in her memoir. "She was a lovely girl and we had some good talks. She, too, was in love with a married man who was quite as famous as Gary. She confided in me that she desperately wanted to marry Bing Crosby. We were in the same boat in more ways than one, but I could not tell her so."[50]

Bing and Dixie would muddle through. Their friends, almost without exception, believed that they never really considered divorce, though the subject would continue to spark rumors in coming years as Dixie drank and Bing wandered, shooting films on location, golfing on distant courses, and indulging in other infatuations—the opera singer Dorothy Kirsten wrote of their 1949 to 1950 friendship, "We actually became quite serious; however, there were two important careers to consider." Yet Bing and Dixie continued to make infrequent public appearances, sharing some genuinely playful moments. The press protected him, sometimes breathlessly. "Talking of Bing," Sheilah Graham prattled after the breakup with Caulfield, "his wife Dixie is joining him in New York this week. It's wonderful that they are so happy now with no problems at all."[51]

But this was months, years, away, and in New York, Spellman notwithstanding, Bing meant to have a little peace, pleasure, and isolation. To most people he seemed hassle-free, though the unevenness of his recordings contradicted that. He saw Joan frequently and attended many shows. It rained a lot but it also snowed, and he liked walking in the snow. One day he attended a brief meeting of the Sister Kenny Foundation at the Plaza, then he walked down Park Avenue to Dobbs, a well-known hat store, and bought a bright yellow woman's hat. He carried it with him a couple of blocks to the racquet and tennis club, where he spent two hours with Vic Hunter, then left him to visit the Caulfield apartment with his present, emerging after an hour with, apparently, a present she had bought him—a big white box, the Barsas observed, contents unknown.

For all his socializing, he could freeze up so that even friends thought him a loner. His eyes glazed over when he was bored or irritated and sometimes when he wasn't. "He could kill with those steel-blue eyes," Nanette Fabray recalled. "He could look at you in a way and you would turn to cement, but I don't think it was intentional. I spent a whole day with Einstein, and there was never anybody more warm and gentle and down to earth than Einstein in his ratty old sweaters. But he had the exact same ocean-water eyes, as cold as ocean water. My husband [the writer and director Ranald MacDougall] said they had to photograph Bing carefully, because his eyes could make him look cold in a way he wasn't." Joan Caulfield, in later life, interrupted an interviewer who implied that Bing did not know how good he was. "He realized exactly who he was. Bing was one of the smartest men I ever met and he tried to play it down and be cool," she said, "but he had a little bit of ice water for blood." The actor Billy Bakewell, who had known Bing years earlier, ran into him at a party that the Caulfields hosted for Patrice Munsel and remembered how outgoing he was that night ("Please call me, we'll get together") and how unavailable he was during the rest of his stay.[52]

A couple of hours before that party, which ended with all the guests going to the Met to see Munsel in *Lucia di Lammermoor,* Bing and Vic returned from a matinee to the Waldorf on a dark rainy afternoon and saw the Barsa sisters. Bing walked straight to them before they could run off.

> "Hello. Aren't you going home to dinner? How are you? Nasty day isn't it? We just went to a show, *Voice of the Turtle.* Have you seen it?"
>
> "No," I said. (The first word either of us had been able to utter up to this point.)
>
> "It's a good show. You should see it. This is Mr. Hunter. This is Miss Barsa and Miss Barsa, sisters. It certainly is an awful day, but you didn't get wet with those, did you?" (He was looking at our galoshes and umbrellas lying side by side in front of us.)
>
> "You didn't get wet!" exclaimed Mr. Hunter, who at this point was near hysteria.
>
> "Well we've got to get ready for dinner. Goodbye. We'll be seeing you." And with those parting words Bing took leave of us in a complete delirium.[53]

Bing spent a great deal of time with Joan, but Joan did not spend as much time with him as the Barsas did, though not even Bing knew it. The next day, a Sunday, Bing went from church to a bar to Radio City Music Hall to finally see *The Bells of St. Mary's*. The Barsa sisters, after unsuccessfully attempting to bribe an usher, snuck through an exit door and strolled into the lobby with a Rockette, then took a forward place in the line that went around the block. Once they were in the theater, they told an usher they needed to find their father in the reserved section and that a vice president of Radio City Music Hall, whom they knew by name, had told them to go right up. They found seats one row behind Crosby. "Every so often he lit his pipe," Mary wrote. "He seemed to have a bottle of liquor in his coat pocket and often laughed throughout the picture. When the picture was over he walked out the front door and in the pouring rain he walked back to the Waldorf, passing the line of people waiting to get into the picture. Few people recognized him—one woman grabbed ahold of his arm. Two girls in the rain asked him for his autograph and he told them this was no place to ask for an autograph to which they replied 'Let's go back to Sinatra!' Near the Waldorf, a little boy, an autograph hound, told him the front door was mobbed and that he'd better go in by the driveway. In gratitude Bing gave him an autograph and dedicated it to him. The boy was thrilled. Bing went in by the driveway." He learned that night that Dixie had taken a fall and was in the hospital. Her caretaker assured him she was all right.[54]

Bing began the last day of the year—cold and rainy—at Decca (the "Ol' Man River" session). In the late afternoon, he and Joan and Vic and Betty met at the Sherry-Netherland Hotel, where a chartered bus arrived for them and a few other people invited by Winthrop Rockefeller to see the year out at the immense Rockefeller estate in Pocantico Hills. He spent the first day of the new year in conference about Kraft, and on January 2, he formally joined the battle with a telegram to J. Walter Thompson's head of broadcasting, John Reber, the man who had brought him to *Kraft Music Hall*:

AS YOU HAVE BEEN HERETOFORE NOTIFIED MY OBLIGATION TO YOU
AND THE KRAFT CHEESE COMPANY TERMINATED AS OF MY LAST BROAD-
CAST OF 1945. THEREFORE I WILL NOT APPEAR ON THE KRAFT CHEESE
RADIO PROGRAM OF JANUARY 3, 1946 OR ANY TIME THEREAFTER UNLESS

IT IS PART OF AN ARRANGEMENT FOR MY FORMAL RELEASE. REGARDS.
BING CROSBY

He left the hotel that afternoon and speed-walked uptown, unaware he was being shadowed. He was glad when he saw them. He did not want to be alone and he did want to talk lawsuit. The remarkably retentive memories of Violet and Mary Barsa were put to the test that evening when they sat down to re-create the day. Without the help of a recording device, they created a singular, persuasive portrait of Crosby in a dialogue caught on the hoof. It is usually obvious when Bing is speaking, but the sisters don't always distinguish between themselves in noting their replies.

"Moments of Bliss," by Mary Claire Barsa, Wednesday, January 2, 1946:

Bing left the Waldorf about 1:30 that day and walked briskly to 92nd Street on Park Ave. It was a very cold day and we followed behind him shivering for all we were worth. At 92nd Street he crossed over to Madison Ave. and went into a Liggett drugstore. Violet and I figured he went into eat so we crossed over to see what was going on but just as we got to the door, out walked Bing. We both shrieked and ran across the street. Bing kept walking straight ahead until he got half way down the next block. Then he stopped and with a swirl of the arm he beckoned to us to come to him. This he did many times for we didn't budge. Finally he crossed the street and started to come toward us, still gesticulating madly. Finally we got up our courage and came over to him.
  "No school?" he said.
  "No it's our vacation," I said.
  "When do you go back?"
  "Monday."
  "Where did you pick me up? You didn't pick me up at the hotel!"
  "Yes."
  "No!"
  "Honestly."
  "You must have thought I was crazy walking so fast. Am I walking too fast for you now?"
  "No."

"Can you walk in those heels?" (looking at Violet's high heels.)

"Yes. I always wear high heels."

"Have you seen any movies lately?"

We laughed and said, "We saw *The Bells of St. Mary's*."

"When?"

"Sunday."

"That's when I saw it."

"I know. We sat right behind you."

"No!"

"Really!"

"Oh, you did not."

"We did so."

"But I sat in a reserve seat. You had to have reserved seats to sit there."

"I know." (Violet then told him of all the trouble we had trying to get into the Music Hall. Bing laughed out loud when he heard about the conscientious usher we tried to bribe.)

"I hope you don't mind our walking with you," I said.

"I asked you to come, didn't I? Besides I am enjoying your company."

[They talked about a country club Bing once played at in New Rochelle and the sisters' schooling, their family's Syrian and Roman Catholic background, their father's negligee business, their married brothers. Bing asked their age; Mary (nineteen) said she was eighteen, and Violet (twenty-seven) said she was twenty-one. Bing said he had thought they were younger than that.]

"You know I liked *The Bells of Saint Mary's* much more than *Going My Way*. I don't usually like the pictures I'm in but I really liked this one. How did you like Bergman?"

"She was good."

"It was sad wasn't it?"

"Well your face was sad at the end."

(Bing laughed.) "You know, I spoke to my kid over the phone the other day. He said he had seen *The Bells* and I asked him how he liked it. 'Oh, it's all right,' he said, 'but the place was full of sobbers!'"

"Did you go to the 21 Club on Christmas?"

"Yes, they gave a party for the good customers there. All the food and drinks were on the house. Boy, I certainly put away a lot of liquor that day!"

"Did you go to the White Mountains on New Year's Eve?"

"The White Mountains?! (He laughed.) Is that what the driver told you? No. A few of us went up to Rockefeller's place in Tarrytown to get away from the smoke and crowd of the cafés. That's right by your place isn't it. We could have driven you home!"

"Gee whiz!"

"How do you get here? [They describe the forty-minute train to Grand Central.] So you like the opera?"

"Yes, I used to be crazy about Ezio Pinza until I heard..."

"That he's a wolf? Yes, I guess he is a fast operator. You'd have to jump out of the window if you were alone with him in the room."

"Well at least now he's married and settled down. Did you ever see him as Mephistopheles?"

"No."

"He's really dreamy."

"How can you have a dreamy devil? I saw another opera, *Lucia di Lammermoor,* the other night."

"Was Lily Pons in it or Patrice Munsel?"

"Patrice Munsel, she's very good."

"Are you going again?"

"I don't know."

"How long are you staying in New York?"

"Oh, about 10 days or two weeks. My brother and my lawyer came in today. We have an awful lot of work to do."

"Everett?"

"Yes. We have an awful lot of work to do."

"It's amazing how you walk along the street and no one recognizes you."

"Oh, they recognize me sometimes when I walk here on Park Ave. But when I walk on 6th Ave. and Broadway they all recognize me. (A few minutes later, two women walked by and he watched them out of the corner of his eye, but they didn't really look at him.) "You're not cold are you? Haven't you got any buttons on your coat? Well, you shouldn't be cold with those! (looking at our bunny fur mittens.)

"Aren't you cold?"

"No." (He opened his coat and revealed a lumber jacket and a yellow scarf.) "See these gloves. They were made out of the hide of an animal from my ranch in Nevada. You give in the hide and they charge $2 to make each pair of gloves." (He stopped to look at a newspaper picture of German war criminals.) "I hope they get them," he said.

"I thought you were in the hospital. It said so in the paper."

"Oh, they say that every day."

"Does it bother you when we follow you around?"

"Oh no, you never bother me. It's those autograph hounds that bother me. There's one boy who stood at the door of the hotel and I swear he had gotten 35 autographs already. I don't know what they do with them. I think they trade in 35 of mine for one of Sinatra's. Don't you think that's what they do? (laughs). I got your letter. Which one of you wrote it?"

"She wrote it. I dictated it," said Violet.

"What are your first names again?"

"I'm Violet."

"I'm Mary."

Whenever there was a lull in the conversation he'd start to whistle "I Apologize." Violet and I would giggle and he'd seem very pleased.

"Nice hats," he said pointing to the ones just like he had bought a few days before for Joan Caulfield. "Tres chic."

We reached 50th Street and with his arm he motioned for us to turn right and proceeded to lead us into Howard Johnson's. We sat at the counter and all ordered hot dogs and hot chocolates.

"You know Howard Johnson's is renowned for its frankfurters. I came in here the other day and Quentin Reynolds was in here. You know, he's the newspaper correspondent, and he said that Howard Johnson's has the best frankfurters around here."

[They asked if Bob Hope was coming to New York. Bing said that he and Hope were friendly but not real friends and didn't socialize much. He explained the policy of reciprocal guest shots and said Bob wanted his sons to appear on his show and promised to return the favor when they were old enough to have their own program. The Barsas showed him pictures of their two-year-old niece.]

"Are your kids going to have a program of their own? I read they were."

"I don't think so. They're very busy."

He left all the change he had in his pocket as a tip and we then thanked him profusely, "It was wonderful! We were so hungry!"

"You could have two frankfurters. You're not sorry you came now are you? You know I'd like to have my car shipped out here and then go back by the southern route."

"That would be nice."

"Yes, but I don't suppose I will. I guess I'll have to go back on the [Twentieth] Century."

A cop came over and asked him if he were in a hurry to cross the street and Bing said no.

"Aren't you ever in a hurry?" Violet asked.

"No."

"I read you were in the hospital," said the cop.

"They say that every day!"

"You should sue them!" retorted the cop.

"Yes, I'll work up a case!"

When we got across the street he said, "I've got some shopping to do now. Then I want you to come up to my room. I have something to give you." Eddie Cantor passed by. He said "Hello, Bing." Bing said "Hello, Edward."

We got to the door of the men's store next to the front door of the Waldorf and Bing was besieged by autograph hounds. Bing asked: "Why don't you go home and read a book and get yourself an education?" A fan asked him to autograph a picture which he said he had stolen from the subway. "Oh, I can't sign that!" Bing exclaimed, but he did anyway. Then as Bing was signing, a store manager came over to Violet and me and told us we couldn't stand there, so Bing, to show him that we were his friends, said "You better stand inside. I'll be with you in a minute." Violet stuck her nose in the air at the manager, who sheepishly muttered, "Excuse me."

We then all went into the store where Bing asked for some bow ties, the kind you tie yourself. They showed him what they had and in a second's time he said, "I'll take these, these, and these." The man asked him if he wanted them delivered, but Bing said "Just put them in a sack." By that time a large crowd of people had gathered in the street, outside the window and peering in. Bing looked up, seemed surprised, pointed, and said "Look at that!" Then he curtsied to his audience. The man in the store asked him if he'd please give the woman an autograph and he did. We walked into the Waldorf. One man he obviously knew said hello and Bing told him to call him and they'd have lunch together. He motioned for us to go into the elevator first and said "Apres vous." When we got to his room the door was open—they had just finished cleaning it.

"Come in," he said to us. He took off his coat and lumber jacket, which revealed a bright red woolen shirt and a yellow tie. In the meanwhile, Violet and I spied a large picture of his 4 kids which he had on the mantelpiece and we went into ecstasies about how cute they were. Also on the mantelpiece was a small snap shot of Bing taken overseas in a uniform and a large picture of Bob Hope in uniform from *Monsieur Beaucaire,* and on it was inscribed, "Always a friend of the Working Man." While we looked at the pictures Bing went into his bathroom and came out with a cigarette lighter. "I thought they gave me two of these," he said apologetically, "but it seems I only have one." He handed it to me and we thanked him profusely. He went into the bedroom and came out with a silver picture frame holding five pictures. "This is what they gave me on the set of *The Bells of St. Mary's.*" Violet said, "Oh, the twins look alike in their pictures."

"They don't look alike. Look over there." (pointing to the picture on the mantel).

Bing got out a record and wrote on it "To Violet and Mary, Bing Crosby." "It's a cowboy number," he said. "Hasn't been released yet so don't give it away now." Next he went through the mass of papers and pictures on his desk and took one and inscribed it, "To my friend Violet, Bing Crosby of Tuscaloosa, Nevada." "It was taken on my ranch," he said. "I suppose you want a picture too, Mary?" he asked.

"Yes please, if you don't mind." At this cue he got down on his hands and knees and went through a pile of papers on the floor in a corner of the room. After a while he came up with another picture and wrote on my picture what he had written on Violet's.

"Well, goodbye now," he said. "Be good!"

"Goodbye, Mr. Crosby. Thank you ever so much for everything."

The next day, at eleven thirty a.m., Crosby answered a rap on his hotel door, and a process server named Steve Brodie said, "Mr. Crosby, I'm glad to see you," as he handed him a summons in the suit by Kraft Foods Company. Bing turned to O'Melveny and Everett and said, "This is it." The injunction filed in New York Supreme Court charged him with breach of a 1937 contract that put him at the company's disposal until 1950. Everett, buttonholed later in the day at the CBS studio where his wife, Florence George, rehearsed for a program, feigned surprise: "But now they'll get it. They asked for it." The die was cast. This would be the year when Bing enjoyed the peak of his popularity while surmounting a nuisance suit in order to attempt a radical change in broadcasting, parleying legal and personal issues with his brother Ted, dissolving his interest in Del Mar, closing his acquisition of a baseball team, finding a new sponsor, and figuring out exactly how a transcribed radio program ought to work; in addition, he continued to make films and records and kept struggling to find the solution to a marriage stretched past the breaking point. The only good news of the day was Dixie's return from the hospital. Four days later, her mother, Nora Wyatt, died suddenly of a heart attack, at the age of sixty-three, leaving Dixie more alone than ever. Bing continued his New York residency for another two weeks.[55]

Amid the daily sessions with his lawyer, brother, accountant, and other interested parties, one of which erupted in "loud voices," he routinely visited the Caulfield home; dined and drank at 21, Leon and Eddie's, Eddie Condon's, the Swiss Grill at the Gotham Hotel; went to the theater; and bought Cokes for the Barsas, who managed to stand in the wings during a performance of an Elmer Rice comedy, *Dream Girl*, attended by the Caulfield family, Crosby, and Hunter. Joan "laughed herself into a delirium" and Bing peeked "through his fingers" and seemed "quite preoccupied with his thoughts." Mr. and Mrs. Caulfield left early, Vic disappeared, and Bing and Joan slipped away together in a taxi. There was an awkward moment late one afternoon as he and Joan walked along East River Drive near Ninety-Sixth Street when a stranger yelled, "That's not Dixie with you," and Bing answered, "That's right." Joan never showed up at the Waldorf unless there was a third person, man or woman, with her. He phoned home regularly for succinct conversations with the boys and a general report from a caretaker named Eleanor. He didn't speak of Dixie to friends, and it's not known how much he spoke to her.

Professionally, the trip ended with two of the most wooden recording sessions of his career and deliverance. After a judge told Kraft that its contract amounted to indentured servitude, O'Melveny orchestrated a deal whereby Crosby recommended *Kraft Music Hall* from early February to early May in exchange for complete release. The long-delayed return to Los Angeles, to Paramount Pictures, to his family, was delayed no longer. He went home on the Twentieth Century.[56]

*　　*　　*

Something important had happened over the previous two months, something that Crosby and most others hardly noticed. Yet it would be remembered long after the crises and negotiations, the pleasures and frustrations that occupied him in this period and in the years to come. It outlived memories of *Kraft Music Hall*, most of his movies, and most of his recordings, and if any of his ardent admirers are inclined to discount this now-commonplace aspect of his work, they can hardly deny that it has ensured his prominence in a cultural pantheon thoroughly corrupted by amnesia. On December 1, Decca introduced the five-disc (ten songs) Bing Crosby album called *Merry Christmas*. It came out just as the three-disc album *Going My Way* completed its second month in the top ten—his first top-ten album—and accumulated extraordinary sales with each passing week. The success of these bulky, expensive compilations came as a surprise, given the millions of singles already sold. Yet *Merry Christmas* counts for more than sales; it set the table for the thematic compilations that flourished in the age of vinyl and launched an international tradition, flinging a compulsory challenge to generations of performers to enter the seasonal sweepstakes.

In 1947, Decca downsized *Merry Christmas* to four discs (expunging "Danny Boy" and "Let's Start the New Year Right"), greatly expanding sales and eventually going gold. On June 18, 1948, Columbia Records introduced the LP—the long-playing, unbreakable disc that revolves 33⅓ times a minute—in ten- and twelve-inch formats. Within eighteen months, thirty Bing Crosby compilation albums hit the market, including the ten-inch disc of *Merry Christmas,* which climbed the top ten, December after December, thirteen times between 1945 and 1960 and continued to sell as reliably, if not in the same quantities, as trees and menorahs; more than fifteen million to date. With the advent of the LP, countless Christmas albums appeared. Yet in nearly seventy-five years, only the 1957 *Elvis' Christmas Album* outsold it. Inevitably, Decca expanded the album as a twelve-inch disc, adding four songs recorded by Crosby in 1950 and 1951, when he was in exceptional voice. On the Hawaiian-themed "Mele Kalikimaka," with the Andrews Sisters, he exalts the pop instinct, surfing the beat with gorgeous lassitude, robust and sly. The holiday repertory is no gimmick for him. From "White Christmas" and "I'll Be Home for Christmas" to "Silver Bells" and "Mele Kalikimaka," the songs Crosby introduced or popularized exemplified the quality that informs all of his finest work; in T. S. Eliot's idiom, "music heard so deeply / That it is not heard at all, but you are the music / While the music lasts."[57]

"Moments of Bliss," by Mary Claire Barsa, Wednesday, January 24, 1946:

> We thought Bing had left for Hollywood so we disconsolately went up to the 6th floor and walked by his room and to our surprise we saw a note in his mailbox. We pulled it out and read: "Mr. Crosby, Mr. Eddie Sutherland called twice and wants you to call him before twelve today. Very important." To our great joy we realized that he was still there so we went down to the lobby and sat. About 2:30 or so he walked out with a brown envelope under his arm. He got in a cab but we didn't follow him. About an hour later he came out of Joan Caulfield's with about 3 books under his arm and no envelope. He walked back to the Waldorf, whistling as he went. On the way a woman grabbed his arm and said "Bing Crosby!!!" He turned around and smiled at her. At the Waldorf he paid his bill downstairs and then went up to his room. Everett and a couple of other men were up there packing for him. After a while Bing came out and tipped the chambermaids and worker at the desk and said: "Aren't you glad to get rid of me? Take good care of my room now." Betty, the chambermaid we made friends with, came over to us very excitedly and told us he had given her $20. She also told us how he had spoken in Italian to her the other day and how floored she was that he knew she was Italian. (She spoke with a thick accent but I guess she didn't realize it). Anyway she went in and told him there were two little girls outside who wanted to say goodbye to him. So he yelled out "Goodbye." The maid, however, tried to drag me in to see him, but I wouldn't go. There was a vacant room right opposite Bing's so Betty let us stay there while she cleaned it and in that way we could see him. Then all of a sudden out walked Everett and we both ran in various directions to hide. (Violet locked herself up in the bedroom and I went into a closet.) About 5:10 Bing and Everett left together but as they had moved down the hall, Betty called out: "Goodbye Mr. Bing

Crosby!" He turned around and said goodbye and then turned
around again (a double take) and said: "Oh, my two good friends
from Pelham," and with that he walked all the way down the hall
and shook hands with each of us. "You're leaving?" was my brilliant question. "Yes," he answered. "When are you coming back?"
Violet asked. "I don't know," he said rather sadly. "Well, goodbye
now." And with that he started to walk down the hall again. Everett seemed completely bewildered. He finally said: "He'll be back
on the air February 7th!" We then went down the driveway and
Bing was standing there with his suitcase waiting for a cab. He
stood there quite some time before he got a cab. When he did, we
ran to Grand Central (it was snowing). By the time we reached
the 20th Century, the train started to pull out and we couldn't see
him.

They didn't see him again until April of 1947. But on December
24, they received the first of thirty-two annual cards in a correspondence that included dozens of letters, notes, gifts, and congratulations on marriages and christenings and Mary's distinguished
career as a professor of biology at Manhattanville College. Sent
airmail and special delivery, the card shows a golden Madonna and
Child and is inscribed DIXIE, BING, AND THE BOYS.

Bing Crosby Wartime Discography

This section includes all studio sessions recorded by Crosby between 1940 and 1946. Alternate or rejected takes are omitted, but a few rejected sessions are included if they were eventually released. The parenthetical information denotes the instrumental leaders and the vocalists and vocal groups accompanying him; bandleaders appear to the left of the slash, and vocal groups (sometimes identified as *chorus*) to the right. Artists who share billing with him—the Andrews Sisters, for example—precede the ensemble leaders. All of these recordings were made for Decca Records.

On most of these recordings and on his weekly radio show, Crosby was accompanied by the John Scott Trotter orchestra. By 1940, the ensemble averaged eighteen to twenty pieces: three or four trumpets, three trombones, four or five saxophones, four violins, and four rhythm. By 1944, the ensemble averaged twenty-six to twenty-eight pieces because Trotter tripled the string section to include eight violins, two violas, and two cellos. He often added a French horn (a signature instrument in the Victor Young ensembles) and a harp. Trotter's personnel remained notably stable in these years, drawing from a reliable pool of Hollywood studio aces:

John Scott Trotter, conductor, arranger. Edward Ehlert, Charles Green, Andy Secrest, Robert Goodrich, Uan Rasey, Billy May (also arranger), Manny Klein, Red Nichols, Charles Griffard, trumpets. Abe Lincoln, Galen Gloyde, Kingsley Jackson, Gus Mayhew, Elmer Smithers, Peter Bielmann, trombones. Arthur Frantz, French horn. Jack Mayhew, Howard White, Lyall Bowen, Joseph Krechter (also arranger), Richard Clark, John Cascales, Morty Friedman, Harold Lawson, saxophones. Sam Freed (also arranger), Henry Castleton, Gerald Joyce, Maxim Sobolewsky, Peter Ellis, Walter Edelstein, Larry Kurkdjie, Raymond Martinez, Nicholas Pisani, Jack Samuels, Jacob Heiderich, Harry Bluestone, Henry Hill,

Howard Halbert, Samuel Cytron, Alfred Lustgarten, Mischa Russell, Alex Kolton, Ray Cerf, violins. Ted Bacon, George Sandell, Julius Toldi, Leon Fleitman, David Sterkin, violas. Karl Rossner, John Sewell, Cy Bernard, Arthur Kafton, Fred Goerner, cellos. Myra Hawley or Vincent Spolidoro, harp. Charles LaVere, piano. Perry Botkin, guitar. Ben Creitz, "Doc" Whiting, or Artie Shapiro, bass. "Spike" Jones or John Cyr, drums.

1940

Feb. 9:	Marcheta	(John Scott Trotter)
	Tumbling Tumbleweeds	(John Scott Trotter)
	If I Knew Then (What I Know Now)	(John Scott Trotter)
	The Girl with the Pigtails in Her Hair	(John Scott Trotter)
Feb. 25:	Devil May Care	(John Scott Trotter)
	The Singing Hills	(John Scott Trotter)
	I'm Waiting for Ships That Never Come In	(John Scott Trotter)
Mar. 22:	Beautiful Dreamer	(John Scott Trotter)
	Jeanie with the Light Brown Hair	(John Scott Trotter)
	Yours Is My Heart Alone	(John Scott Trotter)
	Sierra Sue	(John Scott Trotter)
Apr. 12:	Meet the Sun Halfway	(John Scott Trotter)
	April Played the Fiddle	(John Scott Trotter)
	I Haven't Time to Be a Millionaire	(John Scott Trotter)
	The Pessimistic Character (with the Crab Apple Face)	(John Scott Trotter)
	The Pessimistic Character (with the Crab Apple Face) (parody)	(John Scott Trotter)
Apr. 15:	Mister Meadowlark	(Johnny Mercer/Victor Young)
	On Behalf of the Visiting Firemen	(Johnny Mercer/Victor Young)
July 1:	Trade Winds	(Dick McIntyre)
	A Song of Old Hawaii	(Dick McIntyre)
	Aloha Kuu Ipo Aloha	(Dick McIntyre)
July 3:	When the Moon Comes over Madison Square	(John Scott Trotter)
	Only Forever	(John Scott Trotter)
July 6:	*Ballad for Americans*	(Victor Young/Ken Darby Singers)
	Part One	
	Part Two	
	Part Three	
	Part Four	

July 10:	Rhythm on the River	(John Scott Trotter)
	That's for Me	(John Scott Trotter)
	I Found a Million Dollar Baby	(John Scott Trotter)
	Can't Get Indiana Off My Mind	(John Scott Trotter)
July 20:	The Waltz You Saved for Me	(Paradise Island Trio)
	Where the Blue of the Night Meets the Gold of the Day	(Paradise Island Trio)
	When You're a Long, Long Way from Home	(Paradise Island Trio)
	When I Lost You	(Paradise Island Trio)
	Paradise Isle	(Paradise Island Trio)
July 23:	Do You Ever Think of Me?	(Victor Young/Merry Macs)
	You Made Me Love You	(Victor Young/Merry Macs)
July 27:	Legend of Old California	(John Scott Trotter)
	Please	(John Scott Trotter)
	You Are the One	(John Scott Trotter)
	Prairieland Lullaby	(John Scott Trotter)
Dec. 3:	Along the Santa Fe Trail	(John Scott Trotter)
	Lone Star Trail	(John Scott Trotter)
	It's Always You	(John Scott Trotter)
	I'd Know You Anywhere	(John Scott Trotter)
Dec. 9:	De Camptown Races	(Victor Young/King's Men)
	Did Your Mother Come from Ireland?	(Victor Young/King's Men)
	My Old Kentucky Home	(Victor Young/King's Men)
	Where the River Shannon Flows	(Victor Young/King's Men)
Dec. 13:	Tea for Two	(Connie Boswell/Bob Crosby)
	Yes Indeed!	(Connie Boswell/Bob Crosby)
	Christmas greeting to Decca employees	(Connie Boswell/Bob Crosby)
Dec. 16:	San Antonio Rose	(Bob Crosby)
	It Makes No Difference Now	(Bob Crosby)
Dec. 20:	You're Dangerous	(John Scott Trotter)
	A Nightingale Sang in Berkeley Square	(John Scott Trotter)
	You Lucky People, You	(John Scott Trotter)
	Birds of a Feather	(John Scott Trotter)
Dec. 23:	Dolores	(Bob Crosby/Merry Macs)

	Pale Moon	(Bob Crosby/Merry Macs)
Dec. 30:	Chapel in the Valley	(Victor Young)
	I Only Want a Buddy, Not a Sweetheart	(Victor Young)
	When Day Is Done	(Victor Young)
	My Buddy	(Victor Young)

1941

May 23:	Who Calls?	(John Scott Trotter)
	Lullaby (Cradle Song, Brahms)	(John Scott Trotter)
	You and I	(John Scott Trotter)
	Be Honest with Me	(John Scott Trotter)
	Goodbye, Little Darlin', Goodbye	(John Scott Trotter)
May 26:	The Waiter and the Porter and the Upstairs Maid	(Mary Martin, Jack Teagarden)
	Birth of the Blues	(Jack Teagarden)
June 14:	Clementine	(John Scott Trotter/Music Maids and Hal)
	The Old Oaken Bucket	(John Scott Trotter/Music Maids and Hal)
	Lights Out 'Til Reveille	(John Scott Trotter)
	The Sweetheart of Sigma Chi	(John Scott Trotter)
June 16:	Sweetly She Sleeps, My Alice Fair	(John Scott Trotter)
	Dream Girl of Pi-K.A.	(John Scott Trotter)
	I Wonder What's Become of Sally?	(John Scott Trotter)
	Old Black Joe	(John Scott Trotter)
	Mary's a Grand Old Name	(John Scott Trotter)
July 5:	Oh! How I Miss You Tonight	(John Scott Trotter)
	Don't Break the Spell	(John Scott Trotter)
	Dear Little Boy of Mine	(John Scott Trotter)
	Nell and I	(John Scott Trotter)
	Danny Boy	(John Scott Trotter)
July 8:	You Are My Sunshine	(Victor Young)
	Ridin' Down the Canyon	(Victor Young)
	Flores Negras (You're the Moment of a Lifetime)	(Victor Young)
	No Te Importe Saber (Let Me Love You Tonight)	(Victor Young)
July 14:	Ol' Man River	(Victor Young)
	Day Dreaming	(Victor Young)
	Darling, Je Vous Aime Beaucoup	(Victor Young)
	The Anniversary Waltz	(Victor Young)
July 30:	Let's All Meet at My House	(Woody Herman)
	Humpty Dumpty Heart	(Woody Herman)

	The Whistler's Mother-in-Law	(Woody Herman/Muriel Lane)
	I Ain't Got Nobody	(Woody Herman)
Oct. 24:	Shepherd Serenade	(Harry Sosnick)
	Do You Care?	(Harry Sosnick)

1942

Jan. 18:	I Want My Mama	(Woody Herman)
	Deep in the Heart of Texas	(Woody Herman)
	I'm Thinking Tonight of My Blue Eyes	(Woody Herman)
Jan. 19:	Sing Me a Song of the Islands	(Dick McIntyre)
	I'm Drifting Back to Dreamland	(Dick McIntyre)
	The Singing Sands of Alamosa	(Dick McIntyre)
	Remember Hawaii	(Dick McIntyre)
Jan. 24:	Miss You	(John Scott Trotter)
	Mandy Is Two	(John Scott Trotter)
	Angels of Mercy	(John Scott Trotter)
	Skylark	(John Scott Trotter)
Jan. 26:	Nobody's Darlin' but Mine	(Victor Young)
	When the White Azaleas Start to Bloom	(Victor Young)
	The Lamplighter's Serenade	(Victor Young)
	Blue Shadows and White Gardenias	(Victor Young)
Jan. 27:	Blues in the Night	(John Scott Trotter/Music Maids)
	Moonlight Cocktail	(John Scott Trotter)
	I Don't Want to Walk Without You	(John Scott Trotter)
Mar. 13:	Lily of Laguna	(Mary Martin/John Scott Trotter)
	Wait Till the Sun Shines, Nellie	(Mary Martin/John Scott Trotter)
Mar. 16:	Got the Moon in My Pocket	(John Scott Trotter)
	Just Plain Lonesome	(John Scott Trotter)
	The Waltz of Memory	(John Scott Trotter)
May 25:	Lazy	(Bob Crosby)
	Let's Start the New Year Right	(Bob Crosby)
	I've Got Plenty to Be Thankful For	(Bob Crosby)
May 27:	I'll Capture Your Heart Singing	(Fred Astaire, Margaret Lenhart/Bob Crosby)
	When My Dreamboat Comes Home	(Bob Crosby)
	Walking the Floor Over You	(Bob Crosby)
May 29:	White Christmas	(John Scott Trotter/Ken Darby Singers)
	Abraham	(John Scott Trotter/Ken Darby Singers)

	Song of Freedom	(John Scott Trotter/Ken Darby Singers)
June 1:	The Bombardier Song	(John Scott Trotter/Music Maids and Hal)
	Easter Parade	(John Scott Trotter)
	Happy Holiday	(John Scott Trotter/Music Maids and Hal)
	Be Careful, It's My Heart	(John Scott Trotter)
June 8:	Adeste Fideles	(John Scott Trotter/Max Terr Mixed Chorus)
	Silent Night	(John Scott Trotter/Max Terr Mixed Chorus)
	Faith of Our Fathers	(John Scott Trotter/Max Terr Mixed Chorus)
	God Rest Ye Merry, Gentlemen	(John Scott Trotter/Max Terr Mixed Chorus)
June 10:	Conchita, Marquita, Lolita, Pepita, Rosita, Juanita Lopez	(Vic Schoen)
	Road to Morocco	(Vic Schoen)
	Ain't Got a Dime to My Name	(Vic Schoen)
June 12:	My Great, Great Grandfather	(John Scott Trotter)
	A Boy in Khaki, a Girl in Lace	(John Scott Trotter)
	Moonlight Becomes You	(John Scott Trotter)
	Constantly	(John Scott Trotter)
July 9:	By the Light of the Silvery Moon	(Eddie Dunstedter)
	But Not for Me	(Eddie Dunstedter)
	Hello Mom	(Eddie Dunstedter)

1943

July 2:	Sunday, Monday, or Always	(Ken Darby Singers)
	If You Please	(Ken Darby Singers)
	Duke the Spook (special issue)	(Jimmy Van Heusen, piano)
July 4:	Medley: Mississippi Mud/ I Left My Sugar Standing in the Rain (test-pressing from the radio broadcast)	(Rhythm Boys Reunion)
Aug. 23:	People Will Say We're in Love	(Trudy Erwin, Sportsmen Glee Club)
	Oh! What a Beautiful Morning	(Trudy Erwin, Sportsmen Glee Club)
Sept. 27:	Pistol Packin' Mama	(Andrews Sisters/ Vic Schoen)
	Vict'ry Polka	(Andrews Sisters/ Vic Schoen)

	Jingle Bells	(Andrews Sisters/ Vic Schoen)
	Santa Claus Is Comin' to Town	(Andrews Sisters/ Vic Schoen)
Oct. 1:	Poinciana	(John Scott Trotter)
	I'll Be Home for Christmas	(John Scott Trotter)
Dec. 29:	It Could Happen to You	(John Scott Trotter)
	September Song	(John Scott Trotter)
	San Fernando Valley	(John Scott Trotter)

1944

Feb. 7:	Swinging on a Star	(John Scott Trotter/ Williams Brothers)
	The Day After Forever	(John Scott Trotter)
	Going My Way	(John Scott Trotter)
Feb. 11:	I Love You	(John Scott Trotter)
	I'll Be Seeing You	(John Scott Trotter)
	Night and Day	(John Scott Trotter)
Feb. 17:	Amor, Amor	(John Scott Trotter)
	I'll Be Seeing You	(John Scott Trotter)
	One Sweet Letter from You	(John Scott Trotter)
	On the Atchison, Topeka, and the Santa Fe	(John Scott Trotter/Six Hits and a Miss)
May 3:	Long Ago (and Far Away)	(John Scott Trotter)
	Like Someone in Love	(John Scott Trotter)
	Begin the Beguine	(John Scott Trotter)
	Dearly Beloved	(John Scott Trotter)
June 30:	A Hot Time in the Town of Berlin	(Andrews Sisters/Vic Schoen)
	Is You Is or Is You Ain't (My Baby)	(Andrews Sisters/Vic Schoen)
July 7:	I'll Remember April	(John Scott Trotter)
	Too-Ra-Loo-Ra-Loo-Ral	(John Scott Trotter)
	Moonlight on a White Picket Fence	(John Scott Trotter)
July 17:	Iowa	(John Scott Trotter)
	Welcome to My Dream	(John Scott Trotter)
	It's Anybody's Spring	(John Scott Trotter)
	Let Me Call You Sweetheart	(John Scott Trotter)
July 19:	Sleigh Ride in July	(John Scott Trotter)
	A Friend of Yours	(John Scott Trotter)
	Would You?	(John Scott Trotter)
July 24:	Just a Prayer Away	(Victor Young, Ethel Smith/Ken Darby Singers)

	My Mother's Waltz	(Victor Young, Ethel Smith/Ken Darby Singers)
	Beautiful Love	(Victor Young)
	Dear Friend	(Victor Young/Ken Darby Singers)
July 25:	Don't Fence Me In	(Andrews Sisters/Vic Schoen)
	The Three Caballeros	(Andrews Sisters/Vic Schoen)
July 26:	(Yip Yip de Hootie) My Baby Said Yes	(Louis Jordan)
	Your Socks Don't Match	(Louis Jordan)
July 31:	You've Got Me Where You Want Me	(Judy Garland/Joseph J. Lilley)
	Mine	(Judy Garland/Joseph J. Lilley)
Oct. 13:	Evelina	(Camarata/chorus)
	The Eagle and Me	(Camarata/chorus)
Dec. 4:	Let's Take the Long Way Home	(John Scott Trotter)
	Out of This World	(John Scott Trotter)
Dec. 8:	There's a Fellow Waiting in Poughkeepsie	(Andrews Sisters/Vic Schoen)
	Ac-Cent-Tchu-Ate the Positive	(Andrews Sisters/Vic Schoen)
	Put It There, Pal	(Bob Hope/Vic Schoen)
	Road to Morocco	(Bob Hope/Vic Schoen)
Dec. 11:	Strange Music (from Grieg)	(John Scott Trotter)
	June Comes Around Every Year	(John Scott Trotter/Girls' Octet)
	More and More	(John Scott Trotter)
Dec. 15:	I Promise You	(John Scott Trotter)
	I Love You (from Grieg)	(John Scott Trotter)
	These Foolish Things	(John Scott Trotter)

1945

Jan. 21:	I'd Rather Be Me	(John Scott Trotter)
	Just One of Those Things	(John Scott Trotter)
	All of My Life	(John Scott Trotter)
Feb. 11:	Siboney	(Xavier Cugat)
	Baia	(Xavier Cugat)
	Hasta Mañana	(Xavier Cugat)
	You Belong to My Heart (Solamente una Vez)	(Xavier Cugat)

Mar. 3:	Why Do I Like You (special issue for St. John's Hospital)	(John Scott Trotter)
	Temptation	(John Scott Trotter)
	Close as Pages in a Book	(John Scott Trotter/ chorus)
	Early American	(John Scott Trotter/ chorus)
Mar. 9:	Connecticut	(Judy Garland/Joseph J. Lilley)
	Yah-Ta-Ta, Yah-Ta-Ta	(Judy Garland/Joseph J. Lilley)
April 18:	If I Loved You	(John Scott Trotter)
	Close as Pages in a Book	(John Scott Trotter)
	I Love You Truly	(John Scott Trotter)
	Just Awearyin' for You	(John Scott Trotter)
June 29:	Along the Navajo Trail	(Andrews Sisters/Vic Schoen)
	Good, Good, Good	(Andrews Sisters/Vic Schoen)
July 3:	Happy, Happy, Happy Wedding Day	(Andrews Sisters/Vic Schoen)
	Betsy	(Andrews Sisters/Vic Schoen)
July 12:	It's Been a Long, Long Time	(Les Paul Trio)
	Whose Dream Are You	(Les Paul Trio)
July 17:	Too-Ra-Loo-Ra-Loo-Ral	(John Scott Trotter)
	The Rose of Tralee	(John Scott Trotter)
	Where the Blue of the Night Meets the Gold of the Day	(John Scott Trotter)
	I'll Take You Home Again, Kathleen	(John Scott Trotter)
July 30:	Home Sweet Home	(Victor Young/chorus)
	Ave Maria	(Victor Young/chorus)
Aug. 7:	I Can't Begin to Tell You	(Carmen Cavallaro)
	I Can't Believe That You're in Love with Me	(Carmen Cavallaro)
Aug. 9:	Save Your Sorrow for Tomorrow	(Eddie Heywood)
	Baby, Won't You Please Come Home	(Eddie Heywood)
Aug. 17:	That Little Dream Got Nowhere	(Eddie Heywood)
Aug. 21:	The Happy Prince	(Orson Welles, Lurene Tuttle/Victor Young)
	Part One	
	Part Two	
	Part Three	
	Part Four	

Aug. 29:	Give Me the Simple Life	(Jimmy Dorsey)
	It's the Talk of the Town	(Jimmy Dorsey)
Sept. 5:	I've Found a New Baby	(Eddie Heywood)
	Who's Sorry Now	(Eddie Heywood)
Sept. 6:	Sweet Lorraine	(Jimmy Dorsey)
	A Door Will Open	(Jimmy Dorsey)
Sept. 10:	In the Land of Beginning Again	(John Scott Trotter)
	Aren't You Glad You're You?	(John Scott Trotter)
	The Bells of St. Mary's	(John Scott Trotter)
Sept. 13:	Day by Day	(Mel Tormé Mel-Tones/ Buddy Cole)
	Prove It by the Things You Do	(Mel Tormé Mel-Tones/ Buddy Cole)
Sept. 14:	Symphony	(Victor Young)
Dec. 4:	Mighty Lak' a Rose	(Lehman Engle, Ethel Smith/Song Spinners)
	The Sweetest Story Ever Told	(Lehman Engle, Ethel Smith/Song Spinners)
Dec. 6:	It's the Same Old Shillelagh	(Bob Haggart/the Jesters)
	McNamara's Band	(Bob Haggart/the Jesters)
	Dear Old Donegal	(Bob Haggart/the Jesters)
	Who Threw the Overalls in Mrs. Murphy's Chowder?	(Bob Haggart/the Jesters)
Dec. 18:	J'Attendrai (I'll Be Yours)	(Camarata)
	Till the Clouds Roll By	(Camarata)
	We'll Gather Lilacs	(Camarata)
Dec. 27:	Sioux City Sue	(Bob Haggart/the Jesters)
	You Sang My Love Song to Somebody Else	(Bob Haggart/the Jesters)
Dec. 31:	All Through the Day	(Camarata)
	Ol' Man River	(Camarata)
	I've Told Every Little Star	(Camarata)

1946

Jan. 16:	Blue (and Broken Hearted)	(Eddie Condon)
	After You've Gone	(Eddie Condon)
	Personality	(Eddie Condon)
Jan. 21:	Pinetop's Boogie Woogie	(Lionel Hampton)
	On the Sunny Side of the Street	(Lionel Hampton)
Jan. 22:	Just My Luck	(Jay Blackton)
	You May Not Love Me	(Jay Blackton)
	They Say It's Wonderful	(Jay Blackton)

Mar. 22:	A Gal in Calico	(John Scott Trotter/ Calico Kids)
May 7:	When Irish Eyes Are Smiling	(John Scott Trotter)
	A Gal in Calico	(John Scott Trotter/ Calico Kids)
	Oh, but I Do	(John Scott Trotter)
	That Tumbledown Shack in Athlone	(John Scott Trotter)
May 11:	(Get Your Kicks on) Route 66	(Andrews Sisters/ Vic Schoen)
	South America, Take It Away	(Andrews Sisters/ Vic Schoen)
May 15:	Gotta Get Me Somebody to Love	(Les Paul Trio)
	Pretending	(Les Paul Trio)
July 13:	Lullaby (theme from Godard's *Jocelyn*)	(Jascha Heifetz, Victor Young)
	Where My Caravan Has Rested	(Jascha Heifetz, Victor Young)
July 18:	All by Myself	(John Scott Trotter)
	Blue Skies	(John Scott Trotter/ chorus)
	You Keep Coming Back Like a Song	(John Scott Trotter/ chorus)
	(Running Around in Circles) Getting Nowhere	(John Scott Trotter/ chorus)
	Everybody Step	(John Scott Trotter)
	A Serenade to an Old-Fashioned Girl	(John Scott Trotter/ chorus)
July 24:	A Couple of Song and Dance Men	(Fred Astaire/John Scott Trotter)
	I'll See You in C-U-B-A	(Trudy Erwin/John Scott Trotter)
	I've Got My Captain Working for Me Now	(John Scott Trotter)
Aug. 1:	The Things We Did Last Summer	(Jimmy Dorsey)
Aug. 9:	When You Make Love to Me	(Victor Young)
	So Much in Love	(Victor Young)
Aug. 15:	The Star Spangled Banner	(Victor Young/chorus)
	Old Ironsides (narration)	(Victor Young/chorus)
Aug. 22:	My Heart Goes Crazy	(Russ Morgan)
	Among My Souvenirs	(Russ Morgan)
	So Would I	(Russ Morgan)
	Does Your Heart Beat for Me?	(Russ Morgan)
Nov. 14:	As Long as I'm Dreaming	(John Scott Trotter)

	Smile Right Back at the Sun	(John Scott Trotter)
	The One I Love	(John Scott Trotter)
Nov. 19:	Country Style	(John Scott Trotter/ Calico Kids)
	My Heart Is a Hobo	(John Scott Trotter)
Dec. 17:	That's How Much I Love You	(Bob Crosby/the Chickadees)
	Rose of Santa Rosa	(Bob Crosby/the Chickadees)

Bing Crosby Wartime Filmography

This section lists all feature films and short subjects made for theatrical release between 1940 and 1946. (A complete filmography, 1930 to 1974, may be found in *Bing Crosby: A Pocketful of Dreams*.) It does not include the two pictures Crosby produced in this period, *The Great John L.* and *Abie's Irish Rose,* in which he does not appear. Credits are given only for those in which he has a substantial role. Unless otherwise noted, all pictures were released by Paramount Pictures.

S = short subject
V = voice only
C = cameo or supporting appearance
HC = Bob Hope movie with Crosby cameo

1940
    Road to Singapore Directed by Victor Schertzinger. Produced by Harlan Thompson. Written by Frank Butler and Don Hartman, from a story by Harry Hervey. Photographed by William Mellor. Songs by Johnny Burke/James Monaco; Burke/Victor Schertzinger. Cast: Bing Crosby, Bob Hope, Dorothy Lamour, Charles Coburn, Anthony Quinn, Jerry Colonna, Judith Barrett, Gaylord Pendleton, Miles Mander.
    "Swing with Bing" (Universal) (S) Directed and produced by Herbert Polesie. Written by Grant Garret. Photographed by Al Wetzel. Music by Johnny Burke/James Monaco. Cast: Bing Crosby, Richard Keene, Bud Ward, Toney Penna, Jimmy Thompson, Arthur W. Bryan, Ty Cobb, Richard Arlen.
    If I Had My Way (Universal) Directed and produced by David Butler. Written by William Conselman and James V. Kern, from a story by Butler, Conselman, and Kern. Photographed by George Robinson. Songs by Johnny Burke/James Monaco. Cast: Bing Crosby, Gloria Jean, Charles

Winninger, El Brendel, Allyn Joslyn, Eddie Leonard, Blanche Ring, Grace La Rue, Julian Eltinge, Trixie Friganza, Paul Gordon, Six Hits and a Miss.

Rhythm on the River Directed by Victor Schertzinger. Produced by William LeBaron. Written by Dwight Taylor, from a story by Billy Wilder and Jacques Théry. Photographed by Ted Tetzlaff. Songs by Johnny Burke/James Monaco. Cast: Bing Crosby, Mary Martin, Basil Rathbone, Oscar Levant, Charley Grapewin, William Frawley, John Scott Trotter, Ken Carpenter, Wingy Manone, Harry Barris.

1941

Road to Zanzibar Directed by Victor Schertzinger. Produced by Paul Jones. Written by Frank Butler and Don Hartman, from a story by Hartman and Sy Bartlett. Photographed by Ted Tetzlaff. Songs by Johnny Burke/James Van Heusen. Cast: Bing Crosby, Bob Hope, Dorothy Lamour, Una Merkel, Eric Blore, Douglass Dumbrille, Iris Adrian, Leo Gorcey, Ernest Whitman, Ken Carpenter.

Birth of the Blues Directed by Victor Schertzinger. Produced by B. G. DeSylva. Written by Harry Tugend and Walter DeLeon, from a story by Tugend. Photographed by William C. Mellor. Songs by B. G. DeSylva/Lew Brown/Ray Henderson; W. C. Handy; Johnny Mercer; Gus Edwards/Edward Madden; others. Cast: Bing Crosby, Mary Martin, Brian Donlevy, Carolyn Lee, Jack Teagarden, Eddie "Rochester" Anderson, Ruby Elzy, J. Carrol Naish, Warren Hymer, Harry Barris, Perry Botkin, Ronnie Cosbey, Hall-Johnson Negro Choir.

"Angels of Mercy" (Red Cross Newsreel, Metrotone News, released by Paramount, MGM, and Twentieth Century–Fox) (S, V); "Angels of Mercy" sung by Bing Crosby.

1942

"Don't Hook Now" (S) Produced by Herbert Polesie and Everett Crosby. Music by Johnny Burke/James Van Heusen. Cast: Bing Crosby, Bob Hope, Ben Hogan, Sam Snead, Jimmy Demaret.

My Favorite Blonde (HC)

Holiday Inn Directed and produced by Mark Sandrich. Written by Claude Binyon, from an idea by Irving Berlin adapted by Elmer Rice. Photographed by David Abel. Songs by Irving Berlin. Cast: Bing Crosby, Fred Astaire, Marjorie Reynolds, Virginia Dale, Walter Abel, Louise Beavers, John Gallaudet, Irving Bacon, Harry Barris.

Road to Morocco Directed by David Butler. Produced by Paul Jones. Written by Frank Butler and Don Hartman. Photographed by William C. Mellor. Songs by Johnny Burke/James Van Heusen. Cast: Bing Crosby,

Bob Hope, Dorothy Lamour, Anthony Quinn, Dona Drake, Vladimir Sokoloff, Mikhail Rasumny, George Givot, Andrew Tombes, Leon Belasco, Dan Seymour, Yvonne De Carlo.

Star Spangled Rhythm (C) Directed by George Marshall. Produced by Joseph Sistrom. Written by Harry Tugend, others. Photographed by Leo Tover. Songs by Harold Arlen/Johnny Mercer. Cast: Bing Crosby, Eddie Bracken, Betty Hutton, Walter Abel, Victor Moore, Bob Hope. Fred Mac-Murray, Mary Martin, Alan Ladd, Dorothy Lamour, Veronica Lake, Ray Milland, Eddie "Rochester" Anderson, William Bendix, Jerry Colonna, Cecil B. DeMille, Gary Crosby, Golden Gate Quartette, Paulette Goddard, Dick Powell, Franchot Tone, Vera Zorina, Katherine Dunham.

1943

Dixie Directed by A. Edward Sutherland. Produced by Paul Jones. Written by Karl Tunberg and Darrell Ware, from a story by William Rankin adapted by Claude Binyon. Photographed by William C. Mellor. Songs by Johnny Burke/James Van Heusen, Dan Emmett. Cast: Bing Crosby, Dorothy Lamour, Marjorie Reynolds, Billy De Wolfe, Raymond Walburn, Grant Mitchell, Lynne Overman, Eddie Foy Jr., Fortunio Bonanova, Carl Switzer, Harris Barris.

1944

Going My Way Directed and produced by Leo McCarey. Written by Frank Butler and Frank Cavett, from a story by McCarey. Photographed by Lionel Lindon. Songs by Johnny Burke/James Van Heusen; Franz Schubert; George Bizet; James Joyce Shannon. Cast: Bing Crosby, Barry Fitzgerald, Frank McHugh, Risë Stevens, Stanley Clements, Jean Heather, Gene Lockhart, James Brown, William Frawley, Porter Hall, Fortunio Bonanova, Carl Switzer, Robert Mitchell Boy Choir.

"The Shining Future" (Warner Brothers) (S, C) Directed by LeRoy Prinz. Produced by Gordon Hollinshead and Arnold Albert. Written by James Bloodworth. Songs by Frank Loesser and Joe Bushkin-John DeVries. Cast: Bing Crosby, Frank Sinatra, Jack Carson, Cary Grant, Benny Goodman, Harry James, Irene Manning, Dennis Morgan, Charles Ruggles. Made for Canada's Sixth War Loan and reissued in an edited version as *The Road to Victory* (1944).

"Swingtime with the Stars" (U.S. Coast Guard) (S) Songs by Harold Arlen/Johnny Mercer; Cole Porter. Cast: Bing Crosby, Leo "Ukie" Sherin, Lieutenant Jimmy Grier and the Eleventh Naval District Coast Guard Band.

Here Come the Waves Directed and produced by Mark Sandrich. Written by Allan Scott, Ken Englund, and Zion Myers. Photographed by

Charles Lang. Songs by Harold Arlen/Johnny Mercer. Cast: Bing Crosby, Betty Hutton, Sonny Tufts, Ann Doran, Gwen Crawford, Noel Neill, Catherine Craig, Marjorie Henshaw, Mae Clarke, Minor Watson, Harry Barris, Yvonne De Carlo, Mona Freeman.

The Princess and the Pirate (Goldwyn/RKO) (HC)

1945

Duffy's Tavern (C) Numerous Paramount players made guest appearances in an adaptation of a popular radio show. Bing Crosby sings a parody of "Swinging on a Star"; Gary, Phillip, Dennis, and Lindsay Crosby appear.

Out of This World (V) Eddie Bracken comedy with songs dubbed by Bing Crosby. Gary, Phillip, Dennis, and Lindsay Crosby appear.

"All-Star Bond Rally" (Twentieth Century–Fox, made for the War Activities Committee and U.S. Treasury Department for the Seventh War Bond Drive) (S, C) Directed by Michael Audley. Cast: Bing Crosby, Frank Sinatra, Bob Hope, Harpo Marx, Betty Grable, Harry James, Linda Darnell, Jeanne Crain.

"Hollywood Victory Caravan" (S, C) (Made for the War Activities Committee and U.S. Treasury Department) Directed by William Russell. Written by Mel Shavelson. Songs by Jimmy McHugh/Harold Adamson. Cast: Bing Crosby, Bob Hope, Betty Hutton, Humphrey Bogart, Alan Ladd, Barbara Stanwyck, Franklin Pangborn, Robert Benchley.

The Bells of St. Mary's (Rainbow/RKO) Directed and produced by Leo McCarey. Written by Dudley Nichols, from a story by McCarey. Photographed by George Barnes. Songs by Johnny Burke/James Van Heusen; Grant Clark/George W. Meyer; Douglas Furber/A. Emmett Adams. Cast: Bing Crosby, Ingrid Bergman, Henry Travers, William Gargan, Ruth Donnelly, Joan Carroll, Martha Sleeper, Rhys Williams, Bobby Dolan, Dickie Tyler, Una O'Connor.

1946

Road to Utopia (filmed 1943 to 1944) Directed by Hal Walker. Produced by Paul Jones. Written by Norman Panama and Melvin Frank. Photographed by Lionel Lindon. Songs by Johnny Burke/James Van Heusen. Cast: Bing Crosby, Bob Hope, Dorothy Lamour, Douglass Dumbrille, Jack LaRue, Robert Barrat, Robert Benchley, Nestor Paiva, Hillary Brooke, Will Wright, Jimmy Dundee.

Blue Skies Directed by Stuart Heisler. Produced by Sol C. Siegel. Written by Arthur Sheekman, from an idea by Irving Berlin. Adapted by Allan Scott. Photographed by Charles Lang. Songs by Irving Berlin. Cast: Bing Crosby, Fred Astaire, Joan Caulfield, Billy De Wolfe, Olga San Juan, Frank Faylen, Victoria Horne.

Notes and Sources

AI   Author interview
AMPAS   Academy of Motion Picture Arts and Sciences—Margaret Herrick
            Library
BCCGU   Bing Crosby Collection, Foley Center Library, Gonzaga University
HCC   Howard Crosby Collection
JWTPR   J. Walter Thompson program reports for *Kraft Music Hall*
KCC   Kathryn Crosby Collection
KGM   Unpublished memoir by Kitty (Lang) Good, recorded and
            transcribed during the 1980s and 1990s. Courtesy of Kitty Good
            and her son, Tim Good.
Lucky   Bing Crosby and Pete Martin, *Call Me Lucky.*
POD   *Bing Crosby: A Pocketful of Dreams—The Early Years,*
            1903–1940
RBT   Interview transcripts for *Remembering Bing*, a 1987 Chicago
            WTTW television documentary produced and written by Jim
            Arntz and Katherine MacMillin; executive producer Glenn
            DuBose.
TIA   Time Inc. Archive
USC   Leo McCarey Archive, University of Southern California

Prelude

1. Bobbe Brox (born Josephine Brock, 1902–1999), of the close-harmony vocal group the Brox Sisters, was Bing Crosby's occasional girlfriend during his years with Paul Whiteman's orchestra (see *POD*, 208–12) and a friend all his life. In February 1928, she married William Perlberg, a booking agent and later a successful film producer (*The Country Girl,* starring Crosby). They were divorced in the 1960s, and in 1969, she married Bing's longtime songwriter Jimmy Van Heusen.

2. Edgerton "Edgie" Hogle, one of Bing's friends in Spokane, managed the Musicaladers (*POD,* 97–98), whose members other than Crosby attended North Central High School, as did he. He later married and moved to Denver, where he worked as a salesman; aside from a 1930s reunion, he disappeared from Bing's life.

3. Bing's mother, Catherine Harrigan Crosby (1873–1964), alone called him Harry all his life. Rinker is Al Rinker (1907–1982), Bing's partner during the

vaudeville, Whiteman, and Rhythm Boys years and later a successful radio producer and songwriter. Bob is Bing's kid brother, the bandleader and vocalist Bob Crosby (1913–1993). Crosby did not get to visit London until 1944. See *POD*, page 186, regarding Ziegfeld's *Whoopee!* The Rhythm Boys did not make a Vitaphone short, though they did do one for Pathé ("Two Plus Fours," *POD*, 224).

4. Nothing is known of Mr. Collins. When this letter was posted (January), Bing had been rejected by the major studios. In February, his radio fame inclined Paramount to approach him about taking a part in its adaptation of Broadway's *Wild Waves*. In April, he and Dixie headed for Los Angeles. In October, the release of the picture as *The Big Broadcast* certified him as a Hollywood film star. Crosby answered fan mail like this all his life.

5. One year later, on June 30, 1938, Bing wrote a balance sheet for the Crosby Investment Corporation. He computed its assets as $790,128.32 (including stocks, bonds, real estate, an investment in Paramount Pictures, a loan to Del Mar Turf Club, and four automobiles—Lincoln roadster, Lincoln sedan, Buick sedan, Ford truck) and its liabilities as $798,128.32 (in capital surplus, bank loans, and taxes). These financial notations and letters are courtesy of his nephew Edward Crosby, the son of his brother Ted Crosby (1900–1973).

1. Meanwhile

1. *Radio and Television Mirror,* July 1940, 25.

2. AI, Gary Crosby. To the description of Bing carrying Dixie to bed, he pointedly added, "That is the only time I ever saw him lay a glove on her," to emphasize that if Bing was unable to openly display affection to his mother, neither was he ever violent with her.

3. AI, Basil Grillo, a fan of Dixie's long before he became Crosby's business manager.

4. AI, Gary Crosby.

5. AI, Jean Halliburton, Dr. Stevens's wife in those years; AI, Dr. Hummer; AI, Alan Fisher; Kitty Good's unpublished memoir (KGM); Hedda Hopper's unpublished sixteen-page work "Dixie Crosby," 1952, AMPAS.

6. AI, Gary Crosby; AI, Pat Burke Matthews; Gary Crosby, *Going My Own Way,* 74.

7. AI, Gary Crosby.

8. See *POD* for details of Dixie's flight. A recent discovery of raw footage from an FDR press conference shows newsreel cameramen and photographers putting their cameras down as he is helped from his wheelchair to a podium, where he holds himself erect with his arms and his leg braces long enough for them to get their pictures. Few knew of George VI's speech impediment before the 2010 movie *The King's Speech.*

9. The *American Weekly,* published from 1896 to 1966, was edited at that time by the science-fiction writer Abraham Merritt, whose lavish fantasies were hardly more fantastical than the image of Joan Crawford fervidly darning socks. St. Johns's article was written in response to the negative publicity generated by the March 1940 divorce of Alice Faye and Tony Martin. St. Johns (1894–1988), a close friend of Hearst who covered several major stories, including the Lindbergh kidnapping and the Huey Long assassination, later wrote a bestseller (*Final Verdict*) about her father, attorney Earl Rogers, the alleged model for Erle Stanley Gardner's Perry Mason.

10. *Life,* Nov. 4, 1940, 65–71.

11. Letter to F. F. Kear, Sept. 21, 1939; letter to John Dallavaux, Nov. 22, 1940, KCC.

12. To clarify addresses: The first Crosby house in Toluca Lake was at 4326 Forman Avenue, below the Ventura Freeway. They built it in 1933. A year later, Kitty Lang purchased her home at 4554 Cartwright Street, a distance of about half a mile from the Crosbys. In 1936, the Crosbys moved to the Colonial mansion at 10500 Camarillo Street, above the Ventura Freeway and a few blocks closer to Kitty's home.

13. Eddie Lang's relationship with Crosby and the circumstances of his death are described in *POD*. Six months after that book was published, David L. Mandell, of the Department of Pediatric Otolaryngology at the Children's Hospital of Pittsburgh, wrote a paper analyzing known facts surrounding the operation; it supports Kitty's conjecture in her memoir—"I feel that a mistake was made but I don't know for sure"—and argues that legal action was warranted. See D. L. Mandell, "Jazz and Otolaryngology: The Death of Guitarist Eddie Lang," *Laryngoscope* 111 (Nov. 2001): 1980–83.

14. KGM.

15. Candy Pearce, "Kitty Good: Reno's Auntie Mame," *Reno Evening Gazette,* Jan. 29, 1971.

16. KGM.

17. Ibid.

18. *Lucky,* 253.

19. Everett "Phez" Taylor began handling divorces in the late 1930s and was still at it in 1973 when he told Associated Press reporter Jurate Kazickas, "Sun Valley divorce is the last resort"; Jurate Kazickas, *Free-Lance Star,* Fredericksburg, Virginia, Mar. 19, 1973.

20. KGM.

21. Ibid.

22. Ibid. The story of the third-party intervention that "saved" the marriage made its way around Hollywood. Gary Crosby thought it was Dr. Sturdevant and not a priest who convinced Bing that alcoholism was an illness, but this seems unlikely, given Bing's ambivalent views on psychiatry. Dr. Hummer turns up in an unproduced teleplay by the writer/director Melvin Frank as the doctor counseling Bing on alcohol, insisting that while Bing had been "just a social drinker," Dixie had an illness that could "never be cured, but *can* be controlled." In the teleplay, which was supposed to be produced by Meta Rosenberg, the wife of Bing's agent George Rosenberg, the conversation is set in 1944, and Hummer suggests divorce, which Bing firmly rejects. This is clearly fiction. (From Frank, "The Crosbys," drafts and research notes, dated from January to July 1984.) Kitty's recollection has the ring of truth; Bing often consulted the Jesuits on personal issues and was never long out of touch with Art Dussault.

23. AI, Howard Crosby.

24. Alton Cook, "Crosby to Skip a Week," *New York World Telegram,* Feb. 10, 1941; *Variety,* Feb. 5, 1941. The actor Don Ameche filled in for him on the February 13 broadcast.

25. Letter from Todd W. Johnson, of Johnson and Johnson, to Harry L. Crosby Jr., Jan. 21, 1941.

26. *New York Daily News,* July 1, 1940. The average annual income in 1940 was $1,368; see www.archives.gov.

27. *Variety,* Dec. 16, 1940.

28. Letter from Johnson, Jan. 21, 1941.

29. Ibid.

30. May 13, 1940, letter to Mrs. E. Schindel, KCC.

31. June 14, 1940, letter from Everett Crosby to Bing, KCC.

32. Frank McNaughton, "Roosevelt Deplores German Bombings," *Pittsburgh Press,* Sept. 19, 1939; "Borah Sees Allies 'Pulling Punches,'" *New York Times,* Sept. 19, 1939. The senator, still in thrall to that delusion, died in January 1940.

33. Press conference, Dec. 17, 1940. His speech exists with small variations in countless books; this version is from Kevin Baker, "Lend Lease," in *American Greats,* ed. Robert A. Wilson and Stanley Marcus (New York: PublicAffairs, 1999), 124. Crosby was born May 3, 1903, but (for reasons detailed in *POD,* 30–31) claimed his birthday was May 2, 1904.

34. Franklin D. Roosevelt, "The Arsenal of Democracy," an address to the White House Correspondents Association. An early publication of it is in the fascinating Quincy Howe, ed., *Pocket Book of the War* (New York: Pocket Books, 1942), 335–53.

35. In 1940, RCA (the parent company of NBC) telecast the presidential election, the Rose Bowl, and an opera and assured the FCC, then investigating its monopolistic practices, that it would market television that year. The network then reversed itself, claiming to hold back because it had learned that CBS figured out how to transmit television in color. The war gave both networks cover for the duration.

36. Kinkle, *The Complete Encyclopedia of Popular Music and Jazz,* vol. 1, 351–75, provides a good overview. Other standards from this remarkable two-year period include "Let There Be Love," "I Hear a Rhapsody," "Oh, Look at Me Now," "This Time the Dream's on Me," "It's a Lovely Day Tomorrow," "A Nightingale Sang in Berkeley Square," "Everything Happens to Me," "Flamingo," "Yes Indeed!" "Violets for Your Furs," "Happiness Is a Thing Called Joe," "Back in the Saddle Again," "The Anniversary Waltz," "Beat Me Daddy (Eight to the Bar)," "Cabin in the Sky," "Will You Still Be Mine," "Can't Get Indiana off My Mind," "Mister Meadowlark," "Only Forever," "Rhythm on the River," "Say 'Si, Si,'" "We Three," "That's for Me," "Too Romantic," "Trade Winds," "Whispering Grass," "Do I Worry," "When the Sun Comes Out," "Easy Street," "Java Jive," "Elmer's Tune," "I Don't Want to Set the World on Fire," "Tis Autumn," "It's Always You," "It's So Peaceful in the Country," "I Hear Music," "Someone's Rocking My Dreamboat," "This Love of Mine," "The Waiter and the Porter and the Upstairs Maid," and "White Cliffs of Dover."

37. Sanjek and Sanjek, *American Popular Music Business,* 75–79.

38. Letter from Everett Crosby to Bing Crosby, June 14, 1940, KCC.

2. Independence

1. Crosby radio interview with John Salisbury, 1976.

2. Universal also exploited infancy with Baby Sandy, a baby girl who played the baby boy in *East Side of Heaven* and who was rushed into another seven pictures playing her true gender. She retired at four, in 1942, after appearing in

Johnny Doughboy, in which sixteen-year-old Jane Withers plays an actress, patterned after Deanna Durbin, who rebels against acting beneath her age. As Gloria Jean's star faded, Universal recruited soprano Susanna Foster, who at eighteen had spent six idle years at MGM and Paramount and who got her big chance in Universal's retelling of *Phantom of the Opera* (1943).

3. *Variety,* Nov. 8 and Nov. 22, 1939, reported a budget of $850,000, with Crosby assuming half. The numbers here are based on Universal's weekly status reports, filed each Friday during the course of filming.

4. As was true of *East Side of Heaven,* Butler credited the original story to his friend and collaborator William Conselman, who almost certainly had nothing to do with *If I Had My Way.* He was hospitalized during filming and died, age forty-three, shortly after the picture opened.

5. AI, Gloria Jean. Butler may have felt a lingering gratitude to Brendel, who costarred in the early pictures that established him as a director: the smash-hit Janet Gaynor and Charles Farrell romance *Sunny Side Up* (1929) and the science-fiction musical *Just Imagine* (1930) set in 1980, when babies are procured from vending machines. Crosby had seen each of the other five vaudevillians onstage between 1925 and 1932.

6. Memo from Larry Crosby to Bing Crosby, Dec. 21, 1939, KCC. The Kyser film was *That's Right, You're Wrong.*

7. According to the Northwest radio announcer Bill Osborn, who knew Crosby over many years, Burke thought the lyric more fitting for Bing than for Sinatra. Ironically, another singer who had early success with it was Dick Todd, the Canadian Crosby sound-alike.

8. *Variety,* "Inside Stuff—Pictures," June 5, 1940, 19.

9. AI, Gloria Jean.

10. University of Southern California Archive, Universal Collection, weekly status reports on *If I Had My Way,* Feb. 16, 1940.

11. AI, Gloria Jean: "I had a scene with El Brendel. We were eating sundaes, and they strapped [Crack] to my slip underneath my dress so it would stay on my shoulder, and it clawed my back and I felt blood running. Butler said, 'Cut, perfect.' I said, 'I don't think so,' and they rushed me to the hospital. El said, 'Why didn't you scream? My God, I don't know how you did that.'"

12. Ibid.

13. This is exactly what happened in 1946 when a manager convinced her not to renew with Universal and embark instead on an international concert tour that would increase her stature. In London, she enchanted an audience with her rendition of "The Lord's Prayer" but was pilloried by the press for criticizing British war debt in singing "Forgive us our debts as we forgive our debtors." She returned to Hollywood a twenty-year-old has-been and her career never recovered. When Universal released the butchered print of *If I Had My Way* in 1946, Gloria Jean was no longer advertised or billed as Bing's costarring equal.

14. AI, Gloria Jean. He also influenced her religious life. Clergymen frequently visited the set as guests of the studio, and Bing would walk over and shake their hands and chat. Gloria once told him he made Catholicism "'so interesting I wish I could be one.' He said, 'Well, you can be one. Later on down the line, you look into it.'" She did and converted.

15. Ibid.

16. AI, Bonnie Schoonover.

17. AI, Gloria Jean. She starred opposite Fields in *Never Give a Sucker an Even Break* (1941).

18. *Time* office memorandum, from Ed Thompson to Dick Pollard, Apr. 17, 1940, TIA.

19. Bing Crosby, "Dave Butler," unpublished manuscript, 1975–1977, KCC.

20. Atkins, *David Butler*, 160.

21. "The Bing Crosby Story," *Modern Screen*, Apr. 1951.

22. Telegram from Bing Crosby to Everett Crosby at the Essex House, New York, Mar. 20, 1940, KCC.

23. *Variety*, "Inside Stuff—Pictures," June 5, 1940, 19.

24. Bing never again worked at Universal, which in 1952 was taken over by Decca—the first time a record company owned a movie studio. By the end of the decade, Music Corporation of America had taken over both companies. Today, Universal controls everything Crosby recorded for Decca and all the movies he made for Paramount before 1950.

25. *Variety*, May 1, 1940.

26. Kaplan, *Frank: The Voice*, 49.

27. The 1954 "Imagination" and the Crosby-Sinatra duets were commercially issued for the first time on a 2010 CD produced by Robert S. Bader and Mark Brodka cannily titled *Bing Sings the Sinatra Songbook*. Sinatra's up-tempo return to the song is on his album *I Remember Tommy*.

28. Boswell spelled her first name as Connie until 1943, when she changed the spelling to Connee. Her niece Chica Minnerly told the author that she made the change either to facilitate signing autographs at army camp shows or for reasons of numerology. Today, she is remembered as Connee Boswell, but in the period covered here, she was known only as Connie Boswell.

29. Ironically, Yellen had written Bing's intended solo number in the film, "Song of the Dawn," which Whiteman gave to another singer after Bing was jailed in a drunk-driving incident. In Kathleen Winsor's relentlessly downbeat 1950 novel *Star Money*, the protagonist Shireen finds herself humming "I'm Waiting for Ships that Never Come In," and her mother intrudes, saying, "You mustn't sing it!" Why, Shireen asks; it's pretty. The mother responds: "No, darling. It isn't pretty. It's very sad—it's a song for middle-aged people. I hope you'll never know what it means—"

30. *Otis Ferguson Reader*, 121.

31. Ibid., 124. One of the most gifted critics of his generation and the only one equally adept at jazz and cinema, Ferguson joined the merchant marine weeks after Pearl Harbor, shipping out in February 1942. On his second outing, a year later, at age thirty-six, he was killed by a German bomber in the Bay of Salerno.

3. Ghosts

1. *RBT*.

2. Jimmie Fidler, *San Francisco Chronicle*, May 16, 1940. Fidler repeatedly "warned Hollywood producers against the peril of anti-Nazi films.... Seven such pictures are either in the cutting rooms or in front of the camera today. What will happen to them in the event of a German victory abroad?" (June 4, 1940).

3. AI, Tony Martin.

4. The legal letter submitted to Crosby for his signature on October 23, 1939, stipulates that the studio will purchase "the story entitled GHOST MUSIC by Billy Wilder and Jacques Thery" only if he agreed to make it the basis of one of his "motion picture photoplays."

5. AI, Irene Heymann.

6. Crowe, *Conversations with Wilder,* 203.

7. Martin, *RBT.*

8. Martin, *My Heart Belongs,* 61.

9. Martin, *RBT.*

10. Ibid.

11. Martin, *My Heart Belongs,* 87.

12. Levant, *Memoirs of an Amnesiac,* 180.

13. *Lucky,* 177.

14. The songwriter Jule Styne told entertainer Michael Feinstein, "He could stash all kinds of stuff, because no one ever said, 'Can I see what's in your fake hand, please?'"

15. Manone, *Trumpet on the Wing,* 164. Bing wrote the introduction to Manone's memoir, which sacrifices history for a relentless series of jokey anecdotes.

16. Ibid., 171.

17. "When the Moon Comes over Madison Square" never caught on, but it is a worthy follow-up to "I'm an Old Cowhand," the song that established Johnny Mercer when Bing added it to *Rhythm on the Range* (1936), and Rodgers and Hart's "Way out West (on West End Avenue)," written for *Babes in Arms* (1937) in the small genre of Easterns.

18. Frank Mittauer, *Los Angeles Daily News,* Aug. 23, 1940. He went on to suggest that Basie's "Negro bandsmen must have been selected for uniformity of color as well as musical ability."

19. *New York Times,* Aug. 29, 1940; *Chicago Tribune,* undated 1940 clip; *Time,* Sept. 9, 1940; *Variety,* Aug. 21, 1940; *Film Daily,* Aug. 20, 1940.

20. Sidney Skolsky, *Hollywood Citizen News,* Aug. 28, 1940.

21. Letter from Lester Santly to George Joy, May 14, 1940, KCC.

22. Ibid.

23. Monaco faced a few difficult years until he teamed with lyricist Al Dubin in 1943 and signed a contract at Fox, at which point he displayed a renewed energy. He received three more Academy Award nominations, including one for a song that sold a million records for Ella Fitzgerald and the Ink Spots ("I'm Making Believe"). In 1945, Bing recorded a song he'd written for *The Dolly Sisters,* "I Can't Begin to Tell You," which instantly raced up the charts. Monaco died of a heart attack at sixty before it reached number one and earned Bing his twelfth gold record.

24. Letter from Larry Crosby to Lester Santly, July 2, 1940, KCC.

4. Prewar Air War

1. Letter from Bing Crosby to Margaret Duffy, Oct. 10, 1939, KCC.

2. *Lucky,* 150.

3. Bing Crosby, "The *Kraft Music Hall:* The Very Beginning," unpublished manuscript, 1975–1977, KCC.

4. Second page of a letter to a fan (unidentified) from Bing Crosby, 1936, KCC. Crosby was not the only one who resisted the studio audience. Fred Allen

was vehement: "The worst thing that ever happened to radio was the studio audience. Somebody like Eddie Cantor brought these hordes of cackling geese in because he couldn't work without a bunch of imbeciles laughing at his jokes" (Nachman, *Raised on Radio,* 103). But Allen never had Crosby's clout to challenge the status quo. It's a safe bet that Allen and Crosby would have been nonplussed by twenty-first-century studio audiences, who are rehearsed to welcome the hosts with screaming ovations, a rush to press the flesh, even a unison chant of the host's first name, tiresome rituals enacted every night.

5. Surprisingly little is known about the man who formulated links between sponsors, ad agencies, networks, and stars; launched major radio careers; and created several classic series during radio's Golden Age. John Uhrich Reber was born in 1893, the son of a congressman, and graduated from Amherst College. After serving in the Naval Reserve during World War I, he worked for J. Walter Thompson, where he became head of radio marketing and eventually a vice president. He pioneered broadcasting as an advertising tool and developed programs for radio and television, including the first network show emceed by a black performer, Louis Armstrong, who for six weeks in 1937 replaced Rudy Vallée as host of *Fleischmann's Yeast Hour.* Reber died in 1955 and was inducted into the Broadcast Hall of Fame in 1958.

6. These are the numbers for January 1940. The categories are based on designations created by Harrison B. Summers for his 1958 survey *A Thirty-Year History of Programs Carried on National Radio Networks in the United States 1926–1956.* Shows were popularly identified by the name of the stars, though some were officially titled after their sponsors' names, so that the Bergen-McCarthy show might be listed as *The Chase and Sanborn Hour* and Jack Benny as *The Jell-O Program*—though rarely in newspapers, which resented the shameless attempts at free plugs. *KMH* didn't include Bing's name in its title, though Crosby was the chief selling point in all its advertising. Newspaper listings usually identified it as "Bing Crosby: Variety" or "Bing Crosby Show." As an example of the consistency in prewar radio, compare the top-twelve shows of January 1941: *Jack Benny, Bergen-McCarthy, Bob Hope, Fibber McGee, Lux Radio Theater, The Aldrich Family, Walter Winchell, Maxwell House Coffee Time* (Frank Morgan and Fanny Brice), *Major Bowes, Kay Kyser, Kraft Music Hall, Truth or Consequences.*

7. Crosby, "The *Kraft Music Hall.*"

8. Ibid.

9. Contract, Sept. 12, 1935, between Crosby Productions and J. Walter Thompson. In an addendum signed the same day, Thompson agreed to "make every effort to keep confidential" the three-thousand-dollar salary, as Bing had been offered more by another sponsor and didn't want it known that he accepted a lower sum out of respect for Thompson's track record. He also agreed not to endorse nonagency products; letter from J. Walter Thompson to Crosby Productions, Sept. 12, 1935, KCC.

10. Letter from John Reber to Everett Crosby, Dec. 2, 1935; telegram from Everett to Reber, same day, KCC.

11. Letter from John Reber to Everett Crosby, Dec. 2, 1935.

12. Letter from H. Calvin Kuhl to Everett Crosby, Jan. 21, 1937, KCC.

13. Agreement, Jan. 29, 1937, between Harry L. Crosby Jr., J. Walter Thompson Company, and Kraft-Phenix Cheese Corporation, KCC.

14. Letter from John U. Reber to Calvin Kuhl, Jan. 29, 1937, KCC.

15. Ibid.

16. Letter to Bing Crosby from H. Calvin Kuhl, cc Everett Crosby, Feb. 1, 1937, KCC.

17. Bing Crosby to H. Calvin Kuhl, cc Everett Crosby, Feb. 1, 1937, KCC.

18. Memo signed by Bing, Mar. 11, 1938, KCC.

19. Contracts between J. Walter Thompson and Harry L. Crosby, June 24 and July 7, 1938, KCC.

20. Memo from Larry Crosby to Bing, June 12, 1939, KCC. Bing similarly refused a munificent offer from William Paley at Columbia Records to leave Decca (set forth in a letter from Larry Crosby to George Joy, July 19, 1940). But Jack Kapp treated Bing generously, with high royalties and bonus payments; *KMH* paid him a lower rate than other major radio stars received.

21. Letters from Margaret Duffy to Bing (undated), and from Bing to Margaret Duffy, Oct. 10, 1939, KCC.

22. James B. Johnson Jr., "Hollywood on the Air," in *Swing*, Apr. 1939.

23. Memo, Larry Crosby to Bing, Mar. 13, 1940, KCC.

24. Oddly, the clause was intended to remain in effect only until December 1941.

25. Memo from Everett Crosby to Bing, July 31, 1940, KCC.

26. "Billy Rose Sez 'ASCAP Should Pull in Belt,'" *Variety,* Feb. 12, 1941, 32.

27. "Bing Crosby Gives Views on BMI," *Variety,* Aug. 14, 1940, 32.

28. In a July 10, 1940, letter to the music publisher George Joy (of Santly-Joy-Select), Larry Crosby wrote: "The cowgirl who wrote it is coming along in pictures but needed money so I gave her $100.00 for half interest, to which I was probably entitled anyway because it's my title and part of the lyrics are mine." Walker, in fact, had no career in pictures, and Larry's boast is unlikely — he is not known to have written any song lyrics. Not surprisingly, Larry insisted that his name *not* appear in the copyright; KCC.

29. "Bing Crosby Sends Girl Singer to Gonzaga Feast," *Spokesman-Review,* May 8, 1940.

30. Willie Nelson, who released *You Don't Know Me: Songs of Cindy Walker* in 2006, said of her, "We had to have heard her music before we could do ours."

31. "Bing Crosby Gives Views on BMI."

32. Alexander Kahn, "Radio Music War Baffles Bing Crosby," *Hollywood Citizen News,* Aug. 13, 1940.

33. Ibid.

34. Cable from Larry Crosby to Bing, Aug. 30, 1940, KCC.

35. "Delivery 'Boy' to Script Writer for Bing Crosby," unidentified Armed Forces publication, 1943.

36. Letter from Bing to Robert Brewster, Nov. 9, 1939. Two weeks before he instructed Thompson to leave Hope alone, Bing signed a waiver allowing Jack Benny's show to broadcast two lines about Bing and eating carrots: "Jack: Mrs. Day, for your information, Caruso never ate a carrot in his life. Neither does Bing Crosby and he's doing all right. Mary: But Crosby feeds carrots to his *horses*" (Memo, Young and Rubicam to Everett Crosby, Oct. 22, 1939, KCC).

37. J. Walter Thompson memo from Bob Brewster to John Reber, Sept. 23, 1940, KCC.

38. Letter from John Reber to Bing, Sept. 26, 1940, KCC.

39. Letter from John U. Reber to "Messrs. Carroll, Brewster, Danker & Lochridge," Oct. 17, 1940, KCC.

40. In a subsequent conversation with Reber, McInnerney confessed that Bob Burns was so overpaid he'd be crazy to accept another contract unless it matched his current rate; soon, Burns and Bing would each be earning five thousand dollars per *KMH* broadcast. Still, McInnerney was willing to raise the subject with Burns and William Morris, recognizing that in terms of public opinion, it was essential for the blame to fall on him and not Bing. Burns did leave *KMH*, after five years, in mid-1941, to launch his own CBS program, *The Arkansas Traveler*. It lasted nine months, whereupon he returned to NBC and enjoyed a successful run of four years with *The Bob Burns Show*. He retired a wealthy man in 1949.

41. Letter from Reber to "Messrs. Carroll, Brewster, Danker & Lochridge," Oct. 17, 1940, KCC.

42. "Crosby Tired of Gab but Sticks," *Variety*, Oct. 23, 1940, 1.

43. "Bing Crosby Agrees to Sing BMI," *Variety*, Feb. 5, 1941, 24; "Bing Crosby Will Sing BMI Songs on the Air," *Down Beat*, Jan. 1, 1941.

44. Penciled by Bing on the payment-due telegram from Butch Tower c/o Lindy's, Nov. 6. 1940, KCC.

45. R. W. Stewart, "Radio and Politics," *New York Times*, Nov. 10, 1940; Green and Laurie, *Show Biz*, 392–93.

46. Ulanov, *The Incredible Crosby*, 240. Ulanov, an influential jazz critic and later a professor of theology, supported Willkie because of his internationalism and decisive stand on civil rights (for which he was eulogized by Eleanor Roosevelt) and thought Bing admired him for much the same reasons.

47. This story was retailed in *POD* (557), for which *mea culpa*. Ulanov thought Crosby issued the statement on the November 7 program, but as Bing did not appear that week, the *POD* account altered the date to November 14. A transcript of the November 14 broadcast, discovered subsequent to publication, refutes that as well. Trade papers of the time do not report any such statement, and it is not mentioned in Thompson interoffice memos.

48. Transcript, Nov. 14, 1940, *Kraft Music Hall* show, American Heritage Center, University of Wyoming, Carroll Archive, box 38.

49. Ibid.; note from Reber to Carroll, stapled to the back of the transcript.

50. Transcript of Dec. 12, 1940, *Kraft Music Hall*, American Heritage Center.

51. AI, Ed Helwick; wire from John Allen and Fred Kellam to David Hulbard, Mar. 22, 1941, TIA.

52. John Allen and Fred Kellam, Mar. 22, 1941, TIA.

53. Ibid.

5. Right All the Way

1. Sheed, *The House that George Built*, 235.

2. Letter from Joseph I. Breen to Rev. Wilfrid Parsons, Oct. 10, 1932, in Doherty, *Hollywood's Censor*, 199.

3. Letter from Breen to Luigi Luraschi, Oct. 11, 1940, AMPAS.

4. Letter from Breen to Luraschi, Nov. 1, 1940, AMPAS.

5. Memo from Luigi Luraschi to Paul Jones, Nov. 20, 1940, AMPAS. Breen went over Luraschi's head to *Zanzibar*'s uncredited executive producer William

LeBaron when he heard in the finished cut a "very loud burp or belch on the part of the African chief," which he ordered "reduced to a minor inoffensive burp or a hiccough." Death spared Breen the trauma of Mel Brooks's *Blazing Saddles*.

6. Based on the 1926 play *Kongo*, Chaney's 1928 silent film was remade in 1932 under the original title with Walter Huston, who created the role on Broadway. Both versions are so immoderately violent and sexually perverse that it is hard not to see the choice of Zanzibar as Hartman's deliberate needling of the PCA.

7. Crosby, *Lucky*, 168.

8. Initially known for comedy scripts, Pirosh went on to fight with distinction in the Ardennes, at Bastogne, an experience he revisited as writer-producer of William Wellman's influential 1949 film *Battleground*; he later developed the television series *Combat*.

9. Script for *Road to Zanzibar*, by Hartman and Pirosh, dated June 26, 1940, AMPAS.

10. Merkel's role as Donna's sidekick Julia was intended as a comeback for Glenda Farrell, but she could not get a release from a Broadway production. The part then went to Minerva Pious, but the producer decided she looked too much like Lamour. Merkel had a long career, supporting everyone from Walter Huston to Elvis Presley. She won a Tony in 1956 for her work in the Broadway adaptation of Eudora Welty's *The Ponder Heart*.

11. In the twenty years preceding *Road to Zanzibar*, Hollywood released more than two hundred movies set in exotic locales, most shot on Hollywood soundstages. In the 1920s, the majority of them involved the South Seas; in the 1930s, the majority involved African jungles. The genre merited a thorough hammering. After Zanzibar, despite Tarzan, the genre waned. The war relocated cinema's jungles to Burma and Bataan, and poverty-row programmers took up the slack, often with zombies or great white hunters provoking the restless natives.

12. Hartman's take came to $37,250, Butler's to $22,750. Uncredited writers included Pirosh ($3,750) and the two gagmen Barney Dean and Louis S. Kaye ($925 each).

13. Contract for *Road to Rio*, which was the original title of *Road to Zanzibar*, 1940, AMPAS.

14. The picture was budgeted at $877,613.23, which Schertzinger and Jones reduced by an impressive 14 percent.

15. Shavelson in Davis, *The Glamour Factory*, 170. See Jacobs, *Christmas in July*, 234, for comments on Jones's contributions to films of Preston Sturges.

16. William Douglass, interviewed by Steven Isoardi for the oral-history project *Central Avenue Sounds*, Department of Special Collections, UCLA Library.

17. "Michigan Grid Ace Declines Pro Ball Chicago," *Los Angeles Evening Herald-Express*, Dec. 19, 1940.

18. It seems odd to refer to them by their character names—Chuck Reardon, Hubert "Fearless" Frazier, Donna Latour—when audiences thought of them as radio familiars: Bing, Bob, and Dottie.

19. In *POD*, the Road pictures are placed within the context of British imperialist adventures, chiefly those of Kipling but also of Conrad, Rider Haggard,

A.E.W. Mason, and others. Yet Melville provides a more exacting template in *Typee* and *Omoo*—stories of paired adventurers and their unpunished retreats from Western civilization that include Melville's caveats on the destructiveness of missionary zeal, a contrast to the imperialist objectives of Kipling's would-be rajahs.

20. In the script, Harry was called Scarface, which explains Leigh Whipper's makeup.

21. Radio programs aimed at military personnel were largely segregated. *Jubilee* represented the Negro wing of Armed Forces Radio Service. A few black performers made infrequent appearances on *Command Performance*, among them Lena Horne, Ethel Waters, Eddie "Rochester" Anderson, the Ink Spots, Ella Fitzgerald, and, most frequently, the Charioteers, who became weekly cast members on *Kraft Music Hall* in 1942. For the Christmas 1942 *Command Performance*, the first AFRS show broadcast in the U.S.—to forge "a link between the servicemen abroad and the folks on the Home Front," according to the Office of War Information (*Variety*, Dec. 30, 1942)—Ethel Waters sang "Dinah" and Crosby sang "Basin Street Blues" with the Charioteers. In 1944, he was the first white performer to appear with Ernie Whitman on *Jubilee*.

22. Holden in Lamour, *My Side of the Road*, 98. Holden, a lifelong Crosby admirer, costarred with him in *The Country Girl* (1954) and narrated the two-hour memorial film telecast by ABC after Crosby's death.

23. Film historian Leonard Maltin has suggested that *What Price Glory?* provided a template for buddy-buddy backbiting after it was adapted as a film in 1926. The popularity of the characters Quirt and Flagg, as played by suave Edmund Lowe (a gay Jesuit-educated leading man and one of Bing's best friends in the 1930s) and gruff Victor McLaglen, was such that audiences demanded sequels, which brought their bickering into the sound era and civilian settings.

24. Crosby, *The Joe Franklin Show*, 1976.

25. Robinson, *Teamwork*, 72.

26. Dwiggins, *Frankie*, 35.

27. Bing and Frank more likely met a year later, on the Metro lot, when Tommy and Frank returned to Hollywood to shoot *Ship Ahoy*. The trumpet player Yank Lawson recalled introducing them at Paramount then, at Sinatra's behest.

28. Louella Parsons, "Good News," *Modern Screen*, Nov. 1943.

29. Sy Oliver in Simon, *The Big Bands Songbook*, 361; AI, Lillian Oliver.

30. AI, Will Friedwald.

31. AI, Janet Waldo. Waldo didn't fare well in the movies, but she enjoyed a renowned career as actor and voiceover performer on radio and television, creating a much-imitated teenage squeal as well as the characters of Corliss Archer and Judy Jetson, among countless others; she was active at least as late as 2011.

32. Simon, *The Big Bands Songbook*, 361.

33. Someone else shouted, "Where's the melody?," Jack's credo, posted in Decca's studios. Bing also sang "Happy Christmas, Decca Folk," to the tune of "Happy Birthday."

34. Sy Oliver's friendship with Bing also renewed his association with Kapp, whom he had worked with in the years when Lunceford was a key Decca artist. After serving two years in the army, Oliver returned to New York and formed

his own band. Kapp called him about writing for Decca, which Sy assumed meant writing for black artists in the company's "race" division (all major labels had one). He recalled (in Smith, *Off the Record*, 20), "I told Jack Kapp I didn't know anything about race records. I said I didn't do that sort of thing. He said, 'I don't want you to do that. I want you to write for all our artists.' That took me aback." Sy told him he would hire black musicians, integrating the studio orchestra. Kapp hesitated a moment and then responded, "I don't care who you use. They all get paid the same. Just get the best person for the job." After Kapp's death, in 1949, as producer and arranger, Oliver helped pilot the label through the mid-1950s.

35. W. R. Burnett, *High Sierra* (New York: Knopf, 1940), 178. The record they listen to is "Little Lady Make Believe," recorded by Bing in 1938, accompanied solely by Eddie Dunstedter's organ.

36. Charles R. Townsend, *San Antonio Rose: The Life and Music of Bob Wills* (Champaign: University of Illinois Press, 1976), 196–97; http://www.texasplayboys.net:Western Swing Discussion Forum, June 24, 2005. The wire recording is presumed lost.

37. *Variety*, Mar. 12, 1941.

38. *Variety*, May 14, 1941.

39. *New York Times*, Apr. 10, 1941.

40. *New Republic*, May 5, 1941, collected in *The Film Criticism of Otis Ferguson*, 355–56.

41. "The Groaner," *Time*, Apr. 7, 1941, 92.

42. Ibid.

6. Coventry

1. *Lucky*, Dictaphone belt 29.

2. *Lucky*, 300.

3. Ibid., 302–3. Dixie was alive when the book was composed and set in type but died before it appeared in print. In the dictation, she was always spoken of in the present tense; that was changed to past tense before publication.

4. Gary Crosby, *Going My Own Way*, 24. In an AI, Gary acknowledged, with a shrug, the plucked feathers, while repeatedly blaming his own memory, explaining that he had been drinking through the 1980s and could not be certain of dates or of whole events described in his book. Ross Firestone, in an interview with the author, agreed: "Gary was kind of blottoed out through a lot of that period." Firestone often relied on Gary's ex-wife Barbara, "who had very good memories of specific things that happened," though obviously not of Gary's childhood events except to the degree that Gary related them to her.

5. James Boswell, *Life of Dr. Johnson* (Oxford: Oxford University Press, 1970), 34. In the same passage, Johnson approves the master's justification for his merciless floggings, which was "And this I do to save you from the gallows."

6. *Lucky*, Dictaphone belt 29.

7. A biographer who wanted to interview one had to promise not to call the other. Gary referred to Phillip as a Nazi. After Gary's death, Phillip gave extensive interviews, demonstrating a mild if discursive temperament except in regard to Gary, whom he reviled. After Phillip's lifetime of pills and alcohol, his memory was no more reliable than Gary's, but he was adamant about what he did recall.

8. Phillip related Dixie's dismissal in an interview with J. Roger Osterholm; e-mail, Nov. 1998. Also, see Gary Crosby, *Going My Own Way,* 25.

9. AI, Gary Crosby.

10. AI, Phillip Crosby.

11. Gary Crosby, *Going My Own Way,* 34.

12. AI, Gary Crosby.

13. Gary Crosby, *Going My Own Way,* 13.

14. AI, Phillip Crosby.

15. Scott Heller, "The Sad Ballad of Bing and His Boys," *People,* Mar. 21, 1983.

16. Ibid.

17. AI, Phillip Crosby; Gary writes of St. John's in *Going My Own Way,* 114.

18. AI, Gary Crosby.

19. Ibid.; AI, Phillip Crosby.

20. Robinson, *My Father—My Son,* 12. Manny's book, suggested and produced by an independent packager and co-authored with the journalist William Dufty, appeared in 1958. It detailed his dejected childhood, run-ins with police, and a suicide attempt.

21. Gary Crosby, *Going My Own Way,* 7.

22. Bosworth, *Jane Fonda: The Private Life of a Public Woman,* 38.

23. AI, Gary Crosby.

24. Gary Crosby, *Going My Own Way,* 47. Bing kept a transcription recording of the broadcast.

25. AI, Gary Crosby; www.imdb.com.

26. AI, Robert K. Dornan. The rabidly right-wing congressman of the '80s and '90s, remembered, if he's remembered at all, for his offensive outbursts (chronicled by Nathan Callahan in *Shut Up, Fag!*), proved decorous and reflective when discussing Bing, "who was always terrific to me," and Gary, who recommended him as a reliable observer.

27. "Bing Crosby Sons' Kidnap Threatened," *Los Angeles Examiner,* Apr. 26, 1939; "Guard 4 Crosby Boys After Kidnap Threats," *Los Angeles Evening Herald,* Apr. 26, 1939; "Crosby Family Heavily Guarded," *Los Angeles Times,* Apr. 27, 1939.

28. *Lucky,* Dictaphone belt 29.

29. AI, Gary Crosby.

30. Ibid.

31. Ibid. They were not the only siblings whose affections she divided. For a couple of years, Georgie worked for the Sinatras. Frank Sinatra Jr. called her "a stern governess, a wonderful woman who was very good with children." His sister Nancy disagreed: "All I will say about Georgie is that she was very, very tough." AIs, Frank Sinatra Jr., Nancy Sinatra.

32. AIs Sheila Lynn, Nancy Briggs, Marguerite Toth (Crosby receptionist), Shirley Mitchell, Pauline Weislow, Alan Fisher (Crosby butler), Dolores Hope (wife of Bob Hope), Flo and Gloria Haley (wife and daughter, respectively, of Jack Haley), Gregory Crosby (Dennis's son), Susan Crosby (Lindsay's wife).

33. Undated letters, apparently from the summers of 1943 and 1944, from Gary, Phillip, and Dennis, KCC.

34. Hugues Panassié's *Le Jazz Hot* argued the idea of black dominance in jazz, in 1934, when many Americans still considered Paul Whiteman the king

of jazz. As late as 1956, an entry in the *World Book Encyclopedia* under *Jazz* read: *See Gershwin, George.*

35. *Lucky,* Dictaphone belt 18. In the published book, Pete Martin also added a paragraph about Teagarden working with Whiteman during Bing's tenure, though he joined the band a couple of years after Bing's departure. Letters and telegrams from Bing to Mercer, 1938 to 1940, Georgia State University Special Collections; AI, Ginger Mercer.

36. Silvers, *This Laugh Is on Me,* 73. DeSylva's three 1940 Broadways shows were *Du Barry Was a Lady, Louisiana Purchase,* and *Panama Hattie,* all subsequently filmed.

37. Lally, *Wilder Times,* 143; AI, Eddie Bracken. According to Bracken, "In my opinion, Preston Sturges was never wrong, except in casting Ella Raines in *Hail the Conquering Hero.* Buddy DeSylva wanted her out of there and fought to get her out. And Sturges was stubborn. He picked her, she's going to play it. They were sharp enemies."

38. Earl J. Morris, "Grand Town Day and Night," *California Eagle,* Jan. 8, 1942.

39. Ironically, DeSylva initially wanted to put Bob Crosby into the body of the film but then nixed the idea, as he looked too much like Bing. Putting him in the montage would have been considered nepotistic.

40. MPAA memos from Joseph Breen to Luigi Luraschi, dated Mar. 22 and 24, Apr. 4, 8, 9, 22, and 29, and May 6, 1941, AMPAS.

41. Harry Tugend mapped the storyline and worked on the script with Bert Lawrence and Walter DeLeon, an ex-vaudevillian who doctored dozens of comedies. Lawrence's name was dropped from the credits, though he signed revised pages throughout the process and was assigned to answer Breen's complaints.

42. MPAA memos; *Lucky,* Dictaphone belt 18.

43. Schertzinger died October 26, 1941, three days before completing *The Fleet's In,* for which he composed, in collaboration with Johnny Mercer, the two songs for which he is best remembered: "Tangerine" and "I Remember You."

44. *RBT.*

45. Transcription discs (usually sixteen-inch platters with excellent sound) were popular during the war. They were licensed exclusively for airplay and could not be marketed commercially.

46. See *POD,* 275–77.

47. Ellington, *Music Is My Mistress,* 166; AI, Herb Jeffries.

48. See *POD,* 353–57.

7. South America, Take It Away

1. *Time,* Sept. 15, 1941.

2. Barnes, *The Crosby Years,* 83. The letter has not been found.

3. Sandrich to Berlin, Feb. 11, 1941, AMPAS.

4. Berlin, *Holiday Inn* files, in Kimball and Emmet, *The Complete Lyrics of Irving Berlin,* 348–49. In the event, Astaire's salary was jacked up to $110,000. Combined with Bing's per-picture rate at $175,000, their combined salaries totaled $285,000 at a time when A-list musicals rarely cost as much as $1 million.

5. Intro to treatment, Apr. 28, 1941, AMPAS.

6. Treatment, Apr. 28, 1941, AMPAS.

7. Berlin to Sandrich, June 3, 1941; Sandrich to William Dozier (undated), AMPAS.

8. *Motion Picture Herald* (Aug. 9, 1941): 31.

9. Petrillo's man Ben Selvin went on to say, "Unrestricted use of records on radio and in juke boxes is the great evil" (*Down Beat,* July 1, 1941).

10. Carroll, *Los Angeles Evening Herald-Express,* Aug. 29, 1941.

11. The provenance of these letters, along with the Todd Johnson tax correspondence in chapter 1 and others, is mysterious. They came into the possession of Al Sutton, a Crosby collector who edited the fanzine *Bingang;* he refused to make them available and, in a letter to the author, vowed to burn them. Instead, he left them to his *Bingang* successor Mark Scrimger, who published most of them in 2002. Sutton told the English writer Ken Crossland that he received them from an unnamed man who worked for Bing Crosby Enterprises in the 1940s. The man claimed Dixie asked him to the house to clear out Bing's desk and that he saved the letters from the trash. This is improbable. It is hard to imagine Dixie tossing love letters, harder still to imagine her asking a stranger to do it or allowing anyone to rifle through Bing's desk. The presence of a letter from her father that she almost certainly never saw and would never have left— no more than Bing—lying in a desk drawer (see chapter 12) renders the story preposterous. Crosby kept thousands of letters from fans, friends, associates, virtually everyone who wrote him, in cartons and folders preserved in his home, his office, and a storage locker. Most correspondence between him and Dixie has not come to light—none of the letters he wrote her from South America are available. An obvious explanation is that most of this correspondence burned in the January 1943 fire that destroyed their home and obliterated his home office. Indeed, as the letters in the Sutton stash come from the two years preceding the fire, it seems likely that they were stolen from the house in late 1942 or by a looter in the immediate aftermath of the fire.

In the letter at hand: David is David Butler and Elsie is his wife. Pat is Pat O'Brien, the actor and vice president of Del Mar. Bess is Bessie Burke, the wife of Johnny Burke. Pat Ross is Alice and Hugh Ross's son. Lin is Lin Howard and Judy is his wife, Judith Barrett, an actress who retired when they married, shortly after she appeared in *Road to Singapore.* Preceptor and La Zonga are Binglin horses.

12. Carroll, *Los Angeles Evening Herald-Express,* Oct. 16, 1941.

13. Smith's Brazilian sojourn was curtailed by Pearl Harbor. She settled in Hollywood and helped to popularize the Hammond console and the Brazilian song "Tico Tico."

14. Letters; other than Lin and Judy Howard and tennis champ Don Budge, the first to win the Grand Slam in a single season, the people and clippings mentioned are unidentified. In the 1940s, Pamona was a common misspelling for Pomona.

15. Carroll, *Los Angeles Evening Herald-Express,* Sept. 18, 1941.

16. "Bing Over with a Bang in the Argentine," *Variety,* Oct. 1, 1941.

17. "Crosby's Cuffo Broadcast a Hit with Argentine," *Variety,* Oct. 15, 1941.

18. Letters.

19. Julie is Dixie's longtime confidante Julie Taurog, who worked in silent films as Julie Leonard before marrying the director Norman Taurog.

20. Ed Sullivan, "Little Old New York (in South America)," *New York Daily News,* Oct. 1941.

21. The story of Rolla, the Urca, and the Brazilian account of Crosby's performance is from João Perdigão and Euler Conradi's *O Rei da Roleta: A Incrível Vida de Joaquim Rolla* (*The King of Roulette: The Incredible Life of Joaquim Rolla*) (Rio de Janeiro: Casa da Palavra, 2012), 260–63, translated for the author by Zuza Homem de Mello.

22. Carroll, *Los Angeles Evening Herald-Express*, Oct. 15, 1941.

23. "Bing of All Trades," *New York Post*, Oct. 22, 1941.

24. Simon, *Glenn Miller*, 300; also see pages 226, 303.

25. Letter from Bing Crosby to Naval Reserve Commission, June 22, 1942, courtesy Dan Morgenstern, Institute of Jazz Studies, Rutgers University.

26. Dorothy Kilgallen, *New York Post*, Oct. 25, 1941.

27. "Bing of All Trades."

8. Happy Holiday

1. AI, Ed Helwick.

2. Carroll, *None of Your Business*, 178.

3. "I Was Fired, So Why All the Bunk? Asks Miss Boswell," *Variety*, Mar. 18, 1942. Boswell did not know that Martin wasn't the only contender for the job. John Reber preferred a *Camel Caravan* singer, Margaret Lenhart. Bing agreed to consider her as an alternative if Martin turned them down.

4. Himmler in Rhodes, *Masters of Death*, 10; Hitler in Clara Leiser, ed., *Lunacy Becomes Us* (New York: Liveright, 1939).

5. "Dixie Sees Another Civil War, but Now It's on Birth of Blues," *Variety*, Oct. 15, 1941, 15.

6. *Variety*, Sept. 3, 1941; Parsons, *Los Angeles Examiner*, Nov. 7, 1941; Barnes, *Liberty*, Nov. 8, 1941; Cameron, *New York Daily News*, Dec. 11, 1941; Crowther, *New York Times*, Dec. 11, 1941.

7. Memo from Luigi Luraschi to Mark Sandrich, attached to the screenplay, AMPAS.

8. Carroll, *Los Angeles Evening Herald-Express*, Dec. 13, 1941.

9. *Lucky*, Dictaphone belt 18.

10. Ibid.

11. Carroll, *Los Angeles Evening Herald-Express*, Dec. 13, 1941.

12. Astaire interviewed at home by Gord Atkinson for his Canadian radio series *The Crosby Years*, c. 1975 (archival CD, vol. 8).

13. Unpublished Abel manuscript, c. 1980, courtesy Jerry O'Connell.

14. Scharf and Freedland, *Composed and Conducted by Walter Scharf*, 85.

15. Hillary Gordon, Chapman's granddaughter, on imdb.com; Colin Briggs, "Marjorie Reynolds: Benevolent Beauty," classicimages.com.

16. In an interview with David Lobosco, Marjorie's daughter, Linda Reynolds, said, "Bing was upset because Mom could not sing and a ghost singer had to be brought in. Bing wanted Mary Martin for the part and since he didn't get his way he was very cold to Mom throughout the filming."

17. Treatment, Apr. 28, 1941, AMPAS.

18. "Naked Aspect," *Time*, Nov. 23, 1942.

19. AI, Paul Weston.

20. Friedwald, *Sinatra!*, 93, 112; AI, Will Friedwald.

21. Berlin might well have known the famous refrain in Villon's "Ballade des Dames du Temps Jadis." At no time was the fifteenth-century poet better known

to Americans than during the early decades of the twentieth century when he appeared on the stage, in film, and at the opera. In a 1933 interview, Crosby named him as one of his three favorite fictional heroes (even though he wasn't actually fictional), along with Robin Hood and Robinson Crusoe. See *POD,* 313.

22. Berlin, *Los Angeles Mirror,* Dec. 21, 1954, in Kimball and Emmet, 351; Crosby, in a privately taped discussion with his friend George Coleman, 1951. Berlin's famous "lever" was a mechanism on his upright piano that enabled him to change keys—altering the relationship between the hammers and the strings—from F-sharp, the only key he composed in.

23. Paul Ackerman, *Billboard,* Jan. 10, 1942.

24. Carroll, *None of Your Business,* 179.

25. AI, Ed Helwick.

26. As the short went into wide distribution weeks later and Crosby recorded "Angels of Mercy" for Decca months later, it is often assumed to be a consequence of Pearl Harbor, rather than a foreshadowing. Berlin copyrighted the song December 9, though he wrote it several months earlier.

27. AI, Gene Lester.

28. AI, Ed Helwick.

29. Ibid.

30. Transcript, *Kraft Music Hall,* Dec. 11, 1941, American Heritage Center, University of Wyoming, Carroll Archive, box 40.

9. Keep Away from Eunuchs

1. H. Allen Smith, "Bing: King of the Groaners, Part 1," *Saturday Evening Post,* Oct. 31, 1942.

2. Paul Ackerman, *Billboard,* Jan. 10, 1942.

3. Kuhl, J. Walter Thompson Company program report, Jan. 1, 1942.

4. Martin, *RBT.*

5. *San Francisco News,* Oct. 17, 1942.

6. Photograph published in *POD.*

7. The Dec. 22, 1941, letter is in Kimball and Emmet, *The Complete Lyrics of Irving Berlin,* 362–63.

8. Carol Brightman, "The Great Adventure," *Nation,* Dec. 8, 1984.

9. Letter from John O'Melveny to Bing, Jan. 15, 1942, KCC.

10. Ibid.

11. Letter from Todd Johnson to Bing, Mar. 5, 1942, KCC.

12. Letter from John O'Melveny to Clay Johnson, Crosby Investment Company, Mar. 10, 1942, KCC.

13. Memo from Bing to Todd Johnson, June 3, 1942, KCC.

14. Letter from Lieutenant Colonel Austin C. Matheny to Bing Crosby, Oct. 7, 1943.

15. Carroll, *Los Angeles Evening Herald-Express,* Jan. 7, 1942.

16. "Crosby Program Beamed to Army in Philippines," *New York Times,* Jan. 30, 1942.

17. *New York Times,* Jan. 26, 1942; "Bing to Bataan," *Time,* Feb. 2, 1942.

18. Bing's more than two dozen cameo appearances in movies and television shows included eight Hope pictures made between 1942 and 1972, some of the cameos in the form of inserted clips from his own films. They are *My Favorite Blonde, They Got Me Covered* (audio only; Paramount and Bing agreed to allow

Samuel Goldwyn the use of no more than five bars from a Crosby recording), *The Princess and the Pirate, My Favorite Brunette, Son of Paleface, Off Limits, Alias Jesse James,* and *Cancel My Reservation.*

19. Mike Levin, "All Recordings Stop Today," *Down Beat,* Aug. 1, 1942.

20. Carmichael's working title for "Skylark" was "Bix Lix."

21. O'Melveny to Crosby, KCC.

22. Darsie L. Darsie, "Green Tee," *Los Angeles Evening Herald-Express,* Feb. 2, 1942.

23. Van Heusen, *RBT.*

24. *Road to Morocco,* MPAA file, AMPAS. The Breen office also asked them to delete *lay* in the line "I'll lay you eight to five," but Paul Jones held firm on that one.

25. The sheet music for "The Road to Morocco" claimed "As sung by Bing Crosby and Bob Hope while riding on a camel in the Paramount Picture, *Road to Morocco,*" but in fact offered the Coney Island lyric heard only on Bing's Decca record. In 1976, a young fan (Neuhaus, "Interview") told Bing that his favorite Road film was *Road to Utopia.* Bing said, "I probably have to agree with you, although *Morocco* may have the best music."

26. Bing Crosby, "My Ten Favorite Vocalists," *Music and Rhythm,* Mar. 1942.

27. Ulanov, *The Incredible Crosby,* 291.

28. Bing Crosby, "People I'm Glad I Met Along the Way," 1976–1977, unpublished, KCC.

29. This despite a spat with Warner Brothers over a guest appearance by Ronald Reagan, who offered to rehearse during his lunch hour. Warner told him *KMH* said he wasn't needed. "This lie did them no good," Kuhl observed; "listeners could tell he wasn't prepared"; Kuhl, J. Walter Thompson Company program report, Apr. 16, 1942.

30. Memo from Luigi Luraschi to Paul Jones, Apr. 28, 1941, AMPAS.

31. The film began as an eight-page story, "The Road to Morocco," by Eddie David and E. A. Ellington, for which Paramount paid one thousand dollars. As nothing in the final script used anything "even infinitesimally" from that story, according to Paramount executive William Dozier (memo dated Mar. 3, 1942), Butler and Hartman were given original screenplay credit. Interim treatments were written by Hartman and Erik Charell, who unsuccessfully filed for credit; AMPAS.

32. A forgotten film that provided a kind of trial run for some of the settings and stunts is *Outlaws of the Desert,* a dispiriting entry in Paramount's Hopalong Cassidy series in which Hoppy travels to Arabia to buy horses.

33. Dona Drake had a singular résumé. Born Eunice Westmoreland in Florida, she initially obscured her background by manufacturing a fake Mexican identity. She performed under several names, achieving success in the 1930s as Rita Rio, leading (or cavorting before) an all-girl swing band, and dancing memorably in *Strike Me Pink* as Mademoiselle Fifi. Her musical career collapsed when her boyfriend, Louis "Pretty" Amberg, was whacked with extreme prejudice: garroted and set on fire. Amberg, who was so ugly a Ringling Brothers scout tried to hire him as the Missing Link, is believed to have killed more than a hundred men. Questioned by the FBI, Rita said she knew nothing of his criminal life. She was considered professionally untouchable by Hollywood

until Dorothy Lamour brought her to Paramount, where she was reborn as Dona Drake. She played supporting roles, including, at the age of forty, another sexy handmaiden in *Princess of the Nile* (1954), after which she retired; her marriage to William Travilla lasted forty-five years.

34. The it's-just-a-movie ending, borrowed by Jerry Lewis for *The Patsy* (1963) and Mel Brooks for *Blazing Saddles* (1974), is one of several instances of *Morocco*'s influence on comedy writers. Billy Wilder appropriated a line for his own road picture, *Some Like It Hot* (1959). Bob: "Why would a guy want to buy a guy?" Bing: "They buy anything, any old junk." Wilder altered *buy* to *marry* and improved the response: "Security!"

35. Atkins, *David Butler,* 200.

36. *Lucky,* Dictaphone belt 34.

37. De Carlo, *Yvonne,* 68; *Time* office memorandum, Aug. 4, 1943. "When I get the day's script in the morning [I] flip it over to see if there's any way I can get through the day without putting on the mucket," Crosby told Pete Martin (*Lucky,* Dictaphone belt 23). "It's really not much of a chore to put it on, but it's got that glue and it makes your forehead itchy."

38. The concept album was introduced in the late 1930s by Decca with compilations like *Music of Hawaii* and *Patriotic Songs for Children,* which collected relevant recordings by various performers, and by the singer Lee Wiley, who recorded songbooks (George Gershwin, Cole Porter, Harold Arlen, and others) for New York's Liberty Music Shops. The first concept albums solely by Crosby, *Cowboy Songs* (1939) and *Favorite Hawaiian Songs* (1940), assembled discs he had made over several years. The first concept album of original music was likely Woody Guthrie's *Dust Bowl Ballads,* produced for Victor in 1940. *Holiday Inn* appears to fall into the category of cast albums, but as we shall see, Kapp insisted on new arrangements rather than replicas of the film versions to create a discrete Crosby experience (unlike Decca's 1943 *Oklahoma!,* which emphasized its fidelity to the Broadway production). As such, it was Bing's first thematic album consisting of new material. The first concept album built on mood rather than subject was probably Frank Sinatra's *The Voice* (Columbia, 1946.) Concept albums flourished in the era of microgroove with such LPs as Duke Ellington's *Liberian Suite* (1948), Ella Fitzgerald's *Ella Sings Gershwin* (1950), Billie Holiday's *Solitude* (1952), Crosby's *Le Bing: Song Hits of Paris* (1953) and the epic *Bing: A Musical Autobiography* (1954), *Louis Armstrong Plays W. C. Handy* (1954), Sinatra's *In the Wee Small Hours* (1955), and *Ella Fitzgerald Sings the Cole Porter Song Book* (1956), after which the deluge.

10. Caravan

1. Irving Mills, lyrics to "Caravan," composed by Juan Tizol and Duke Ellington.

2. AI, Gene Lester. Lester had been warned by George Watman, a New York publicist who handled Bing's first CBS radio series in 1931. Watman told him to say hello, and Lester made a point of dropping his name—"George told me to do right by you"—as he showed him his hirsute flashbulb.

3. *Kraft Music Hall,* Jan. 18, 1945.

4. Telegram from Crosby to Freeman, Feb. 9, 1944, KCC.

5. Letter to Harry L. Crosby from Major Arthur C. Farlow, acting chief, Special Service Division of the War Department, Aug. 31, 1942, KCC.

6. Porter Hall in *Cagney on Cagney*, 108. Most statistics are from "Holly-wood Group Shows War Work," *New York Times*, Dec. 16, 1942.

7. Hope and Shavelson, *Don't Shoot, It's Only Me*, 63–64; Hyatt, *Hollywood Victory Caravan*, 93–96.

8. The official itinerary included twelve cities (DC, Boston, Philadelphia, Cleveland, Detroit, Chicago, St. Louis, St. Paul, Minneapolis, Des Moines, Dallas, and Houston), but several performers added a last-minute, smaller version of the show in San Francisco.

9. James McClellan in *Minneapolis Morning Tribune*, May 11, 1942.

10. *Lucky*, 277.

11. *Cagney by Cagney*, 108–9. Cagney used two researchers to shore up his memory and they gave him an incorrect venue for this performance, Soldier Field instead of Chicago Stadium. Bing did give an important performance at Soldier Field a year later before a crowd of 130,000, but Cagney wasn't present for that.

12. Patty De Roulf, unidentified newspaper story, 1942, in Macfarlane, *Bing Crosby Day by Day*, 193–94.

13. Ibid.

14. Crosby, interview with S. R. "Dick" Mook, *Silver Screen*, Sept. 1942.

15. Hope, *Confessions of a Hooker*, 136.

16. Keyes, *Scarlett O'Hara's Younger Sister*, 54.

17. James Harvey, *New York Review of Books*, June 30, 1998.

18. Lahr, *Notes on a Cowardly Lion*, 252.

19. Nunnally Johnson, who wrote the screenplay for a couple of Joan Bennett's pictures, adopted her myopia for Marilyn Monroe's character in the 1953 film *How to Marry a Millionaire*.

20. James Gray, *St. Paul Pioneer Press*, May 10, 1942.

21. *Houston Chronicle*, May 13, 1942.

22. Lahr, *Notes on a Cowardly Lion*, 253.

23. Herb and Midge Polesie, "Dixie, the Athlete," unpublished manuscript, written at Bing's request while he was working on *Call Me Lucky* and forwarded by him to Pete Martin, Dec. 29, 1952.

24. Associated Press, "Crosby First Movie Star to Race Horse," May 18, 1942; letters from Bing Crosby to Billy Post, May 29, June 3, Aug. 3, 1942, KCC.

25. Gary Crosby, *Going My Own Way*, 19; AI, Phillip Crosby.

26. Undated letters, evidently written during the Victory Caravan, as that's when Zoltan Korda's film *Jungle Book* played Los Angeles. Bing had that picture's star, Sabu, on *KMH* shortly before he left for the tour (KCC).

27. A Paramount Pictures press release filed as "Biography of Bing Crosby," dated December 1942 and credited to "woolfenden el," described him as the "richest man in Southern California and laziest man in the world." Setting out to "winnow the facts from the chaff," it gave a date of birth that was off by two years, claimed he nicknamed himself the Groaner, could "very definitely" read music (he very definitely could not), and starred on a radio show on—believe it or not—CBS (AMPAS).

28. Letter from Irving Berlin to Mark Sandrich, July 10, 1942, AMPAS.

29. The myth of the eighteen-minute session probably first appeared in Thompson's *Bing* (95), unsourced and coupled with the plainly false assumption that he did it in one take. Two takes survive; the first was rejected because

Bing dropped the word *your* from the last line, "And may all your Christmases be bright."

30. AI, Alan Duncan.

31. Booklet for *Holiday Inn,* Decca album no. A-306.

32. AI, Vic Schoen.

11. Friends

1. "Bing Crosby Best Paid Actor in Hollywood," *Hollywood Citizen News,* June 26, 1942.

2. Harrison Carroll, *Los Angeles Evening Herald-Express,* July 27, 1942; AI, Jean Halliburton, who was married to Stevens from 1939 to 1959; AI, Carole Jackson, their daughter; AI, Esther Reichenbaum, manager of patron history during the 1940s and 1950s, Waldorf Astoria, New York.

3. AI, Phil Harris.

4. AI, Jean Halliburton. Arnold Stevens's former wife, who went back to her maiden name after they divorced, died in 2011, at ninety-five. Arnold Stevens, whose career declined after their 1959 divorce, died in 1972, at age sixty-nine. One of the last papers he wrote, while he was affiliated with a rehab clinic, argued that alcohol does not destroy brain cells.

5. Ibid.

6. *Lucky,* Dictaphone belt 14. In the published *Lucky,* Bing attributes the line about her shoes to Bessie, to show she could kid about herself. In the transcript, he says Johnny said it of her patronizingly and often.

7. AI, Jean Halliburton; AI, Rory Burke.

8. Larry Crosby signed Friday to a management contract in 1939 after she won a college singing contest. When she compromised the co-ed image by getting married, he canceled her contract. Friday claimed that the Crosbys blackballed her until she complained to their mother, who got them to lift the ban. She later worked with Jack Webb, who asked her permission to name his *Dragnet* character Joe Friday.

9. *Lucky,* Dictaphone belt 14.

10. Ibid. During the interview, Martin asked, "What does a smuck [sic] mean?" Bing answered, "Oh, a louse."

11. Letter from Lieutenant P. G. Farley and three others to Bing Crosby, Sept. 3, 1943; letter from Bing Crosby to Farley and "the balance of your gay group," Sept. 22, 1943.

12. Ibid. In telling Martin of the anti-Semitism, Bing quipped, "I don't know whether you can use a story like that—a racial thing. Make it colored." They laughed and omitted the story from *Call Me Lucky.*

13. Silvers, *This Laugh Is On Me,* 135; AI, Jean Halliburton.

14. AI, Rory Burke; AI, Jean Halliburton. Jean became a writer and editor for *Los Angeles Magazine.*

15. Al, Jean Halliburton.

16. Ibid. The word *periodic* and, indeed, the tortures of alcoholism would be more widely discussed two years later with the publication of Charles Jackson's powerful novel *The Lost Weekend,* which contained the line "He was a periodic drinker, with intervals of sobriety between."

17. AI, Trudy MacKenzie (aka Jinny Erwin and Trudy Erwin).

18. Al, Jean Halliburton.

19. Jean Halliburton, "Bing and Dixie Crosby," unpublished manuscript.

20. AI, Pauline Weislow.

21. AI, Jean Halliburton.

22. AI, Jean Halliburton; AI, Gary Crosby.

23. AI, Walter Scharf.

24. AI, Bill Goodwin, quoting his mother, Philippa, on Bing's philandering; AI, Pauline Weislow; AI, Jean Halliburton; KGM.

25. AI, Shirley Mitchell; AI, Gene Lester; *Photoplay,* June 1943, 50.

26. AI, Dolores Hope.

27. Judy Schmid, "Music Maid Alice Sizer Ludes Sings Bing's Praises," a 2007 interview posted on Facebook in 2011, when she was ninety-four.

28. Kyser's biographer Steven Beasley found this in a 1943 radio review: "It was a chilly 'hello' Kay Kyser gave Ginny Simms backstage at a COMMAND PERFORMANCE program, and the two had to be persuaded to be photographed together." Kyser retired at forty-five and devoted the next thirty-five years to his family and Christian Science. It has become commonplace to refer to Kyser's show as the *Kollege of Musical Knowledge,* but in its day, he used the conventional spelling.

29. AI, Trudy MacKenzie; Kyser hired one other singer along with Erwin, Dorothy Dunn.

30. Dinah Shore interview videotaped, but not used, for a documentary by Bryan Johnson, 1991. In the Apr. 1943 issue of *American Magazine,* Shore told a reporter that when Bing approached her, he said, "I like your singing and I've wanted to meet you," which sent her into a spin; she had to "rush out of the studio to get some fresh air." The reporter was "shocked" when Bing remarked, "There's nothing square about Dinah," until he learned that *square* was a jive term that meant "corny"; he wasn't using *square* in the sense of "honest, on the square." He figured the new slang "derives from the old-fashioned square dances."

31. Letter from Jinny Erwin to Crosby, Mar. 28, 1942, KCC.

32. Letter from Dinah Shore to Crosby, Mar. 28, 1942, KCC.

33. Trudy MacKenzie said in an author interview that Crosby "was very good about corresponding," but that his letters had been burned in a fire that destroyed her home in 1970.

34. Letter from Jinny Erwin to Bing, Apr. 7, 1942. The Lucky Strike cut-ins refer to Kyser's quiz show.

35. Mark Scrimger, liner notes, *Bing Crosby: The War Years* (Broadway Intermission, 129).

36. Mackenzie, *Command Performance, USA*; Pairpoint, *"And Here's Bing"*; Kiner and Reade, "Bing Crosby: A Bio-Discography"; Baker, *Bing Crosby Discography.* Crosby walked out on his *KMH* contract in the summer of 1945, so the number of *KMH* shows (135) is lower than if he had done his usual fall season.

37. Bing Crosby, interview by John Salisbury, 1976.

38. Dinah Shore interview, videotaped for a documentary by Bryan Johnson, 1991.

39. Ibid.

40. Gary Crosby, *Going My Own Way,* 53; Herb and Midge Polesie, "Dixie, the Great Mother," unpublished manuscript.

41. "Better Breaks for Negroes in H'wood," *Variety*, Mar. 25, 1942; Hall Johnson letter to Albert Lewis in Fordin, *The Movies' Greatest Musicals*, 75; Cripps, *Slow Fade to Black*, 376; Bosley Crowther, *New York Times*, May 9, 1942.

42. In 1944, the cultural critic Gilbert Seldes made the pertinent observation (in *Esquire*) that Crosby's *Ballad for Americans* lacks Paul Robeson's nobility but that in the passage where Uncle Sam declares himself a composite of every nationality, race, and religion, Bing is "supreme."

43. AI, Skitch Henderson. In her memoir, Esther Williams described Johnston as a "con man" who surrounded himself with groupies and read aloud to them the intimate parts of love letters from a famous paramour: "God, I thought to myself, that's my leading man!" Williams, *The Million Dollar Mermaid*, 152–53. In an interview with the author, Eddie Bracken recalled that Johnston had a decent voice, "but his ego destroyed him. Bing hated him."

12. Home Fires

1. "Inn's In—B'way All Out," *Variety*, Aug. 5, 1942, 12.

2. Silvers, *This Laugh Is On Me*, 146–48.

3. *Tacoma News*, Aug. 7, 1942.

4. Silvers, *This Laugh Is On Me*, 146–48.

5. *Wyoming Eagle*, Aug. 12, 1942, reprinted in Macfarlane, *Bing Crosby Day by Day*, 237.

6. *Variety*, June 17, 1942, 8; *Time*, Aug. 31, 1942; Bosley Crowther, "Irving Berlin's Holiday Inn, Co-Starring Bing Crosby and Fred Astaire, Has Navy Benefit Premiere at Paramount," *New York Times*, Aug. 5, 1942; Kate Cameron, *New York Herald Tribune*, Aug. 5, 1942. Cameron, too, admired "Abraham" as "a modern spiritual."

7. S. J. Woolf, "Sergeant Berlin Re-Enlists," *New York Times*, May 17, 1942.

8. Parish, *The Encyclopedia of Ethnic Groups in Hollywood*, 56.

9. An entrepreneur named Kemmons Wilson was so stirred by *Holiday Inn* that in 1952, he borrowed the title to create America's most successful hotel chain.

10. Letter from Irving Berlin to Mark Sandrich, July 10, 1942, AMPAS.

11. Letter from Irving Berlin to Mark Sandrich, July 31, 1942, AMPAS.

12. Telegram from Irving Berlin to Mark Sandrich, Sept. 14, 1942, AMPAS.

13. Letter from Irving Berlin to Mark Sandrich, Nov. 2, 1942, AMPAS.

14. Letter from Everett N. Crosby to Jack Kapp, Sept. 17, 1942, KCC.

15. Letter from Irving Berlin to Mark Sandrich, Nov. 2, 1942, AMPAS.

16. *Time*, Nov. 23, 1942.

17. Sandberg, *Chicago Times*, Dec. 1942, in Kimball and Emmet, *Complete Lyrics of Irving Berlin*, 351.

18. Atkinson, *Gord Atkinson's Showbill*, 200. Atkinson, the Canadian broadcaster, recorded countless hours with and about Crosby.

19. Letter from E. N. Crosby to T. H. McInnerney, Aug. 21, 1942, KCC.

20. *Grand Rapids Herald*, Sept. 13, reprinted in Macfarlane, *Bing Crosby Day by Day*, 241.

21. Letter from Henry Morgenthau Jr. to Crosby, Oct. 1, 1942, KCC.

22. AI, George Coleman; Nathaniel Crosby, *Eighteen Holes with Bing*, 58.

23. Letter from Fred Corcoran to Larry Crosby, Oct. 20, 1942, KCC.

24. Letter from Elmer Davis to Crosby, Oct. 27, 1942; letter of acceptance from Crosby to Francis Kepple, Joint Army and Navy Committee, Nov. 18, 1942; letters from Crosby to Herbert Lindsley ("missionary work"), Nov. 9, 1942, and Private John P. Decker, U.S. Naval Hospital, Mare Island, Nov. 27, 1942, KCC. In his syndicated column "Jimmie Fidler in Hollywood," on August 8, 1943, Fidler wrote: "Hollywood will be surprised to learn that Bing Crosby for eight months has been special consultant to the Hollywood OWI office, censoring entertainment for service men." This last part is plainly absurd; there is no suggestion of "censoring" in the OWI correspondence.

25. *New York Age*, Nov. 22, 1942.

26. Bosley Crowther, *New York Times*, Nov. 12, 1942.

27. "Broadcast over Public Address System on U.S.S. *Joseph T. Dickman* to Crew and Soldiers Bound for North Africa," Oct. 28, 1942, American Heritage Center, University of Wyoming, Carroll Archive, box 64.

28. Letter from Morales to Crosby, Dec. 22, 1942; letter from Crosby to Morales, Mar. 23, 1943, Carroll Archive, box 64.

29. AI, Trudy MacKenzie. She began her contract on the show that aired February 4, 1943, the week after the guest star had been Ginny Simms.

30. Gary Crosby, *Going My Own Way*, 73.

31. Memo from Ed Eberle to B. G. DeSylva, Nov. 4, 1942, AMPAS.

32. Letter from E. E. Wyatt to Crosby (box 42, Del Mar, Calif.), Nov. 29, 1942, courtesy Mark Scrimger. Dixie almost certainly never saw or knew of this letter.

33. Letter from "Dixie & Bing" to recipients including Hazel and Ted Crosby (HCC) and Mr. and Mrs. Carroll Carroll, Carroll Archive.

34. Kuhl, J. Walter Thompson Company program report, Dec. 24, 1942.

35. *Variety*, Dec. 30, 1942.

36. General Walton wrote him: "My dear Mr. Crosby: We feel very honored to have had you for our Christmas show and certainly do appreciate all the trouble you went to in arranging to come here"; Dec. 28, 1942, KCC.

37. *Lucky*, Dictaphone belt 14; AI, Pauline Weislow; AI, Bill Goodwin Jr. The Goodwin children were two-year-old Jill and eleven-month-old Bill Jr. Bill grew up to be an eminent jazz drummer and music producer, associated chiefly with the great alto saxophonist Phil Woods, who married Bill's sister, Jill.

38. *Lucky*, Dictaphone belt 14.

39. AI, Pauline Weislow. Most newspaper accounts reported that the dog belonged to the Crosby boys. They also reported Bing's golf partner that day was Fred Astaire.

40. "Disastrous Fire Sweeps Home of Bing Crosby," *Los Angeles Times*, Jan. 4, 1943.

41. *Lucky*, 168.

42. AI, Jean Halliburton; AI, Dolores Hope.

43. Letter from Bing Crosby to Lieutenant Saul C. Weislow, Mar. 18, 1943, KCC.

44. Elizabeth W. Adkins, archives manager of Kraft General Foods, letter to author, Nov. 20, 1992; Jack Richardson, western division manager of NBC Radio-Recording, letter to Everett Crosby, Sept. 1, 1943.

45. Survey of basement (Apr. 17, 1939) and record of installation (undated), F. Roy Tisdall, Fire-Gard Corporation, KCC.

13. Divertissement

1. *Dixie* files, AMPAS.

2. Claude Binyon's original screenplay was rewritten by Karl Tunberg and Darrell Ware, among others.

3. "South Recalls Actual Origin of 'Dixie' Tune As Link to Crosby Pic," *Variety*, Sept. 1, 1943, 23. The story of the Snowden brothers is told in Howard Sacks and Judith Sacks, *Way Up North in Dixie* (Washington, DC: Smithsonian Institution Press, 1993). The 1976 gravestone for Ben and Lew Snowden, set by the American Legion, reads "They taught 'Dixie' to Dan Emmett."

4. T. C. DeLeon, *Belles, Beaux and Brains of the 60's* (New York: G. W. Dillingham, 1907), 359. The reporter who documented this dialogue was the drama critic and editor of the *New York Clipper*, T. Allston Brown, who wrote a short history of "Ethiopian Minstrelsy."

5. Oscar Wilde, "The Critic as Artist"; Bert Williams, http://black-face.com/Bert-Williams.htm; AI, Bob Hope.

6. William Faulkner, "A Rose for Emily." For a taste of how minstrelsy was marketed, one need only consult the large catalog of joke books published in New York beginning in 1879 by Henry J. Wehman. The cover of a volume from 1897 reads: *Wehman's Black Jokes, for "Blue Devils." Chock Full of Darkey Fun! Colored Philosophy and Nigger Witticisms. Consisting of Plantation and "High Life" Stories—Highfalutin Sermons, Die-Away Songs.—Ivory Opening Jokes, Complicated "Conunderfums" and an endless variety of sable wit, showing up the peculiarly laughable character of "Sambo" in the strongest "colors." Fully Illustrated with Near One Hundred Pictorial "Black Jokes."* These books, with altered titles (*Wehman's Minstrel Sketches Conundrums and Jokes*), were in print in the 1930s and probably long after. Compare these to the relatively judicious title of Wehman's 1891 volume *Yankee, Hebrew and Italian Dialect Readings & Recitations*. Iterations of minstrel jokes and songs are still heard today.

7. For a picture ostensibly concerned with the history of black show business, *Stormy Weather* is undermined by Twentieth Century–Fox's inexplicable omission of second-line credits, even that of the featured vocalist Mae Johnson. If their names are now obscure, their works survive: Flournoy Miller's *Shuffle Along* was revived on Broadway in 2016); Herb Jeffries's Westerns were restored for the Blu-ray anthology *Pioneers of African American Cinema*, and Johnny Lee (the voice of Brer Rabbit in Disney's *Song of the South*) played the lawyer Calhoun in the televised *Amos 'n' Andy*.

8. *Life*, July 5, 1943.

9. These numbers are based largely on information in *The American Film Institute Catalogs* covering the years 1931 to 1950. Relevant films that opened between 1940 and 1946 include *Adventures of Mark Twain, After Midnight with Boston Blackie, Babes on Broadway, Billy the Kid's Fighting Pals, Born to Sing, Boss of Rawhide, Boston Blackie's Rendezvous, The Captive Heart, Carolina Moon, Coney Island, "Cooks and Crooks," Dance Girl Dance, The Daring Young Man, Dixie, The Dolly Sisters, Gentleman Jim, Here Come the Waves, Holiday Inn, If I Had My Way, Irish Eyes Are Smiling, The Jolson Story, Kisses for Breakfast, "Ye Olde Minstrels," The Lonesome Trail, The Man in Grey, The Meanest Man in the World, The Merry Monahans, "Minstrel Days," Minstrel Man, "Minstrel Parade," Mister Big, Mokey, The Naughty Nineties, People Are Funny, "Plantation Melodies," Redhead from Manhattan, Rhapsody in Blue, Saratoga*

Trunk, Show Business, "Show Business at War," *The Spoilers, Stormy Weather,* "Swanee Showboat," *There Goes Kelly,* "Three Pests in a Mess," *They Meet Again, This Is the Army, Thundering Trails, The Time, the Place and the Girl, The Vanishing Virginian,* "Uncivil War Birds," "Unusual Occupations No. 3," *Up in the Air, West of Cimarron, White Cargo, Wild Man of Borneo, Yankee Doodle Dandy, Young People, Ziegfeld Follies.*

Significantly, the long-standing radio favorite *Amos 'n' Andy* enjoyed a revival in the year of *Dixie,* 1943, but with the innovation of an integrated cast— indeed, it hired more black actors than appeared in any other "white" show. In February, the fifteen-minute series, which debuted in 1929, left the air to reemerge in October as a weekly thirty-minute series with the new cast. Its Hooper rating soared from a low 9.4 in January 1943 to 17.1 in January 1944 and continued to rise, peaking in January 1948 at 23.0, the highest rating for any comedy program on the air.

10. Archer Winsten quoted in Irving Hoffman's column in the *Holly-wood Reporter,* June 29, 1943, concerning the unanimously favorable reviews earned by *Dixie* in every publication in New York and Los Angeles, including the leftist *PM.*

11. Nat Hentoff, "Bing Crosby Is Coming to Town," *New York Daily News,* Dec. 5, 1976, 12.

12. Sallye Bell, *Pittsburgh Courier,* Jan. 8, 1938, in Sampson, *Swingin' on the Ether Waves,* 248–50.

13. AI, Lena Horne: "Black people liked Bing Crosby very much. They liked Billy Eckstine, too, who was younger, but they liked Crosby."

14. John O'Melveny, interviewed by M. Gleason, *Fortune,* Aug. 7, 1946, TIA. See *POD,* 78–87, for a more extensive discussion of minstrelsy and Crosby's relationship to it and to Jolson.

15. *Variety,* June 30, 1943, 8.

16. *Swanee River* was the second of three Foster biopics. The others were produced as low-budget programmers: *Harmony Lane* in 1935 and *I Dream of Jeanie* in 1952, the last with a plot taken from *Mississippi* and a minstrel show as accurate and discomfiting as the one in *Dixie.*

17. Bobby Newcomb, "Hints to the Amateur Minstrel," *Tambo His Jokes and Funny Sayings* (New York: Wehman Brothers, 1882). Coincidentally, Newcomb died on tour in Tacoma, Crosby's birthplace.

18. *Hollywood Reporter,* June 29, 1943. In June 2014, Dan Emmett's home, a tourist attraction in Mount Vernon, Ohio, was gutted by fire, thought to be the work of an arsonist.

19. *Variety,* June 30, 1943, 10–11.

20. Memo from Joseph Breen to Luigi Luraschi, Sept. 21, 1942, AMPAS.

21. Sampson, *Swingin' on the Ether Waves,* 475.

22. "Crosby Tells Why Hams Are Scarce," *Omaha World Herald,* Feb. 7, 1943.

23. Gubar, *Racechanges,* 54. Initially, the "transference" song in *Dixie* was "Deep River," but the producer worried that audiences would not know it and changed it to the more familiar "Swing Low, Sweet Chariot"; Kate Cameron, *New York Daily News,* June 24, 1943.

24. Yellow script of *Dixie* by Karl Tunberg and Darrell Ware, dated Sept. 17, 1942, AMPAS.

25. Irving Hoffman, *Hollywood Reporter,* June 29, 1943.

26. Although no one appears to have noted it, the one possible upside of the strike is that it helped shore up the diminished supply of shellac and encouraged the use of vinyl. This may explain why FDR did not interfere with the musicians' strike until 1944, when rationing of the former was no longer an issue and the transition to the latter had been accomplished. When he did ask Petrillo to back down, he received a long petulant refusal. Still, the strike ended shortly thereafter.

27. A few additional numbers were never issued on V-Disc or anything else. One apocryphal story has Crosby recording a V-Disc with guitarist Tony Mottola. When Mottola played a wrong chord, Bing, under his breath—as no one heard him until the playback—said, "Tony, take your fucking gloves off." This disc, title unknown, has apparently not survived.

28. This song was a favorite of the alto saxophonist Paul Desmond, who habitually improvised variations on it. When he wrote "Take Five" for the Dave Brubeck Quartet, he had trouble coming up with a middle section. Someone mockingly said, "Just play 'Sunday, Monday, or Always.'" That's what Desmond did; the bridge to "Take Five" converts the first five notes of "Sunday, Monday, or Always" into a rhythmically altered four-note riff.

29. Letter from Bing Crosby to Private Grey Morgan of the 905th Signal Depot Company, Sept. 9, 1943, KCC.

30. "298,946 Paid Bing Crosby," *Philadelphia Inquirer,* June 9, 1943.

31. *PIC,* Nov. 23, 1943.

14. Just an Old Cowhand

1. Letters from Bing Crosby to Private Grey Morgan of the 905th Signal Depot Company, Sept. 9, 1943, and to Lieutenant Saul C. Weislow, Mar. 15, 1943, KCC; AI, Gary Crosby.

2. *Los Angeles Times,* Mar. 17, 1943; "Crosby to Appear at Camp Roberts," *San Diego Union,* Mar. 12, 1943; letter to Lieutenant Saul C. Weislow, Mar. 15, 1943, KCC.

3. Marva Peterson, "House of Memories," original publication unknown, reprinted in *Bingang,* Dec. 1993, 38–42.

4. AI, Gary Crosby.

5. AI, Alan Fisher; Alan Shipnuck, "The Westside Six," *Sports Illustrated,* Aug. 21, 1995; Bing Crosby, unpublished ms, KCC. The Crosby-Benny exchange is thought by some to have originated as an ad-lib moment on radio.

6. AI, Phillip Crosby; AI, Gary Crosby.

7. *Variety,* June 30, 1943.

8. When a star of Crosby's caliber was mentioned in a movie (for example, Jimmy Durante in *Two Girls and a Sailor* brags that he got a particularly egregious musical note from "Bing Crosby, and was he glad to get rid of it"), a formal release had to be obtained.

9. *Memphis Press-Scimitar,* May 24, 1943, reproduced in Macfarlane, *Bing Crosby Day by Day,* 254.

10. *Variety,* July 7, 1943; *Time,* July 19, 1943.

11. Rinker, who worked for the William Esty Agency, wrote more than two dozen songs, none of them major hits. But the height of his achievement as a composer came in 1953, when he set a cycle of Robert Burns poems to music

for Jo Stafford's marvelous recording *Songs of Scotland*, arranged by Paul Weston. Rinker later cowrote "Ev'rybody Wants to Be a Cat," the highlight of Disney's *The Aristocats* (1970), sung by Scatman Crothers and Phil Harris. Harris recorded it as a pop single.

12. Jack Wade, "Easy Ace," *Modern Screen*, June 1943; letter to author from Jack Ellsworth, formerly a Marine Corps combat correspondent stationed at Oak Knoll Naval Hospital in Oakland to interview combat veterans, Jan. 31, 2001; press release from the Office of Assistant Director Public Relations for the United States Marine Corps (West Coast Area), signed "shiebler," 1944.

13. AI, Vic Schoen.

14. Ibid. The instrumentation here is four rhythm and five winds. The rhythm section has pianist Charlie LaVere, guitarist Perry Botkin, bassist Artie Shapiro, and drummer Nick Fatool, all jazz veterans who earned good wages in John Scott Trotter's radio orchestra and the segregated enclave of Hollywood studio musicians. The winds consist of two trumpets (George Wendt, Robert Goodrich), two reeds (clarinetist Archie Rosate, baritone saxophonist Mort Friedman), and trombone (Peter Bielmann). For the September 29 session, Rosate was replaced by Jack Mayhew, a Paul Whiteman alumnus and Trotter regular.

15. "Music in the News," *Billboard*, Nov. 27, 1943, quoted in Nimmo, *The Andrews Sisters*, 162–63.

16. Ibid.

17. AI, Vic Schoen.

18. Murrells, *Million Selling Records*, 37.

19. Letter from Brick Miller of KTAR to Mrs. Albert Kahn, Mar. 23, 1943; letter from Shirley Ross to Bing Crosby, Apr. 4, 1943; letter from Bing Crosby to Mrs. B. Ross, Oct. 11, 1943, KCC. Another private recording from the same month involved a lead sheet mailed to him by a navy seaman stationed in the South Pacific. Crosby recorded and broadcast it shortwave so that the amateur songwriter could hear his song (*Tune-In*, Nov. 1943).

20. The U.S. government did not share that concern. A year later, in December 1944, one of Crosby's *KMH* performances of "I'll Be Home for Christmas" was coupled with "White Christmas" to create the most requested of all V-Discs.

21. Maxene Andrews, interviewed by Mark Scrimger and Bob Pasch, 1992, transcribed by the author. An edited version appeared in *Bingang*, Dec. 1992.

22. Ibid.

23. AI, Vic Schoen.

24. Lincoln Barnett, "Bing, Inc.," *Life*, June 18, 1944, reprinted with an introduction about meeting Crosby in Barnett, *Writing on Life*, 180–99. Faÿ's *Franklin: The Apostle of Modern Times* was a bestseller in 1929 in France and the United States. At the time of their lunch, unbeknownst to Crosby and Barnett, Faÿ was collaborating with the Nazis in Vichy, where he was known for his murderous hatred of Freemasons; he was tried and imprisoned in 1946. Van Doren's prizewinning *Benjamin Franklin* (1938) is periodically reprinted.

25. S. R. Mook, "Candid Closeup of Bing Crosby," *Screenland*, 1943. The story's teaser reads "An interview with Bing Crosby is harder to get than a pair of nylons!"

26. Ibid.

27. Ibid. Similar themes, including his middle-class status, aired in Kay Proctor, "Play Truth or Consequences with Bing Crosby," *Photoplay*, June 1943.

28. Smith, *Life in a Putty Knife Factory*, 260–64.

29. Crosby genealogy, see *POD*, 625; Mary Greene, "Relax and Get Rich," *Radio Life* 7, no. 24 (1943); AI, Alan Fisher.

30. Mary Lanigan Healy, "He Takes It Easy the Hard Way," *Vincentian*, Feb. 1943; AI, Tony Bennett.

31. Jordan Rane, "Spotlight: Mary Crosby," *Cowboys and Indians* (July 2009): 124–29.

32. Theodore Roosevelt, *Ranch Life and the Hunting Trail* (New York: Century, 1899), 24.

33. Schneider, *Bing on the Road to Elko*, 30–31; *Lucky* transcript, unnumbered.

34. *Lucky*, Dictaphone belt 32.

35. Ibid.

36. *Lucky*, 55; letter from Postmaster Mary C. McNamara to Bing, Apr. 12, 1943; *Lucky*, Dictaphone belt 32.

37. AI, Jean Halliburton.

38. *Lucky*, Dictaphone belt 32.

39. Ibid.; Rane, "Spotlight: Mary Crosby."

40. Gary Crosby, *Going My Own Way*, 88.

41. Ibid., 101.

42. Ibid., 91.

43. *Lucky*, Dictaphone belt 29.

44. *Lucky*, Dictaphone belt 27.

45. Gary Crosby, *Going My Own Way*, 100.

46. Letter from Gary Crosby to Bing and Dixie, 1943, KCC.

47. Gary Crosby, *Going My Own Way*, 94–98.

48. Ibid., 98–99.

49. Letter from Gary Crosby to Bing and Dixie, 1943, KCC.

50. This phrase plays on the 1933 song "Annie Doesn't Live Here Anymore," which, coincidentally or not, was the first major hit by Johnny Burke (music by Harold Spina).

51. Henry King was a society band leader who specialized in non-jazz dance music at chic hotels. Bing arranged for him to perform in the 1945 Paramount comedy *Out of This World*, featuring Bing's dubbed vocals for Eddie Bracken and a cameo appearance by the four Crosby boys. Jane Pickens, originally of the Pickens Sisters, had a solo career in theater and on television before turning to philanthropy and politics; she ran unsuccessfully as the conservative candidate against New York's congressman (later mayor), Ed Koch.

52. Letter to Bing and Dixie from Doris Eacret, Aug. 13, 1943, KCC. Charles Howard was the owner of Seabiscuit and father of Bing's racing partner Lin Howard (see *POD*, 468–69).

53. Letters from Gary Crosby, 1943, KCC.

54. Letter to Gary from Doris Eacret, Oct. 2, 1943, KCC.

15. The Leo McCarey Way

1. *The Odyssey*, book 8. In truth, William Broome is said to have translated this section.

2. Bing Crosby, "Leo McCarey— 1898–1969," July 20, 1969, reprinted in *Action!*, Sept. 1969.

3. Laughton in "Paramount Pictures Biographies" (press release signed by De Vane), Apr. 1936, AMPAS; Renoir in Wakeman, *World Film Directors,* 747; Hecht, *A Child of the Century,* 396, 482. Wes Gehring refers to the Shaw correspondence in *Leo McCarey: From Marx to McCarthy* (xix, 141), without sourcing. These letters have evidently not survived.

4. Dore Schary in McGilligan, *Film Crazy,* 197. Schary said he devised plot points for *Love Affair* (1939) and that McCarey paid him but denied him screen credit as co-author of the story. Schary's complaint was, at least in part, demonstrably untrue. He claimed Leo had contributed only a title yet wanted a solo story credit. In fact, McCarey shared that credit with Mildred Cram, a well-known writer of the era, famous for storylines with mystical or religious themes.

5. Letter from Leo McCarey to Charles Oliphant, chief counsel for Bureau of Internal Revenue, June 1949: "[The large studios] manufacture pattern pictures that to my mind are run off a belt"; USC.

6. McCarey reported his 1944 income as $1,113,035, which earned him the widely reported title of "Employee of the Year"; see, for example, "Show World Tops Salaries for 1944," *New York Times,* June 17, 1946.

7. McCarey remade *Love Affair* in 1957 as *An Affair to Remember,* using, scene for scene, the original script, yet creating a different modality in line with the actors. The remake introduced his one successful song, the Academy Award–nominated "Our Love Affair," for which he received a co-lyricist credit with Harold Adamson. Harry Warren composed the melody.

8. Crosby, "Leo McCarey."

9. His modesty increased exponentially. During a flurry of television and radio appearances he made in 1976, he said to Joe Franklin, "Well, it was just Bing Crosby with his collar turned around. But there was no acting in that, really. It was a pleasant guy who sang some nice songs"; to Jack O'Brien, "I played the same part all the time"; and to John Salisbury, "I think the part carried me. Or the director [who] just had me do things. I didn't know what I was doing, just did what they said."

10. Leo shaved two years off his birth year, and most reference works continue to use 1898, although that would make him a practicing lawyer before he was twenty years old. His widow, Stella McCarey, who surely rankled at going through life being thought of as his senior by four years (she didn't hedge her birth year, which was 1894), had *1896* chiseled on his tombstone. Leo himself gave the correct date in his 1947 appearance, under oath, before the House Un-American Activities Committee.

11. Ward, *Unforgivable Blackness,* 45. Ward vividly portrays the senior McCarey and the world in which he operated.

12. Ibid., 48.

13. "Boxing Proves Most Favored Athletic Sport," *Los Angeles Herald,* Dec. 20, 1908.

14. Capra, *The Name Above the Title,* 41; Gehring, *Leo McCarey,* 3; "Boxer Lost to Wolgast in 1912 Double Knockout," *New York Times,* June 26, 1957.

15. McCarey's Catholic-themed films are *Love Affair* (1939), *Going My Way* (1944), *The Bells of St. Mary's* (1945), *An Affair to Remember* (1957), and *Satan Never Sleeps* (1962). The Greene novels are *Brighton Rock* (1938), *The Power and the Glory* (1940), *The Heart of the Matter* (1948), *The End of the Affair*

(1951), *A Burnt-Out Case* (1960). One can make a case for Catholic tropes in other McCarey and Greene works, but they are most literally treated in these.

16. Bogdanovich, *Who the Devil Made It*, 384.

17. Ibid., 386.

18. Richard W. Bann, "Leo McCarey at Hal Roach Studios," www.laurel-and-hardy.com/archive/articles/1998-10-mccarey-long.html.

19. Capra, *The Name Above the Title*, 40.

20. McKeever, "The McCarey Touch," 5.

21. Schulberg's son, the writer Budd Schulberg, avenged McCarey by citing him as an example of brilliant visual economy in his 1941 novel *What Makes Sammy Run?* (chapter 8), changing his name to Ray MacKenna and his apprenticeship to "the Mack Sennett two-reel comedy school."

22. McCarey to the director Edward Dmytryk, who edited *Ruggles of Red Gap* and *Love Affair*, cited in McKeever, "The McCarey Touch," 28.

23. Philip K. Scheuer, *Los Angeles Times*, May 28, 1944.

24. Wiley and Bona, *Inside Oscar*, 82.

25. Hanson, *American Film Institute Catalog: Feature Films, 1931–1940*, 1242.

26. George Schaefer to Leo McCarey, Sept. 30, 1939, USC.

27. First report, traffic accident, file no. 72144, approximately 6:15, Nov. 17, 1939, intersection of Citrus and Alosta, Azusa District. Files by Deputies Max E. Bayha and Robert G. Fry, San Dimas Station.

28. Crosby, "Leo McCarey."

29. Telegram from McCarey to Ned E. Depinet, RKO Pictures, Nov. 19, 1942, USC; Bogdanovich, *Who the Devil Made It*, 420.

30. Of these projects, only *Here Come the Waves* was made with Crosby. *All Around Town*, scripted by two *Dixie* writers, Karl Tunberg and Darrell Ware, became 1945's *Bring on the Girls* with Veronica Lake and Sonny Tufts. *California* was made in 1947 with Ray Milland and Barbara Stanwyck. *Stallion Road* was taken off the schedule long enough for Stephen Longstreet to write a novel of that name, which he adapted as a 1947 film with Ronald Reagan and Alexis Smith, directed by Crosby's friends Jimmy Kern and (uncredited) Raoul Walsh.

31. Atkins, *David Butler*, 189–90.

32. David Butler, interviewed by M. Gleason, Aug. 4, 1946, TIA; Harrison Carroll, *Los Angeles Evening Herald-Express*, Mar. 18, 1943.

33. Atkins, *David Butler*. The test survives and is easily found online. Warner eventually made *The Story of Will Rogers* in 1952, starring Will Rogers Jr.

16. Padres

1. Robert Bresson, *Notes on the Cinematographer*, trans. Jonathan Griffin (Los Angeles: Green Integer, 1997), 23.

2. Leo to Bing in Pete Martin, "Going His Way," *Saturday Evening Post*, Nov. 11, 1946, 15.

3. Letter from Bing Crosby to Lieutenant Allan S. Hayes Jr., Apr. 5, 1945, KCC.

4. *Lucky*, Dictaphone belt 18.

5. Letter from Crosby to Hayes.

6. McCarey, draft of affidavit for the IRS, Dec. 1949, USC; Bogdanovich, *Who the Devil Made It*, 422.

7. Several Hollywood movies had featured Catholic priests (Joe Breen was faulted for religious favoritism), but their duties invariably consisted of accompanying bad men to the electric chair, praying for the surcease of natural disasters, or founding Boys Town.

8. Letter from Leo McCarey to Charles Oliphant, chief counsel for Bureau of Internal Revenue, June 1949.

9. *Lucky*, Dictaphone belt 18.

10. McCarey affidavit. McCarey's participation in *Going My Way* projects ended before the television adaptation; in settling his postwar IRS bill, he sold the story rights to Paramount.

11. *Variety*, Apr. 14, 1943.

12. To Bing Crosby from Mrs. T. N. McClure Sr., Colfax, Washington, Apr. 15, 1943, KCC; "Berlin Radio Uses Feminine Voice on American Troops," *Riverside Daily Press*, Apr. 16, 1943; Harrison Carroll, *Los Angeles Evening Herald-Express*, Apr. 13, 1943.

13. Hedda Hopper, *San Francisco Chronicle*, May 5, 1943. If she got her synopsis directly from McCarey, which is more than likely, he may have been slyly taunting her; Hopper was known as a right-wing bigot opposed to America's intervention in the war, Social Security and other New Deal programs, and civil rights. The two later found common cause in anti-Communism but not on other social issues.

14. *Variety*, May 5, 1943, 6.

15. The playwright Emmet Lavery, a recent hire at RKO best known for *The Magnificent Yankee*, tried to attach himself to the McCarey project with a story about the young priest battling gangsters. In 1962, Lavery wrote the pilot and four more episodes for the television series *Going My Way;* RKO Inter-Department Communication from Emmet Lavery to Leo McCarey, May 6, 1943, USC.

16. McCarey holograph, eight pages scrawled in pencil at the request of his attorney to defend himself against the IRS, 1949 or 1950, USC.

17. Martin, "Going His Way"; openbuildings.com/buildings/st-monica-catholic-church-santa-monica-profile-26977.

18. Lloyd C. Douglas, "*The Padre* Story Treatment," June 17, 1943, AMPAS.

19. Frank Cavett, "Outline, *The Padre*," May 18, 1943, AMPAS.

20. *Memphis Press-Scimitar*, May 24, 1943; Macfarlane, *Bing Crosby Day by Day*, 253–56.

21. The conversion also cleared the air after Larry Crosby offered the idle track to an aircraft plant and had his hand slapped by attorney general Robert W. Kenny, who declared that the state, not the turf club, had that right.

22. Bryan Field, "Don Bingo Wins Suburban as 47,083 at Belmont Bet $2,699,153, World Record," *New York Times*, June 1, 1943.

23. Letter from Bing Crosby to Sergeant Marjorie T. Lutkin, July 12, 1944; letters from John A. Clark of the Aircraft Division of Bechtel to Crosby and Carlton Duffus in the Treasury Department, June 7, 1943; letter from E. E. Wilson to Crosby, June 4, 1943; Bob Rule, *Nashville Banner,* June 3, 1943, KCC.

24. Bing to Everett, June 2 and June 3, 1943, KCC.

25. "Bing Shoots a 73 over Broadmoor," *Omaha Evening World-Herald*, June 10, 1943; Louella O. Parsons, *Los Angeles Examiner*, June 10, 1943.

26. Grace Moore to Leo McCarey, June 11, 1943, USC. One might like to think she didn't work out because McCarey learned of her infamous 1933

vaudeville clause prohibiting any "colored act" from sharing her bill. She added it to her contract because she considered it humiliating for Mary Garden to share top billing with the Mills Brothers. Loew's read the clause and refused to book her. There is no evidence that this played any role in the *Going My Way* decision, but it may be relevant to note that the Tennessee Nightingale, who averaged a picture a year in the 1930s when opera singers were a regular component of *KMH*, never appeared on a Crosby broadcast.

27. AI, Risë Stevens and Walter Surovy; Risë Stevens to Leo McCarey, June 23, 1943, USC. Surovy, a canny agent with one client, had himself been a stage star in Austria before the war.

28. Martin, "Going His Way."

29. AI, Risë Stevens.

30. Bogdanovich, *Who the Devil Made It*, 426.

31. McCarey holograph. In a 1976 radio interview with John Salisbury, Crosby was asked about Burke's story. He said, "That's what Johnny Burke told me, but he's such a great writer and he's so inventive that I really doubt the veracity of that. But it sounds reasonable. I did say something like that, different times, to the kids."

32. McCarey Papers, box 12, USC; memo from William Dozier to various executives on screenwriters, July 2, 1943; letter from William Dozier to Henry Ginsberg on "lending" Frank Butler to McCarey "at same salary we are paying Butler [$1,850 a week]," July 15, 1943.

33. McCarey Papers, box 12, USC; memo from Bill Blowitz to William Dozier, cc'd to McCarey, with alternate titles, June 14, 1943; Paramount telegram to New York requesting title search, July 12, 1943; telegram from New York on availability of *Going My Way*, July 20, 1943; memo, Luigi Luraschi to William Flannery, on St. Dominic's name, July 22, 1943; telegram from New York granting title and requesting song "Going My Way," July 27, 1943.

34. Memos from William Meiklejohn to Leo McCarey, July 23 and 26, 1943, and to Jacob Karp, Aug. 3, 1943, USC.

35. Though best remembered for his work in monochrome, he won his Academy Award for the virtuoso requirements of the leaden spectacle *Around the World in 80 Days*.

36. Scripts by Frank Butler, Aug. 3 and Aug. 13, 1943, AMPAS.

37. Letter from McCarey to Oliphant, June 1949; Bing Crosby, "Leo McCarey—1898–1969," July 20, 1969, reprinted in *Action!*, Sept. 1969.

38. Memos from William Dozier to Jacob Karp, Aug. 18, 1943; Dozier to McCarey, Aug. 24, 1943, AMPAS.

39. Letter from Joseph Breen to Luigi Luraschi, Aug. 12, 1943, AMPAS. McCarey was fond of Luraschi, the tireless middleman between filmmakers and censors. In *Make Way for Tomorrow*, a close-up of the lobby buzzers in a principal character's apartment building lists him as a tenant.

40. Ibid.; letter from Luraschi to McCarey, Aug. 11, 1943, AMPAS.

41. Luraschi interoffice memos Aug. 9 through Aug. 13, 1943; memo from Breen to Luraschi, Aug. 17, 1943, AMPAS.

42. Starr, *The Dream Endures*, 257–58.

43. Interoffice memo from Luigi Luraschi to Leo McCarey, Aug. 13, 1943; letter from Luraschi to McCarey and Frank Butler detailing changes suggested by Father Devlin, Aug. 19, 1943; letters from Auxiliary Bishop Joseph T. McGucken

to Joseph Breen, Aug. 19, 1943, and from Breen to McGucken, Aug. 20, 1943, AMPAS.

17. Swinging on a Star

1. Barney Dean, background interview with M. Gleason, Aug. 1946, TIA; AI, Phil Harris. Harris said, "Barney Dean was a good guy, very witty, and all of us had one of those kinds of guys around. They were what you call leg men. They'd do anything for you. Everybody loved Barney. He was [Bing's] right-hand man."

2. AI, Risë Stevens.

3. Burns, *Gracie,* 64; Bellamy in Harvey, *Romantic Comedy,* 269; Menjou and Musselman, *It Took Nine Tailors,* 230–32.

4. *Lucky,* Dictaphone belt 19.

5. *Lucky,* Dictaphone belt 18.

6. *Lucky,* Dictaphone belt 19.

7. One that McCarey had to delete centered on the wonder drug penicillin, introduced in the United States in 1942. A year later, the antibiotic was in such demand and in such short supply, he was advised not to promote it; *Hollywood Citizen News,* Sept. 21, 1943.

8. Memo from Luraschi to McCarey, Aug. 16, 1943, AMPAS.

9. McCarey relished the preceding scene between Gene Lockhart and Barry Fitzgerald, two of the finest character actors of the era. They had appeared together in Michael Curtiz's *The Sea Wolf* (1941), playing a suicidal alcoholic and a vile informer, respectively—nothing like the subtle comedy here.

10. AI, Risë Stevens.

11. Agee, *Film Writing,* 398. Fitzgerald's jabbering created problems for McCarey when he viewed the dailies and realized that some of his lines were unintelligible. During postproduction looping sessions, Fitzgerald dubbed some two dozen lines; see "Suggested Line Replacements," memo from Loren Ryder to Leo McCarey and others, Dec. 11, 1943, AMPAS.

12. Cal York, "Barry Fitzgerald," *Movieland,* Jan. 1945; AI, Risë Stevens.

13. *Lucky,* Dictaphone belt 18.

14. When Carol is introduced, she is in the custody of a policeman, played by Tom Dillon, who is a dead ringer for McCarey.

15. It's probably a stretch to connect 1940s tokenism to McCarey's years with Hal Roach, whose Our Gang comedies also had a single black cast member. A more relevant indication of racism in wartime America is the fact, according to the American Film Institute, that "half of all first run theaters refused to book" *Stormy Weather.*

16. In 1994, the superb cabaret singer Mary Cleere Haran recorded a definitive interpretation of "Going My Way" for her album *This Heart of Mine.* She sings the sixteen-bar verse, omitted from the film, and, like Crosby, makes a half note of *full.* A product of 1960s San Francisco, she once described (AI) the lyrics as "sort of druggy."

17. They offer O'Malley a place in the publishing firm in the Frank Cavett script of Apr. 28, 1943, AMPAS.

18. Wire from Leo McCarey to Edward Ziegler, Aug. 25, 1943, USC.

19. The first melodic phrase of the refrain ("A mule is an animal with long funny ears") morphed into a familiar jazz lick after the tenor saxophonist Wardell Gray interpolated it into his 1949 blues "Twisted" and the singer Annie

Ross added lyrics. To the "Swinging on a Star" lick, she wrote: "I heard little children were supposed to sleep tight," adding, "That's why I drank a fifth of vodka one night." Over the years, the song inspired parodies, including one by Crosby and another by Frank Sinatra in his 1957 film *The Joker Is Wild*. Sammy Cahn said that Sinatra wanted his own animal song to sing with children. Cahn and Van Heusen obliged with their Oscar-winning "High Hopes" for the 1959 film *A Hole in the Head*. Sinatra's single stalled at number thirty, but the song became a phenomenon as John Kennedy's campaign theme, with Sinatra singing the revised lyrics; AI, Sammy Cahn. Van Heusen's widow was the former Bobbe Brox; see the first letter in this volume's prelude.

20. LeRoy, *Take One*, 175. In 1939, the Vatican contacted the Crosby office directly on behalf of Pope Pius, who requested an autographed photo of Bing, inscribed to him, "for his gallery in the Vatican broadcasting room." Larry Crosby relayed the request to Bing in a memo (Apr. 22, 1939, courtesy Ed Crosby) and suggested that instead of sending the usual press photo, they use one of the entire family.

21. AI, Risë Stevens.

22. Ibid. An astute fan wrote to Crosby about a similar scene in which Jenny asks Chuck to autograph a copy of his song "Going My Way." What, the writer wondered, did Chuck inscribe "that made her look at you and you at her the way you did?" Crosby wrote back candidly that McCarey "wanted to establish in the audience's mind the feeling that there had been some relationship between the two people before O'Malley entered the Priesthood. This was a delicate thing to handle, so he thought if he could convey this by inferring that what the Priest wrote on the manuscript was something obviously sentimental, no one would be offended. Risë's reaction was the key to the scene. Actually I think I wrote, 'What time do we eat?'" Letter from Joan Pratt to Bing Crosby, Jan. 31, 1945; letter from Crosby to Pratt, May 24, 1945, KCC.

23. AIs, Risë Stevens and Walter Surovy.

24. Ibid.

25. AI, Risë Stevens; Paramount memos from Louis Lipstone to Sidney Justin, Sept. 10, 1943, USC, and Sam Frey to Bernard Goodman, Mar. 13, 1944, AMPAS.

26. AI, Risë Stevens; Crichton, *Subway to the Met*, 163; Adelaide Kerr, *Miami Daily News*, Dec. 30, 1952.

27. Letter from Frank Cavett to William Dozier, Sept. 23, 1943; memo from Dozier to Leo McCarey, same date, asking if "you care to reopen the credit matter" or "let it stand as it is"; USC.

28. McCarey details this grievance in his letter to Charles Oliphant, chief counsel for the Bureau of Internal Revenue, June 1949. To be clear, the title of the film equals 100 percent, against which the other percentages are measured.

29. "Main Title Billing" and "Notes on Main Title Billing," Sam Frey, Nov. 29, 1943; handwritten memo to Mr. Carn, undated, AMPAS; AI, Risë Stevens.

30. One moviegoer was so incensed by the absence of her credit that the production office researched her contract and responded: "Please be sure that no slight was intended in this regard. Had Miss Reynolds asked for screen credit, she would have received it"; letter from Don Rowland to Mrs. May Prince, Feb. 28, 1945, AMPAS. In 1951 she appeared, uncredited, as Aunt Amy in one of Frank Capra's Crosby pictures, *Here Comes the Groom*.

31. Agee, *Film Writing,* 397.

32. Judy Garland, quoted in *Movie Radio Guide,* Nov. 1943.

33. Harrison Carroll, *Los Angeles Evening Herald-Express,* Dec. 21, 1943; https://www.pacificwrecks.com/aircraft/b-24/41-23836.html.

34. Telegrams, Morgenthau to Crosby and Crosby to Morgenthau, Aug. 31, 1943; letter from Treasury Department to Crosby, Sept. 20, 1943; letter from Vincent Callahan, director of advertising, press, and radio for the Treasury Department, to Crosby, Oct. 2, 1943; letters from Major Thomas C. Ferguson to Crosby, Oct. 15 and Dec. 29, 1943; letter from Crosby to Ferguson, Oct. 27, 1943, KCC.

35. The story about the songwriting seaman (identity unknown) first appeared in *Tune-In,* Nov. 1943. The projector was reported by Jimmy Starr, *Los Angeles Evening Herald-Express,* Nov. 9, 1943. Letter from aerographer's mates Jack E. Davis and Dick Loughney to Bing, Oct. 25, 1943; letter from Bing to Jack E. Davis, Nov. 19, 1943; letter to Crosby from J. F. Skane "for the crew of the U.S.S. *Tumult,*" Feb. 22, 1944, KCC.

36. "Bing Crosby Makes Canadian Loan Short," *Lewiston Evening Journal,* June 17, 1944; letter from James Lorimer Ilsley to Crosby, Oct. 8, 1943; letter from J. J. Fitzgibbons to Barney Balaban, Oct. 8, 1943.

37. "California Fire Razes 115 Houses," *New York Times,* Nov. 8, 1943; Harrison Carroll, *Los Angeles Evening Herald-Express,* Nov. 20, 1943.

38. John Steinbeck, *New York Herald Tribune,* July 20, 1943.

39. AI, Ed Helwick; letter from Crosby to Helwick, Dec. 7, 1943; letter from Harrie Wood to Crosby, Feb. 25, 1944, KCC.

40. AI, Ed Helwick.

41. Ibid.; letter to Helwick, Dec. 7, 1943; letter to Silvers, Jan. 24, 1944, KCC.

42. Letter from Jack O'Melveny to Crosby, Dec. 29, 1944, KCC.

43. Florabel Muir, *Hollywood Citizen News,* Apr. 12, 1945.

44. "Crosby Seeks Coliseum Pro Grid Franchise," *Hollywood Citizen News,* Dec. 3, 1943; Lawton Carver, "Bing Crosby Must Give Up Horses or Pro Grid Idea," *Greensboro (NC) Record,* Jan. 14, 1944; letter from Bing's brother Ted to their father, Harry, Jan. 24, 1944 ("[I] suppose by this time you have sold the Del Mar place"), KCC.

45. "Eisenhower Choice Linked to Stalin," *New York Times,* Dec. 28, 1943. A solid account of the Tehran meeting can be found in Jon Meacham, *Franklin and Winston* (New York: Random House, 2003).

46. Spada, *More Than a Woman;* Macfarlane, *Bing Crosby Day by Day,* 265; *Radio Daily,* Jan. 5, 1944.

47. Thompson, *Bing,* 113; Geoff Boucher, *Los Angeles Times,* May 6, 2007. See also Starr, *Embattled Dreams,* 204.

48. The *KMH* version of "San Fernando Valley" and hundreds of other legally dubious releases of radio performances are periodically reissued on CD and can usually be found on YouTube.

18. Put It There, Pal

1. Letter from Bing Crosby to Phil Silvers, Jan. 24, 1944, KCC.

2. James Lindsley, "Crosby-Hope-Lamour Trio Face Fateful Fork in Road," *Sunday Oregonian,* Dec. 12, 1943.

3. Signed Paramount memo of Crosby's acceptance of Lamour, Nov. 17, 1943, KCC.

4. Rick Lyman, "Norman Panama, 88, Half of Duo Who Wrote Many Film Comedies," *New York Times*, Jan. 27, 2003.

5. Letter from Jack McGowan to Paul Jones, May 11, 1943. The earliest commentary on the Panama-Frank script is a long production memo from Luigi Luraschi, Jan. 15, 1943 (at which time *Utopia* was scheduled to shoot between Nov. 26 and Dec. 24). He requested deletions of various phrases: "freeze the ears off a brass elephant," "now they're furnishing dames," "we're Mohammedans," "lousy," and "praise the Lord and pass the ammunition," among others. Subsequent *Utopia* scripts are dated July 12, 1943; Oct. 15, 1943; and Nov. 26, 1943, AMPAS.

6. Unsigned "Notes to Mr. DeSylva on ROAD TO UTOPIA, Oct. 9, 1943, AMPAS; H. Allen Smith in Harrison Carroll, *Los Angeles Evening Herald-Express*, Nov. 29, 1943; Billy Altman, *Laughter's Gentle Soul: The Life of Robert Benchley* (New York: Norton, 1997), 348.

7. Memo from Luraschi to Paul Jones, Oct. 25, 1943, AMPAS.

8. *Film Daily*, Dec. 5, 1945. This was not the first instance of Crosby's genetic hardiness. In the 1936 cartoon "Let It Be Me," a spats-wearing cock named Mr. Bingo seduces a capon, whose later brood includes a crooning chick off the old block. See *POD*, 279.

9. Letters from Larry Crosby to Joseph Breen, Feb. 22, 1946, and from Breen to Crosby, Feb. 27, 1946. Memo from Breen to Luigi Luraschi, Feb. 22, 1946, AMPAS.

10. Hope, *Don't Shoot, It's Only Me*, 94–97.

11. Sidney Skolsky, "Watching Them Make Pictures," *Hollywood Citizen News*, Dec. 21, 1943.

12. Frank in Norman, *The Film Greats*, 211; Thompson, *Bing*, 125; Lamour, *My Side of the Road*, 140.

13. Letter to Silvers; AI, Hazel Sharp (in later years she was known by her middle name, Diane, and her married name, Notestine); Jimmy Starr, *Los Angeles Evening Herald-Express*, Jan. 28, 1944; Harry Crocker, *Los Angeles Examiner*, Feb. 5, 1944.

14. The Santa Ana evening is drawn from two accounts by Zuma Palmer, *Hollywood Citizen News*, Feb. 17 and Feb. 18, 1944.

15. Letter from F. C. O'Keefe to Bing Crosby, dated Friday 1944, KCC. One of the possible replacements, recommended by Larry Crosby, was the gifted Dolly Dawn, who turned the George Hall Orchestra into Dolly Dawn and Her Dawn Patrol, but she liked being her own boss and turned down the offer.

16. Levinson, *September in the Rain*, 74.

17. Harrison Carroll, *Los Angeles East Herald-Express*, Apr. 12, 1944. Sandler's "Eli, Eli" is not to be confused with the postwar song of the same name, far better known today, derived from a poem by the courageous Jewish Hungarian paratrooper Hannah Szenes who was tortured and shot by the Nazis in 1944. For the McCarey idea, see Dorothy Manners, *Los Angeles Times*, July 3, 1946. A complete print of the 1946 *Abie's Irish Rose* may be viewed at the Library of Congress.

18. AI, Hazel Sharp.

19. Hope, *Have Tux, Will Travel*, 161.

20. Thompson, *Bing*, 124; Lamour, *My Side of the Road*, 141. Among countless other books that thoughtlessly recycle the story is an essay collection by

Gary Giddins called *Natural Selection,* 42. In the words of Father O'Dowd, "Don't trust anyone."

21. AI, Bob Hope. A few days after the Hope interview, when queried about the incident, Norman Panama laughed. "Where did you hear that? I think there is some confusion here. We did do a picture with lions and giraffes, and the lion hadn't worked for a while and it came out of its cage, went straight for the trainer. But Bob wasn't in that. I think he's confused." The *Life* story (Aug. 19, 1946), timed to the release of *Utopia,* included photographs of Rosie and Beebe roller-skating in New York.

22. AI, Panama; Roy Hoopes, *When the Stars Went to War,* xx; AI, Bob Hope.

23. AI, Hazel Sharp.

24. Ibid.

25. Ibid.

26. Ibid.

27. *Billboard,* Jan. 8, 1944, 21.

28. AI, Hazel Sharp.

29. Indeed, *Down Beat* (Apr. 1, 1944) reviewed it as if Crosby were a pal and beyond criticism: "Harry sings...as always, with nice phrasing and perfect interpretation." See Brackett, *Interpreting Popular Music,* 39. The ultimate upbeat version was recorded by Sinatra and Sy Oliver for the 1961 album *I Remember Tommy.*

30. The June 15, 1944, show is one of several *KMH* broadcasts that have been released in their entirety on CD.

31. Frederick C. Othman, *Hollywood Citizen News,* Feb. 24, 1944; Harrison Carroll, *Los Angeles Evening Herald-Express,* Feb. 24, 1944.

32. Letter quoted in Starr, *Embattled Dreams,* 179. This section is largely drawn from *Embattled Dreams,* chapter 6; Hoopes, *When the Stars Went to War,* chapter 9; and Mitchell and Torrence, *The Hollywood Canteen.*

33. AI, Tom and Florence Smith. In 2003, the Smiths drove three hours from Greenfield Center to Vestel, where they had learned Kathryn Crosby would be signing her book *My Last Years with Bing,* just so he could tell her this story. Her publicist Judy Schmid kindly asked Smith for his phone number. Crosby sang "Night and Day" only once on the air between 1941 and 1953, on April 20, 1944, two weeks after meeting Tom Smith.

34. "Crosby Film Bound Over to Next Season," *Variety,* Mar. 22, 1944, 11.

35. Louella Parsons, *Los Angeles Examiner,* Mar. 16, 1944; Hedda Hopper, "Hollywood," *New York Daily News,* Mar. 17, 1944; *Variety,* Mar. 8, 1944; Jimmy Starr, *Los Angeles Evening Herald-Express,* Apr. 22, 1944.

36. Zuma Palmer, "Radio," *Hollywood Citizen News,* Apr. 13, 1944.

37. Letters quoted in Thornton Delehanty, *New York Herald Tribune,* July 16, 1944; *Billboard,* Sept. 9, 1944, 45. The comic strip was syndicated on August 27, 1944, by which time no one needed a caption to identify the film.

38. Letter from Al Wilkie to Leo McCarey, May 4, 1944, USC.

39. Barnes, *New York Herald Tribune,* May 3, 1944; Bosley Crowther, *New York Times,* May 3, 1944; Eileen Creelman, *New York Sun,* May 3, 1944; Alton Cook, *New York World Telegram,* May 3, 1944; Archer Winsten, *New York Post,* May 3, 1944; Kate Cameron, *New York Daily News,* May 3, 1944; *Newsweek,* May 15, 1944; Agee, *Film Writing,* 397. Agee toned down his fervor in the subsequent review he published in the more intellectual and political *Nation:* "A

rather saccharine story about priests, has a gentle, engaging performance by Bing Crosby, a very full and fine one by Barry Fitzgerald, and a general leisure and appreciation of character which I think highly of" (Agee, *Film Writing,* 112).

40. A. H. Weiler, "'Going My Way' Sets Record—Giant Mural for the Roxy," *New York Times,* July 16, 1944.

41. "'Going My Way' Soaring," *Box Office Digest,* May 17, 1944.

42. *Variety,* July 26, 1944; "For 3rd Time in 23 Years, Dallas Pic Held 2nd Wk.—It's 'Way,'" *Hollywood Reporter,* undated clip, 1944; "'Way' Brings Audience to Feet," *Hollywood Reporter,* July 5, 1944; "Over 100,000 Saw Bing's New Play," *Spokesman-Review,* Aug. 22, 1944.

43. MacLeish in his speech of Mar. 19, 1942, when he became director of the Office of Facts and Figures, forerunner of the Office of War Information; Horten, *Radio Goes to War,* 52; Dwight D. Eisenhower, foreword to Carson, *Home Away from Home.*

44. Jacques Lourcelles, *Dictionnaire du cinéma: les films* (Paris: Lafont, 1992), quoted in translation in Tag Gallagher, "Going My Way," http://www.screeningthepast.com/2014/12/going-my-way/.

45. Roosevelt's D-day prayer can be found at //www.fdrlibrary.marist.edu/aboutfdr/d-day.html.

46. Rogers quoted in Weiler, "'Going My Way' Sets Record"; "McCarey's 'Way' Breaks 2,420 Theater Records to Date," *Hollywood Reporter,* Aug. 28, 1944; letter from Y. F. Freeman to Rainbow Productions and Leo McCarey, Dec. 20, 1944, USC.

47. Letter from Hutton to Crosby, Apr. 21, 1944; letter from Lamour, Apr. 19, 1944, KCC.

48. Jerry Wexler, an editor at *Billboard* and subsequently one of the most influential producers and executives in the record industry, coined the term *rhythm and blues* to replace the objectionable *race* as a ratings category.

49. Jordan derived the band's name from his drummer Walter Martin's use of timpani. Jordan changed it to Tympany, and he kept the Five even after the group became a sextet and then a septet.

50. Lipsitz, *Rainbow at Midnight,* 315.

51. A 1971 interview with Louis Jordan, quoted in Chilton, *Let the Good Times Roll,* 106.

52. Ibid., 107.

53. Certification for Harry Lillis Crosby, Headquarters, Port Terminals, NYPE, Aug. 14, 1944; letter from Bob Hannegan to Crosby, Aug. 15, 1944, KCC.

19. Heer Shpreekht Bing CROS-by

1. Robert Kotlowitz, *Before Their Time,* 192. This chapter and the one that follows are much indebted to the research of Malcolm Macfarlane.

2. Carolyn Schneider, the daughter of Bing's sister, Mary Rose, "Uncle Bing Sings for Uncle Sam," Nov. 9, 2012. http://mesquitelocalnews.com/sections/opinion/guest-columnist/uncle-bing-sings-uncle-sam.html. Data concerning USO fatalities is notoriously unreliable, as the agency withholds that information. The estimated number of deaths range from twenty-eight (Lowell Matson, "Theatre for the Armed Forces in World War II," *Educational Theatre Journal* 5, no. 1 [Mar.

1954]: 1–11) to thirty-seven (Hoopes, *When the Stars Went to War,* 194) and do not include performers who were killed outside of USO parameters or nonperformers killed in USO transport, like those on the Pan Am Clipper.

3. Special Service Section, ed., *Stand-By* 1, no. 2 (Aug. 18, 1944).

4. Crosby, *Call Me Lucky,* 290; *Lucky,* Dictaphone belt 30; Stafford, *The Ile de France,* 137–38; *Stand-By* 1, no. 7 (Aug. 23, 1944).

5. *Lucky,* Dictaphone belt 23. Pete Martin asked him to tell the story about the paratrooper, having been urged to do so by Wally Westmore. Bing shrugged. "Oh, well, it's the kind of story I don't know whether it will improve much in the telling. It's something you'd have to see." The February 5, 1945, *Cavalcade of America* radio show included it as the sole anecdote of the outbound voyage. (Jeanne Darrell: "Just a minute, Bing. Don't tell us you're skipping the trip across the Atlantic." Crosby: "Well, I didn't think it was…" Darlene Garner: "Oh, he's still embarrassed about the paratrooper." Joe DeRita: "That boy sure had the Groaner on the ropes, didn't he, kids?")

6. Stafford, *The Ile de France; Stand-By* 1, no. 7 (Aug. 23, 1944).

7. Again, the numbers are estimates even when they seem extremely precise. The lower numbers here are in Carson, *Home Away from Home* (1946), 130, and the higher ones are in Coffey, *Always Home* (1991), 26. Both books were officially sanctioned by the USO.

8. Carson, *Home Away from Home* 109, 117–18.

9. Letter from Lynn Vass to Crosby, Sept. 19, 1944; Private Robert Byrnes Jr. wrote his parents, who forwarded the letter to Bing: "He is the perfect host, the same suave M.C. clad in a fatigue hat, one of our field jackets, battered but clean trousers rolled at the bottom, careless tennis shoes, and EGAD! a loud yellow tie with springs appearing here and there on it" (Third Army, France, Sept. 26, 1944, KCC). The Associated Press syndicated a story that began, "Bing Crosby asserts civilian individuality in neckties even on the war front" (Sept. 13, 1944).

10. *Stand-By* 1, no. 7 (Aug. 23, 1944).

11. Bing Crosby, typed pages and holographs, KCC.

12. *San Francisco Examiner,* Aug. 7, 1944; "Crosby Croons for Oak Knoll," *Oak Leaf,* Aug. 19, 1944.

13. Transcript of "The Road to Berlin," *Dupont Cavalcade of America,* broadcast February 5, 1945.

14. Letter from William Morrow to Crosby, Aug. 10, 1944, KCC; "The Road to Berlin," *Dupont Cavalcade of America.*

15. Bing Crosby, typed pages and holographs, KCC.

16. Ed Stone, "Bing Croons a Swathe Through France," *Stars and Stripes,* Sept. 25, 1944.

17. Janet Fife-Yeomans, "Reporter's Career of John Burney Began with Bing Crosby," *Sydney Daily Telegraph,* June 30, 2009.

18. Sterling, *Encyclopedia of Radio,* 1362–64. A civilian at the start of his service, Kirby was made colonel by 1944; he also received the Order of the British Empire and the 1944 Peabody Award for "Yankee ingenuity on a global scale." In 1948, Kirby and Gorham each published memoirs, *Star-Spangled Radio* and *Sound and Fury,* respectively. See also American Forces Information Service, American Forces Radio and Television Service, *History of AFRTS: The First Fifty Years,* https://archive.org/stream/AFRTSTheFirst50Years/AFRTSThe First50Years_djvu.txt.

19. Dennis M. Spragg, "The Allied Expeditionary Forces Programme," Glenn Miller Archive, University of Colorado, Boulder, updated March 2017, 12.

20. These included an hour-long adaptation of *Going My Way* and an appearance on the perdurable *Children's Hour*.

21. Memo from Maurice Gorham to Colonel Kirby, Aug. 23, 1944, BBC Archive, Ex File R27/4/1, 1942–1946, American Artists.

22. Sidney Skolsky, *Hollywood Citizen News,* Aug. 28, 1944.

23. AI, Jack Russin; AI, Jake Hanna, who heard the story first from Russin, an old friend, and later from Crosby, with whom he played drums on his 1970s concert tours.

24. The golf date is thought to have been where Bing met and became friends with Commander Raymond Guest, a naval hero and breeder of horses who headed the London section of the OSS and later served as Lyndon Johnson's ambassador to Ireland.

25. Details and dialogue relating to the Queensberry performance are based on a transcript of a recording made that evening and on interviews conducted with Madden, Williams, Shelton, and Crosby for the BBC Radio2 series *The Bing Crosby Story,* part 7, "On the Air," first broadcast May 20, 1973. Some of the interview material appears in a slightly altered form and without attribution in Thompson, *Bing,* 118–21. This account differs from Thompson's chiefly in its reliance on the 1944 recording, which was not available to him.

26. Russin told the author that he was actually just a private and that Bing had impulsively promoted him to first class.

27. Ray Sonin, "Bing Went the Strings of Our Hearts!," *Melody Maker,* Sept. 2, 1944, 3. A front-page story in the same issue, "He's Here! Bing Crosby Arrives," begins: "Bing Crosby is here! The world's greatest popular singer— stated to pull down £225,000 a year—has arrived in this country to entertain the troops, and the 'Melody Maker' takes a modest bow for being the very first paper to report that he was coming. In last week's issue we told you he would be arriving any day now, and that he would broadcast to Home listeners. Our information was pretty good. He arrived a day after the 'M.M.' was issued and he duly sang to Home listeners in 'Variety Band Box' last Thursday. A full report of the broadcast by our Editor, who watched it being recorded, is on page 3 of this issue."

28. Shelton, interviews for *The Bing Crosby Story.* A number of online sites now give Anne Shelton's birth year as 1923, but the later date she insisted upon in this account and everywhere else (1928) is consistent with the trajectory of her career.

29. *The Bing Crosby Story.*

30. Ibid.

31. Ibid.; *Melody Maker,* Sept. 2, 1944.

32. Crosby in Thompson, *Bing,* 121.

33. Kirby and Harris, *Star-Spangled Radio,* 214. *Melody Maker* inexplicably reported that he sang eight songs from the window at Kettner's, which did not and could not have happened, but that was nothing compared to what Hollywood columnists did with the story. Jimmie Fidler, who once admitted to a Senate subcommittee that he didn't necessarily see the movies he reviewed, wrote (in *Screen Romances,* Dec. 1945), "He sang for an hour and a half." But the *New York Times* (in "Crosby Halts London Traffic," Aug. 28, 1944) and

Time (in Sept. 1944) reported that he sang only "Pennies from Heaven," which is what Crosby always said.

34. Kirby and Harris, *Star-Spangled Radio*, 223–24. *Melody Maker* story echoed his estimate of thousands outside Kettner's.

35. Kirby and Harris, *Star-Spangled Radio*, 223–24; Fussell, *The Boys' Crusade*, 18–22; George Orwell, "As I Please," *Tribune*, Dec. 3, 1943, and Dec. 17, 1943; *Melody Maker*, Sept. 2, 1944.

36. Gorham, *Sound and Fury*, 156.

37. Way, *The Big Bands Go to War*, 23; letter from George Melachrino to Bing, Aug. 31, 1944, KCC. Crosby's other recordings on the program were "Swinging on a Star" and "With a Song in My Heart." While writing his Glenn Miller biography, George Simon asked Bing if he would contribute a recollection of their wartime experiences. Crosby recounted the story of his first night at Kettner's, but in this version, instead of stumbling through the dark with just Brod Crawford, he was now accompanied by Brod and Glenn. He might have confused the two visits to Kettner's, but more likely he found a facile way to answer Simon's request—the twice-told anecdote says nothing about Miller.

38. This account is largely drawn from Bryan Cornell's "American Broadcasting Station in Europe," in Sterling, *Encyclopedia of Radio*, 95–97.

39. Robert Musel's story was published in countless newspapers with such headlines as "Der Bingle Goes to Work in Der Tottering Wehrmacht," *PM New York*, Sept. 4; "Allies Hurl Der Bingle at Nazis' Eager Ears," *New York Daily News*, Sept. 3; and "Songs by Bing Crosby New U.S. Secret Weapon," *Los Angeles Times*, Sept. 4, 1944. Bing's brief broadcast was beamed to Norway first, then to Germany. Did Musel attend the session, as he claimed, or did he write the story based on subsequent (exclusive) interviews with Crosby and others? There is no evidence to doubt him, but the second possibility may explain generalities in his report, such as his failure to identify songs, his mistake about the French songs (see page 425), his three-day delay in filing the story, and the odd fact that no other reporter covered it.

Will Yolen, the chief of radio news for the Office of War Information, conveyed the story's success in a letter to Oliver W. Nicoll, director of Program Operations, who sent it to Bing at his London address several days after he left for France. Crosby told the Hollywood columnist May Mann (*Screen Stars*, Dec. 1944), "I didn't hear the 'Der Bingle' story until I returned to America."

40. The original version with Crosby's emendations, KCC.

41. The entire text of the message is as follows: *Hallo, Deutsche Soldaten. Hier spricht Bing Crosby: Ich komme soeben aus Amerika, dem Lande, wo niemand sich vor der Gestapo fuerchten muss, wo jedermann die Freiheit hat, zu sagen und zu schreiben, was er denkt. Ich komme aus dem Lande Lincoln's, wo es keine Herren, und keine Knechte gibt. Ich hoffe, dass unsere Rechte und unsere Freiheiten auch bald wieder in Ihrem Lande Einzughalten werden. Dafuer kaempfen wir Amerikaner! Aber ich bin nicht hier, um zu Euch zu predigen sondern um fuer Euch ein paar Lieder zu singen.* The complete phonetic transliteration appears in Kirby and Harris, *Star-Spangled Radio*, 233–34.

42. May Mann, "Bing's G.I. Jaunt," *Screen Stars*, Dec. 1944.

43. Privin in Simon, *Glenn Miller*, 380; Crosby in Way, *The Big Bands Go to War*, 182; Madden in Thompson, *Bing*, 122. This broadcast was thought lost for nearly forty years, but a beat-up copy was found in the early 1980s.

44. Crosby's script for "The American Band of the A.E.F. under the Direction of Glenn Miller," KCC; Simon, *Glenn Miller*; Madden in Way, *The Big Bands Go to War*, 181.

45. Way, *Big Bands Go to War*, 216–17. With Bing appearing wigless everywhere, reporters were suddenly liberated to state the obvious. The lede in one syndicated story (*Evening Sun*, Baltimore, Mar. 20, 1944) read, "Now that it is known that Bing Crosby wears a small toupee before the camera, it can be told that" nearly a decade earlier, a child actor (Edith Fellows) had "un-toupeed" him with a seltzer bottle at a cast party.

46. W. J. MacQueen-Pope in Marshall, *Top Hats and Tails*, 150.

47. Ibid.

48. The most complete account, notwithstanding errors regarding the members of Crosby's troupe, is in Hedtke, *The Freckleton, England, Air Disaster*. In 1977, shortly before his death, Crosby kicked off his British tour in Preston, the first time he had played in northwestern England since 1944.

49. Jim Dodson, "The Magic of Lytham & St. Annes," ThePilot.com, July 22, 2012. Crosby evidently took seriously the imposed silence; the incident is unmentioned in his diary except for the note "At Wharton [*sic*] (Modification center)."

50. Hedtke, *The Freckleton, England, Air Disaster*, 123.

51. "Remembering the Freckleton Air Disaster of 1944," BBC Lancashire, Aug. 7, 2009, http://news.bbc.co.uk/. Also "The Day Freckleton Wept," in Macfarlane, *Bing Crosby Day by Day* at www.bingmagazine.co.uk.

52. Hedtke, *The Freckleton, England, Air Disaster*, 124.

53. Unless otherwise noted, all of Crosby's daily observations are from his diary, KCC.

54. Saul B. Schwartz, first lieutenant, group historian, "War Diary of the 381st Bomb Group (H)," Sept. 1944, http://www.381st.org/Unit-Histories/War-Diaries/381st-Bomb-Group-War-Diary.

55. Joseph Oravec, "City Desk Notes," unidentified newspaper, Oct. 1977. Bing's nephew Howard Crosby once asked him about the most difficult thing he had done. He said it was going out alone at the end of the shows in Europe in 1944 to sing "White Christmas."

56. Brown, quoted in Macfarlane, *Bing Crosby Day by Day*, 281–82.

20. Somewhere in France

1. Letter from Ernest Hemingway to Marlene Dietrich, June 27, 1952, quoted in Wieland, *Dietrich and Riefenstahl*, 407.

2. Unless otherwise noted, Crosby's observations throughout this chapter are drawn from his diary, KCC.

3. Ed Stone, "Bing Croons a Swathe Through France," *Stars and Stripes*, Sept. 25, 1944.

4. Astaire, *Steps in Time*, 272–73; Pogue, *Pogue's War*, 206–7.

5. *Lucky*, Dictaphone belt 30.

6. Ibid. In the last years of his life, he told his friend the Canadian broadcaster Gord Atkinson (*Showbill*, 201) that "White Christmas" generated "rather lugubrious atmosphere. . . . But I guess in retrospect that it was a glad kind of sadness."

7. *Lucky*, Dictaphone belt 30.

8. Unsigned letter, copied and sent to Bing by its recipient, Sybil Burg, Oct. 31, 1944, KCC.

9. The field-hospital recording is not known to exist and may not have aired.

10. http://www.jazzwax.com/2010/02/interview-dave-brubeck-part-1.html.

11. Letter from Captain Charles Donatelli to Peg Donatelli, Sept. 8, 1944, published in *Bing* 162 (Winter 2012). On November 29, 1944, Crosby wrote him: "Dear Captain, You are certainly a nice fellow to remember your promise and send me the pictures taken at Melun when our little show appeared there for the 3rd Replacement Depot. Incidentally, they are very fine pictures. If you have any extra prints of the one in which the comedian, myself and the little girl appear, the one in which she appears alone with the accompanist, and the one with the four performers together, I know they would appreciate copies. If there is any way I can serve you here in Hollywood, feel free to call upon me. Hope you and your pals soon get out of the mud of France, and back home where you long to be. Sincere regards, Bing."

12. Mrs. Eleanor Lucas of Assonet, Massachusetts, sent Bing the first pages of a lengthier letter from infantryman James Lucas, probably written in Meaux, with a short note, dated October 16, 1944: "Dear Mr. Crosby, Enclosed is a letter from my husband which speaks for itself. You've done so much for the men of the combat div. I just want to thank you from the bottom of my heart." She enclosed two prints each of three snapshots: Bing alone, Bing and Joe DeRita, Bing and Jeanne Darrell, encouraged to do so by her husband, as "Bing said that if anyone who took pictures would like them autographed to send two copies to Bing Crosby Paramount studios, Hollywood and he would sign them." He kept one set and evidently sent the other back (KCC).

13. Edward W. Beattie, "At Third Army Front," United Press, Sept. 11, 1944.

14. Letter from First Lieutenant Julius D. Weiner to Headquarters, Sept. 8, 1944.

15. Harrison Carroll, *Los Angeles Evening Herald-Express,* Sept. 4 and Oct. 4, 1944; Louella Parsons, *Los Angeles Examiner,* Sept. 5 and Sept. 23, 1944, and several others; newspaper accounts of Bing's letters sound like public relations plants and retail misinformation. Also see Carroll Carroll collection, American Heritage Center, University of Wyoming, box 64, "1944."

16. Crosby apparently coined (and exclusively used) this phrase. Celanese is a chemical company that manufactured cheap fabrics used to make airplane wings and clothing, material that often involved polyester, which was introduced by British inventors in 1941 and inspired the classic 1951 Alec Guinness comedy *The Man in the White Suit.* Thus "nicotine my celanese" means "singe my suit."

17. Letter from Crosby to Leo McCarey, 1944, USC.

18. "Memories of Colonel Reginald Stowe, Battery C of the 161st Field Artillery Battalion (35th Infantry Division)," *Septembre 1944, Bing Crosby à Vézelise,* http://espacedememoire.fr/crosby.html.

19. "Bing Back, Tells of Exciting Eight-Week Tour," *New York Sun,* Oct. 12, 1944.

20. References that do not come from Crosby's diary notes are from U.S. Army, "The Cross of Lorraine: A Combat History of the 79th Infantry Division, June 1942–December 1945," *World War Regimental Histories* 39 (1946), http://digicom.bpl.lib.me.us/ww_reg_his/39. See also "History of the 314th Infantry Regiment: September 1944, Unit Journal, 3rd Battalion, 314th Infantry," http://www.privateletters.net/history_sep44.html.

21. May Mann, "Bing's G.I. Jaunt," *Screen Stars,* Dec. 1944, 61; *New York Times,* Sept. 29, 1944; *Variety,* Oct. 11, 1944.

22. Letter from Robert J. Mauney to National Headquarters of the American Legion in Indianapolis after reading a letter to the editor from Judy Schmid encouraging readers to "visit us at www.BingCrosby.com," Dec. 16, 2009. Courtesy Judy Schmid.

23. Stuart Muskin, interview by Leo Adam Biga, "By Land, by Sea, by Air, Omaha Jewish Veterans Performed Far-Flung Wartime Duties," May 2011, https://leoadambiga.com/2011/05/22/.

24. A colonel wrote his wife, "Then he sang 'Sweet Leilani.' It just about tore the heart out of my body. I hung on every word. He times the humorous side of his show so that when we were about to weep the comedian followed. His 'White Christmas' had us all in tears as did 'Aloha' and 'If I Had You.' I talked to him and he said he would phone you when he went thru New York." Letter from Colonel John Arthur Weeks to Betty E. Weeks, transcribed and sent by her to Crosby in a letter that begins, "My dear, Mr. Crosby, I cannot thank you enough for finding time to phone me and deliver Colonel Weeks's message. Now I can take a deep breath and carry on for a while longer" (Oct. 11, 1944, KCC).

25. "Partial History of the XX Corps United States Third Army, 23 August 1944–1 January 1945," http://www.90thdivisionassoc.org/90thdivisionfolders/mervinbooks/XX/XX01.pdf. Sergeant John F. Milliken of the Twentieth Corps wrote to his uncle F. M. Bingham, a paving contractor in Beverly Hills, a meticulous description of this performance, which Bingham forwarded to Crosby. In a letter dated November 14, Bing wrote directly to Milliken, thanking him for his "very exact detail," which gave him a "big kick" in recalling the occasion: "I remember the show, because you mention me clipping daisies with the make-shift golf club." These are excerpts:

A slow rain that had been falling all day withdrew behind some capricious clouds and rolled lazily across the horizon. As the sun broke thru GI's came out of the bushes and gathered in a clearing to see a current USO show touring our present area. The show was scheduled to start 1600 (four in the afternoon) and started promptly at that time. We all knew well in advance that the star was Bing Crosby. It was a motley group that had gathered for this occasion—headquarters clerks that had been behind a typewriter all day, cooks fresh from the kitchen, guards that had been patrolling in the mud all day, men just back from the front, mechanics swathed in grease and nurses from a nearby medical unit.

An impromptu stage had been set up on the rear of a truck. Canvas tarp, once the property of the Germans, formed a cover and backdrop. In front of the stage a USO orchestra assembled and started off the show with a few lively numbers. Small tents were on the sides as dressing rooms. The men sat on the wet ground or on their helmets, each with their weapons at their side. Even though the star of the show was not supposed to be seen previous to his entrance several of the fellows had the opportunity of seeing his familiar form behind the tents swinging at an imaginary golf ball with an old limb.

At the conclusion of a number by the band, Crosby casually sauntered around the truck and on to the stage amid a rousing burst of applause. This illustrious Hollywood figure was garbed in his usual careless style of dress. He wore khaki trousers, a GI jacket, an OD [olive-drab] muffler that appeared to have been thrown around his neck instead of placed. A herringbone twill fatigue hat rested indifferently on the back of his head. A pair of brown service shoes with a generous coating of mud completed his attire. The applause continued and increased with vigor as Crosby unconsciously revealed bright yellow socks.

In his nonchalant manner he opened the program by ribbing Bob Hope.... After a few minutes of chatter all of which was mirth provoking he went into "San Fernando Valley" with accompaniment by accordion and guitar. At the end of the song the ovation was tremendous. His line of chatter and jokes continued as he built up an introduction for a comedian that had recently returned from a tour of the South Pacific — [a] fat little fellow with a big cigar and a little brown derby. [...]

Bing then spoke in behalf of the entire troupe, saying how glad they were to be here and doing their part in entertaining the soldiers. He said the soldiers shouldn't be applauding him, but that he should be applauding them and that he did and so did the folks back home.

Parts of this may seem mediocre to the blasé people back home, but for us GI's over here, used to mud, sweat and monotony, it was a definite relief. The end of the show was just an intermission for us, because the entire troupe retired to our section where they remained for dinner. They came in the tent and were briefed on the situation and everybody conversed with each other. On leaving the situation map [DeRita] assured the men of our section that the war would soon end as he had just changed the map. After dinner they all climbed in the back of a truck and drove off in the night (KCC).

26. According to the daily history of the 1103 (see http://www.150th.com/reports/sept44.htm), the battalion was engaged at this point in maintenance and drainage in an area between Chambrey and Grémecey, an hour or so southeast of Metz and well outside the ambit for the Crosby itinerary on September 24. Chambley-Bussières, the location for an American air base, was a ten-minute drive from the troupe's next stop, near Onville. Crosby entertained members of the 1103 that day, but given the size of the audience, it undoubtedly contained elements of other units.

27. "Bing Crosby Lost Way, Got Behind Nazi Lines," *New York Herald Tribune*, Oct. 13, 1944.

28. Joan Younger, "Bing 'Captures' a German Town," *Marietta Daily Journal*, Oct. 18, 1944; Stanley Hirshson, *General Patton* (New York: HarperCollins, 2002), 535.

29. *Lucky*, Dictaphone belt 31. Bing told the story to Pete Martin with the proviso that he would clean up the language if he used it in *Call Me Lucky*. In the original transcript, Martin or an assistant typed "sock of ———." Martin didn't use the story at all.

30. Letter from Patton to Crosby, Oct. 11, 1944, KCC.

31. The online unit histories of evac hospitals provided by the WW2 US Medical Research Centre are exemplary; the Twelfth Evac history is at https://www.med-dept.com/unit-histories/12th-evacuation-hospital.

32. Dwight Eisenhower, *Crusade in Europe* (New York: Doubleday, 1948), 279: "It was literally possible to walk for hundreds of yards at a time, stepping on nothing but dead and decaying flesh."

33. https://www.med-dept.com/unit-histories/34th-evacuation-hospital.

34. Mann, "Bing's G.I. Jaunt."

35. *Abie's Irish Rose*, 1946; *The Bing Crosby Show*, 1954. A fine account of the five directors and their war work is Mark Harris's *Five Came Back: A Story of Hollywood and the Second World War* (New York: Penguin, 2014).

36. Crosby was enchanted by the famous hotel and its proprietor, Marie-Louise Ritz, the widow (as of 1918) of the illustrious César Ritz. "Though she must be eighty [in fact, she was almost seventy-eight] she still is active in their management. Small, chic, she speaks excellent English. And I would have loved to have seen her handling the Heinies." He admired the hotel's spirited efficiency despite the shortages, which extended to the bar on the rue Cambon side: "Some gin but no Scotch or bourbon."

37. Cassidy, *Dinah!*, 87.

38. *Lucky*, Dictaphone belt 31; Mann, "Bing's G.I. Jaunt."

39. Ibid. "There's Eisenhower's signature. Got his autograph. Funny story about Eisenhower that isn't in the [address] book. I might tell it now. It was used in the newspaper years ago but I don't think they'll remember it," Crosby said to Pete Martin as he showed him the journal and told him about the encounter. He evidently tore out the signed page at a later date.

40. Ibid.

41. After Bing told the story about Eisenhower to Pete Martin in 1952, they had this exchange. Crosby: "I don't know how much of that you can use but..." Martin: "Well, I think Eisenhower wouldn't mind being involved, especially if he wins." Bing: "Yeah. You don't have to say his car was parked in front of any whorehouse." Martin: "'Odd places.'" Crosby: "'Odd places,' that's good enough. 'Odd places' for a five-star general could mean anything. It could mean little bistros or honkytonk cafés." In *Call Me Lucky* (296), the wittier phrase they devised is "a few gay spots where the General wouldn't normally have been featured."

42. *Lucky*, Dictaphone belt 31. When Bing edited the transcript, he made a KMH-type joke of the story, inserting: "Johnny Ray never put on a more lugubrious performance." Martin deleted the entire episode from *Call Me Lucky*. Bing stayed in touch with the de Ricous, visiting them on his subsequent trips to France.

43. AI, Pleas McNeel Jr. (McNeel's son).

44. Astaire, *Steps in Time*, 279; *Call Me Lucky*, 292. Crosby and Pete Martin put this at the beginning of the USO tour rather than the end.

45. *Lucky*, Dictaphone belt 24; AI, George Coleman, a longtime friend, business associate, and traveling companion, who heard him tell it several times.

21. A Little Touch of Harry in the Day

1. Gilbert Seldes, "The Incomparable Bing," *Esquire*, Feb. 1944, 38. Seldes translates the French phrase as "the man of normal human instincts" and adds parenthetically, "That's our Bing."

2. May Mann, "Bing's G.I. Jaunt," *Screen Stars*, Dec. 1944; Louella O. Parsons, "In Hollywood," *New York Journal American*, Nov. 19, 1944.

3. Letter from Crosby to Walter Winchell, Nov. 14, 1944, KCC.

4. "Der Bingle Has Come Back to Us," *P.M.*, Oct. 13, 1944, 14.

5. Ibid.

6. Letter from members of the Medical Detachment to Crosby, Oct. 14, 1944; letter from Crosby to the medics, Nov. 13, 1944, KCC.

7. Letter from Maxwell Fox to Bing Crosby, Oct. 12, 1944. Crosby wrote him back on the train en route to the West Coast, which prompted Fox to reply (in a Dec. 2, 1944, letter) that his "gracious" note was particularly appreciated "because no other star has taken time to write us a note of that kind." Crosby wrote in the margin "a good man," with an arrow pointing to Fox's name, before filing the correspondence, KCC.

8. Earl Wilson, "A Slight Political Essay: Bing's Not for Dewey!," *New York Post*, Oct. 13, 1944. Bing's brother Everett may have encouraged the Dewey committee to use Bing's name. He sent a letter to Bing at the Waldorf containing the seeds of paranoia that infected Hollywood after the war. No evidence of a response from Bing exists. The relevant passage reads: "There has been some terrific activity out here in an organization known as the 'Hollywood for Dewey Committee' which all your friends have joined. I believe one of the head Dewey men will contact you regarding this, and regarding your support. It's quite an organization and they have really gone to work to get Dewey in, and are working in a real sensible and constructive manner. Since its organization another group was organized here, as the 'Hollywood is for Roosevelt' group, including in its membership all of the Hollywood Communists, and headed by Jack Warner and Sam Goldwyn"; Oct. 3, 1944, KCC.

9. Reprinted in Bill Mauldin, *Up Front* (New York: Henry Holt, 1945), 132. The dispatch Mauldin refers to was syndicated by International News Service, Oct. 13, 1944.

10. Letter from Harold T. O'Hara to Bing Crosby, from Germany, Oct. 28, 1944, with *Raiders of the 9th*, Oct. 28, 1944, KCC.

11. Letter from Crosby to O'Hara, Nov. 24, 1944, KCC.

12. Undated letter from Crosby to Eisenhower, written on City of San Francisco Streamliner stationery, Dwight D. Eisenhower Library, courtesy Barbara Constable, archivist.

13. Letter from Eisenhower to Crosby, Oct. 28, 1944; letter from Crosby to Eisenhower, Nov. 27, 1944.

14. "Crosby Will Cancel Bob Hope's Ballot," *Omaha World-Herald*, Oct. 30, 1944.

15. Details of the trip are outlined in Bob Crosby's undated (but evidently prepared in May or June of 1945) "Memo to Bing Crosby, Subject, Tour of Pacific, Proposed," and in letters from Captain T. J. O'Brien, Bureau of Naval Personnel, to Crosby, June 1, 1945, and from Henry Ginsberg to Captain O'Brien, July 5, 1945, the latter proposing a departure date of September 15 and promising confirmation in early August. The trip was initially reported in an AP story on October 24, 1944. The Crosby-Harding letters are dated Dec. 27, 1944, Jan. 1, 1945, and Apr. 3, 1945; KCC.

16. W. H. Mooring, *Picturegoer*, Apr. 14, 1945, courtesy Malcolm Macfarlane.

17. Associated Press, filed in Hollywood, syndicated with small variations, e.g., "Crosby Hails Vets' Morale," *Los Angeles Examiner*, Nov. 10, 1944, and "Bing Crosby Home from War Fronts," *New York Sun*, Nov. 10, 1944.

18. He developed this endearing hobby in the 1950s as an extension of earlier endeavors at songwriting. He once wrote, "I really think I'd trade anything I've ever done if I could have written just one hit song" (Thomas, *Harry Warren and the Hollywood Musical*, 2). Upon returning from a safari, tournament, or extended holiday, he composed verses about the participants, each set to a

different evergreen melody and tied together as a medley. Accompanied by one or two musicians, he recorded them in a studio, pressed enough discs for everyone in the party, and sent them out as mementos.

19. See *POD*, 550–51.

20. *Lucky*, Dictaphone belt 31. Martin rephrased Bing's writing, to little effect—"Once in a while, I've been asked what has been the most satisfying and rewarding experience in my career. The answer is readily available"—and fleshed out the passage with conversational anecdotes; *Call Me Lucky*, 290.

21. This is from one of ten letters he wrote to each member of the Ninety-Fifth Bomb Group, 336th Squad, which flew Big Bing.

22. These excerpts are from letters written by Bing Crosby between September 1944 and early 1945; KCC.

23. Letter from Captain George L. Booth, transport commander, SS *Mormac-moom*, to Crosby (addressed to Mr. Bing Crosby, Wherever You Are, c/o Postmaster, NY, NY), June 30, 1945. Crosby penciled atop the page: "nice letter."

24. Dinah Shore, videotaped interview by Bryan Johnson, 1991.

25. Frank S. Nugent, "At Home with the Crosby Team," *New York Times Magazine*, Mar. 4, 1945; letter from John McCormack to Hiram L. Sloanaker, *Boston Sunday Post*, June 26, 1944. Sloanaker forwarded McCormack's letter to Crosby; the underscoring is McCormack's (KCC).

26. Gilbert Seldes, "The Incomparable Bing," *Esquire*, Feb. 1944, 38.

27. Unsigned editorial by Barry Ulanov, "Der Bingle," in *Metronome*, Oct. 1944; Carroll Carroll, "Bing Crosby," a liner essay in *Bing Crosby, a Collection of Early Recordings*, vol. 2, 1944; "World-Wide Groaner," *Time*, Mar. 26, 1945, 88.

28. "Bing's Crooning 'Hypnotizes' Snake in New Guinea," *Baltimore Evening Sun*, Oct. 25, 1944; AI and correspondence, Kenneth Larson, who published the "Blue Skies" story in a 2001 issue of "The Cub of the Golden Lion," the publication of the 106th Infantry Association; AI, Peter Rahill, who thought the "Silent Night" story appeared in a New York newspaper (no such story has been found, but other veterans recalled hearing a similar tale). The broadcaster was Royal Arch Gunnison Jr. of the Mutual Network whose transcribed report was sent to Crosby by a Mutual executive, Lewis Allen Weiss, on May 16, 1944.

29. R. E. Leiser, "Hope, Crosby, Cantor Headline Christmas Season Entertainment," *Dry Dock*, Dec. 23, 1944; letters from Captain M. D. Willcutts, U.S. Naval Hospital, to Bing Crosby, Dec. 26, 1944; Erskine Johnson, *Los Angeles Daily News*, Dec. 27, 1944; letter from Colonel Harry D. Offutt, Hoff General Hospital, to Bing Crosby, Dec. 23, 1944; Richard K. Bellamy, *Milwaukee Journal*, Dec. 26, 1944; "Road Show Realizes Goal of $10,000,000," *Hollywood Citizen News*, Dec. 30, 1944.

30. The seven number ones were "San Fernando Valley," "I Love You," "I'll Be Seeing You," "Swinging on a Star," and, with the Andrews Sisters, "Is You Is or Is You Ain't My Baby," "A Hot Time in the Town of Berlin," and "Don't Fence Me In."

31. McCarey won the New York Film Critics prize on the sixth ballot, owing to heavy competition. His main rivals were Preston Sturges (*Hail the Conquering Hero*) and Billy Wilder (*Double Indemnity*), but other notable contenders included Otto Preminger (*Laura*) and Vincente Minnelli (*Meet Me in St. Louis*). In the acting category Crosby tied for second place with Alexander Knox in *Wilson*. The Redbook Annual Motion Picture Awards had to finesse the prize. The magazine's rules prohibited selecting a film that wasn't initially chosen as

one of their twelve pictures of the month. The magazine's Hollywood columnist Thornton Delehanty, in what Buddy DeSylva jeered as "the mistake of his life," ignored *Going My Way.* So they presented the cup to "Bing Crosby, Barry Fitzgerald, and Leo McCarey for the acting and directing of *Going My Way.*" The cup was delivered to DeSylva's office, but he sent it to McCarey, "as you are responsible for all the directing and at least ninety per cent of the good acting....Wear it in good health!" In a postscript, he wrote, "I owe you a case of scotch and other valuables which you used as bribes recently. Let me know what this all amounts to and I shall reimburse you at once—although I can never repay you for your efforts." Letter from B. G. DeSylva to Leo McCarey, Jan. 18, 1945, USC. In the *Down Beat* poll, Crosby received 2,406 votes, as compared to 1,606 for Sinatra and 680 for Dick Haymes. The GI Oscars were reported in *Yank Magazine,* June 8, 1945, and the *New York Times,* Dec. 7, 1945; the other recipients were Leo McCarey, Rita Hayworth, Eddie Bracken, Jennifer Jones, and *Going My Way.* The certificate of the India Film Journalists' Association was sent to Crosby; KCC.

32. William R. Weaver, "The Money Making Stars of 1944," *Motion Picture Herald* 157, no. 13 (Dec. 30, 1944): 12–15. Crosby's fifteen poll appearances place him at number seven in the poll's all-time list, going from 1932 to 2013, after John Wayne, Clint Eastwood, Tom Cruise, Gary Cooper, Tom Hanks, and Clark Gable.

33. Gomery, *The Hollywood Studio System,* 93. Relying on the June 1947 *Fortune,* Gomery gives Paramount's net profit for 1945 as $18 million. In 1946, it was a to-date unparalleled $44 million, as compared with $22 million at Fox, $19 million at Warner, $18 million at MGM, and $12 million at RKO.

22. Dial O for O'Malley

1. Alyce Canfield, "Almost Everything Went His Way," *Liberty,* May 26, 1945; Kenneth Rhodes, "The Magic of McCarey," *Photoplay,* Apr. 1947; letter from Father Pat Duffy to Leo McCarey, Sept. 26, 1944, USC.

2. Louella O. Parsons, *Los Angeles Examiner,* Sept. 14, 1944; a Sept. 1, 1944, interoffice memo from William Dozier at RKO says that Ketti Frings will confer with a nun in South Bend for five or six days, spend a week in Chicago (for research), and then go to New York for an unpaid leave of absence at her request.

3. Louella O. Parsons, *Los Angeles Examiner,* Feb. 25, 1945.

4. Selznick's various demands are detailed in McKeever, "The McCarey Touch." Their total value is calculated in "Ingrid Bergman," an unsigned tribute in *Look,* Feb. 19, 1946, 38.

5. Bergman played a streetwalker in *Dr. Jekyll and Mr. Hyde,* an adulteress in *Casablanca,* a Creole prostitute in *Saratoga Trunk,* a socialite nearly driven mad in *Gaslight,* a guerrilla in *For Whom the Bell Tolls,* and a psychiatrist in *Spellbound.* Her definitive party-girl role, in *Notorious,* followed *The Bells of St. Mary's.* She reminded Selznick of his disapproval of *Bells* in a 1947 letter in Rudy Behlmer, *Memo from David O. Selznick* (New York: Viking, 1972), 366–67. The "I shall register" comment is in Bergman and Burgess, *Ingrid Bergman,* 182.

6. In a December 20, 1944, letter to the partners in Rainbow Productions, Y. Frank Freeman wrote, "Under date of Sept. 18th, 1944, I gave a statement to Mr. McCarey, stating that in my opinion GOING MY WAY, on a conservative estimate,

would gross not less than $5,000,000, in the United States and Canada, by December 31, 1945. It is now apparent the figures given in my letter of Sept. 18th were ultraconservative. As of the week ending December 16th, the picture has actually grossed, in the United States and Canada, $5,900,000, and by December 31st this gross [would] seem to be in excess of $6,000,000." He estimated an additional $1.5 million for 1946 and an ultimate total of between $9 and $10 million; USC.

7. Canfield, "Almost Everything Went His Way"; letter from Leo McCarey to Charles Oliphant. Cronin's telegram to William Dozier, dated Sept. 24, 1944, is a Pecksniffian marvel—unctuous, boastful, glib, and dismissive: I RECENTLY SAW "GOING MY WAY" AND WAS GREATLY MOVED LIFTED UP CARRIED AWAY AND GENERALLY EXHILARATED BY IT AT THE SAME TIME INTRIGUED REGARDING ITS GENESIS. I THINK IN ALL MODESTY I COULD BE OF SERVICE TO MR. MCCAREY IN SHAPING A FINE SEQUEL TO THIS SPLENDID PICTURE. HOWEVER WHILE GENUINELY ENTHUSIASTIC AND DEEPLY HONORED BY YOUR INVITATION I FEEL THAT THE MATERIAL RECOMPENSE FOR THIS KIND FOR [sic] RKO MUST NECESSARILY FALL BELOW THE HIGH RETURN WHICH ACCRUES FROM MY INDEPENDENT WRITING AND AS I PLAN TO GET IN A NEW NOVEL THIS WINTER I AM AFRAID I MUST SAY NO TO ALL YOUR ENTICEMENTS BUT I DO SO WITH REAL REGRET AND WITH THE RENEWED EXPRESSION OF MY WARM REGARD FOR YOU. In forwarding it to McCarey, Dozier wrote, "I see no reason to belabor the point further with him, do you?"; USC.

8. *Call Me Lucky*, 123.

9. Letter from Bing Crosby to Harry Ray, Nov. 27, 1944, KCC.

10. "Biography of B. G. DeSylva," Paramount Pictures publicity, revised June 1945; "DeSylva in Deal with Paramount," *Motion Picture Herald* (July 1, 1944). His last two productions, both successful, were *The Stork Club* and *Two Years Before the Mast*.

11. DeSylva himself broke the story when he asked his wife to testify about the onerous financial demands made by his former mistress Marie Ballentine. This entanglement had long legal ramifications. In 1956, six years after DeSylva's death, Ballentine's suit to establish her son's participation in DeSylva's songwriting copyrights reached the Supreme Court. Justice Harlan decided that, as "there is no federal law of domestic relations," the court must defer to California law, which allows an "illegitimate" child (when acknowledged by the father) to inherit. In 2013, Justice Kennedy adapted the logic of this precedent to overturn the Defense of Marriage Act; absent a "federal law of domestic relations," the court must defer to New York law, which allows same-sex marriage. See "Florabel Muir, "Buddy DeSylva's Pride in Offside Fatherhood Stirs Up a Court Mess," *New York Sunday News*, Apr. 13, 1947; Louella Parsons, "DeSylva Sues Over Child," *Milwaukee Sentinel*, Apr. 6, 1947 (Parsons uniquely and repeatedly called the sailor Moskocivota); "Hi Court Upsets Tradition; Illegitimate Tots, Widows Share Royalties Equally," *Variety*, June 12, 1956; "DeSylva Son in Song Pact," *Los Angeles Examiner*, Dec. 30, 1955. The link between *DeSylva v. Ballentine* (1956) and *United States v. Windsor* (2013) is explored in David Kluft, "Why Don't You Marry the Girl? How the 1909 Copyright Act Helped Bring Down DOMA," July 9, 2013, and "Copyright Law: The Silent © in Same-Sex Marriage," June 29, 2015, http://www.trademarkandcopyrightlawblog.com.

12. Frank S. Nugent, "At Home with the Crosby Team," *New York Times Magazine*, Mar. 4, 1945; "Duffy's Tavern Sprouts a Quintet of Crosbys," unidentified clipping, 1945.

13. The performers taking turns with Crosby on "Swinging on a Star" are Sonny Tufts, Billy De Wolfe, Dorothy Lamour, Cass Daley, Diana Lynn, and Betty Hutton; for *Duffy's Tavern* grosses, see *Variety*, Oct. 3, 1945, and Oct. 31, 1945.

14. Harrison Carroll, *Los Angeles Evening Herald-Express*, Dec. 5, 1944; Erskine Johnson, *Los Angeles Daily News*, Dec. 19, 1944.

15. Bracken and Bing become friendly after Buddy DeSylva, who loved Bracken's spot-on impersonation of FDR, threw a party on a day when the president was scheduled to speak. At the appointed time, DeSylva quieted the room and pretended to switch on a radio while actually cueing a recording of Bracken. Nobody realized it was phony until they heard lines like, "In the Pacific we are pushing the Japs around from the Aleutians to New Guinea. We are going to give these Japanese cocksuckers just what they deserve" and "Eleanor once said I should have been doing to her what I have been doing to the home front." Bing cracked up and asked for a copy, which he played for friends who dropped by his office. Bracken gave a copy to Kentucky's senator Happy Chandler to give to FDR, who (Chandler assured Bracken) also thought it hilarious; AI, Eddie Bracken.

16. Ibid.; "Crosby's Four Sons Scorn Crooner, Collect $50,000," *Los Angeles Herald Examiner*, June 24, 1945; Sidney Skolsky, "Watching Them Make Pictures," *Hollywood Citizen News*, Sept. 6, 1944; *Song Hits*, Mar. 1945, 8.

17. Undated letter from J. Cooper and R. J. Tallman of NROTC unit at University of Washington to Bing Crosby; letter and script page from Dodie Heath of Samuel Goldwyn to Betty Eastman, Feb. 12, 1945; letter (and script page) from Crosby to Cooper and Tallman, Feb. 14, 1945, KCC. In an earlier scene, Hope's character, Sylvester, tells a guard his last name is Crosby, adding, "I can't help it. That's the name they gave me."

18. Coleman, *The Hollywood I Knew*, 144. "The only thing I knew about Betty Hutton," Coleman recalled of the film, "was that "she was blond, loud, and obviously knew someone important in the front office." That was Buddy DeSylva, who gave her a role on Broadway and brought her to Hollywood, where he signed her to Paramount and Capitol Records.

19. In 1953, Wilde received the Legion of Merit and became the WAVES' fourth director. Letter from Mark Sandrich to Louise K. Wilde, Mar. 24, 1944 (their extensive correspondence is at AMPAS); Jean Ebbert and Marie-Beth Hall, *Crossed Currents: Navy Women in a Century of Change* (Washington, DC: Batsford Brassey, 1999); "Capt. Louise Wilde Dies, Ex-Director of WAVES," *Washington Post*, Dec. 11, 1979.

20. Dorothy Manners, *Los Angeles Examiner*, Feb. 9, 1945; Otis L. Guernsey Jr., *New York Herald Tribune*, Dec. 28, 1944.

21. Fussell, *Thank God for the Atom Bomb*, 24; Agee, *Film Writing*, 160; Bosley Crowther, *New York Times*, Dec. 28, 1944.

22. It isn't known why Dixie was taken to St. Vincent's instead of St. John's Hospital in Santa Monica, where Hummer had worked for forty-five years and which was closer to the Crosby house in Holmby Hills.

23. The roll of Father's Day winners is now sadly amusing, as we know more about some of these fathers than did the jurors, thanks mostly to accounts by their children. In 1945, the other recipients were Harry Truman (Father of the Year), Jack Benny (Radio Father), and Frederic March (Stage Father). Only presidents and entertainers made the cut, but General Eisenhower received

special commendation as "outstanding father of the war"; Freda Dudley, "No. 1 Pop," *Movie Stars Parade,* Oct. 1945; Nancy Winslow Squire, "Crosby Quintette," *Modern Screen,* Nov. 1945; Frank S. Nugent, "At Home with the Crosby Team," *New York Times Sunday Magazine,* Mar. 4, 1945; Dick Mook, "A Day with Bing's Boys," *Screenland,* undated (1945).

24. AI, Gary Crosby; Gary Crosby, *Going My Own Way,* 114; AI, Phillip Crosby.

25. AI, Jack Haley Jr.

26. Louella O. Parsons, "In Hollywood," *New York Journal American,* Nov. 19, 1944; Louella O. Parsons, "Bing—As I Know Him," *Photoplay,* Dec. 1944; "Duffy's Tavern Sprouts a Quintet of Crosbys," unidentified clipping, 1944 or 1945.

27. Letters from Bing Crosby to Lieutenant Ab Young, U.S. Naval Reserve, Jan. 11 and July 12, 1944, KCC; letter from Bing Crosby to Clarence Mattei, undated, likely 1944. Mattei, a friend of Crosby's since the 1930s, died in his Santa Barbara studio in 1945.

28. Lincoln Barnett, "Bing, Inc.," *Life,* June 18, 1944, 86.

29. Letter from Bing Crosby to Lucille Armstrong, July 10, 1971; Louis Armstrong Archive, Scrapbook 72, Louis Armstrong House and Archives at Queens College.

30. Pete Martin, "Going His Way," *Saturday Evening Post,* Nov. 30, 1946; Bogdanovich, "Leo McCarey Interviewed."

31. Letter from Joseph Breen to Earl Rettig, secretary, Rainbow Productions, Mar. 7, 1945, AMPAS.

32. Leo McCarey, *The Bells of St. Mary's,* master file 3349, AMPAS; Gordon, "Father Chuck," 72. "In the Land of Beginning Again," by George Meyer ("For Me and My Gal," "There Are Such Things") and Grant Clarke ("Am I Blue," "Second Hand Rose") had not been popularly recorded since 1919. Louis Armstrong recalled it as the theme song Fate Marable's band played on Mississippi steamboats in that era.

33. *Lucky,* Dictaphone belt 19.

34. Kobal, *People Will Talk,* 469, 478; letter from Leo McCarey to William Dozier, Dec. 28, 1944; letter from Dozier to Joe Nolan, Jan. 15, 1945, USC; Louella Parsons, "In Hollywood," *Los Angeles Examiner,* Jan. 13, 1946.

35. Albert Camus, *The Fall (La Chute),* trans. Justin O'Brien (New York: Knopf, 1957): *"Vous savez ce qu'est le charme: une manière de s'entendre répondre oui sans avoir posé aucune question claire."*

36. "*The Bells of St. Mary's* Story Summary," AMPAS. The doctor's order, ludicrous in the context of the film, oddly prefigures the insistence, in 1952, of Dixie's doctor that Crosby not tell his wife of her incurable cancer. After the film premiered, the United States Chamber of Commerce sent a memo to RKO with the subject line: "The medical fallacies of 'The Bells of St. Mary's'" (memo from Howard Strong, secretary, Health Advisory Council, to Joyce O'Hara, Mar. 8, 1946, AMPAS). It reads in part:

Sister Benedict (Ingrid Bergman) is found to have an active case of tuberculosis. She is permitted to continue to teach and mingle with the children until the end of the school year. She is seen also moving furniture and exerting herself in other ways. This is unsound both from the standpoint of her own cure and from the standpoint of the protection of those with whom she is associated. The fact that she has tuberculosis is carefully kept from her, which is fallacious, for she can care for herself properly only by knowing of the existence of the disease and taking proper precautions.

After commencement, she is sent to Arizona either to teach in another school or to care for old people in a home. The medical profession has pretty much abandoned the idea of sending a patient to a high and dry climate as a means of cure. A sanitarium nearby is usually equally or more satisfactory. Furthermore, no person with active tuberculosis should be permitted to continue her work but should be given proper rest and other treatment. And of course no person with active tuberculosis should continue to teach children or care for older people and expose them to the disease.

Leo McCarey's response is not known.

37. The February 14, 1945, "Rough Draft" script, delivered to cast and crew little more than a week before the shooting began, is at AMPAS and is not to be confused with the "cutting continuity" script of October 8, 1945, which replicates the finished film. Rainbow Productions leased the rights for two novelizations. The first, by Viña Delmar, ran in the November 1945 Cosmopolitan. Delmar, who co-authored the scripts for Make Way for Tomorrow and The Awful Truth, based her work on the February draft; it has no "Dial O for O'Malley." The novelization based on the completed film, by George Victor Martin (who wrote the novel Our Vines Have Tender Grapes), was published by Grosset and Dunlap in 1946 and reprinted for a dozen years. Both versions were written for adolescents and trivialize the material.

38. Rhodes, "The Magic of McCarey," Gallagher, Screening the Past; Bogdanovich, "Leo McCarey Interviewed."

39. Ingrid Bergman and Bill Davidson, "I Am Not Doing Penance for Anything," Collier's, Oct. 26, 1956, 36. The title refers to a televised request by Ed Sullivan for his viewers to vote on whether she had done sufficient "penance" to appear on his program. When the vote went against her, Steve Allen presented her on his show in the same time slot; Bergman and Burgess, Ingrid Bergman, 183. Larry Adler, the mouth-organ virtuoso who had an affair with Bergman in the summer of 1945, believed that when Crosby ignored her, she turned to McCarey (AI).

40. Lucky, Dictaphone belt 19. For Marion Davies's similar repasts, see POD, 332.

41. Crosby, radio interview with John Salisbury, 1976.

42. Cooper told a columnist, "On that picture, Ingrid loved me more than any woman in my life loved me. The day after the picture ended, I couldn't get her on the phone" (Arce, Gary Cooper, 188); letter of understanding between Paramount Pictures and Harry L. Crosby Jr., Nov. 16, 1944.

43. A year later, Zanuck compared Wilson unfavorably with the propaganda of Joseph Goebbels ("You Can Sell Almost Anything but Politics or Religion Via Pix—Zanuck," Variety, Mar. 20, 1946). Wilson lost two million dollars but picked up seven Oscars, the same number as Going My Way.

44. Lucky, Dictaphone belt 19; New York Times, Mar. 16, 1945.

45. Sidney Skolsky, Hollywood Citizen News, Mar. 17, 1945; Lucky, Dictaphone belt 19; Crosby, interview by Gord Atkinson for radio series The Crosby Years, part nine, 1975; Jimmy Starr, Los Angeles Evening Herald-Express, Mar. 16, 1945; Harrison Carroll, Los Angeles Evening Herald-Express, Mar. 19, 1945.

When Crosby and Cooper re-created the Oscar moment for a newsreel, the dialogue was accompanied by much laughter. Cooper: "It is the greatest pleasure I've ever had to present to you the best acting award for 1944 for your wonderful, superb performance..." Crosby: "Superb?" Cooper: "Superb!" Crosby: "Oh, my heavens." Cooper: "That is the best word I can think of at the moment...in *Going My Way*." Crosby: "Thank you very much, Gary. I couldn't be more surprised if I won the Kentucky Derby, really."

46. Gerry Day, "*Going My Way* Reflects Trend in Religious Films," *Hollywood Citizen News*, Mar. 17, 1945; undated letter from Stanwyck to Crosby, 1945, KCC.

47. Edgar Ulmer, quoted in Gallagher, *Screening the Past*; AI, Gary Crosby.

48. Letter from Margaret Gledhill of AMPAS to Bing Crosby, Mar. 21, 1945, KCC.

23. Nothing but Bluebirds

1. Several American home-front writers registered a sometimes ominous thrumming of things to come; novelists included the realistic war writer turned Western elegist Harry Brown, the chronicler of addiction and carnal confusion Charles Jackson, the social renegade Isabel Bolton, the Catholic apostate Harry Sylvester, and the diviner of reactionary mind control Darwin Teilhet. Most of their work is virtually forgotten, and the fading of Roi Ottley's work is particularly confounding. Ottley attained widespread recognition in 1943 for *New World A-Coming*, his eloquent account of black America, and in the following year for his war reporting. *New World A-Coming*, which inspired the Duke Ellington concerto *New World A-Comin'*, augurs James Baldwin's exhortations and Albert Murray's cultural celebrations and remains a powerful call for America to fulfill its promise of a multiracial Arcadia.

2. AI, Violet Brown.

3. Louella Parsons, *Los Angeles Examiner*, Apr. 27 and Apr. 30, 1945. In a conversation with the author, Bergman's eldest daughter, Pia Lindström, said that the bracelet was not among her late mother's personal effects.

4. *Lucky*, Dictaphone belt 19; Thompson, *Bing*, 112.

5. *Lucky*, Dictaphone belt 19; McCarey's version is similar to Crosby's and Pete Martin included it in his "Going His Way," *Saturday Evening Post*, Nov. 11, 1946. Bergman's telling begins, "Actually, I played an extra gag on Bing and Leo at the end of the picture"; Bergman and Burgess, *Ingrid Bergman*, 183–84.

6. Ironically, RKO's participation is deleted from every known print of *The Bells of St. Mary's*. In 1957, after the rights were sold to the television distributor National Telefilm Association, RKO's tower logo was removed and a gray band inelegantly stamped on the title card to block out the credit reading "Released by RKO Radio Pictures."

7. Sanjek, *American Popular Music*, 276. *Blue Skies* grossed about $5.7 million; in addition to participating in the profits, Berlin earned his standard ASCAP royalties on all those songs. For the Berlin credit demand, see AMPAS.

8. Harrison Carroll, *Los Angeles Evening Herald-Express*, May 29, 1945; "JWT, Crosby Come to Grips Today," *Variety*, Aug. 22, 1945, 30; "Crosby Warm to Idea of Recording Weekly Air Stint, May Cue Broad Move Against Webs Waxing Tabu," *Variety*, Aug. 29, 1945, 25; "Decish Due This Week on Bing's Kraft Scram," *Variety*, Aug. 29, 1945, 36.

43. AI, Gary Stevens, who briefly worked for Kenny's advertising agency Bozell and Jacobs.

44. O'Toole, *Branch Rickey in Pittsburgh*, 32–33; M. Gleason to Sid Olson (for *Fortune*, Jan. 1947), TIA.

45. Maurice Bernard, "Del Mar Attracts Top Spring Fields," *Los Angeles Times*, July 10, 1945; "8,823 Fans at Del Mar," *Los Angeles Times*, July 12, 1945; Bob Thomas, *Hollywood Citizen News*, Nov. 3, 1945; "Bing, Bob Series?," *Los Angeles Times*, Aug. 10, 1946; "Sale of Pirates for $2,250,000 to McKinney Syndicate Completed," *New York Times*, Aug. 9, 1946; "The Great Throat— Bing Crosby: First in Films, First on the Air, and First on the Phonographs of His Countrymen," *Fortune*, Jan. 1947.

The 1960 World Series made front-page news again in 2010 after a pristine kinescope of the seventh game was found in the cellar of Crosby's Hillsborough home by Robert Bader, an executive of Bing Crosby Enterprises. Kathryn Crosby recalled that Crosby had been too nervous to watch the game, so he hired a company to film it off a television monitor. The Crosbys flew to Paris, where they listened to it on shortwave. Bing watched the kinescope when they returned and placed it in the vault, where it remained for fifty years. See Richard Sandomir, "In Bing Crosby's Wine Cellar, Vintage Baseball," *New York Times*, Sept. 2, 2010.

46. Edward J. Crosby's *The Story of the Washington Water Power Company and Its Part in the History of Electric Service in the Inland Empire, 1889–1930 Inclusive* is referenced at the free online encyclopedia of Washington State history, www.historylink.org/File/11211. See *POD* for Ted's stories, 67–68, and the writing of *Bing*, 244–50.

47. AI, Howard Crosby; letter from Larry Crosby to Ted Crosby, Feb. 20, 1946, HCC.

48. Letter from Bing Crosby to Ted Crosby, Nov. 5, 1945, HCC.

49. Ibid.; letter from Harry Crosby to Ted Crosby, June 21, 1944; letter from Mary Rose Crosby to Ted Crosby, undated, late 1945, HCC.

50. AI, Howard Crosby.

51. Day letter from Ted Crosby to Larry Crosby, undated, Jan. or Feb. 1946, HCC; "Crosby Boys (Bing, E, J) Take $10,000 Spat to Court," *Washington Times Herald*, Mar. 9, 1946; "Bing Stops Stock Sale by Brother," *Washington Post*, Mar. 9, 1945; "Bing Wins Court Battle," *Washington Daily News*, Mar. 9, 1945; "Bing Crosby Wins Injunction," *New York Sun*, Mar. 9, 1945; "Non-Crooning Crosby Counter-Charges Bing," *Washington Times-Herald*, Mar. 14, 1945; "Ted Crosby Claims Damages in Stock Sale Fight with Bing's Firm," *Washington Star*, Mar. 15, 1946.

52. In 1960, hoping to end the feud, Bing's wife, Kathryn, invited Ted and Margaret to a party celebrating Mother Crosby's ninetieth (in fact, eighty-seventh) birthday. Upon learning of Ted's presence, Catherine refused to attend the reception, but Kathryn forced her hand. Bing also berated his wife for inviting Ted: "He did something that I can never forgive." Yet after Bing's mother's death, in 1964, he did forgive. "Everett was in the hospital in New York with cancer, plus a leg amputation from diabetes," Howard Crosby recalled, "and Bing couldn't go to visit, so he called [Howard's dad] and asked if he could visit Ev and represent the family. From then on, all was well." World Publishing Company royalty statement in account with Ted Crosby, July 15, 1946; Kathryn

Crosby, *My Last Years with Bing,* 149–53. Howard Crosby pointed out that in the family photograph taken at the party, "My mother hid behind Uncle Everett so as not to be seen!"

53. AI, Violet Brown; Sidney Skolsky, *Hollywood Citizen News,* Oct. 22, 1945; Louella Parsons, *Los Angeles Examiner,* June 6, 1945; Jimmy Starr, *Evening Herald-Express,* Sept. 5, 1945; "O'Halloran's Luck" was adapted for television in 1949 and 1961 but was never a feature film.

54. Louella O. Parsons, *Los Angeles Examiner,* Aug. 22, 1945; Lowell E. Redelings, "The Hollywood Scene," *Hollywood Citizen News,* Aug. 22, 1945; Virginia MacPherson, *Hollywood Citizen News,* Oct. 22, 1945.

24. A Long, Long Time

1. Christopher Logue, *War Music: An Account of Homer's Iliad* (New York: Farrar, Straus and Giroux, 2015), 138.

2. *Call Me Lucky,* 288–89; *Lucky,* Dictaphone belt 24.

3. *Lucky,* Dictaphone belt 24. The published version is in *Call Me Lucky,* 289.

4. Letter from Bing Crosby to "My dear friends" Violet and Mary Barsa, Aug. 17, 1953; AI, Violet Brown.

5. AI, Violet Brown; *Call Me Lucky,* 288.

6. AI, Violet Brown; AI, Pamela Crosby Brown; Barsa, "Moments of Bliss," Jan. 11, 1946.

7. Violet Brown made the diary, written in longhand, available to the author; AI, Gary Stevens. Stevens, an old acquaintance (*POD,* 263) who worked in the New York office of Bozell and Jacobs, recalled that Crosby usually took a second room at the inconspicuous Shelton Hotel, across the street from the Waldorf. But if he took a second room in December 1945, he probably chose the Gotham Hotel, seven blocks from the Waldorf. The Barsas followed him there four times and, though they waited around, never saw him leave.

8. "The Crosby Story," *Billboard,* Oct. 26, 1946.

9. Letter from John O'Melveny to Bing Crosby, Nov. 29, 1945, KCC.

10. *Lucky,* Dictaphone belt 31: "I had been the unlucky recipient of a sour apple four or five times. I probably haven't been very cooperative because I don't like to take pictures all the time and I get a bit weary of giving out the same interview all the time—'Where were you born?'—so I probably haven't been very cooperative and got a rotten apple. But I saw they were going to have their annual Christmas party at the Beverly Hills [hotel], a hundred or a hundred fifty of them, mostly California women. So I got the studio wardrobe department to fix me a Santa Claus suit and the beard and the hat, boots, everything, and presents. I went there and handed out presents, and they were baffled by who it was until someone tipped them off. And I haven't got a sour apple since."

11. *Newsweek,* Jan. 26, 1946, 66.

12. Crosby's *Down Beat* victory in 1944 was so lopsided (with 2,406 votes), that Hal Halley, in his *Hollywood Citizen News* Swing Time column (Jan. 3, 1945), cited it as evidence that Frank Sinatra (1,606 votes) and Dick Haymes (680) were "old stuff." In 1945, however, Crosby edged out Sinatra by a mere 110 votes, with Haymes still in third, and in 1946, Sinatra prevailed over Crosby and, in third place, Perry Como. When Sinatra abruptly tumbled from the top tier, he was supplanted by Billy Eckstine; *Look,* Feb. 20, 1945, and Jan. 15,

Interviews and Bibliography

The primary interviews on which this work is based were conducted by the author or by research associates. Interviews were also made available by John McDonough (Frank Capra, Matty Malneck, and Al Rinker), James T. Maher (John Scott Trotter), and Mark Scrimger and Bob Pasch (Maxene Andrews). Numerous interviews with Bing Crosby and others, taken from various broadcasts and publications, are identified in the source notes. The names of the author interviews (AI) are as follows.

Scott Ables, Anna Maria Alberghetti, Steve Allen, Mike Alpert, Bill Angelos, Army Archerd, Bob Bakewell, Danny Bank, Ken Barnes, Marti Barris, Rose Baylis, Tom Bell, Milt Bernhart, Charles M. Black, Ann Blyth, Victor Borge, Jimmy Bowen, Eddie Bracken, Buddy Bregman, Nancy Briggs, Earl Brown, Les Brown, Pamela Crosby Brown, Violet Brown, Bud Brubaker, Pat Stanley Burke (Matthews), Rory Burke, Fran Bushkin, Joe Bushkin, Red Buttons, Bill Challis, Saul Chaplin, Barrie Chase, Doc Cheatham, Rosemary Clooney, Alan Cohen, Dawn Coleman, George Coleman, Perry Como, Frank Converse, Alex Cord, Deborah Crosby, Sister Dolores "Dixie" Crosby, Gary Crosby, Gregory Crosby, Harry Crosby, Howard Crosby, Janet Crosby, Kathryn Crosby, Mary Frances Crosby, Nathaniel Crosby, Phillip Crosby, Susan Crosby, Blythe Danner, Fred DeCordova, Bob DeFlores, Alan Dell, Norman Dewes, Kurt Dieterle, Dante DiPaolo, Ivan Ditmars, Ray Dolby, Father John W. Donahue, S.J., Donfeld (Donald Feld), Robert Dornan, Gordon Douglas, Richard Drewitt, Ted Durein, Don Eagle, Harry "Sweets" Edison, Blake Edwards, Trudy Erwin, Nanette Fabray (MacDougall), Robert Farnum, José Feliciano, Bob Finkel, Alan Fisher, Ray Flaherty, Rhonda Fleming, Father Patrick J. Ford, S.J., Sister Mary Francis, Mona Freeman, John Frigo, Jack Fulton, Milt Gabler, Beverly Garland, Leslie Gaylor, Mitzi Gaynor, Dick Gibson, Bill Goodwin, Jill Goodwin, Johnny Grant, Coleen Gray, Hy Grill, Basil Grillo, Bob Haggart, Florence Haley, Gloria Haley, Jack Haley Jr., Jean Halliburton, Pete Hammar, Jake Hanna,

Bill Harbach, Phil Harris, Kitty Carlisle Hart, Edmund Hartman, Ed Helwick, Eddie Henderson, Skitch Henderson, Sid Herman, Ray Herzog, Jim Hillburn, Milt Hinton, Walter Hogue, Celeste Holm, Bob Hope, Dolores Hope, George J. Hummer, Marsha Hunt, Jack Hupp, Carole Jackson, Gloria Jean, Carl Jefferson, Herb Jeffries, Hank Jones, Hal Kantor, Frieda Kapp, Mickey Kapp, Quentin Kelly, Joseph H. King, Robert Kipp, Buz Kohan, Miles Krueger, Mort Lachman, Duncan Lamont, Burton Lane, Johnny Lange, Peggy Lee, Gene Lester, Howard Levine, Lou Levy, Judy Lewis, Frank Liberman, Rich Little, Jay Livingston, Alice Ludes, A. C. Lyles, Sheila Lynn, June MacCloy (Butler), Murdo MacKenzie, Michael G. McDonald, James T. Maher, John Mandel, Carolyn Manovill, Gerald Marks, Tony Martin, Billy May, Ginger Mercer, Don Mike, Henry Miller, Donald Mills, Geoff Milne, Shirley Mitchell, Lyle Moore, Pete Moore, Tom Moore, John Mullin, Lillian Murphy, Farlin Myers, David Nelson, Miriam Nelson, Sheree North, Red Norvo, Robert O'Brien, Jerry O'Connell, Donald O'Connor, Lillian Oliver, Nancy Olson, Bill Osborn, Norman Panama, Marty Pasetta, John Patrick, Les Paul, William Perlberg Jr., Elsie Perry, Jerry Pickman, Terry Polesie, Dorothea Ponce, Joey Porter, Mike Post, Leslie Raddatz, Fred Reynolds, Carole Richards, Julia Rinker, Max Roach, Bob Roberts, Kenneth Roberts, Buddy Rogers, Roy Rogers, Lina Romay (O'Brien), Iris Flores Schirmer, Vic Schoen, Mozelle Seger, Nick Sevano, Hazel Sharp (Diane Notestine), Melville Shavelson, Artie Shaw, James Sheldon, Virgil H. Sherill, Vivian Sherwood, Bob Sidney, Kevin Silva, Frank Sinatra Jr., Nancy Sinatra, Ann Slater, Daniel G. Smith, Francis X. Smith, Johnny Smith, Michael Smith, Paul Smith, Kay Starr, Gary Stevens, Risë Stevens, Gloria Stuart, Ralph Sutton, Jim Tainsley, Norma Teagarden (Friedlander), Todd Thomas, Noble Threewitt, Elaina Thurston, Mel Tormé, Marguerite (McGhee) Toth, Arthur Tracy, Barry Ulanov, Mickey Van Gerbig, Bobbe Van Heusen, Felisa Vanoff, Betty Caulfield Vietor, Helen Votachenko, Robert Wagner, Janet Waldo, Ray Walston, Pauline Weislow, Sandy Wernick, Paul Weston, Charlie Whittingham, Spiegel Wilcox, Max Wilk, Joe Williams, Jane Wyman.

Books and Selected Articles About Bing Crosby

Baker, J. Richard. *A Bing Crosby Discography.* bingmagazine.co.uk/bing magazine/crosby.html, 2011.

Barnes, Ken. *The Crosby Years.* New York: St. Martin's, 1980.

Bauer, Barbara. *Bing Crosby.* New York: Pyramid Publications, 1977.

Bishop, Bert, and John Bassett. *Bing: Just for the Record.* Gateshead, England: International Crosby Circle, 1980.

Bookbinder, Robert. *The Films of Bing Crosby.* Secaucus, NJ: Citadel Press, 1977.

Crosby, Bing, with Pete Martin. *Call Me Lucky.* New York: Simon and Schuster, 1953.

Crosby, Gary, with Ross Firestone. *Going My Own Way.* New York: Doubleday, 1983.

Crosby, Kathryn. *Bing and Other Things.* New York: Meredith Press, 1967.

———. *My Life with Bing.* Wheeling, IL: Collage, 1983.

———. *My Last Years with Bing.* Naples, FL: Collage, 2002.

Crosby, Nathaniel, and John Strege. *Eighteen Holes with Bing: Golf, Life, and Lessons from Dad.* New York: Dey Street Books, 2016.

Crosby, Ted. *The Story of Bing Crosby.* Cleveland: World, 1946.

Crosby, Ted, and Larry Crosby. *Bing.* Los Angeles: Bolton, 1937.

Edwards, Anne. "Bing Crosby: The Going My Way Star in Rancho Santa Fe." *Architectural Digest* (April 1996).

Giddins, Gary. *Bing Crosby: A Pocketful of Dreams—The Early Years, 1903–1940.* Boston: Little, Brown, 2001.

Grudens, Richard. *Bing Crosby: Crooner of the Century.* Stony Brook, NY: Celebrity Profiles Publishing, 2003.

Hamann, G. D., ed. *Bing Crosby in the 40's.* Hollywood: Filming Today, 1997.

———. *Bing Crosby Covering All Bases.* Hollywood: Filming Today, 2002.

———. *Bing Crosby 1940–1944.* Hollywood: Filming Today, 2005.

———. *Bing Crosby 1945–1949.* Hollywood: Filming Today, 2005.

Macfarlane, Malcolm. *Bing Crosby Day by Day.* Kent, England: Scarecrow Press, 2001. Updated at www.bingmagazine.co.uk/bingmagazine/1903-1935 .htm.

Marill, Alvin H. "Bing Crosby Photographed as Pleasingly as He Sang." *Films in Review* (June–July 1968).

Mello, Edward J., and Tom McBride. *Crosby on Record.* San Francisco: Mello's Music, 1950.

Mielke, Randall G. *Road to Box Office: The Seven Film Comedies of Bing Crosby, Bob Hope and Dorothy Lamour.* Jefferson, NC: McFarland, 1997.

Mize, J.T.H. *Bing.* Chicago: Who Is Who in Music, 1946.

Morgereth, Timothy A. *Bing Crosby: A Discography, Radio Program List and Filmography.* Jefferson, NC: McFarland, 1987.

Neuhaus, Mel. "Interview: Bing Crosby." *Laser Marquee* (November 1994).

O'Connell, Sheldon, with Gord Atkinson. *Bing: A Voice for All Seasons.* Tralee, Ireland: Kerryman, 1984.

Osterholm, J. Roger. *Bing Crosby: A Bio-Bibliography.* Westport, CT: Greenwood Press, 1994.

Pairpoint, Lionel. *"And Here's Bing!" Bing Crosby: The Radio Directories.* Gateshead, England: International Crosby Circle, 2000.

Prigozy, Ruth, and Walter Raubicheck. *Going My Way: Bing Crosby and American Culture.* Rochester, NY: University of Rochester Press, 2007.

Reynolds, Fred. *The Road to Hollywood.* Rev. ed. Bristol, England: John Joyce, 1988.

———. *The Crosby Collection, Part Two: 1935–1941.* Self-published, 1991–1997.

———. *The Crosby Collection, Part Three: 1942–1950.* Self-published, 1991–1997.

Ruhlmann, William. "Swing (on a) Star: The Road to Bing Crosby." *Goldmine* (December 24, 1993).

Schneider, Carolyn. *Bing on the Road to Elko.* Las Vegas: Stephens Press, 2009.

Schneider, Carolyn, with Lin Anderson. *Me and Uncle Bing.* Las Vegas: Xlibris, 2005.

Shepherd, Donald, and Robert F. Slatzer. *Bing Crosby: The Hollow Man.* New York: St. Martin's, 1981.

Staff. "Bing Crosby: He Is Still Falling Uphill." *Time,* April 7, 1941.

———. "Going His Way Is a Nation's Habit After Twenty Years of Crosby Song." *Newsweek,* January 28, 1946.

———. "The Crosby Story." *Billboard,* October 26, 1946.

———. "The Great Throat: Bing Crosby, First in Films, First on the Air, First on the Phonographs of His Countrymen." *Fortune,* January 1947.

Taylor, Vernon Wesley. "Hail KMH!" (six parts). *The Crosby Voice,* Bing Crosby Victorian Society, 1984–1986.

Thomas, Bob. *The One and Only Bing.* New York: Grosset and Dunlap, 1977.

Thompson, Charles. *Bing.* New York: David McKay, 1976.

Ulanov, Barry. *The Incredible Crosby.* New York: Whittlesey House, 1948.

Wiggins, F. B., and Jim Reilly. *The Definitive Bing Crosby Discography from 78s to CDs.* Self-published, 2014.

Wolfe, Norman. *Troubadour: Bing Crosby and the Invention of Pop Singing.* Gateshead, England: International Crosby Circle, 2005.

Zwisohn, Laurence J. *Bing Crosby: A Lifetime in Music.* Los Angeles: Palm Tree Library, 1978.

Selected Bibliography

Aberdeen, J. A. *Hollywood Renegades: The Society of Independent Motion Picture Producers.* Los Angeles: Cobblestone, 2000.

Adler, Larry. *It Ain't Necessarily So.* New York: Grove Press, 1984.

Agee, James. *Film Writing and Selected Journalism.* New York: Library of America, 2005.

Andrews, Maxene, and Bill Gilbert. *Over Here, Over There: The Andrews Sisters and the USO Stars in World War II.* New York: Zebra Books, 1993.

Arce, Hector. *Gary Cooper.* New York: William Morrow, 1979.

Armstrong, Louis. *Satchmo: My Life in New Orleans.* New York: Prentice Hall, 1954.

———. *Swing That Music.* London: Longmans, Green, 1936.

Astaire, Fred. *Steps in Time.* New York: Harper and Row, 1959.

Atkins, Irene Kahn, ed. *Arthur Jacobson.* Metuchen, NJ: Directors Guild of America and Scarecrow Press, 1991.

———. *David Butler.* Metuchen, NJ: Directors Guild of America and Scarecrow Press, 1993.

Atkinson, Gordon A. *Gord Atkinson's Showbill.* Carp, Ontario: Creative Bound, 1996.

Bach, Bob, and Ginger Mercer. *Our Huckleberry Friend: The Life, Times, and Lyrics of Johnny Mercer.* Secaucus, NJ: Lyle Stuart, 1982.

Bailey, Beth L. *From Front Porch to Back Seat.* Baltimore: Johns Hopkins University, 1989.

Balio, Tino. *Grand Design: Hollywood as a Modern Business Enterprise, 1930–1939*. Berkeley: University of California Press, 1993.

Barnett, Lincoln. *Writing on Life: Sixteen Close-Ups*. New York: William Sloane Associates, 1951.

Barnouw, Erik. *A Tower in Babel*. New York: Oxford University Press, 1966.

———. *The Golden Web*. New York: Oxford University Press, 1968.

Barrett, Mary Ellin. *Irving Berlin: A Daughter's Memoir*. New York: Simon and Schuster, 1994.

Basie, Count, with Albert Murray. *Good Morning Blues*. New York: Da Capo, 1995.

Basinger, Jeanine. *The Star Machine*. New York: Knopf, 2007.

Beck, Jerry, and Will Friedwald. *Looney Tunes and Merrie Melodies*. New York: Henry Holt, 1989.

Bell-Metereau, Rebecca. *Hollywood Androgyny*. New York: Columbia University Press, 1993.

Bennett, Tony, and Will Friedwald. *The Good Life*. New York: Pocket Books, 1998.

Benny, Jack, and Joan Benny. *Sunday Nights at Seven: The Jack Benny Story*. New York: Warner Books, 1990.

Benny, Mary Livingstone, and Hilliard Marks with Marcia Borie. *Jack Benny*. New York: Doubleday, 1978.

Berg, A. Scott. *Goldwyn*. New York: Knopf, 1989.

Berger, Edward. *Bassically Speaking: An Oral History of George Duvivier*. Metuchen, NJ: Institute of Jazz Studies and Scarecrow, 1993.

Bergman, Ingrid, and Alan Burgess. *Ingrid Bergman: My Story*. New York: Dell, 1981.

Bergreen, Laurence. *As Thousands Cheer: The Life of Irving Berlin*. New York: Viking, 1990.

———. *Louis Armstrong: An Extravagant Life*. New York: Broadway Books, 1997.

Bernstein, Matthew. *Walter Wanger: Hollywood Independent*. Berkeley: University of California Press, 1994.

Bérubé, Allan. *Coming Out Under Fire*. Chapel Hill: University of North Carolina Press (reprint), 2010.

Blake, Richard A. "The Sins of Leo McCarey." *Journal of Religion and Film* 17, no. 1 (2013). digitalcommons.unomaha.edu/jrf/vol17/iss1/38.

Blesh, Rudy. *Combo: U.S.A.* Philadelphia: Chilton, 1971.

Bloom, Ken. *Hollywood Song*. 3 vols. New York: Facts on File, 1995.

Blumenthal, Ralph. *The Stork Club*. Boston: Little, Brown, 2000.

Bogdanovich, Peter. "Leo McCarey Interviewed." Beverly Hills: American Film Institute, 1975.

———. *Pieces of Time*. New York: Arbor House, 1973.

———. *Who the Devil Made It*. New York: Knopf, 1997.

Bordman, Gerald. *American Musical Theatre: A Chronicle*. New York: Oxford University Press, 1986.

Bordwell, David. *The Way Hollywood Tells It*. Berkeley: University of California Press, 2006.

———. *The Rhapsodes: How 1940s Critics Changed American Film Culture*. Chicago: University of Chicago Press, 2016.

Bordwell, David, Janet Staiger, and Kristin Thompson. *The Classical Hollywood Cinema*. New York: Columbia University Press, 1985.

Bosworth, Patricia. *Jane Fonda: The Private Life of a Public Woman*. Boston: Houghton Mifflin Harcourt, 2011.

Brackett, David. *Interpreting Popular Music*. Rev. ed. Berkeley: University of California Press, 2000.

Brooks, Elston. *I've Heard Those Songs Before*. New York: Morrow, 1981.

Brown, James Good. *The Mighty Men of the 381st: Heroes All*. Salt Lake City, UT: Publishers Press, 1984.

Brown, Richard Howard. *I Am of Ireland*. Lanham, MD: Roberts Rinehard (reprint), 1995.

Burns, George. *Gracie: A Love Story*. New York: G. P. Putnam's Sons, 1988.

Buxton, Frank, and Bill Owen. *The Big Broadcast 1920–1950*. Rev. ed. New York: Viking, 1966.

Cagney, James. *Cagney by Cagney*. Garden City, NY: Doubleday, 1976.

Cahn, Sammy. *I Should Care*. New York: Arbor House, 1974.

Callender, Red, and Elaine Cohen. *Unfinished Dream*. London: Quartet Books, 1985.

Capra, Frank. *The Name Above the Title*. New York: Macmillan, 1971.

Carmichael, Hoagy. *The Stardust Road*. New York: Rinehart, 1946.

Carroll, Carroll. *None of Your Business, or My Life with J. Walter Thompson*. Toronto: Cowles, 1970.

Carroll, Michael Thomas. *Popular Modernity in America*. New York: State University of New York Press, 2000.

Carson, Julia M. H. *Home Away from Home: The Story of the USO*. New York: Harper and Brothers, 1946.

Cassidy, Bruce. *Dinah!* New York: Franklin Watts, 1979.

Catechism of the Catholic Church. Libreria Editrice Vaticana. Liguori: Liguori Publications, 1994.

Chandler, Charlotte. *Nobody's Perfect: Billy Wilder, a Personal Biography*. New York: Simon and Schuster, 2002.

Chaplin, Saul. *The Golden Age of Musicals and Me*. Norman: University of Oklahoma Press, 1994.

Chilton, John. *Who's Who of Jazz*. Rev. ed. New York: Da Capo, 1972.

———. *Stomp Off, Let's Go! The Story of Bob Crosby's Bob Cats and Big Band*. London: Jazz Book Service, 1983.

———. *Let the Good Times Roll: The Story of Louis Jordan and His Music*. London: Quartet, 1992.

Clarke, Donald. *Wishing on the Moon: The Life and Times of Billie Holiday*. New York: Viking, 1994.

Clooney, Rosemary, with Joan Barthel. *Girl Singer*. New York: Doubleday, 1999.

Clooney, Rosemary, with Raymond Strait. *This for Remembrance*. Chicago: Playboy Press, 1977.

Coffey, Frank. *Always Home: Fifty Years of the USO*. McLean, VA: Brassy's, 1991.

Cohan, Steve, and Ina Rae Hark, editors. *The Road Movie Book*. London: Routledge, 1997.

Cole, Maria, with Louie Robinson. *Nat King Cole: An Intimate Biography*. New York: William Morrow, 1971.

Coleman, Herbert, and Judy Lanini. *The Hollywood I Knew: A Memoir, 1916–1988*. Metuchen, NJ: Scarecrow Press, 2003.

Condon, Eddie. *We Called It Music*. Rev. ed. New York: Da Capo, 1988.

Conrad, Barnaby. *Name Dropping: Tales from My Barbary Coast Saloon*. New York: Harper Collins, 1994.

Coppula, Christopher A. *Jimmy Van Heusen: Swinging on a Star*. Nashville: Twin Creek, 2014.

Coslow, Sam. *Cocktails for Two*. New Rochelle, NY: Arlington House, 1977.

Couffer, Jack. *Bat Bomb*. Austin: University of Texas Press, 1992.

Cray, Ed. *General of the Army: George C. Marshall, Soldier and Statesman*. New York: Cooper Square Press, 1990.

———. *Ramblin' Man: The Life and Times of Woody Guthrie*. New York: Norton, 2004.

Crichton, Kyle. *Subway to the Met*. New York: Doubleday, 1959.

Cripps, Thomas. *Slow Fade to Black*. New York: Oxford University Press, 1977.

Cronkite, Kathy. *On the Edge of Darkness*. New York: Doubleday, 1994.

Crosby, John. *Out of the Blue*. New York: Simon and Schuster, 1952.

Crossland, Ken, and Malcolm Macfarlane. *Late Life Jazz: The Life and Career of Rosemary Clooney*. New York: Oxford University Press, 2013.

Crowe, Cameron. *Conversations with Wilder*. New York: Knopf: 1999.

Crowther, Bruce, and Mike Pinfold. *The Jazz Singers*. Poole, England: Blanford Press, 1986.

Curtis, Jenny. *Bob Hope*. New York: Metrobooks, 1999.

Dance, Stanley. *The World of Earl Hines*. New York: Scribner's, 1977.

———. *The World of Swing*. New York: Scribner's, 1974.

Dardis, Tom. *Some Time in the Sun*. New York: Scribner's, 1976.

Davies, Marion. *The Times We Had*. Indianapolis: Bobbs-Merrill, 1975.

Davis, Ronald L. *The Glamour Factory*. Dallas: Southern Methodist University, 1993.

De Carlo, Yvonne, with Doug Warren. *Yvonne*. New York: St. Martin's, 1987.

Decker, Todd. *Music Makes Me: Fred Astaire and Jazz*. Berkeley: University of California Press, 2011.

DeLong, Thomas A. *Pops: Paul Whiteman, King of Jazz*. Piscataway, NJ: New Century Publishers, 1983.

Dexter, Dave, Jr. *Playback*. New York: Billboard Publications, 1976.

Dick, Bernard F. *Engulfed: The Death of Paramount Pictures and the Birth of Corporate Hollywood*. Lexington: University Press of Kentucky, 2001.

———. *City of Dreams: The Making and Remaking of Universal Pictures*. Lexington: University Press of Kentucky, 1997.

Dmytryk, Edward. *It's a Hell of a Life, but Not a Bad Living*. New York: New York Times Books, 1978.

Doherty, Thomas. *Hollywood's Censor*. New York: Columbia University Press, 2007.

Donaldson, Ellen, ed. *The Walter Donaldson Songbook*. Winona, MN: Hal Leonard, 1988.

Dunning, John. *On the Air: The Encyclopedia of Old-Time Radio*. New York: Oxford University Press, 1998.

Dwiggins, Don. *Frankie: The Life and Loves of Frank Sinatra*. New York: Paperback Library, 1961.

Eames, John Douglas. *The Paramount Story*. New York: Crown, 1985.

Eberly, Phillip K. *Music in the Air.* New York: Hastings House, 1982.

Edmonds, I. G. *Paramount Pictures and the People Who Made Them.* San Diego: A.S. Barnes, 1980.

Eisenberg, Evan. *The Recording Angel.* New York: McGraw-Hill, 1987.

Ellington, Duke. *Music Is My Mistress.* Garden City, NY: Doubleday, 1973.

Emerson, Ken. *Doo-Dah! Stephen Foster and the Rise of American Popular Culture.* New York: Simon and Schuster, 1997.

Epstein, Daniel Mark. *Nat King Cole.* New York: Farrar, Straus and Giroux, 1999.

Erenberg, Lewis A. *Swingin' the Dream.* Chicago: University of Chicago, 1998.

Evanier, David. *All the Things You Are: The Life of Tony Bennett.* Hoboken, NJ: Wiley, 2011.

Ewen, David. *Great Men of American Popular Song.* Englewood Cliffs, NJ: Prentice Hall, 1972.

Fein, Irving A. *Jack Benny: An Intimate Biography.* New York: G. P. Putnam's Sons, 1976.

Ferguson, Otis. *The Film Criticism of Otis Ferguson.* Edited by Robert Wilson. Philadelphia: Temple University, 1971.

———. *In the Spirit of Jazz: The Otis Ferguson Reader.* Edited by Dorothy Chamberlain and Robert Wilson. New York: Da Capo, 1982.

Feuer, Jane. *The Hollywood Musical.* Bloomington: Indiana University Press, 1993.

Fidelman, Geoffrey Mark. *First Lady of Song: Ella Fitzgerald for the Record.* New York: Carol Publishing, 1994.

Finler, Joel W. *The Hollywood Story.* New York: Crown, 1988.

Fisher, Eddie. *Eddie: My Life, My Loves.* New York: Harper and Row, 1981.

Fleischer, Richard. *Just Tell Me When to Cry.* New York: Carroll and Graf, 1993.

Fontaine, Joan. *No Bed of Roses.* New York: William Morrow, 1978.

Fordin, Hugh. *The Movies' Greatest Musicals.* New York: Frederick Ungar, 1984.

Forrest, Helen, with Bill Libby. *I Had the Craziest Dream: Helen Forrest and the Big Band Era.* New York: Coward, McCann and Geoghegan, 1982.

Fowles, Jib. *Starstruck.* Washington, DC: Smithsonian Institution Press, 1992.

Fox, Ted. *In the Groove: The People Behind the Music.* New York: St. Martin's, 1986.

Frank, Gerold. *Judy.* New York: Da Capo (reprint), 1999.

Frank, Rusty E. *Tap!* Rev. ed. New York: Da Capo, 1990.

Franklin, Joe. *Encyclopedia of Comedians.* New York: Bell, 1979.

Franklin, Joe, with R. J. Marx. *Up Late with Joe Franklin.* New York: Scribner's, 1995.

Freidel, Frank. *Franklin D. Roosevelt: A Rendezvous with Destiny.* Boston: Little, Brown, 1990.

Fried, Albert. *FDR and His Enemies.* New York: St. Martin's, 1999.

Friedwald, Will. *Jazz Singing.* New York: Scribner's, 1990.

———. *Sinatra! The Song Is You.* New York: Scribner's, 1995.

———. *A Biographical Guide to the Great Jazz and Pop Singers.* New York: Pantheon, 2010.

Furia, Philip. *Ira Gershwin: The Art of the Lyricist*. New York: Oxford University Press, 1996.

Fussell, Paul. *The Boys' Crusade*. New York: Modern Library, 2003.

———. *Thank God for the Atom Bomb*. New York: Summit, 1988.

Gabbard, Krin. *Jammin' at the Margins*. Chicago: University of Chicago, 1996.

Gabler, Neal. *Winchell: Gossip, Power, and the Culture of Celebrity*. New York: Knopf, 1994.

Gallagher, Tag. "Going My Way." *Screening the Past*. screeningthepast .com/2014/12/going-my-way.

Garnett, Tay, with Frieda Dudley Balling. *Light Your Torches and Pull Up Your Tights*. New Rochelle, NY: Arlington House, 1973.

Gehring, Wes D. *Leo McCarey: From Marx to McCarthy*. Lanham, MD: Scarecrow Press, 2005.

Geist, Kenneth L. *Pictures Will Talk: The Life and Films of Joseph L. Mankiewicz*. New York: Scribner's, 1978.

Gelatt, Roland. *The Fabulous Phonograph*. Philadelphia: J. B. Lippincott Company, 1954.

Giddins, Gary. *Riding on a Blue Note*. New York: Oxford University Press, 1981.

———. *Satchmo: The Genius of Louis Armstrong*. New York: Da Capo, 2001.

———. *Natural Selection: Gary Giddins on Comedy, Film, Music, and Books*. New York: Oxford University Press, 2006.

———. *Warning Shadows: Home Alone with Classic Cinema*. New York: Norton, 2010.

Gioia, Ted. *The History of Jazz*. New York: Oxford University Press, 1997.

———. *The Jazz Standards*. New York: Oxford University Press, 2012.

Goldberg, Isaac, and Edward Jablonski. *Tin Pan Alley*. Rev. ed. New York: Frederick Ungar, 1961.

Goldenson, Leonard H., with Marvin J. Wolf. *Beating the Odds*. New York: Scribner's, 1991.

Goldman, Herbert G. *Jolson: The Legend Comes to Life*. New York: Oxford University Press, 1988.

———. *Banjo Eyes: Eddie Cantor and the Birth of Modern Stardom*. New York: Oxford University Press, 1997.

Gomery, Douglas. *The Hollywood Studio System*. London: BFI/Palgrave, 2005.

Goodman, Ezra. *The Fifty-Year Decline and Fall of Hollywood*. New York: Simon and Schuster, 1961.

Gordon, Mary. "Father Chuck: A Reading of *Going My Way* and *The Bells of St. Mary's*, or Why Priests Made Us Crazy," in Thomas J. Ferraro, *Catholic Lives, Contemporary America*. Durham, NC: Duke University Press, 1997.

Gorham, Maurice. *Sound and Fury: Twenty-One Years in the BBC*. London: Percival Marshall, 1948.

Gottlieb, Robert, and Robert Kimball, ed. *Reading Lyrics*. New York: Pantheon, 2000.

Goulden, Joseph C. *The Best Years, 1945–1950*. New York: Atheneum, 1976.

Gourse, Leslie. *Louis' Children*. New York: William Morrow, 1984.

Green, Abel, with Joe Laurie Jr. *Show Biz: From Vaude to Video*. New York: Henry Holt, 1951.

Green, Stanley. *Encyclopedia of the Musical Film*. New York: Oxford University Press, 1981.

Green, Stanley, and Burt Goldblatt. *Starring Fred Astaire*. New York: Dodd, Mead, 1973.

Gross, Ben. *I Looked and I Listened*. New York: Random House, 1954.

Gubar, Susan. *Racechanges: White Skin, Black Face in American Culture*. New York: Oxford University Press, 1997.

Hale, Lee, with Richard D. Neely. *Backstage with the Dean Martin Show*. Arcadia, CA: Dean Martin Fan Center, 1999.

Halliwell, Leslie. *Mountain of Dreams*. New York: Stonehill, 1976.

Hamann, G. D., ed. *Music in the Films, 1938–1941, Dr. Bruno David Ussher*. Hollywood: Filming Today, 2001.

———. *Clarence Muse in the 30's*. Hollywood: Filming Today, 1996.

Hamm, Charles. *Yesterdays*. New York: Norton, 1979.

Hanson, Patricia King, ed. *The American Film Institute Catalog: Feature Films 1931–1940*. Berkeley: University of California Press, 1993.

———. *The American Film Institute Catalog: Feature Films 1941–1950*. Berkeley: University of California Press, 1999.

Harmon, Jim. *The Great Comedians*. Garden City: Doubleday, 1970.

Harrill, Paul. "Leo McCarey." *Senses of Cinema* 23 (2002). sensesofcinema .com/2002/great-directors/mccarey/.

Harvey, James. *Romantic Comedy in Hollywood from Lubitsch to Sturgis*. New York: Knopf, 1987.

Hecht, Ben. *A Child of the Century*. New York: Simon and Schuster, 1954.

Hedtke, James R. *The Freckleton, England, Air Disaster*. Jefferson, NC: McFarland, 2014.

Heimann, Jim. *Out with the Stars*. New York: Abbeville Press, 1985.

Hemming, Roy, and David Hajdu. *Discovering Great Singers of Classic Pop*. New York: Newmarket Press, 1991.

Hill, Constance Valis. *Tap Dancing in America*. New York: Oxford University Press, 2010.

Hinton, Milt, and David G. Berger. *Bass Line*. Philadelphia: Temple University Press, 1988.

Hirschhorn, Clive. *The Hollywood Musical*. New York: Crown, 1981.

Hoopes, Roy. *When the Stars Went to War*. New York: Random House, 1994.

Hope, Bob. *They Got Me Covered*. Self-published, 1941.

Hope, Bob, with Pete Martin. *Have Tux, Will Travel*. New York: Simon and Schuster, 1954.

Hope, Bob, with Dwayne Netland. *Confessions of a Hooker*. New York: Doubleday, 1985.

Hope, Bob, with Melville Shavelson. *Don't Shoot, It's Only Me*. New York: G. P. Putnam's Sons, 1990.

Horten, Gerd. *Radio Goes to War*. Berkeley: University of California Press, 2002.

Howard, John Tasker. *Stephen Foster: America's Troubadour*. New York: Crowell, 1934.

Hunt, Marsha. *The Way We Wore*. Fallbrook, CA: Fallbrook Publishing Group, 1993.

Hyatt, I. Joseph. *Hollywood Victory Caravan*. Self-published, 2015.

Hyland, William G., *The Song Is Ended*. New York: Oxford University Press, 1995.

Inman, David. *The TV Encyclopedia*. New York: Perigee Books, 1991.

Irvin, Sam. *Kay Thompson*. New York: Simon and Schuster, 2002.

Jablonski, Edward. *Harold Arlen*. Boston: Northeastern University Press, 1996.

———. *Irving Berlin: American Troubadour*. New York: Henry Holt, 1999.

Jacobs, Diane. *Christmas in July: The Life and Art of Preston Sturges*. Berkeley: University of California Press, 1992.

Jacobs, Dick. *Who Wrote That Song?* White Hall, VA: Betterway, 1988.

Jasen, David A. *Tin Pan Alley*. New York: Donald I. Fine, 1988.

Jasen, David A., and Gene Jones. *Spreadin' Rhythm Around: Black Popular Songwriters, 1880–1930*. New York: Schirmer Books, 1998.

Jones, John Bush. *The Songs That Fought the War*. Waltham, MA: Brandeis University Press, 2006.

Jones, Max. *Talking Jazz*. New York: Norton, 1987.

Jones, Max, and John Chilton. *Louis: The Story of Louis Armstrong*. Boston: Little, Brown, 1971.

Kaminsky, Max, with V. E. Hughes. *My Life in Jazz*. New York: Harper and Row, 1963.

Kanter, Hal. *So Far, So Funny*. Jefferson, NC: McFarland, 1999.

Kaplan, James. *Frank: The Voice*. New York: Doubleday, 2010.

———. *Sinatra: The Chairman*. New York: Doubleday, 2015.

Karney, Robin, ed. *Chronicle of the Cinema*. New York: DK Publishing, 1995.

Kashner, Sam, with Nancy Schoenberger. *A Talent for Genius: The Life and Times of Oscar Levant*. New York: Villard Books, 1994.

Kay, Eddie Dorman. *Box-Office Champs*. New York: Portland House, 1990.

Kempton, Murray. *Part of Our Time*. New York: Simon and Schuster, 1955.

Kendall, Elizabeth. *The Runaway Bride*. New York: Cooper Square Press (reprint), 2002.

Kennedy, David M. *Freedom from Fear*. New York: Oxford University Press, 1999.

Keyes, Evelyn. *Scarlett O'Hara's Younger Sister*. Secaucus, NJ: Lyle Stuart, 1977.

Kimball, Robert, and Linda Emmet. *The Complete Lyrics of Irving Berlin*. New York: Knopf, 2001.

Kimball, Robert, Barry Day, Miles Krueger, and Eric Davis. *The Complete Lyrics of Johnny Mercer*. New York: Knopf, 2009.

Kinkle, Roger D. *The Complete Encyclopedia of Popular Music and Jazz: 1900–1950*. 4 vols. New Rochelle, NY: Arlington House, 1974.

Kirby, Edward M., and Jack W. Harris. *Star-Spangled Radio*. Chicago: Ziff-Davis, 1948.

Kirsten, Dorothy. *A Time to Sing*. Garden City, NY: Doubleday, 1982.

Knight, Arthur. *Disintegrating the Musical: Black Performance and American Musical Film*. Durham, NC: Duke University Press, 2002.

Kobal, John. *People Will Talk*. New York: Knopf, 1985.

Kotlowitz, Robert. *Before Their Time*. New York: Knopf, 1997.

Lahr, John. *Notes on a Cowardly Lion*. New York: Ballantine, 1970.

Lally, Kevin. *Wilder Times: The Life of Billy Wilder*. New York: Henry Holt, 1996.

Lamour, Dorothy, with Dick McInnes. *My Side of the Road*. Englewood Cliffs, NJ: Prentice Hall, 1980.

Laurie, Joe, Jr. *Vaudeville*. New York: Henry Holt, 1953.

Lax, Roger, and Frederick Smith. *The Great Song Thesaurus*. New York: Oxford University Press, 1989.

Lee, Peggy. *Miss Peggy Lee*. New York: David I. Fine, 1989.

Lejeune, C. A. *The C.A. Lejeune Film Reader*. Manchester, England: Carcanet, 1991.

Leonard, Hal, ed. *I'll Be Seeing You: 50 Songs of World War II*. Milwaukee: Hal Leonard, 1995.

LeRoy, Mervyn, with Dick Kleiner. *Mervyn LeRoy: Take One*. New York: Hawthorn Books, 1974.

Lester, Gene, with Peter Laufer. *When Hollywood Was Fun!* New York: Birch Lane Press, 1993.

Levant, Oscar. *A Smattering of Ignorance*. New York: Doubleday, Doran, 1940.

———. *Memoirs of an Amnesiac*. New York: G. P. Putnam's Sons, 1965.

Levine, Lawrence W. *Black Culture and Black Consciousness*. New York: Oxford University Press, 1977.

———. *Highbrow/Lowbrow*. Cambridge, MA: Harvard University Press, 1988.

Levinson, Peter J. *Trumpet Blues: The Life of Harry James*. New York: Oxford University Press, 1999.

———. *September in the Rain: The Life of Nelson Riddle*. New York: Billboard Books, 2001.

———. *Puttin' On the Ritz: Fred Astaire and the Fine Art of Panache*. New York: St. Martin's, 2009.

Lewis, Judy. *Uncommon Knowledge*. New York: Pocket Books, 1994.

Lhamon, W. T., Jr. *Raising Cain: Blackface Performance from Jim Crow to Hip Hop*. Cambridge, MA: Harvard University Press, 1998.

Linet, Beverly. *Ladd: A Hollywood Tragedy*. New York: Arbor House, 1979.

Lingeman, Richard R. *Don't You Know There's a War On?* New York: G. P. Putnam's Sons, 1970.

———. *The Noir Forties: The American People from Victory to Cold War*. New York: Nation Books, 2012.

Lipsitz, George. *Rainbow at Midnight: Labor and Culture in the 1940s*. Urbana: University of Illinois Press, 1994.

Lott, Eric. *Love and Theft: Blackface Minstrelsy and the American Working Class*. New York: Oxford University Press, 1993.

Lowry, Ed, with Charlie Foy. *Joe Frisco*. Edited by Paul M. Levitt. Carbondale: Southern Illinois University Press, 1999.

Loza, Steven. *Barrio Rhythm*. Urbana: University of Illinois Press, 1993.

MacDonald, J. Fred. *Don't Touch That Dial!* Chicago: Nelson-Hall, 1979.

MacGillivray, Scott, and Jan MacGillivray. *Gloria Jean: A Little Bit of Heaven*. Lincoln, NE: iUniverse, 2005.

Mackenzie, Harry. *Command Performance, USA! A Discography*. Westport, CT: Greenwood, 1996.

Maltin, Leonard. *Selected Short Subjects*. New York: Da Capo, 1972.

———. *The Great American Broadcast*. New York: Dutton, 1997.

Manchester, William. *The Glory and the Dream*. Boston: Little, Brown, 1974.

Manone, Wingy, with Paul Vandervoort II. *Trumpet on the Wing*. Garden City, NY: Doubleday, 1948.

Marmorstein, Gary. *Hollywood Rhapsody*. New York: Schirmer Books, 1997.

Marshall, Michael. *Top Hats and Tails: The Story of Jack Buchanan*. London: Elm Tree Books, 1978.

Martin, Mary. *My Heart Belongs*. New York: Quill, 1984.

Martin, Pete. *Pete Martin Calls On...* New York: Simon and Schuster, 1962.

Marx, Arthur. *The Secret Life of Bob Hope*. New York: Barricade Books, 1993.

Mast, Gerald. *Can't Help Singin'*. Woodstock, NY: Overlook Press, 1987.

Mattfield, Julius, ed. *Variety Music Cavalcade*. New York: Prentice Hall, 1952.

May, Larry. *The Big Tomorrow: Hollywood and the Politics of the American Way*. Chicago: University of Chicago Press, 2000.

McBride, Joseph. *Frank Capra*. New York: Simon and Schuster, 1992.

McCabe, John. *Mr. Laurel and Mr. Hardy*. New York: Doubleday, 1961.

McCarthy, Albert. *Big Band Jazz*. London: G. P. Putnam's Sons, 1974.

McGilligan, Patrick. *Backstory*. Berkeley: University of California Press, 1986.

———. *Film Crazy: Interviews with Hollywood Legends*. New York: St. Martin's, 2000.

McGilligan, Patrick, and Paul Buhle. *Tender Comrades: A Backstory of the Hollywood Blacklist*. New York: St. Martin's, 1997.

McKeever, Jerome M. "The McCarey Touch: The Life and Films of Leo McCarey." PhD diss., Case Western Reserve University, 2000.

Menjou, Adolphe, and M. M. Musselman. *It Took Nine Tailors* (New York: McGraw-Hill, 1948).

Mezzrow, Mezz, and Bernard Wolfe. *Really the Blues*. New York: Random House, 1946.

Mitchell, Lisa, and Bruce Torrence. *The Hollywood Canteen*. Duncan, OK: BearManor, 2012.

Mize, J.T.H., ed. *The International Who Is Who in Music*. 5th ed. Chicago: Who Is Who in Music, 1951.

Mordden, Ethan. *The Hollywood Studios*. New York: Simon and Schuster, 1988.

Morgenstern, Dan. *Living with Jazz*. New York: Pantheon, 2004.

Mueller, John. *Astaire Dancing*. New York: Knopf, 1985.

Murray, Ken. *Life on a Pogo Stick*. New York: Holt, Rinehart and Winston, 1960.

Murray, William. *Del Mar: Its Life and Good Times*. Del Mar, CA: Del Mar Thoroughbred Club, 1988.

Murrells, Joseph. *Million Selling Records from the 1900s to the 1980s*. New York: Arco, 1984.

Nachman, Gerald. *Raised on Radio*. New York: Pantheon, 1998.

Nasaw, David. *Going Out*. New York: Harper Collins, 1993.

———. *The Chief: The Life of William Randolph Hearst*. Boston: Houghton Mifflin, 2000.

Nash, Gerald D. *World War II and the West*. Lincoln: University of Nebraska Press, 1990.

———. *The American West Transformed*. Bloomington: University of Indiana Press, 1985.

Nathan, Hans. *Dan Emmett and the Rise of Early Negro Minstrelsy*. Norman: University of Oklahoma Press, 1962.

Neal, Patricia. *As I Am*. New York: Simon and Schuster, 1988.

Nelson, Miriam. *My Life Dancing with the Stars*. Albany, GA: BearManor, 2009.

Netland, Dwayne. *The Crosby: Greatest Show in Golf*. Garden City, NY: Doubleday, 1975.

New York Times Directory of the Film. New York: Arno Press/Random House, 1971.

Nicholson, Stuart. *Reminiscing in Tempo: A Portrait of Duke Ellington*. Boston: Northeastern University Press, 1999.

Nimmo, H. Arlo. *The Andrews Sisters*. Jefferson, NC: McFarland, 2004.

Nolan, Frederick. *Lorenz Hart: A Poet on Broadway*. New York: Oxford University Press, 1994.

Norman, Barry. *The Film Greats*. London: Hodder and Stoughton, 1985.

Nugent, Elliott. *Events Leading Up to the Comedy*. New York: Trident, 1965.

O'Brien, Pat. *The Wind at My Back*. Garden City, NY: Doubleday, 1964.

O'Neill, Eileen, ed. *The Thalians: Stars and Stripes*. San Bernardino, CA: Franklin, 1976.

O'Toole, Andrew. *Branch Rickey in Pittsburgh*. Jefferson, NC: McFarland, 2000.

Ottley, Roi. *New World A-Coming: Inside Black America*. Cleveland: World (reprint), 1945.

Parish, James Robert. *The Paramount Pretties*. New Rochelle, NY: Arlington House, 1972.

———. *The Encyclopedia of Ethnic Groups in Hollywood*. New York: Facts on File, 2003.

Parish, James Robert, and Lennard DeCarl. *Hollywood Players: The Forties*. New Rochelle, NY: Arlington House, 1976.

Parish, James Robert, and Michael R. Pitts. *Hollywood Songsters*. 3 vols. New York: Routledge, 2003.

Patterson, James T. *Grand Expectations*. New York: Oxford University Press, 1996.

Peary, Danny, ed. *Close Ups: The Movie Star Book*. New York: Simon and Schuster, 1978.

Penna, Toney, with Oscar Fraley. *My Wonderful World of Golf*. New York: Centaur House, 1965.

Perito, Nick. *I Just Happened to Be There*. Las Vegas: Xlibris, 2004.

Perry, Jeb H., ed. *Variety Obits*. Metuchen, NJ: Scarecrow Press, 1980.

Pimlott, John. *The Historical Atlas of World War II*. New York: Henry Holt, 1995.

Pitrone, Jean Maddern. *Take It from the Big Mouth*. Lexington: University Press of Kentucky, 1999.

Pleasants, Henry. *Serious Music and All That Jazz*. New York: Simon and Schuster, 1969.

———. *The Great American Popular Singers*. New York: Simon and Schuster, 1974.

Poague, Leland A. *The Hollywood Professionals: Billy Wilder and Leo McCarey.* Vol. 7. San Diego: A. S. Barnes, 1980.

Pogue, Forrest C. *Pogue's War: Diaries of a WWII Combat Historian.* Lexington: University Press of Kentucky, 2001.

Pye, Michael. *Moguls.* New York: Holt, Rinehart and Winston, 1980.

Quirk, Lawrence J. *Bob Hope: The Road Well-Traveled.* New York: Applause, 1998.

Rhodes, Richard. *Masters of Death.* New York: Knopf, 2002.

Roberts, John Storm. *The Latin Tinge.* New York: Oxford University Press, 1979.

Roberts, Mary Beth, ed. *The Famous Musical Publishing Companies Professional Song Guide.* New York: Famous Music, 1993.

Robinson, Earl, with Eric A. Gordon. *Ballad of an American.* Lanham, MD: Scarecrow Press, 1998.

Robinson, Edward G., Jr., and William Dufty. *My Father—My Son.* New York: Frederick Fell, 1958.

Robinson, Jeffrey. *Teamwork: Cinema's Greatest Comedy Teams.* London: Proteus, 1982.

Rogin, Michael. *Blackface, White Noise.* Berkeley: University of California Press, 1998.

Rosen, Jody. *White Christmas: The Story of an American Song.* New York: Scribner's, 2002.

Rosten, Leo C. *Hollywood.* New York: Harcourt, Brace, 1941.

Rourke, Constance. *American Humor.* New York: Harcourt Brace Jovanovich, 1931.

———. *The Roots of American Culture.* New York: Harcourt, Brace and World, 1942.

Rust, Brian. *Jazz Records 1897–1942.* Rev. ed. New Rochelle, NY: Arlington House, 1978.

———. *The American Dance Band Discography 1917–1942.* New Rochelle, NY: Arlington House, 1975.

———. *The American Record Label Book.* New York: Da Capo, 1984.

Sackett, Susan. *Hollywood Sings!* New York: Billboard Books, 1995.

Sampson, Henry T. *Swingin' on the Ether Waves.* 2 vols. Lanham, MD: Scarecrow, 2005.

Sanders, Coyne Steven, and Tom Gilbert. *Desilu: The Story of Lucille Ball and Desi Arnaz.* New York: William Morrow, 1993.

Sanford, Herb. *Tommy and Jimmy: The Dorsey Years.* New Rochelle, NY: Arlington House, 1972.

Sanjek, Russell. *American Popular Music and Its Business.* Vol. 3 (1900–1984). New York: Oxford University Press, 1988.

Sanjek, Russell, and David Sanjek. *American Popular Music Business in the 20th Century.* New York: Oxford University Press, 1991.

Sarris, Andrew. *The American Cinema: Directors and Directions 1929–1968.* New York: Dutton, 1968.

———. *You Ain't Heard Nothin' Yet.* New York: Oxford University Press, 1998.

Satchell, Tim. *Astaire.* London: Century Hutchinson, 1987.

Scharf, Walter, and Michael Freedland. *Composed and Conducted by Walter Scharf.* London: Valentine, Mitchell, 1988.

Schatz, Thomas. *The Genius of the System*. New York: Pantheon, 1988.

———. *Boom and Bust: Hollywood in the 1940s*. New York: Scribner's, 1997.

Schickel, Richard. *Film on Paper*. Chicago: Ivan R. Dee, 2008.

———. *Good Morning, Mr. Zip Zip Zip*. Chicago: Ivan R. Dee, 2003.

———. *His Picture in the Papers*. New York: Charterhouse, 1973.

Schoenberg, Wilfred P. *Gonzaga University Seventy-Five Years 1887–1962*. Spokane, WA: Gonzaga University, 1963.

Schuller, Gunther. *The Swing Era*. New York: Oxford University Press, 1989.

Sears, Richard S. *V-Discs: A History and Discography*. Westport, CT: Greenwood, 1980.

———. *V-Discs: First Supplement*. Westport, CT: Greenwood, 1986.

Seldes, Gilbert. *The Seven Lively Arts*. New York: Harper, 1924.

———. *The Great Audience*. New York: Viking, 1950.

———. *The Public Arts*. New York: Simon and Schuster, 1956.

Shacter, James D. *Piano Man: The Story of Ralph Sutton*. Chicago: Jaynar Press, 1975.

Shapiro, Nat, and Nat Hentoff. *Hear Me Talkin' to Ya*. New York: Dover (reprint), 1966.

Shaughnessy, Mary Alice. *Les Paul*. New York: William Morrow, 1993.

Shaw, Arnold. *Let's Dance*. New York: Oxford University Press, 1998.

———. *The Jazz Age*. New York: Oxford University Press, 1987.

Sheed, Wilfrid. *The House That George Built*. New York: Random House, 2007.

Sheldon, James. *Before I Forget*. Duncan, OK: BearMedia, 2011.

Shindler, Colin. *Hollywood Goes to War*. London: Routledge and Kegan Paul, 1979.

Shipman, David. *The Story of Cinema*. New York: St. Martin's, 1982.

Shorris, Sylvia, and Marion Abbott Bundy. *Talking Pictures*. New York: New Press, 1994.

Sikov, Ed. *On Sunset Boulevard: The Life and Times of Billy Wilder*. New York: Hyperion, 1998.

Silvers, Phil, with Robert Saffron. *This Laugh Is on Me*. Englewood Cliffs, NJ: Prentice Hall, 1973.

Simon, George T. *The Best of the Music Makers*. Garden City, NY: Doubleday, 1979.

———. *The Big Bands Songbook*. 4th ed. New York: Schirmer Books, 1981.

———. *Glenn Miller*. New York: Thomas Y. Crowell, 1974.

Sklaroff, Lauren Rebecca. *Black Culture and the New Deal*. Chapel Hill: University of North Carolina Press, 2009.

Skretvedt, Randy. *Laurel and Hardy: The Magic Behind the Movies*. Beverly Hills: Past Times Publishing, 1987.

Slide, Anthony. *The Vaudevillians*. Westport, CT: Arlington House, 1981.

———. *Inside the Hollywood Fan Magazine*. Jackson: University Press of Mississippi, 2010.

Smith, Anthony Burke. *The Look of Catholics: Portrayals in Popular Culture from the Great Depression to the Cold War*. Lawrence: University Press of Kansas, 2010.

Smith, H. Allen. *Life in a Putty Knife Factory*. Garden City, NY: Doubleday, Doran, 1943.

Smith, Jay D., with Len Gutteridge. *Jack Teagarden*. New York: Da Capo, 1960.

Smith, Joe. *Off the Record*. New York: Warner Books, 1988.

Snowden, Clinton A. *History of Washington*. Vol. 2. New York: Century History Company, 1909.

Sobol, Louis. *The Longest Street*. New York: Crown, 1968.

Spada, James. *Grace: The Secret Lives of a Princess*. Garden City, NY: Doubleday, 1987.

———. *More Than a Woman: An Intimate Biography of Bette Davis*. New York: Bantam, 1993.

Spoto, Donald. *Notorious: The Life of Ingrid Bergman*. New York: HarperCollins, 1997.

Stafford, Don. *The Ile de France*. New York: Appleton Century Crofts, 1960.

Starr, Kevin. *The Dream Endures: California Enters the 1940s*. New York: Oxford University Press, 1997.

———. *Embattled Dreams: California in War and Peace, 1940–1950*. New York: Oxford University Press, 2002.

Sterling, Christopher H. *Encyclopedia of Radio*. 3 vols. New York: Routledge, 2004.

Stowe, David W. *Swing Changes: Big Band Jazz in New Deal America*. Cambridge, MA: Harvard University Press, 1994.

Stratemann, Klaus. *Louis Armstrong on Screen*. Copenhagen: JazzMedia, 1996.

Stratton, David H., ed. *Spokane and the Inland Empire*. Pullman: Washington State University Press, 1991.

Strom, Robert. *Miss Peggy Lee*. Jefferson, NC: McFarland, 2005.

Sudhalter, Richard M. *Lost Chords*. New York: Oxford University Press, 1999.

Summers, Harrison B. *A Thirty-Year History of Programs Carried on National Radio Networks in the United States 1926–1956*. Salem, NH: Ayer Company (reprint), 1986.

Swindell, Larry. *The Last Hero: A Biography of Gary Cooper*. New York: Doubleday, 1980.

Taylor, Robert Lewis. *W. C. Fields: His Follies and Fortunes*. New York: Doubleday, 1949.

Taylor, Theodore. *Jule: the Story of Composer Jule Styne*. New York: Random House, 1979.

Thomas, Bob. *King Cohn*. New York: McGraw-Hill, 1990.

Thomas, Tony. *Harry Warren and the Hollywood Musical*. Secaucus, NJ: Citadel Press, 1975.

Toll, Robert C. *Blacking Up: The Minstrel Show in Nineteenth-Century America*. New York: Oxford University Press, 1974.

———. *The Entertainment Machine*. New York: Oxford University Press, 1982.

———. *On with the Show*. New York: Oxford University Press, 1976.

Tormé, Mel. *My Singing Teachers*. New York: Oxford University Press, 1994.

Tucker, Mark, ed. *The Duke Ellington Reader*. New York: Oxford University Press, 1993.

Tuttle, Frank. *They Started Talking*. Boalsberg, PA: BearMedia, 2005.

Vallée, Rudy, and Gil McKean. *My Time Is Your Time*. New York: Obolensky, 1962.

Vallée, Rudy. *Vagabond Dreams Come True*. New York: E. P. Dutton, 1930.

————. *Let The Chips Fall...* Harrisburg, PA: Stackpole Books, 1975.

Van der Merwe, Peter. *Origins of the Popular Style.* New York: Oxford University Press, 1989.

Wakeman, John, ed. *World Film Directors.* Vol. I, *1890–1945.* New York: H. W. Wilson, 1987.

Walsh, Raoul. *Each Man in His Time.* New York: Farrar, Straus and Giroux, 1974.

Ward, Geoffrey C. *A First-Class Temperament: The Emergence of Franklin Roosevelt.* New York: Harper and Row, 1989.

————. *Unforgivable Blackness: The Rise and Fall of Jack Johnson.* New York: Knopf, 2004.

Ward, Larry Thomas. *Truth, Justice, and the American Way: The Life and Times of Noel Neill.* Los Angeles: Nicholas Lawrence Books, 2003.

Waring, Virginia. *Fred Waring and the Pennsylvanians.* Urbana: University of Illinois Press, 1997.

Watkins, Mel. *On the Real Side.* Rev. ed. Chicago: Lawrence Hill Books, 1999.

Way, Chris. *The Big Bands Go to War.* Edinburgh, Scotland: Mainstream, 1991.

Welles, Orson, and Peter Bogdanovich. *This Is Orson Welles.* New York: Harper Collins, 1992.

Wertheim, Arthur Frank. *Radio Comedy.* New York: Oxford University Press, 1979.

Westmore, Frank, and Muriel Davidson. *The Westmores of Hollywood.* Philadelphia: Lippincott, 1976.

Wexler, Jerry, with David Ritz. *Rhythm and the Blues.* New York: Knopf, 1993.

Whitburn, Joel. *Pop Hits Singles and Albums 1940–1952.* Menomonee Falls, WI: Record Research, 2002.

————. *Pop Memories 1890–1954.* Menomonee Falls, WI: Record Research, 1986.

————. *Top R&B Singles 1942–1988.* Menomonee Falls, WI: Record Research, 1988.

White, John I. *Git Along, Little Dogies.* Urbana: University of Illinois Press, 1989.

Whiteman, Paul. *Records for the Millions.* New York: Hermitage Press, 1948.

Wieland, Karin. *Dietrich and Riefenstahl.* New York: Liveright, 2015.

Wilder, Alec, with James T. Maher. *American Popular Song.* New York: Oxford University Press, 1972.

Wiley, Mason, and Damien Bona. *Inside Oscar.* New York: Ballantine Books, 1986.

Wilk, Max. *They're Playing Our Song.* New York: Atheneum, 1973.

Williams, Esther, with Digby Diehl. *The Million Dollar Mermaid.* New York: Simon and Schuster, 1999.

Williams, Martin. *Jazz Masters in Transition 1957–69.* New York: Macmillan, 1970.

Wood, Robin. *Sexual Politics and Narrative Film: Hollywood and Beyond.* New York: Columbia University Press, 1998.

Young, Jordan R. *Spike Jones Off the Record.* Beverly Hills: Past Times Publishing, 1984.

Zierold, Norman. *The Moguls.* Los Angeles: Coward-McCann, 1969.

Zoglin, Richard. *Hope.* New York: Simon and Schuster, 2014.

Zukor, Adolph, with Dale Kramer. *The Public Is Never Wrong.* New York: G. P. Putnam's Sons, 1953.

Unpublished Manuscripts

Frank, Melvin. "The Crosbys: Bing and Dixie." Teleplay. Courtesy of his daughter Elizabeth Frank.

Good, Kitty. Untitled memoir by the widow of Eddie Lang, taped by her son Tim Good. Courtesy of Kitty and Tim Good.

Gordon, Julia M. "What a Life: The Eddie Bracken Story." Life of the actor by his granddaughter, written on a senior fellowship from Dartmouth. Courtesy of Eddie Bracken and Julia M. Gordon.

Kiner, Larry F., and Graham C. Reade. "Bing Crosby: A Bio-Discography." The most comprehensive account of Crosby recordings, this is the only one that accesses union contracts to display orchestral personnel. Updated as of 2003. Courtesy Larry Kiner and Graham Reade.

McDonough, John. "Decca: 60th Anniversary History." Commissioned by MCA. Courtesy of John McDonough.

Porter, Joey. "Never Been So Lost." Screenplay by the son-in-law of Harry Barris. Courtesy of Joey Porter and Marti Barris.

Rinker, Al. "The Bing Crosby I Knew." Written memoir. Courtesy of his daughter Julia Rinker, and widow, Elizabeth Rinker.

Taylor, Doreen. Untitled memoir of dancer Doreen Wilde, taped by her granddaughter Alison McMahan. Courtesy of Alison McMahan.

Fan Magazines and Websites

Bing. The primary vehicle for all things Crosby is published in the UK by International Club Crosby, which, with the American Club Crosby, is the world's oldest fan club. The magazine began in 1950 and continues to turn out three professional-looking and art-directed issues per year, edited by Malcolm Macfarlane, aided by Michael Crampton and, in the United States, F. B. Wiggins. Information is available at bingmagazine.co.uk.

Bingang. An organ of Club Crosby, published between 1936 and 2003, when it merged with *Bing.* A vast resource to which the Crosby office occasionally contributed, it became scholarly in its last fifteen years under the editorship of Mark Scrimger and Wayne Martin.

Bingcrosby.com is the official Bing Crosby website, operated through the Crosby estate.

Derbingle.blogspot.com is a handsomely designed virtual museum of American popular culture, with particular attention paid to Crosby, curated by Jon Oye.

Google.com/site/crosbyfanworld/home is the home of Crosby Fan World, with many links.

Acknowledgments

You can encourage a blindfolded man as much as you
like to stare through the cloth, but he will never see a
thing [until] you remove the blindfold.
—Franz Kafka, *The Castle* (1926)

*The biographer arrived at the village late one evening and stared
upward at the gated estate shrouded in a darkening fog. He found
lodging and in the morning applied unsuccessfully for admittance to
the mansion. He stayed for nine years, making inquiries, interviewing everyone who had known or worked with the master, never losing
hope that the gates might open. Shortly after the biographer published a life of the man's early years, the mansion suddenly erupted
with light shining from every turret, as the portals parted and the
luminous widow, the keeper of the flame, emerged to receive the
biographer. As he passed into the courtyard, he could hear behind
him a village band playing "Please Don't Talk About Me When I'm
Gone" as the fog dispersed, and he heard himself roaring, "I can see!"*

Cut! And yet it kind of felt like that after *Bing Crosby: A Pocketful
of Dreams, The Early Years, 1903–1940* came out in early 2001 and
Kathryn Crosby invited me to stay at the family's Hillsborough
home and sift through her husband's papers. She had understand-
ably resisted earlier entreaties, given the kind of rubbish published
about Crosby in the 1980s. But now I was free to burrow into filing
cabinets, desk drawers, and boxes packed with letters, memos, contracts, photographs, Dictaphone belts, and more. After a few days,

as I haplessly pointed to the stacks of papers I had yet to digest or note down and wanted to photocopy, she left the room and returned with a suitcase; I could send them back when I was finished, she said. Months later, traveling to New York to visit her grandchildren, Kathryn asked me to meet her at her son Harry's apartment. She had found something I might find useful: unmediated transcripts, marked up in Bing's hand, of the interviews that made up the bulk of his 1953 memoir, *Call Me Lucky*.

It got even better.

Several years later, the Crosby estate hired the writer and documentarian Robert S. Bader to curate its archive; he is currently vice president of HLC Properties, Ltd. In addition to producing Crosby CDs and a documentary, he uncovered the long-forgotten kinescope reels of the 1960 World Series clincher between Bing's victorious Pittsburgh Pirates and the New York Yankees, and a warehouse with thousands of documents. Robert informed me that the family would make them available to me after they were vetted. My researcher, Amy Schireson, regularly visited his office to photocopy them and dispatched FedEx cartons over the course of a year. Thank you, Robert and Amy.

In short, although this book is unauthorized, it could not have been written or even conceived without the access provided by the unfailingly gracious Kathryn Crosby, who requested nothing in return. It was this access that spurred me to tear up my original outline and drafts and write a book about Crosby in the context and crucible of the home front. Kathryn, what can I say?

The great photographer Herman Leonard once told me you have to train yourself to be lucky. No training on my part triggered a chance subway encounter between two strangers: Pamela Crosby Brown, a godchild of Bing Crosby's, and David McCain, an expert on the Boswell Sisters. As luck would have it, David mentioned my work in progress and Pam went home and told her mother, Violet Brown (née Barsa), urging her to share her story with the biographer she had heard about. Violet was warm and funny but slightly mortified about the stalking she and her sister, Mary, played at in the 1940s. Still, over time, she shared her memories, correspondence, and the diary she helped her sister to write. After Violet's death, Pamela drove to my home, her trunk filled with scrapbooks documenting thirty-plus years of the Crosby-Barsa connection. Pam gave me a key to Crosby's two-month stay in New York—the sojourn with which I planned to close the circle of this story.

The following acknowledgments are intended as a continuation of those in the preceding volume.

As ever, I cannot overstate my gratitude to everyone—especially the friends, relations, colleagues, and acquaintances of Bing Crosby—listed in the now expanded Interviews and Bibliography. I remain equally indebted to curators and librarians previously mentioned, to whom I thankfully add Barbara Hall, research archivist of the Margaret Herrick Library of the Academy of Motion Picture Arts and Sciences. In addition to providing the detailed "report from our database" on the materials I requested, she accommodated my work there and, asked to recommend a researcher to continue in my absence, suggested Amy Schireson. My thanks also to Ginny Kilander, the associate faculty archivist of the American Heritage Center at the University of Wyoming, which has gathered a bottomless treasure of showbiz lore.

The materials that the then-director Ned Comstock and Leith Adams led me to at USC's Film and Television Archive were indispensable in writing about Leo McCarey, as was the AFI McCarey collection. Edward Crosby, Bing's nephew, provided me with letters that went into the Prelude. His half brother Howard supplied letters between their father (Ted) and Bing; his own explication of the legal mess that entangled them; and an occasional, much-appreciated bourbon.

Zuza Homem de Mello, a legendary chronicler of Brazilian music, and his wife, Ercilia Lobo, guided my wife, Debbie, and me through São Paulo and translated from Portuguese accounts of Crosby's 1941 South American journey. Mark Brodka, an attorney and the husband of Mary Frances Crosby, explained the dark forces of music contracts and royalties. My mentor Dan Morgenstern, who brought the Institute of Jazz Studies at Rutgers to life, discovered Crosby gems and inspired me by example. The maestro of American biography Robert Caro steeled my spine when I made the decision to pursue a volume entirely on the war years, and his wife and researcher,

Ina Caro, eased my way into the world of presidential libraries. Liz Dutton, the music editor at Alexander Street Press, made available the "rough draft" script for *The Bells of St. Mary's*. Paul Doherty, a voice-over artist and the co-head of CESD Talent Agency, expedited interviews with such clients as Shirley Mitchell and the magical, twinkle-voiced Janet Waldo and made available numerous rare television shows involving Crosby and Hope. The indefatigable Hollywood researcher G. D. Hamann expanded his volumes on Crosby, directing me to countless obscure newspaper stories.

I've written before of the generosity and keenness of Crosby fans who volunteered to do whatever they could, which amounted to quite a lot. Malcolm Macfarlane, the editor of the fan magazine *Bing*, whose own exhaustive research provided me with a blueprint, pulled my coat to books, articles, photos, tapes, and people I would not have known about, and he never failed to provide prompt replies to my queries. Mark Scrimger will finally see the uses to which I put some of his most precious discoveries. The illustrator and website curator Jon Oye has been a trusty correspondent about Crosby matters for over a decade. My thanks to F. B. Wiggins, not least for introducing me to Jean Halliburton, and to Steven Lewis for maintaining the Bing Crosby Internet Museum. I particularly thank my shrewd and generous friend Judy Schmid, who created a couple of web pages in my name that otherwise would not exist, bestowed upon me cartons of memorabilia and hundreds of Crosby photographs, answered countless queries, and, during a brief period in my employ, achieved in record time a level of organization I could only marvel at.

I mourn the passing of several people who contributed mightily to my understanding of Crosby, extending amity far beyond the call of biographical collusion. Hail and farewell to three marvelous friends, Rosemary Clooney, who opened a great many doors beyond her own; Mary Cleere Haran, an almanac of musical insight and solid research; and the great curmudgeon Richard Schickel, the perfect foil for arguing about anything cinematic. Jean Halliburton (formerly Mrs. Arnold Stevens) remained a superb raconteur until the end. It meant a great deal to Ed Helwick, who abandoned radio to teach high school, and Michael G. McDonald (former executive at Minute Maid) for me to appreciate Crosby in full. The effervescent Ruth Prigozy, a professor of English at Hofstra who specialized in F. Scott Fitzgerald and popular singers, launched the seminal 2002 conference "Bing! Crosby and American Culture." My stylish aunt Esther Reichenbaum, sharp as a croupier until the end (at age 101), managed Patron History at the Waldorf Astoria through the war and after.

I continue to grieve, as do all who knew her, over the loss of Elora Charles, who came to work for me in 2000 and stayed for nearly fourteen years, until illness suddenly overtook her at age forty-one. Her contribution to this work was thoroughgoing: she did yeoman's research (how many days did we emerge seasick from libraries, after hours of scrolling through microfiche), conducted follow-up interviews, checked dozens of transcriptions against original tapes to certify every word, typed up my unreadable notes, and invariably provided a robust second opinion to my assumptions and uncertainties. Elora was a multilingual classicist and an amateur vocalist, strong, uncompromising, acerbically witty, resolutely loyal.

Professional salvation arrived in the person of Marlon Calliste, a computer wizard and innovator who built my PC from scratch, with three monitors on which I am now hopelessly dependent. He assisted me for five years, picking up where Elora left off, and even inventoried my library between Crosby-related tasks. Lee Rothchild, who assisted me in the early stages, is now keeping a major corporation on track yet still finds time to supervise my speaking gigs.

I am grateful for the kindnesses and friendship of Patricia Bosworth, Geoffrey Ward, Debra Grace Winer, and William P. Kelly, who as president of the CUNY Graduate Center encouraged me to accept the directorship of the Leon Levy Center for Biography, where I was assisted by Michael Gately and schooled in fine points of biography by each of our gifted fellows and an illustrious board.

With apologies to those inadvertently omitted, I thank Michael Feinstein, a full-time archivist when he isn't a full-time performer; Matthew C. Hanson, the archivist of the Franklin D. Roosevelt Presidential Library; Barbara Constable, the archivist of the Dwight D. Eisenhower Library; Neal Hotelling, the director of licensing and special products for Pebble Beach Company; Alan C. Duncan (son of the orchestrator Ted Duncan); Rosemary Riddle Asara (daughter of Nelson Riddle) and Keith Pollack of the Nelson

Riddle Archive at the University of Arizona; the pianist Larry Vukovich, who forwarded a Crosby-related broadcast from KMPX in San Francisco; David A. Chubb, a friend to and a chronicler of the audio engineer John Mullin; Robert R. Phillips, whose trove of materials on Crosby's involvement with tape transcription may be found at ethw.org/First-Hand:Bing_Crosby_and_the_Recording_Revolution; Nigel Algar of the British Film Institute; Georgette Zwertlin, formerly of the Waldorf Astoria; and William F. Abbott, Jessica Barrett, Nell Payne Benson, Joel Blumberg, Ricky Calliste, William G. Clotworthy, Bernard Dick, Keefe Ferrandini, Bill Greffen, Jerry W. Jones, Malcolm Leo, Leonard Maltin, Father Bob Murphy, Filipp Nicolosi, David O'Rourke, Ron Roose, Bonnie Schoonover, Don Smith, Steven C. Smith, Tom and Florence Smith, David Torreson, and Bob Walden. My continued gratitude to Paul Bresnick, who talked me into taking on Crosby; Will Friedwald, whose research helped me break the ice; and Robert Christgau, who once wrote: "Credit [Bing Crosby's] decency and intelligence and you can comprehend the attractions of an American dream that deserves better than the exploitation to which it's still subjected by ruling-class cynics he would have seen through in a minute."

A lot has changed at Little, Brown and Company in the years since Sarah Crichton shepherded Bing Crosby: A Pocketful of Dreams into print, except for Michael Pietsch (now the CEO of Hachette Book Group) and the dedicated proficiency of its entire staff. Editors come and go; writers plod on. I was plodding obliviously when this project landed with my editor John Parsley, who, with the support of the publisher Reagan Arthur, gave me the go-ahead to pursue the idea of a wartime narrative. (Earlier responses included "No," and "For Chrissake, Gary, he isn't Churchill," concerning which my agent Georges Borchardt wisely advised me to keep plodding.) John reeled me in chapter by chapter, always encouraging, and brought in Charlie Conrad, who suggested cuts that I grumpily took very seriously, to the tune of 42,000 words—fewer than he suggested, but none that I would now wish on any reader. When John accepted a gig at another publishing tabernacle, Reagan assured me his replacement would be the "best possible editorial match" and made good on her word with Phil Marino, whose unwavering support made the shift smooth and auspicious. The transition was greatly facilitated by assistant editor Gabriella Mongelli. I am grateful for the reassurances of Judith Clain and Craig Young.

The most fun I have had with Track Changes was a consequence of working with copyeditor Tracy Roe, who was introduced to me as "brilliant and funny and our very best" and yet exceeded expectations, scouring sentences for any hint of unruliness and fact-checking with an apparently effortless skill. Jayne Yaffe Kemp has been a bulwark of stability, coordinating production with eagle eyes and promptly responding to my every peep. My thanks to her team, including Melissa Mathlin, Gail Cohen, and Kay Banning; the designers Judy Wingerter and Julianna Lee; and the postproduction team, Elizabeth Garriga, Sabrina Callahan, and Pamela Brown.

I am as proud to be represented by Georges Borchardt, Inc., as I am to have the friendship of Georges and Anne Borchardt. Much of this book was written during four stays at the MacDowell Colony. My thanks to Cheryl Young, David Macy, Blake Tewksbury, and every other soul associated with this paradisiacal retreat. I am eternally grateful for the loving support of Norman and Helen Halper.

Our daughter, Lea, was three when I began this road trip and eleven when the first volume was published. There followed years of "Will you finish before I graduate middle school...high school...college?" I did finish before she earned her MPA, in part because she worked to bring order to my office, as she had previously done for hurricane and earthquake survivors here and abroad. She has the biggest heart of anyone I have ever known, except for her mother. Deborah Halper has lived through every page of this book, accepting for too long the semimonastic life of a writer who worked through weekends. She's never been less than fully engaged, utterly supportive, and quick to find the solution to every situation. Debbie has kept me going in part because she's never doubted the value of the work. This book is dedicated to Debbie, Lea, and my ninety-seven-year-old mother. They earned it.

Index

Frank, Melvin, 231, 375–77, 379, 385, 601n22
Franklin, Benjamin, 289–90, 627n24
Frawley, William, 57, 72, 84, 86, 326, 343–44, 353
Frazier, George, 551–52, 553
"Freedom," 160
Freeman, Y. Frank: and Bing's independent production company, 367; and Bing's publicity photos, 192; on *Birth of the Blues,* 154; and Eddie Bracken, 493; and Buddy DeSylva, 130, 141, 325; and *Dixie,* 252; as head of Paramount Pictures, 129, 321, 491; and Bob Hope, 378; and Leo McCarey, 325–26, 337, 342, 399, 489; and *Road to Morocco,* 188–89; and *Road to Utopia,* 380; and *Star Spangled Rhythm,* 231
Friday, Pat, 214, 620n8
"Friendly Tavern Polka, The," 135
Frings, Ketti, 488, 649n2

Gable, Clark, 19, 83, 192, 295, 485
Gabler, Milt, 259, 552, 553, 555, 556, 660n25
Gallico, Paul, 98, 466
Gander, Wayne "Goose," 445–46
Ganzer, Alvin, 337, 385
Garbo, Greta, 489, 513
Garfield, John, 66, 328, 391
Garland, Judy, 34, 123, 269, 360–61, 365, 369, 550, 552
Garner, Darlene, 405, 412, 639n5
Gemora, Charles, 96, 385
General Electric radio show, 45
George, Florence, 245, 578
George VI (king of England), 15, 600n8
German American Bund, 27
Germany: Allied occupation of, 424; occupation of France, 433–34, 435, 437, 439, 440, 443–44, 446, 448, 450–57, 470; unconditional surrender of, 514, 522; and World War II, 24, 153–54, 327, 370, 414

Gershwin, George, 127, 131, 209, 281
"Get on the Road to Victory," 362
Ginsberg, Henry, 474, 490, 491, 516, 519
GI Oscars, 484, 518–19
"Girl with the Pigtails in Her Hair, The," 46
"Give Me the Simple Life," 555
"God Bless America," 163, 174, 242
"God Rest Ye Merry, Gentlemen," 242, 369
Goebbels, Joseph, 173, 425
Going Hollywood, 507
"Going My Way," 351–52, 387–88, 400, 422, 425, 448, 633n16, 634n22
Going My Way: and Academy Awards, 354, 394, 396, 399, 484, 490, 508–11, 546; adaptations of, 640n20; awards for, 484–85, 648–49n31; Bing's filming of, 215, 303, 304, 307, 309, 321, 326, 342, 343, 344–46, 349, 356–57, 360–61, 362, 363; Bing's film persona in, 307, 310, 335, 348–50, 394, 396, 482, 488, 504; and Buddy DeSylva, 130, 335, 372, 393, 396, 510; *Dixie* compared to, 273; locations for, 337; Leo McCarey's negotiations for, 325–26, 337, 342, 359; plot of, 307, 324–25, 326, 328, 329, 330–31, 334, 335–36, 341, 345, 346–50, 354–56, 503, 504, 505, 634n22; and postproduction work, 358; premiere of, 394–95; promotion of, 390, 393–96; release of, 372, 393, 394, 399; and screen credits, 358–60; sneak preview of, 373–74, 393; songs of, 329, 337, 341, 350–55, 394, 397, 403, 509, 580; start date for, 302, 337, 338–39; and Risë Stevens, 334–37, 339, 343–45, 349, 351–53, 356–60, 396, 634n22; success of, 397–98, 399, 405, 485, 487, 493, 516,

About the Author

GARY GIDDINS was a longtime columnist for the *Village Voice* and director of the Leon Levy Center for Biography at the City University of New York Graduate Center. He received the National Book Critics Circle Award, the Ralph J. Gleason Music Book Award, and the Bell Atlantic Award for *Visions of Jazz: The First Century* in 1998. His other books include *Bing Crosby: A Pocketful of Dreams— The Early Years, 1903–1940*, which won the Ralph J. Gleason Music Book Award and the ARSC Award for Excellence in Historical Sound Research; *Weather Bird: Jazz at the Dawn of Its Second Century*; *Faces in the Crowd*; *Natural Selection*; *Warning Shadows: Home Alone with Classic Cinema*; biographies of Louis Armstrong and Charlie Parker (winner of the American Book Award); and, with Scott DeVeaux, the widely used textbook *Jazz*. He has won an unparalleled six ASCAP–Deems Taylor Awards, a Guggenheim Fellowship, and a Peabody Award in Broadcasting. He lives with his wife, Deborah Halper, in New York.